P9-BJB-628

INTRODUCTION TO
COUNSELING
AND GUIDANCE

INTRODUCTION TO
COUNSELING
AND GUIDANCE

SECOND EDITION

ROBERT L. GIBSON
MARIANNE H. MITCHELL

Indiana University

MACMILLAN PUBLISHING COMPANY
New York
COLLIER MACMILLAN PUBLISHERS
London

To Our Parents—for a lifetime of guidance

Flora Lewis Gibson   Helen Metzger Mitchell

Alva Jason Gibson   Frank Henry Mitchell

Copyright © 1986, Macmillan Publishing Company, a division of Macmillan, Inc.

Printed in the United States of America

All rights reserved. No part of this book may be reproduced or transmitted in any form or by any means, electronic or mechanical, including photocopying, recording, or any information storage and retrieval system, without permission in writing from the publisher.

Earlier edition, entitled *Introduction to Guidance*, copyright © 1981 by Macmillan Publishing Co., Inc.

Macmillan Publishing Company
866 Third Avenue, New York, New York 10022

Collier Macmillan Canada, Inc.

Library of Congress Cataloging in Publication Data

Gibson, Robert Lewis.
  Introduction to counseling and guidance.

  Rev. ed. of: Introduction to guidance. c1981.
  Includes index.
  1. Counseling. I. Mitchell, Marianne Helen. II. Gibson,
Robert Lewis. Introduction to guidance.
III. Title.
BF637.C6G48 1986   158'.3   85-8809
ISBN 0-02-341800-1

Printing: 3 4 5 6 7 8 Year: 6 7 8 9 0 1 2 3 4 5

ISBN 0-02-341800-1

Credits

The authors would like to thank the following publishers for granting them the use of the material listed below.

ACADEMIC PRESS, INC.: Figure 10–1, p. 329, from *Behavior Modification in the Natural Environment* (p. 47) by R. G. Tharp and R. Wetzel. Copyright © 1969 by Academic Press, Inc., N.Y. Used by permission.

ALLYN AND BACON, INC.: Figures 2–1, 6–1, and 6–2, pp. 29, 163, and 164, from *Group Counseling: A Developmental Approach,* 3rd ed., (pp. 6–9, 27–28) by G. M. Gazda. Copyright © 1984 Allyn and Bacon, Boston, MA. Used by permission.

AMERICAN ASSOCIATION FOR COUNSELING AND DEVELOPMENT: Figure 3–1, p. 47, from "Dimensions of Counselor Functioning," *Personnel and Guidance Journal (P&GJ)* (*52*, p. 355) by W. H. Morrill, E. R. Oetting, and J. C. Hurst, © 1974. Tables 3–4 and 3–5, p. 52, from "Counselor Role and Function: An Appraisal by Consumers and Counselors," *P&GJ* (*61*, p. 598) by F. A. Ibrahim, B. J. Helms, and D. L. Thompson, © 1983. Tables 4–2, 4–3, 4–4, 4–5, and 4–6, pp. 84, 85, 86(2), and 87, from "The Counseling-Community Psychologist in the CMHC: Employer Perceptions," *Counselor Education and Supervision Journal* (*17*, 246–250) by D. L. Randolph, © 1978. Figure 4–1, p. 88, and Table 4–8, p. 88, from "Counselors as Community Psychologists," *P&GJ* (*54*, pp. 512 and 514) by R. K. Goodyear, © 1976. Extract on pp. 92–94 from "Role of the Employment Counselor," *Journal of Employment Counseling* (*12*, pp. 148–149, 152–53) by the National Employment Counselors Association, © 1975. Table 5–1, p. 127, from "Classification of Counseling and Therapy Theorists, Methods, Processes, and Goals: The E-R-A Model," *P&GJ* [*59*(5), pp. 263–265] by L. L'Abate, © 1981. Table 5–4, p. 131, from "Continuum of Counseling Goals: A Framework for Differentiating Counseling Strategies," *P&GJ* (*62*, p. 20 and 38) by P. Bruce, © 1984. Extract on pp. 151–152, from "Module I: Demographic Aspects of Aging: Implications for Counseling," in *Counseling the Aged: A Training Syllabus for Educators* (pp. 23–24) (M. L. Ganikos, editor) by R. Blake and D. Peterson, © 1979. Table 6–1, p. 181, from "Group-focused Counseling: Classifying the Essential Skills," *P&GJ* (*60*, pp. 302–305) by S. J. Gill and R. A. Barry, © 1982. Figure 9–4, p. 309, from "The College Check List," *Vocational Guidance Quarterly* [*9*(2), pp. 121–123] by R. L. Gibson, © 1960–1961. Extract on pp. 330 and 334 from "Consultation Theory and Process: An Integrated Model," *P&GJ* (*56*, p. 335 and 337) by D. Kurpius, © 1978. Extract on pp. 331–332 from "The Role of the Consultant: Content Expert or Process Facilitator?" *P&GJ* (*56*, pp. 340–342) by E. H. Schein, © 1978. Extract on pp. 347–348 from "Implementing Theme-focused Prevention: Challenge for the 1980's," *P&GJ* (*62*, pp. 511–512) by D. J. Drum © 1984. Table 11–1, p. 350, from "Primary Prevention Through a Campus Alcohol Education Project," *P&GJ* (*62*, p. 526) by R. K. Conyne, © 1984. Extract on pp. 353–354 from "Nutritional Counseling: A Humanistic Approach to Psychological and Physical Health," *P&GJ* (*61*, p. 22) by D. Martin and M. Martin, © 1982. All copyright © American Association for Counseling and Development. Reprinted with permission.

BASIC BOOKS, INC.: Table 4–10, p. 100, from *Americans View their Mental Health* (Table 10.3, p. 307) by Gerald Gurin, Joseph Veroff, and Sheila Feld. © 1960 by Basic Books, Inc., Publishers. Reprinted by permission of the publisher.

BROOKS/COLE PUBLISHING CO.: Extracts on pp. 16, 18, 35, 341–342, and 383, from *Community Mental Health: A General Introduction*, 2nd ed. by B. L. Bloom. Copyright © 1984, 1977 by Wadsworth, Inc. Figure 5–4, p. 153, from *The Counseling Experience: A Theoretical and Practical Approach* (p. 106) by M. E. Cavanagh. Copyright © 1982 by Wadsworth, Inc. Figure 8–6, p. 257, from *You and Me: The Skills of Communicating and Relating to Others* by G. Egan. Copyright © 1977 by Wadsworth, Inc. All reprinted by permission of Brooks/Cole Publishing, Monterey, CA 93940.

WM. C. BROWN COMPANY PUBLISHERS: Table 9–4, pp. 89–90, from *Practical Counseling in the Schools*, 2nd ed. (Table 14.2, p. 439) by Gary S. Belkin. © 1975, 1981 Wm. C. Brown Publishers, Dubuque, Iowa. All rights reserved. Reprinted by permission.

BURGESS PUBLISHING COMPANY: Figures 3–6 and 3–7, p. 71, from *Guidance: A Longitudinal Approach* (pp. 43 and 44) by H. L. Blanchard and L. S. Flaum. © 1968 Burgess Publishing Company, Minneapolis, MN.

HARVARD BUSINESS REVIEW: Figure 10–2, p. 335, from "Consulting Is More than Giving Advice," *Harvard Business Review* [*60*(5), p. 122] by A. N. Turner. Copyright © 1982 by the President and Fellows of Harvard College; all rights reserved.

THE HAWORTH PRESS, INC.: Extract on pp. 97–98 from "Critical Transitions over the Family Lifespan: Theory and Research," *Marriage and Family Review* [*6*(1/2), pp. 50–52] by H. Mederer and R. Hill. © The Haworth Press, Inc., 75 Griswold St., Binghamton, NY 13904.

HOUGHTON MIFFLIN COMPANY: Table 4–7, p. 87, and Figure 5–2, p. 132, from *Counseling: An Introduction,* 2nd ed., (Figure on p. 8 and Table on p. 10) by J. J. Pietrofesa, A. Hoffman, and H. H. Splete. Copyright © 1984 Houghton Mifflin Co. Extracts on pp. 163, 174, 175, 176, 177, and 178, from *Group Counseling: Theory and Process,* 2nd ed. (pp. 95, 398–399, 491, 502, 513, and 531) by J. C. Hansen, R. W. Warner, and E. M. Smith. Copyright © 1980 Hougton Mifflin Co. Extract on pp. 188–189, from *The World of the Contemporary Counselor* (pp. 34–35) by C. Gilbert Wrenn. Copyright © 1973 Houghton Mifflin Co. Extracts on pp. 220, 236 (Table 8–1), and 267, from *Fundamentals of Individual Appraisal: Assessment Techniques for Counselors* (pp. 285, 369, and 446) by B. Shertzer and J. D. Linden. Copyright © 1979 Houghton Mifflin Co. Table 9–2, p. 290, from "Youth in Exploration and Man Emergent" in *Man in a World at Work* (p. 216) by Robert J. Havighurst (Henry Borow, editor). Copyright © 1964 Houghton Mifflin Co. Table 9–3, p. 292, *Theories of Occupational Choice and Vocational Development* (p. 44) by J. Zaccaria. Copyright © 1970 Houghton Mifflin Co. All used with permission.

LITTLE, BROWN AND COMPANY: Tables 9–1 and 9–4, pp. 285 and 293, from *Career Guidance and Counseling Through the Life Span: Systematic Approaches,* 2nd ed., (pp. 36 and 107) by E. L. Herr and S. H. Cramer. Copyright © 1984 by Little, Brown and Co. By permission of Little, Brown and Co.

PRENTICE-HALL, INC.: Table 5–3, p. 130, from *Therapeutic Psychology: Fundamentals of Counseling and Psychotherapy,* 4th ed. (pp. 33–34) by L. M. Brammer and E. L. Shostrom, © 1982. Figure 5–3, p. 133, *The Helping Relationship: Process and Skills,* 3rd ed. (p. 41) by L. M. Brammer, © 1985. Table 5–5, p. 144, *Counseling and Psychotherapy: Skills, Theories, and Practice* (pp. 80, 170, 171–182) by A. E. Ivey and L. Simek-Downing, © 1980. Unnumbered Table on pp. 312–313, from *Career Information* (pp. 183–184) by R. H. Fredrickson, © 1982. All reprinted by permission of Prentice-Hall, Inc., Englewood Cliffs, N.J.

SAGE PUBLICATIONS, INC.: Figure 5–6, p. 156, from "Counseling Psychologists in Business and Industry," *The Counseling Psychologist* [*10*(3), p. 13] by J. E. Toomer. Copyright © 1983 by Sage Publications, Inc. Reprinted by permission.

SPRINGER PUBLISHING COMPANY, INC.: Figure 5–5, p. 153, and Table 5–6, p. 154, from *Counseling Adults in Transition* (p. 68 and 108) by N. K. Schlossberg. Copyright © 1984 Springer Publishing Co., Inc.

CHARLES C THOMAS, PUBLISHER: Figure 8–5, p. 253, from *Personal and Interpersonal Appraisal Techniques* (p. 66) by M. A. Kiley, 1975. Courtesy of Charles C Thomas, Publisher, Springfield, IL.

JOHN WILEY & SONS, INC. PUBLISHERS: Extracts on pp. 81, 82, 336, 376, 398–399, and Table 4–1, p. 83, from *Community Counseling: A Human Services Approach,* 2nd ed. (146, 173, 184, 195–196, and Table 7.2 on p. 195) by J. A. Lewis and M. D. Lewis. Copyright © 1983 John Wiley & Sons, Inc. Figure 7–3, p. 203, and Table 7–2, p. 204 from *Measurement and Evaluation in Psychology and Education,* 4th ed. (pp. 133 and 117) by R. L. Thorndike and E. Hagen. Copyright © 1977 John Wiley & Sons, Inc. Reprinted by permission of John Wiley & Sons, Inc.

PREFACE

This book is primarily designed for use in introductory counseling and guidance courses and in related fields for those who seek a comprehensive overview of counseling services. The reader will find here a broad general discussion rather than the in-depth treatment that students majoring in counseling can anticipate later in their specialized preparatory courses.

The objectives of this book are to provide the reader an overview and general understanding of (a) historical perspectives and current activities of counselors, (b) the role and function of the counselors in a variety of settings, (c) techniques utilized by counselors, and (d) the organization of counseling programs.

Although counselors in both school and nonschool settings adhere basically to the same principles and practices, it is recognized, through special attention in Chapter 3 (schools) and Chapter 4 (community and agency), that counselors are functioning in a variety of settings. We therefore believe that those interested in counseling in both school and nonschool settings will find this book an appropriate introduction.

The initial chapters lead the reader from the historical background of the counseling movement through traditional and current activities. These activities are then translated into the counselor's role and function in both school and nonschool settings (Chapters 3 and 4). Chapter 5 focuses on the primary and distinguishing activity of counselors—individual counseling. Chapters 6 through 10 discuss other basic activities of counselors (assessment through standardized and nonstandardized techniques, career counseling, group counseling, and consultation). Chapter 11 discusses the current trends for increased counselor attention to prevention and wellness. The final chapters (12 and 13) deal with the developing and managing of counseling and guidance programs and their improvement through accountability, evaluation, and research.

As an introductory text, we have tried to write and revise this book in a relatively informal style in the hope that it may be readable and enjoyable as well as informative. Your comments, suggestions, and reactions will be most welcome.

Finally, we would like to acknowledge all of those who have contributed directly and indirectly to the undertaking and completion of this book. These include, of course, the helpful staff of the Macmillan Publishing Company, particularly our editor, Mr. Lloyd C. Chilton, and our production supervisor, Hurd Hutchins. We would also like to acknowledge the valuable comments of our anonymous reviewers, and we are extremely grateful to the many considerate authors and publishers who granted us permission to quote from their publications. It is also appropriate to acknowledge the many useful suggestions from our departmental colleagues at Indiana University and our fellow counselor educators who volunteered their time and comments for our guidance. We have also been appreciative of the critical comments of our graduate students (who undoubtedly had in mind the well-being of their counterparts of the future).

We are particularly thankful for the patient and persistent assistance of our graduate assistants, Ms. L. Lynn Krebs and Ms. Patricia J. Parrett. In conclusion, we would like to acknowledge our close friends and families, who have endured "the worst of times" and are now looking forward to "the best of times."

R. L. G.
M. H. M.

CONTENTS

CHAPTER 4

COUNSELORS IN COMMUNITY AND AGENCY SETTINGS   79

CHAPTER 5

INDIVIDUAL COUNSELING   107

CHAPTER 6

GROUP TECHNIQUES FOR COUNSELORS   161

CHAPTER 7

STANDARDIZED TESTING AND HUMAN
ASSESSMENT   193

CHAPTER 8

NONSTANDARDIZED TECHNIQUES FOR HUMAN ASSESSMENT   229

CHAPTER 9

COUNSELING FOR CAREER PLANNING AND DECISION MAKING   277

CHAPTER 10

THE COUNSELOR AS DEVELOPMENTAL AND EDUCATIONAL CONSULTANT   327

CHAPTER 11

PREVENTION AND WELLNESS   345

CHAPTER 12

PROGRAM MANAGEMENT, DEVELOPMENT, AND LEADERSHIP   361

CHAPTER 13

ACCOUNTABILITY, EVALUATION, AND RESEARCH   393

APPENDICES   413

INTRODUCTION TO
COUNSELING
AND GUIDANCE

CHAPTER 1

HISTORICAL PERSPECTIVES

Introduction: Counseling—A Response to Human Needs

Many of you have recently made a decision to prepare for careers as counselors; some of you may be considering such a decision; still others of you may be interested in the field of counseling because you are in or are preparing to enter various careers in which some introductory knowledge of this field may be helpful. In this process you probably asked yourself, Why have I selected this field or this career? Your friends and family may have asked similar questions of you. On occasion, you also may have even thought, Why do I have to work? Both are age-old questions that are vital to society and that have been discussed and researched extensively over the years.

Perhaps an equally important question but one that is not raised quite as frequently or researched as extensively is, Why do certain careers exist? What were the factors that led to their demand and creation? The answers to these questions are fairly obvious concerning such fields as medicine and law, for the need for and role of physicians and lawyers in society have been clearly and universally recognized since the earliest recordings of civilizations. Less clear to many, however, are the need for and role of less well-known occupations, such as ornithologists, demographers, and cytotechnologists. Although a popular understanding and acceptance of the need for and role of all careers are not necessary or expected, it would appear helpful to those studying the general areas encompassed by counseling to understand the nature of the societal needs to which counseling and counselors are responding and, in turn, to understand the nature of those responsibilities and responses.

It is therefore appropriate in an introduction to the field and profession of counseling to begin by examining some of the historical antecedents leading to the development of counseling programs and the professional careers they represent. This first chapter presents a brief historical review of these developments. You, the reader, may determine whether counseling and counselors are a response to human needs or just another fancy that will pass when the need is examined more closely and critically.

Our Heritage from the Past

It is quite possible that the historically earliest, although unconfirmed, occasion in which humankind went in search of a counselor was when Adam reaped the

1

consequences of his eating the apple in the Garden of Eden. There is no proof of this early beginning to counseling, but there is an abundance of evidence that persons throughout the ages have sought the advice and counsel of others believed to possess superior knowledge, insights, or experiences.

Perhaps the first counterparts of the present-day counselor were the chieftains and elders of the ancient tribal societies to whom youths turned or were often sent for advice and guidance. In these primitive societies the tribal members shared fundamental economic enterprises such as hunting, fishing, and agriculture. No elaborate career guidance programs were developed—or needed—because occupational limitations were usually determined by two criteria: age and sex. Later, as skills became more recognizable and important to societies, the occupational determinant of inheritance became common. Thus, potters passed on the secrets and skills of their trade to their sons, as did the smiths and carpenters. Women passed on their skills to their daughters; however, their occupational opportunities were limited. A study of early primitive life can lead one to conclude that most of the conflicts existing in present-day society regarding career decision-making were absent. This absence of a career decision-making dilemma, however, should not be interpreted to mean that workers did not enjoy or take pride in a "job well done." Even from the earliest evidence of humankind's existence, it appears that pride and pleasure resulted from developing and demonstrating one's skills—in developing one's "human potential."

In the early civilizations, the philosophers, priests, or other representatives of the gods and religions assumed the function of advising and offering counsel. The historical origins of "developing one's potential" may be identified in the early Grecian societies, with their emphasis on developing and strengthening individuals through education so that each could fulfill a role reflecting their greatest potential for themselves and their society. It was believed that within the individual there were forces that could be stimulated and guided toward goals beneficial to both the individual and the community. Of these early Greek "counselors," Plato more than any other person is generally recognized as one of the first to organize psychological insights into a systematic theory. Belkin (1975) noted that Plato's interests

> were varied, and he examined the psychology of the individual in all of its ramifications: in moral issues, in terms of education, in relation to society, in theological perspective, and so on. He dealt with such questions as "What makes a man virtuous—his inheritance, his upbringing, or his formal education" (Meno), "How can children be most effectively taught" (Republic), and "Which techniques have been successfully used in persuading and influencing people in their decisions and beliefs" (Gorgias). But it is not the specific questions themselves that prove important to counselors, but, rather, the method that Plato used to deal with these questions, a method which, more than any other in the history of human thought, sets the way for the counseling relationship. It is a dramatic method, in which profound questions are dealt with through the dynamics of very real human interactions, a method in which the characters are as important as the things they say. (p. 5)

The second great counselor of the early civilizations was Plato's student, Aristotle, who made numerous and significant contributions to what was to become the field of psychology. One of these major contributions was his study of people interacting with their environment and with others. Also Hippocrates and other Greek physicians offered the opinion that mental disorders were diseases originating from natural causes. The treatments of physicians (bleeding, purging, and so forth) were hardly humane except by comparison.

Later, in ancient Hebrew society, individuality and the right of self-determination were assumed. The early Christian societies emphasized, at least in theory if not always in practice, many of the humanistic ideals that later became basic to democratic societies and, in this century, to the counseling movement.

Philosophers who were also educators, such as Luis Vives (1492–1540), recognized the need to guide persons according to their attitudes and aptitudes. Foreshadowing the more recent women's equity movement and the earlier women's liberation movement, "Vives in his *De subventione pauperum* (Bruges, 1526) even demanded that girls should be prepared for useful occupations" (Mallart, 1955, p. 75).

In the Middle Ages, attempts at counseling increasingly came under the control of the church:

> By the early Middle Ages the duty of advising and directing youth had become centered in the parish priest. At that time education was largly under church jurisdiction. Sporadic efforts at placement of youth in appropriate vocations occurred during the rise of European kingdoms and the subsequent expansion of the colonial empires (Gibson and Higgins, 1966, p. 4).

Books stating that they were to be used to help youths in the choice of an occupation began to appear in the 17th century (Zytowski, 1972). One notable effort by the Italian Tomasco Garzoni was nearly 1,000 pages and treated various professions and occupations in great detail. His publication *La Piazza Universale ai Tutti le Professioni del Mundo* (The Universal Plaza of all the Professions of the World) had 24 Italian editions and was also translated into Latin, German, and Spanish. Zytowski labeled it the *Occupational Outlook Handbook* of the 16th and 17th centuries (Zytowski, 1972, p. 448).

In the 17th century a number of picture books also appeared depicting different occupations. One of the more popular publications was Powell's *Tom of All Trades; Or the Plain Pathway to Preferment,* published in 1631 in London. "Powell gives much information on the professions and how to gain access to them, even suggesting sources of financial aid and the preferred schools in which to prepare" (Zytowski, 1972, p. 447).

Also during this time, Rene Descartes (1596–1650) and others began to study the human body as an organism that reacted or behaved to various stimuli. These studies were to be forerunners for later more accurate and scientific psychological studies.

In the 18th century Jean Jacques Rousseau (1712–1778) "suggested that the growing individual can best learn when he is free to develop according to his natural impulses; he advocated permissiveness in learning and learning through doing" (Gibson and Higgins, 1966, p. 4). At approximately the same time, the famous Swiss educator Johann Pestalozzi (1746–1827) "expressed the belief that society could be reformed only to the extent that the individual in that society was helped to help *himself* develop" (Gibson and Higgins, 1966, p. 4).

For centuries, however, many with mental illnesses, as did those with physical illnesses, went underground and retreated. While the wealthy could afford the attention of physicians, most mentally ill patients were almost always treated in the home. Those poor who received any treatment at all were treated in hospitals run by religious orders. For the first 75 years of this new nation, the United States of America, few public facilities existed for the treatment of the mentally ill.

The newly independent United States did have leading citizens with a "counseling viewpoint." "One of its most versatile citizens, Thomas Jefferson, called for a plan to recognize and educate its male youth as a source of national leadership" (Gibson and Higgins, 1966, p. 4). The second president of the United States, John Adams, called for laws for the liberal education of youths, especially of the lower class of people and that no expense for this purpose could be thought extravagant.

The most famous American educator of the 19th century, Horace Mann, included in his *Twelfth Annual Report* a notation of the advantages of the American common school system, advantages that were to be conducive to the development of programs of counseling and guidance in American education in the next century. Mann reported that "in teaching the blind and the deaf and dumb, in kindling the latent spark of intelligence that lurks in an idiot's mind, and in the more holy work of reforming abandoned and outcast children, education has proved what it can do by glorious experiments" (Johansen, Collins and Johnson, 1975, p. 280). Horace Mann also believed that education should have as one of its objectives the reform of society, and he continuously stressed this view in his reports to the Massachusetts Board of Education.

In the wake of the political scandals of the Grant administration and other evidence of the decay of Christian morals, methods of moral instruction and moral education became significant in the later 1800s. In 1872, the noted educator A. D. Mayo (1872) stated that morality and good citizenship were indistinguishably intermingled and that moral education in the public schools should be based on concepts, principles, and models drawn from the Christian tradition of American society.

During this period, the biologist Herbert Spencer (1820–1903) set forth his concept of *adjustment* (Hinshaw, 1942). This biological concept held that forms of life that do not adapt to their environment eventually become extinct. From this, Spencer concluded that perfect life consisted of perfect adjustment. In other words, biological adjustment is a criterion of life. Adaptive behavior is that which maintains life.

Also important to the scientific study of behavior and of special significance to the eventual emergence of counseling as a psychologically based profession was the emergence of the field of psychology itself during the latter part of the 19th century. Preceded by physicists and physiologists who were conducting experimental investigations leading to reliable information on physical and physiological aspects of behavior, similar investigations launched psychology as a separate science in the late 1800s, with the formal beginnings of psychology as a separate science occurring in 1879 when Wilhelm Wundt opened his Psychological Institute at the University of Leipzig. This was the beginning of the movement toward a systematic inquiry into human behavior rather than aimless and often biased observation. The next 100 years would witness the emergence

of psychology as a recognized discipline with its own distinct areas of specialization, inquiry, and training.

The emergence of psychiatry as a specialty of medicine was another important and relevant development of this period. This led to a decline in the support of moral treatment for mental disorders, since psychiatry advocated organic
treatment for organic causes. During this same period, the state mental hospital
movement, led by Dorothea Dix, resulted in the development of these institutions and the removal of much of the care for at least the seriously mentally ill
from local communities (Goshen, 1967).

As America entered the 20th century, its society was growing more complex,
and finding one's appropriate place within it and adjusting to it was becoming
increasingly complicated. Many adults were turning to such traditional sources
of advice, guidance, and counsel as their family physcian, minister, or employer.
However, it would appear that the 20th century was ripe for a considered and
genuinely scientific approach to meeting many human needs. The time was
"now" for the development of counseling and other psychologically oriented
programs to meet these needs. Let us now examine how these emerged in
schools and institutional and agency settings in this century.

The Development of Counseling and Guidance in American Education

History is often made when a person with an idea coincides with a need and an
opportunity. In 1908, Frank Parsons organized the Boston Vocational Bureau
to provide vocational assistance to young people and to train teachers to serve
as vocational counselors. These teachers were to aid in the selection of students
for vocational schools and were to assist students in choosing a vocation wisely
and making the transition from school to suitable work. Soon thereafter, Parsons (1909) published *Choosing a Vocation,* a predecessor to this and other basic
books in the field. In this publication he discussed the role of the counselor and
techniques that might be employed in vocational counseling. This publication
was divided into three areas: personal investigation, indu trial investigation, and
the organization and the work. Parson's book is interesting reading even today,
and few would find fault with what he considered to be three factors necessary
for the wise choice of a vocation:

> (1) a clear understanding of yourself, your aptitudes, abilities, interests, ambitions,
> resources, limitations, and other causes; (2) a knowledge of the requirements and con-
> ditions of success, advantages and disadvantages, compensation, opportunities, and
> prospects in different lines of work; and (3) true reasoning on the relations of these
> two groups of facts. (p. 5)

Parsons goes on to suggest that in initiating the personal investigation, the
client should first make an extensive self-study by answering questions on a
"schedule of personal data." The counselor then fills in the details by reading
between the lines. Parsons suggests that this will give clues to possible defects

such as defective verbal memory and slow auditory reactions. Such a client would make a poor stenographer, or as he puts it, "would have difficulty becoming an expert stenographer" (p. 7). The inventory suggested by Parsons includes such items as "How far can you walk? Habits as to smoking? Drinking? Use of drugs? Other forms of dissipation? How often do you bathe?" An unusual feature of the intake interview was the observations Parsons suggested regarding the physical appearance of the client:

> While I am questioning the applicant about his probable health, education, reading, experience, et cetera, I carefully observe the shape of his head, the relative development above, before, and behind the ears, his features and expression, color, vivacity, voice, manner, pose, general air of vitality, enthusiasm, et cetera.
>
> If the applicant's head is largely developed behind the ears, with big neck, low forehead, and small upper head, he is probably of an animal type, and if the other symptoms coincide, he should be dealt with on that basis. (p. 7)

Parsons advocated getting the client to see himself or herself exactly as others do and to give the client recommendations about methods that can be used for self-improvement—for example, reading suitable books to develop analytical power. Parsons also recommended using biographies of famous people and finding commonalities with the client in biographical details as a form of inspiration.

Parsons also insisted that counselors be thoroughly familiar with all relevant details concerning job opportunity, the distribution of demand in industries, and courses of study. A detailed analysis should be made of industrial opportunities for men and women. This would include location and demand, work conditions, and pay. A similar detailed approach was to be given to opportunities in vocational schools.

Parsons also explained the need to train vocational counselors. This training was to be accomplished in one to three terms, and the applicants were to have some relevant occupational background and maturity. In addition to sound judgment, character, and maturity, Parsons believed the vocational counselor should have:

1. A practical working knowledge of the fundamental principles and methods of modern psychology.
2. An experience involving sufficient human contact to give him an intimate acquaintance with human nature in a considerable number of its different phases; he must understand the dominant motives, interests, and ambitions that control the lives of men, and be able to recognize the symptoms that indicate the presence or absence of important elements of character.
3. An ability to deal with young people in a sympathetic, earnest, searching, candid, helpful, and attractive way.
4. A knowledge of requirements and conditions of success, compensation, prospects, advantages, and disadvantages, etc., in the different lines of industry.
5. Information relating to courses of study and means of preparing for various callings and developing efficiency therein.
6. Scientific method—analysis and principles of investigation by which laws and causes are ascertained, facts are classified, and correct conclusions drawn. The

counselor must be able to recognize the essential facts and principles involved in each case, group them according to their true relations, and draw the conclusions they justify. (Parsons, 1909, pp. 94–95)

Parson's pioneer efforts and publications were popular and succeeded in identifying and launching a new helping profession—the guidance counselor. Today, Parsons is generally referred to as the "father of the guidance movement in American education," but he probably did not envision the growth of the movement from the several dozen counselors he trained to the more than 50,000 counselors functioning in schools alone 70 years later.

By 1913, the fledgling "guidance" movement (as it was initially called) had grown sufficiently in numbers and specialization to warrant the organization of the National Vocational Guidance Association and to initiate, 2 years later, the publication of the first guidance journal, appropriately titled *Vocational Guidance.* The term *guidance* was the popular or "in" designation for the counseling movement in schools for well over 50 years. However, in recent generations guidance has been increasingly viewed as an outdated label. Additionally, the early years of the movement had a vocational orientation that was primarily concerned with those aspects of youth guidance dealing with vocational choice, preparation, and placement. (Sixty years later, many of the same characteristics would once again be reasserted in the career education and guidance movements.) Hence, in these early years the movement was often referred to as one of "vocational guidance."

According to Rockwell and Rothney (1961), other early leaders in the guidance movement in America were Jessie B. Davis, Anna Y. Reed, Eli W. Weaver, and David S. Hill. Their contributions should also be noted.

Davis's approach was based on self-study and the study of occupations. His descriptions of counseling (Rockwell and Rothney, 1961) seemed to suggest that students should be "preached to" about the moral value of hard work, ambition, honesty, and the development of good character as assets to any person who planned to enter the business world. In their discussion of early pioneers of the guidance movement, Rockwell and Rothney (1961) suggested:

Davis's position within the social gospel philosophy was enhanced by his use of the "call" concept of the ministry in relation to the way one should choose a vocation. When an individual was "called," he would approach it with the noblest and highest ideals which would serve society best by uplifting humanity. (p. 351)

In the same era, Anna Reed was an admirer of the then prevailing concepts and ethics of the business world and the free enterprise system. She believed that guidance services could be important to the Seattle school system as a means of developing the best possible educational "product." Contrary to today's philosophy, she placed the system's (business world) needs above those of the individual. As a result, the guidance programs she developed were designed to judge a person's worth by the employability of that individual.

Another early leader, Eli Weaver, succeeded in establishing teacher guidance committees in every high school in New York City. These committees worked actively to help youths discover their capabilities and learn how to use those capabilities to secure the most appropriate employment (Rockwell and Rothney, 1961).

The fourth of these early pioneers, David S. Hill, was a researcher in the New Orleans school system who used scientific methods to study people. Because his research studies pointed out the wide diversity in student populations, he advocated and worked for a diversified curriculum complemented by vocational guidance. He viewed this model as most appropriate if the individual student were to develop fully.

In the first quarter of the 20th century, two other significant developments in psychology profoundly influenced the school guidance movement. These were the introduction and development of standardized, group-administered psychological tests and the mental health movements.

The French psychologist Alfred Binet and his associate Theodore Simon introduced the first general intelligence test in 1905. In 1916, a translated and revised version was introduced in the United States by Lewis M. Terman and his colleagues at Stanford University, and it enjoyed widespread popularity in the schools. However, when the United States entered World War I and the armed services sought a measure that would enable them to screen and classify inductees, the first so-called group intelligence measure, the Army Alpha Test, was subsequently administered to thousands of draftees. The possibilities of applying these and other psychometric techniques to pupil assessment resulted in the rapid development and expansion of standardized testing in education in the decade immediately following World War I.

The 1920s was a lively decade in many ways. That noble experiment, prohibition, was launched; in turn, such names as Al Capone and "Baby Face" Nelson appeared in the nation's newspaper headlines. Socially, the jazz age, flappers, and bathtub gin were in vogue. For the professional educator, the progressive movement ensured a lively educational era as well. This movement, the thought of which would influence the further development of a people-oriented philosophy, stressed the uniqueness and dignity of the individual pupil, emphasized the importance of a humanistic (current label) classroom environment, and suggested that learning occurred in many ways. Many of today's counselors would have embraced the progessive education suggestions that pupils and teachers should plan together, that the child's social environment should be improved, that the developmental needs and purposes of the student should be considered, and that the psychological environment of the classroom should be a positive, encouraging one.

Organized guidance programs began to emerge with increasing frequency in secondary schools in the 1920s and more often than not modelled themselves after college student personnel programs with titles of deans—separately for boys and girls, of course—and with similar accompanying functions of discipline, school attendance, and related administrative responsibilities. As a result, many programs of this decade began to have a remedial emphasis, as pupils who experienced academic or personal difficulties were sent to their deans who sought to help them modify their behavior or correct their deficiencies. Nevertheless, a counselor of the mid-1920s, if projected by a time capsule into a school counselor's meeting 60 years later, could converse easily with his present-day counterparts—at least to the point of their concerns and involvement in vocational or career counseling, the use of the standardized testing instruments, assistance to students with their educational planning, the need for a more humanistic school environment, and their role as disciplinarians and quasi-administrators.

It is also probable that the elementary school movement had its beginnings in the mid-1920s and early 1930s, stimulated by the writings and efforts of William Burnham. Faust (1968) indicated that Burnham emphasized the important role of the teacher in the mental health of children in the elementary school. Efforts to develop guidance in elementary schools during this period were scarcely noticeable, but a few notable programs were undertaken. One of these, in Winnetka, Illinois, established a department of elementary counseling with resource personnel for guidance. These personnel included (although not all on a full-time basis) psychiatrists, psychometrists, psychologists, an educational counselor, a psychiatric social worker, and supporting clerical services. Their basic responsibilities were counseling, child study, psychotherapy, pupil analysis, parental assistance, and referrals.

By the end of the 1920s, it was evident that the early guidance pioneers believed there was a need for guidance services and believed that the school was the proper institution for the delivery of these services. Some even believed that pupil guidance should encompass all grades.

While in the 1930s the American public debated the policies of FDR and the threat of Hitler to world peace, the "guidance" movement continued to develop to the point that it was becoming increasingly popular as a topic for discussions and debate in educational circles. Questions and criticisms concerning guidance activities were increasingly noted in the professional literature of the era. Educational associations appointed committees to study the movement, and many issued reports with descriptions and definitions of guidance and guidance services. The New York State Teachers Association published a report in 1935 in which guidance was defined as "the process of assisting individuals in making life adjustment. It is needed in the home, school, community, and in all other phases of the individual's environment" (p. 10).

As in the 1960s, when concern was often expressed about the interchangeability of the words *guidance* and *counseling*, in the 1930s a similar concern was expressed over the interchangeability of the terms *student personnel* and *guidance*. Adding to the confusion, leading spokespeople for the movement during that period, such as John Brewer (1932), used the terms *education* and *guidance* synonomously.

Sarah M. Sturtevant (1937) sought to deal with some of these growing concerns by addressing some of the questions regarding the developing secondary school guidance movement. These included What do we mean by the guidance movement? What are the essentials of a functioning guidance program? What personnel and what qualifications should guidance workers have for a good guidance program? and the inevitable question, What are the costs of individualizing education?—questions that would not be outdated more than 45 years later.

During the late 1930s, and early 1940s, the trait-factor approach to counseling became increasingly popular. This often-labeled "directive" theory received stimulus from the writings of E. G. Williamson (*How to Counsel Students: A*

Manual of Techniques for Clinical Counselors, McGraw-Hill Book Company, 1939) and others. Whereas critics of this measurement-oriented approach claimed it was rigid and dehumanizing, Williamson stressed its worth:

> You are trying to improve your understanding by using data with a smaller probable error of estimate, such as test data—instead of judgments, which have a much larger probable error of estimate: variability. (Ewing, 1975, p. 84)

Also during the 1930s, possible directions for guidance in the elementary school were put forth by the child study movement, which took the position that it was the teacher's role to provide guidance for each pupil in the self-contained classroom. Publications by Zirbes and others described the ways in which the learning experiences of children could be guided. The intensive study of each child was recommended with the objective of understanding how children achieved or failed to achieve certain developmental tasks. This approach was a popular one that found some following at the secondary school level and ultimately led to the suggestion of "every teacher a guidance worker." (Shane, Shane, Gibson and Munger, 1971).

As the country emerged from World War II, the counseling and guidance movement appeared to be taking on new vitality and direction. A significant contributor to this new direction with an impact on counseling in both school and nonschool settings, was Carl R. Rogers, who had set forth a new counseling theory in two significant books, *Counseling and Psychotherapy* (1942) and a refinement of his early position, *Client-Centered Therapy* (1951). In his publication *Counseling and Psychotherapy,* Rogers offered nondirective counseling as an alternative to the older, more traditional methods. Rogers also stressed the client's responsibility in perceiving his or her problem and enhancing the "self." This self theory soon was labeled nondirective because it appeared to be the opposite of the traditional counselor-centered approach for dealing with client problems. Rogers's suggestion that the client assume the major responsibility for solving his or her own problem rather than the therapist solving the client's problem provoked the first serious theoretical controversies in the school guidance and counseling movement. Rogers' follow-up publication, *Client-Centered Therapy* (1951), was the result of this continued research and application effort. The book promoted the semantic change from nondirective to client-centered counseling, but, more importantly, placed increased emphasis on the growth-producing possibilities of the client. Perhaps more than any other person, Rogers has influenced the way in which American counselors interact with clients. Furthermore, his view of the client as an equal and his positive view of a person's potential seemed more consistent with the American way of life and democratic traditions than did the European-based theories.

> The extent of [Rogers's] influence was most marked by the overnight replacement of testing by counseling as the key guidance function. In turn, counseling would rise to such eminence in the next few years that it would compete and contend with guidance in regard to the use of counselor's time and the overall purpose of counseling and guidance. *What began as an adjunct tool of guidance would now raise a challenge for ascendency in its own right.* (Aubrey, 1977, p. 292)

Over the years Rogers continued to research, test, revise, and challenge others to test his theory. In summary, it might be analogous to compare Carl Rogers's impact and contributions to the counseling movement in this century with Henry Ford's contribution to the development of the automotive industry.

Another dimension to the techniques of counselors of the late 1940s and one to which Rogers, again, was a significant contributor was *group counseling*. Others, utilizing research data gathered by the armed services and their investigations into small group dynamics, developed a theoretical framework within which school counselors could integrate the skills and processes of individual counseling with the dynamic roles and interactions of the individual in a group setting.

Other opportunities also appeared on the horizon for the counseling and guidance movement. Feingold (1947), writing in *School Review,* called for a new approach to guidance. He indicated that guidance counselors cannot stop with mere educational direction—they must go beyond that goal, must provide guidance, "not only for the annointed, but for those pupils who really need it—the pupils who run afoul of rules and regulations" (p. 550). Feingold and others also called for "guidance of the whole child," an outgrowth of the child study movement of the 1930s. Three years later, Traxler (1950), writing in the same publication, identified emerging trends in guidance:

1. More adequate training of guidance personnel.
2. Guidance as an all-faculty function.
3. Closer cooperation with home and community agencies.
4. Orderly accumulation and recording of individual information.
5. Use of objective measures.
6. Differential prediction of success on the basis of test batteries that yield comparable scores in broad areas.
7. Increased interest in improved techniques in the appraisal of personal qualities of pupils and the treatment of maladjustment.
8. Trend toward "eclectic" guidance (rather than direction/nondirective).
9. Recognition of the relationship between remedial work and guidance.
10. Improved case study techniques.
11. Availability and better use of occupational-educational information. (pp. 14–23)

In 1957, the Soviet Union made headlines around the world by successfully launching the first earth satellite, Sputnik I. An indirect but nevertheless significant result of this accomplishment was the "lift-off" of the counseling and guidance movement into orbit in the United States. This came about through legislation resulting from the public's criticism of education and its failure to supply trained personnel for careers deemed vital for the national well-being. This legislation, labeled the National Defense Education Act, passed in September, 1958, became a most important landmark in American education, as well as one of great significance to the guidance movement, for its acknowledgement of the vital link between our national well-being, personnel needs, and education. This act provided special benefits for youth guidance in five of its ten titles or sections. Of these, perhaps Title V was the key to the upsurge in counseling and guidance program development. Gibson and Higgins (1966) indicated that this title provided for "(1) grants to states for stimulating the establishment and maintenance of local guidance programs, and (2) grants to institutions of higher education for the training of guidance personnel to staff local programs" (p. 7).

Gibson and Higgins go on to point out that 6 years later (September, 1964), the impact of the act could be detected in announcements from the United States Department of Health, Education and Welfare, which pointed out that the act had, in that short period of time, achieved the following:

National Defense Education Act (Sept. 1958)

1. Made grants to states of approximately $30 million, thereby helping bring the number of full-time high school counselors from 12,000 (one for every 960 students) in 1958 to 30,000 (one for every 510 students) in 1964.
2. Through the end of the 1964–1965 academic year, supported 480 institutes designed to improve counseling capabilities, which were attended by more than 15,700 secondary school counselors and teachers preparing to become counselors.
3. From 1959 to 1964, made it possible for 109 million scholastic aptitude and achievement tests to be given to public secondary school students and over 3 million to private secondary school students.
4. Helped 600,000 students obtain or continue their college education with federal loans.
5. Trained 42,000 skilled technicians to meet critical manpower needs.
6. Granted 8,500 graduate fellowships, a first step toward meeting the need for many more college teachers. (p. 7)

Stimulated by this rapid growth in counseling and guidance, standards for the certification and prerformance of school counselors were developed and upgraded; the criteria used by accrediting associations for school guidance program evaluation were strengthened; and noticeable progress was made in counselor training. Many writers in the field were to note that guidance had come of age—that there was a "new era."

For example, Donovan (1959) wrote about a new era for guidance in which he pointed out that "the testing expert and professional counselor enter the picture to give scientific aid in getting each child in touch with those teachers and courses best calculated to free his abilities" (p. 241). His writings and those of others further discussed the movement from an era of mass education to one in which each child was treated as an individual with "counseling personnel becoming indispensable auxiliaries to administrators and teachers" (p. 241).

The following year, Klopf (1960) called for an expanding role for the high school counselor. He pointed out that "as populations increase, schools will become larger and taxes become greater in most communities. Instructional services will increase in communities, but guidance programs may not increase accordingly" (p. 418). He suggested that new uses and approaches to homeroom group guidance, small discussion groups, and group counseling needed to be explored. He also suggested that guidance workers should view themselves not only as counselors but as individuals concerned with total learning, including the personal and social relations of the student:

If he has a knowledge of individual behavior, the social structure of the school and the community, and awareness of the world of today and the future, this in all the ongoing activities of the school he should share. (p. 418)

In the 1960s one of the most important developments for the school counseling and guidance movement was the "Statement of Policy for Secondary School Counselors" (1964), which was developed and approved as an official policy statement by the American School Counselors Association (ASCA). This effort to specify the role and function of the school counselor involved more than 6,000 school counselors plus teachers, school administrators, and other educators.

C. Gilbert Wrenn's classic contribution of the 1960s, *The Counselor in a Changing World,* also examined the counselor's role in a society with changing ideas about human behavior and changing schools. Wrenn (1962) noted the growing complexity of the counselor's task:

> It is not enough for the counselor to understand youth in isolation, as it were. More than ever before, the counselor must understand not only the student, but himself and his adult contemporaries as they attempt to adjust to a rapidly changing technology and world order. (p. 8)

C. Harold McCully (1965) implied that if school counselors were to move toward bona fide professionalization, "they cannot afford do define their function on the basis of a retrospective analysis of what counselors have done in the past as technicians" (p. 405). He forecast needed new directions in which the counselor functioned as a consultant and agent for change, directions that would require substantive study of the dynamics of cultural and social change.

By the 1970s the school guidance counselor had inherited a series of stereotypes, the value and validity of which had to be determined. What historians recorded about guidance in the 1970s attested to their concern for these stereotypes and their behavior in dealing with them. These stereotypes were:

> *The Stereotype of Responsibility.* The belief by parents and others that counselors have certain responsibilities such as ensuring that the student takes the "right" courses, selects the appropriate college, takes necessary standardized examinations, meets application deadlines, and so forth.

> *The Stereotype of Failure.* The belief that the counselor is responsible for keeping individuals from failing—that the counselor is a buffer between success and failure. As a predictor of outcomes that determine decisions, the counselor can assess risks and chances for success or failure.

> *The Stereotype of Occupational Choice.* Perhaps more consistent and widespread than another is the view of the counselor as the person who can tell a student what occupation to enter—who can make this "once-in-a-lifetime" decision for individuals. After all, the counselor is the one with the various interest and aptitude tests and occupational fields—and one is constantly referred to as the person to see about industrial, armed services, and educational recruitment materials. (Munson, 1971, pp. 16–17)

In 1973, the Report of the National Commission on the Reform of Secondary education published its report with 32 recommendations for the improvement of secondary education. Although the majority of these held implications for the functioning of the secondary school counselor, the following were of particular importance:

Recommendation Number 6: Bias in Counseling
Counselors should insure that all students regardless of sex or ethnic background are afforded equal latitude and equally positive guidance in making educational choices.

Recommendation Number 9: Career Education
Career education advisory councils, including representatives of labor, business, community, students, and former students, should be established to assist in planning and implementing career education programs in comprehensive high schools.

Career awareness programs should be initiated as an integral part of the curriculum to assure an appreciation of the dignity of work.

Opportunities for exploration of a variety of career clusters should be available to students in grades eight to ten.

In grades eleven and twelve, students should have opportunities to acquire hard skills in a career area of their choice. This training should involve experience in the world outside school and should equip the student with job-entry skills.

Recommendation Number 10: Job Placement
Suitable job placement must be an integral part of the career education program for students planning to enter the labor force upon leaving school. Secondary schools should establish an employment office staffed by career counselors and clerical assistants. The office should work in close cooperation with the state employment services. Agencies certifying counselors for secondary schools should require such counselors to show experience in job placements as a condition for granting initial certification.

Recommendation Number 12: Alternative Paths to High School Completion
A wide variety of paths leading to completion of requirements for graduation from high school should be made available to all students. Individual students must be encouraged to assume major responsibility for the determination of their educational goals, the development of the learning activities needed to achieve those goals, and the appraisal of their progress. (pp. 15–17)

During the mid-1970s and early 1980s, a number of developments influenced counselors in schools and frequently in other settings as well. As noted in more detail in Chapter 13, the accountability movement of this period resulted in many school counseling programs developing more relevant data-based programs, usually based on objective needs assessments. A major publication of this period, *Guidance and Counseling in the Schools* (1979), was the outgrowth of a national survey directed by Dr. Edwin L. Herr and jointly sponsored by the American Personnel and Guidance Association* and the Counseling and Guidance Office of the United States Department of Education. While state certification laws have in recent generations governed the credentialing of counselors in schools in all states, school counselors also became increasingly interested in the movement to license counselors for practice outside school settings. By 1985 16 states had passed legislation to license counselors (Alabama, Arkansas, Flor-

*American Personnel and Guidance Association officially changed its name to the American Association for Counseling and Development (AACD) in 1983.

ida, Georgia, Idaho, Maryland, Mississippi, Missouri, Montana, North Carolina, Ohio, Oklahoma, South Carolina, Tennessee, Texas, and Virginia) and others were preparing to follow suit. In 1983, the presidentially appointed National Commission on Excellence in Education issued their report, entitled *A Nation at Risk,* which cited as its primary evidence the decline in standardized achievement test results and resulted in recommendations for longer school days, more effective school discipline, a return to basics, and more. While there were no specific references to school counseling programs, many inferences for such programs could be drawn.

The Development of Institutional and Agency Counseling Programs

The mental health movement, like the vocational guidance movement, owed much of its impetus in the early 1900s to the efforts of one man. This man was Clifford Beers, who was neither a physician nor a psychologist, but was for a number of years a patient in a mental institution suffering from schizophrenia. During his confinement Beers (1908) wrote:

> I soon observed that the only patients who were not likely to be subjected to abuse were the only ones least in need of care and treatment. The violent, noisy, and troublesome patient was abused because he was violent, noisy and troublesome. The patient too weak, physically or mentally, to attend to his own wants was frequently abused because of that very helplessness which made it necessary for the attendants to wait upon him. Usually a restless or troublesome patient placed in the violent ward was assaulted the very first day. This procedure seemed to be a part of the established code of dishonor. The attendants imagined that the best way to gain control of a patient was to cow him from the first. In fact, these fellows—nearly all of them ignorant and untrained—seemed to believe that 'violent cases' could not be handled in any other way. (pp. 164–165)

In another statement, Beers (1908) wrote:

> Most sane people think that no insane person can reason logically. But that is not so. Upon unreasonable premises I made most reasonable deductions, and at that time when my mind was in its most disturbed condition. Had the newspapers which I read on that day which I supposed to be February 1st borne a January date, I might not then, for so long a time, have believed in special editions. Probably I should have inferred that the regular editions had been held back. But the newspapers I had were dated about two weeks ahead. Now if a sane person on February 1st receives a newspaper dated February 14, he will be fully justified in thinking something wrong, either with the publication or with himself. But the shifted calendar which had planted itself in my mind meant as much to me as the true calendar does to any sane businessman. During the seven hundred and ninety-eight days of depression I drew countless incorrect deductions, and essentially the mental process was not other than that which takes place in a well-ordered mind. (pp. 57–58)

These and similar descriptions aroused the public to initiate humanitarian reforms and scientific inquiry into the problems of mental illnesses and their treatment. With the help of a few psychologists of the time, such as William

James and Adolph Meyer, the mental hygiene movement was launched to educate the general public on a better appreciation of the plight and treatment of disturbed persons (Shane, Shane, Gibson, and Munger, 1971, p. 39).

At the same time the viewpoint that persons are products of both their environment and their heredity was re-emerging. As a result, a new type of institution for dealing locally with mental illness was gaining support. This institution was to become the forerunner of our present-day community mental health center. It was called a psychopathic hospital.

According to Bloom (1984):

> It was to be located in the community, and it was to provide treatment rather than custodial care. The rationale for the psychopathic hospital was based on a set of what were then quite radical ideas. First, it was believed that patients should be identified and treated soon after the onset of their disorder. Second, it was believed that patients should not be isolated from their families, friends, and other sources of support. Third, it was believed that patients' families could provide very useful information to those persons responsible for the patients' treatment and that such information would be far easier to obtain if the treatment facility were in the community. Finally, the psychopathic hospital was designed to stimulate in local physicians an increased interest in the problem of mental illness. (p. 15)

During the same time, community after-care services for former psychiatric patients began to emerge, and local hospitals began to develop psychiatric diagnostic and out-patient clinics. Community efforts also increased to raise the standards of treatment and prevention of mental disorders and to establish local clinics for disturbed children. As the American public became increasingly aware of the extent and impact of mental illness, the possibility of preventive or early treatment began to be discussed.

World War I not only stimulated the development and post-war usage of standardized group psychological tests, it also resulted in two acts significant to the development of one of the early specializations in counseling, rehabilitation counseling. The first of these, the Civilian Vocational Rehabilitation Act (Public Law 236, 1920), was followed in 1921 by Public Law 47. The latter created the Veteran's Bureau and provided, among other benefits, a continuation of vocational rehabilitation services for veterans, including counseling and guidance:

> The counseling provided for veterans was one of the most important features of the Veteran's Administration's vocational rehabilitation and education program. It had been observed early in the vocational rehabilitation program for the disabled veterans of World War I that good vocational counseling and guidance was of crucial importance. The lesson was not overlooked in the legislation for World War II veterans and in the implementation of that legislation. All Public Law 16 trainees were required to select their vocational objectives only after formal vocational evaluation and counseling. Those training under Public Law 346 could receive counseling services if they requested them. (Obermann, 1965, p. 190)

The term *rehabilitation counselor*, however, did not appear in professional literature until the late 1930s. Since then, rehabilitation counseling has generally come to be recognized as basically psychological counseling that specializes in the rehabilitation of persons with physical as well as social and emotional problems. In the history of its development, the practice of rehabilitation counseling seems to have gone through several models, described by Jacques (1969, p. 17) as

1. Vocational agent, trainer, or worker model.
2. Vocational counselor or coordinator of services model.
3. Psychotherapeutic model.
4. Community-centered team counselor model.

The quarter century from 1904 to 1929 was a period of rapid growth in solid scientific research in many different areas. As Mueller (1979) reported:

> While there may have been an overly optimistic view of the fruits of mathematization and postulational procedures, it was a period in which the foundations for such techniques as factor analysis, test theory, scaling, etc., were broadly expanded. In areas such as physiological and sensory psychology, human and animal learning, and social and abnormal psychology, the empirical bases of psychology as science were made as firm in that period as they have ever been. This period established psychology as a provable science, not just an "in-principle" science. (p. 20)

During the first half of this century, the community mental health movement reflected a great deal of diverstiy and encompassed both ideological and practical features. Jeger and Slotnick (1982) noted that:

> As a philosophy, it has its roots in the fields of social psychiatry and public health, which recognized the iatrogenic effects of institutionalization, redefined "mental illness" as a social problem, advocated alternatives to hospitalization and called for community change for purposes of preventing mental health problems. As a methodology, community mental health refers to specific programs that sought to translate this ideology into practice. (p. 15)

After World War II a series of federal legislative acts defined the mandates of agencies and in so doing provided operational definitions of community mental health practices. The federal government's first major entrance into the public mental health arena began with the passage of the National Mental Health Act of 1946, which established the National Institute of Mental Health, thus announcing the federal government's interest and involvement in public mental health.

During and immediately after World War II, counselors again found increasing opportunities in the Veteran's Administration vocational rehabilitation and educational services as these were rapidly expanded to accommodate the needs of U.S. Armed Services personnel and ex-service personnel.

In the 1950s, another counseling speciality began to emerge in the form of marriage and family counseling. Although historically this movement appeared to have been initiated in the early 1930s, the dramatic post-World War II increase in the separation and divorce rate of young couples led to rapid developments in marital therapy. In the 1960s, dramatic increases in new styles of coupling, marriage, and living together further stimulated interest in providing professional counseling assistance to couples and families.

Also during the 1960s and 1970s, increases in substance abuse and increased public awareness of the extent and seriousness of the problem at all age levels led to research, the development of training programs, and the growth of another area of specialization for counselors. Special attention to preparing specialists for correctional counseling and counseling the elderly reflected a concern for the needs of these populations as well.

This period also saw a rapid expansion of community mental health services. In 1955 Congress passed a Mental Health Study Act, which established a joint commission on mental illness and health. This study resulted in a report entitled "Action for Mental Health" (1961), which led in 1963 to the Community Mental Health Centers Act (Public Law 88–164) (Jeger and Slotnick, p. 16–17).

The initial 2,000 centers were expected to provide five essential services:

1. Inpatient (for short-term stays);
2. Outpatient;
3. Partial hospitalization (i.e., day and/or night hospitals);
4. Emergency care (i.e., 24-hour crisis services); and
5. Consultation (i.e., indirect service) and community education (i.e., prevention).

In order for a center to be considered "comprehensive," five additional services were required: (a) diagnostic; (b) rehabilitation; (c) precare and aftercare; (d) training; and (e) research and evaluation (Jeger and Slotnick, p. 17).

> The Community Mental Centers Amendments of 1975 (Public Law 94–63) redefined the notion of a comprehensive community mental health center from the five minimum and five optional services to a mandated set of twelve services. They include the five originally established as "essential" plus seven additional services: (1) special services for children (diagnosis, treatment, liaison, and follow-up); (2) special services for the elderly; (3) preinstitutional screening and alternative treatment (as pertains to the courts and other public agencies); (4) follow-up for persons discharged from state mental hospitals; (5) transitional living for persons discharged from state mental hospitals; (6) alcoholism services (prevention, treatment, and rehabilitation); and (7) drug abuse services (prevention, treatment and rehabilitation). In addition to expanding the mandated number of services, the 1975 amendments also obligated centers to allocate 2 percent of their operating budgets for program evaluation.
>
> The mandated delivery of these twelve services was modified in the Community Mental Health Extension Act of 1978 (Public Law 95–622). Specifically, new centers were required to provide six services (inpatient, outpatient, emergency, screening, follow-up of discharged inpatients, and consultation/education), and were allowed to phase in gradually the remaining six of the twelve services over their initial 3 years of operation (i.e., partial hospitalization, children's services, elderly services, transitional halfway houses, alcohol abuse, and drug abuse services. (Jeger & Slotnick, 1982, p. 17)

In considering all the various provisions for services mandated by legislation during the past 17 years, we can convey the spirit of the community mental health movement. The ten characteristics delineated by Bloom (1984) as differentiating community mental health from "traditional" clinical practice can serve to identify both the ideological and operational aspects of the movement:

- First, as opposed to institutional (i.e., mental hospital) practice, the community provides the practice setting.

- Second, rather than an individual patient, a total population or community is the target; hence the term "catchment area" to define a given center's area of responsibility.
- A third feature concerns the type of service delivered, that is, offering preventive services rather than just treatment.
- Continuity of care among the components of a comprehensive system of services constitutes the fourth dimension.
- The emphasis on indirect services, that is, consultation, is the fifth characteristic.
- A sixth characteristic lies in the area of clinical innovations—brief psychotherapy and crisis intervention.
- The emphasis on systematic planning for services by considering the demographics of a population, specifying unmet needs, and identifying "high-risk" groups represents a seventh characteristic.
- Utilizing new person-power resources, especially nonprofessional mental health workers, constitutes the eighth dimension.
- The ninth dimension is defined in terms of the community control concept, which holds that consumers should play central roles in establishing service priorities and evaluating programs.
- Finally, the tenth characteristic identifies community mental health as seeking environmental causes of human distress, in contrast to the traditonal intrapsychic emphasis.

Although a majority of community mental health workers might agree that these characteristics reflect the orientation of community mental health, there is much less agreement on the emphasis of these concepts in practice. (Bloom, 1984, pp. 3–8)

In the 1980s, significant federal legislation in the form of the Mental Health Systems Act passed Congress and was signed into law by President Carter. In addition to continuing many of the provisions of the original act, other provisions broadened the scope of care for disturbed children and adolescents. The election of President Reagan in 1980, however, led to new economic policies at the federal level, which included repealing the budgetary authorizations of this act. As a result, in the 1980s, states and local communities have increasingly been called upon to assume the financing of mental health care facilities and programs.

Summary: Implications of the Past for the Present and Future

In retrospect, we have examined the need for humankind from the time of Adam down through the ages for advice and counsel, to understand themselves and their relationships to their fellow human beings, and to recognize and develop their own potential. In responding to these needs, the chieftains and elders of the ancient tribal societies were perhaps the first forerunners, the ancient counterpart, of the present-day counselor. Later, in the early civilizations, the philosophers, priests, or other representatives of the gods were seen in roles offering advice and counseling. Often "treatment" for the mentally ill was cruel, even when administered by physicians. The role of religion in the counsel and advice of the young in particular, but not exclusively, continued through the Middle Ages, supplemented by sporadic efforts of talent identification and development and even planned career placement. From the Middle Ages onward, teachers also were increasingly expected to provide "guidance" for their pupils—often of the most directive kind. To supplement these efforts, books began to appear with increasing frequency from the 18th century onward that focused on providing advice and counsel to youth in meeting many of the problems of the times, especially those concerning occupational choice. Meanwhile, many leading statesmen, philosophers, scientists, and educators were laying a philosophical groundwork that would eventually support and nurture an embryonic movement to establish psychology as a science and academic discipline in its own right, with an impact on school and community settings.

The school counseling and guidance movement, which for many years was unique to American education, in its beginnings had a vocational guidance emphasis but was shortly to be influenced by a multitude of other movements, especially psychological testing, mental health, and progressive education. Later in the 20th century, the interdisciplinary character of the movement was further emphasized through influences from such movements as group dynamics, counseling psychology, education of the gifted, career education, and placement.

The public or community aspects of the mental health movement initially focused on home confinement and treatment, if at all. An early significant development was the establishment of mental hospitals, characterized in the United States in the 19th century, by state support for the establishment of state mental hospitals. However, at the turn of the century (1908), the mental health movement was stirred by the writings of Clifford Beers, and local mental health treatment centers began to emerge. These community after-care services were the forerunners of the present-day community mental health centers.

Three significant legislative acts that were to further stimulate the counseling movement were the Civilian Vocational Rehabilitation Act (1920), the Mental Health Study Act (1955), and the Community Mental Health Centers Act (1963). Later in this century, public need led to the development of specializations in marriage and family, substance abuse, corrections, and elderly counseling.

Over the years the movement has not been without its pioneers and heroes. Of course, the great humanistic teachers of history—Christ, Mohammed, Buddha—and far-sighted leaders such as Plato, Aristotle, Pestalozzi, Rousseau, and Charlemagne would have been charter members and undoubtedly elected officers of any counseling association of their time in history. In the United States, one can easily envision the Franklins, Jeffersons, Lincolns, and Roosevelts receiving honorary life memberships in the American Association for Counseling and Development for the contributions to the eventual growth of the movement. But the real heroes have been persons such as Parsons, Beers, Davis, Reed, Weaver, and Hill—those early, persistent, and farsighted pioneers of the movement, whose efforts were later recognized and advanced and then further enriched by the giants of the last half of the 20th century—Carl R. Rogers, E. G. Williamson, and C. Gilbert Wrenn.

It is said that a movement must have a cause and leadership to survive. This brief review of some historical highlights of the development of counseling and guidance in the United States should indicate to you that neither has been lacking. As the past illuminates the future, it is possible to predict that regardless of the wonderful scientific and technological advances that await humankind in the generations ahead, many persons, young and old, will search out the counsel and advice of the trained, while others will still seek self and other understandings for the development of their potential or the solution of their problems. Let us therefore proceed to the next chapter to examine an introduction to the activities of the trained professional counselor.

References

Aubrey, R. F. (1977). Historical development of guidance and counseling and implications for the future. *Personnel and Guidance Journal, 55,* 288–295.

Beers, C. (1908). *A mind that found itself.* New York: Longmans Green, and republished by Doubleday, 1953.

Belkin, G. S. (1975). *Practical counseling in the schools.* Dubuque, IA: William C. Brown.

Bloom, B. L. (1984). *Community mental health: A general introduction.* (2nd ed.). Belmont, CA: Brooks/Cole.

Brewer, J. M. (1932). *Education as guidance.* New York: Macmillan.

Donovan, C. F., S. J. (1959) A new era for guidance. *School and Society, 87,* 241.

Ewing, D. B. (1975). Direct from Minnesota—E. G. Williamson. *Personnel and Guidance Journal, 54,* 77–87.

Faust, V. (1968). *The history of elementary school counseling: Overview and critique.* Boston: Houghton Mifflin.

Feingold, G. A. (1947). A new approach to guidance. *School Review, 4,* 542–550.

Ford Foundation. (1972). *A foundation goes to school.* New York: Author.

Gibson, R. L., & Higgins, R. E. (1966). *Techniques of guidance: An approach to pupil analysis.* Chicago: Science Research Associates.

Goshen, C. E. (1967). *Documentary history of psychiatry: A sourcebook on history principles* (pp. 501–504). New York: Philosophical Library.

Hinshaw, R. P. (1942). The concept of adjustment and problems of norms. *Psychological Review, 49,* 284–292.

Jacques, M. E. (1969). *Rehabilitation counseling: Scope and services.* Boston: Houghton Mifflin.

Jeger, A. M., & Slotnick, R. S. (1982). *Community mental health and behavioral-ecology: A handbook of theory, research and practice.* New York: Plenum.

Johansen, J. H., Collins, H. W., & Johnson, J. A. (1975). *American education* (2nd ed.). Dubuque, IA: William C. Brown.

Klopf, G. (1960). The expanding role of the high-school counselor. *School and Society, 88,* 417–419.

Mallart, J. (1955). The history of the guidance movement: Western civilization–Spanish origins. In R. K. Hall & J. A. Lauwerys (Eds.), *Yearbook of education—1955.* Cleveland, OH: William Collins & World.

Mayo, A. D. (1872). Moral instruction in common schools. *National Education Association Journal of Addresses and Proceedings.* 11–24.

McCully, C. H. (1965). The counselor: Instrument of change. *Teachers College Record, 66,* 405–412.

Mueller, C. G. (1979). Some origins of psychology as science. In M. R. Rosenzweig & L. W. Porter (Eds.), *Annual review of psychology, Vol. 30* (pp. 9–29). Palo Alto, CA: Annual Reviews, Inc.

Munson, H. L. (1971). *Foundation of developmental guidance.* Boston: Allyn & Bacon.

National Commission on the Reform of Secondary Education. (1973). *The Reform of Secondary Education.* New York: McGraw-Hill.

New York State Teachers Association. (1935). Guidance in the secondary school. *New York State Teachers Association Educational Monograph #3.* New York: Author.

Obermann, C. E. (1965). *A history of vocational rehabilitation in America.* Minneapolis: T. S. Denison.

Parsons, F. (1909). *Choosing a vocation.* Boston: Houghton Mifflin.

Rockwell, P. J. & Rothney, J. W. M. (1961). Some social ideas of pioneers in the guidance movement. *Personnel and Guidance Journal, 40,* 349–354.

Rogers, C. R. (1942). *Counseling and psychotherapy.* Cambridge, MA: The Riverside Press.

Rogers, C. R. (1951). *Client-centered therapy.* Boston: Houghton Mifflin.

Shane, J. G., Shane, H. G., Gibson, R. L., & Munger, P. F. (1971). *Guiding human development: The counselor and the teacher in the elementary school.* Worthington, OH: Charles A. Jones.

Sturtevant, S. M. (1937). Some questions regarding the developing guidance movement. *School Review, 14,* 347–356.

Traxler, A. E. (1950). Emerging trends in guidance. *School Review, 58,* 14–23.

Williamson, E. G. (1939). *How to counsel students: A manual of techniques for clinical counselors.* New York: McGraw-Hill.

Wrenn, C. G. (1962). *The counselor in a changing world.* Washington, D.C.: American Personnel and Guidance Association.

Zytowski, D. G. (1972). Four hundred years before Parsons. *Personnel and Guidance Journal, 50,* 443–450.

CHAPTER 2

TRADITIONAL AND CURRENT
ACTIVITIES OF COUNSELORS

Introduction

In the study of any profession, it is appropriate to ask "What is the profession of . . . (i.e., counseling)?" and "What do they (i.e., counselors) do?" The objective of this chapter is to respond to those questions. In this chapter, then, we begin by examining counseling as a helping profession and proceed to identify activities through which the professional counselor carries out his or her responsibilities.

Counseling as a Helping Profession

In examining counseling as a profession, we begin by identifying counseling as a helping profession; a concept that forms the basis for the role and function of the counselor in today's society. A "helping" profession may be described as one in which the members are especially trained and licensed or certificated to perform a unique and needed service for the fellow human beings of their society. Helping professionals serve; they are recognized by the society as the sole professional providers of the unique and needed services. The helping professions include medicine, law, dentistry, education, psychology, and social work. Each of these professions has the roots of its development and existence in the nature of humankind and the nature of society, past and present. It is on these bases that services are determined and programs for providing these services are developed. The paragraphs that follow briefly review some of the basic concepts of humankind and society as a basis for the helping profession in general and the profession of counseling in particular.

In the instance of the helping professions, including counseling, it is appropriate to begin with the very foundation of their existence—namely, the human client. This client has certain distinguishing characteristics that provide a basis for the profession of counseling and the institutions and agencies through which this profession contributes its special knowledge and skills to the development of peoples and societies. Although any attempt to characterize such a versatile and ever-changing species as human beings is fraught with peril, we have and do possess certain stable yet unique traits that set us apart from other living species. In the main these are what we might term the "privileges" of the human race. They provide not only the basis or focus of our "being," but the basis for our "doing" as well. They also suggest roles that human beings can play in helping their fellow human beings. These distinguishing characteristics include the following:

- Humans are among the weakest species at birth.

We are born without the genetically imprinted behaviors possessed by many forms of life. Young animal life in the forests and jungles of the world can survive without adult help; young human life cannot. Our early survival—for years—is dependent solely upon the attention, care, and affection of others. The human need for love and care and the degree to which it is provided becomes a critical basis for the lifelong adjustment or lack of it for the individual.

- Humankind has the greatest potential for growth and development of all the species.

The brain itself triples in physical size, and multiples even more in capacity. This brainpower, coupled with a surplus of energy (over all other species) gives us almost limitless possibilities. The realization of human potential does not, however, rest with the individual alone, but is dependent on many environmental variables and assistance in recognizing and developing one's potential.

- Humankind has the highest level of communication skills, skills that enable us to express our thoughts in detail to many others; skills to teach our language to others (even other animal species at certain levels), skills that enable us to record, to send, and to receive.

These dual capacities, sending and receiving, in both word and gesture, form the bases for human relationships skills and for love and affection, which in turn forms the primary stimulus for the human race. This ability to relate to others thus becomes the core of a happy, well-adjusted life.

- The human species exhibits a wider range of differences than any other.

These differences not only clearly distinguish each human from every other human, but also multiply the potential of the society and stimulate the advancement of civilizations. The concept of individual differences provides the rationale for client analysis in the helping professions.

- Human beings manipulate and are manipulated by their environment.

Thus, the behavior of a human being cannot be adequately understood apart from the environmental context within which it occurs. Thus, environmental analysis is becoming increasingly important to the professional counselor.

- Humankind is the only living organism that captures the time stream.

We can recall the past, act in the present, and plan for the future. This gives humans the capability for building on their past experiences, avoiding past mistakes, anticipating the future, and planning for the development of their potential.

- Humankind has the ability to reason and to gain insight.

These twin factors enable us to make reasoned choices among alternatives and to change. This aptitude for planned individual change is significant in the important arenas of individual development and social adjustment (relationships with one's peers). Our ability to understand ourselves and act rationally also contributes to the maturing process.

From images of the human species, McCully (1969) drew inferences for counseling and other helping relationships as follows:

1. All men at birth possess the potential for the distinguishing characteristics of the human species; and
2. The environmental conditions the individual experiences from birth on may either nourish or suppress their realization. (pp. 134, 135)

In light of these premises, it is appropriate to suggest at even this early point in our discussions that a fundamental basis for counseling program development must be rooted in our understanding of the characteristics of all our clientele, including their needs, plus an understanding of the environment that shapes their characteristics and needs. For counselors, this implies learning in human growth and development and our sociocultural foundations.

It is also important to recognize the role of societal needs and expectancies in the development and functioning of a profession. The brief historical review in Chapter 1 indicated some of the social influences on our profession.

Traditional Activities

The historical review of the counseling movement in Chapter 1 noted the contributions of the many disciplines and influences that have consistently been adding and expanding its areas of emphasis. Noted were eras of vocational or career guidance, mental health, standardized testing for client analysis, education as guidance, group activities, and the identification and college placement of the gifted. Other "movements of the times" included the community mental health agency movement, the counseling psychology movement, the development of specialized counseling programs for rehabilitation, substance abuse, correctional, marriage and family, and elderly counseling, the re-emphasis of the impact of environment on the individual's growth and development, and a currently renewed emphasis on preventive intervention. However, despite the relatively short period of time that counseling has existed as a profession, certain traditional activities, basic principles, and identifiable patterns of program organization have emerged. An understanding of these can provide some insights into the not infrequently asked question, "How come counselors do what they do the way they do it?" Since many of the early training programs emphasized school counselor preparation, many of the influential texts had this orientation as well. These authors tended to discuss counselor functions in terms of "services." For example, over 25 years ago, Froehlich (1958, pp. 13–21) in discussing counseling and guidance services to pupils in schools identified basic services to pupils in groups and individually, services to the instructional staff, services to the administration, and research services. Hatch and Costar (1961) also noted that "it seems more desirable to think of the guidance program as a program of services—services which can be defined, recognized, administered, and evaluated. It is then possible to define a guidance program as a program of services specially designed to improve the adjustment of the individual for whom it was organized" (p. 14). They went on to suggest that:

- Guidance services are for all concerned.
- Guidance services are for all school levels.
- Guidance services are primarily preventive in nature.
- The teacher plays a major role in the guidance program.
- The program of guidance services needs trained personnel.
- The program of guidance services requires coordination.
- The guidance program uses and improves on present practices.
- Guidance services are not an added activity.
- Guidance services are a group of facilitating services.
- The training background of guidance workers presupposes certain elements.

They concluded their first chapter by identifying the following services as desirable for a school counseling program:

- Pupil inventory service.
- Information service.
- Counseling service.
- Placement service.
- Follow-up and evaluation service.

Zeran and Riccio (1962) identified basic services as analysis of the individual, counseling, placement, and follow-up and informational services (pp. 3–5). Gibson and Higgins (1966) noted that although semantics and labels varied, the basic services were usually identified as pupil analysis, individual counseling, informational activities, group guidance, placement and follow-up, and evaluation and research (p. 8). Shertzer and Stone (1981) enumerated components of guidance programs in schools as follows: an appraisal component; an informational component; a counseling component; a consulting component; a planning, placement, and follow-up component; and an evaluation component. Blocher and Biggs (1983) noted in their discussion of counseling in community settings that counseling psychologists engage in individual and small group counseling around concerns involving educational and vocational planning, personal problem solving and decision-making, family problems, and other activities related to personal growth, prevention, consultation, and, at times, as a psychological educator (pp. 15–17). They noted that assessment strategies must be developed and mastered that permit an understanding of individuals as they interact in natural environments. Finally, counselors must understand processes of human development as they apply to both individuals and social organizations.

In summary, these and numerous other authors point toward certain traditional or basic activities for counselors across all settings, although emphasis may vary, of course. Those prominently identified include individual assessment, environmental assessment, individual counseling, group counseling and guidance, career development, placement, and follow-up. Recently, preventive intervention has also received renewed attention. These are discussed briefly in the paragraphs that follow. Later chapters discuss these and related activities in greater detail.

Individual Assessment

Individual assessment is that activity which seeks, through systematic assessment efforts, to identify the characteristics and potential of every client. This activity is based on the fundamental premises that persons are similar in some ways but different in others and that techniques for assessing these similarities and differences should be a part of the counselor's professional repertoire. This activity is often considered a primary skill of the professional counselor because it provides a data base for more readily understanding the person in the counseling setting, the effective planning of group counseling activities that reflect the client interests and needs, the development of responsive career and human potential development programs, and the organization of systematic placement and follow-up programs. Often referred to as individual inventory, assessment, or appraisal, this activity promotes the client's self-understanding, as well as better understandings by counselors and other helping professionals. This activity received initial stimulus as a result of the standardized testing movement. Even today, standardized test results are the most frequently used objective data in individual analysis. Other popular and traditional techniques are observation and observation reports, self-reporting techniques such as the autobiography, and, in recent years, an increasing use of values clarification techniques. It should be noted that other helping professional specialists also have diagnostic skills and responsibilities. For example, a school counselor will often consult with school psychologists and psychometrists as specialists in psychological assessment, including individual testing, and with school social workers as specialists in environmental and case study analysis. Chapters 7 and 8 will discuss these and other techniques for human resource assessment in greater detail.

Counseling

Individual counseling, since the early days of the counseling movement, has been identified as the core activity through which all the other activities become meaningful. Counseling is a one-to-one helping relationship that focuses upon a person's growth and adjustment and problem-solving and decision-making needs. It is a client-centered process that demands confidentiality. This process is initiated by establishing a state of psychological contact or relationship between the counselor and the counselee and progresses as certain conditions essential to the success of the counseling process prevail. These include counselor genuineness or congruence, respect for the client, and an empathic understanding of the counselee's internal frame of reference. Although each counselor will, in time, develop his or her own personal theory to guide personal practice, established theories provide a basis for examination and learning. It must also be mentioned that effective counseling not only requires counselors with the highest levels of training and professional skills, but a certain type of person as well. Counseling programs will suffer in effectiveness and credibility unless counselors exhibit the traits of understanding, warmth, humaneness, and positive attitudes toward humankind. Chapter 5 will discuss individual counseling in greater detail.

Group Counseling and Guidance

In recent generations groups have become increasingly popular as a means of providing organized and planned assistance to individuals for a wide range of needs. Counselors provide such assistance through group counseling or group guidance. In schools, students have been organized into groups for what might be called guidance purposes since long before any counseling or guidance label was bestowed on the activity. The organization of courses and group meetings to dispense primarily occupational information can be traced back to before the evolution of the counseling movement. Homeroom grouping served a guidance as well as an administrative function long before being labeled as such. However, in 1934, a textbook by H. C. McKown bore the title *Home Room Guidance*. With the increasing importance and attention given to extracurricular activities in schools in the 1920s and 1930s, there were some who suggested these activities also were a type of group guidance experience. Although various activities, from time to time, have been given the label *group guidance,* the most consistent definition of this service is one that views it as an activity designed to provide individuals with information or experiences that promote their career or educational understandings and personal social growth and adjustment. Some traditional group guidance activities that have become familiar to most high school students are career days, college days, and orientation days.

In recent generations, group counseling has also been viewed as a basic but different activity than group guidance. Whereas group guidance focuses on providing information and developmental experiences, group counseling tends to focus more on the problem solving and adjustment needs of persons through a process very similar to individual counseling. Gazda (1984) makes distinctions between group guidance and group counseling in the school setting as follows:

Group Guidance

Group guidance was organized to prevent the development of problems (see Figure 2–1). The content included educational-vocational-personal-social information not otherwise systematically taught in academic courses. The typical setting was the classroom. Typical class size ranged from approximately twenty to thirty-five. Providing accurate information for use in improved understanding of self and others was the direct emphasis in group guidance; attitude change frequently was an indirect outcome or goal. The leadership was provided by a classroom teacher or a counselor who utilized a variety of instructional media and group dynamics concepts in motivating students and in obtaining group interaction. Instructional media included unfinished stories, puppet plays, movies, films, filmstrips, guest speakers, audio and videotaped interviews, student reports, and the like. (p. 6)

Group dynamics concepts referred to the process employed in group guidance, such as sociodramas, buzz groups, panels, and other related techniques.

In addition to the classroom-size unit in which group guidance was provided by either the teacher or counselor, group guidance was also implemented in junior and senior high schools through units taught in courses such as social studies, language arts, and home economics. A third means of implementing group guidance was through credit courses (for example, psychology, senior problems, occuaptions). With the increasing interest and need for direct teaching/training in life skills, one can predict an increase in courses that are guidance in nature (courses in psychological education, consumer skills, family management, interpersonal relationships).

[Gazda's] recommendations would provide an impetus for increasing direct teaching of nonacademic content and skills (life skills) in elementary, secondary, higher education, and community mental health agencies. Life-skills training, therefore, replaces group guidance for elementary age children, as well as the whole age spectrum. (pp. 6–7)

Group Counseling

Whereas the goal of group guidance is to provide students with accurate information that will help them make more appropriate plans and life decisions and in this sense is prevention oriented, group counseling is growth engendering and prevention and remediation oriented [See Figure 2–1]. Group counseling is prevention oriented in the sense that the counselees or clients are capable of functioning in society but may

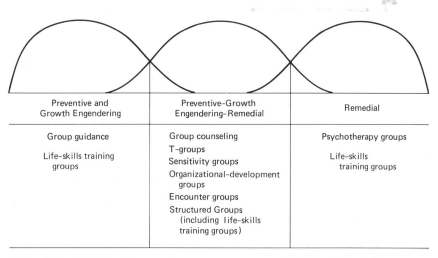

Preventive and Growth Engendering	Preventive-Growth Engendering-Remedial	Remedial
Group guidance Life-skills training groups	Group counseling T-groups Sensitivity groups Organizational-development groups Encounter groups Structured Groups (including life-skills training groups)	Psychotherapy groups Life-skills training groups

Figure 2–1. Relationships among group processes. *(Gazda, 1984, p. 6.)*

be experiencing some "rough spots" in their lives. If counseling is successful, the rough spots may be successfully smoothed with no serious personality defects incurred.

Group counseling is growth engendering insofar as it provides the participants incentive and motivation to make changes that are in their best interest (that is, the participants are motivated to take actions that maximize their potential through self-actualizing behaviors).

Group counseling is remedial for those individuals who have entered into a spiral of self-defeating behavior but who are nevertheless capable of reversing the spiral without counseling intervention. However, with counseling intervention, the counselee is likely to recover, and recover more quickly and with fewer emotional scars.

Although the content of group counseling is very similar to group guidance—including educational, vocational, personal, and social concerns—a number of other factors are quite different. First, *group guidance* is recommended for *all* students on a regularly scheduled basis; *group counseling* is generally recommended only for those who are experiencing continuing or temporary problems that information alone will not resolve.

Group guidance makes an *indirect* attempt to change attitudes and behaviors through accurate information or an emphasis on cognitive or intellective functioning; group counseling makes a *direct* attempt to modify attitudes and behaviors by emphasizing total involvement. Group guidance is applicable to classroom-size groups, whereas group counseling is dependent upon the development of strong group cohesiveness and the sharing of personal concerns, which are most applicable to small, intimate groups. (pp. 7–8)

We might conclude that group guidance activities are most likely to be found in schools. Group counseling will be popular in agency and institutional settings and utilized somewhat, though not as frequently as group guidance, in school settings, while group psychotherapy will most frequently occur in clinics and agency or institutional settings. Group counseling and other group responsibilities of the counselor will be discussed in greater detail in Chapter 6.

Career Assistance

Counselors in both school and nonschool settings are called upon to provide career planning and adjustment assistance to clients. In some agencies, such as community career centers and career centers for special populations, the focus is almost exclusively on the career needs of individuals. Counselors in government employment offices and rehabilitation services have an obvious responsibility to provide career counseling and guidance. Even those counselors in more broadly based programs such as community agencies, secondary schools, and institutions of higher education are expected to provide for the career-oriented needs of the populations they are designed to serve.

Since their earliest inception, both the school guidance movement and the counseling psychology movement have had a strong vocational influence. Traditionally, this activity has been viewed as one in which standardized tests were used for career assessment and planning; descriptive materials and media were accumulated, organized, and then disseminated through planned group activities, as well as used in individual advising and counseling.

For many years in school settings this activity was referred to as the information service (providing occupational and educational information). In the 1970s the concept of this basic service was broadened and a new—now more appropriate—label assigned: career guidance. This term seemed more compatible with the rapidly developing career education movement and also represented in the minds of many (but not all) a broadening of the school counseling program's responsibility in the career development of school-aged youths. This approach is a developmental one that suggests certain experiences and understandings at each stage of one's growth that will provide for the building of appropriate foundations for later career planning and decision-making. Currently, the availability of various computer-based programs and other technological advances are significantly changing the career assistance resources available to counselors and how they use them in interactions with those they serve.

Consultation

Consultation as an acitivity engaged in by counselors is a process for helping a client through a third party or a process for helping a system improve its services to its clientele. The former is usually labeled *triadic consultation* and is popular in working with parents of troubled children or teachers with problem pupils. The latter, appropriately labeled *process consultation,* focuses primarily on the processes that an agency or institution may be using to carry out its mission. Thus, consultation is a form of outreach in which counselors function as team members to assist individual clients or systems that serve clients. In community and other agency settings, consultation is receiving increased attention as a way of preventing severe mental illnesses. In school settings, especially elementary schools, the counselor is being increasingly used as a consultant to teachers and parents. Consultation is discussed in greater detail in Chapter 10.

Placement and Follow-up

Placement and follow-up have more traditionally been a service of school counseling programs with an emphasis on educational placement in courses and programs. In actual practice this has meant that many school counselors have had responsbility for student scheduling, a not unconsuming task and one that has been viewed with considerable controversy as an administrative rather than a counseling function. Another aspect of educational placement are those activities associated with the college admissions of the college-bound. The other obvious component of the placement service—employment placement—has had much less emphasis and planning in schools as the authors of this text discovered in a national survey of school placement activities (Gibson, Mitchell, Stockton, Gerster, and Shafe, 1977). This type of placement seeks to match students seeking part-time or regular employment with available jobs. Follow-up activities are a means of assessing the effectiveness of a program's placement activities. Placement and follow-up activities have taken on increasing importance in schools in which there is increased emphasis on career education and planning. Of course, employment counselors and rehabilitation counselors are very active in the placement and follow-up of their clients. Counselors in all settings should use follow-up procedures for assessing counseling outcomes.

Research

Research is necessary to the advancement of the profession of counseling. It provides a major source of empirically based hypotheses relevant to the ultimate goal of implementing effective counseling. It is a means for producing additional knowledge in our field, for providing factual data to reinforce or guide the counselors' professional judgments, and for seeking answers to questions and issues of professional concern. Research results and the research process are important to program managers and other counselors who find it advantageous to have factual data to reinforce or guide their professional judgment. Whether one is an active researcher or not, a counseling professional cannot afford to ignore or gloss over the important research in the field. It is important to recognize that different client populations, more diverse and usually more intense client problems, plus greater variation in staff backgrounds and hence, treatment approaches, offer counselor researchers the opportunity for unique and significant research investigations. It should be noted that the Community Mental Health Center Amendment of 1975 provides an emphasis on research with local application. Research is discussed in more detail in Chapter 12.

Evaluation and Accountability

While evaluation and accountability are not synonymous terms, they are interrelated and counselors and counseling programs are expected to engage in both. Evaluation is a means or process for assessing the effectiveness of the counselor's activities. It is fundamental to the verification and improvement of professional and program performance. The use of the term *accountability* is an outgrowth of demands that schools and other tax-supported institutions and agencies be held accountable for their actions. In other words, some evidence of accomplishments must be provided in return for tax investments. Accountability also implies that these accomplishments must be provided in return for tax investments. Accountability also implies that these accomplishments be relevant to the purpose for which the agencies or organizations were established. Accountability establishes a basis for relevance, effectiveness, and efficiency. In this context, evaluation can be viewed as a component of the accountability model.

Prevention Strategies

The last 20 years have seen a substantial number of reports on important studies that examined the promotion of mental health through primary prevention using a social psychological perspective. These include the Hahnemann Group (Spivak and Shure, 1974), the Connecticut Group (Allen et al., 1976), Project Aware (Thomas-Rountree and Woodruff, 1982) and the Rochester Pilot Program (1976–1977) (Weissberg and Gesten, 1982). The protective factors that operate in children's responses to stress and disadvantage have also been used to profile "invulnerable," that is, stress-resistant, children (Rutter, 1979; Garmezy et al., 1979). These and other studies suggest that a most attractive alternative to traditional remedial mental health practices is primary prevention, which seeks to prevent the occurrence of the disorder in the first place. Such an alternative suggests a shift in focus to the settings and life conditions that shape early adaptation. In this regard, the school and the family are those social institutions that most profoundly affect early human development. Increasingly, this focus is on the school as a vital ongoing shaping force with organizational advantages for the initiation and development of mental health programs for primary prevention.

Thus, for society there are potential benefits to be derived from devising programs in schools that facilitate positive mental health interacting with a mastery of cognitive development. Since the basic human needs, both sociological and psychological, are to a large measure met either successfully or unsuccessfully in the major institutions of the society with which one associates, the nation's schools for our growing youth become a resource for not only intellectual achievement, but institutions which, in a larger and more important sense, shape the entire societal group, subject to its experiences. As such, the schools have a major role in the promotion of positive mental health. In this effort, a significant contribution can be made through effective primary intervention strategies.

Community and other mental-health-oriented agencies are becoming active in working with families to "head off" anticipated stresses, as well as in working with other stress-prone groups, such as divorced individuals, widows and widowers, and so forth. We can anticipate that counselors in a wide range of settings will be increasingly called upon to develop and implement prevention strategies for serving their clientele.

Basic Principles

Principles tend to form a philosophical framework within which programs are organized and activities are developed. They are guidelines that are derived from the experiences and values of the profession, and they are representative of the views of the majority of the profession's membership. As such, they become fundamental assumptions or a system of beliefs regarding a profession and its role, function, and activities.

For Schools

Here are some principles that suggest that school counseling programs can make their contributions more effectively when:

1. School counseling and guidance programs are designed to serve the developmental and adjustment needs of *all* youth.

2. Pupil guidance is viewed as a process that is continuous throughout the child's formal education.

3. Trained professional counseling personnel are essential for ensuring professional competencies, leadership, and direction. (This does not imply that paraprofessionals cannot make worthwhile contributions.)

4. Certain basic activities are essential to program effectiveness, and these must be specifically planned and developed if they are to be effective.

5. The school counseling program must reflect the uniqueness of the population it serves and the environment in which it seeks to render this service; thus, like individuals, each school guidance program will be different from other programs.

6. Relevant to the preceding, the school counseling program bases its uniqueness on a regular and systematic assessment of the needs of the student clientele and of the characteristics of the environmental setting for the program.

7. The school counseling program is concerned with the total development of the students it serves.

8. An effective instructional program in the school requires an effective program of pupil counseling and guidance. Good education and good guidance are interrelated. They support and complement each other to the student's advantage.

9. Relevant to statement 7, teacher understanding and support of the school counseling program is significant to the success of such programs.

10. The school counseling program is accountable. It recognizes the need to provide objective evidence of accomplishments and the value of those accomplishments.

11. The school counselor is a team member. The counselor shares a concern and programs for youths with psychologists, social workers, teachers, administrators, and other educational professionals and staff.

12. The school counseling program recognizes the right and capability of the individual to make decisions and plans.

13. The school counseling program recognizes and respects the worth and dignity of the individual—*every* individual.

14. The school counseling program recognizes the uniqueness of the individual and the individual's right to that uniqueness.

15. The school counselor is a role model of positive human relations—of unbiased, equal treatment.

It may be concluded that although counseling is a relatively young profession, counselors are developing traditions, establishing their role and worth, and will cope resourcefully and imaginatively with the demands of the future. The following represent some reflections related to traditions, activities, and effective counseling program organization and functioning.

For Community Agencies

Counseling programs in community and other institutional or agency settings represent a wide range of approaches for delivering the services of this helping profession to the citizenry. The development and implementation of these services is based on certain underlying assumptions and basic principles.

The basic assumption that community involvement is essential for relevant and accountable community mental health agencies has implications for the basic principles of those agencies that are community-based. Bloom (1984) has suggested seven such principles for the guidance of professional personnel employed in community mental health agencies as follows (these might be paraphrased slightly for noncommunity based mental health agencies):

Principle 1: Regardless of where your paycheck comes from, think of yourself as working for the community.

Principle 2: If you want to know about a community's mental health needs, ask the community.

Principle 3: As you learn about community-mental-health-related needs, you have the responsibility to tell the community what you are learning.

Principle 4: Help the community establish its own priorities.

Principle 5: You can help the community decide among various courses of action in its efforts to solve its own problems.

Principle 6: In the event that the community being served is so disorganized that representatives of various facets of the community cannot be found, you have the responsibility to find such representatives.

Principle 7: You should work toward the equitable distribution of power in the community. (pp. 429–431)

Summary and Conclusions

Most of the basic principles and traditional activities enumerated here have, as Chapter 1 suggested, an historical relationship with the development of the counseling movement. Although the organization of these activities into program formats differs across the various settings, the mention of the importance of individual assessment, one-to-one counseling, group activities, providing of information and placement, and follow-up would evoke a ringing round of applause from our professional forefathers. Additionally, in recent generations we have come to view consultation as an expected professional service, and the current emphasis on prevention indicates it will be a major role for counselors in the future.

1. Traditions are the hallmarks of a profession. They are often seen as indices of the professional maturity of a discipline and are often synonomous with the guiding principles for a profession. They represent guidelines for newcomers (and reminiscences for the "old timers") to the profession. They become powerful determinants of the profession's goals and actions, and, in time, become extremely resistant to elimination or alteration. Thus, although there are those who have and will call from time to time for drastic

change—even elimination of counseling programs in some settings—it is not the fundamental beliefs or traditional activities of the counselor that must change, but rather how the activity is interpreted or viewed and carried out that will determine the merits of a counseling program in any setting.

2. Relevancy is a key to the success or failure of a program's activities and services. For example, it is doubtful that the counseling skills and understandings that we, your authors, possessed when we first entered the profession would be relevant to the demands of today's youths, and it is certain that both the concept of careers and the career information at our disposal then would not be in any way relevant today. As C. Gilbert Wrenn stressed in his classic book *The World of the Contemporary Counselor* (1973), "the need of the counselor is to attempt to understand contemporary youth and the world in which they live" (p. 3). That is relevancy—seeing and understanding the environment that surrounds our clients, as well as our clients.

We move down from this broad overview of counselor activities to more specifically examine how counselors may function in school settings (Chapter 3) and community and agency settings (Chapter 4).

References

Allen, G. J. et al. (1976). *Community psychology and the schools.* Hillsdale, NJ: Lawrence Erlbaum Associates.

Blocher, D. H., & Biggs, D. A. (1983). *Counseling psychology in community settings.* New York: Springer.

Bloom, B. L. (1984). *Community mental health: A general introduction* (2nd ed.). Belmont, CA: Brooks/Cole.

Froehlich, C. P. (1958). *Guidance services in schools* (2nd ed.). New York: McGraw Hill.

Garmezy, N. (1978). DSM III: Never mind the psychologists—is it good for the children? *Clinical Psychologist,* (Spr-Sum), *31* (3–4), 1, 4–6.

Gazda, G. M. (1984). *Group counseling: A developmental approach* (3rd ed.). Boston, MA: Allyn & Bacon.

Gibson, R. L., & Higgins, R. E. (1966). *Techniques of guidance: An approach to pupil analysis.* Chicago: Science Research Associates.

Gibson, R. L., Mitchell, M. H., Stockton, R., Gerster, D., & Shafe, M. (1977). *The dissemination and implementation of effective concepts and practices in placement and follow-up services for school guidance programs.* State of Indiana.

Hatch, R. N., & Costar, J. W. (1961). *Guidance services in the elementary school.* Dubuque, IA: William C. Brown.

McCully, C. H. (1969). *Challenges for change in counselor education.* (Compiled by L. L. Miller.) Minneapolis, MN: Burgess.

McKown, H. C. (1934). *Home room guidance.* New York: McGraw-Hill.

Rutter, M. (1980). School influences on children's behavior and development: The 1979 Kenneth Blackfan Lecture, Children's Hospital Medical Center, Boston. *Pediatrics,* (Feb.), *65* (2), 208–220.

Shertzer, B., & Stone, S. C. (1981). *Fundamentals of guidance* (4th ed.). Boston: Houghton Mifflin.

Spivack, G., & Shure, M. B. (1974). *Social adjustment of young children.* San Francisco: Jossey-Bass.

Thomson-Rountree, P., & Woodruff, A. E. (1982). An examination of Project Aware: The effects on children's attitudes toward themselves, others and school. *Journal of School Psychology,* (Spring), *20*(1), 20–31.

Weissberg, R. P., & Gesten, E. L. (1982). Considerations for developing effective school-based social problem solving (SPS) training programs. *School Psychology Review, 11*(1), 56–63.

Wrenn, C. G. (1973). *The world of the contemporary counselor.* Boston: Houghton Mifflin.

Zeran, F. R., & Riccio, A. C. (1962). *Organization and administration of guidance services.* Skokie, IL: Rand McNally.

CHAPTER 3

THE SCHOOL COUNSELORS' ROLE AND FUNCTION

Introduction

It is important for counselors in any work setting to be aware of what services school counselors and school counseling programs provide. It is therefore a purpose of this chapter to orient potential counselors, including those interested in school settings, to:

1. The training of counselors.
2. Certifying that counselors are professionally prepared.
3. The role and function of counselors and their supporting professionals in differing educational settings.

Training Programs for Counselors

As previously noted, counseling and guidance programs in schools are an educational development of this century, and they have, until recent years, been unique to the United States and Canadian educational systems; the same is true of training programs for counselors. Similarly, since the initial years of the National Defense Education Act (1958–1960), there has been a rapid growth in both the number and size of counselor training programs. The supporting facts indicate that in 1964 there were 327 institutions of higher education supporting counselor preparation programs with 706 faculty. Hollis and Wantz (1983) reported that by 1983 this number of programs had increased to 506 with 3,064 faculty. Thus, if you had entered a counselor training program in 1964, you could have anticipated a training staff of slightly more than two full-time faculty members; however, if you delayed your entry until 1983, you could expect, on the average, a staff of six full-time faculty members.

Because many of you reading this text may already be enrolled in programs of counselor education, it is quite possible that the initial discussion of this chapter will serve only to remind you to see your advisor about the course work that lies ahead or how your own program may differ or be similar to others. We are certain, however, that you recognize the significant relationships between what you are trained to do and your role and function once you are on the job. Also, as Thomas (1973) noted in *The Schools Next Time:*

> Control of the lower schools (elementary and secondary) by the colleges is again obvious when one remembers that all certified school personnel are college trained; they cannot be licensed without such training. Teachers, counselors, and administrators are all encultured with the biases of academia. (p. 216)

As a means of putting into perspective who functions at what level and with what training or expertise, see Table 3–1, which indicates that persons with appropriate *experience* or *training* and the *skills* to communicate can function at the advice-giving level. In the school setting, for example, all teachers and most staff would qualify as *advisors* for many occasions and should serve in this important role in the school's program of pupil guidance. At the second level, special training to at least the master's degree level is required, and it is this training that provides the school counselor with special expertise as a counselor, an expertise that sets the counselor apart from other professionals in the school setting and establishes his or her unique qualifications to interact with or on behalf of students in meeting their routine development, adjustment, planning, and decision-making needs. The third level represents the highest levels of professional training available and usually terminates with an earned doctorate. As practicing counselors, these professionals are most frequently used as resource personnel for referrals and consultation. Their clients are usually those with serious personality disorders who require intensive and long-term counseling. In addition to counseling, these higher-trained counselors may also seek careers in research or university teaching.

Additional insights into the relationship between levels of training and the counselor's role and function as represented by initial employment may be noted by an examination of Table 3–2. As may be noted from Table 3–2, it is clear that the majority of master's degree graduates find their initial employment in elementary, middle/junior, or senior high schools.

In examining the content of training programs available, one cannot help but note course content consistency among master's programs across the United States and Canada. A great deal of this conformity in the United States is undoubtedly the result of state certification patterns for school counselors, which reflect, with little deviation, an expectancy of training to perform the traditional basic services noted in Chapter 2.

Table 3–1. Levels of Training and Responsibility

Level	Training	Responsibility
First	Appropriate educational and/or experience background.	Advising; information giving.
Second	Master's degree in counseling and guidance.	Developmental and normal adjustment counseling.
Third	Doctorate in counseling and guidance or counseling psychology.	Serious personality disorders.

Table 3-2. Initial Placement of Graduates by Degree Levels and Settings (1983 Data)

Five Majors By Settings	Initial Employment Setting	Doctorate			Master's			Baccalaureate		
		N	Av %	Rank	N	Av %	Rank	N	Av %	Rank
College, University, Postsecondary Settings	Higher Education Academic Areas	69	24.4	2	63	11.8	8	2	6.5	11
	Counseling Positions	57	19.9	4	124	11.6	9	3	13.3	7
	Other	25	17.6	5	65	16.1	5	0	0	14
Community Agencies	Corrections Institutions	27	8.7	12	148	8.5	11	17	11.5	8
	Diagnostic Centers	13	8.2	13	75	7.4	12	8	6.4	12
	Employment Agencies	4	11.8	11	91	6.2	14	7	10.7	9
	Hospitals	50	11.9	10	139	10.5	10	14	10.6	10
	Mental Health Clinics	77	28.6	1	231	21.5	2	19	24.5	5
Marriage & Family	Marriage & Family Counseling Centers	46	14.0	8	131	15.6	7	7	30.7	3
Rehabilitation	Rehabilitation Agencies	32	15.0	7	145	20.0	3	12	46.5	1
Schools	Elementary Schools	14	12.6	9	160	16.8	4	8	17.5	6
	Jr & Sr Highs	26	15.8	6	189	34.2	1	5	28.2	4
	Vocational & Trade	6	3.5	14	64	7.3	13	1	5.0	13
Other	Other	27	20.1	3	30	16.0	6	3	38.3	2

Source: Hollis and Wantz, 1983, p. 56.

41

A number of counselor training institutions also offer a specialist or sixth-year degree. In many states this degree qualifies one with appropriate experience for director or supervisor of guidance or director of pupil personnel services certificates. The current trend toward a two-year master's degree will probably result in the elimination of the specialist degree in many institutions. Brown and Pate (1983) suggested that this trend will go far to establish a distinction between those who want some level of human relations training and those who have a commitment to a career.

Approximately 130 counselor training institutions in the United States and Canada offer programs leading to an earned doctorate. These programs tend, according to the nature of the program, to prepare their candidates for positions on university counselor education faculties, in colleges and university counseling centers, for rehabilitation counseling, student personnel work in higher education, mental health clinics, and other agency or institutional settings. Some may also elect to enter private practice. Variations in program emphasis and preparation patterns are more commonplace than at the master's level. Also, in many institutions, several counselor education or related programs may exist because of specialized training, (i.e., departments of counselor education, rehabilitation counseling, and so forth).

The Credentialing of School Counselors

Today, *counselor* seems to be used with ever-increasing frequency in a variety of settings. There are home buyer counselors, financial counselors, landscape counselors, used car counselors, and diet counselors. There are also counselors who may be distinguished from the first group on the basis of certification or legal licensure. These include legal counselors, investment counselors, psychological counselors, and school guidance counselors. Differences between licensure and certification will be discussed later in this chapter. The licensure or certification indicates tht the holder has successfully completed and has been examined on learning and experience criteria recommended by the representative professional organizations and the appropriate licensing boards or agencies. The late C. Harold McCully, in his discussion "The School Counselor: Strategy for Professionalization," (1962) suggested eleven characteristics of a profession. These included the statement that:

> A profession is an occupation in which the members of a corporate group assure minimum competence for entry into the occupation by setting and enforcing standards for selection, training, and licensure or certification. (p. 682)

Advantages

There are advantages to some sort of a credentialing process, including:

1. *It provides a measure of protection for the public against those who would masquerade as possessing certain skills and trainings.* A number of years ago, an

article in the old *Look* magazine entitled, "Beware of the Psycho-Quacks," gave examples of the various guises for preying on the public under counseling and psychological titles. Many have read the book or seen the movie, "The Great Imposter," in which one individual assumed a variety of professional careers and proceeded to prosper in one after the other. Although these and other similar reports sometimes amuse and often attract sympathetic admirers for those who have "beat the system," very few people would knowingly like to be treated by a physician who is not a physician, represented by a lawyer who is not a lawyer, or counseled by a counselor who is not a counselor. The implications of these examples are appropriate reminders of the need for some sort of a procedure that protects the public against professional misrepresentation and fraud.

2. *It provides, at the very least, minimally accepted training and experience requirements.* Credentialing and training requirements (and experiences) are closely interrelated. This interrelationship provides for a common core of learning experiences and achievement expectancies. These are related to the profession's concept of preparatory standards for entry into the profession. This is not only helpful to candidates considering entry into training programs and protects them from misleading training schemes, but also provides some reassurance for employers as well as the general public who use the services.

3. *It can provide a legal base for the protection of the membership of the profession.* Because credentialing suggests standards that benefit the public, law-making bodies are prone to provide the profession and its membership with certain legal forms of protection. For example, individuals cannot legally practice medicine without a license, and lawyers legally have the right of privileged communication with their clients. In many states, the right to enter private practice in such fields as psychology and professional counseling is limited by law.

4. *It may provide a basis for special benefits.* In addition to legal benefits, credentialed professionals may also qualify for certain financial benefits. Physicians' and laywers' fees may qualify for insurance payments. Physicians, including psychiatrists, also qualify for national health insurance payments such as Medicaid. Psychologists may also qualify as mental health providers for insurance payments in some states. Credentialed school counselors have, on occasion, been qualified to receive special training grants to increase their qualifications. Because credentialing qualifies individuals for membership in professional organizations, they become eligible for the benefits such memberships provide. These may include special training opportunities, publications, and group insurance programs.

There are two common methods used to credential practitioners of a profession such as counseling. These are certification and licensure. Differences between certification and licensure have been described by Forster (1977):

> *Certification:* This is a process of recognizing the competence of practitioners of a profession by officially authorizing them to use the title adopted by the profession. Certification can be awarded by voluntary associations, agencies, or by governmental bodies, some of which are recognized by state laws. In school counsel-

ing, certification is usually handled by an office within the state government's department of education or its branch for executing public instruction matters. Certification officials commonly check transcripts for evidence that the applicant has completed required courses from preparation programs that are known to be acceptable.

Licensure: This is a process authorized by state legislation that regulates the practice and the title of the profession. Because of its legislative base, licensure subjects violators to greater legal sanctions than does certification. Licensure is generally considered to be more desirable when a substantial proportion of a profession's practitioners are in private practice, because of the broader coverage and greater potential for using sanctions against violators. Licensure boards are usually established with quasi-legislative power to make rules and examine applicants who seek licenses. (p. 573)

Another activity that has significance for the credentialing process, whether it be certification or licensure, is accreditation. *Accreditation,* according to Forster (1977) is a process

whereby an association or agency grants public recognition to a school, institute, college, university, or specialized program of study that has met certain established qualifications of standards as determined through initial and periodic evaluations. "Program approval" is another name for accreditation. In some professions, graduates of accredited preparation programs are considered credentialed. Sometimes a registry is used by a profession to list graduates of accredited programs. (p. 573)

Most programs preparing school counselors are accredited by their regional accrediting associations. Counselor training programs in schools or colleges of education may also have accreditation by the National Council for Accreditation of Teacher Education (NCATE), and programs both within and outside of education may qualify for approval by the Council for Accreditation of Counseling and Counseling Related Programs (CACREP), which is affiliated with the American Association for Counseling and Development. Programs preparing counseling psychologists may seek accreditation by the American Psychological Association. In addition, many state departments of public instruction accredit higher education training programs within their jurisdictions.

The Issue of Licensure

During the 1970s, credentialing became one of the major issues facing the counseling profession. Although school counselor certification existed in all states before 1970, the issue of licensure became of greater concern as the American Psychological Association moved to secure legal recognition of the more or less exclusive right of psychologists and those trained in psychological counseling programs to engage in and identify themselves in practice as counselors. Many counselors trained in counselor education programs viewed this as limiting their options to primarily school or certain agency settings. A major focus of the legislative efforts of the American Psychological Association has been to establish psychology as a profession to provide health services (and as previously noted, qualifying them for insurance reimbursements).

In the 1980s the American Personnel and Guidance Association, renamed the American Association for Counseling and Development in 1983, became increasingly active in providing certification options for counselors through their certification arm, the National Board for Certified Counselors. A national examination has been developed and a national registry of mental health care providers published listing those who have met the specified qualifications for training, experience, and examination. The content areas of the NBCC (National Board for Certified Counselors, Inc.) examination reflect the knowledge and skills necessary to carry out the traditional activities supporting the role and function of the counselor. These are

- Appraisal of persons.
- Group dynamics, processing and counseling.
- Human growth and development.
- Lifestyle and career development.
- Professional orientation.
- Research and evaluation.
- Social and cultural foundations.
- The helping relationship.

Concurrently, the American Association for Counseling and Development has been politically active in securing legal recognition for counselors licensed through the National Board for Certified Counselors. A number of states currently have licensure (16 in 1985) with success anticipated in more states in the remaining 1980s. As part of the growing trend toward licensure, other counseling groups such as marriage and family, drug, alcohol, and rehabilitation counselors are now licensed or certified in many states. Since there are a variety of training programs that, despite different orientations, can lay claim to training counselors, such as counseling psychology, school counselors, marriage counselors, rehabilitation counselors and others, the movement toward licensure has been rightfully or wrongly viewed in many instances as an effort to limit and restrict the practice of counseling to those who come from a particular training background.

In general, it is the view of most of those in the counseling profession that the movement toward licensure is one that in the long run will protect both the public and the profession. The issues primarily center on what training for what role and function and under whose jurisdiction or approval.

Certification and the School Counselor

As previously mentioned, all states require certification for those who would perform as school counselors. In general, these requirements are very similar across states and account for the considerable degree of reciprocity whereby candidates certified in one state may be eligible for certification in another state. For example, the vast majority of certification programs require a counselor's minimal completion of a master's degree. Also, most certification patterns require the completion of course work appropriate to the basic guidance services. That includes courses in appraisal or, sometimes, standardized testing, occupational and educational information, career guidance or career development, individual counseling, group guidance and counseling, and a course in either principles of guidance or organization of school guidance programs. In addition, some sort of supervised practicum experience is typically required. The majority of states also require prior teaching experience of from one to three years. An increasing number of states have, in recent years, however, amended their certification requirements to provide for an alternative experience to teaching, such as in internship.

It is probably a "chicken or egg" situation to attempt to determine whether training influences practice or vice versa, and it is not the intent of this chapter to bias that argument. We have, by choice, discussed training and resulting certification first. In the paragraphs that follow, counseling practices in various educational settings will be discussed. One may take note of the relationship between these practices and training patterns previously presented. It should be emphasized that this discussion is a brief overview only, and greater detail and specificity will be provided later.

The Role and Function of Counselors in School Settings

An Overview

The counselor's role and function by educational levels for school settings, as described in official American School Counselor Association statements for the elementary, middle/junior high schools, secondary schools, and postsecondary institutions are presented in Appendices A through D.

However, as Baker (1981) notes:

> In discussion of the counselor's role, only a few things can be concluded. These are that many counselors define their role in terms of the functions they perform, that there is variation in the kinds of functions performed by counselors in the schools of this nation, and that counselors have been encouraged to consider several different primary roles over the years—therapeutic counselor, client advocate or change agent, administrator, vocational guidance specialist, psychoeducator, etc. These changing notions about primary roles for counselors have been more frustrating than sustaining for many counselors. The frustration seems to be associated with the relative helplessness that school counselors feel in attempting to establish their own role. (p. 247)

A popular view of the role and function of the school counselor (but also appropriate to counselor functioning in a variety of nonschool settings as well) is suggested by the cube depicted in Figure 3–1. This figure indicates with whom the counselor will work, what the purpose of the counselor's involvement will be, and the methods or techniques that will be used. The architects of the cube, Morrill, Oetting, and Hurst (1974), in their discussion of the dimensions of counselor functioning described their model:

> *Counseling interventions* comprise all counselor functions designed to produce changes in clients, groups, or institutions. This article introduces a model that pro-

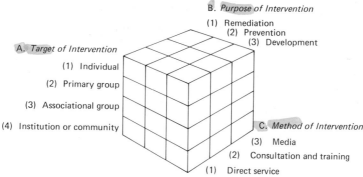

Figure 3–1. Counseling interventions. *(Morrill, Oetting, and Hurst, 1974, p. 354.)*

vides for the descriptions and categorization of a very broad range of possible counseling interventions. The figure presents a model of the three dimensions to be discussed. This model permits the identification and classification of a variety of counseling programs or counseling approaches and thereby serves as a means of categorizing and describing the potential activities of the counselor in a variety of settings. The three dimensions described are the intervention target, purpose, and method.

The Target of the Intervention
Interventions may be aimed at (a) the individual, (b) the individual's primary groups, (c) the individual's associational groups, or (d) the institutions or communities that influence the individual's behavior.

The Purpose of the Intervention
The purpose may be (a) remediation, (b) prevention, or (c) development.

The Method of Intervention
The method of reaching the target population may be through (a) direct service, which involves direct professional involvement with the target; (b) consultation with and training of other helping professionals or paraprofessionals; or (c) indirect interventions utilizing media, i.e., computers, programmed exercises, books, television, and other media.

Any intervention has these three dimensions: who or what the intervention is aimed at, why the intervention is attempted, and how the intervention is made. (p. 355)

The variety in school settings, of course, will account for some differences in the ways counselors may carry out their roles. There are, however, some common influences determining the role and function of counselors, regardless of the setting. The first of these is what might be called professional constants or determinants that tend to indicate what is appropriate and not appropriate to the counselor's role and function. These include guidelines and policy statements of professional organizations, licensing or certification limitations, accreditation guidelines and requirements, and the expectancies of professional training programs. In addition to these professional constants, there are also those personal factors that inevitably influence role and function. These include the interest of the counselor, such as what he or she likes to do versus what he or she does not like to do; what he or she gets encouraged to do and is rewarded for doing by the school, community, or his or her peers; what the counselor has resources to do; what the counselor perceives as the appropriate role and function for a given setting; and finally, how life in general is going for the counselor. The counselor's attitudes, values, and experiences both on and off the job can influence how he or she views the job.

It has also been increasingly noted in recent years that counselors and other professional helpers are coming to grips with the facts that traditional roles and delivery systems in human services may have imposed real limitations on their ability to deal directly and effectively with the critical needs of clients. We would also note the current call for counselors and counseling programs to become increasingly active in preventive interventions. Thus, as we further view the role and function of counselors, we are seeking to integrate for you, our reader, not only those concepts that have proven themselves over the years, but also current and promising directions that seem necessary for the counselor to remain a viable entity in the school setting.

The Elementary School Counselor

The characteristics of the elementary pupil and the elementary school dictate certain characteristics in program organization that distinguish elementary school counseling programs from those in secondary schools and at other educational levels. It therefore follows that the elementary school counselor's role and function will also reflect these differences. The differences, however, are not so much in what the elementary school counselors do, but in how they do it. For example, counselors and other elementary school specialists must work closely and effectively with classroom teachers. This provides a natural relationship for an emphasis on consultation and coordination. In addition to counseling, coordination, and consulting functions, the elementary school counselor has responsibilities for the orientation, assessment, and career development needs of pupils.

Counselor. Although one-to-one counseling in the elementary school may take correspondingly less of the counselor's time than counseling at other levels, the counselor should be available to meet individually or in groups with children referred by teachers or parents or identified by the counselor or other helping professionals as in need of counseling. The counseling process recognizes where individual pupils are in their growth and development and the implications of this for counseling practice.

Consultant. As a consultant, the counselor may confer directly with teachers, parents, administrators, and other helping professionals to help an identified third party such as students in the school setting. In this role, the counselor helps others to assist the student-client in dealing more effectively with developmental or adjustment needs.

Coordinator. Elementary school counselors have a responsibility for the coordination of the various guidance activities in the schools. Coordinating these with ongoing classroom and school activities is also desirable. As the only building-based helping professional, the elementary school counselor may be called upon to coordinate the contributions of school psychologists, social workers, and others. Other coordination activities could include intraschool referrals and interagency referrals.

Agent of Orientation. As a human development facilitator, the elementary school counselor recognizes the importance of the child's orientation to the goals and environment of the elementary school. It is important that the child's initial education experiences be positive ones, and it is in this regard that the counselor may plan group activities and consult with teachers to help children learn and practice the human relationship skills necessary for their adjustment in the togetherness enforced by the school setting.

Assessment. The counselor in the elementary school can anticipate being called upon to interpret and often gather both test and nontest data. To the counselor will also fall the task of putting these data into focus to not only see but be able to interpret the child as a total being. Beyond the traditional data used for pupil understanding, the counselor should also understand the impacts of culture, the sociology of the school, and other environmental influences that are determinants of pupil behavior.

Career Developer. The importance of the elementary school years as a foundation for later significant decisions of the child underscores the desirability of planned attention being given to the elementary pupil's career development. Although the responsibility for career education planning rests with the classroom teachers, the elementary school counselor can make a major contribution as a coordinator and consultant in developing a continuous, sequential, and integrated program.

Agent of Prevention. In the elementary school, there are early warning signs of future problems for young children. These include learning difficulties, general moodiness (unhappiness, depression), and acting-out behaviors (fights, quarrels, disruptions, restlessness, impulsivity, and obstinacy) (Finkel, 1976). Conyne (1983), Dodge (1983), and others have cited a body of evidence that has accumulated to demonstrate that children who cannot adjust during their elementary school years are at high risk for a variety of later problems. Elementary school counselors will be increasingly called upon and challenged to develop programs that seek to anticipate, intervene in, and prevent the development of these problems.

Some additional insights into the role and function of the elementary school counselor may also be provided by examining the results of a study conducted by the North Central Association of Schools and Colleges (1977). This study, which sampled or interviewed more than 180 elementary school teachers, administrators, supervisors, and counselors, concluded that the elementary school counselor's priority activities should focus on (in descending order) individual counseling, group guidance (including counseling) activities, and consultation with teachers and parents. Other high priority activities recommended by these elementary school practitioners included parent counseling, behavior

Table 3-3. Rank Ordering of Elementary School Counselor Activities As Assigned by 183 Elementary School Educators*

Rank	Activity	Mean
1	Individual Counseling	8.4
2.5	Consultation with Teachers	7.7
2.5	Group Counseling	7.7
4	Consultation with Parents	7.4
5	Behavior Modification	6.5
6	Parent Counseling	6.4
7	Values Clarification Activities	5.7
8	Assessment Activities	4.6
9	Career Guidance	3.8
10	Middle/Senior High School or Secondary School Placement and Follow-up	3.7
11	Research and Evaluation	3.2

*Rank ordered on a scale of zero to ten with ten being the highest and zero being of no priority.

modification, values clarification activities, and career development. Table 3-3 shows, in rank order, a priority of counselor activities in the elementary schools as viewed by this sample of elementary educators.

As the role and function of elementary school counselors has begun to clarify, so have the demands for counselors in elementary schools. For example, a national survey conducted in 1967 indicated that there were 3,837 elementary school counselors in 48 states. Less than 10 years later, a 1976 study indicated approximately 10,770 counselors employed in public elementary schools in 50 states. Although the study pointed out that 15 percent of these counselors were working in more than one elementary school, it is important to note the near tripling of the number of elementary school counselors in less than 10 years as noted by Myrick and Moni (1976). Continued growth in the number of elementary school counselors is expected well into the 1980s.

The Middle/Junior High School Counselor

In the 1970s there was a trend from the elementary, junior, senior high school organizational concept to the elementary, middle, senior high school concept. These changes have not been without their attending controversies, but the middle school in concept and function may not really be all that different from the more traditional junior high school. For example, many contend that the junior high school was originally conceived as an institution to meet the developmental and transitional needs of youths from puberty to adolescence, from elementary to secondary school. Early in the middle school movement, it was suggested that a rationale for the middle school concept was based on data indicating that modern youths reach physical, social, and intellectual maturity at a younger age than did previous generations and that the junior high school may no longer meet the developmental needs of these students. Regardless of whether a school system adopts a middle school type of intermediate school or stays with the more traditional junior high school, it would appear that either institution will reflect such characteristics as (a) providing for the orientation and transitional needs of students; (b) providing for the developmental needs of students who, as a group, are moving toward adolescence; and (c) providing for the educational and social developmental needs of their student populations. In such a setting, middle or junior high school counselors will be actively involved in:

Student Orientation. This would include the initial orientation of entering students and their parents to the programs, policies, facilities, and counseling activities of their new school and later, their pre-entry orientation to the high school they will attend upon completion of their junior high or middle school program.

Appraisal or Assessment Activities. In addition to typical school record and standardized test data, counselors may increasingly encourage the use of observation and other techniques to identify emerging traits of individual students during this critical development period. Values clarification activities may also be increasingly used for assessment and developmental purposes during this time.

Counseling. Both individual and group counseling should be used by school counselors at this level. In practice, it appears that middle and junior high school counselors tend to use group counseling more frequently than individual counseling.

Consultation. Counselors will provide consultation to faculty, parents, and, on occasion, school administrators regarding the developmental and adjustment needs of individual students. Counselors will also consult with other members of the school system's pupil personnel services team.

Placement. Counselors are usually involved in course and curricular placement of pupils, not only within their own schools, but also cooperatively with their counterparts in the feeder secondary schools.

The Secondary School Counselor

Of all the educational levels in which counselors serve, the secondary school is the one in which counselors and the general educational public (teachers, pupils, parents) are most likely to have some consistent understanding of "what the school counselor does." Although the role and function of the secondary school counselor has changed and expanded over the years, it is clearly the most traditional and most readily identified, even though the role of secondary school counselors has been more frequently and seriously challenged than that of their elementary or collegiate counterparts. However, despite these challenges, there have not been and likely will not be any drastic or "overnight" changes. Secondary school counseling programs in the future will still be built around the traditional basic services. Although the emphasis and techniques will undoubtedly change, counseling as a professional activity in schools will never have the opportunity to "start from scratch" again. It is anticipated that the role and function of the secondary school counselor will continue to be built around these traditional expectancies:

1. Assessment of the pupil's potential and other characteristics.
2. Counseling the pupil.
3. Group counseling and group guidance activities.
4. Career development, guidance, and informational activities.
5. Placement, follow-up, and accountability evaluation.
6. Consultation with teachers and other school personnel, parents, pupils in groups, and appropriate community agencies.
7. Needs assessment for program direction.

These expectations are, for the most part, confirmed in greater detail in a study of counselor roles and function conducted by Ibrahim, Helms, and Thompson (1983) and participated in by both "consumers" and counselors. This study examined the role and function of counselors based on the American School Counselor Association statement adopted in 1977.

As may be noted by examining Tables 3–4 and 3–5 all four groups rated most of the activities with a mean of 2.0 or higher, indicating a general consensus that these activities and functions were important components of a counselor's role. The notable exceptions included functions listed under research (student characteristics, new programs, newsletter publication), and staff consulting (conducting guidance activities in the classroom); counselors saw research and staff consulting as less important than the administrators. The administrators, on the other hand, ranked the majority of functions higher in importance than any of the other groups. In fact, the perceptions of the degree of importance of these items varied significantly between the groups and some generalizations can be made regarding these differences. Counselors and administrators considered the following functions of greater importance than did parents or the busi-

Table 3–4. Sample Stratification on the Standard Metropolitan Statistical Areas and Number of Full-Time Counselors in Each School

	Urban		Suburban		Rural		Total	
Counselors	Percent needed	Actual number	Percent needed	Actual number	Percent needed	Actual number	Percent needed	Actual number
1–3	1	1	17	4	17	4	35	9
4–6	15	3	16	4	8	2	39	9
7–10	17	4	8	2	1	1	26	7
Total	33	8	41	10	26	7	100	25 schools

Source: Ibrahim, Helms, & Thompson, 1983, p. 598.

Table 3-5. Importance of Counselor Functions as Perceived by Parents (P), Counselors, (C), Administrators (A), and the Business Community (B)

Role and Function	Means[a]				
	P	C	A	B	F-Ratio
Program development					
Develop objectives for the secondary school guidance and counseling program	NA[b]	2.640	2.842	NA	2.73
Plan several activities to achieve the above objectives	NA	2.488	2.789	NA	4.5*
Plan specific evaluation method for each of the program activities	NA	2.286	2.210	NA	9.48
Provide in-service training programs for school staff	NA	2.130	2.167	NA	0.05
Counseling					
Provide individual counseling services for personal problems and concerns	2.346	2.723	2.550	2.309	13.11**
Provide group counseling services for personal problems and concerns	1.813	2.200	2.050	1.900	13.24**
Provide individual counseling services for educational problems and concerns	2.734	2.792	2.950	2.907	3.30**
Provide group counseling services for educational problems and concerns	2.059	2.392	2.579	2.268	12.64**
Provide individual counseling services for vocational problems and concerns	2.529	2.641	2.789	2.791	4.58**
Provide group counseling services for vocational problems and concerns	2.003	2.368	2.500	2.286	15.38**
Provide counseling services for parents to help them understand their children	1.916	2.212	2.158	2.154	6.97**
Provide information to students about the content of school courses to aid them in course selection	2.797	2.733	2.800	2.727	1.08
Pupil appraisal					
Keep a record of student test results and academic progress	NA	2.414	2.526	NA	0.46
Plan, carry out, and interpret achievement, ability, and interest-testing programs to assess students	NA	2.423	2.421	NA	0.14
Explain the results of testing to students and teachers	NA	2.470	2.526	NA	0.14
Educational and occupational planning					
Provide students with information about careers	2.734	2.634	2.600	2.884	3.92**
Provide students with information about educational opportunities after high school	2.741	2.682	2.789	2.909	2.7*
Conduct guidance activities in the classroom such as career development, self-awareness, and decision making, along with classroom teacher	2.295	2.126	2.200	2.605	5.83**
Help teachers plan and implement teaching units where materials and concepts are related to guidance, that is career development, self-awareness, decision making	2.352	2.050	2.111	2.512	9.51**
Provide testing to help students make career choices	2.387	2.256	2.400	2.500	2.2

Table 3-5. (cont.)

Role and Function	Means[a]				
	P	C	A	B	F-Ratio
Referral					
Refer students with special needs to the appropriate community agency	2.470	2.641	2.650	2.537	3.82**
Placement					
Assist graduating students and dropouts in getting jobs	2.122	2.057	2.000	2.000	0.78
Assist students in school to get part-time jobs	1.950	1.975	1.765	1.721	1.85
Conduct group guidance sessions for students in resume writing, completing job applications, job interviewing skills, and job application follow-up strategies	2.264	2.057	1.800	2.659	12.01**
Assist students to make educational plans for the future such as selecting a college, career training programs, etc.	2.656	2.723	2.700	2.930	4.46**
Parent help					
Counsel with parents on problems their children are encountering	2.236	2.527	2.250	2.317	7.54**
Help resolve family conflicts around career and educational choices with parents and students	1.928	2.224	2.222	2.000	7.02
Staff consulting					
Consult with teachers in areas such as student motivation, student behavior, educational adjustment, classroom management, and teaching strategies	NA	2.422	2.263	NA	1.57
Consult with school psychologist on specific cases	NA	2.644	2.632	NA	0.06
Conduct guidance activities in classroom along with classroom teacher	NA	1.731	1.944	NA	1.92
Research					
Conduct research studies on students characteristics (abilities, attitudes, interests, etc.) for various publics, i.e., teachers, administrators, the business community	NA	1.535	1.722	NA	1.03
Conduct research on new programs for implementation in school system	NA	1.689	2.000	NA	2.84
Publish newsletter for students, parents, and teachers	NA	1.975	2.000	NA	0.02
Public relations					
Keep public (parents, students, and teachers) informed of available guidance programs	2.355	2.605	2.600	2.286	8.55**
Plan and conduct orientation programs	2.108	2.442	2.650	2.105	17.03**
Inform community agencies of students' needs and available guidance programs	2.098	2.221	2.316	1.951	3.26*
Plan and coordinate parent-teacher meetings pertaining to guidance programs	2.062	2.290	2.400	2.413	6.93**

*p < .05
**p < .01
[a]Means are based on the following rating scale: 3 = Very important, 2 = important, 1 = unimportant.
[b]NA denotes these groups were not asked to respond to these items.
Source: Ibrahim, Helms, & Thompson, 1983, p. 598.

ness community: counseling, parent help, and public relations. Parents and the business community rated the following functions higher in importance: educational and occupational planning and referral.

Some interesting differences were also noted on specific sections rated only by counselors and administrators. Administrators consistently perceived the majority of the functions listed in program development, pupil appraisal, staff consulting, and research as of greater importance than did counselors. The difference between the means, however, was statistically significant for only one of the 13 functions included in the four sections—to plan several activities to achieve guidance and counseling objectives.

The roles and functions of the secondary school counselor are not dissimilar from those of counselors in the elementary and middle/junior high schools; it should be emphasized that the differences occur in how counselors in the secondary school discharge their role and function and in the different emphases appropriate to the secondary school setting. For example, the emphasis at the secondary school level shifts drastically from the preventive to the remedial in dealing with many common counseling concerns. Many of these concerns are now potentially serious life problems, such as addiction to drugs and alcohol, sexual concerns, and interpersonal relationship adjustments. Furthermore, there is less client emphasis on preparing for decisions and more emphasis on making decisions. These include immediate or impending career decisions or further education decisions; decisions relevant to relationships with the opposite sex and perhaps marriage; and decisions involved in developing personal values systems.

In addition to these different emphases in contrast to counseling needs at other educational levels, there are indications that counselors anticipate more emphasis on consultation and on a broader understanding of the impact of environment on students' behavior; a shifting emphasis towards a closer relationship with the classroom teacher in the school environment, as opposed to the traditional "medical" model (where the client in need comes to the office for a "prescription") and, finally, a change in emphasis from reactive to proactive and change agent in both the school and the community.

Counselors in Vocational Schools

The image and the significance of vocational education changed markedly in the 1970s. Once regarded as a "dumping ground" for the unwilling or unable student (with facilities usually appropriate to this image), vocational education programs have made a dramatic turnaround in recent generations. Today they are some of the finest educational facilities in the country and are attracting students at all ability levels and are preparing them for jobs that are in demand. School counselors need to become aware of both the nature of vocational education programs and the opportunities available to those who complete them. Additionally, counselors in preparation need to recognize some differences in the role and function of the counselor in the vocational school.

Counselors in Higher Education

A wide variety of counseling services are available to students in programs of higher education across the United States and Canada. Some of these counselors function in specialized facilities such as career centers and college admissions and placement offices. The majority of counselors, however, are employed in university counseling, mental health, or psychological service centers. These centers typically offer personal, academic, and vocational counseling, although group counseling has increased in popularity in recent years. Many of these centers are interdisciplinary in terms of staffing.

A noticeable trend in the activities of college counseling center programs is their move to assist larger numbers of students on their campuses through such activities as outreach programs, special workshops, residence hall groups, and peer counseling. On some campuses, counselors are also becoming more active in consultation with their faculty peers, campus administrators, and leaders of student organizations.

Teacher and Administrator Roles in the School Counseling Program

The Role of the Classroom Teacher

Although it seems heresy to the counseling profession, it has been and could continue to be possible for schools to exist without the benefit of counselors. Many students possibly would not achieve their potential, solve their problems, or make appropriate decisions and plans, but nonetheless most of them would learn, would progress, and would be viewed as educated. It is also possible for schools to exist without the presence of an even more prominent member—the school principal. Although teachers would be even more overburdened with administrative responsibilities, and their teaching effectiveness would undoubtedly suffer, students would still be taught, would still learn, perhaps at a slower rate, would still graduate, even without the principal's handshake, and would be viewed as educated. Schools without teachers, however, cease to be schools. They become, instead, detention centers, social clubs, or temporary shelters, but they are not schools, and any learning that takes place would be both incidental and accidental. It therefore becomes obvious, and has been since the beginning of schooling, that the teacher is the key and most important professional in the school setting. Teacher support and participation are crucial to any program that involves students. The school counseling program is no exception. It is therefore important to examine the role and function of the classroom teacher in this program, recognizing, of course, that differences may be anticipated at differing educational levels and in different educational settings.

Role as a Listener-advisor

Most classroom teachers see their pupils every day, five days a week, for at least 45 minutes per day on the average of 180 school days per year, often for several years, all of which represents a staggering amount of contact time exceeded by no other adults except parents, and that exception does not always hold true. The inevitable result is that the teacher, more than any other professional in the school setting, is in the position to know the students best, to communicate with them on an almost daily basis, and to establish a relationship based on mutual trust and respect. The teacher thus becomes the first line of contact between the student and the school counseling program; a contact in which the teacher will frequently be called upon to serve in a listening-advising capacity.

Role as a Referral and Receiving Agent

The classroom teacher is, inevitably, the major source of student referrals to the school counselor. Because the counselor's daily personal contacts with students are necessarily limited, the counselor's personal awareness of students needing counseling is similarly limited. The counseling program must therefore depend upon the alertness of the teaching faculty to ensure that students with counseling needs will not go unnoticed and uncounseled. School counselors need to encourage their teacher colleagues to actively "search" for these students, since much evidence exists to suggest that only "the tip of the iceberg" has been touched in our efforts to identify all students with serious counseling needs. Of course, it may not be enough to simply identify the students to a counselor. In many instances, the teacher must orient and encourage the student to seek counselor assistance. Nor does the teacher's responsibility necessarily end when the student has entered a counseling relationship. The teacher may still be involved, if only in the role of supporting the student's continuation with the counseling process. Teachers may also anticipate a role as a receiving agent, not only for those students they have referred but for others in their classes as well. In such situations, the teacher in a sense "receives" the counseled student back into the classroom environment and, it is hoped, supports and reinforces the outcome of the counseling. The importance of this reinforcer role cannot be overemphasized.

Role as a "Human Potential Discoverer"

Each year teachers witness a talent parade through their respective classes. Although teachers may lack sufficient training, experience, or versatility to identify the special talents of the vast majority of students, most teachers have the expertise to identify those who may have some special talents for their own particular career specialty. That expertise multiplied across the many career specialties represented in most school programs represents a near army of talent scouts that should ensure the probability that each student will have his or her talents and potentials identified and his or her development encouraged and assisted. This teacher role as a discoverer of human potential is significant in fulfilling not only a mission of the school counseling program, but also in meeting the responsibility of education to the individual and to society.

Role as a Career Educator

Closely related to the foregoing is the teacher's central role in the school's career education program. Because career education is recognized as a part of the total education of the student, it is important to also recognize the classroom teacher's responsibility to incorporate and integrate career education into teaching subject matter. Career education cannot succeed without career guidance and vice versa. It therefore follows that the success of the career guidance program is tied to the success of the career education program, a success that rests largely with the classroom teacher.

The career education responsibilities of the teacher include the developing of positive attitudes and respect for all honest work, a challenging responsibility in view of the many adult-imposed biases with which the student is constantly confronted. Additionally, the teacher must promote the parallel development of positive student attitudes towards education and its relationship to career preparation and decision making. Students must also have the opportunity to examine and test concepts, skills, and roles and to develop values appropriate to their future career planning. The security of the classroom group provides an ideal setting for these experiences.

Role as a Human Relations Facilitator

The potential for success of any school counseling program depends to a considerable degree upon the climate or environment of the school, an environment that is conducive to the development and practice of positive human relations. The influence of the classroom teacher on that environment is dominant, as ably expressed by Haim Ginott:

> I have come to the frightening conclusion
> I am the decisive element in the classroom
> It is my personal approach that creates the climate
> It is my daily mood that makes the weather
> As a teacher I possess tremendous power to make a child's life miserable or joyous
> I can humiliate or humor, hurt or heal
> In all situations it is my response that decides whether a crisis will be escalated or de-escalated, and a child humanized or dehumanized. (Gross and Gross, 1974, p. 39)

Among the research emphasizing the importance of a favorable classroom and school environment for learning is that reported in Benjamin Bloom's book *Human Characteristics and School Learning* (1976). Bloom suggests that it is possible for 95 percent of the students to learn all that the school has to teach at or near the same achievement level. His research indicates that most students will be very similar in both learning and their motivation to learn when they are provided the favorable conditions or environment for learning. On the other hand, his research also demonstrates that when the environment in the classroom is unfavorable, differences occur that widen the gap between high and low achievers. In this role as a human relations facilitator, the classroom teacher has the opportunity to be a model to demonstrate positive human relations. The teaching and practicing of these skills should occur as a regular procedure in the classroom as the teacher plans and directs group interactions that promise positive human relationship experiences for each individual participant.

Role as a Counseling Program Supporter

Someone once said, "Counselors are the most human of all humans." Be that as it may, counselors, as all humans, need and respond to the encouragement and support of their fellow beings. Therefore, a significant contribution that the classroom teacher can make to the school counseling program is one of counselor encouragement and support and the creation of a motivating environment. Support can be especially influential in determining how pupils view and use the services of the school's counseling program. Teachers' reactions also do not go unnoticed by school administrators and supervisors. Of course, it is also to be hoped that evidence of teacher support for counseling will extend to parent contacts and out into the community as well.

Despite the importance of the classroom teacher in any school counseling program at any educational level, evidence indicates that in far too many settings, the classroom teacher is still only incidentally involved in the program. Many classroom teachers may feel uncertain about the goals of their school programs and may feel a lack of communication and involvement in the counseling programs. In such situations, the student is the real loser, and both the counselor and the teacher must share the blame. Because the school counseling program is the responsibility of counselors, they must initiate communications and interaction with their teaching faculties, they must actively pursue teachers' involvement and assistance, and they must exemplify their claim to human relations expertise. They must also recognize that although most teachers are willing to accept their role in the school counseling program, as many studies have indicated, they may lack some understanding of what that role and function is. Of course, not all teachers will or can be "all things," as suggested in this section. Hopefully, most can and will accept many of these roles, however. These role opportunities also can be enhanced by preparing teachers to recognize, accept, and enjoy their roles in the school counseling program. Unfortunately, most teachers do not seek and are not required to take coursework in counseling and guidance and therefore are limited in realizing their full potential as team members.

The Role of the Chief School Administrator

Whether a building principal or a university president, the chief on-site administrator is potentially (and usually) the most singularly important person in the development of any educational program in their respective setting. Most staff members of schools (including principals and college presidents) think of chief administrators in terms of power—what the chief administrators permit them to do and not to do. Previous studies (Gibson, Mitchell, and Higgins, 1983, p. 76) have noted that administrative support was ranked in the highest priority category in the establishment and development of school guidance programs. Other studies earlier reported by Griffiths (1964) have noted that program development and change are far more likely to succeed if stimulated from the top rather than from the bottom up. These emphasize the significant role the school principal and other educational leadership can and should play in any program of counseling within their jurisdiction. This role may be appropriately expressed through leadership, consultation, advice, and resource support. Some of the characteristics of these activities follow.

Role as a Program Leader and Supporter

The leadership behavior of the school principal in behalf of the school counseling program is a major determinant of the program's prospects for success. Because school administrators represent the educational leadership in both the school and the community, they have the responsibility of giving clear, open, and recognized support for the school program. This will include responsibilities for communicating program characteristics, achievements, and needs to school boards and others within the educational system and to the tax-supporting public.

Role as a Program Consultant and Advisor

The chief school administrator has the best overview of all activities and planning within the institution. This position enables the chief administrator to make a valuable contribution to the school counseling program as advisor and consultant on school needs that can be served by the school program, school policies that affect counseling program functioning, resolution of problems encountered by the program, and procedures or directions for program development and improvement.

Role as a Resource Provider

Chief school administrators are usually responsible for the institution's budget—its makeup and utilization. In this role, they provide advice and direction to all school programs regarding budget expectations, staffing possibilities, facilities, and equipment. They may also be aware of possible external resources such as state or federal funding, which the school counseling program may wish to explore.

The Counselor and Relationships with Other Helping Professions

As already noted, one of the school counselor's important roles is as a team member. Unlike the gifted athlete who may have to limit membership to one team, the counselor may play on several teams. One of the most important and logical of these is the pupil personnel services or helping professions team. This team typically includes the school psychologist, social worker, speech and hearing specialists, and health personnel. To work effectively with each other, members of these teams must understand the expertise and responsibilities of their team members and how they support each other. These brief descriptions present only a superficial overview. Unfortunately, most training programs do little in the way of interdisciplinary planning or training. Therefore, it becomes the responsibility of the school counselor and other helping professionals to initiate and develop positive, cooperative working relationships consistent with the team concept.

The School Psychologist

In 1980 it was estimated that there were more than 9,000 school psychologists practicing in the United States and Canada. These psychologists were prepared in approximately 150 training programs. In the 1970s and 1980s, the number of school psychologists increased as a result of state and federal laws mandating equal educational opportunities for the handicappped. Because school psychology has its historical antecedents in clinical psychology, the school psychologist is heavily trained in the use of such clinical tools as those which measure the mental and personality characteristics of the individual. In the school setting, they work with individual children to assess learning and emotional problems, and they consult with teachers, administrators, and parents regarding individual pupils. Gregersen (1977) noted that ten common roles for school psychologists, as described in the literature, include:

1. Psychometrician.
2. Clinician/counselor/therapist.
3. Diagnostic-prescriptive consultant.
4. Mental health consultant.
5. Educational evaluator/consultant.
6. Researcher.
7. Organizational development specialist/social system analyst.
8. Administrator-supervisor.
9. Community liaison.
10. In-service trainer.

> Obviously, many of these roles or broad categorical definitions of activities are not mutually exclusive. In fact, most school psychologists in practice tend to fill more than one role and, at different times, are involved with most of these activities. Obviously, when a classroom teacher seeks consultation or assistance in dealing with a classroom problem, whether it emanates from an individual child or from some broader instructional difficulty, the adequacy of the information or assistance that s/he receives is dependent on the kind of role or nature of service which the school psychologist provides. (Gregersen, 1977, p. 6)

Counselors may often find it desirable to refer students to the school psychologist for clinical diagnosis, whereas on the other hand, the school psychologist will often identify, through his or her diagnostic evaluations, pupils in need of counseling.

Also as Cristiani and Sommers (1978) noted:

with the present movement in special education to reintegrate handicapped children into the regular classroom, the counselor's role in the school takes on an exciting, yet challenging, new meaning. Whereas traditionally counselors have been concerned with the child's psychological and emotional adjustment and the impact of the child's emotional life on his or her readiness to learn, the integration of handicapped children will require that the counselor be prepared to respond to a wider range of behavior problems.

Therefore, the school counselor will work directly with the school psychologist and special educators as well in offering direct counseling and psychological support services to handicapped children and the classroom teachers teaching such children. Counselors and school psychologists will also find themselves members of teams that consult with the parents of handicapped children.

The School Social Worker

Social work has been defined by Crouch (1979) as "the attempt to assist those who do not command the means to human subsistence in acquiring them and in attaining the highest possible degree of independence." The school social worker provides helping services for those children who are unable to make proper use of their educational opportunities and who find it difficult to function effectively in the school environment. In this role, the social worker is a referral source for those children who appear to have emotional or social problems that are handicapping their learning and social adjustment to school. The school social worker has special interviewing and case work skills that are used within a school–child–parent context. The school social worker also is usually the pupil personnel services team member who works closest with community agencies and nonschool professional helpers, such as physicians, lawyers, and ministers. Meares (1977) reported a study (May, 1977) that ranked the importance of the tasks performed by school social workers. Four major interrelated priority activities were identified:

> (1) *clarifying* the nature of the child's problem and the parameters of social work services, (2) *assessing* the child's specific problem, (3) *facilitating* better relationships among school, community, and pupils, and (4) *educational counseling* with the child and his parents. Most activities emphasize the importance of the liaison role. Thus, there has been a transition from the primarily clinical casework approach to serving children in schools to that of home-school-community liaison and educational counseling with the child and his parents. (p. 198)

The school social worker is an important member of the school services team. Counselors and other helping professionals may depend on the social workers to provide broader and deeper understanding of the child, especially in regard to the home environment and the nature of the pupil's behavioral problems.

School Health Personnel

Most school systems employ professional health services personnel, at least on a part-time basis. Most common are the school nurse and the dental hygienist, and a number of school systems also employ school physicians. Your personal recall of these helping professionals may consist of memories of immunization shots, opening your mouth to say "Ah," the taste of the tongue-depressor, and the admonition of the dental hygienist when she discovered a cavity. Such recalls are fairly characteristic of the role of these providers of basic, preventive health services for all school children. These professionals also identify children who need special medical treatment or referrals for the correction or alleviation of defects. Counselors will find these medical specialists a resource for referrals and a help in determining whether or to what extent physical ailments or defects are an obstacle to a student's anticipated development or adjustment.

Psychiatrists

Psychiatrists are physicians with specialized training in the treatment of behavioral abnormalities. As physicians, psychiatrists are permitted by law to use drugs and other physical means of treatment for mental problems. Counselors often suggest to parents that they refer their son or daughter to a psychiatrist if it is suspected that the child may have an emotional disturbance requiring the use of medication. Many psychiatrists perform an important consultative role to pupil personnel workers, as well.

Patterns of Counseling Program Organization in Educational Settings

Because it was noted earlier in this chapter that school counseling programs must reflect the differences in their populations and settings, it is appropriate to assume that these differences will also result in differing organizational structures for programs. Consequently, it must be recognized that there are many successful yet differing patterns of program organization for all educational levels. Furthermore, these structures differ according to the educational levels (elementary, middle, secondary, or higher education) they serve. This chapter attempts to briefly illustrate only a few of the more traditional and popular program formats.

Organizational Patterns in Elementary Schools

As has been already noted in discussions of the historical development of guidance in American education, counseling programs are just beginning to emerge in the elementary schools of this country, despite the fact that there have been supporters of this concept for more than 50 years. Because there are no established, traditional organizational formats with which the subject of elementary counseling programs might be comfortably introduced, let us examine some possible considerations.

In determining appropriate approaches to program organization and development in the elementary school, elementary educators have considered those characteristics and goals of the elementary school, especially those that highlight the special role of the elementary school as an educational institution. These include the missions of orienting the elementary school child to the educational environment and providing the elementary school pupil with the basic educational-developmental experiences that are essential for future development. Other special characteristics of the elementary school are also important as considerations in the organization and development of their counseling programs, including the following:

1. Most elementary schools are homeroom-teacher-centered. The elementary pupil in a self-contained classroom has one teacher for most of the school day, and he is with this teacher for at least one academic year. As a result, pupil and teacher get to know each other better in the elementary school than in schools at higher levels.
2. There is an emphasis on learning through activity. Physical activity and exercises related to learning are characteristic of the elementary school.
3. The elementary school pupil is a member of a reasonably stable group. Although some school populations are relatively transient, it is common for a child to be with the same group of fellow pupils for most of each school year and, in many elementary school situations, with many of the same children throughout his elementary years.
4. Elementary schools are usually smaller and less complex than secondary schools.
5. Parental interest and involvement are generally greater at the elementary level. (Gibson and Higgins, 1966, p. 14)

Further reflected in the educational approach and structure of the elementary school are the characteristics of the elementary school children. It must be noted by anyone who has ever set foot in an elementary school that there is no such thing as the "typical" elementary school pupil. And parents and teachers who interact with these children on a daily basis can further testify to the difficulties of characterizing this age group. It is therefore appropriate to suggest that the common characteristic all elementary youths share is that no two are alike. Despite this, it is not inappropriate to briefly note some broadly recognized needs and characteristics of this youthful population, even though there have been and will continue to be innumerable studies made and volumes written about the needs of children:

> As a basis for guidance in the elementary school, we will view these needs from two standpoints: (1) those basic needs which continuously demand satisfaction, and (2) those developmental needs which must be met during different life stages.
>
> Man's basic needs have been presented by Maslow in a hierarchy or priority ordering of needs in which the higher-order needs will emerge only when the lower-order needs have been fairly well satisfied. In his discussions, Maslow has pointed out that

the best way to repress the higher motivation of man is to keep him chronically hungry, insecure, or unloved. According to Maslow's theory, as the teacher and counselor view the elementary pupil and his ability to become self-actualized and develop his potential, the teacher or counselor must be concerned with, and aware of, the degree to which the pupil's lower-order needs are being met.

The developmental needs of humankind, according to his life stage, have been well presented by Havighurst (1953) in his popular "developmental tasks." Counselors and teachers in the elementary school should take note of the following developmental tasks for middle childhood:

1. Learning physical skills necessary for ordinary games.
2. Building wholesome attitudes toward oneself as a growing organism.
3. Learning to get along with age mates.
4. Learning an appropriate masculine or feminine social role.
5. Developing fundamental skills in reading, writing, and calculating.
6. Developing concepts necessary for everyday living.
7. Developing conscience, morality, and a scale of values.
8. Achieving personal independence.
9. Developing attitudes toward social groups and institutions.

The presentations of Maslow and Havighurst stress both the personal and the cultural nature of the needs of children as they grow and develop. There is also an implied "developmental task" for educational programs—the task of providing learning experiences appropriate to the needs, both basic and developmental, of the elementary school child.

In addition to the needs of children, plans for counseling in the elementary school should take into consideration the following characteristics of the student.

1. He or she is experiencing continuous growth, development, and change.
2. He or she is constantly integrating experiences.
3. He or she is relatively limited in the ability to verbalize.
4. His or her reasoning powers are not fully developed.
5. His or her ability to concentrate over long periods of time is limited.
6. His or her enthusiasm and interest can be easily aroused.
7. His or her decisions and goals serve immediate purposes—he or she does not yet make long-range plans.
8. He or she displays feelings more or less openly.

The implications of these characteristics and needs for programs of counseling in the elementary school must be reflected in both counseling program structure and counselor role and function. (Gibson, 1972, pp. 19–20)

On the basis of these identifiable characteristics of the elementary school and of the characteristics and needs of elementary school students, it is evident that any program in the elementary school that focuses on the student, to be successful, must have not only the approval of but also significant involvement of the faculty; it must be teacher-centered. Furthermore, close and frequent contact with parents must be anticipated, especially in the primary years. It is also clear that any program that relies too heavily on "talking at" the elementary school student, even when supplemented with films and other media or material aids, is doomed to failure. The elementary school is activity-oriented, and the counseling program in this setting must "do as the Romans do." Finally, the elementary years are noted as developmental years. The elementary school guidance program must therefore respond accordingly with a developmental rather than a remedial emphasis, an emphasis that suggests, for example, less individual adjustment counseling and more developmental group guidance activities.

Organizational Patterns in the Secondary School

Since their early, sometimes timorous, and sometimes tenuous beginnings in the 20 years after Parsons through their experimental growth years of the 1930s and 1940s into the boom years of the 1950s and 1960s, school programs of counseling and guidance have been almost the exclusive property of the American high school. Although different influences and emphases in both the secondary school and the counseling and guidance movement have often altered concepts of program structure and function, the movement maintained a steady growth in both numbers and professionalization through the 1970s and developed recognizable images of program structure, role, and function. These, however, may also be more readily understood if one renews acquaintance with the characteristics of the secondary school (so well eulogized in *Is There Life After High School*, Keyes, 1976) and with the high school student as well.

Although adolescence is identified as that period between puberty and adulthood, nothing defies standard definition or description more than the adolescent. They are as varied, unpredictable, and uncontrollable as their peer group permits. They give meaning to the expression "generation gap," of which many adolescents are proud and, before it's over, for which many adults are thankful. Most persons view their adolescent years as different from those of today. They probably were, for adolescents today not only exhibit a wide variation in individual characteristics, but the group characteristics also seem to change rapidly from generation to generation. As an extreme example, many may recall that some of their grandparents seemed to go directly from childhood to work and adulthood. They completed their 8 to 10 years of schooling and went to work as farmers, miners, and so forth. Today, some youths stretch their adolescence into their 20s, resisting growing up, or accepting responsibility, and rejecting independence. For all who are concerned with youth during these magical years, for those who may hope to "ease their passage," it is important to recognize some of the characteristics of adolescents:

1. It is a period of continuous physical growth, not the least of which is the awakening of sexual impulses. Girls discover boys, and boys discover girls who discover boys. "Puppy" love becomes a serious crush that becomes "undying love" (at least for the moment).
2. It is a period of movement towards maturity with all its implications for independence, responsibility, and self-discipline; a period often very trying to parents who want to keep little Janie tied to her mother's apron strings or Johnnie still passing the football to old "butter fingers" Dad.

3. Reveling in their newly acquired independence and the discovery of their rapidly developing abilities to reason and hypothesize, many adolescents exaggerate their ability to solve "the problems of the world" and those that are personal for them. At the same time, many become critical of adult solutions to social problems, of their life-styles, and of their values but deny that adults are in a position to evaluate life among the adolescents.

4. Furthermore, with the acquisition of the privileges of adulthood—independence, responsibility, and self-direction—there is a movement from childish to adult forms of expression, reaction, and behavior. For better or worse, adult behavior is mimicked and often exaggerated.

5. Self-selected (not adult-imposed) peer group memberships are important to the adolescent. The peer group becomes the center of most of their significant social-recreational activities and, in the eyes of many parents (and many authorities as well), their initial sex education "program." Also, while demanding their independence from parents and other adult controls, adolescents in turn may surrender much of their independence and individuality to peer group conformity.

6. It is a period when they seek direction, a set of values, and their own personal identity. The latter demands treatment as an individual—a demand that the home and the school often appear to overlook. In the quest for this new identity, the adolescent encounters, with peers, many of the common problems of this journey. Although a multitude of studies have investigated the priority concerns of youths, most of these tend to be outdated immediately after their publication. Recognizing this limitation, we would use three categories to classify a consensus of common adolescent problems from current studies.

   A. *Developing as a social being.* This includes problems of one-to-one personal relationships, particularly dating, love, sex, and marriage. It also involves group living and acceptance and, in general, the development of human relationship skills.

   B. *Developing as a unique being.* The adolescent is concerned with the development and recognition of the uniqueness of individuals. It is a time when they are seeking to develop their own value system and often find they face value conflicts. Anxieties are often created as a result of constant demands to "measure up" made by evaluative testing and other appraisal techniques that appear to standardize them. They are also concerned when they fail to gain parental or other support for their "new self."

   C. *Developing as a productive being.* In this regard, youths are concerned with their educational adjustments and achievements, their career decisions, future educational directions, impending financial needs, and employment prospects. Many become concerned because school is not providing them with a marketable skill. Others feel that staying in school is delaying earning a living.

Let us now briefly note some of the significant characteristics of the secondary school, because these characteristics are important considerations in the organization of all programs, including those of counseling. Although there are, of course, many exceptions to any attempt to characterize schools at any level, the following are generally appropriate for many secondary schools in the United States and Canada.

1. Secondary schools are generally large, complex institutions populated by a heterogeneous student body. The size and complexity of the secondary school have implications for both counseling program development and program activities. Since the larger student bodies tend to be more heterogeneous, often representing many cultural minority groups, the identification of these groups and the response to their needs can represent a major challenge to the program.

2. Secondary school faculties represent a variety of academic specialities. The secondary school faculty member tends to concentrate on a particular subject area. As a result, the secondary school faculty represents a variety of specializations, which provides a reservoir of resources that the school counseling program may use in the career, educational, and personal-social development of students.

3. Secondary school years are important decision-making years for the individual student. During a student's secondary schooling, he or she is usually confronted with at least two lifetime influencing decisions. The first of these decisions that many youths make during this period of time is whether to complete their secondary schooling. Various dropout studies indicate that approximately one fourth of our high school youths make the decision to leave school before finishing their secondary school program. In addition, many students make important decisions regarding careers or choice of college. The wide variety of course offerings and activities available in most secondary schools prompts a nearly continuous series of minor decisions for the students as well. They may also be confronted with significant personal decisions regarding sex and marriage, use of tobacco, alcohol and drugs, and friends and friendship.

4. Secondary schools are subject-matter oriented. Schedules and classes tend to be formal and rigidly organized in many secondary schools, with considerable emphasis on academic standards, homework, and grades (rather than personal growth). Emphasis on standardized test achievements and school discipline can be expected. The homeroom that many students have experienced in the elementary school years ceases to exist in most high schools, except as an administrative checkpoint. As a result, at a time when students are accelerating their development as social beings, the secondary school structure often tends to inhibit this growth and development by placing them in a series of formal, academically oriented subject-matter class experiences. At the same time, many schools fail to provide students with an organized scheduled group (such as homeroom) where they might develop social skills and attitudes. This suggests a challenge to the subject-matter teacher and the counselor to work cooperatively to incorporate social development experiences into the academic program.

5. School spirit, or esprit de corps, is usually more evident in secondary schools than in any other educational institution. This school spirit is usually

reflected in the quest for winning athletic teams, championship bands, and other public indications of excellence. Often the competition among students for participation in significant school events is keen. Social divisions may often arise between those who have "made it" and those who have not in terms of these activities. On the positive side, however, school spirit in competitive activities can often be a potential factor in motivating students to remain in school, in making them seek higher academic achievements, and in promoting pride in the school. In recent years there have been frequent suggestions and efforts to increase the visibility of academic competition as well.

6. The school principal is the single most influential person in the secondary school setting. Decisions, policy development, and practices all emanate or are subject to the approval of the school principal. Unlike the elementary school principal, the secondary principal is frequently assisted by several assistant principals, supervisors, department heads, and specialty chairs. In addition, probably no other person is so significant in establishing the tone or atmosphere of the school and its inhabitants.

Although the adolescent and the adolescent's school share many characteristics in common, there are also wide variations among both secondary schools and secondary school populations. Counseling programs in secondary schools seem to reflect these ambivalences as counselors engage in many of the same basic activities but within a variety of organizational structures. Figures 3–2 through 3–5 present four of the more traditional organizational models of school counseling programs. Figures 3–6 and 3–7 take note of one characteristic—school size—and how that factor can influence the organizational framework within which school guidance programs function. For example, larger schools in larger school systems may have resource specialists and specialized services (computer and data processing, test scoring) available in the administrative offices of the school system. These resources are available to supplement the efforts of the local building counselors. On the other hand, small schools

Figure 3–2. Class counselor model.

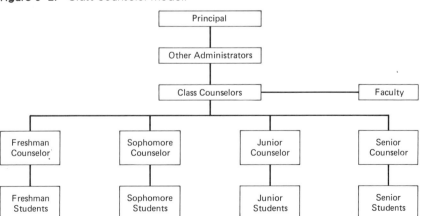

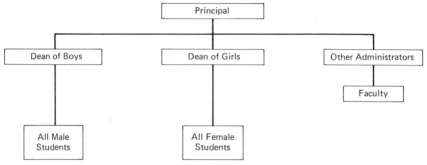

Figure 3–3. Separate deans model.

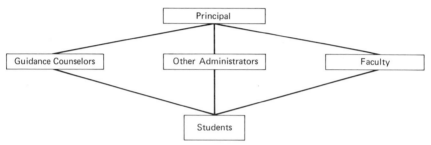

Figure 3–4. Guidance counselor (generalist) model.

may often have to share counseling and other specialized personnel. These personnel may operate out of the central administrative offices of the school system and be available on certain days to each school that shares their assignment.

Organizational Patterns in Institutions of Higher Education

Although the popular view from the "Ivory Tower" seems to most frequently focus on the football stadium, the pretty coeds, and, sometimes (but rarely) the distinguished professor, a serious look at most college and university campuses

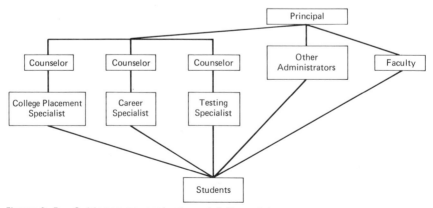

Figure 3–5. Guidance counselor (specialist) model.

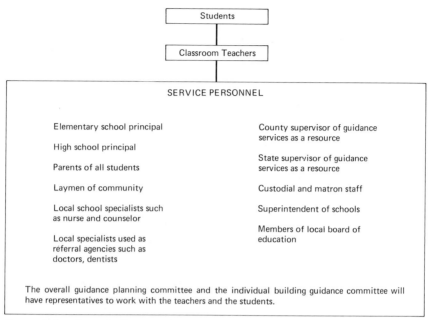

Figure 3–6. Organization chart for the small school guidance program. *(Blanchard, H. L., & Flaum, L. S., 1968, p. 43.)*

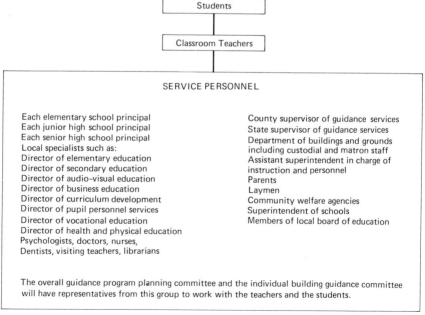

Figure 3–7. Organization chart for the large school guidance program. *(Blanchard, H. L., & Flaum, L. S., 1968, p. 44.)*

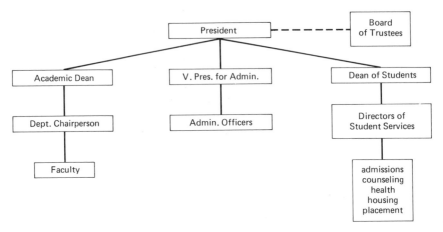

Figure 3–8. Organization chart for a four-year college.

confirms the existence of counselors and attending programs of counseling and other student personnel services. As might be anticipated, these programs are as unusual or as traditional as the institutions they represent. The burgeoning junior and community college movement appears to be developing programs that often suggest "open marriage" between elements of secondary school counseling programs and traditional university student personnel services programs. Four-year colleges and universities maintain, although often with interesting innovations, programs based on traditional student personnel services models—programs in which counseling services are freqeuntly provided through campus counseling centers or clinics, residential counselors, and career counseling offices. Figure 3–8 illustrates an organizational chart for a four-year college, with counseling services provided as a part of the student services of the college or university. Figure 3–9 displays counseling services as a unit of a large university program.

Future Directions for School Programs of Counseling

All of us engage in predicting the future. Much of our speculation on what lies ahead is, of course, short-range—we predict that the weather will be better tomorrow, the price of coffee will go up again next month, or the football team will be a winner next fall.

While predicting the future is fun, it is also risky, especially if one is bold enough to put these speculations in print. However, despite the many uncertainties attending even the most scientific efforts—and there are highly reputable scientific institutes engaged in such studies today—no less than in the past, we read our horoscopes in the daily paper, have our palms read or our handwriting analyzed, read with interest the annual New Year's predictions of those "gifted" with visions of the future, and note that books such as Toffler's *Future Shock* (1970) and *The Third Wave* (1980) become international best sellers.

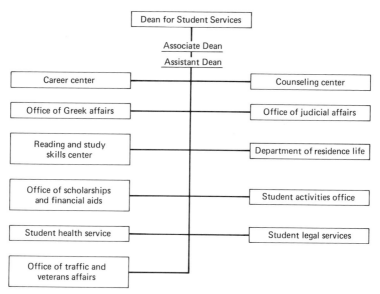

Figure 3–9. Organization chart for student services division in a large university *(Indiana University)*.

Although the high level of interest in knowing what the future holds in store for us and our societies does not appear to have diminished over the centuries, both the nature and the need for future insights have undergone significant change. We have noted the emergence since World War II of a "futuristic" science, with an emphasis on scientific, data-based, and computer-assisted forecasting, and the development of organizations such as The Institute for the Future (Middletown, Connecticut) and the World Future Society (formed in Washington, D.C. in 1966). The need for some form of reasonably accurate future forecasting has become increasingly evident.

One indicator that change will probably take place in product, activity, or organization is strong and significant criticism of their present state. For example, even those who "see no evil, hear no evil, speak no evil" are well aware of the volume and intensity of critical charges leveled at education over the years, criticims that have and will continue to promote change in the future. It is therefore appropriate to note, as one predictor of future change, that during the past decade, school programs of counseling have also come under frequent attack. Included have been suggestions that school programs of counseling and related counselor education programs must remodel to provide for more relevant and effective roles and functions in the decades ahead or disappear from the American educational scene. Counselors should be aware that as far back as 1971 the Gallup poll on education in that year revealed that out of 16 proposals for economizing in education, counselor removal was ranked fourth in priority. During the same year, Cook (1971) expressed it well in his *Guidance for Education in Revolution,* when he suggested the following:

> Guidance is at a crossroads as we begin the decade of the 1970s. The path travelled thus far has brought the guidance counselor out of the shadows of teaching and into

relatively high visibility as a professional person in his own right. But visibility creates special perils and responsibilities that are not so evident when a profession is young and seeking an identity. For the past several years school counseliing has been wrapped in an identity crisis, struggling with the question, "What is our role?" Now the signs point to an increasing likelihood that more and more the question will be raised by those outside the profession of school counseling, including those who hold the tightening purse strings of education, "Is what you are doing effective, making any difference in the lives of pupils, and do you even know what you are supposed to be doing." (p. 517)

A report of the June, 1972, National Advisory Council on Vocational Education called upon the field of counseling and guidance to initiate significant changes that would, in effect, increase the effectiveness of counseling youths for today's world of work.

Another critical study, *The Nationwide Study of Student Career Development* by Prediger, Roth, and Noeth (1973), reported a sharp contrast between youths' needs for career planning and the help received. This study confirmed that youths were seriously deficient in knowledge about the world of work and career planning and that they were unable to cope with the career development tasks posed by society during the difficult high-school–to–post-high-school transition and placement period. Prediger and colleagues recommended the reorientation of the traditional school counseling model to provide increased as well as more realistic assistance in career guidance and placement.

In 1978, a significant study reported by the North Central Association of Colleges and Schools sought to identify "those activities that will be emphasized in school guidance programs of the future." This study sampled 1,280 administrators, teachers, and counselors representing 616 different secondary schools. Recommendations resulting from this study were:

1. Counselors must get out of their offices—must become more active and visible in the school and community.
2. Counselors must function more as counseling service personnel and less as therapists.
3. Counselors must become more attuned to characteristics and needs of ethnic minority groups.
4. Counselors must become more cognizant of the need to overcome sex biases in their practices.
5. Counselors must become more skillful in their public relations, including communications with school staff, students, and parents.
6. Counselors must become more conscious of their local environment and its resources for enrichment of all aspects of the school counseling program.
7. Counselors cannot ignore student behavior. Both teachers and parents expect counselors to be concerned with unacceptable behavior, its causes, and modification.
8. Counselors, as all others in the educational system, must be accountable.
9. There is a need for counseling programs at all educational levels. Currently, the biggest deficit exists at the elementary school level.
10. Counselor training programs must become more selective and conscientious in their admissions practices.

11. Counselor training programs must become more relevant and field-based, as well as conscious of the needs and new directions of schools.

Increased emphasis on basics was called for by President Reagan's 1984 Task Force on Education, and we can therefore anticipate another "return to basics" movement for this decade. However, defining the basics will prove to be one of the most difficult issues that the schools will face, because the schools will serve as arenas in which various groups will do battle for their values (Apple, 1983). At the same time that schools are being called on to return to no-nonsense basics, give greater attention to student discipline and management, and measure student growth through standardized achievement testing, they are competing for the attention of youths with the continuing challenges from television and home computers and, shortly, challenged by a new innovation, robotics. The balancing of basics, behavior controls, technology, and humaneness will be one of the great challenges for education in the coming years (Apple, 1983, p. 322).

And what about the future for school counselors and their counseling programs in the remainder of this 20th century? We believe the future indicators give us some clues.

We would begin by recognizing that a "new wave" of counselors will be entering our schools in the last 15 years of this century as many of the N.D.E.A. (National Defense Education Act) trained counselors of the 1960s move into retirement. This, coupled with the increased demand—a nationwide trend—for elementary school counselors, will result in an acceleration in employment opportunities for counselors in schools.

It is evident that this new generation of counselors must be computer competent and alert to the technological advancements of "the information age" that have implications for their practice. As in the past, counselors will continue to counsel and consult and give attention to the career development needs of student populations, but there will be a greater program emphasis on prevention and early intervention. Counselors of the 1990s will also be expected to be more professionally competent in assessing differing environments (i.e., community, school, and so forth) and their impact on their clients.

Finally, we believe that our school counselors of the future increasingly will be called on to engage in research in their settings to hasten the solutions to many of our constant and worrisome youth problems, such as substance abuse, vandalism, delinquency and crime, dropping out, and underachievement. Only through an all-out professional effort involving those "on the scene" can we hope to make real headway in dealing with these problems. We believe our profession will rise to this challenge in the remaining years of this century.

Summary and Conclusions

An article in *Better Homes and Gardens* noted that "if you graduated from high school before 1960, chances are the only school counselors you have known are your child's" (Daly, 1979, p. 15). This chapter assumes that most of those who graduated from high school after 1960 also knew little about how their counselors were trained or licensed and had little familiarity with their role and function. It is perhaps this very lack of understanding that has led the counseling professionals in the past decade to move more energetically into the public communications arena to "tell what they're about," to upgrade their training, and to seek protection of their profession from unqualified intruders through certification and licensure. Much has been accomplished in a short period of time if one considers that at the turn of this century there were no counselors in schools. More than 80 years and 80,000 school counselors later, we can identify tremendous progress in training, certification, and practice.

Counselor training today is available at the master's, specialist, and doctoral levels, with the possibility of undergraduate and postdoctoral courses as well. All states specify some type of counselor preparation or certification for employment in school settings, with the exception of postsecondary institutions. These requirements in general reflect role and function expectancies. Differing characteristics of various school levels, settings, and clientele, by necessity, result in variations in that role and function. However, school counselors cannot "go it alone." They must view themselves as "member players" on the school "team" and work for the cooperation and contributions of teachers, administrators, and other helping professionals who are vital to the success of any school counseling program.

Finally, we noted that school counselors and school counseling programs must be able to adapt to the demands of the future if they are to become or remain relevant and valuable to the populations they are intended to serve. This is, of course, no less true for counselors functioning in various community and agency settings. Chapter 4 will describe counselors in these various settings.

References

Apple, M. (1983). Curriculum in the year 2000: Tensions and possibilities. *Phi Delta Kappan, 64,* 321–326.

Baker, S. B. (1981). *School counselor's handbook: Guide for professional growth and development.* Boston, MA: Allyn & Bacon.

Blanchard, H. L., & Flaum, L. S. (1968). *Guidance: A longitudinal approach.* Minneapolis, MN: Burgess.

Bloom, B. S. (1976). *Human characteristics and school learning.* New York: McGraw-Hill.

Brown, J. A., & Pate, R. H., Jr. (1983). *Being a counselor.* Belmont, CA: Brooks/Cole.

Conyne, R. K. (1983). Two critical issues in primary prevention: What it is and how to do it. *Personnel and Guidance Journal, 61,* 331–340.

Cook, D. R. (1971). *Guidance for education in revolution.* Boston: Allyn & Bacon.

Cristiani, T., & Simmons, P. (1978). The school counselor's role in mainstreaming the handicapped. *Viewpoints in Teaching and Learning, 54*(1), 20–28.

Crouch, R. C. (1979). Social work defined. *Social Work, 24,* 46–48.

Daly, M. (1979). How good is your child's school counselor? *Better Homes and Gardens, 57*(2), 15–22.

Dodge, K. (1983). Promoting social competence in school children. *Schools and Teaching, 1.*

Finkel, N. J. (1976). *Mental illness and health: Its legacy, tensions, and changes.* New York: Macmillan.

Forster, J. R. (1977). What shall we do about credentialing? *Personnel and Guidance Journal, 55,* 573–576.

Gibson, R. L. (1972). *Career development in the elementary school.* Columbus, OH: Charles E. Merrill.

Gibson, R. L., & Higgins, R. E. (1966). *Techniques of guidance: An approach to pupil analysis.* Chicago: Science Research Associates.

Gibson, R. L., Mitchell, M. H., & Higgins, R. E. (1983). *Development and management of counseling programs and guidance services.* New York: MacMillan.

Gregersen, G. D. (1977). What to expect from your school psychologist: Some reasons why you might not get it. *Viewpoints, 53*(1), 1–14.

Griffiths, D. E. (1964). Administrative theory and change in organizations. In M. B. Miles (Ed.), *Innovations in education* (pp. 425–436). New York: Teachers College Press.

Gross, B., & Gross, R. (1974). *Will it grow in a classroom.* New York: Dell.

Havighurst, R. J. (1953). *Human development and education.* New York: Longmans, Green and Co.

Hollis, J. W., & Wantz, R. A. (1983). *Counselor preparation 1983: Programs, personnel, trends* (5th ed.). Muncie, IN: Accelerated Development.

Ibrahim, F. A., Helms, B. J., & Thompson, D. L. (1983). Counselor role and function: An appraisal by consumers and counselors. *Personnel and Guidance Journal, 61,* 597–601.

Keyes, R. (1976). *Is there life after high school?* Boston: Little, Brown & Co.

McCully, C. H. (1962). The school counselor: Strategy for professionalization. *Personnel and Guidance Journal, 40,* 681–689.

Meares, P. A. (1977). Analysis of tasks in school social work. *Social Work, 22,* 196–201.

Morrill, W. H., Oetting, E. R., & Hurst, J. C. (1974). Dimensions of counselor functioning. *Personnel and Guidance Journal, 52,* 354–359.

Myrick, R. D., & Moni, L. (1976). A status report of elementary school counseling. *Elementary School Guidance and Counseling, 10,* 156–164.

National Advisory Council on Vocational Education. (1972). *Counseling and guidance: A call for change* (6th Report). Washington, D.C.: Author.

North Central Association of Schools and Colleges, Counseling and Guidance Committee. (1977). [Study of the elementary school counselor role.] Unpublished data.

Prediger, D., Roth, J. D., & Noeth, R. J. (1973). *Nationwide study of student career development: Summary of results.* (Research Report No. 61). Iowa City, IA: American College Testing Program.

Thomas, D. R. (1973). *The schools next time.* New York: McGraw-Hill.

Toffler, A. (1970). *Future shock.* New York: Random House.

Toffler, A. (1980). *The third wave.* New York: Random House.

CHAPTER 4

COUNSELORS IN COMMUNITY AND AGENCY SETTINGS

Introduction

Many of you may eventually consider employment as counselors in community, agency, or other "nonschool" professional situations. The objective of this chapter is to acquaint you with the counselor's role and function in a variety of these settings. These include community mental health agencies, employment and rehabilitation agencies, correctional settings, crisis prevention centers, and marriage and family practice.

The training of counselors for these various settings shares a great deal with the training of school counselors, and in the past there was little distinction in many master's degree level training programs with the possible exceptions of practicum and internship settings and a few specialized courses. However, new standards for the preparation of counselors in specialty areas as officially indicated by appropriate professional organizations has resulted in an increase in specialized courses. In some training programs counselors may be trained in separate departments or in programs with distinctly different emphases. Even greater distinctions will be noted at the doctoral degree level, where preparation tends to focus on one's anticipated professional work setting. The similarities and dissimilarities in both training and on-the-job functioning may be noted by examining the definitions appropriate to the profession in three professional organizations representing trainers and practitioners in the field of counseling. These are the American Association for Counseling and Development, the American Mental Health Counselors Association, and the American Psychological Association.

The description of professional counseling proposed by the American Association for Counseling and Development (formerly the American Personnel and Guidance Association) Licensure Committee (1978) is

> counseling procedures include but are not restricted to the use of counseling methods and psychological and psychotherapeutic techniques, both verbal and non-verbal, which require the application of principles, methods, procedures of understanding, predicting and/or interpreting tests of mental abilities, aptitudes, interests, achievement, attitudes, personality characteristics, emotion or motivation; informational and community resources for career, personal or social development, group and/or placement methods and techniques which serve to further the goals of counseling; and

designing, conducting and interpreting research on human subjects or any consultations on any item above. (p. 20)

The American Mental Health Counselors Association Certification Committee in 1978 defined the professional counselor as one who is involved in

> the process of assisting individuals or groups, through a helping relationship, to
> achieve optimal mental health through personal and social development and adjust-
> ment to prevent the debilitating effects of certain somatic, emotional and intra- and/
> or inter-personal disorders.

By the American Psychological Association (1967) definition, the practice of
psychology (including counseling psychology) is

> rendering to individuals, groups, organizations, or the public a psychological service
> involving the application of principles, methods and procedures of understanding,
> predicting and influencing behavior, such as the principles pertaining to learning,
> perception, motivation, thinking, emotions and interpersonal relationships; the meth-
> ods and procedures of interviewing, counseling, and psychotherapy; of constructing,
> administering and interpreting tests of mental abilities, aptitudes, interests, attitudes,
> personality characteristics, emotions, and motivation; and of assessing public opinion.
>
>   The application of said principles and methods includes but is not restricted to:
> diagnoses, prevention, and amelioration of individuals and groups; hypnosis; educa-
> tional and vocational counseling; personnel selection and management; the evalua-
> tion and planning for effective work and learning situations; advertising and market
> research; and the resolution of interpersonal and social conflicts. (pp. 1098–1099)

It should be noted that these organizations in their definitions stress developmental as well as remedial activities. Whereas for many years the image of
the counselor tended to be that of a remedial agent, it is clear that the present
and future orientation of the counseling professions places an increasingly significant emphasis on developmental services. This emphasis was encouraged by
Kagan (1977) in his presidential address to Division 17 of the American Psychological Association, in which he said:

> So-called "normal" people no longer are content to seek help only when they are
> vocationally uncertain, depressed, grieving or unable to grieve, preorgasmic or impo-
> tent. They want prevention and enrichment. They want the wherewithal to anticipate
> and deal with the many major personal and interpersonal events of living—they want
> a tool kit along with the car, so that they themselves are able to effect maintenance
> and repairs when things don't run smoothly. There is a need and a demand for self-
> directed personal and vocational exploration programs, personal and marital enrich-
> ment programs, mental health check-ups, and preventive maintenance programs.
> There is a need for participation of counselors on health teams with workers from
> other professions and for the further development and dissemination of structured
> learning experiences in human interaction as a part of secondary school curriculum
> and in medical, law, and nursing school programs. These too soon will be very much
> in demand. Also needed are family counseling and family interaction education
> courses as a routine part of termination of long-term hospital care or prison confine-

ment. Another exciting area for us is the teaching of mutual counseling skills for people to become colleague counselors for each other—physicians, dentists, police. All this I see as the immediate future—the long-range possibilities are mind-boggling, and let's be conservative and stay with the immediate future for now. (p. 5)

Lewis and Lewis (1983) also sounded a similar challenge in regard to community counseling when they wrote:

Educational programs should be made available to the entire community being served. These programs can involve two distinct thrusts: (1) educating community members *about* mental health, and (2) providing experiences that can enhance community members' own development and prevent the occurrence of serious problems. Programs dealing with mental health itself as a subject matter should help to clarify what is presently known about the positive factors that encourage health and effectiveness in everyday living. They should attempt to eliminate the lay person's assumption that mental problems always involve some kind of illness that comes from within the individual. They should, instead, encourage recognition of the notion that mental health cannot really be understood without an understanding of the relationships between individuals and their environments. This kind of program might help to erase the stigma that is all too often placed on people who have needed intensive assistance with psychological problems in the past.

Educational programs should attempt to increase understanding of the dynamics of mental health and mental illness and should also define the kind of contribution that the mental health agency is trying to make. This can help community members to set their own mental health goals and to become more actively involved in the planning and evaluation of the services that are offered. (p. 196)

Blocher and Biggs (1983), in discussing counseling psychology in community settings, defined counseling psychology as a

subdiscipline of the science of psychology and a speciality in the practice of professional psychology. As a discipline, counseling psychology draws upon and contributes to psychological knowledge, particularly in the following domains:

1. Vocational behavior, including the development of vocational interests, attitudes, values, and aptitudes and their relationship to vocational satisfaction and effectiveness.
2. Human cognition and cognitive development and their relationships to problem-solving, decision-making, and judgment.
3. Human learning and behavior change particularly in their relationships to the acquisition, transfer, and maintenance of coping and mastery behaviors through the life span.
4. Human communication and interpersonal behavior especially within family and other primary group settings that influence developmental processes.
5. The nature of optimal person-environment fit, especially in family, educational, work, and other community settings as these impinge upon the health, happiness, and continuing growth of members.

As a professional practitioner, the counseling psychologist draws upon the science of human behavior to help people in a variety of settings and situations. The counseling psychologist engages in individual and small-group counseling around a variety of concerns involving educational and vocational planning, personal problem-solving and decision-making, family problems, and other activities related to the enhancement of personal growth and effectiveness. Such counseling also focuses on the prevention, removal, or remediation of obstacles to personal growth as these exist in the interaction between the individual and the environment.

The counseling psychologist also engages in consultation with individuals, organizations, and institutions in the society to help enhance the quality of physical, social, and psychological environments as these affect the growth of those who work, study, or live within them.

The counseling psychologist often engages in training a variety of people in basic interpersonal and life skills that can improve their functioning in significant social roles. The counseling psychologist also functions at times as a psychological educator who shares with a variety of others important psychological skills and knowledge needed to help them function more effectively in helping situations and to move to higher levels of personal and social development. (pp. 15–16)

Thus, as we proceed to examine the role of the counselor in a variety of nonschool settings, we would emphasize that the nonschool counselor will and should be dealing with the developmental and growth needs of clients as well as the more traditional remedial and adjustment concerns.

Community Mental Health Agencies

Community mental health agencies provide counseling services for the general population within a specified geographic locale. Many community mental health agencies have been initiated under the provisions of the Community Mental Health Act of 1963, which provides initial funding for such centers that must be developed following the guidelines of the National Institute of Mental Health. These agencies were designed to provide preventive community mental health services. Typically, such centers offer inpatient and outpatient services, emergency services, and educational and consultation services. Many centers also provide partial hospitalization services, diagnostic services, and precare and aftercare in the community through programs of home visitations, foster home placement, and halfway houses.

Lewis and Lewis (1983) believe that the community mental health concept has great potential,

> because agencies dealing with specific "catchment areas" have the opportunity to develop well-coordinated human services and, at the same time, to recognize environmental situations and assist in organizing the local population to deal with them. This can occur in a small agency dedicated to out-patient care, or in a major mental health center providing comprehensive services to meet a variety of mental health needs. (p. 195)

A multifaceted approach that such agencies might attempt to implement is illustrated in Table 4-1.

Table 4-1. Community Counseling in Community Mental Health Agencies

	Community Services	**Client Services**
Direct	Educational programs concerning the nature of mental health Educational programs encouraging community involvement in planning and evaluating services Educational programs to enhance effective mental health development and prevent psychological problems	Ongoing counseling and rehabilitation programs Assistance with problems of living Crisis intervention
Indirect	Assistance in organizing local community to bring about needed environmental change Class advocacy in behalf of individuals such as former or present mental patients Organizing and planning for alternatives to hospitalization	Linkage with support systems and helping network Advocacy in behalf of individual clients Attempts to secure placements more appropriate than hospitalization Consultation with helping network

Source: Lewis & Lewis, 1983, p. 195.

The Agency Team

In most community mental health agencies, counselors are employed as team members with other helping professionals. These typically include psychiatrists, clinical psychologists, and psychiatric social workers. Psychiatrists are usually considered to be the leaders of the team, inasmuch as they have a medical background and may perform physical examinations, prescribe drugs, and admit people to hospitals in the treatment of behavior abnormalities. In addition to basic medical training, certification as a psychiatrist typically requires 3 years of residency in a psychiatric institution plus 2 years of further practice.

Counseling or clinical psychologists are prepared in programs that require a minimum of 3 academic years of full-time resident graduate study. Although emphases in programs will vary somewhat from institution to institution and depend on whether one is trained in a clinical or counseling psychology program, the psychologist receives general training in basic psychology, counseling and psychotherapy, psychological assessment, and psychological research. Some, such as Schofield (1966), report that the difference between clinical and counseling psychology has never been enterly clear, but distinctions do exist:

> there appear, however, to be some important distinctions which warrant continued separation, albeit with close cooperation. The tools which each use most typically (for example, different kinds of psychological tests) are different enough to warrant separate, although overlapping, training programs, and the problems presented by their clients are also different enough to justify different practicum and internship experiences. (p.122)

A tentative distinction might be that clinical psycyologists tend to work with behavioral abnormalities and personality reorganization, whereas counseling psychologists emphasize increased understanding of the adjustment problem of normal persons (Jordaan, Myers, Layton, and Morgan, 1968).

Psychiatric social workers are trained minimally to the master's degree level in 2-year programs. One year of this program is devoted to supervised internship in a clinical or hospital setting. Social workers are trained to give assistance to people in the community who are experiencing economic or other problems. This assistance is facilitated through welfare and other programs. The psychiatric social worker, however, is more frequently found in hospital or community mental health settings. In such settings, they may gather data regarding patients and their families and often will work with the patient's family in assisting the client's adjustment. In many community mental health centers, psychiatric social workers may also conduct treatment of a nonmedical nature.

A study by Randolph (1973) presented data of interest to those counselors in training who may be interested in possible employment in community mental health and other community settings. His study identified skills that were important in providing counseling, therapy, and consultation; testing, diagnosis, and research; and dealing with the specialized personality and personal qualities

Table 4–2. Ratings of Major, Department Title, Licensure, and Psychology Course Work Items

Item No.	Item	Mean Rating	Average Rank in 76 Items
55	Course in abnormal psychology	1.32	3
56	Course in personality theory	1.35	5
57	Course in learning theory	1.43	9
60	Course in developmental psychology	1.56	14
31	Hold degree from a psychology department	1.57	16
59	Course in behavior modification	1.60	19
58	Course in social psychology	1.60	19
34	Trained as a clinical psychologist	1.62	21
75	Licensed as a psychologist	1.63	22.5
66	Course in child development	1.69	26
35	Trained as a counseling psychologist	2.07	36
70	Course in physiological psychology	2.18	41
36	Trained as a community psychologist	2.22	43
76	Licensed as a school psychologist	2.32	47
37	Trained as a psychiatric social worker	2.44	51
74	Trained in social and rehabilitation services	2.45	52.5
65	Course in vocational development theory	2.48	54
32	Degree from a social-work department	2.51	56.5
39	Trained as a social worker	2.63	60
33	Degree from a counseling and guidance department	2.78	63
41	Trained as a school psychologist	2.81	64
40	Trained as a community counselor	2.89	66
38	Trained as a correctional counselor	3.17	73

Source: Randolph, 1973, p. 246.

TABLE 4–3. Ratings of Counseling, Therapy, and Consultation Items

Iten No.	Item	Mean Rating	Average Rank in 76 Items
1	Skill in individual therapy and counseling	1.15	1
22	Skill in providing therapy and counseling services for families	1.34	4
2	Skill in group therapy and counseling	1.41	6.5
9	Training in crisis intervention	1.50	11
21	Skills in providing consultative services for families	1.53	13
3	Skill in using supportive and reflective techniques	1.63	22.5
10	Training in mental health consultation for prevention	1.66	24
5	Skill in using behavioral therapy techniques	1.88	31
4	Skill in using reality therapy techniques	2.02	34
6	Skill in using Gestalt therapy techniques	2.05	35
20	Skill in providing play therapy for children	2.10	38
8	Skill in using transactional analysis techniques	2.23	46
7	Skill in using rational therapy techniques	2.45	52.5
24	Skill in providing vocational and career counseling	2.51	56.5
71	Training in biofeedback	2.59	58
72	Training in alphagenics	2.91	67

Source: Randolph, 1973, p. 247.

desired. The results of his study, representing 117 directors of community mental health facilities, are presented in Tables 4–2, 4–3, 4–4, 4–5, and 4–6.

For example, the most important overall skill desired in the preparation of counselors (among those surveyed) can be noted in Table 4–3 as skill in individual therapy and counseling. The most important skill in the area of testing, diagnosis, and research and, overall, the second most desirable skill that counselors should possess was skill in the diagnosis of psychopathologic conditions. The third most important item in the study and the highest rated item in Table 4–2 is a course in abnormal psychology.

Counseling in the Agency Setting

Counselors in community settings deal with widely diverse populations and a wide variety in both the type and nature of human concerns. These range from continuous developmental needs of people to crises requiring immediate emergency attention. Table 4–7 presents a description by Pietrofesa, Hoffman, and Splete (1984) of the general types of counseling situations with which community agency counselors deal.

Table 4–4. Ratings of Testing, Diagnosis, and Research Statistics Items

Item No.	Item	Mean Rating	Average Rank in 76 Items
15	Skill in diagnosis of psychopathology	1.23	2
13	Skill in administering individual mental tests for clinical-diagnostic purposes	1.49	10
62	Course in the Weschsler	1.51	12
12	Skill in administering individual mental tests for educational screening	1.57	16
14	Skill in administering projective personality tests	1.57	16
63	Course in the Binet	1.68	25
64	Course in testing for learning disabilities	1.74	27
61	Course in experimental psychology	1.90	32
68	Course in statistics	2.12	39
19	Skill in administering, scoring, and interpreting group-administered tests	2.27	45
16	Skill in conducting and publishing scientific research	2.37	49
67	Course in computer programming	2.73	61
73	Experience in conducting experiments with rats	3.01	71

Source: Randolph, 1973, p. 248.

Table 4–5. Ratings of Specialized Populations and Settings Items

Item No.	Item	Mean Rating	Average Rank in 76 Items
30	Specialized training in dealing with marital and sex problems	1.94	33
28	Specialized training in dealing with alcohol abuse	2.16	40
29	Specialized training in dealing with drug abuse	2.21	42
26	Experience in working with disadvantaged Blacks	2.33	48
53	Specialized training in working with institutionalized mental patients	2.43	50
54	Specialized training in working with geriatric populations	2.49	55
49	Specialized training in special education and retardation	2.60	59
52	Specialized training in working with noninstitutionalized public offenders	2.74	68.5
51	Specialized training in working with institutionalized public offenders	2.84	65
27	Experience in working with native Americans	2.92	68.5
69	Course(s) in a foreign language(s)	2.92	68.5
50	Specialized training in working with the physically disabled	2.99	70
25	Fluency in speaking Spanish	3.09	72

Source: Randolph, 1973, p. 249.

Table 4-6. Ratings of Personality, Personal Qualities, and Miscellaneous Items

Item No.	Item	Mean Rating	Average Rank in 76 Items
11	Training in intake-interviewing techniques	1.41	6.5
44	Good oral and written communication skills	1.42	8
47	Communicate high degree of personal warmth	1.60	19
23	Knowledge of community resources for referral of clients	1.82	28
18	Skill in organization and administration of helping services	1.87	29.5
42	Neat personal appearance	1.87	29.5
46	Skill in publicizing and public relations	2.09	37
17	Skill in grant and proposal writing	2.24	44
48	Communicate coolness or aloofness in interpersonal relations	4.35	74
43	Sloppy, unkempt personal appearance	4.44	75
45	Poor oral and written communication skills	4.63	76

Source: Randolph, 1973, p. 250.

Table 4-7. General Types of Counseling Situations

Type	Time Lines	Possible Concerns	Possible Counselor Activities
Crisis	immediate	suicidal drug anxiety rejection by lover	personal support direct intervention gather additional support individual counseling or refer to appropriate clinic or agency
Facilitative	varies (short to long term)	job placement academic problems marriage adjustment	individual counseling including: reflection of content and feelings informing interpreting confronting directing activities
Preventive	specific time span (depending on the program)	sex education self-and career awareness drug awareness	information giving referral to relevant programs individual counseling regarding program content and process aiding values clarification reviewing decision making
Developmental	continuous (over lifespan)	developing positive self-concept in the elementary school mid-career change acceptance of death and dying	individual counseling regarding: personal development in conjunction with significant others and environmental placement

Source: Pietrofesa, Hoffman, & Splete, 1984, p. 10.

Table 4–8. Counselor Activities at Each Level of Intervention

Primary	Secondary	Tertiary
Deliberate psychological education	Crisis counseling (drug & alcohol related, acute emotional upheavals, vocational choice point crisis)	Vocational rehabilitation of emotionally disturbed
Career education		Supportive therapy
Parent education	Marriage & family counseling	
Death education		
Sex education	Sex therapy	
Consultation/supervision	Brief therapy, individual & group	
Paraprofessional training	Developmental counseling	
	Long-term therapy	

Source: Goodyear, 1976, p. 514.

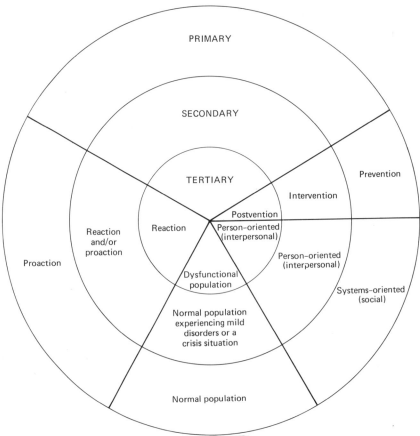

Figure 4–1. Levels of psychological interventions. *(Goodyear, 1976, p. 512.)*

In further examining the professional activities of counselors in community settings, Goodyear (1976) noted three levels of psychological intervention: primary, secondary, and tertiary. These may be noted in Table 4–8 and Figure 4–1.

In addition to community mental health agencies, a variety of what might be labeled alternative and nontraditional yet related community counseling services have developed over the past several generations. These nontraditional service centers have had a variety of titles, but most of them can be categorized under the labels of hot lines or crisis centers, "drop in" or open-door centers, and specialized counseling centers such as those catering to drug and alcohol abusers, young adults, or the aged.

Hot lines or crisis phones have been one of the most popular and older alternative services offered. They are frequently staffed by nonprofessionals or paraprofessionals with, in some settings, professional volunteers available or a professional supervisor on call. Usually hot lines or crisis phones are designed to provide sympathetic and helpful listeners and reliable information for dealing with such common concerns as drug overdoses, suicide, spouse abuse, alcoholism, and mental breakdown.

It is obviously desirable that crisis situations be handled by trained, professional counselors wherever possible:

> [These] crisis situations can be related to suicide attempts, unwanted pregnancy, death of a loved one, divorce, hospitalization, job relocation, new family member, loss of job, imprisonment, infidelity, retirement, drug addiction, or financial problems. Regardless of the nature of the crisis, the counselor needs to accept the situation and maintain personal poise and self-assuredness. This type of confidence can help to reduce the anxiety on the part of the client, as the counselor models responsibility for the client at this time. Through reassurance and expression of hope to the client, the counselor can deal with this immediate situation and then, in the future, aid the client in a developmental sense. (Pietrofesa, Hoffman, and Splete, 1984, p. 9)

In Table 4–9 are some suggestions made by Belkin (1981) for counselor behavior in a crisis situation.

Table 4–9. Do's and Don'ts in Crisis Intervention Counseling

Do's	Don'ts
1. Remain calm and stable. Prepare yourself psychologically for the turbulence of emotion that is soon to flow from the client.	1. Don't try to "cheer up" the client, to tell him that his problems are not as bad as they seem, to reassure him unless he specifically requests these types of interventions (which is, by the way, the exception rather than the rule).
2. Allow the client full opportunity to speak. Attempt to determine the type of crisis, its precipitating forces, and its severity. Interrupt only when it is for the client's benefit, never to relieve yourself of distressing feelings being induced by the client.	2. Don't ask the suicidal client to abandon his plans. Always make such a request a temporary delay.

Table 4–9. (cont.)

Do's	Don'ts
3. When indicated, ask object-oriented questions. These should, if asked properly, have a calming effect upon the client. If they fail to have such an effect, the counselor should consider the possibility that he is asking ego-oriented questions.	3. Don't attempt to solve the total personality adjustment difficulty. Some counselors make the error of minimizing the crisis itself and attempting to get the client to speak about more "fundamental" things.
4. Deal with the immediate situation rather than its underlying, unconscious causes that may be left for later. "In the crisis period," Brockopp (1973) points out, "the person is open to change; the sooner we can work with him, the more likely we are able to minimize the possible deterioration of the personality and to develop an effective solution which will improve the personality functioning of the individual."	
5. Have readily available local resources to assist the counselor: community, medical, legal, etc.	

Source: Belkin, 1981, p 439.

Open-door or drop-in centers provide havens for persons who need a place to come to and, in larger cities, to get off the streets—a place where they can feel secure and recieve sympathetic attention and counseling assistance. Some of these centers, actually provide minimal accommodations where a person can "sleep it off." For the most part, however, they simply provide an opportunity for the person to face emergency counseling assistance. In many of these centers, record-keeping is at a minimum and clients may not even be required to give their name or other personal data unless they wish.

In a number of more populous communities, various specialized counseling service centers are on the increase. Kelly, Franklin, and Jackson (1976) report that these centers tend to focus on special clientele, defined either by the nature of the problem, such as alcohol or drug addiction, spouse abuse, marital relations, or sexual information; by age classifications, such as the elderly, retired, or youths and young adults; by special racial considerations, and, on occasion, by religious denominations. These speciality centers tend to be staffed by a mixture of professionals, paraprofessionals, and volunteers. Facilities are equally diverse. For example, the Norfolk, Virginia Redevelopment and Housing Authority has established a system of community-based counselors who function with aids to assist individuals and families living in eleven public housing parks in that city. These counselors and their aides give support to residents in crisis situations and provide the information they need to cope with their problems, including the rules and regulations of the housing authority. Counseling activities tend to focus particularly on strengthening families.

O'Brien and Lewis (1975), in describing their community adolescent self-help center, point out that in this alternative to the traditional community mental health agency,

> members work on their own behalf, striving to control their futures and change those conditions that affect their lives. Members also gain a sense of prestige, self-esteem, and responsibility as positions of leadership and control within their organizations are made available to each of them. Self-help centers narrow the social distance between the care giver and the recipient by empowering members and equipping them with the tools and information necessary to meet their needs. (p. 213)

The functioning of this particular center, referred to as "the City," was described by O'Brien and Lewis (1975):

> The City is run much of the time by student staff volunteers who manage the center; they coordinate activities, engage in crisis counseling, and handle discipline problems and referrals. They have the authority to open or close the center as they deem necessary, and they assist the senior staff in deciding what programs and activities should be initiated and funded. (p. 213)

Employment Counseling

In 1933, the Department of Labor established the Employment Security offices that were to provide job placement and attending advising or counseling functions for the unemployed. Counseling was more specifically provided for in the G.I. Bill of 1944, which provided job counseling for veterans returning from World War II. By the 1960s, the Department of Labor was encouraging the states to upgrade their counselors to the professional or master's degree level of training:

> In the fall of 1970, the Manpower Administration initiated a massive inservice training program for selected employment service personnel. Originally, 88 colleges and universities in 33 states participated in the training program. Approximately 2,500 employment service personnel were initially involved in the training. The training was intended to increase the overall skill level of the trainees in dispensing employability assistance to those persons comprising the client population of the U.S. Public Employment Service. It was assumed by Manpower officials and participating university faculty that training in basic counseling skills and the behavioral sciences would improve the general quality of service rendered the public by employment service workers. (Phelps, Peer, and Canada, 1973, pp. 173–174)

Within the Department of Labor, an employment counselor is defined as one who performs counseling duties and who meets the minimum standards for employment counselor classification.

Brown and Feit (1978) described the services that an employment counselor should offer:

> The employment counselor needs to be aware of and familiar with a number of placement service skills. These would include (1) securing job leads, (2) recording job specifications, (3) referring clients to employers, (4) assessing client level of motivation,

(5) assessing client readiness for employment (Goeke and Salomone, 1979) as well as (6) surveying of job opportunities. (pp. 176–183)

The Employment Service also employs a number of counselor trainees who work under the close supervison of an employment counselor or an employment counseling supervisor. To qualify as a trainee, one must have

1. Completed a baccalaureate degree in one of the behavioral or social sciences, such as pscyhology, education, and sociology, which shall include a minimum of 15 semester hours (graduate or undergraduate) in counseling-related courses.
2. An expressed interest in becoming an employment couselor.
3. Demonstrated the ability to assist people in a counseling type of relationship (such as helping individuals to resolve employment or employment-related problems) in such settings as the employment service, a community action agency, vocational rehabilitation agency or schools.
4. The ability to complete successfully the necessary in-service, on-the-job, and out-service training programs for counselors. (J. Haner, Counselor Supervisor, Indiana Employment Security Division. Personal communication, August, 1978).

Although the focus of employment counselors, as with other employees of the employment security offices, is appropriate job placement of its clientele, the counselors are expected in the process to counsel clients on personal problems and assist them in developing attitudes, skills, and abilities that will facilitate their employment. Counselors are also involved in data gathering from their clients and in the administration and interpretation of standardized tests. Employment counselors tend to consider the National Employment Counselors Association (a division of the American Association for Counseling and Development, formerly the American Personnel and Guidance Association) as their professional organization. In 1975, this organization issued a position paper on the "Role of the Employment Counselor":

Rationale for Employment Counseling

As with counselors in other work settings, the employment counselor is a member of the counseling profession, differing from other members only in terms of the work setting and the nature of the problems presented by the clientele served. The employment counselor generally assists persons who are faced with an immediate problem related to employment, usually involving job choice, job change, or job adjustment. Since counselees come to the employment counselor's attention as a result of applying for a job, they are often referred to as "applicants." In providing the needed assistance the employment counselor considers factors both within and outside the counselee, such as psychological, physical, and socioeconomic factors that bear on the counselee's current status and that may have some effect on his or her future. Thus the employment counselor is concerned with the individual's potential and actual strengths and weaknesses, and with helping the counselee to understand the physical, mental, and emotional growth processes of individuals, but he or she must also understand these processes to use human service facilities and job opportunities for the benefit of the counselee.

The employment counselor believes that each person should have equal opportunity to develop and use individual talents for the betterment of self and the community, and that this is a developmental, lifelong process in which any number of institutions and other individuals, including the employment counselor, may play significant roles.

The employment counselor believes that work represents a meaningful expression of the individual's self-concept and values, and that individuals have the capacity to change, to grow, and to make intelligent decisions. However, the increasing complexity of the industrialized work world, constantly evolving through technological change, makes it increasingly difficult for the individual, without assistance, to make decisions regarding the choice of an occupation and preparation for it. Through the counseling process, the counselee is helped to achieve better understanding of self and of the occupational world, and to relate individual interests and talents to the demands of various occupational outlets. Thus employment counseling is an important element of the total spectrum of manpower services. For those in need of this service, it becomes an integral component of the placement process and a prerequisite to suitable job placement. Throughout the employment counseling process, the belief in freedom of choice is basic.

The employment counselor believes that there are situations in which active intervention by the counselor, or client advocacy, is an essential additional component of effective counseling. When successful individual adjustment is obstructed by environmental factors, and when the counselee is unable to effect needed change, the counselor has an obligation to act on the counselee's behalf, within the limits of applicable law, regulation, and policy. (pp. 148–149)

The National Employment Counselors Association (1975) has presented the following basic competencies that the employment counselor must develop in order to carry out employment counseling responsibilities effectively:

Employment Counselor Competencies

Relationship skills. The ability to establish a trusting, open, and useful relationship with each counselee, accurately interpreting feelings as well as verbal and nonverbal expressions, and conveying to the applicant this understanding and whatever pertinent information and assistance is needed.

Individual and group assessment skills. The ability to provide ongoing assessment in individual and group settings involving the appraisal and measurement of the counselee's needs, characteristics, potentialities, individual differences, and self-appraisal.

Group counseling. The ability to apply basic principles of group dynamics and leadership roles in a continuous and meaningful manner to assist group members to understand their problems and take positive steps toward resolving them.

Development and use of career-related information. The ability to develop and use educational, occupational, and labor market information to assist counselees in making decisions and formulating occupational plans.

Occupational plan development and implementation. The ability to assist the counselee in developing and implementing a suitable employability plan that helps move the jobseeker from current status through any needed employability-improvement services, including training and related supportive services, into a suitable job.

Placement skills. The ability to ascertain and to communicate understanding of employers' personnel needs, to make effective job development contacts, and to assist the counselee in presentation of qualifications in relation to the employer's needs.

Community relations skills. The ability, based on extensive knowledge of the important service delivery systems in the community, to assist counselees in obtaining the services needed.

Work load management and intra-office relationships skills. The ability to coordinate the various aspects of the total counseling program in the employing agency, resulting in a continuous and meaningful sequence of services to counselees, agency staff, and the community.

Professional development skills. The ability, based on interest in furthering professional development, to engage in activities that promote such development individually and within the profession, and to demonstrate by example the standards and performance expected of a professional employment counselor. (pp. 152–153)

Correctional Counseling

Practitioners of correctional counseling are employed in various law enforcement settings, ranging from those involved with first-time juvenile probationary offenders to persons incarcerated in penal institutions. Counselors in these settings usually have training backgrounds in counseling, psychology, sociology, or forensic studies. Their duties include counseling and interviewing; the use of various analytical techniques, including the use of standardized testing; referrals; parole recommendations; and placement. In some juvenile institutional settings, counselors may be employed as "live in advisors." Counselors working with youthful juvenile offenders work closely with police officers and other juvenile authorities. For example, Collingwood, Williams, and Douds (1976) described two major goals of such a program in Dallas, Texas, as diverting juveniles from the juvenile justice system, and reducing re-arrests/recidivism (p. 435). In this program, police officers as well as counselors were used in helping roles, with both working in an integrated manner within the department:

> The model adopted to implement the program was Carkhuff's (1971) Human Resource Development (HRD) model, which emphasizes the physical, intellectual, and emotional skills of helper and helpee. The model was applied to the selection and training of police and counseling staff and to the training-as-treatment methods employed with the juvenile offenders. (p. 435)
>
> Youths referred to the counseling unit were able to significantly increase their physical, intellectual, and emotional skills while in the program. Also, they appeared able to apply the skill improvement to improved functioning in certain outcome areas. (p. 436)

Examples of counselors functioning in juvenile correctional institutions may be found in the differential treatment approach of the Kennedy Youth Center of Morgantown, West Virginia, and the Indiana Boys' School, Plainfield, Indiana. These and other similar institutions utilize the differential treatment approach, which seeks to take into account individual differences in matching

inmates with counseling staff on the basis of personality or behavioral categories. In other correctional settings, counselors function as key agents in converting closed, traditional punitive systems into those that are more positive,
helping, and rehabilitative. In these settings, the emphasis is on the formation
of positive interpersonal climates and open lines of communication among the
various members of the prison community, including inmates and correctional
officers, or guards. An example of such an activity is described in an article by
Wittmer, Lanier, and Parker (1976) in which prison officers (guards) in Florida
participated in a race relations training program with an emphasis on
communications.

Rehabilitation Counseling

History reflects the admiration that society has always held for those who have
overcome physical handicaps to achieve notable success. The man (Franklin D.
Roosevelt) who was paralyzed by polio in both legs at 39, but later became President of the United States of America and a wartime world leader; the girl
(Helen Keller) who was deaf and blind from the age of 2, but became a successful author and lecturer; the deaf musician (Ludwig van Beethoven), or the
amputee actress (Sarah Bernhardt)—to name but a few—are examples of
achievement over physical adversity. Clifford Beers, who was mentioned in
Chapter 1, is an example of individual triumph over mental illness. The
achievements of these and others, despite their handicaps, were notable, but
history has failed to record the tragic losses in human potential that were
allowed to occur because of lack of attention, other than medical, for the disabled. Since World War II, however, the expansion of rehabilitation counseling
into public agencies has provided a dramatic increase in opportunities for the
handicapped to receive special counseling assistance in overcoming their
disabilities.

The functions of a rehabilitation counselor enumerated by Muthard and Salomone (1969) in terms of eight major classes of role behavior have often been
considered to be a definitive description of rehabilitation counselor role behavior (Berven, 1979). These eight classes of role behavior include: (a) placement;
(b) affective counseling; (c) group procedures; (d) vocational counseling; (e)
medical referral; (f) eligibility-case finding; (g) test administration; and (h) test
interpretation.

Rehabilitation counselors work with disabled clients in overcoming deficits
in their skills. Rehabilitation counselors may work with a special type of client
such as the deaf, blind, the mentally ill, or the physically handicapped or, in
some settings, the rehabilitation counselor may deal with all of these plus other
types of handicapped and disabled as well. The rehabilitation counselor's work
is often done in close cooperation with physicians or psychiatrists. In this
regard, Lamb and Associates (1971) indicated that although the counselor needs

> to take into account what goes on in psychotherapy and how the client's illness, per-
> sonality problems, and pathological family relationships affect his ability to function
> and his capacity to work, the rehabilitation counselor, in his interaction with a client,
> is committed to the *now* and *from here on* and to working to strengthen the healthy

portion of the client's ego. The counselor needs to see the client as he is functioning now in his environment, and where modifications can help him to get where he is or should be going vocationally. (p. 29)

The counselors' role is a complex one in which they provide a broad range of psychological and career-oriented services and work with and often coordinate the efforts of community agencies in their client's behalf:

A major role which most definitely distinguished rehabilitation counselors from workers in other helping professions is that of being a resource person. The counselor must have a wide knowledge of the occupations, including an intimate knowledge of how and under what circumstances they are practiced. Counselors must be aware of groupings of jobs so that skills which are transferable can be utilized in vocational planning. Further, the counselor develops an in-depth working knowledge of the particular personality traits that are required or contraindicated for specific jobs, so that he can help his client make an appropriate choice. The counselor must bring together the individual needs of the client and all the reasonable possibilities open to him. (Lamb and Associates, 1971, p. 41)

The rehabilitation counselor as a resource person also seeks to encourage the optimum adjustment and development of the handicapped:

In his role as resource person, the counselor must be familiar with nearby schools and training institutions and be able to evaluate their usefulness to particular clients. Further, he needs to be aware of funding sources of all kinds so that training is available to those who cannot finance it themselves.

Beyond this, a counselor must keep up with the state of the labor market in his locale so that clients are not preparing for unmarketable or outmoded occupations.

He must assess clients' past work experiences to find those which are particularly marketable now. The search can be as exciting as a detective story, depending upon the attitude and creativity of the counselor.

When clients are ready for employment, the counselor becomes a teacher. He helps clients to learn the most effective way of seeking a job. He shows them how to fill out applications, how to enhance their chances of passing entry tests, how to prepare a resume, if one is necessary, and how to behave in employment interviews to maximize their chances of success with emphasis on alternate behaviors in differing circumstances. (Lamb and Associates, 1971, pp. 42–43)

Although rehabilitation counseling was originally provided by private services, since World War II the field has been largely preempted by the Veterans Administration and by state departments of vocational rehabilitation, the latter assisted by the Vocational Rehabilitation Administration in the Department of Health, Education, and Welfare. Most of the rehabilitation counseling within the Veterans Administration is conducted by counseling psychologists and within the state agencies by rehabilitation counselors. (Lewis, 1970, p. 231).

Marriage and Family Counseling

Although the marriage vows read "until death us do part," the high divorce rate in this country in recent decades indicates that thousands of couples have decided they cannot wait until their entry into eternity to part. In addition, thousands of other couples suffer through phases of their marriages or seek adjustment to marriage difficulties by means other than separation or divorce. Although not based on empirical studies, the report by the popular advice columnist Ann Landers that the top four on her readers' ten most common problems concern marriage and family may also be symptomatic of the need.

Certainly, there is an abundance of statistical empirical evidence indicating that family discord and divorce is continuing to increase. The stresses of the actual divorce process for spouses and children and the later adjustment requirements for all involved are well documented and include such problems as the feelings of failure that often accompany divorce, and other emotions such as anger, regret, and depression are also commonplace. There is also the problem of adjustment in terms of separation, child rearing where children are concerned, and single parent roles. In addition to these emotional and psychological stresses, there are also those practical concerns that center on the legal issues and financial responsibilities for persons in divorce or separation. Also, the adjustment problems of children in the divorcing of parents cannot be overlooked. Concerns about loyalty, parental dating, and custody can have severe psychological consequences, especially when coupled with the feelings of guilt and the devalued self-concept commonplace in children of divorce.

We can conclude that the traditional image of the "home" and "family" as a cozy nest of love, security, togetherness, and never-ending happiness has been severely battered (as have many of its inhabitants) in recent generations. The need for counselors who can effectively counsel outside the one-to-one relationship, who can work in this new dimension—the family or family system— has evolved. Yet, providing effective counseling assistance to families and couples in today's complex and stressful society is a challenging and often difficult task, frequently complicated by advice from nonprofessionals, cultural traditions, and environmental pressures. (In fact, Prochaska and McCrady (1978) noted that "most therapists are about as poorly prepared for marital therapy as most spouses are for marriage." p. 1.)

It is only within the past several decades that marriage and family therapy has emerged as a counseling speciality. While individual counseling focuses on the individual person and his or her concerns, family therapy tends to focus on "the family system." Even if only one member of the family is being counseled, if the counseling is concerned primarily with the family system, it can be viewed as family counseling. Family therapy focuses upon the communications process, power balances and unbalances, influence processes, structures for conflict resolution, and the current functioning of the familiy system as a system. The goal of family therapy is not simply to effect change in an individual within the family, but rather, to effect change in the structure of the family and the sequencing of behavior among its members (Okun and Rappaport, 1980, p. 37).

The theoretical and empirical contributions of Rhona Rapoport (1963, 1964) in her work on normal family crises and family structure have clarified the process of transition and adjustment. Rapoport noted the close parallels between the responses to the hardship-bearing stressor events of the family crisis studies and the normal developmental challenges requiring family reorganization which punctuate the family's life span. Termed "normal crises of transition" because they are encountered by all families bearing children, she identified them in sequence as (1) the crisis of getting married; (2) the crisis of parenthood; (3) the crisis of deparentalization; (4) the crisis of leavetaking or launching; and (5) the crisis of retirement. She invoked crisis theory to account for the behavior of families as they moved through "points of no return" from one crisis to the next. If the crisis is handled advantageously, it is assumed that the result is some kind of maturation or development. If the crisis is not handled well, old tensions may be renewed and new conflicts may arise. It should be noted that the developmental crises carry no stigma, no label of deviancy, which characterize a number of the crises depicted in the family crisis literature. Hill (1973) offered a tentative way of operationalizing Rapoport's concept of critical transition to generate stages of family development. He noted that stages of development, by definition, were marked by multiple sharp changes in the family's role complex. Most families can sustain one or two changes in their role scripts but are forced into major reorganization if there is a pile-up of role complex changes. Hill singled out three types of structural events which might be expected to be stressful and hypothesized that, if they recurred within the same period of time, they would precipitate a critical transition demarcating a new stage of development:

1. Changes in numbers of family members (accessions and losses of spouse and/or children, return of divorced and widowed adult children).
2. Age composition changes:
   Changes in age norm content due to individual developmental status change, school status change, and so on of:
   oldest child
   middle child
   youngest child
3. Major status changes of:
   Cohabitating, engaged, married, divorced, widowed statuses
   Childless, parenthood, stepparenthood, grandparenthood, emptynesthood statuses
   Changes in conjunctive roles affecting priorities in role cluster and role sets:
      Entering and leaving school (Fa, Mo, Ch)
      Entering labor force, changing careers, and leaving labor force (Fa, Mo, Ch)
      Entering and leaving military service (Fa, Mo, Ch)
      Entering and leaving hospital as patient (Fa, Mo, Ch)
   Residential status and location changes:
      Renter, homeowner, renter
   Network affiliation changes. (Mederer and Hill, 1983, pp. 50–52)

In recent years, three major approaches to marriage and family counseling have been identified:

   1. The first of these major foci for family counseling could be termed the Communications Approach. This approach is centered on the task of teaching family members to communicate more effectively and so increasing the sensitivity and awareness of family members to each other's needs and concerns. Treatment models based upon this approach have been described by therapists such as Satir (1964) and Gordon (1970).
   Family counseling interventions within this approach emphasize structured communications exercises, direct analyses of family communications processes, and teaching of models of communication based upon open and honest two-way communication. The communication approach to family counseling is based upon a

number of fundamental concepts and assumptions about social interaction processes. (Blocher and Biggs, 1984, p. 250)

2. The structural approach to counseling of families is a logical extension of the application of general systems theory to the study of family life. In a sense, the structural approach looks at family functioning in terms of basic organizational principles. Family structure refers to the pattern of roles, relationships, rules and responsibilities established for accomplishing family tasks. (Blocher and Biggs, 1984, p. 256)

Counseling interventions drawn from this [general systems] research tend to emphasize the family as a hierarchical system with parents or parent surrogates being responsible for the managerial or executive functions. In families experiencing difficulties, the exercise of these functions is often observed to be confused and inappropriate. In particular, many such families are found to involve children in parental conflict to the detriment of both the child's emotional well-being and the overall effectiveness of the family.

Treatment generally includes a careful analysis of family decision-making processes and prevailing ways of handling conflict. Parents are often taught child-management techniques and attitudes that clearly differentiate between the roles and responsibilities of children and parents. Children are encouraged to play age-appropriate roles and to stay out of parental conflict situations as much as possible.

Family counselors in this model serve, in a sense, as organizational consultants who analyze family interaction processes and present new and more effective organizational arrangements. (Blocher and Biggs, 1984, p. 257)

3. A third basic approach to family counseling concerns what can be called family community transactions (Bronfenbrenner, 1979). This approach is especially relevant to the counseling psychologist in community practice in that it focuses on the degree to which families are able to utilize and contribute to needed resources that exist in the community.

. . . Research [has supported] an approach to providing family services which has been developed that is sometimes called "family networking." This approach emphasizes helping to break down barriers between families and community resources. It often involves building positive, cooperative relationships between parents and teachers. It may concentrate on helping families relate positively to neighbors or to restore extended family relationships. It may involve helping to organize support or action groups around the specific needs of single parents, tenants, insecure neighborhoods, or others. The approach may help families utilize the services of already organized community groups such as Parents Without Partners, Big Brothers, Big Sisters, or other community resources. (Blocher and Biggs, 1984, pp 258–259.)

An outgrowth of the increased recognition of the extent of marital problems has been the development of a specialty area within the field of marriage counseling. This group, represented by the American Association of Marriage and Family Therapy, includes memberships from diverse professional preparation backgrounds, including psychiatrists, psychologists, law, and the ministry. Another representative organization of this group is the National Council on Family Relations. The focus of marriage counseling, as noted,

deals primarily with a disordered relationship between two persons. The husband and wife must not, of course, be ignored as individuals, but their interaction is of chief concern to the marriage counselor. If it becomes evident that the root of the difficulty lies in adjustment problems of one or both of the parties, the emphasis shifts to them as individuals, and the concern for the relationship is temporarily abandoned.

If either of the individuals appears to have deep-seated emotional problems which are contributing to the marital disruption, he will generally be advised to seek individual psychotherapy. Some marriage counselors undertake this responsibility themselves, but most prefer to refer the client elsewhere. If, at a later time, marriage counseling for the couple seems warranted, it can be resumed. By the same token, the marriage counselor should feel free to refer to other professionals, such as a lawyer or physician, when their specialized knowlege may be of value to his clients.

The goal of marriage counseling is not, as many persons would suppose, the preservation of the marriage. As with any counseling, the client must be free to make his own decisions; it is the counselor's responsibility to help him think things through rationally, and thoroughly, so that he can live with the decision he makes. (Lewis, 1970, pp. 234, 235)

In states that have enacted laws regulating the practice of marriage and family counseling, a doctorate plus appropriate experience is most frequently required for licensure in this area.

Pastoral Counseling

From the standpoint of sheer numbers and geographic coverage, pastoral counseling provides a significant mental health resource. Not only are clergy members generally available to listen to the concerns and personal problems of their parishioners, but it appears that they are frequently the first source to which people in trouble turn. For example, the study illustrated in Table 4–10 indicated that as many as 42 percent of the population may consider their clergy as their first choice for mental health assistance. In recognition of the mental health function of the clergy, many theological training programs include courses in pastoral counseling, related psychology, and general counseling sub-

Table 4–10.   Where People Go for Help*

Source of Help	Percent
Clergyman	42
Doctor	29
Psychiatrist (or psychologist): private practitioner or not ascertained whether private or institutional	12
Psychiatrist (or psychologist) in clinic, hospital, other agency; mental hospital	6
Marriage counselor; marriage clinic	3
Other private practitioners or social agencies for handling psychological problems	10
Social service agencies for handling nonpsychological problems (e.g., financial problems)	3
Lawyer	6
Other	11

*Of the 2,460 people interviewed in a national survey, 345 had sought professional help for a personal problem. The sources of help and the percentage of time each source was sought are presented here. Because some respondents gave more than one reply, the total comes to more than 100 percent.

Source: Gurin, Veroff, & Feld, 1960, p. 307.

jects. Special programs have also been developed in clinical pastoral education for theology students and clergy desirous of further training. Although many of these specialized programs are comparatively short-term, others provide intensive training in clinical settings. Additionally, clergy members are increasingly enrolling in regular preparation programs in counselor education.

Gerontology Counseling

The "greying of America" is the phrase frequently used to note the dramatic increase in our "older" population. The U.S. Bureau of the Census Current Population Reports noted that the group 65 years of age and older constitutes approximately 11 percent of our total population, contrasted to 4.1 percent in 1900, with predictions of continued increases well beyond the turn of the century. With increased representation in our population has also come an increased sensitivity to the needs, including counseling, of this special population. Also, as this group becomes more politically potent and active, the aged themselves are demanding the same range of social services and attention to their needs that are provided for other age groups.

In addition to the older Americans themselves, their employers have also indicated increased concern regarding their adjustment to retirement. A poll of the top 1,000 companies in America in 1980 by Research and Forecast, Incorporated (Black, 1981) found that 42 percent of the chief executives of these companies believed that preretirement counseling was a high priority for their employees. Thirty-seven percent confirmed that such programs were in progress while another 22 percent were planning future programs. In recognition of the increased demand for counselors with special knowledge and skills to function effectively in this area, the American Association for Counseling and Devleopment (formerly the American Personnel and Guidance Association), developed, under a grant from the Administration on Aging, U.S. Department of Health, Education, and Welfare, a training syllabus for counselor educators, *Counseling the Aged* (Ganikos, 1979). This publication provided an expanse of basic information about aging with major emphasis on those aspects particularly relevant to counselors.

As more people live longer, they are often required to move into untested roles. The greater the difference in role and the less knowledge beforehand about this role, the more marginal that person will feel (Schlossberg, 1984). Without clear-cut expectations in many areas of their lives, older people may frequently feel confused by the role shifts brought on by aging or retirement. Counseling can assist such persons in coping with these and other adjustment and development needs.

Future Directions

In 1980, *The Counseling Psychologist* had a special theme issue (Volume 8, Number 4) entitled "Counseling Psychology in the Year 2000." In this issue Whiteley concluded:

In order to have an increased impact in the changed world of 2000 A.D., counseling psychology will have to enlarge its substantive bases to include environmental psychology and environmental planning; life-span developmental psychology including aging, developmental tasks, and transitions between phases of life; the psychology of men and women, the growth of men and women within relationships, sex roles, parenting, sexuality, and child rearing; more refined approaches to building a psychological sense of community; assertion training and social organization self-renewal; psychobiology; information and computer science; and, finally, systematic study of the expected future and its alternatives. (p. 7)

Ivey (1980) suggested:

For the future, one can predict a counseling psychologist who will be skilled in one-to-one counseling but will be more interested in teaching what he or she knows to others via the psychoeducational model. And, with each individual or group with whom the counseling psychologist works, the emphasis will be first on the transactions, then on the environment. Where necessary, individual counseling interventions will be initiated, but more often systemic and planned interventions to facilitate change and growth in BOTH the person and the environment may be expected.

Underlying this model will be an increased awareness of the decisional model underlying the structure of the helping interview, planned change in institutions or environmental services, and the decisional process of the client. Decision making is not new, but our understanding of the process will lead to many new discoveries. Facilitating the decisional process will be computer-assisted counseling and computer modeling of alternative futures. Aiding in this process will be an increased awareness of the linguistic frames that organize the helping process. Awareness of cultural and social differences will increase. (p. 15)

Leona Tyler (1980) discussed the implications for the year 2000:

It means that counseling psychology (and counseling psychologists) will be dealing with the significant *reality problems* of that day, just as they have been oriented toward the reality problems of the 40s, 50s, 60s, and 70s.

What are these reality problems of 2000 likely to be? (Fortunately, I can treat this as an academic exercise). No one really knows, of course, but it is useful to speculate. Here are my speculations concerning those trends that are likely to involve counseling psychologists:

1. The single-cycle sequence of family life, education, work, and labor-force retirement will break down. *Education will be a life-long process,* interspersed and interacting with work and family.
2. There will be more explicit attention to a broader scope of *life skills.* Just as we now have organized training in educational skills and job skills, so there will be organized training in family skills, community skills, recreational skills, and so on.
3. Mental health will be a recognized aspect of our total health system. Just as we go to the dentist twice a year and have an annual medical exam, so we will periodically go to the psychologist for a "psychological check-up."

In all of the above, counseling psychologists, with their history of dealing with the normal, everyday reality problems of the entire spectrum of age and level of adjustment will have an increasingly important role to play. They will be located in a variety of settings—educational institutions, government, community and social agencies, and private business and industry. And if psychology ever develops a "general practitioner," (as I think it will) professional training in counseling psychology will be the best preparation for this role. (p. 22)

As we progress through the exciting era of high technology, the technological explosion could threaten to isolate the individual. However, Naisbitt in his popular publication *Megatrends* (1982) expressed the view

> that whenever new technology is introduced into society there must be a counterbalancing human response—that is, high touch—or the technology is rejected. (p. 40)

In other words, he suggests "we must learn to balance the material wonders of technology with the spiritual demands of our human nature" (p. 40).

Naisbitt (1982) also notes that we are in a transition from a goods-producing to a service-producing to an information-producing society. This will result in rapid shifts in the career world with the implication that people must learn to adjust and plan for multiple careers. This implies also that people must learn to get along with others (p. 47).

The implications and opportunities for counselors in the future can include increased opportunities in the development and promotion of human relations and communications skills and career counseling through the life span. Of course, counselors must upgrade their own professional skills to keep abreast of the many changes and new demands for their services.

Summary

You have a problem, and you need to see a counselor, but you are no longer in school and besides, your old school counselor is too busy with the current student body. So what are your options? This chapter has suggested a number of these opportunities both for employment as counselors and assistance for clients in nonschool settings.

Community mental health agencies are perhaps the most versatile in terms of their readiness to deal with a wide range of developmental as well as remedial needs. Also, the staffing of these agencies is usually more diverse, often including professionals trained in medicine and social work as well as psychology. If one is seeking less conventional settings, many communities have crisis centers, "hot line" counseling, open-door agencies, centers for human growth and other nontraditional approaches to providing mental health services.

If your problem is one of career decision making or job placement, you might want to seek the assistance of a government employment office counselor (unlike private employment agencies, government employment offices charge no fees and are more likely to employ trained counselors). Additionally, career counseling centers, both government and nongovernment sponsored, are available in a number of communities. These specialized centers are also popular on college campuses.

Of course, if you are confined to a correctional institution, your only option may be your institutional counselor. Unfortunately, in many such institutions counseling personnel may not be employed.

For assistance in overcoming a physical or mental handicap, rehabilitation counselors can be a valuable resource because they have received special training to work with the developmental needs of the handicapped. Veterans can seek such assistance through the Veterans Administration, of course, and other "rehab" counselors may be found in community and other governmental agencies and hospitals. A small number are in private practice.

If your problem is marriage- or family-related, there can be help for you too. Marriage and family counseling is a growing area of specialization. Like many of your friends and neighbors, you may turn to your family clergy. The likelihood is increasing that your minister, priest, or rabbi will have received some counseling preparation in his or her ministerial studies, or will have some assistant specially trained to provide counseling services. Another source of counseling assistance, if you are by chance a member of the armed services, would be your service counselor. If you are among our older readers, or when you do enter the "golden years," specialized counseling assistance may also be available to you to help you plan for your retirement or other needs.

A final option, one that would probably cost you more dollars, is to seek out a counselor in private practice. Large population centers, university-oriented communities, and upper socioeconomic suburbs are the more likely habitats of the private practitioners. Obviously, evidence of appropriate training, such as licensure, is important for private practitioners.

Having examined the historical development of our profession, the activities of counselors and their role and function in various school and nonschool settings, we now move to a more detailed examination of specific counselor services and activities. We shall begin in the next chapter with our most important skill and service—individual counseling.

References

American Mental Health Counselors Association. (1978). *Certification Committee Report.* Unpublished manuscript.

American Personnel and Guidance Association. (1978). *Licensure Committee Action Packet.* Washington, D.C.: Author.

American Psychological Association Committee on Legislation. (1967). A model for state legislation affecting the practice of psychology. *American Psychologist, 22,* 1095–1103.

Belkin, G. S. (1981). *Practical counseling in the schools* (2nd ed.). Dubuque, IA: William C. Brown.

Berven, N. L. (1979). The roles and functions of the rehabilitation counselor revisited. *Rehabilitation Counseling Bulletin, 23,* 84–88.

Black, E. (1981). Preparing for life after work. *American Way, 14*(1), 32–37.

Blocher, D. H., & Biggs, D. A. (1983). *Counseling psychology in community settings.* New York: Springer.

Brown, D., & Feit, S. S. (1978). Making job placement work. *Vocational Guidance Quarterly, 27,* 176–183.

Collingwood, T. R., Willams, H., & Douds, A. (1976). An HRD approach to police diversion for juvenile offenders. *Personnel and Guidance Journal, 54*, 435–437.

Ganikos, M. L., editor (1979). *Counseling the aged.* Washington, D.C.: American Personnel and Guidance Association.

Goodyear, R. K. (1976). Counselors as community psychologists. *Personnel and Guidance Journal, 54*, 512–516.

Gordon, T. (1970). *Parent effectiveness training: The no-lose program for raising responsible children.* New York: Wyden.

Gurin, G., Veroff, J., & Feld, S. (1960). *Americans view their mental health.* New York: Basic Books.

Kagan, N. (1977). Presidential address. Division 17, *The Counseling Psychologist, 7* (2), 4–9.

Ivey, A. E. (1980). Counseling 2000: Time to take charge! *The Counseling Psychologist, 8* (4), 12–16.

Jordaan, J. P., Myers, R. A., Layton, W. L., & Morgan, H. H. (1968). *The counseling psychologist.* New York: Teachers College Press, Columbia University.

Kelly, E. W., Franklin, V. S., & Jackson, G. C. (1976). Counseling in public housing. *Personnel and Guidance Journal, 54*, 521–523.

Lamb, H. R., and Associates. (1971). *Rehabilitation in community mental health.* San Francisco: Jossey, Bass.

Lewis, E. C. (1970). *The psychology of counseling.* New York: Holt, Rinehart, & Winston.

Lewis, J. A., & Lewis, M. D. (1983). *Community counseling: A human services approach (2nd ed.)* New York: John Wiley & Sons.

Mederer, H., & Hill, R. (1983). Critical transitions over the family life span: Theory and research. *Marriage and Family Review, 6* (1/2), 39–60.

Muthard, J. E. & Salomone, P. R. (1969) The roles and functions of the rehabilitation counselor. *Rehabilitation Counseling Bulletin, 13*, 81–168.

Naisbitt, J. (1982). *Megatrends: Ten new directions transforming our lives.* New York: Warner.

National Employment Counselors Association (with abstract by A. Horwitz). (1975). Role of the employment counselor. *Journal of Employment Counseling, 12*, 148–153.

O'Brien, B. A., & Lewis, M. (1975). A community adolescent self-help center. *Personnel and Guidance Journal, 54*, 212–217.

Okun, B. E., & Rappaport, L. (1980). *Working with families: An introduction to family therapy.* Belmont, CA: Duxbury.

Phelps, R. J., Peer, G. G., & Canada, R. M. (1973). Training employment personnel in basic counseling skills. *Journal of Employment Counseling, 10*, 173–179.

Pietrofesa, J. J., Hoffman, A., Splete, H. H., & Pinto, D. V. (1984). *Counseling: An introduction* (2nd ed.). Boston: Houghton Mifflin.

Pietrofesa, J. J., Hoffman, A., Splete, H. H., & Pinto, D. V. (1984). *Counseling: Theory, research and practice* (2nd ed.). Skokie, IL: Rand McNally.

Randolph, D. L. (1973). The counseling-community psychologist in the CMHC: Employer perceptions. *Counselor Education and Supervision, 17*, 244–253.

Satir, V. M. (1964). *Conjoint family therapy: A guide to theory and techniques.* Palo Alto, CA: Science and Behavior Books.

Schlossberg, N. K. (1984). *Counseling adults in transition.* New York: Springer.

Schofield, W. (1966). Clinical and counseling psychology: Some perspectives. *American Psychologist, 21*, 122–131.

Tyler, L. E. (1980). The next twenty years. *The Counseling Psychologist. 8* (4), 19–21.

Whiteley, J. M. (1980). Counseling psychology in the year 2000 A.D. *The Counseling Psychologist, 8* (4), 2–8.

Wittmer, J., Lanier, J. E., & Parker, M. (1976). Race relations training with correctional officers. *Personnel and Guidance Journal, 54*, 302–306.

CHAPTER 5

INDIVIDUAL COUNSELING

Introduction

Counseling is, of course, the single most important activity in which counselors engage. They are called counselors not because they give tests, provide career planning information, or consult with teachers and parents, but because they counsel. Counseling is a skill and process distinguished from advising, directing, perhaps listening sympathetically, and appearing to be interested in many of the same concerns as professional counselors. To introduce you to this topic, the objectives of this chapter are to (a) orient the reader to traditional and popular theories of counseling; (b) introduce and briefly discuss the counseling process, and (c) examine some basic counseling skills.

Individual counseling has, since the early days of the movement into both school and nonschool settings, been identified as the heart of any program of counseling services. All other professional activities of the counselor lead to this most important function. Test results, career information, and autobiographies are all relatively meaningless if they do not provide information that enhances the effectiveness of the counseling process.

A popular definition identifies individual counseling as a

personal, face-to-face relationship between two people, in which the counselor, by means of the relationship and his special competencies, provides a learning situation in which the counselee, a normal sort of person, is helped to know himself and his present and possible future situations so that he can make use of characteristics and potentialities in a way that is both satisfying to himself and beneficial to society, and further, can learn how to solve future problems and meet future needs. (Tolbert, 1972, p. 9)

Blackham (1977) suggests that "counseling is a unique helping relationship in which the client is provided the opportunity to learn, feel, think, experience, and change in ways that he or she thinks is desirable" (p. 7). Shertzer and Stone (1980) define counseling as "an interaction process which facilitates meaningful understanding of self and environment and results in the establishment and/or clarification of goals and values for future behavior" (pp. 19–20). Cottle and Downie (1970) define counseling as "the process by which a counselor assists a client to face, understand, and accept information about himself and his interaction with others, so that he can make effective decisions about various life choices" (p. 1).

107

Stefflre and Grant (1972) indicated:

counseling denotes a professional relationship between a trained counselor and a client. This relationship is usually person-to-person, although it may sometimes involve more than two people, and it is designed to help the client understand and clarify his view of his life space so that he may make meaningful and informed choices consonant with his essential nature in those areas where choices are available to him. This definition indicates that counseling is a process, that it is a relationship, that it is designed to help people make choices, that underlying better choice-making are such matters as learning, personality development, and self-knowledge which can be translated into better role perception and more effective role behavior (p. 15)

These are but a few of the many definitions available to students of counseling. There are semantic differences, of course, but most definitions begin by suggesting that individual counseling is a one-to-one relationship involving a trained counselor and focuses on some aspects of a client's adjustment, developmental, or decision-making needs. This process provides a relationship and communications base from which the client can develop understanding, explore possibilities, and initiate change. In this setting, it is the skill of the counselor that makes positive outcomes possible. The counselor's skills and knowledge provide the appropriate framework and direction that maximizes the client's potential for positive results. Untrained and unskilled helpers, regardless of their best intentions, cannot duplicate the functions of the professional counselor.

Theories of Counseling

Having previously suggested that the various definitions of counseling differ little in actual meaning, one might assume that all counselors function similarly in like situations; that, like so many robots, we would all respond similarly, interpret client information in the same manner and agree on desired outcomes in specific counseling situations. Thus, a chapter on counseling techniques might read like a "Betty Crocker Cook Book" in which recipes were specified for the kinds of situations and the kinds of outcomes desired for these situations. Of course, nothing could be further from the truth. As definitions vary in counseling, the approaches that professional counselors use vary even more. While the variety of these approaches may, at times, confuse the beginning student and the general public as well, it is fair to say that unlike Betty Crocker recipes, there are a variety of approaches which have proven useful in the provision of counseling services to various populations. These approaches are usually distinguished and described under their theoretical labels.

Theoretical models for counseling have their origins in the values and beliefs of persons who, in turn, have converted these into a philosophy and a theoretical model for counseling. These values and beliefs form a rationale for what one does, how one does it, and under what circumstances.

As Brammer (1985) noted:

> theorizing refers to a rational rather than a feeling function. Helpers need a guiding theory to help them make sense of the complex helping process. Of course, people can help others ... without a thought about theory, but if they are going to work systematically in a helping function, they need some "hooks" on which to hang their experiences and some frame of reference for gaining perspectives on their work and improving their services. (p. 139)

Of course, for the established theories, research has played an important part in bridging the gap through verifying or "proving" theoretical premises:

> The application of counseling theory is quite different from the application of theory in the physical sciences. Physical theories can be applied with little regard for the element of human interaction, but counseling theory, which is applied in the give and take between and among persons, must be integrated into the counselor's philosophy and personality. To apply theory in counseling as one applies it in the physical sciences would result in a view of oneself and the client as objects, with the consequent loss of the human element so essential to the success of a counseling relationship. (Boy and Pine, 1982, p. 38)

This progress from values to practice is depicted in Figure 5–1.

In the next section of this chapter, brief descriptions of some of the popular counseling theories will be presented. It should be stated, however, that these and other recognized theories in the field of counseling provide only a base that the practicing counselor will modify in order to suit the unique situation in which he or she functions and his or her unique personality for, as Boy and Pine (1982) noted, "A counselor's theory of counseling is a reflection of the counselor as a person; that is, what the counselor IS as a person is demonstrated in his or her application of a theory" (p. 38). In other words, every counselor evolves his or her own unique counseling style, but in this process he or she is guided by his or her knowledge and understanding of the acceptable and researched models available to his or her professional field.

Psychoanalytic Theory

For beginning counselors, the study of psychoanalytical theory is more important from an historical perspective rather than as a model for adoption. The

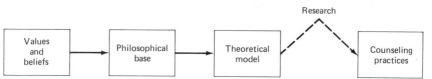

Figure 5–1. Bridging the gap from theory to practice. *(Shane, Shane, Gibson, & Munger, 1971, p. 215.)*

psychoanalytical approach requires extensive training, so it is presented here for informational purposes only:

> Psychoanalysis historically has had three different meanings. First, it is a system of psychology derived from Sigmund Freud which stresses particularly the role of the unconscious and of dynamic forces in psychic functioning; second, it is a form of therapy which uses primarily free association and relies on the analysis of transferences and resistance; and third, it is sometimes used to differentiate the Freudian approach from neo-Freudian approaches within the field of psychoanalysis proper. (Fine, 1973, p. 1)

> *Psychoanalysis* is a system of psychology derived from the discoveries of Sigmund Freud. Originating as a method for treating certain psychoneurotic disorders, psychological analysis has come to serve as the foundation for a general theory of psychology. Knowledge derived from the treatment of individual patients has led to insights into art, religion, social organization, child development, and education. In addition, by elucidating the influence of unconscious wishes and feelings on the physiology of the body, psychoanalysis has made it possible to understand and treat many psychosomatic illnesses. (Arlow, 1979, p. 1)

> In Freud's view, the development of personality, including the various defense mechanisms and how an individual uses them, is largely dependent on the course of her or his psychosexual development. Much of this development occurs during the first five years of life, after which there is a period of relative calm for six years. Then, during adolescence the process becomes very active once again. Another of Freud's major assumptions is that at any point in a person's development a person moves through an orderly sequence in which one body area gives way to another; the order of this sequence is the same for everyone. The third major assumption is that failure to complete this normal sequence will result in serious personality problems. (Hansen, Stevic, and Warner, 1982, p. 30)

Psychoanalytic theory views the structure of personality as separated into three major systems; the id, the ego, and the superego. Hereditary factors are represented by the id, which functions in the inner world of one's personality and is thus largely unconscious. The id is usually viewed as the original system of personality that is inherent and present at birth. Many believe that the id is ruled by the "pleasure principle," and thus it seeks to avoid tension and pain, seeking instead gratification and pleasure. As Corey (1982) noted, it is "the spoiled brat of personality" (p. 10).

The ego is viewed as the only rational element of the personality. The ego also has contact with the world of reality. Becasue of this contact with reality it controls consciousness and provides realistic and logical thinking and planning.

The superego represents the conscience of the mind and operates on a principle of moral realism. It represents the moral code of the person, usually based on one's perceptions of the moralities and values of society. As a result of its role, the superego in a sense is responsible for providing rewards, such as pride and self-love, and punishments, such as feelings of guilt or inferiority to its owner.

In this triangle, the superego, because it resides largely in the subconscious, is most aware of the impulses of the id and seeks to direct the ego to control the id. As a result, psychoanalytic theory views tension, conflict, and anxiety as inevitable in humans and that human behavior is therefore directed toward reduction of this tension. In the psychoanalytical context, then, the reduction of tension becomes a major goal of counseling. Because personality conflict is present in all people, nearly everyone can benefit from professional counseling.

Individual Psychology

The works of Adler have had a profound impact on many therapists, acknowleged by persons such as Albert Ellis, Victor Frankl, Rudolf Dreikurs, Rolla May, and William Glasser. Individual Psychology is often called Adlerian therapy, since its initial developer was Alfred Adler, a colleague of Freud who disagreed with Freud on some basic issues, which led him to resign and to break away entirely from Freud's circle.

Individual Psychology sees the person as a unity, an indivisible whole and focuses on the unique individuality of persons (Manaster and Corsini, 1982). Adler's view of humans offered a refreshingly optimistic focus. At the core of his theory was the belief that there exists within the human being an innate drive to overcome perceived inferiorities and to develop one's potential, to self-actualize, and that given a healthy environment, this growth will take place.

What is it that keeps a person from moving in a fast and easy manner toward this full realization of self? For Adler it was feelings of inferiority. A person permits himself or herself to experience these feelings through three sources: (a) our biological dependency and dependency in general as infants, (b) our image of ourselves in relationship to the grandeur of the universe, and (c) organ inferiority. The drive within ourselves, however, enables us to compensate for these feelings and strive for superiority and perfection.

Adler's theory is sometimes referred to as socioteleological, for as has been noted, it sees persons as constantly in the process of striving toward goals. This is not done, however, in isolation but with other people. This concept, called *Gemeinschaftsgefühl*, usually translated as "social interest," is central to the growth and actualization of the individual person as well as of the good of the society. Because social interest is viewed as an innate aptitude, it must be consciously developed over time (Manaster and Corsini, 1982). Social interest or developing one's ability to give and take is accomplished through the "Life Tasks" in which all human beings participate. These include (a) occupation, (b) society, and (c) sex (Mosak, 1979). When a person comes for therapy, it is in one or more of these areas that he or she is experiencing incongruence and discomfort. The counseling process then is seen as a means by which the therapist and counselee work together in order to help the counselee develop awareness as well as healthier attitudes and behaviors in order to function more fully in society on the more useful side of life. Developing social interest is seen as the salient variable of one's mental health.

The Adlerian counseling process involves four stages: (a) establishing relationship, (b) diagnosis, (c) insight/interpretation, and (d) reorientation. In the first session the counselor establishes a relationship with the client through a subjective/objective interview in which the client is helped to feel comfortable, accepted, respected, and cared about. Through an "objective" component of the interview, the client is encouraged to explain what specifically has helped him or her determine the need for counseling. The client is asked to discuss how things are going in each of the life task areas. Also during this first session the counseling process is explained and discussed with the client. The diagnostic-stage involves the "life-style interview," a formal assessment procedure that looks at such things as family constellation, perceptions of self in relationship of siblings, perceptions of parents, early recollections, and recurrent dreams. The interpretation phase is the time during which the counselor and the client develop insight from the lifestyle interview into the client's "basic mistakes" by analyzing and discussing the convictions, goals, and movement that the client developed early in life and the ensuing thought, emotional, and behavioral patterns and attitudes. The reorientation stage is perhaps the most critical, for it is in this stage that the therapist helps the counselee to move from "intellectual" insight to actual development and expression of healthier attitudes and behaviors. Here the client—with the support, encouragement, and direction from the counselor—actively pursues changing unhealthy ways of thinking, feeling, and behaving to ways that are more satisfying and healthy for himself or herself and society.

Client-Centered Theory

Client-centered (now frequently referred to as person-centered) counseling is another historically significant and influential theory. This theory was originally developed and described by Carl R. Rogers as a reaction against what he considered the basic limitations of psychonanalysis. As a result of his influence, this particular approach is often referred to as "Rogerian counseling":

> This person-centered approach focuses on the client's responsibility and capacity to discover ways to more fully encounter reality. Clients, who know themselves best, are the ones to discover more appropriate behavior for themselves.
>
> The person-centered approach emphasizes the phenomenal world of the client. With accurate empathy and an attempt to apprehend the client's internal frame of reference, therapists concern themselves mainly with the client's perception of self and of the world.
>
> Rogers proposes the hypothesis that certain attitudes on the therapist's part (genuineness, nonpossessive warmth and acceptance, and accurate empathy) constitute the necessary and sufficient conditions for therapeutic effectiveness. Person-centered theory holds that the therapist's function is to be immediately present and accessible to the client and to focus on the here-and-now experience created by their relationship. (Corey, 1982, p. 82)

In understanding the client or person-centered approach to counseling, it is helpful to be aware of the personality basis for this theory, as presented by Rogers (1959a) in the form of 19 propositions. The lead statements for each of these propositions are:

1. Every individual exists in a continually changing world of experience of which he is the center.

2. The organism reacts to the field as it is experienced and perceived. This perceptual field is, for the individual, "reality."

3. The organism reacts as an organized whole to this phenomenal field.

4. The organism has one basic tendency and striving—to actualize, maintain, and enhance the experiencing organism.

5. Behavior is basically the goal-directed attempt of the organism to satisfy its needs as experienced, in the field as perceived.

6. Emotion accompanies and in general facilitates such goal-directed behavior, the kind of emotion being related to the seeking versus the consummatory aspects of the behavior, and the intensity of the emotion being related to the perceived significance of the behavior for the maintenance and enhancement of the organism.

7. The best vantage point for understanding behavior is from the internal frame of reference of the individual himself.

8. A portion of the total perceptual field gradually becomes differentiated as the self.

9. As a result of interaction with the environment, and particularly as a result of evaluational interaction with others, the structure of self is formed—an organized, fluid, but consistent conceptual pattern of perceptions of characteristics and relationships of the "I" or the "me," together with values attached to these concepts.

10. The values attached to experiences and the values which are a part of the self structure, in some instances, are values experienced directly by the organism, and in some instances are values introjected or taken over from others, but perceived in distorted fashion, *as if* they had been experienced directly.

11. As experiences occur in the life of the individual, they are either (a) symbolized, perceived, and organized into some relationship to the self; (b) ignored because there is no perceived relationship to the self-structure; (c) denied symbolization or given a distorted symbolization because the experience is inconsistent with the structure of the self.

12. Most of the ways of behaving which are adopted by the organism are those which are consistent with the concept of self.

13. Behavior may, in some instances, be brought about by organic experiences and needs which have not been symbolized. Such behavior may be inconsistent with the structure of the self, but in such instances the behavior is not "owned" by the individual.

14. Psychological maladjustment exists when the organism denies to awareness significant sensory and visceral experiences, which consequently are not symbolized and organized into the gestalt of the self-structure. When this situation exists, there is a basic or potential psychological tension.

15. Psychological adjustment exists when the concept of the self is such that all the sensory and visceral experiences of the organism are, or may be, assimilated on a symbolic level into a consistent relationship with the concept of self.

16. Any experience which is inconsistent with the organization or structure of self may be perceived as a threat, and the more of these perceptions there are, the more rigidly the self-structure is organized to maintain itself.

17. Under certain conditions, involving primarily complete absence of any threat to the self-structure, experiences which are inconsistent with it may be perceived, and examined, and the structure of self revised to assimilate and include such experiences.

18. When the individual perceives and accepts into one consistent and integrated system all his sensory and visceral experiences, then he is necessarily more understanding of others and is more accepting of others as separate individuals.

19. As the individual perceives and accepts into his self-structure more of his organic experiences, he finds that he is replacing his present value *system*—based so

largely upon introjections which have been distortedly symbolized—with a continuing organismic valuing process. (pp. 483–524)

In the counseling relationship, six conditions account for personality change in the client. These were presented by Rogers (1959a, 1967):

1 .Two people (a therapist and a client) are in psychological contact. (1967, p. 73)
2. The client is experiencing a state of anxiety, distress, or incongruence.
3. The therapist is genuine (truly himself or herself) in relating to the client.
4. The therapist feels or exhibits *unconditional positive regard* for the client.
5. The therapist exhibits *empathetic understanding* of the client's frame of reference and conveys this understanding to the client.
6. The therapist *succeeds* to a minimum degree in communicating empathetic understanding and unconditional positive regard to the client. (1959a, p. 213)

Some of the changes expected from a successful utilization of this approach are:

The person comes to see himself differently.
He accepts himself and his feelings more fully.
He becomes more self-confident and self-directing.
He becomes more the person he would like to be.
He becomes more flexible, less rigid, in his perceptions.
He adopts more realistic goals for himself.
He behaves in a more mature fashion.
He changes his maladjustive behaviors, even such a long-established one as chronic alcoholism.
He becomes more acceptant of others.
He becomes more open to the evidence, both to what is going on outside of himself, and to what is going on inside of himself.
He changes in his basic personality characteristics in constructive ways. (Rogers, 1959b, p. 232)

Thus, the client-centered model is optimistic or positive in its view of humankind. Clients are viewed as being basically good and possessing the capabilities for self-understanding, insight, problem solving, decision making, change, and growth.

The counselor's role is that of a *facilitator* and *reflector.* The counselor facilitates a counselee's self-understanding and clarifies and reflects back to the client the expressed feelings and attitudes of the client. Information-giving for problem-solving in a client-centered context is not usually considered a counselor responsibility. The client-centered counselor also would not seek to direct the mediation of the counselee's "inner world," but, rather, would seek to provide a climate in which the counselee could bring about change in himself or herself.

In recent years, another label, *self-theory,* has been increasingly used instead of the traditional client-centered, nondirective, or Rogerian labels. This has probably resulted from the emphasis on enhancement of the self, the capacity of one's self, self-actualization and self-perceptions. Regardless of one's choice of label, this theory, originated by Rogers, continues to exert its influence on the field of counseling.

Behavioral Theory

Behavioral theory and conditioning can be traced directly from Pavlov's 19th century discoveries in classical conditioning. Important foundations for the behavioral approach later were discovered from the system of psychology called behaviorism, founded by American psychologist John B. Watson (1913) and expressed initially in his article "Psychology as the Behaviorist Views It."

Significant research and publication on the subject were conducted by Watson, Thorndike, and others, but it was not until B. F. Skinner systematically refined and developed his principles of behaviorism that the behavioral theory moved toward its current popularity. The behaviorist views behavior as a set of learned responses to events, experiences, or stimuli in a person's life history. The behaviorist believes that behavior can be modified by providing appropriate learning conditions and experiences. The experimental origins of the behaviorist's approach explain their indifference to concepts that cannot be empirically observed or measured. Thus, rather than being concerned with the emotional dynamics of behavior characteristics of the insight approaches of either Freudians or Rogerians, the behaviorist focuses on specific behavioral goals, emphasizing precise and repeatable methods.

For the behaviorist, counseling involves the systematic use of a variety of procedures that are intended specifically to change behavior in terms of mutually established goals between a client and a counselor. The procedures employed encompass a wide variety of techniques drawn from knowledge of learning processes. Current leaders in behavioral psychology, John D. Krumboltz and Carl Thoreson (1966), place these procedures into four categories:

1. *Operant Learning.* This approach is based on the usefulness of reinforcers and the timing of their presentation in producing change. Reinforcers may be concrete rewards or expressed as approval or attention.
2. *Imitative Learning.* This approach facilitates acquisition of new responses by exposure to models performing the desired behaviors.
3. *Cognitive Learning.* This technique fosters learning of appropriate responses by simply instructing the client how he may better adapt.
4. *Emotional Learning.* Involves substitution of acceptable emotional responses for unpleasant emotional reactions, using techniques derived from classical condition. (pp. 13–20)

Behaviorists also believe that stating the goals of counseling in terms of behavior that is observable is more useful than stating goals that are more broadly defined, such as self-understanding or acceptance of self. This means that counseling outcomes should be identifiable in terms of overt behavior changes. Krumboltz (1976) suggests three criteria for counseling goals:

1. The goals of counseling should be capable of being stated differently for each individual client.

2. The goals of counseling for each client should be compatible with, though not necessarily identical to, the values of his counselor.
3. The degree to which the goals of counseling are attained by each client should be observable. (pp. 172–173)

Three examples of behavioral change appropriate to counseling are the altering of behavior that is not satisfactory; the learning of the decision-making process; and problem prevention. Krumboltz (1976) indicates that the consequences of the behavioral statements of counseling goals would include the following:

1. Counselors, clients, and citizens could more clearly anticipate what the counseling process could and could not accomplish.
2. Counseling psychology would become more integrated with the mainstream of psychological theory and research.
3. The search for new and more effective techniques of helping clients would be facilitated.
4. Different criteria would have to be applied to different clients in assessing the success of counseling. (pp. 175–176)

Blackham and Silberman (1980) developed an operant paradigm consisting of six steps as follows:

1. Define and state operationally the behavior to be changed.
2. Obtain a baseline or operant level of the behavior that is considered desirable to promote or change.
3. Arrange the learning or treatment situation so that the desirable behavior will occur.
4. Identify potential reinforcers.
5. Shape and/or reinforce the desired behavior.
6. Maintain records of the reinforced behavior to determine whether response strength or frequency has increased. (pp. 33–35)

Counselors utilizing behavioral theory assume that the client's behavior is the result of conditioning. The counselor further assumes that each individual reacts in a predictable way to any given situation or stimulus, depending on what has been learned.

Horan (1979) declared that the goal of behavioral decision-making counseling is obviously the making of a decision. Behavioral counselors assume that a favorable outcome is more likely if the client engages in a number of preparatory behaviors before choosing. The counselor's major tasks are to stimulate and reinforce these client behaviors.

Patterson (1980) suggested:

The goal of behavior therapy is the development of a complete set of psychological principles to apply to an individual patient from the initial presentation of the patient's complaint to his or her discharge. This requires systematic methods of collecting information to appraise the patient's difficulties and to reach decisions about a treatment program. The behavioristic framework requires that the therapist (1) locate the problem and (2) translate the initial complaint into a language and a set of questions appropriate for available behavioral technology. (pp. 225–226)

5 Rational Emotive Therapy

As is often the case, a person, for instance, Carl R. Rogers, is associated with the formulation and development of a theory, in this case client-centered therapy. A comparatively recent example is the rational emotive therapy (R.E.T.) movement developed by Albert Ellis. This theory is based on the assumption that people have the capacity to act in either a rational or irrational manner. Rational behavior is viewed as effective and potentially productive, whereas irrational behavior results in unhappiness and nonproductivity. Ellis assumes that many types of emotional problems result from irrational patterns of thinking. This irrational pattern may begin early in life and be reinforced by significant others in the individual's life as well as by the general culture and environment. According to Ellis, people with emotional problems develop belief systems that lead to implicit verbalizations or self-talk resting on faulty logic and assumptions. And what a person tells himself is intimately related to the way he feels and acts.

The basic foundation of Ellis's theorizing is contained in his ABCDE paradigm. Blackham (1977) briefly explained Ellis's paradigm:

> *A* refers to an external event to which a person is subjected. *B* refers to a sequence of thoughts or self-verbalizations in which the person engages in response to the external event. *C* connotes the feelings and behaviors that result from *B*. *D* indicates the therapist's attempt to modify the sequence of thoughts or self-verbalizations. *E* refers to the presumed affective and behavioral consequences resulting from intervention by the therapist. (p. 152)
>
> The main purposes of R. E. T. counseling are to (1) demonstrate to the client that self-talk is the cause of disturbance, and (2) re-evaluate this self-talk in order to eliminate it and subsequent illogical ideas. (Peitrofesa, Hoffman, Splete and Pinto, 1984, p. 136)

In summary,

> R.E.T. is an approach to counseling that is based on the assumption that most people in our society develop many irrational ways of thinking. These irrational thoughts lead to irrational or inappropriate behavior. Therefore, counseling must be designed to help people recognize and change these irrational beliefs into more rational ones. The accomplishment of this goal requires an active, confrontive, and authoritative counselor who has the capacity to utilize a whole variety of techniques. (Hansen et al., 1982, p. 173)

The R.E.T. therapist does not believe that a personal relationship between the client and counselor is a prerequisite to successful counseling. In fact, the therapist may frequently challenge, provoke, and probe the irrational beliefs of the client. In the relationship the counselor is viewed more as a teacher and the client as a student. As a result, procedures may include not only teaching and related activities such as reading or other assignments, but also questioning and challenging, even confrontation tactics, contracts, suggestions and persuasion. R.E.T. can be applied not only to individual therapy but also to group therapy, marathon encounter groups, marriage counseling, and family therapy. He mentions that Ellis wrote that "R.E.T. has inspired a large number of publications

we are emotional beings.

and studies on its application to the treatment of anxiety, depression, hostility, character disorder, and psychosis; to problems of sex, love, marriage; to child rearing and adolescence; and to assertion training and self-management" (Corey, 1982, p. 180).

Reality Therapy

Another theory of counseling that has gained popularity in recent decades is that of reality therapy, largely developed by William Glasser. Glasser's approach is a fairly straightforward one that places confidence in the counselee's ability to deal with his or her needs through a realistic or rational process. From a reality therapy standpoint, counseling is simply a special kind of teaching or training that attempts to teach an individual what he should have learned during normal growth in a rather short period of time.

Glasser (1984) suggested that reality therapy is

> applicable to individuals with any sort of psychological problem, from mild emotional upset to complete psychotic withdrawal. It works well with behavior disorders of the aged and the young, and with drug- and alcohol-related problems. It has been applied widely in schools, corrections institutions, mental hospitals, general hospitals, and business management. It focuses on the present and upon getting people to understand that they choose essentially all their actions in an attempt to fulfill basic needs. When they are unable to do this they suffer, or cause others to suffer. The therapist's task is to lead them toward better or more responsible choices that are almost always available. (p. 320)
>
> Reality therapy stipulates that people have two basic needs, which if unfulfilled cause pain. They are: *"The need to love and be loved and the need to feel that we are worthwhile to ourselves and to others."* (Glasser, 1965, p. 10). The need to feel love and be loved includes all forms of affection from friendship to parental love. Every person needs to feel love throughout life. It is necessary both to love someone and to feel loved. When we are unable to fulfill our need for love, we suffer from anxiety, self-blame, depression, and anger and possibly withdraw from society. (Pietrofesa, Hoffman, Splete, and Pinto, 1984, p. 150)

Reality therapy focuses on present behavior and, consequently, does not emphasize the client's past history. When using this approach, the counselor functions as a teacher and a model. "Reality therapy is based on the premise that there is a single psychological need that is present throughout life: the need for identity, which includes a need to feel a sense of uniqueness, separateness, and distinctiveness. The need for identity, which accounts for the dynamics of behavior, is seen as universal among all cultures." (Corey, 1982, p. 186)

Reality therapy is based on the anticipation that the client will assume personal responsibility for his or her well-being. The acceptance of this responsibility, in a sense, helps a person to achieve autonomy or a state of maturity whereby he or she relies on his or her own internal support. Whereas many of the counseling theories suggest that the counselor should function in a noncommittal way, reality therapists praise clients when they act responsibly and indicate disapproval when they do not. Reality therapy has direct implications for school situations. Glasser first became concerned about children's learning and behavior problems while he was working with delinquent girls at the Ventura Schools for Girls of the California Youth Authority. He noted the almost universal history of school failure among these girls, and this finding led him to the public schools as a consultant. Glasser (1965) developed the concepts for helping children in problem solving that he described in his book *Reality Therapy.*

As he continued his work in the public elementary schools, he became convinced that the stigma of failure permeated the atmosphere in most schools and had a damaging effect on most children in schools. The elimination of failure in the school system and the prevention, rather than merely the treatment, of delinquency became two of his goals.

Glasser (1969) believes that education can be the key to effective human relating, and, in his book *Schools Without Failure,* he proposed a program to eliminate failure, emphasize thinking instead of memory work, introduce relevance into the curriculum, substitute discipline for punishment, create a learning environment where children can maximize successful experiences that will lead to a success identity, create motivation and involvement, help students develop responsible behavior, and establish ways of involving the parents and the community in the school. (Corey, 1977, p. 158)

Corey (1977) summarizes the reality approach as

an active, directive, didactic, cognitive behavior-oriented therapy. The contract method is often used, and when the contract is fulfilled, therapy is terminated. The approach can be both supportive and confrontational. "What" and "how," but not "why" questions are used. (p. 49)

It is important to make a plan through which the client can improve his or her behavior. This plan should lead to behavior that enables the client to gain satisfaction and, even at times, favorable recognition as well.

Transactional Analysis

Transactional analysis is a cognitive-behavioral approach that assumes a person has the potential for choosing and for redirecting or reshaping his or her own destiny. It is designed to help a client review and evaluate early decisions and to make new, more appropriate choices:

Transactional analysis stresses understanding the transactions between people as a way to understand the different personalities that comprise each of us. Each of these personalities behaves in a distinct pattern and at various times is in control of the person. When one of the personalities (ego states) is in rigid control and is unwilling to relinquish that control at appropriate times, it is said to be pathological (Pietrofesa, Hoffman, Splete, and Pinto, 1984, p. 92).

Thus, transactional analysis (TA) places a great deal of emphasis on the ego, which, from a TA viewpoint, consists of three states: parent, adult, and child:

The first step of any prospective counseling relationship is for the counselor to observe and begin the classification of ego states, one reason being that a counseling contract—even in a crisis situation—can be made only with the adult ego state. The first step in establishing a TA group is the teaching of the recognition of ego states. (Mellecker, 1976, p. 199)

An essential technique in TA counseling is the contract that precedes each counseling step. This contract between counselor and counselee is a way of training or preparing people to make their own important decisions.

Dusay and Steiner (1971) believed that the contract must meet the following requirements:

1. Both the counselor and the client, through Adult-Adult transactions, must mutually agree on the objectives.
2. The contract must call for some consideration. The counselor gives professional skill and time as his consideration. In some agency situations the client gives money, in others he signs a contract that commits his time and effort as his consideration.
3. The contract defines the competencies of both parties. On the part of the counselor, it means stating that he does have the skill to help with this problem; on the part of the client, it means that he is of mind and age sound enough to enter the contract.
4. Finally, the objective(s) of the contract must be legal and within the ethical limits adhered to by the counselor. (Hansen et al., 1982, p. 83)

In addition to the contract technique, TA also utilizes questionnaires, life scripts, structural analysis, role playing, analysis of games and rituals, and "stroking." Although not a counseling technique, TA sessions are tape-recorded in their entirety.

At each stage of counseling the decision to go ahead is squarely up to the counselee. (This is the way the counselor protects himself or herself from implications that the counseling is being forced on the counselee.) The counselor may specify conditions to client participation in contracts, such as requiring the counselee to define, in advance, what advantage might ensue from their joint effort.

Transactional analysis, of course, focuses on the indivudual, but it is a procedure for counseling persons within a group setting. TA counselors feel that the group setting facilitates the process of providing feedback to persons about the kind of transactions in which they engage. The counseling group, then, represents a microcosm of the real world. In this setting, the individual group members are there to work on their own objectives and the counselor is there in the role of the group leader.

Gestalt Counseling

Gestalt psychology is defined by Webster (1976) as

the study of perception and behavior from the standpoint of the organism's response to configurational wholes with stress on the identity of psychological and physiological events and rejection of atomistic or elemental analysis of stimulus, percept, and response. (p. 952)

Gestalt counselors believe that people always act to organize stimuli into total pictures or wholes. A leader in the development of this theoretical approach was Frederick (Fritz) Perls (1894–1970). The focus of this theory is on an awareness of experiences in the here and now. Several of the principles that have been developed to explain this process were stated by Hansen et al. (1982):

> *Principle of Closure:* When we perceive a figure that is incomplete, our mind acts to finish the figure and perceives it as complete.
>
> *Principle of Proximity:* The relative distance of stimuli from each other within the perceptual field determines how they are seen.
>
> *Principle of Similarity:* The similarity of stimuli in the perceptual field causes us to group them together. (p. 115)

Each of these three principles illustrates how the human mind seeks to make sense from the vast array of stimuli in the phenomenal field by pulling things together. The important point is that the stimuli have meaning only as they are organized in the mind by the individual (pp. 115–116).

Passons (1975) lists eight assumptions about the nature of humans that act as the framework for Gestalt counseling:

1. Individuals are composite wholes made up of interrelated parts. None of these parts—body, emotions, thoughts, sensations, and perceptions—can be understood outside the context of the whole person.
2. Individuals are also part of their own environment and cannot be understood apart from it.
3. People choose how they respond to external and internal stimuli; they are actors, not reactors.
4. People have the potential to be fully aware of all their sensations, thoughts, emotions, and perceptions.
5. Individuals are capable of making choices because they are aware.
6. Individuals have the capacity to govern their own lives effectively.
7. People cannot experience the past and the future; they can experience only themselves in the present.
8. People are neither basically good nor bad. (p. 117)

Gestalt counseling has as its major objective the integration of the person. In popular terminology, this might be called "getting it all together." Perls (1948) wrote:

> The treatment is finished when the patient has achieved the basic requirements: a change in outlook, a technique of adequate self-expression and assimilation, and the ability to extend awareness to the verbal level. He has then reached that state of integration which facilitates its own development, and he can now be safely left to himself. (p. 585)

In order to achieve this togetherness, the counselor seeks to increase the client's awareness. As a result, the counselor functions in a way that provides the client with an atmosphere conducive to the discovery of client needs, what the client has lost because of environmental demands, and a setting in which the client can experience the necessary discovery and growth:

> To facilitate this process, counselors utilize the most important tool they have: themselves. A counselor, fully aware of herself in the now, engages the client in a here and now interaction. The counselor does not interpret, probe, preach about reality; rather she interacts with the client in the now. (Hansen et al., 1982, p. 124)

Integrated Theories

In recent years we have seen continued efforts to not only reinforce and expand on the many traditional theories of counseling, but, additionally, to develop new multidimensional and integrated models. One of these, Actualizing Counseling and Psychotherapy, presented by Brammer and Shostrom (1982), represents a creative synthesis approach to counseling theory and human growth. Actualizing counseling is based upon the following assumptions:

1. Each person is a *unique human being* seeking actualization even though he or she shares much "human nature" in common with others. A better term is Buber's "particularity" principle, a unique "thou" seeking to be realized.
2. While the actualizing principle has a futuristic quality in the "becoming" sense, it takes place in the *moment-to-moment* growth process. Hence, the "here and now" becomes the temporal focus of the process.
3. Human behavior is not determined by events (external and internal) as much as by one's own cognitive representations of events.
4. While much of human behavior is determined by personal history and forces beyond one's control, the actualizing process assumes that one's future is largely undetermined and one has wide ranges of *freedom to choose.*
5. The assumption of freedom places corresponding *responsibility* on the person for his or her own actualizing. One cannot depend upon others or blame others for one's growth or lack of it. Even though growth takes place in a social context, each person alone is responsible for his or her own life.
6. While some primitive behaviors are reflexive, hence largely genetically determined, and some are the result of chemical and neurological changes, a fundamental assumption of actualizing counseling is that *social behavior is learned* and changes in behavior follow an active learning process.
7. Most human learning is not automatic but, rather, is mediated through cognitive processes such as symbolic coding and selective attention.
8. Actualization is achieved primarily in *social interaction* with a counselor, teacher, minister, group, friend, or family; but it also can be achieved through self-help methods, such as meditation and imagery. Social interaction becomes the main vehicle for conditions of actualization, such as honesty with feelings, awareness of self, freedom of expression, and trust in one's self and others.
9. A reciprocal interaction takes place between thoughts, emotions, and actions such that a change in one tends to bring about a change in the others. Each person decides intentionally which modality begins the change process—thought, feeling, or action. To go from intention to action the person must move beyond awareness and intention to commitment.

10. Each personality contains the paradoxical state of *polar opposites* which are expressed and forced to awareness and action in the actualizing process. Examples are dependence and independence, affection and aggression, support and criticalness. (Brammer and Shostrom, 1982, pp. 80–81)

Ivey (1980) noted that

all counseling approaches and techniques are ultimately concerned with freeing people from immobility or blocking (tight or excessively loose constructs, polarities, splits, discrepancies between idealized and real self, etc.). The model of freedom underlying all theories implies the ability of people to generate new sentences or constructs to commit themselves more intentionally in the world. (p. 170)

The major assumptions and their corollaries of this theoretical framework, labeled Intentional Counseling, as developed by Ivey (1980) are:

Assumption 1. All helping approaches and techniques are ulitmately concerned with freeing people to generate a maximum number of verbal and nonverbal sentences and constructs, thus freeing them for more intentional action.

Corollary I.A. Different theories are concerned with generating different sentences and constructs among their clientele.

Corollary I.B. As a result of counseling or therapy with counselors of differing theoretical orientations, clients tend to generate sentences resembling those of their therapists or counselors.

Assumption II. Different psychotherapy approaches and techniques will be of more or less effectiveness with people who present alternative types of treatment problems, who come from varying cultural backgrounds, or who have special histories of person–environment transactions.

Corollary II.A. A major task of counseling and psychotherapy over the next several years will be to determine the specific methods and techniques which are likely to be most suitable with different clients who present different issues.

Corollary II.B. The intentional counselor and therapist of the future will demonstrate competence in several existing theoretical models and be able to generate her or his own personal sentences, constructs, and general theory concerning the counseling process.

Corollary II.C. If counseling and therapy programs are differentially effective with different people, it then follows that some counselors and therapists, theories, and methods may at times be destructive to the client.

Assumption III. The counseling and psychotherapeutic interview may be considered analogous to the decision-making process of problem definition, generation of alternatives, and commitment for action.

Corollary III.A. If the decisional process is indeed critical for an understanding of the interview process, creativity on the part of the therapist or counselor is required to help free old and inefficient patterns of client thinking.

Corollary III.B. There is a variety of styles of decision-making. However, the intentional, vigilant mode appears to be most effective. It requires constant openness to new alternatives and ability to maintain commitment and direction.

Corollary III.C. Counseling and psychotherapy can be viewed as creative acts. The therapist with the client examines data from the client's life, and together they reorganize pieces and create new sentences, new constructs, and new meanings.

Assumption IV. All counselors and therapists use the attending and influencing microskills. However, each counselor has her or his own unique blend of these skills.

Corollary IV.A. Therapists and counselors of different theoretical persuasions tend to use different skill patterns.

Corollary IV.B. Different patterns of skill usage will present themselves in varying cultural groups. Skill usage appropriate in one culture may be less effective in another.

Assumption V. A counselor or therapist may make the main theme of counseling interventions focus on the client, on themselves, on significant others, on the problem of topic, on the immediate interaction, or on the cultural-environmental context. Given any single client, any of these, solely or in combination, may be appropriate.

Corollary V.A. Virtually all counseling theories focus on the individual and fail to integrate cultural-environmental issues into the interview systematically.

Corollary V.B. It may be anticipated that a reasonable blend of focusing on the several possible dimensions will be increasingly emphasized as person–environment transactions and their importance is recognized.

Assumption VI. Empathy may be considered a foundation stone of effective, intentional counseling. However, empathy and its subcomponents (immediacy, concreteness, genuineness) manifest themselves differentially in the several theories of counseling.

Corollary VI.A. Empathy is demonstrated in various forms among different cultural groups and individuals. What is appropriate for one group or individual may not be appropriate for another.

Corollary VI.B. Primary empathy, or the accurate hearing of another, is manifested through the attending skills; additive empathy, or the reasoned sharing of self and theory with the client, is demonstrated through influencing skills.

Assumption VII. The nonverbal language of the interview can be as important as or, in some cases, more important than the verbal content. The manifestations of nonverbal language in the interview vary from theory to theory, from culture to culture, and from individual to individual.

Assumption VIII. A person's mode of being in the world is represented by both nonverbal and verbal sentences. It is important to recognize that words and sentences drawn from key constructs form the core of most counseling approaches.

Corollary VIII.A. A useful way to measure movement in counseling and therapy is by examining sentences generated by the client before, during, and after the therapy process.

Corollary VIII.B. The client may be expected to come to the interview presenting a surface structure sentence describing her or his problem. A task of the counselor is to examine the deep structure to determine underlying meanings of the client's original statement.

Corollary VIII.C. Despite the best efforts of counselors and therapists to facilitate clients in generating their own sentences and constructs, there is evidence that clients tend to assume language and thought patterns similar to those of their therapists.

Assumption IX. Incongruities, discrepancies, and double messages in verbal and nonverbal behavior may be considered primary issues in all theories of counseling and psychotherapy. The resolution of synthesis of incongruities may be said to be a central goal of all theoretical orientations.

Corallary IX.A. Although different theories identify and label incongruities differently, all cope with these discrepancies similarly at a structural level.

Corollary IX.B. Cultural, sexual, social status, socioeconomic, and other environmental variables, which in themselves are incongruous, are seldom considered as issues for examination of incongruities in most theories of counseling and psychotherapy.

Assumption X. Basic to the understanding of the client and the counseling process is the person–environment transaction and the effect that each has on the other.

Corollary X.A. The counselor or therapist is an environment which the client experiences, and the client is an environment which the therapist experiences. Through their interaction, client and therapist affect and change one another.

Corollary X.B. For the most intentional counseling and psychotherapy, it is desirable to match clients and counselors in growth-producing combinations.

Corollary X.C. The counselor or therapist who is most skilled in a variety of skills and theoretical persuasions and who is knowledgable about many cultural issues is most likely to be able to provide help to the greatest variety of clientele.

Assumption XI. The underlying purpose of assessment and diagnosis is to understand how the client construes, organizes, and acts on the world. Whether by interview, test, or other means, the counselor seeks to understand the client's unique constructions and representations in order to determine the most suitable program of help.

Corollary XI.A. An important part of the assessment of any client is an examination of her or his key constructs for representing the world.

Corollary XI.B. An equally important part of any systematic assessment program is the counselor's awareness of her or his own personal construct system and worldview and how it is possible to influence the client consciously into the therapist's worldview.

Corollary XI.C. Both counselor and client in their transaction also have transactions with the larger cultural and environmental context in which they work. Through lack of awareness of how large system issues relate to personal development, the counselor is potentially guilty of symbolic violence and of supporting institutional or societal goals which oppress the client.

Assumption XII. The psychological theories of counseling and therapy may be considered systematic formulations for construing the world, as developed by capable individuals. While these theories have demonstrated utility, none of them should be considered definitive. Rather, it is the task of the professional counselor and therapist to know as many theories as possible—their similarities and differences—and to select out of each theory whatever seems most helpful to a particular client. Each counselor can become her or his own general theorist. (Ivey, 1980, pp. 171–182)

Corollary XII.A. "Man can enslave himself with his own ideas and then win his freedom again by reconstruing his life."(Kelly, 1955, p. 21)

Corollary XII.B. "A system of knowledge and belief results from the interplay of innate mechanisms, genetically determined maturation processes, and interaction with the social and physical environment. The problem is to account for the system constructed by the mind in the course of this interaction. The particular system of human knowledge that has so far lent itself most readily to such an approach is the system of human language." (Chomsky, 1971, p. 21)

Corollary XII.C. The first act of a teacher is to introduce the idea that the world we think we see is only a view, a description of the world. Every effort of a teacher is geared to prove this point to his apprentice. But accepting it seems to be one of the hardest things we can do; we are complacently caught in our particular view of the world, which compels us to feel and act as if we knew everything about the world. A teacher, from the very first act he performs, aims at stopping that view. (Castaneda, 1974, p. 230)

Assumption XIII. One useful route toward development of a general theoretical approach in counseling and psychotherapy is in acquiring skills and understanding in the decisional process and microskills of attending and influencing, as well as in developing skills in empathic qualities, verbal and nonverbal language of therapy, person–environment transaction, and effective client assessment. (Ivey, 1980, 171–182)

Eclectic Counseling

The eclectic approach to counseling is one of long-standing tradition and equally long-standing controversy. It originally provided a safe, middle-of-the-road theory for those counselors who neither desired nor felt capable of functioning as purely directive or nondirective counselors. Defenders of the theory, on the other hand, suggested eclecticism as an approach that allowed each individual to construct his or her own theory by drawing on established theories. It has often been suggested that the eclectic counselor can choose the best of all counseling worlds. However, the many theoretical models currently available can be confusing in the absence of a model for theory and technique selection. One such classification system is presented in Table 5–1. Another model, but using the same categories of emotionality, rationality, and activity (Ulrici, L'Abate, and Wagner, 1980, p. 264), is noted in Table 5–2.

Tolbert (1972) noted several assumptions appropriate to the eclectic approach:

Table 5-1. A Classification of Psychotherapy Theorists, Goals, and Processes According to an E-R-A Model (from Frey & Raming, 1979)

	Emotionality	**Rationality**	**Activity**
Theorists	Rogers Perls Frankl	Berne Ellis Alexander Kelly Sullivan	Dreikurs Wolpe Dollard & Miller
Goals	Awareness and acceptance of self in conflict and of inner resources Awareness of negative feelings	Strengthening of ego functioning Awareness of negative thoughts	Transfer of therapy Symptom removal Learning to respond and to control the environment
Processes	Acceptance Support of client's autonomy	Recognition and interpretation of the unconscious material Manipulation of client anxiety	Active initial questioning Reeducation about emotional conflicts

Source: L'Abate, 1981, p. 264.

One of the most critical assumptions has to do with the effect of the counselor as a person in the counseling relationship. If one's counseling is viewed as a "personal trait" (Lister, 1964; Shoben, 1966), and it seems that it should be, then an approach is unique for the individual counselor and tied to his way of relating to others. To take this a step further, it may be inferred that he could not expect to help others unless his counseling approach were, in fact, a utilization of himself as a real person in a human relationship.

A second assumption is that the counselor has a thorough knowledge of the necessary ingredients for personal theory building. These are himself, existing counseling approaches, theories of learning and personality development, and perceptions of others. Without these, it is difficult of conceive of any kind of meaningful and consistent approach being developed.

A third assumption has to do with the underlying consistency of the counselor in interpersonal relations. In developing a personal theory, could the counselor include different sorts of basic attitudes and methods—to use an extreme example, could he be "democratic" some times and "autocratic" at others? Arbuckle (1966) points out that: "If . . . what are called methodologies are actually qualities of the individual counselor, it is difficult to see how the counselor could be eclectic" (p. 229). But an *eclectic orientation* is quite different from an eclectic counseling approach: "There is a vast difference, however, between an eclectic *orientation*, which surely every professional counselor should have, and without which there will be provincialism or even downright ignorance of counseling, and an eclectic *method of counseling*" (Arbuckle, 1966, p. 231). The counselor should be consistent in his basic approach to others; he should have, however, a broad knowledge of counseling approaches. This concept of eclecticism is apparent in Arbuckle's (1966) illustration: "The consistency of the client-centered counselor, for example, comes simply because he has found, eclectically and pragmatically, that this is the means of operation in which he is comfortable, and in which he is most effective" (p. 232).

Lister (1967) takes the same position in describing the possibilities of "theoretical eclecticism": "The primary advantage of theoretical eclecticism is that it enables the counselor to work out for himself an internally consistent, coherent rationale for his counseling behavior. . . . He may develop a point of view more personally meaningful than any existing orthodox position. . . . He may conceptualize the counseling process in a way that meshes comfortably with his own life style" (pp. 288–291). This suggests that the counselor would desirably have a consistency in human relations, in contrast to the "technical eclectic" who concentrates on selecting "techniques" that seem to work but have no sound theoretical framework (Lister, 1967).

A final assumption is that a counselor is capable of developing a personal style that is better for him than other formal approaches. An eclectic counselor makes this assumption, implicitly or explicitly. He should be aware, however, that his approach may have serious deficiencies which he does not realize and which he does nothing to correct (Lister, 1967) (p. 79).

Brammer and Shostrom (1982) recommended that each counselor and psychotherapist must ultimately develop a point of view that is uniquely his or her own. They went on to state:

Developing one's own view is a very demanding lifelong task. In addition to knowing current theories of personality structure and behavior change, counselors must know

Table 5–2. Classification of Intervention Methods According to the E-R-A Model (from Ulrici, L, Abate, & Wagner, 1980, p. 264)

Emotionality	Rationality
Methods focus on experimental exercises that differentiate feeling states of solitude and solidarity.	Methods focus on the development of conscious understanding that supports reality based controls.
1. Developing interpersonal awareness through individual exercises of mediation fantasy trips, imaginary dialogues, here-and-now awareness.	1. Teaching new facts, concepts, and theories through lectures, readings, and discussions.
2. Developing awareness of interpersonal relationships through interactional task of role play, sculpting, etc.	2. Relating past influences to present functioning through cognitive recreation of past events (e.g., psychoanalytic dialogues, genograms, and rational reevaluations).
3. Developing bodily awareness through physical exercises of creative movement and interpersonal body contacts.	3. Developing insight to differentiate feelings from actions through analysis of one's present and past relationships (e.g., working through transference, understanding defense operations, and ego controls).
4. Teaching skills of interpersonal sensitivity and communication through lectures, readings, demonstrations, and practice exercises.	4. Teaching skills of rational thinking and ego control through lectures, discussions, and practice at rational problem solving and decision making.

Table 5-2 (cont.)

Activity	
Behavioral	**Systemic**
Methods focus on the application of scientific principles to shape and control behavior.	Methods focus on adjusting dimensions of cohesion and adaptability that maintain family functioning.

Behavioral:

1. Solving behavioral problems through experimental analysis—quantifying behavior, determining controls, and implementing interventions.
2. Teaching and increasing desired behavior and extinguishing ⁎ unappropriate behavior through techniques of:
   a. respondent conditioning (e.g., stimulus pairing, desensitization)
   b. operant conditioning (e.g., positive reinforcement, punishment.)
3. Teaching desired behavior through social learning (e.g., modeling, films).
4. Increasing and maintaining behavior through evaluative feedback.
5. Practice application of learned behavior through role play and simulated exercises.
6. Implementing desired behavior or its approximation through behavioral tasks performed in daily context.
7. Teaching behavioral principles through lectures, models, and practice exercises.

Systemic:

1. Establishing appropriate boundaries for cohesion and autonomy through:
   a. directives given in session (e.g., interactions, blocking others, bringing members of the social network)
   b. behavior assignments for daily context (e.g., rituals, paradoxical exercises, age-appropriate tasks, activities to support coalitions or limit enmeshment).
2. Restructuring operations in response to situational stress or developmental change through:
   a. assigning linear tasks to directly change operations (e.g., rescheduling, assigning family duties)
   b. assigning paradoxical tasks that emphasize operations problems. (e.g., role reversals, behavioral extremes).

their own assumptions about the nature of man and the process of knowing, their own values and views of the good life, and their models of the mature well-functioning person. This goal is accomplished through self-study of client–counselor relationships and personal therapeutic experiences resulting in increased self-understanding. These understandings and assumptions are then related to one's goals for counseling, which in turn are matched with strategies and methods to reach those goals most effectively. One borrows from other theorists in the sense that one stands on their shoulders to reach higher levels of understanding and effectiveness in practice. Then, one synthesizes these pieces incrementally into a unified system which is comfortable and effective in a particular setting. Finally, one tests the theory in practice and formulates hypotheses which can be tested experimentally. The results then are incorporated into one's system, or one revises the system. (p. 38)

Brammer and Shostrom (1982) also believed that

Counselors and psychotherapists can take one of three positions: identify with one of the theories already published and tested in practice, develop an eclectic position, or strive for a personalized creative synthesis of theory and practice. [These positions are summarized in Table 5–3.] (p. 33–34)

Table 5–3. Comparison of Basic Approaches to Theory Building

Established Single Theory	Eclectic Approaches	Creative Synthesis
	Main Characteristic	
Integrated set of assumptions related directly to strategy and method	Strategies and methods from several approaches applied selectively to clients	Application of broad and varied strategies and methods related to a synthesized theory evolved and "owned" by the practitioner
	Examples	
Freud's Psychoanalytic Theory Rogers' Client-Centered Theory	Thorne's Integrative Psychology Lazarus's Structural Eclecticism	Assagioli's Psychosynthesis Shostrom's Actualizing Therapy
	Advantages	
Ready-made system of assumptions Extensive experience and data base Consistency of theory and method	Collection of various methods Flexibility of choice on methods Wide agency application of methods	Continues synthesizing, extending, and amplifying personal system Discourages competition Fosters therapist's identity with own views
	Limitations	
Tendency toward restricted view of data Often a closed system Encourages hero worship Fosters competition and divisiveness	Encourages uncritical choosing De-emphasizes integrative theorizing Tends toward faddism Additive collection of what works for now Imitative and limited creativity	A continuous lifelong task Tends to be idealistic Futuristic—ahead of its time Requires continuous creativity Requires trust in self Risky—requires standing on one's own
	Illustrative Comments by Practitioners	
"Client-centered theory speaks to me." "Ellis is my hero." "I dig Freud." "I am analytic." "I stick with the tried and true."	"I use what works." "I'm flexible." "I try many methods." "I like TA methods but not the basic assumption." "Everyone says something important."	"I'm constantly reevaluating my ideas." "I develop my own theory to fit me." "I try to keep open and take some risks." 'I trust my own observations and judgments."

Source: Brammer & Shostrom, 1982, p. 34.

Goals of Counseling

Another approach to viewing the various theoretical models may be by examining goals in relationship to theories. Table 5–4 presents a framework in the form of

> a dynamic, developmental continuum of counseling goals that allows systematic inclusion of several of the more viable counseling models currently on the scene. This continuum of goals is related to and is an extension of Maslow's (1970) hierarchy of human needs, and it is based on Maslow's assumption that "lower-order" or primary needs (in this case, counseling goals) have priority over "higher-order" or secondary needs (i.e., counseling goals).

The chart in Table [5–4] outlines the continuum moving from the top (primary goals/needs) to the bottom (secondary goals/needs). It is proposed that client goals/needs that are most basic (at the top of the continuum) need to be addressed in counseling before a client can work effectively on higher level goals/needs (at the bottom of the continuum). The continuum is seen as fluid, however, and a counselor might well be working up and down the continuum at different times with a client. (Bruce, 1984, p. 259)

Obviously, counseling goals may also be more simply classified in terms of counselor goals and client goals or in terms of the immediate, intermediate, or

Table 5–4. Continuum of Counseling Goals

Counseling Process Goals	Corresponding Counseling Process Models	Maslow's Hierarchy of Needs, Expanded (Physiological Needs)
Ego Development (Inception) Anxiety reduction Personal adjustment	Clinical/analytical model Ego psychotherapy	Security/safety needs Dependency ego defenses
Socialization Role/self identity Social adjustment Behavior change	Behavioral counseling Behavior modification Reality therapy	Belongingness needs affiliation identification character development
Developmental Competence Resolving developmental conflicts and challenges Coping/mastery Problem solving Decision making Self-sufficiency	Developmental counseling Adlerian counseling Transactional analysis Rational-emotive therapy Problem solving Decision making	(Developmental/cognitive needs) to know and understand, curiosity
Self-esteem Self-awareness Self-acceptance Self-confidence Congruence of self	Client-centered/relationship counseling	Esteem needs values development
Self-realization Actualizing potential: Intellectual, emotional, Social, spiritual.	Gestalt counseling Existential counseling	Actualization needs

Source: Bruce, 1984, p. 260.

long-range goals of therapy. Regardless of how one chooses to classify counseling goals, it is obvious that counseling, like all other meaningful activities, must be goal driven, must have a purpose, must seek to attain an objective.

The Counseling Process

Having briefly introduced some of the popular counseling theories, let us now move on to examine the translation of these theories into action. This "action" is frequently referred to as the counseling process. This process is usually specified by a sequence of interactions or steps. Although various authors will conceptualize these stages or phases differently with differences usually resulting from different theoretical models, there is considerable agreement that initially the process is concerned with relationship establishment, followed by some method of problem identification and patterns of exploration leading to planning for problem solution and remediation and concluding with action and termination. Blackham (1977) identified the stages in the counseling process as follows: (1) problem identification and relationship establishment stage, (2) exploration and analysis stage, (3) implementation stage, and (4) termination stage. Pietrofesa et al. (1984) presented the therapeutic process as depicted in Figure 5–2.

A brief description of each of these stages will be helpful.

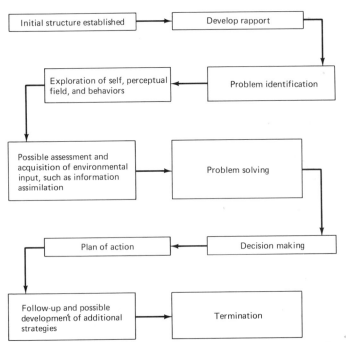

Figure 5–2. Commonalities between counseling and psychotherapeutic processes. *(Pietrofesa, Hoffman, Splete & Pinto, 1984, p. 8.)*

Relationship Establishment

As often stated in definitions, counseling is a relationship. Furthermore, it is defined as a helping relationship. It therefore follows that if it is to be a relationship that is helpful, the counselor must take the initiative in the initial interview to establish a climate conducive to mutual respect, trust, free and open communication, and understanding in general of what the counseling process involves.

Within a formal context, Brammer (1985) asserted that this relationship takes the form of an interview—a structured helping relationship to which many variables contribute. Figure 5–3 illustrates these variables.

Although responsiblity will later shift increasingly to the client, at this stage the responsibility for the counseling process rests primarily with the counselor. Among the techniques the counselor may use are those designed to relieve tensions and open communication. Both the counselor's attitude and verbal communcations are significant to the development of a satisfactory relationship. In the latter instance, all of the counselor's communication skills are brought into play. These include attentive listening, understanding, and feeling with the client. As Egan (1982) described it, the counselor's goal in this stage is attending: " ... the way you orient yourself physically and psychologically to clients. ..." (p. 59).

Among the factors that are important in the establishment of this counselor-client relationship are positive regard and respect, accurate empathy, and genuineness. These conditions imply counselor openness, an ability to understand and feel with the client, and valuing the client. As Hackney and Cormier (1979) inferred, this constructive

> counselor–client relationship serves not only to increase the opportunity for clients to attain their goals, but also serves as a potential model of a good interpersonal relationship, one that clients can use to improve the quality of their other relationships outside the therapy setting. (p. 8)

Counselors must keep in mind that the purpose of a counseling relationship is to meet, insofar as possible, client needs (not counselor needs). The counseling process within this relationship seeks to assist the client in assuming the responsibilities for his or her problem and its solution. As viewed by Okun (1976):

> a helping relationship that benefits the helpee is a two-way mutual learning process between two (or more) people. The relationship is dependent for its effectiveness upon the helper possessing the skill to communicate his or her understanding of the

Figure 5–3. The helping relationship in the interview. *(Brammer, 1985, p. 41.)*

helpee's feelings and behaviors and the ability to apply appropriate helping strategies in order to facilitate the recipient's self-exploration, self-understanding, problem-solving, and decision-making, all of which lead to constructive action on the part of the helpee. (p. 16)

The establishment of a relationship that is seen as helpful to the client must be achieved early in the counseling process, inasmuch as this will often determine whether or not the client will continue.

Eisenberg and Delaney (1977) suggested the essential goals of the initial counseling interview are

For the Counselor:

Stimulate open, honest, and full communication about the concerns needing to be discussed and the factors and background related to those concerns.

Work toward progressively deeper levels of understanding, respect, and trust between self and client.

Provide the client with the view that something useful can be gained from the counseling sessions.

Identify a problem or concern for subsequent attention and work.

Establish the "gestalt" that counseling is a process in which both parties must work hard at exploring and understanding the client and his or her concerns.
Acquire information about the client that relates to his or her concerns and effective problem resolution.

For Most Clients:

Stimulating self-examination.

Generating some specific task for the client to do, or some specific issue to think about before the next counseling session. (p. 75)

Problem Identification and Exploration

Once an adequate relationship has been established, clients will be more receptive to the in depth discussion and exploration of their concerns. At this stage, clients assume more responsibility, because it is their problem and it is their willingness to communicate as much of the nature of the problem to the counselor that will determine to a large extent the assistance the counselor can give.

During this phase, the counselor continues to exhibit attending behavior and may place particular emphasis on such communication skills as paraphrasing, clarification, perception checking, or feedback. The counselor may question the client, but the questions are stated in such a way as to facilitate the continued exploration of the client's concern. Questions that would embarrass, challenge, or threaten the client are avoided. During this stage, the counselor is seeking to distinguish between what might be called surface problems and those that are more complex. The counselor is also seeking to determine if the stated problem is, in fact, the concern that has brought the client to the counselor's attention. This may be a time for information gathering. The more usable information the counselor has, the greater the prospects of accurate assessment of the client needs. It is therefore helpful for counselors to recognize the various areas of information that must be tapped:

> The information index in Figure 5–4 represents the main sources of information for the counselor.
>
> Continuum A–B represents the time dimension. Information about the person's past helps the counselor understand how the person got where he or she is. Information about the present indicates how well the person is functioning currently, and information about the future tells the counselor who the person wishes to become. As these pieces of information are brought together, they can give a reasonably good picture of who the person is and why the person is seeking help.
>
> Continuum C–D reflects the importance of getting both intrapsychic and interpersonal information. Intrapsychic information consists of learning about the person's perceptions of reality; his inner conflicts and how they are handled; the relationship between who the person is, thinks he is, and wants others to think he is; as well as the person's beliefs, values, and hopes. Interpersonal information comprises the dynamics involved in how the person relates with others, whether these relationships are satisfying or dissatisfying to the person or to the people with whom he or she relates.
>
> Continuum E–F denotes what the person thinks and feels about herself, others, and relevant events. It is not only important to know the content of the person's thoughts and feelings, but to recognize how they interact and perhaps conflict. For example, when asked how she viewed her father, a woman repsonds "I have nothing but the utmost respect for him." When she is asked how she *feels* about her father, she replies "I resent him more than words can say."
>
> The information index highlights cautions in information gathering. Typically, people seeking help lure counselors into talking about the past, discussing interpersonal relationships, and focusing on ideas. The counselor who is successfully lured will have a fragmented and inaccurate picture upon which to make a clinical evaluation. (Cavanagh, 1982, p. 106)

During this stage, some counselors may use appraisal techniques such as standardized tests for problem diagnosis. Subproblems of the problem may also be identified. During this stage, the client not only explores experiences and behaviors, but also may reveal feelings and the relationship of concern to the way he or she is living life in general. The counselor, on the other hand, is seeking to secure as much relevant data as possible and to integrate it into an overall picture of the client and his or her concern. The counselor also shares these perceptions with the client. A goal of this stage is for both the counselor

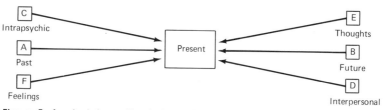

Figure 5–4.   An information index. *(Cavanagh, 1982, p. 106.)*

and the client to perceive the problem and its ramifications similarly. Another goal of the counselor during this stage is to help the client develop a self-understanding that recognizes the need for dealing with a concern—the need for change and action.

Obviously, this is a busy stage of the counseling process. As Blackham (1977) described it:

> Much of the real work of counseling takes place in the second stage, where exploration and client analysis become intensive. Facilitative conditions are created that enable clients to explore and understand the basis of their problems, and procedures are formualted to resolve them. Some problem-solving activity may be initiated, but the bulk of this activity, along with the implementation of change procedures, takes place in stage three.

The goals and guidelines for this stage are as follows:

1. Explore and analyze each problem area.
2. Specify client problems behaviorally and state them in a form that makes them possible to resolve. Problems are stated in terms of client behavior that can be learned or changed in the context of the person's present life circumstances.
3. Analyze each problem in terms of variables that influence or maintain it. For example, if the client has a behavior or interpersonal problem, identify the significant people in the client's life and analyze the interactions or contingencies (stimulus–response–consequence relationships) that maintain the inappropriate response.
4. Determine the severity of client problems and make arrangements for referral if they are beyond the counselor's competence.
5. Arrange client problems in terms of priorities; decide which problem will be worked on first.
6. Extend the facilitative conditions that best promote problem exploration, client understanding, and problem-solving activity.
7. Recognize and deal effectively with transference, countertransference, and resistance.
8. Formulate procedures that will resolve client problems effectively or promote the desired behavior change. (pp. 201, 203)

Successful counseling and therapeutic outcomes are not only a function of method and counselor's characteristics. Client problems and characteristics may also play an important role. Both clinical experience and research seem to suggest that counseling prognosis tends to be more positive under the following conditions:

1. Client problems are recent rather than long-standing, and the client has some expectation of improvement.
2. The symptoms the client exhibits and the degree of distress or anxiety present are handicapping or incapacitating.
3. The client voluntarily seeks help and is willing to explore problems and invest time and effort to change.
4. The client has normal intelligence or higher, has adapted reasonably well in the past, and his present family or circumstances of living do not negate or jeopardize counseling or change efforts.
5. The client's problem has no hereditary, constitutional, or endocrine basis.
6. The client's problems or symptoms do not produce major secondary gains. That

is, the client's nonadaptive behavior should not provide excessive personal gratification or be intentionally encouraged or reinforced by significant others.

7. The client has experienced some satisfying interpersonal relationships in the past with parents or parent figures and is able to form an appropriate relationship to the counselor. (pp. 196–197)

Planning for Problem Solving

Once the counselor has determined that all relevant information regarding the client's concern is available and understood and once the client has accepted the need for doing something about a specific problem, the time is ripe for developing a plan to solve or remediate the concern of the client.

At this point, effective goal setting becomes the vital part of the counseling activity. Indicated here are seven specific criteria from Dyer and Vriend (1977) for judging effective goal setting in counseling:

1. Mutual agreement on goals is vital.
2. Goal specificity promotes goal achievement.
3. On-target goals are relevant to the self-defeating behavior of the goal setter.
4. Effectively set goals are achievable and success-oriented.
5. Effectively set goals are quantifiable and measurable.
6. Effectively set goals are behavioral and observable.
7. Goals have been effectively structured when a client understands them and can restate them clearly. (pp. 470–471)

Dyer and Vriend (1977) went on to suggest that the counselor can ask the following evaluative questions:

> Am I helping this client to set goals that are: (1) High in mutuality? (b) Specific in nature? (c) Relevant to the client's self-defeating behavior? (d) Achievable and success-oriented? (3) Quantifiable and measurable? (f) Behavioral and observable? (g) Understandable and repeatable? (p. 471)

In the further development of this plan, the counselor recognizes that the client will frequently not arrive at basic insights, implications, or probabilities as fast as the counselor will. However, most counselors will agree that it is better to guide the client toward realizing these understandings himself or herself, rather than just telling the client outright. To facilitate the client's understanding, the counselor may use techniques of repetition, mild confrontation, interpretation, information, and, obviously, encouragement.

The outcome of this process is aimed at allowing the client to identify as many solutions as possible, project the consequences of each solution, and finally set the priorities of these solutions.

Solution Application and Termination

In this final stage, the responsibilities are clear-cut. The client has the responsibility for applying the determined solution, and the counselor, for determining the point of termination. In the first instance, the counselor has a responsibility to encourage the client's acting on his or her determined problem solution. During the time that the client is actively engaged in applying the problem solution, the counselor will often maintain contact as a source of followup, support, and encouragement. The client may also need the counselor's assistance in the event things do not go according to plan. Once it has been determined, however, that the counselor and the client have dealt with the client's concern to the extent possible and practical, the process should be terminated. As noted before, this responsibility is primarily the counselor's, although the client has the right to terminate at any time. The counselor usually gives some indication that "the next interview should just about wrap it up," and may conclude with a summary of the main points of the counseling process. Usually, the counselor will leave the door open for the client's possible return in the event unexpected additional assistance is needed. Because counseling is a learning process, the counselor hopes that the client has not only learned to deal with this particular problem, but has also learned problem-solving skills that will decrease the probability of the client's need for further counseling in the future.

In concluding this section on the counseling process, we are aware of our frequent reference to the client's "problem" and we would like to remind our readers that problems are not always based in perceived inadequacies or failures requiring remediation and restorative therapy. Clients can have equally pressing needs resulting from concerns for developing their human potential—for capitalizing on their strengths. In these instances the emphasis is on development, growth, or enhancement rather than remediation.

Counseling Skills

Thus far in this chapter we have discussed the importance of the counselor having a theoretical framework within which to function and a knowledge of the process or stages through which client counseling moves. Equally important are the skills that the counselor must possess to apply a given theory and implement the process.

The skills of counseling have their roots in both theory and process and have been reinforced through both practice and research. The counselor acquires these skills through both learning and practice. We have grouped these under the categories of communications skills, diagnostic skills, motivational skills, and management skills, recognizing that there will be overlap and interrelations among these as well as between skills and process.

Communications Skills

Nonverbal Communications Skills

All of us communicate nonverbally. Through the use of facial expressions, body posture, and physical movement we send messages, usually intended but infrequently not. We also usually "read messages" that others communicate to us in a similar manner. In our society, nonverbal language is a popular means of communication and in counseling, a social interaction process, nonverbal communication is important to both the counselor and the counselee. For example, from the onset and throughout the counseling process, visual clues will influence the client's perception of the counselor. As noted earlier in this chapter, one of the nonverbal ways in which the counselor deals with this factor is by exhibiting attending behavior, by communicating nonverbally, "I am interested in you and your concerns, I respect you and I'm going to give you my undivided attention, etc." Attending behaviors accomplish several purposes:

1. *Communication of Individual Attention.* Attending behaviors communicate nonverbally, "I am listening to you and only you." They can act as a reinforcement for the clients to continue to speak.
2. *Communication of Respect.* Counselors, by attending, communicate respect for the client, as if to say, "What you say is so important, I will attend to you."
3. *Modeling of Effective Behavior.* Counselors can act as models for their clients. Through their modeling behavior, counselors are afforded the opportunity to demonstrate effective interpersonal skills for clients. After several sessions, counselors will often report how clients have altered their own attending behaviors. With the modeling concept, counselees learn to utilize attending behaviors outside the counseling framework.
4. *Improvement of Counselor Discrimination.* Good attending behaviors can actually help counselors focus on the client. It helps to maintain alertness and to provde for more effective discrimination. (Pietrofesa, Hoffman, Splete, and Pinto, 1984, pp. 270–271)

Gazda, Asbury, Balzer, Childers, and Walters (1977) categorized nonverbal behaviors into four modalities. It should be emphasized that nonverbal behaviors are highly idiosyncratic; interpretation of these clues must be tentative and based on the context in which they are sent.

1. Nonverbal Communication Behaviors Using Time

Recognition
Promptness or delay in recognizing the presence of another or in responding to his or her communication

Priorities
Amount of time another is willing to spend communicating with a person
Relative amounts of time spent on various topics

2. Nonverbal Communication Behaviors Using the Body

Eye contact (important in regulating the relationship)
Looking at a specific object
Looking down
Steady to helper
Defiantly at helper ("hard" eyes), glaring
Shifting eyes from object to object
Looking at helper but looking away when looked at

Covering eyes with hand(s)
Frequency of looking at another

Eyes
"Sparkling"
Tears
"Wild-eyed"
Position of eyelids

Skin
Pallor
Perspiration
Blushing
"Goose bumps"

Posture (often indicative of physical alertness or tiredness)
"Eager," as if ready for activity
Slouching, slovenly, tired looking, slumping
Arms crossed in front as if to protect self
Crossing legs
Sits facing the other person rather than sideways or away from
Hanging head, looking at floor, head down
Body positioned to exclude others from joining a group or dyad

Facial expression (primary site for display of affects; thought by researchers to be
subject to involuntary responses)
No change
Wrinkled forehead (lines of worry), frown
Wrinkled nose
Smiling, laughing
"Sad" mouth
Biting lip

Hand and arm gestures
Symbolic hand and arm gestures
Literal hand and arm gestures to indicate size of shape
Demonstration of how something happened or how to do something

Self-inflicting behaviors
Nail biting
Scatching
Cracking knuckles
Tugging at hair
Rubbing or stroking

Repetitive behaviors (often interpreted as signs of nervousness or restlessness but
may be organic in origin)
Tapping foot, drumming or thumping with fingers
Fidgeting, squirming
Trembling
Playing with button, hair, or clothing

Signals or commands
Snapping fingers
Holding finger to lips for silence
Pointing
Staring directly to indicate disapproval

Shrugging shoulders
Waving
Nodding in recognition
Winking
Nodding in agreement, shaking head in disagreement

Touching
To get attention, such as tapping on shoulder
Affectionate, tender
Sexual
Challenging, such as poking finger into chest
Symbols of camaraderie, such as slapping on back
Belittling, such as a pat on top of head

3. Nonverbal Communication Behaviors Using Vocal Media

Tone of voice
Flat, monotone, absence of feelings
Bright, vivid changes of inflection
Strong, confident, firm
Weak, hesitant, shaky
Broken, faltering

Rate of speech
Fast
Medium
Slow

Loudness of voice
Loud
Medium
Soft

Diction
Precise versus careless
Regional (colloquial) differences
Consistency of diction

4. Nonverbal Communication Behaviors Using the Environment

Distance
Moves away when the other moves toward
Moves toward when the other moves away
Takes initiative in moving toward or away from
Distance widens gradually
Distance narrows gradually

Arrangement of the physical setting
Neat, well-ordered, organized
Untidy, haphazard, careless
Casual versus formal
Warm versus cold colors
Soft versus hard materials
Slick versus varied textures
Cheerful and lively versus dull and drab

"Discriminating" taste versus tawdry
Expensive or luxurious versus shabby or spartan

Clothing (often used to tell others what a person wants them to believe about him/
    her)
Bold versus unobtrusive
Stylish versus nondescript

Position in the room
Protects or fortifies self in position by having objects such as desk or table between
    self and other person.
Takes an open or vulnerable position, such as in the center of the room, side by
    side on a sofa, or in a simple chair. Nothing between self and other person.
Takes an attacking or dominating position. May block exit from area or may
    maneuver other person into boxed-in position.
Moves about the room.
Moves in and out of other person's territory.
Stands when other person sits, or gets in higher position than other person.

(Gazda et al., 1977, pp. 89–92)

Verbal Communications Skills

Strange as it may seem, we will initiate our discussion of verbal communications
skills by discussing listening. Listening, however, is a prerequisite to effective
verbal communicating. Listening also is implied in attending behavior, but
because of its importance, we would emphasize the point again. Cavanagh
(1982) made the point that

> Listening is the basis of a counselor's effectiveness. The one behavior that effective
> counselors do most is listen. Without listening, counselors cannot know who the per-
> son in counseling really is and, without this knowledge, cannot help him or her.
> Unfortunately, listening is one of the most difficult behaviors in which human beings
> participate. (p. 194)

Effective listening enables counselors to adroitly manipulate their verbal counseling skills. These include the use of attending responses that indicate to the
client that you are listening (i.e., "I understand," "I see") and what we might
label as "stimulus responses," those that encourage the client to continue to
comment (i.e., "Can you tell me more about that?" "Could you clarify that for
me?" "Please continue if you wish"). Effective listening is mandatory for feedback, another important verbal (as well as nonverbal) communication skill.
Feedback is the verbalization of the counselor's perceptions and reactions to the
client's behaviors, feelings, concerns, actions, expressions, and so forth. And it
offers the client the opporunity in turn to feedback—react—perhaps validate or
expand on the counselor's feedback. It offers the counselor the opportunity to
periodically summarize and validate what has transpired and ensure that both
counselor and counselee are accurately "receiving" each others messages,
before moving further in the counseling process.

Also important in verbal communcations is the art of questioning. Skill in
questioning involves timing, wording, and type of questions. The skillful counselor does not inject questions that will stop, alter or "slow down" a client's open

discussion of a concern. Questions are injected to keep the discussion moving (i.e., "Why do you think they reacted that way to your behavior?"); to clarify (i.e., "What do you mean?; Am I right in understanding you, etc.?"); and to validate (i.e., "How do you know? Give me an example."). The type of question used should be appropriate to the desired outcome from asking it. Open questions (i.e., "How did you feel about that?") provide opportunities for the client to express feelings, provide greater detail, and gain new insights) while closed questions (i.e., "Will you go back next week?") gets an answer rather than an evasive or rambling reply. The counselor may also decide when to use direct questions (i.e., "Tell me, are you an alcoholic?") or nondirect questions (i.e., "What do you think about alcoholism today?"), which do not directly identify the client with a problem or issue.

Effective communication is also facilitated by knowing what not to do. George and Cristiani (1986) listed these barriers to communications:

1. Giving advice
2. Offering solutions
3. Moralizing and preaching
4. Analyzing and diagnosing
5. Judging or criticizing
6. Praising and agreeing; Giving positive evaluations
7. Reassuring (p. 125)

Diagnostic Skills

Other chapters in this book document both the importance and the basic techniques of diagnosis. We would simply indicate in this section on counseling skills that effective counseling requires skill in accurately diagnosing and understanding the client, client concerns, and the relevant environmental influences. Counselors must therefore be skillful in the use of both standardized psychological measures and nonstandardized techniques for diagnosis.

Motivational Skills

The goals of counseling usually represent some form of behavior or attitudinal change. Client movement toward counseling goals will often be dependent on the skill of the counselor in motivating the client. This may require a sensitivity to cues that stimulate motivation for the client, or it may require the use of influence (see Table 5-5). Ivey (1980) was of the opinion that

> When the counselor becomes an active participant in the interview, the counselor can influence the process of change. The counselor has her or his repertoire of experiences, training, insights, perceptions, and theories of human growth with which to enrich the client and produce growth. Influencing skills are those through which the counselor shares himself or herself. When the counselor shares with the client, the interview becomes a process of interpersonal influence. (p. 80)

Table 5–5. Influencing Skills

Skill	Description	Use in Interview
Directive	Telling the client what to do; giving directions.	Leads client to participate in the therapeutic exercise such as fantasy or role-playing; may be used to tell client what to do following interview.
Expression of content	Giving advice; providing instructions; giving opinions; sharing information; making suggestions; providing client feedback; threat; reassurance	Brings data from counselor's experience or knowledge; means of communicating facts.
Expression of feeling	Counselor shares own emotions, states, and attitudes.	Facilitates client sharing of emotions, states, and attitudes; distinguishes emotions from cognition.
Influencing summary	Stating main themes of counselor's statements over period of time.	Means of checking perceptions; brings together separate thoughts and feelings; provides structure; gives opportunity for reflection.
Interpretation	Renaming and relabeling client's thoughts, feelings, and behaviors from a theoretical perspective.	Provides alternate frame of reference for viewing behavior; understanding, and bringing change, often through client insight.
Self-disclosure	Counselor shares own feelings, thoughts, experiences, and life with client; a special variety of expression of content and expression of feeling.	Builds client/counselor rapport; mutuality of relationship; modeling of interpersonal openness; facilitates client self-disclosure and self-exploration.
Direct-mutual communication	Counselor and client focus on their interaction as perceived and felt, and share with each other their experience of the other.	Promotes analysis of transference relationship; provides insight into selves of client and counselor; facilitates development of deep relationship.

Source: Ivey, 1980, p. 80.

Management Skills

We conclude our discussion of the counseling skills that counselors should possess by noting the importance of the counselor's "management" of the coun-

seling process. This includes, first of all, attention to the environment and physical arrangements where the counseling takes place. Once the counseling process begins, the counselor has the responsibility for managing this process; keeping it moving, "on-track," and progressing. A sense of both timing and time management are important. An awareness of the client's well-being and managing the process in this context is another kind of management task. Management also means managing your own contributions to the process; recognizing and working within your professional limitations. Finally, determining the point and method of termination plus any follow-up and evaluation are primarily the counselor's reponsibilities.

Special Counseling Populations

Counselors in nearly all settings deal with a variety of individual problems and concerns. Because increasing attention is being given to certain problem areas, it seems appropriate to note several of these "special" counseling situations. These include alcohol and drugs, sex, marriage and family, retirement and aging, women, and ethnic minorities.

Substance Abusers

Increases in the use of alcohol and drugs and the ill effects of the abuse of these substances are well publicized. Persons are considered abusers of any substance when it is used to the extent that it causes or threatens damage to the individual or society or both. While a variety of classification systems may be used, the American Psychiatric Association recognizes the following types of alcoholism:

Episodic excessive drinking. If alcoholism is present and the individual becomes intoxicated as frequently as four times a year, the condition should be classified here. Intoxication is defined as a state in which the individual's coordination or speech is definitely impaired or his behavior is clearly altered.

Habitual excessive drinking. This diagnosis is given to persons who are alcoholic and who either become intoxicated more than twelve times a year or are recognizably under the influence of alcohol more than once a week, even though not intoxicated.

Alcoholic addiction. This condition should be diagnosed when there is direct or strong presumptive evidence that the patient is dependent on alcohol. If available, the best directive evidence of such dependence is the appearance of withdrawal symptoms. The inability of the patient to go one day without drinking is presumptive evidence. When heavy drinking continues for three months or more it is reasonable to presume addiction to alcohol has been established. (Kinney and Leaton, 1978, p. 42)

Drug abusers may be classified for treatment purposes by the drugs they use. These are:

Depressants—(barbiturates, narcotics, tranquilizers, other sedatives)
Stimulants—(amphetamine, cocaine, caffeine)
Mind-altering drugs—(PCP, LSD, glue, other hallucinogens)
Marijuana and hashish (Ohio Alcoholism Counselor Credentialing Commission, p. 4)

Let us examine the counselor's role in the community and rehabilitation agency and school settings that either seek to prevent or engage in the treatment of these abuses.

In discussing the counselor's role, Belkin (1975) suggested the activities and program may be divided as follows:

1. Preventive
   a. Understanding the problem.
   b. Creating a drug education program.
   c. Making available to students adequate information.
2. Therapeutic
   a. Working with drug users.
   b. Maintaining ongoing patterns of facilitative communication.
3. Administrative and legal
   a. Cooperating with system-wide efforts.
   b. Working with the community.
   c. Maintaining communication and feedback with law enforcement authorities. (p. 349)

The counselor in this setting should be actively involved in all three phases of this work, especially the preventive phase. He or she should have a thorough and well-grounded understanding of the drug problem. He or she should also be engaged in a continual interaction with teachers, sharing understandings, learning from them, and helping to implement within the school a viable drug education program (Belkin, 1975, p. 349).

In working in community treatment centers, Page, Smith, and Beamish (1977) indicated that

it is important for professional counselors to consider several things when a treatment center is established in an agency or a community setting. A concrete working philosophy developed by the staff, and a staff committed to this philosophy, are mandatory. Staff training sessions need to be conducted before residents enter the program. A constructive and cooperative liaison with the sponsoring agency should be developed. Means to facilitate staff communication need to be initiated. A plan to foster positive public relations can prevent many problems. It is important to formulate an effective way to evaluate the success of the program. (p. 183)

In many programs, both individual and group counseling are used. In some settings, counseling teams have been found to be effective for group counseling. It is also obviously important that counselors who work with drug and alcohol abuse have more than a superficial knowledge of the causes, symptoms, and potential outcomes of the problem. Furthermore, in many individual situations, medical treatment may be needed, and referral to or "teaming" with a psychiatrist may be necessary.

Counselors in all settings therefore need to be aware of the resources available for the treatment of substance abuse clients. These may include emergency clinics, specialized centers, hospital care (both in-patient and out-patient), halfway houses, crisis centers, and special assistance groups such as Alcoholics Anonymous and Narcotics Anonymous. Counselors working with such populations generally have a specialized knowledge of the pharmacological, physiological, psychological, and sociocultural aspects of the use of alcohol and drugs.

Women

In recent generations, considerable attention has been focused upon the effects of sex role stereotyping with its detrimental effects, particularly on women, yet, according to Ohlsen (1983):

> there are many obstacles that block women from realizing their full potential as human beings. Today's woman has been socialized to live in a world which no longer has the same demands as the world of yesterday. The obstacles are multidimensional and complex; some are outside of the woman's control, i.e., sex, race, ethnicity, and social stereotypes. Others she can directly influence if she is able to interpret her life experiences in such a way that she becomes empowered to appreciate herself as a whole being. She can learn how to use these resources to influence change in her personal and career relationships. (p. 242)

Although federal and state legislation has sought to promote opportunities for women to achieve their potential by stimulating legal equality of the sexes, there is abundant evidence that women are still encountering problems in achieving their sex-role identity and career destinies without the impediments of sexual bias. In career decision making alone, Feller (1978) wrote that

> from early infancy onward, such sex-role stereotyping has profound effects on the manner in which the individual perceives herself/himself in relation to the environment. Self-concepts, values, attitudes, interests, needs, and goals all develop in response to the influence of sex-role differentiation (or equality). (p. 4)

Maccoby and Jacklin (1974) pointed out that some of the most common sex-role stereotypes accepted within American society are:

1. Females are more susceptible to persuasion than males.
2. Females have lower self-esteem.
3. Females excel in rote learning and simple repetitive tasks, while males perform better in tasks that require higher-learning cognitive processing and the inhibition of previously learned responses.
4. Males are more analytic.
5. Females are more affected by heredity; males, by the environment.
6. Females lack achievement motivation.
7. Females are more fearful, timid, and anxious.
8. Males are more active; females are passive.
9. Males are more competitive.
10. Males are dominant; females are dependent.

11. Females are more compliant.
12. Females demonstrate more nurturing behavior.
13. Females are more emotional.
14. Males are more aggressive.
15. Females have greater verbal ability; males have greater mathematical ability.

According to the extensive research review reported by Maccoby and Jacklin, only two* of these stereotypes have been supported by empirical evidence; however, all have popular support in American society. Thus, the counselor's role in counseling women is often further complicated by not only the woman's perception of what is appropriate for her, but also society's suggestion that her opportunities are limited by her sex. Another complicating factor in counseling women is the multiple role expectations held for women. Counselors must be particularly alert not to reinforce these biases through sexist behavior or verbalization. With increasingly greater numbers of women seeking counseling, especially in periods of career planning and decision making, there is a need to be alert that sexist counseling does not limit their career opportunities.

Rawlings and Carter (1977) suggested the following guidelines for nonsexist counseling:

1. The therapist is aware of his or her own values.
2. There are no prescribed sex-role behaviors.
3. Sex-role reversals in life-style are not labeled pathological.
4. Marriage is not regarded as any better an outcome of therapy for a female than for a male.
5. Females are expected to be as autonomous and assertive as males; males are expected to be as expressive and tender as females.
6. Theories of behavior based on anatomical differences are rejected.
7. The therapist does not use the power of his or her position to subtly reinforce or punish clients for exhibiting "appropriate" or "inappropriate" feminine or masculine behaviors.
8. Diagnoses are not based on a client's failure to achieve culturally prescribed sex-role behaviors.
9. Sex-biased testing instruments are not used. (pp. 51–53)

The counselor has the responsibility to help women understand their own values, abilities, aptitudes, and interests and to utilize these to develop their fullest potential. In so doing, the counselor must, as always, function as a non-biased, non-stereotyping helper.

Ethnic Minorities

In the past two decades, special attention has been focused on the societal and legal rights of ethnic minority members of our society. Stimulated by the Civil Rights movement of the 1960s and the social activism of various groups during that period, society became increasingly aware of the plight and disadvantages

*Only numbers 14 and 15 are supported by research.

imposed upon minorities. In attempting to correct these inequities, especially within the educational system, counselors were often expected to assume significant roles. However, in many instances, counselors failed to perceive the differences in perceptions, values, and cultural heritages that characterized ethnic minority group members in the society. As a result, counselors often failed to relate effectively to and meet the needs of the minority client.

Ridley (1978) believed that

> Evidence of differential treatment offered to minority group clients is indicated by several major factors: (a) the types of treatment provided, (b) the duration of the treatment experience, and (c) the attitudes of the therapist and client toward the movement and outcome of the therapeutic endeavor. Historically, these inequities have been attributed to racism in the profession, and even though old treatment paradigms utilized in the past have given way to new therapeutic modalities, a comprehensive review of the literature suggests that the consequences in terms of racism remain essentially unchanged—the preferential treatment of majority group clients over minority group clients. (p. 43)

Recognizing the problem, the question must be raised, "What can counselors do to interact effectively in the counseling relationship with minority counselees?" (assuming the counselor is not a minority member). Belkin (1981) suggested that counselors' understanding of nine special situations that he found commonly expressed by minority group members in a New York City school system will enable them to understand better and interact more effectively with the minority group client. These nine needs are

1. The Minority Group Client (MGC) needs to feel that he is perceived as an individual, rather than only as a member of a group.
2. The MGC wants to be able to retain his own identity as well as to function within the context of the larger society.
3. The MGC may tend to perceive the white counselor as being white above all other perceptions. This implies that whatever general stereotypical feelings about white he has will be projected onto the counselor.
4. The MGC needs a sense of social mobility; he wants to be able to feel that he has an opportunity to rise above his present station in life. Often this hope has been tempered by the realization of the severe restraints that poverty imposes upon social advancement.
5. The MGC wants the emotional freedom to be able to express his own prejudices toward white people. He wants to be able to feel that the white counselor will not be overly threatened by this expression.
6. The MGC wants the school, through its curriculum, its teachers, and its rules to relate to his world rather than to the world of "whitey."
7. The MGC sees things happening around him over which he feels no control. He wants to be better able to control his world, and thus his own destiny, but he is lacking many of the educational and psychological tools necessary for doing so.
8. The MGC often has less opportunity than his white counterpart to discuss home and family life problems. His loyalty to his family may deter him from discussing these with an outsider.
9. The MGC may see the school as the primary social institution (which he considers oppressive and nonresponsive) and be inclined to act out his rage and anger within the school environment. (Belkin, 1981, pp. 455–456)

In a *Personnel and Guidance* editorial in 1978, Derald Wing Sue proposed a list of characteristics that distinguish culturally effective counselors. His descriptions, in brief, are

1. Culturally effective counselors understand their own values and assumptions of human behavior and recognize that those held by others may differ.
2. Culturally effective counselors realize that "no theory of counseling is politically or morally neutral."
3. Culturally effective counselors understand that external sociopolitical forces may have influenced and shaped culturally different groups.
4. Culturally effective counselors are able to share the world view of their clients rather than being culturally encapsulated.
5. Culturally effective counselors are truly eclectic in their counseling, using counseling skills because of their appropriateness to the experiences and lifestyles of the culturally different. (Arredondo-Dowd and Gonsalves, 1980, p. 657)

Obviously, understanding alone will not accomplish the task. The counselor must learn to communicate both verbally and nonverbally in a manner and style that is recognizable and comfortable for the client. The counselor must convey his or her own attitude of acceptance and respect for the ethnic minority client, and the counselor must genuinely feel this respect if he or she is to successfully convey it.

Arredondo-Dowd and Gonsalves (1980, p. 659) profiled the attitude of the culturally effective counselor:

Attitudes

1. All persons possess certain intellectual, emotional, linguistic, sociocultural, and physical capabilities and potentials that they bring to counseling and that should be developed and enhanced during the process.
2. Equal opportunities are available to all persons.
3. Cultural discontinuity may affect the self-identity of individuals (Elliston, 1977).
4. Non-English languages are valid, structured systems of communication, with legitimate functions in various social contexts.
5. An individual's culture is the basis for learning to function as a social being.

Competencies	*Skills*
1. Counseling	1. Teaching
2. Cultural	2. Helping
3. Linguistic	3. Bilingual
4. Pedagogical	4. Life

Older Adults

In the 1980s we are being increasingly made aware that our population is growing older and living longer and more actively and becoming another special population for counseling services. As Blake and Peterson (1979) wrote, "when facts about the life conditions of older people are added to the facts of numbers of people involved, the apparent needs for counseling and service opportunities for counselors seem obvious." (p. 22)

From available data, Blake and Peterson (1979) drew eleven conclusions regarding the counseling of the aged:

1. Since the older old people (those over 75 years of age) are the fastest increasing part of the 65+ population, the demands for physical health services will be very great. These are the most expensive services, and the bulk of available funds for older people is most likely to go in that direction, rather than for retirement adjustment or other such programs oriented more toward the younger old. Since the physical needs are more obvious, counseling-type needs may require more action from counseling organizations if they are to be recognized and counselors' potential contributions better known.

2. When facts about the geographical distribution of older people are considered, we can see that all communities will have some older residents. (Even if there is an apartment building or block that has no older residents, there are almost certain to be many sons and daughters of older people. Some of these sons and daughters have concerns for their parents and often are involved in very serious problems related to them.) Demographic data or living patterns also suggest that some areas have proportionately more older people than other areas and have different demographic trends. This suggests a need for identification of local data for planning in relation to local situations; over-reliance on national data or trends may be quite inappropriate.

3. Since the life expectancy of men is less than that of women, the potential clientele, generally speaking, will be women. The concerns of older women need special emphasis in the training of counselors and the design of service delivery. The greater number of older women may make it relatively easy to obtain funding for women-oriented programs. On the other hand, there is a considerable number of older men, and counseling as well as other service groups should guard against the neglect of these persons who might otherwise become a forgotten minority within a minority.

4. Services for "lonely" persons, or those living alone, are especially likely to have female clientele. There are more older women than men, and more of the older men are married than older women. This is because men tend to marry younger women, and more older men remarry than do older women. Proportionately, there are more older single women than men.

5. Most counseling for older people will be through public rather than private fee services. This is even more true of the older population than it is for the rest of the adult population and results from the substantially worsened financial condition of older people in general.

6. Existing counseling services such as the employment service or vocational rehabilitation can expect their client populations to be increasingly older. This suggests the possible need for additional aging-specific training of counselors in these programs. Such training may be needed for increased self-awareness of beliefs and values, possible special counseling techniques, referral sources, and possibly other factors particular to working with older people.

7. Counseling programs aimed at serving the general population of older persons can expect most potential clients to be physically able to travel to the serivce. But no program for older people can be truly inclusive unless it also has a capacity for having home delivery of service and a capacity for providing transportation assistance for those who require it. Five percent of the noninstitutionalized older

population is homebound and another 14 percent needs some human or mechanical aid in getting about.

8. The age to which older persons, on the average, can expect to live is greater than that for persons just born or that of the population in general. Data on life expectancy at birth are not appropriate for use with older persons. Counselors can better assist middle-aged or older clients in life planning by using the most relevant demographic data available. Counselors can help allay the mistaken beliefs about life expectancy that some older clients or their families may have.

9. Demographic data differ substantially between sexes and among racial groups. This implies that at least in some instances sex- and race-specific data are more helpful for clear understanding than general data. General demographic data are not always accurate in reflecting the condition of specific subgroups within the population, and counselors sometimes need group-specific data.

10. In all respects except age itself, older people are as different from each other as from any other group. In fact, the differences between people may be accentuated with age and the indicators of central tendency less meaningful. In wealth and health, for example, the differences among the old are the most extreme of any age group. Only among the old are found both newlyweds and couples who have been married for 60 years. Counselors are accustomed to viewing people as individuals, but there is no group for which this is more essential than for the extremely diverse older population.

11. Mental health problems of older adults are of such magnitude that the best hope for substantial improvement is to change the general psychosocial milieu in which we age. This suggests that counselors should be social activists working against factors such as ageism that mitigate against mental health. It also suggests a training role for professional counselors fostering an improved quality of relationships between older persons and those with whom they are in contact; children, friends, neighbors, and providers of all kinds of services. The level of self-help within the community of older persons can be raised by using appropriately prepared counselors as trainers for large numbers of peer counselors. (pp. 23–24)

For most older Americans, one of the significant transitions of that period of their life is the move from work to retirement. For many retirees, adjusting to life without work is difficult because they feel a loss of status; workers are more valued in our society than nonworkers; for many it means a loss of planned involvement with other people; and some have developed so few supplemental leisure time/recreational activities that life suddenly becomes boring or meaningless because they have excess time on their hands. But there is promise of a better transition for these older adults and this promise appears to rely heavily on counseling. A corporate viewpoint may be expressed in an article by Black (1981) in the publication of American Airlines, *American Way*, which pointed out:

> The era of sending out a retiring employee with a handshake, a gold watch, and a subscription to a senior-citizens magazine may be gone forever. Employees are asking for more, and many companies are responding. During the past two years preretirement counseling as an employee benefit has appeared at companies across the country. Benefits departments are either administering preretirement counseling programs, planning to do so, or feeling guilty about not getting around to it. (p. 33)

Schlossberg (1984), in discussing adults (including retirees) in transition, depicted the process in Figure 5–5.

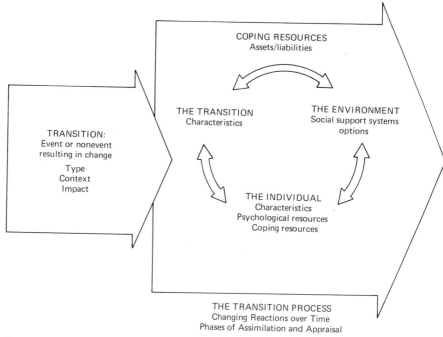

Figure 5–5. The individual in transition. *(Schlossberg, 1984, p. 68.)*

She then described a detailed look at the process as outlined in Table 5–6.

In their discussion of counseling with the elderly living in public housing, Leung and Eargle (1980) concluded that

> Counselors who work with the elderly must (a) be aware of specific circumstances in the living environment of the elderly, (b) be aware of the particular psychological factors of anxiety, loss, and interpersonal struggles of the elderly client, (c) be aware of the need to carefully build a trusting relationship, and (d) be able to adapt general counseling techniques to specific concerns important to the elderly. With an increasing population of elderly persons, there will be an increasing need for counselors who are able to work with the elderly. Counselors need to become sensitive to the needs of the elderly and prepare themselves to serve this important segment of today's society. (p. 445)

Counselors will thus have the opportunities to meet, primarily through community services, the needs of another distinct and worthy segment of our population. Counselors working with older clients must again exhibit acceptance, openness, and respect of clients and their values. Even the oldest client must be permitted to look ahead and plan for a different future if this is the client's desire.

Business and Industry

The decades of the 1970s and 1980s have witnessed a steady broadening of the opportunities for counselors to function in a variety of settings. This is due in

Table 5–6. The Individual in Transition: A Detailed Look

The Transition (event or nonevent resulting in change)		Coping Resources (balance of assets and liabilities)		The Transition Process (reactions over time for better or for worse)
Type Anticipated Unanticipated Nonevent Chronic hassle **Context** Relationship of person to transition Setting in which transition occurs **Impact** Relationships Routines Assumptions Roles	**Variables Characterizing the Transition** *Event or nonevent characteristics* Trigger Timing Source Role change Duration Previous experience with a similar transition Concurrent stress *Assessment*	**Variables Characterizing the Individual** Personal and demographic characteristics Socioeconomic status Sex role Age and stage of life State of health Psychological resources Ego development Personality Outlook Commitments and values Coping responses Functions: Controlling situation, meaning, or stress Strategies: Information seeking, direct action, inhibition of action, intrapsychic behavior	**Variables Characterizing the Environment** Social support Types: intimate, family unit, friendship network, institution Functions: affect, affirmation, aid, feedback Measurement: convoy Options Actual Perceived Utilized Created	**Phases of Assimilation** Pervasiveness Disruptions Integration, for better or for worse **Appraisal** Of transition, resources, results Of preoccupation *vs.* life satisfaction

Source: Schlossberg, 1984, p. 108.

154

part to organizations, agencies, and special populations recognizing that they share needs and concerns in common with other populations and settings where these needs and concerns are recognized and dealt with. Increasingly, business and industrial organizations, and their work forces, have been recognizing that they may benefit, from both a corporate and individual viewpoint, from programs of counseling assistance. Cristiani and Cristiani stated (1979) that "many companies are providing direct counseling services, at least at the corporate level, to help employees with a variety of problems" (p. 167). Toomer (1983) reported a survey of the primary work settings of 1,000 counseling psychologists in which 2.94 percent were employed in manufacturing (business settings). An additional 7.84 percent were employed in consulting (individual or firms). Forrest (1983) also noted that Employee Assistance Programs (EAPS) in business and industry are increasing, transforming, and offering new and expanded work opportunities for counselors. He noted that the essential components for an effective EAP program as described in the literature by Busch (1981), Dickman and Emener (1982), and Good (1982) include

1. Early intervention and crisis assistance
2. Self-referral, peer referral, supervisory referral
3. Confidentiality and easy access
4. Management/leadership/union support
5. Supervisor and union representative training
6. Written policies distributed to all participants
7. Insurance involvement
8. Treatment separated from work evaluation
9. Staffing by trained helping professionals
10. Breadth of service components
11. Follow-up and evaluation

The immediate implications for counselors in all work settings relate to employment opportunity, treatment availability, and issues of territoriality. (Forrest, 1983, p. 106)

Certainly counselors can provide worthwhile programs to facilitate the career development and placement or replacement of workers and management personnel. Personnel training, especially in human relationship and communications skills, is another area of promise. Retirement counseling, to be discussed in the next section, is also an area of potential counseling service.

Toomer (1982) suggested possible roles and functions in business and industry as outlined in Figure 5–6.

Cristiani and Cristiani (1979) felt that it is

apparent that counselors could become a vital part of many business and industrial organizations. The problem seems to be one of lack of information and resources. Should this be the case, here are a few additional suggestions to those with counseling backgrounds for approaching jobs in the industrial or business setting.

1. Become familiar with the American Society for Training and Development (ASTD); read the ASTD Journal and attend meetings of local chapters. This is an excellent way to meet those people who have interests similar to yours and who are working in the field. They may be able to give you specific suggestions about

approaching the job market in your location, possibly providing leads and contacts in your area.

2. Conduct library research in the area of training and development; become familiar with readings by major business authors.

3. Take business courses in industrial psychology and management. Strengthen your background in the behavioral sciences if needed.

4. Do not be intimidated by employers who try to discourage you because of your lack of experience in the business world. You have the essential skills and expertise that are part of training and development in the business community. The first person to convince is yourself! (p. 169)

Summary

Counseling is the heart of the counselor's activity. Although there is general agreement in broadly defining counseling, a variety of theoretical concepts have emerged over the years. Traditional approaches such as psychoanalytic and

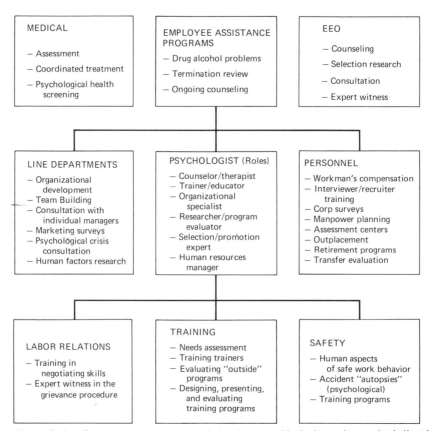

COUNSELING PSYCHOLOGIST IN BUSINESS AND INDUSTRY
ROLES AND RELATIONSHIPS

MEDICAL
— Assessment
— Coordinated treatment
— Psychological health screening

EMPLOYEE ASSISTANCE PROGRAMS
— Drug alcohol problems
— Termination review
— Ongoing counseling

EEO
— Counseling
— Selection research
— Consultation
— Expert witness

LINE DEPARTMENTS
— Organizational development
— Team Building
— Consultation with individual managers
— Marketing surveys
— Psychological crisis consultation
— Human factors research

PSYCHOLOGIST (Roles)
— Counselor/therapist
— Trainer/educator
— Organizational specialist
— Researcher/program evaluator
— Selection/promotion expert
— Human resources manager

PERSONNEL
— Workman's compensation
— Interviewer/recruiter training
— Corp surveys
— Manpower planning
— Assessment centers
— Outplacement
— Retirement programs
— Transfer evaluation

LABOR RELATIONS
— Training in negotiating skills
— Expert witness in the grievance procedure

TRAINING
— Needs assessment
— Training trainers
— Evaluating "outside" programs
— Designing, presenting, and evaluating training programs

SAFETY
— Human aspects of safe work behavior
— Accident "autopsies" (psychological)
— Training programs

Figure 5–6.   Counseling psychologist in business and industry: roles and relationships. *(Toomer, 1982, p. 13.)*

client-centered theories are still popular, but in recent generations, the behavioral, the rational-emotive therapy theory, the reality therapy theory, and the integrative theory have attracted their followings. However, as noted in concluding our discussion of theory, counselors may still opt for the eclectic approach, one that gives the option of selecting from any and all the existing theories.

The counseling process initially focuses upon relationship establishment, then seeks to identify and explore the client's problem with the objective of establishing client goals. The process then proceeds to the planning and problem-solving stage and, finally, to the applying of the solution and termination of the counseling relationship. Although these stages tend to blend one into the other, they serve as a guide to a logical sequence of events for the counseling process. The effective application of the process is dependent upon the basic counseling skills required of the counselor.

In recent generations, increasing attention has been given to the counselor's responsibility and need for special preparation in dealing with special populations and special problems.

As Kennedy (1977) suggested

for most who can learn to listen to others and can employ psychological counseling techniques successfully, the task of being a professional counselor is not an achievement but a never-ending process. (p. 336)

Recent generations have also noted increased usage of group counseling and other group techniques by counselors. These will be discussed in the next chapter.

References

Arlow, J. A. (1979). Psychoanalysis. In R. J. Corsini (Ed.), *Current psychotherapies* (2nd ed.), (pp. 1–43). Itasca, IL: F. E. Peacock.

Arredondo-Dowd, P. M., & Gonsalves, J. (1980). Preparing culturally effective counselors. *Personnel and Guidance Journal, 58,* 657–661.

Belkin, G. S. (1975). *Practical counseling in the schools.* Dubuque, IA: William C. Brown.

Belkin, G. S. (1981). *Practical counseling in the schools* (2nd ed.). Dubuque. IA: William C. Brown.

Black, E. (1981). Preparing for life after work. *American Way, 14*(1), 32–37.

Blackham, G. J. (1977). *Counseling: Theory, process and practice.* Belmont, CA: Wadsworth.

Blackham, G. J., & Silberman, A. (1980). *Modification of child and adolescent behavior* (3rd ed.). Belmont, CA: Wadsworth.

Blake, R., & Peterson, D. (1979). Module I: Demographic aspects of aging: Implications for counseling. In M. L. Ganikos (Ed.), *Counseling the aged: A training syllabus for educators* (pp. 1–27). Washington, D. C.: American Personnel and Guidance Association.

Boy, A. V., & Pine, G. J. (1982). *Client-centered counseling: A renewal.* Boston: Allyn & Bacon.

Brammer, L. M. (1985). *The helping relationship: Process and skills* (3rd ed.). Englewood Cliffs, NJ: Prentice-Hall.

Brammer, L. M., & Shostrom, E. L. (1982). *Therapeutic psychology: Fundamentals of counseling and psychotherapy* (4th ed.). Englewood Cliffs, NJ: Prentice-Hall.

Bruce, P. (1984). Continuum of counseling goals: A framework for differentiating counseling strategies. *Personnel and Guidance Journal, 62,* 259–263.

Busch, E. J., Jr. (1981). Developing an employee assistance program. *Personnel Journal, 60,* 708–711.

Castaneda, C. (1974). *Tales of power.* New York: Simon & Schuster.

Cavanagh, M. E. (1982). *The counseling experience: A theoretical and practical approach.* Belmont, CA: Brooks/Cole.

Chomsky, N. (1971). *Problems of knowledge and freedom.* New York: Vintage.

Corey, G. (1977). *Theory and practice of counseling and psychotherapy.* Monterey, CA: Brooks/Cole.

Corey, G. (1982). *Theory and practice of counseling and psychotherapy* (2nd ed.). Monterey, CA: Brooks/Cole.

Cottle, W. C., & Downie, E. M. (1970). *Preparation for counseling* (2nd ed.). Englewood Cliffs, NJ: Prentice-Hall.

Cristiani, T. S., & Cristiani, M. F. (1979). The application of counseling skills in the business and industrial setting. *Personnel and Guidance Journal, 58,* 166–169.

Dickman, F., & Emener, W. G. (1982). Employee assistance programs: Basic concepts, attributes and an evaluation. *Personnel administration, 27*(8), 55–62.

Dusay, J. M., & Steiner, C. (1971). Transactional analysis in groups. In H. I. Kaplan and B. J. Sadock (Eds.), *Comprehensive Group Psychotherapy.* Baltimore: Williams & Wilkins.

Dyer, W. W., & Vriend, J. (1977). A goal-setting checklist for counselors. *Personnel and Guidance Journal, 55,* 469–471.

Egan, G. (1982). *The skilled helper: Model, skills, and methods for effective helping* (2nd ed.). Monterey, CA: Brooks/Cole.

Eisenberg, S., & Delaney, D. J. (1977). *The counseling process* (2nd ed.). Chicago: Rand McNally.

Feller, J. L. (1978). *Impact of sex-role stereotypes and biases on the vocational development and counseling of women.* Unpublished manuscript. Indiana University, Bloomington.

Fine, R. (1973). Psychoanalysis. In R. J. Corsini (Ed.), *Current psychotherapies,* (pp. 1–33). Itasca, IL: F. E. Peacock.

Forrest, D. V. (1983). Employee assistance programs in the 1980's: Expanding career options for counselors. *Personnel and Guidance Journal, 62,* 105–107.

Frey, D. H., & Raming, H. E. (1979). A taxonomy of consulting goals and methods. *Personnel and Guidance Journal, 58,* 26–33.

Gazda, G. M., Asbury, F. R., Balzer, F. J., Childers, W. C., & Walters, R. P. (1977). *Human relations development: A manual for educators.* Boston: Allyn & Bacon.

George, R. L., & Cristiani, T. S. (1986). *Counseling: Theory and practice.* Englewood Cliffs, NJ: Prentice-Hall.

Glasser, W. (1984). Reality therapy. In R. J. Corsini (Ed.), *Current psychotherapies* (3rd ed.), (pp. 320–353). Itasca, IL: F. E. Peacock.

Good, L. (1982). *The employee assistance program from school district 1.* Wheatland, WY: Southeast Wyoming Mental Health Center.

Hackney, H., & Cormier, L. S. (1979). *Counseling strategies and objectives* (2nd ed.). Englewood Cliffs, NJ: Prentice-Hall.

Hansen, J. C., Stevic, R. R., & Warner, W. R., Jr. (1982), *Counseling: Theory and process* (3rd ed.). Boston: Allyn & Bacon.

Horan, J. J. (1979). *Counseling for effective decision making.* North Scituate, MA: Duxbury.

Ivey, A. E., with Simek-Downing, L. (1980). *Counseling and psychotherapy: Skills, theories, and practice.* Englewood Cliffs, NJ: Prentice-Hall.

Kelly, G. (1955). *The psychology of personal constructs.* New York: W. W. Norton.

Kennedy, E. (1977). *On becoming a counsellor: A basic guide for non-professional counsellors.* Dublin: Gill and Macmillan.

Kinney, J., & Leaton, G. (1978). *Loosening the grip: A handbook of alcohol information.* St. Louis: C. V. Mosby.

Krumboltz, J. D. (1976). Behavior goals for counseling. In G. S. Belkin (Ed.), *Counseling directions in theory and practice* (pp. 171–178). Dubuque, IA: Kendall/Hunt.

Krumboltz, J. D., & Thoreson, C. B. (1966). *Revolution in Counseling: Implications of behavioral science.* Boston: Houghton Mifflin.

L'Abate, L. (1981) Classification of counseling and therapy theorists, methods, processes and goals: The E-R-A model. *Personnel and Guidance Journal, 59*(5), 263–265.

Leung, P., & Eargle, D. (1980). Counseling with the elderly living in public housing. *Personnel and Guidance Journal, 58,* 442–445.

Maccoby, E. E., & Jacklin, C. N. (1974). *The psychology of sex differences, Vol. 1.* Stanford, CA: Stanford University Press.

Manaster, G. S., & Corsini, R. J., (1982). *Individual Psychology: Theory and practice.* Itasca, IL: F. E. Peacock.

Mellecker, J. (1976). Transactional analysis for non-TA counselors. In G. S. Belkin (Ed.), *Counseling: Directions in theory and practice.* Dubuque, IA: Kendall/Hunt.

Mosak, H. H. (1979). Adlerian psychotherapy. In R. J. Corsini (Ed.), *Current psychotherapies* (2nd ed.), (pp. 44–94). Itasca, IL: F. E. Peacock.

Ohlsen, M. M. (1983). *Introduction to counseling.* Itasca, IL: F. E. Peacock.

Okun, B. F. (1976). *Effective helping: Interviewing and counseling techniques.* North Scituate, MA: Duxbury.

Page, R. C., Smith M., & Beamish, P. (1977). Establishing a drug rehabilitation center. *Personnel and Guidance Journal, 56,* 180–183.

Passons, W. R. (1975). *Gestalt approaches in counseling.* New York: Holt, Rinehart & Winston.

Patterson, C. H. (1980). *Theories of counseling & psychotherapy* (3rd ed.). New York: Harper & Row.

Perls, F. (1948). Theory and technique of personality integration. *American Journal of Psychotherapy, 2,* 565–586.

Pietrofesa, J. J., Hoffman, A., Splete, H. H., & Pinto, D. V. (1984). *Counseling: An introduction* (2nd ed.). Boston: Houghton Mifflin.

Rawlings, E. I., & Carter, D. K. (Eds.). (1977). *Psychotherapy for women: Treatment toward equality.* Springfield, IL: Charles C. Thomas.

Ridley, C. R. (1978). Cross-cultural counseling: A multivariate analysis. *Viewpoints in Teaching and Learning,* (Journal of the School of Education, Indiana University), *54*(1), 43–50.

Rogers, C. R. (1959a). A theory of therapy, personality and interpersonal relationships as developed in the client-centered framework. In S. Koch (Ed.), *Psychology: A study of science, Vol. 3* (pp. 184–256). New York: McGraw-Hill.

Rogers, C. R. (1959b). Significant learning: In theory and in education. *Educational Leadership, 16,* 232–242.

Rogers, C. R. (1965). *Client-centered therapy.* Boston: Houghton Mifflin.

Rogers, C. R. (1967). The conditions of change from a client-centered viewpoint. In B. G. Berenson and R. R. Carkhuff (Eds.), *Sources of gain in counseling and psychotherapy.* New York: Holt, Rinehart & Winston.

Schlossberg, N. K. (1984). *Counseling adults in transition.* New York: Springer.

Shane J. G., Shane, H. G., Gibson, R. L., & Munger, P. F. (1971). *Guiding human development: The counselor and the teacher in the elementary school.* Worthington, OH: Charles A. Jones.

Shertzer, B., & Stone, S. C. (1980). *Fundamentals of counseling* (3rd ed.). Boston: Houghton Mifflin.

Stefflre, B., & Grant, W. H. (1972). *Theories of counseling* (2nd ed.). New York: McGraw-
Hill.

Tolbert, E. L. (1972). *Introduction to counseling* (2nd ed.). New York: McGraw-Hill.

Toomer, J. E. (1983). Counseling psychologists in business and industry. *The Counseling
Psychologist, 10*(3), 9–18.

Ulrici, D., L'Abate, L., & Wagner, V. (1981). The E-R-A model: A heuristic framework
for classification of social skills training programs for couples and families. *Family
Relations, 30*(2), 307–315.

Watson, J. B. (1913). Psychology as the behaviorist views it. *Psychological Review, 20,*
159–170.

CHAPTER 6

GROUP TECHNIQUES FOR COUNSELORS

Introduction

The rugged individualist has been extolled over the years in American history. The sagas and accomplishments of Daniel Boone, Davey Crocket, "Wild Bill" Hickok, Wyatt Earp, Buffalo Bill, Susan B. Anthony, Charles Lindbergh, and others have been told and retold. Additionally, in recent years, nearly all have been further immortalized by TV series recalling their feats. We still pay certain homage today to the "lone wolf" who can make it alone, ignore the system, or shun the spotlight. Perhaps one of the reasons we so admire this rugged individualist is that we recognize it is almost impossible to go it alone in today's group-oriented, group-dominated, and group-processed society.

The objectives of this chapter are therefore to (a) identify the various types of group settings used by counselors to assist their clients, and (b) introduce the process and values of group counseling, group guidance, and values clarification techniques.

Suggestions of the influence and dependence on groups may result from an examination of the individual's functioning in today's society. Such an examination leads to the following conclusions:

1. Humans are group-oriented. People are meant to complement, assist, and enjoy each other. Groups are natural for these processes to occur.
2. Humans seek to meet most of their basic and personal-social needs through groups, including the need to know and grow mentally; thus, groups are a most natural and expeditious way to learn.
3. Consequently, groups are most influential in how a person grows, learns, and develops behavioral patterns, coping styles, values, career potentials, and adjustment techniques.

For counselors, teachers, and others who work with groups in leadership, facilitative, and teaching capacities, it can further be assumed that

1. An understanding of the influences and dynamics of groups can help further assessments and understandings of the individuals.

2. An understanding of the organization and utilization of groups can help in the teaching and guidance of others.
3. Group counseling may be more effective for some people and some situations than individual counseling.

Definitions and Explanations

In any study of groups, particularly of an introductory nature, it is important at the onset to clarify and define the various labels that have come into popular usage in the areas of group couseling and guidance. Any attempt to clarify and define various terms common to the study of groups in counseling requires a definition or explanation of what is meant by the term *group*. Webster's *Third New World International Dictionary* (Unabridged) defines a group as "a number of individuals bound together by a community of interest, purpose, or function."

However, within and across the professional disciplines engaged in the study and practice of groups, there are wide variations in defining a group. To narrow the definition of group for discussion here, it should be noted that counseling groups are characterized by interaction. They are functional or goal-oriented groups. Aggregate groups without interaction of the members are not functioning groups.

Counselors may view various group activities as occurring at three levels. These are the guidance level, the counseling level, and the therapy level. In brief, the levels may be defined as follows:

Group Guidance.   Group guidance is group activities that focus on providing information or experiences through a planned and organized group activity. Examples of group guidance activities are orientation groups, career exploration groups, and college visitation days. Gazda (1984) notes that group guidance is organized to prevent the development of problems. The content could include educational, vocational, personal, or social information, with a goal of providing students with accurate information that will help them make more appropriate plans and life decisions.

Group Counseling.   Group counseling is the routine adjustment or developmental experiences provided in a group setting. Group counseling focuses on assisting counselees to cope with their day-to-day adjustment and developmental concerns. Examples might focus on behavior modification, developing personal relationship skills, concerns of human sexuality, values or attitudes, or career decision-making.

Gazda (1984) suggests that group counseling can be growth engendering insofar as it provides participation incentives and motivation to make changes that are in the clients' best interests. On the other hand, it is remedial for those persons who have entered into a spiral of self-defeating behavior but who are, nevertheless, capable of reversing the spiral with counseling intervention.

Group Therapy. Therapy groups provide intense experiences for people with serious adjustment, emotional, or developmental needs. Therapy groups are usually distinguished from counseling groups by both the length of time and the depth of the experience for those involved. These levels are presented in chart form in Figure 6–1.

Ohlsen (1977) noted that whereas counselors devote most of their time to helping clients learn to recognize and cope early with self-defeating behaviors and to master developmental tasks, psychotherapists devote most of their time to remediation for emotionally disturbed persons.

Gazda's continuum, describing relationships among the group processes, is a clarifying one and is presented in Figure 6–2.

T-Groups. T-groups are derivatives of training groups. They represent the application of laboratory training methods to group work.

> Golembiewski and Blumberg (1970) indicate that the T-group may be considered a laboratory in the following ways: (1) It attempts to create a miniature society; (2) it is geared toward working with processes that emphasize inquiry, exploration, and experimentation with behavior; (3) it is oriented toward assisting its members to learn; (4) it stresses developing a psychologically safe atmosphere to facilitate learning; and (5) group members determine what is to be learned, even though a trainer is usually available for guidance. (Hansen, Warner, and Smith, 1980, p. 95)

T-groups are relatively unstructured groups in which the participants become responsible for what they learn and how they learn it. This learning experience also usually includes learning about how people function in groups and about one's own behavior in groups. A basic assumption appropriate to T-groups is that one learns more effectively when he or she establishes authentic relationships with others.

Sensitivity Groups. In actual practice, the label sensitivity group appears to be applied so frequently and broadly as to be almost meaningless. In a more technical sense, however, a sensitivity group is a form of T-group that focuses on personal and interpersonal issues, upon the personal growth of the individual. There is an emphasis in sensitivity groups on self-insight, which means that the central focus is not the group and its progress, but, rather, the individual member.

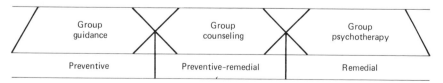

Figure 6–1. Relationship among group guidance, group counseling, and group therapy. (Gazda, 1971, p. 9.)

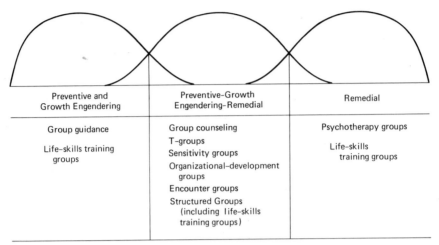

Preventive and Growth Engendering	Preventive-Growth Engendering-Remedial	Remedial
Group guidance Life-skills training groups	Group counseling T-groups Sensitivity groups Organizational-development groups Encounter groups Structured Groups (including life-skills training groups)	Psychotherapy groups Life-skills training groups

Figure 6–2. Relationships among group processes. *(Gazda, 1984, p. 6.)*

Encounter Groups. Encounter groups are also in the T-group family, although they are more therapy-oriented. These intensive, small group experiences, according to Eddy and Lubin (1971), emphasize

> personal growth through expanding awareness, exploration of intrapsychic as well as interpersonal issues, and release of dysfunctional inhibitions. There is relatively little focus on the group as a learning instrument; the trainer takes a more active and directive role; and physical interaction is utilized. Other modes of expression and sensory exploration such as dance, art, massage, and nudity have been tried on occasion as part of the encounter experience. (p. 627–628)

Rogers (1967) defined an encounter group as one that stresses personal growth through the development and improvement of interpersonal relationships via an experiential group process. Such groups seek to release the potential of the participant:

> In an intensive group, with much freedom and little structure, the individual will gradually feel safe enough to drop some of his defenses and facades; he will relate more directly on a feeling basis (come into a basic encounter) with other members of the group; he will come to understand himself and his relationship to others more accurately; he will change in his personal attitudes and behavior; and he will subsequently relate more effectively to others in his everyday life situation. (Rogers, 1967, p. 262)

Extended encounter groups are often referred to as marathon groups. The marathon encounter group uses an extended block of time in which massed experience and accompanying fatigue are used to break through the participants' defenses.

Mini-groups. Although technically two or more people can constitute a group, the use of the term *mini-group* has become increasingly popular in recent years to denote a counseling group that is smaller than usual. A mini-group usually consists of one counselor and a maximum of four clients. Because of the smaller number of participants, the potential exists for certain advantages resulting from the more frequent and direct interaction of its members. Mercurio and Weiner (1975) indicated that

> because of the increased dynamics that seem to occur in a group of this limited size, members of the mini-group are less able to withdraw or hide, and interaction seems to be more complete and responses fuller. . . . Mini-groups may either function as the singular treatment focus or be used in conjunction with individual counseling. (p. 227)

Group Process and Group Dynamics.   Two terms commonly used in describing group activities are *process* and *dynamics.* Although often used interchangeably, they do have different meanings when used to describe group counseling activities. The beginning counseling student should note that *group process* is the continuous, ongoing movement of the group toward achievement of its goals. It represents the flow of the group from its starting point to its termination. It is a means of identifying or describing the stages through which the group passes.

Group dynamics, on the other hand, refers to the social forces and interplay operative within the group at any given time. It is descriptive of the interaction of a group, which may include a focus on the impact of leadership, group roles, and membership participation in groups. It is a means of analyzing the interaction between and among the individuals within a group. Group dynamics is also used on occasion to refer to certain group techniques such as role playing, decision making, "rap" sessions, and observation.

Organizational Development Groups.   Organizational development groups have become very popular in business and industry.

> Golembiewski (1972) has characterized Organizational Development (OD) as follows: OD basically reflects a variety of group-oriented strategies for conscious and deliberate change in social systems. In essence, changes in group level phenomena such as social norms and values are seen as the primary motivators of organizational change, via their influence on the behaviors of individuals. (p. 13)
>
> In other words, OD specialists diagnose communication and interaction problems within and between work units in educational, governmental, and industrial settings. (Gazda, 1984, p. 10)

Group Counseling

More than 80 years ago, the psychologist William James (1890) wrote:

> We are not only gregarious animals liking to be in sight of our fellows, but we have an innate propensity to get ourselves noticed and noticed favorably, by our kind. No more fiendish punishment could be devised, were such a thing physically possible,

than that one should be turned loose in society and remain absolutely unnoticed by all the members thereof. (p. 293)

James, as well as others, have noted over the years the importance of human relationships in meeting basic needs and influencing the personality development and adjustment of persons. For most people, the vast majority of these relationships are established and maintained in a group setting, and for many, daily routine adjustment problems and developmental needs also have their origins in groups.

Counseling, as a facilitative science, has a helping relationship base, which must also be a human relationship. Because the most frequent and common human relationship experiences occur in groups, groups also hold the potential to provide positive developmental and adjustment experiences for many people. The following paragraphs examine some of the potential values of group counseling and how these values are realized. The careful selection of participants and formations of groups and the skillful utilization by the counselor of appropriate group techniques are also discussed.

Values of Group Counseling

Group counseling is not a team sport. The goal is not to have a winning group. The goal of group counseling is the achievement of the goals, the meeting of needs, and the providing of an experience of value to the individual members who constitute the group. The following are some of the opportunities that may be provided by group counseling:

1. Exploration, with the reinforcement of a support group, of one's developmental and adjustment needs, concerns, and problems, may be provided. Groups can provide a realistic social setting where the client can interact with peers who not only are likely to have some understanding of the problem or concern that the client brings to the group, but will, in many instances, also be sharing the same or a similar concern. The counseling group can provide the sense of security needed by the group members to spontaneously and freely interact and to take risks, thus promoting the likelihood that the needs of each of the members will be touched upon and that the resources of peers will be utilized. The old saying that "misery loves company" may in fact provide a rationale for group counseling. One is more comfortable in sharing a problem with others who have similar experiences and may also be more motivated to change under these conditions.
2. Group counseling may provide the client with an opportunity to gain insights into his or her own feelings and behavior. Yalom (1975), in discussing the group as a social microcosm, stated that "a freely interactive group, with few structural restrictions, will, in time, develop into a social microcosm of the participant members" (p. 29). He then went on to point out that, given enough time in the group setting, clients will begin to be themselves, to interact with others, and to create the same interpersonal universe they have experienced, including the display of maladaptive, interpersonal behavior to

the group. Yalom also pointed out that corrective emotional experiences in groups may have several components, including:

> Reality testing which allows the client to examine the incident with the aid of consensual validation from other members.
>   A recognition of the inappropriateness of certain interpersonal feelings and behavior or of the inappropriateness of certain avoided interpersonal behaviors.
>   The ultimate facilitation of the individual's ability to interact with others more deeply and honestly. (p. 28)

As the client gains new insights into behaviors and feelings as a result of interactions with members of the counseling group, influences on self-concept formation may also occur. Because of the significant influence of self-concept in one's personal-social adjustment, perception of school and career decision making, the opportunity to bring about positive change in self-concept through new insights provided by the group counseling experience is a value not to be overlooked.

3. Group counseling provides clients with an opportunity to develop positive, natural relationships with others. The personal interactions that take place within the group counseling structure provide an excellent and continuous opportunity for the group member to experiment with and learn to manage interpersonal relations. This includes developing sensitivities to others, their needs, and feelings. It also provides opportunities to learn of the impact one's behavior has on others. Thus, through the group process and its interactions and sharing of experiences, the client may learn to modify earlier behavior patterns and seek new, more appropriate behaviors in situations that require interpersonal skills.

4. Group counseling provides opportunities for the client to learn responsibility to self and others. Becoming a member of a counseling group implies the assumption of responsibilities. Even when there are initial tendencies to avoid the assumption of responsibility for one's behavior, for contributions to the group's interactions, or one's "assignment" within the group, these avoidance techniques will usually fade away as group relationships develop and group goals are established.

Selection of Group Members

All of us have had experience in organizing groups. When we select group members for a social occasion we pick out good old Charlie because he is a laugh a minute; Diane, because she gets along with everybody; Harry in case we need some serious conversation, and Olga, because she is a good listener. On the other hand, if the purpose of the group is a more serious one, such as planning a neighborhood park, we might choose Rosalie because of her "know-how" with flowers and shrubbery; Jim because he is a landscaping expert; Jane because of her architectural skills, and Jerry because of her proven fund-raising abilities. In each instance, people are usually selected because they can contribute something to the group and its interaction. Although group counseling focuses upon the need of the individual, the importance of group membership to the achievement and adjustments of individuals in the group cannot be overestimated. Group member selection is one key to a successful counseling group. The following are possible criteria for the selection of group members: (a) common interest; (b) volunteer or self-referred; (c) willingness to participate in the group process; and (d) ability to participate in the group process.

A popular criterion for group selection may be a common interest of the potential members in a similar problem, concern, or issue. According to Dinkmeyer and Caldwell (1970):

> The homogeneous group, centered around a common problem or feeling, may possess a sense of unity in their mutual concerns, but also, they may lack the opportunity to react to normal youngsters who do not suffer from their handicap. As will be shown later, those in a predicament need to be able to gain insight from others who are competent in the area where they are lacking. In the beginning process of selection, however, some thought should be given to those most in need of resolving a particular kind of problem, then the rest of the group can be built around that focus. However, there should be enough of a heterogeneous make-up to provide a varied feedback to the members. Homogeneous groups can only be so on a particular variable. To select groups upon the basis of a common problem is a crisis-oriented approach rather than a developmental one, and not usually workable. It is the *interaction,* not the problem, that is important. Further, a group above all needs to be *balanced* so that no one factor or type of individual is too dominant to allow free interaction. (pp. 148–149)

A number of authors—Wagner (1976); Bates, Johnson, and Blaker (1982); and Ohlsen (1977)—believe that the best group member is a self-referred group member. Group counseling should be an option chosen by the group participants. Choice guarantees the protection of the client's rights. It also further enhances the motivation for counseling should the client decide to be in a counseling group. On the other hand, Ohlsen (1977) suggested:

> Many clients who at first appear to be poor bets (and have not volunteered) can become good treatment risks when the treatment is described for them; their questions about it are answered; they are encouraged to explore alternative sources for help; they are permitted to decide for themselves whether to participate; and they accept the responsibility for convincing themselves and their counselor that they can discuss their problems openly, define precise behavioral goals, and encourage fellow clients to learn desired new behaviors. Perhaps even the reluctant client, including the resisting type, can be helped when he or she is included in a group in which most clients are strong enough to prevent her from interfering with the development of (or from destroying) therapeutic group norms. If, however, one is to profit from counseling, she must not be forced to participate. (pp. 20–21)

In the selection of potential group participants the following questions might be proposed as a basis for determining selections:

1. Do you have a concern or difficulty you want to discuss in the group?
2. Are you willing to talk about it?
3. Are you willing to listen and to help others? (Dinkmeyer and Caldwell, 1970, p. 149)

In some instances, potential group members may lack the ability or desire to communicate with others or to relate to and assist others. From a temperament viewpoint, not everyone will be a suitable group member. In short, a person must possess certain abilities or aptitudes if he or she is to profit from the group experience and contribute to it as well.

Hardy and Cull (1974), noting that there are any number of procedures used by counselors to form a group, suggested that inviting clients to participate once the counselor has become familiar with the individual and his or her concerns, is a procedure that is by far the most realistic and professionally sound. They then went on to recommend that the invitation to join the group will

> be extended, or not, only after a personal interview with the prospective group member, with the emphasis in the interview being on what the student may gain through this kind of experience. The counselor explains the student's role, that of giving help to members in the group as well as receiving help from the group members and the counselor, should he decide to participate. Confidentiality with respect to the content of the group sessions should be stressed, and the prospective group member will need to commit himself to maintaining strict confidentiality for the duration of the group sessions, as well as after the group has terminated. (p. 9)

Hardy and Cull (1974) added that by using this interview invitation approach,

> the counselor has (1) made an assessment of the probable needs of the students who comprise the group; (2) assessed the probable contributions the student will make to the group; (3) set the parameters with respect to the personality composition of the group; (4) ascertained the probable extent to which each student would benefit from the group experience; and (5) established in his mind the probable goals for the group. (p. 10)

During the process of the screening interviews for possible group membership, the counselor may want to specify the "ground rules" group members are expected to follow. Gazda (1984) presented the following as an example:

1. Set a goal or goals for yourself before you enter the group, or at the very latest, as early as you can isolate and define your direction of change. Revise these goals as clarification and/or experience dictates.
2. Discuss as honestly and concretely as you can the nature of your trouble, including the successful and unsuccessful coping behaviors you have employed.
3. When you are not discussing your own difficulties, listen *intently* to the other group members and try to help them say what they are trying to say and to communicate your understanding, caring, and empathy for them.
4. Maintain the confidentiality of all that is discussed in the group. (There are no exceptions to this rule other than those things that pertain to you only.)
5. Be on time and attend regularly until termination of the group (if a closed group) and until you have met your goals (if the group is open ended).
6. Give the counselor the privilege of removing you from the group if the counselor deems it necessary for your health and for the overall benefit of the group.
7. Concur that all decisions affecting the group as a whole will be made by consensus only.

8. Inform the group counselor in private, before the group is constituted, of individuals who would for various reasons constitute a serious impediment to your group participation. (I feel that the "cards should be stacked in the counselee's favor" as much as possible; therefore those individuals who could inhibit the counselee should be excluded from the group if at all possible.)
9. You may request individual counseling interviews, but what is discussed in these interviews should be shared with the group at the appropriate time and at the discretion of the counselor and yourself.
10. When fees are involved, concurrence on amounts and payments schedules is made with the counselor before counseling begins. (pp. 27–28)

Another consideration in the formation of the counseling group is "what should the size of the group be to get the best results?" Yalom (1975) noted that his own experience and a consensus of the clinical literature implies that the

ideal size of an interactional therapy group is approximately seven, with an acceptable range of five to ten members. The lower limit of the group is determined by the fact that a critical mass is required for an aggregation of individuals to become an interacting group. When a group is reduced to a size of four or three, it often ceases to operate as a group; member interaction diminishes, and therapists often find themselves engaged in individual therapy within the group. Many of the advantages of a group—the opportunity for broad consensual validation, the opportunity to interact and to analyze one's interaction with a large variety of individuals—are compromised as the group size diminishes.

The upper limit is determined by sheer economic principles; as the group increases in size, less and less time is available for the working through of any individual's problems. (pp. 284–285)

Luft (1984) also wrote that

The influence of the sheer number of persons contained in a group is entangled with other variables such as the purpose of the group and the composition of the membership. A few generalizations can be made on the basis of specific studies. Cohesion tends to be weaker and morale tends to be lower in larger groups than in comparable smaller ones. How often groups meet varies inversely with size and duration and directly with closeness of feelings (Coleman and James, 1961; Fischer, 1953; Tannenbaum, 1962).

Two-person and three-person groups have unique characteristics with reference to closeness of feeling and power as interaction factors (see especially Theodor Caplow's *Two Against One*). Thomas and Fink (1961) also report that, for most kinds of tasks or problems where group discussion is desirable, a five-person group appears to be an optimal size. Hare (1976) presents a summary of research bearing on group size. Referring to work by Bales and Borgatta (1965), Hare notes, "as size increases, there is a tendency toward a more mechanical method of introducing information (by round robin procedure, for example), a less sensitive exploration of the point of view of the other, and a more direct attempt to control others and reach solution whether or not all group members indicate agreement" (p. 226). Consistent with these findings is Simmel's (1955) observation, "a group upon reaching a certain size must develop forms and organs which serve its maintenance and promotion, but which a smaller group does not need. On the other hand . . . smaller groups have qualities, including types of interaction among their members, which inevitably disappear when the groups grow larger" (in Nixon, 1979). (p. 23)

Group Leadership

In his book, *Leadership,* James M. Burns (1978) refers to the activity of leadership as "that most observed and least understood phenomenon," a viewpoint that few would dispute. The nature and quest for leadership at all levels and across all settings has been a continuing challenge to humankind. However, Burns's suggestion that "true leaders emerge from, and always return to, the wants and needs of their followers" (Goodwin, 1978, p. 48) appears to have some relevance for leaders of counseling groups.

An earlier and similar theme was suggested for group counseling leaders by Bates and Johnson (1972):

> a counseling group draws definition from its leader. It will be only as good as the leader, as good as his skills and as good as the being of the leader himself. A person may be competent in the technical aspects of group leadership, but if he himself is not a "good" human being, his groups can become destructive . . . it is important that he (the leader) is a nourishing human being. Such a nourishing leader thrives on joyous human interaction and is a self-nourisher who will generate his own enrichment rather than feeding off group members. In other words, the group counselor's primary concern is the welfare of all the clients which comprise the group and it is to this and this end only that he directs his skills and energies. (p. 43)

Within this framework of the group counselor as a leader-member-nourisher, what are the leadership responsibilities or functions? Helen Driver (1958), an early leader in the group counseling movement, identified leadership techniques for the group counselor:

1. Support; giving commendation; showing appreciation.
2. Reflection: mirroring feelings.
3. Clarification: making meanings clear, showing implications of an idea.
4. Questioning: bringing out deeper feelings, inviting further response.
5. Information: providing data for examination, serving as a resource person, teaching.
6. Interpretation: explaining the significance of data, using analogy.
7. Summary: asking for client summary first, pointing out progress, alternatives (pp. 100–102).

In preparation for group leadership responsibility, Stockton (1980) reviewed the importance of training in four areas:

> (1) didactic knowledge (e.g., potential group leaders should understand theories of group counseling, ethical principles, research); (2) individual clinical skills such as those involving assessment, interpreting nonverbal behaviors, ability to use self-disclosure, confrontation and other standard therapeutic tools; (3) knowledge of group dynamics, most particularly developing a keen sense of the importance of timing and knowing how to pace a variety of specific group leader techniques and interventions; and (4) achieving a healthy personality oneself. (p. 57)

Bates, Johnson, and Blaker (1982) specified four responsibilities of leadership as (a) traffic directing (helping members become aware of behaviors that facilitate or inhibit open communications), (b) modeling, (c) acting as an interaction catalyst, and (d) communications facilitator (pp. 95–117).

Rutan and Alonso (1978) specified guidelines to help group leaders become more aware of ongoing process issues occurring in group meetings:

1. Building an hypothesies. It may be helpful for the counselor to speculate about possible outcomes and reactions in advance. Such speculation may help the leader to become better prepared to function in his or her role as a group leader.
2. Take your time. The old saying that "haste makes waste" is one that group leaders should keep in mind. It is important to guard against responding too quickly and attempting to move a group too rapidly toward possibly erroneously preconceived goals.
3. Note the beginning. Initial behavior and words of individuals comprising the group can be of particular significance as well as possibly forecasting the theme that the group will follow.
4. Think analogies. It is important for the group leader to also be aware of the covert meanings of group discussions and actions. Observable behavior may often be analogous to deeper, more hidden content.
5. Keep the presenting problem and client background in mind at all times. It is important that the group leader not lose track of the context within which each individual functions and views his problem. Thus, an understanding of each group member's background assists the counselor in keeping appropriate perspectives.
6. Formulate a summary. It is often suggested that the counselor begin identifying materials for a final summary statement from the very beginning of each meeting. The nature of the summary statement can be significant, too, in making effective transition between meetings, as well as in the final termination of the group.

The group counselor, in the leadership role, must also take on the responsibility when the occasion dictates, of intervening in the group interaction. Such interventions, whether initiated by the counselor or by group members, help to keep the group participants goal-oriented. Vriend and Dyer (1973) believed that the group counselor can productively take responsibility for initiating or causing an intervention when:

1. A group member speaks for everyone.
2. An individual speaks for another individual within the group.
3. A group member focuses on persons, conditions, or events outside the group.
4. Someone seeks the approval of the counselor or a group member before and after speaking.
5. Someone says, "I don't want to hurt his feelings, so I won't say it."
6. A group member suggests that his problems are caused by someone else.
7. An individual suggests that "I've always been that way."
8. An individual suggests, "I'll wait, and it will change."
9. Discrepant behavior appears.
10. A member bores the group by rambling. (pp. 171–182)

Ohlsen (1977) noted the group counselor's facilitative behaviors:

1. Developing readiness.
2. Relationship building.

3. Relationship maintenance.
4. Problem identification.
5. Definition of counseling goals.
6. Definition of criteria to appraise client's growth.
7. Resistance.
8. Countertransference.
9. Feedback.
10. Termination. (p. 39)

An examination of these suggestions for group leadership indicates the group counselor's responsibility for the structure, conduct, and general overseeing of the group sessions. It should also be mentioned that conscientious group leaders do not become involved in group activities beyond their depth of professional preparation. Group counseling emphasizes factors of associations rather than deep emotional disturbances. The counselor's depth of psychological understanding and skill in group dynamics are individual considerations in the level of group counseling that he or she undertakes. For those counseling groups that focus on specific and narrow concerns, such as family relations, human sexuality, or substance abuse, it is obviously desirable that the counselor-leader have some special understanding of the topic.

Group Process

The elements of the group counseling process share much in common with those identified with individual counseling. These may be separated into their logical sequence of occurrence.

The Establishment of the Group

The initial group time is used to acquaint the new group membership with the format and processes of the group, to orient them to such practical considerations as frequency of meetings, duration of group, and length of group meeting time. Additionally, the beginning session is used to initiate relationships and open communications between the participants. The counselor also may use beginning sessions to answer questions that clarify the purpose and processes of the group. The establishment of the group is a time to further prepare members for meaningful group participation and to set a positive and promising group climate.

The group counselor must remember that in the initial group sessions the general climate of the group may be a mixture of uncertainty, anxiety, and awkwardness. It is not uncommon for group members to be unfamiliar with one another and uncertain regarding the process and expectancies of the group regardless of previous explanations or the establishing of "ground rules." As Gruen (1977) stated:

they are, therefore, fearful about whether they may eventually be excluded because they may not "fit in." Furthermore, they are concerned about who else is to be included or excluded. In this way, they can figure out the group boundaries and then learn whom to attend to and whom to ignore. Members are apt to watch others as well as themselves for clues about proper behavior that invites acceptance by the group and especially by the leader. Since the group and the whole therapy climate is uniquely new to them, they want to be safe and secure. They do not want to create waves or stand out as potentially unacceptable. Hence, they discuss "safe topics"—if they talk at all—such as the weather or events outside the group. Many of these topics were acceptable in the (social) groups they have known in the past. If they talk about their problems at all, they will initially do so in a stereotyped way. (p. 13)

It is important for the counselor to take positive steps to reduce the initial anxieties of group members. Hansen et al. (1980) emphasized that

the counselor should be able to comprehend and be empathic with a variety of life-styles and be able to relate to clients who express their personalities in various ways. The counselor should be aware of current events in business, science, and social and political areas that affect the well-being of clients. The counselor must know her own needs, sensitivities, motivations, frustrations, deprivations, and vulnerabilities. The counselor must know how to defend against anxiety and be capable of spontaneous participation with minimal countertransferences. The counselor should be aware of the social impression he or she makes. The counselor must communicate an accept-ing attitude. The counselor should be free of prejudices and permit others to express doubts and anger toward him or her. Group therapists should not become unduly frustrated when clients are slow to change because of resistances or are overly sensi-tive to members' criticism and complaints. The group counselor serves as a model and, therefore, should be emotionally expressive. The counselor should be able to experience and express warmth, caring, respect, support, as well as negative feelings of anger, fear, and resentment. When expressing negative feelings, counselors have to have insight into themselves and the impact of such expressions on helping the group resolve issues. The counselor must maintain personal security and identity apart from his or her need for group support. This permits the group members to develop identity and independence as well as to rely on the group as a vehicle for that process. (pp. 398–399)

Identification (Group Role and Goal)

Once an appropriate climate has been established that at least facilitates a level of discussion, the group may then move toward a second, distinct stage—that of identification. In this stage, a group identity should develop, the identification of individual roles should emerge, and group and individual goals established. These may all emerge simultaneously or develop at different paces. They are, however, significant at this stage of the group counseling process. It is also important to make operational the group counseling goals.

Most of us have few undirected, nongoal-oriented activities in our typical everyday plan of action. Those who work with groups frequently, whether in teaching or other capacities, can well predict the outcome if one were to appear before such a group with the question, "How would you like to spend your time today?" At worst, chaos would result, and at best, considerable time would be lost before determining how the group could best utilize the time available.

Goal setting is no less important in group counseling than in any other activ-

ity that seeks to be meaningful. The early identification of goals in group counseling will facilitate the group's movement toward a meaningful process and
outcomes. These goals are most readily identified and implemented when they
are specified in behavioral terms. Ryan (1973) discussed this point:

> Goal-setting in group counseling is the process of setting goals to implement the
> group counseling process. Goal-setting is accomplished by defining group goals and
> subgoals, which are implemented in individual behavioral objectives, and by ordering
> the objectives according to priority needs and contribution to the group goals. (p. 57)

Hansen et al. (1980) pointed out that it is also important to make operational
the group counseling goals:

> Group goals are operationalized when broad statements of intent for the group are
> analyzed into cognitive, affective, and behavioral dimensions, which in turn can be
> described as behavioral objectives for individual members. Behavioral objectives
> include specific, pertinent, obtainable, measurable, and observable behavior that will
> result from planned intervention. She [referring to T. A. Ryan] suggests that opera-
> tionalizing group goals has four advantages that increase the likelihood of counseling
> success: (1) operationalized goals produce more homogeneity in the group's shared
> interest; (2) operationalized goals contribute to more realistic expectations; (3) oper-
> ationalized goals lead to more highly motivated members because they know what
> they are working for; (4) operationalized goals make the group members more inter-
> dependent as they are able to see how goals for other members fit into their objectives
> as well (pp. 490–491)

They further indicated that

> there are certain problems in the process of goal setting for a group. The importance
> of a particular group goal for any individual in the group may be influenced by his
> individual needs. Obviously, goal setting is a part of the counseling process which
> must be accomplished jointly by the counselor and the group members. If a counselor
> establishes the goals for the group, he may not be aware of the individual subgoals.
> Other members in the group may not be aware of each other's individual goals under-
> neath the umbrella of the general goal for the group. The extent to which group goals
> implement personal goals will vary from time to time throughout the group. Despite
> these difficulties involved in the goal setting process, however, it is one of the most
> important aspects to success in group counseling. (p. 491)

It is also important for counselors to be aware of the probable, or, at least
possible, conflict and confrontation during this stage of the group's development. Yalom (1975) labeled this second phase as "the conflict, dominance-
rebellion stage." Yalom wrote that it is a time when

> the group shifts from preoccupation with acceptance, approval, commitment to the
> group, definitions of accepted behavior, and the search for orientation, structure, and
> meaning to a preoccupation with dominance, control, and power. The conflict char-
> acteristic of this phase is between members or between members and the leader. Each
> member attempts to establish for himself his preferred amount of initiative and
> power, and gradually a control hierarchy, a social pecking order, is established. (p.
> 306)

Hansen et al. (1980) described this second stage as one in which the group members manifest their dissatisfaction with the operation of the group. It is a period of time following the initial acquaintance period when

> members are frequently frustrated in their attempts to evolve new patterns of behavior through which to work toward group goals. The discrepancy between individuals' real selves and their stereotyped images of the group may lead to conflict. Group members may challenge others' reactions to them and insist on their own rights. Some conflict may erupt when certain issues are discovered to be more complex than the group members originally perceived. The process of conflict and confrontation also occurs as group members begin to perceive and experience difficulty implementing changes in behavior. (p. 502)

They further noted that

> in many counseling groups Stage Two may not emerge early or may be avoided completely unless there is enough commitment to the group so that the members will risk open confrontation. In fact, the conflict may not be expressed openly but through passive resistance. The members may remain silent rather than confront each other or the counselor. Open conflict and confrontation is not often seen in group counseling conducted in school settings or other short-term counseling situations in which the counselor is perceived as an authority figure.
>
> Without working through this phase and establishing appropriate norms of behavior, only a superficial level of cohesiveness can develop. As the group members work through their differences of opinions about appropriate behavior for each other and the counselor, they are able to accept the real person rather than the stereotyped image. This can lead to a greater feeling of identity with the group. It is important to recall that even when the group moves into a cohesive stage, it may regress to periods of conflict and confrontation.
>
> The necessity for working through the stage of conflict and confrontation cannot be emphasized too strongly. For groups to evolve from a superficial to a more truly effective level of functioning, this painful and difficult period must be experienced and dealt with successfully. (pp. 391–392)

When conflicts and confrontations, as previously described, do occur, a more cohesive group usually emerges, with resulting increased openness in communication, consensual group action and cooperation, and mutual support among the members. A concern at this point may also be the tendency of some group members to withdraw. Stockton, Barr, and Klein (1981) warned that not only does the group member lose but premature termination can result in negative effects on the group from which the member has dropped. Initial work stages of the group require membership stability in order to develop therapeutic potential from group treatment, and loss of members makes this task more difficult.

Productivity

In the third stage of the group's development, a clear progression towards productivity is noted. As the group has achieved some degree of stability in its pattern of behaving, the productivity process can begin. Also, because the members are now more deeply committed to the group, they may be ready to reveal more of themselves and their problems.

This is the period of problem clarification and exploration, usually followed by an examination of possible alternate solutions:

> The established group now directs itself toward individual as well as group goals, attempting to produce something of a general and lasting value. In a counseling group the task may be to develop insight into personal and interpersonal processes and to affect constructive personality change. (Hansen et al., 1980, p. 531)

The emphasis of this stage is on recognizable progress toward the group's and individual members' goals. In this process, however, each group member is exploring and seeking an understanding of self, situation, and problem or concern, and each member develops a personal plan integrating these understandings. The three subphases of this stage may be (a) assessment, (b) understanding, and (c) planning. The group structure tends to be functional.

In group counseling productivity can be frequently translated as successful problem solving. Group counseling thus often becomes a process seeking to promote change. Johnson and Johnson (1982) specified four concerns in problem solving:

> (1) determining the actual or current state of affairs; (2) specifying the desired state of affairs; (3) determining the best means of moving the group from the actual to the desired state of affairs; and (4) doing so. Problem solving requires both an idea about where the group should be and correct information about where it is now. Every group, furthermore, can be evaluated on the basis of its problem-solving adequacy. *Problem-solving adequacy* has four elements: (1) general agreement about the desired state of affairs; (2) structures and procedures for producing, understanding, and using relevant information about the actual state of affairs; (3) structures and procedures for inventing possible solutions, for deciding upon and implementing the best solution, and for evaluating its effectiveness in having permanently eliminated the problem; and (4) accomplishing these three activities without deteriorating—preferably while augmenting—the effectiveness of the group's problem-solving capabilities. (p. 401)

Although group strategies may be selected by the group for any or all of these phases, it is important that they make sense to each member in terms of their individual needs. The counselor may note that progress is being made when progress can be seen. Of course, progress is not always constant during this time, and occasionally regression, stagnation, or even confusion may occur. Certainly it is appropriate that

> Whenever the group does not know what it is doing, it ought to stop and find out. This does *not* mean that the group ought to argue over its objectives, but rather, that it ought to describe to itself what it is doing. In unclear situations, there is actually discrimination against the participation of some members. When a person knows what the group is doing, then he also knows how to participate, and if he does not participate, it is reasonable to assume that he has nothing to contribute. But when a person does not know what the group is doing, he does not know how to participate,

and he is blocked. Therefore, with every change in the nature of the group's activity, it is well to be sure the member roles are redefined. (Thelan, 1954, p. 288)

The necessity for working through the stage of conflict and confrontation cannot be emphasized too strongly. For groups to evolve from a superficial to a more truly effective level of functioning, this painful and difficult period must be experienced and dealt with successfully. (pp. 391–392)

It is also on these occasions that the counselor is alert to prevent process problems from handicapping progress and group achievement. Often, a simple reminder by the counselor of the stated goals or objectives of the group can prevent activities or discussions that tend to sidetrack members or the group as a whole from maintaining progress. However, because of the relationships and the group climate previously established, groups should overcome these difficulties and regain their productivity. As Hansen et al. (1980) noted:

Because interpersonal bonds are strong, evaluation, criticism, discussion, and re-evaluation can be undertaken. The group directs itself to members as objects since subjective relations have been established. Members view individual behavior in the group with greater objectivity. They show a greater ease in making decisions and more flexibility in controlling group processes. Because they have learned to relate to others as social entities, role structure is not an issue. Members can adopt and play roles that will enhance the effectiveness of the group. (p. 531)

During this phase, the problem or concern should be clarified to everyone's satisfaction and ownership should be verified. This clarification includes a thorough understanding of the nature of the problem and its causes. It is only when this has been achieved that resources for problem solutions can be realistically examined. This phase may be successfully concluded when all possible solutions have been considered and examined in terms of their consequences. These solutions should be practical or capable of being realized (obtainable), and the final choice of a solution should be made only after appropriate considerations and discussion. It should be emphasized that this is not the time for snap judgments and hurried commitments. At this point, then, the group members have examined themselves and the problem as it applies to them and have explored these considerations in considerable depth; have looked at possible solutions and their consequences; have determined the course of action that appears most appropriate; and are ready to move into the next stage, one in which they will try out or experiment with their chosen solution. In this process, they have, by making their own decisions, also established their ownership of the problem and the chosen solution.

Realization

At the point at which the members of the group recognize the inappropriateness of past behaviors and begin to try out their selected solutions or new behaviors to implement in practice their decisions, progress is being made toward realization of their individual goals. At this time, responsibility has been established with the individual members to act upon their own decisions. The counselor encourages the sharing of individual experiences and goal achievement *both* within and outside the group. Although general success with the new behaviors may provide sufficient reinforcement for many members to continue, for others a support base of "significant others" outside the group should now be developed to facilitate a maintenance of the change once the counseling group is terminated. In school settings, counselors might, for example, consult with parents and teachers to implement this strategy.

Termination

Most of us have experienced occasions of regret and even sorrow when temporary groups to which we have belonged reach the break-up point. Regardless of the purpose for which the group is organized, we may try to prolong its eventual dissolution by promising get-togethers, planning social activities, and in general agreeing that "this has been too much fun to let it end." On many such occasions, casual strangers have become the best of friends in relatively short periods of time, and the threatened termination of the relationships is at least psychologically resisted.

For these same reasons, members may resist the termination of a counseling group. The very nature of counseling groups, with their emphasis on interpersonal relationships, open communication, trust, and support, promises the development of a group that the membership may want to continue indefinitely. It is therefore important from the very beginning that the group counselor emphasize the temporary nature of the group and establish, if appropriate, specific time limitations. The counselor also reminds the group, as the time approaches, of the impending termination. This does not mean that the counselor alone is responsible for determining the termination point of a group. Although the counselor may, of course, assume this responsibility, termination may also be determined by the group members or by the group members and the counselor together.

Termination, like all other phases or stages of the group counseling experience, also requires skill and planning on the part of the counselor. Termination is obviously most appropriate when the group goals and the goals of the individual members have been achieved and new behaviors or learnings have been put into practice in everyday life outside the group. The group will also be ready to terminate when, in a positive sense, it has ceased to serve a meaningful purpose for the members. Under less favorable circumstances, groups may be terminated when their continuation promises to be nonproductive, harmful, or when group progress is slow, and long-term continuation might create overdependency on the group by its members.

Members may be terminated from a group at any time during the group's existence. Members who are disruptive, who seriously handicap the other members, who may be more effectively assisted through individual counseling, or who personally desire to terminate are not uncommon subjects for individual terminations. Group counselors should be aware that this is a common happening, especially in the beginning stages of a group, when several members may voluntarily terminate. It is important that the counselor accept this as a matter of course and refrain from exerting pressure on such persons to remain in the group. At the same time, however, the counselor may indicate a willingness to see the person(s) on an individual basis.

The point of termination is a time for review and summary by both counselor and clients. With some groups, time will be needed to work through the feelings of the members regarding termination. Even though strong ties may have developed and there are pressures from the group to extend the termination time, those pressures must be resisted, and the group must be firmly, though gently, moved toward the inevitable termination.

An excellent summary of essential counseling skills related to stages of the group process was presented by Gill and Barry (1982) (Table 6–1).

Group Guidance Activities

In a broad, general context, group guidance is probably as old as formal schooling. Good teachers through the years have used groups for what today would be called pupil guidance purposes. In schools group guidance activities have been designed to provide information to students in groups or experiences beyond those associated with the day-to-day learning activities in the classroom. In nonschool settings as well as schools, group activities have been planned to provide information, skill-building, opportunities for personal growth and development, orientation, and assistance in decision-making.

Values

Over the years certain values have been attributed to group activities of a guidance nature.

Facilitating Personal Development. Certain experiences that lead to personal development can take place only in the group setting. These include the opportunity to learn and play certain roles, such as group leader, group follower, or member, the development of patterns of cooperation with others, and the learning of group communication skills.

Stimulation of Learning and Understanding. According to Lifton (1972), it is fairly well accepted that clients will incorporate information when the information is presented in a way that enables them to use the facts with a minimum of transfer until they are secure enough to allow themselves to perceive the situation broadly and when they have perceived that the information is necessary to achieve a goal important to them. He then points out that in group settings people are seeking two kinds of information: that about themselves and their relationships with others, and information about the external world. Group guidance activities are important in providing learning and understand-

Table 6-1   Classification System for Group-Focused Counseling Skills

Stage I	Stage II	Stage III
Group Formation: Facilitating Cooperation Toward Common Goals Through Development of Group Identity	*Group Awareness:* Facilitating a Shared Understanding of the Group's Behavior	*Group Action:* Facilitating Cooperative Decision-Making and Problem-Solving

Group Formation: Facilitating Cooperation Toward Common Goals Through Development of Group Identity
1. *Norming.* Stating explicitly the expected group behavior
2. *Eliciting Group Responses.* Inquiries or invitations to members that encourage comments, questions, or observations.
3. *Eliciting Sympathic Reactions.* Inquiries or invitations to members that encourage disclosure of experiences or feelings similar to those being expressed.
4. *Identifying Commonalities and Differences.* Describing comparative characteristics of participants.
5. *Eliciting Empathic Reactions.* Inquiries or invitations to members that encourage reflection of one member's expressed content or feeling.
6. *Task Focusing.* Redirecting conversation to immediate objectives; restating themes being expressed by more than one member.

Group Awareness: Facilitating a Shared Understanding of the Group's Behavior
1. *Labeling Group Behavior.* Identifying and describing group feelings and performance.
2. *Implicit Norming.* Describing behavior that has become typical of the group through common practice.
3. *Eliciting Group Observations.* Inquiries or invitation to members that encourage observations about group process.
4. *Eliciting Mutual Feedback.* Inquiries or invitations to members that encourage sharing of perceptions about each other's behavior.
5. *Identifying Conflict.* Labeling discordant elements of communication between members.
6. *Identifying Nonverbal Behavior.* Labeling unspoken communications between members (facial expression, posture, hand gestures, voice tone and intensity, etc.)
7. *Validating.* Requesting group confirmation of the accuracy of leader or members' perceptions.
8. *Transitioning.* Changing the group's focus on content or feelings being expressed.
9. *Connecting.* Relating material from group events at a particular time or session to what is happening currently.
10. *Extinguishing.* Ignoring, cutting-off, or diverting inappropriate talk or actions of members.

Group Action: Facilitating Cooperative Decision-Making and Problem-Solving
1. *Identifying Group Needs.* Asking questions and making statements that clarify the want and needs of the group.
2. *Identifying Group Goals.* Asking questions and making statements that clarify group objectives.
3. *Attributing Meaning.* Providing concepts for understanding group thought, feelings, and behavior.
4. *Eliciting Alternatives.* Providing descriptions of possible courses of action and inviting members to contribute alternatives.
5. *Exploring Consequences.* Inquiries or invitations to the group that evaluate actions and potential outcomes.
6. *Consensus Testing.* Requesting group agreement on a decision or course of action.

Source: Gill and Barry, 1982, p. 304.

ing relevant to career and career decision making, educational planning and decision making, and personal-social adjustments and decision making.

Advantages of Group Interaction.   By actively participating in groups organized for guidance purposes, members have the opportunity to broaden their scope of understanding regarding the subject or purpose for which the group is organized. Additionally, participants should grow in their understanding of group interactions and dynamics as well as understanding their own behavior in groups.

Economy.   Although groups should not be organized for guidance purposes solely on the basis of economy, it must be recognized that where effectiveness in terms of outcome is not lessened, the saving of both counselors' and clients' time through the use of groups can be of considerable value.

Organizing Group Guidance Activities

All of us have experienced being participants in some type of group activity, social or otherwise, that has been organized on the spur of the moment. Occasionally these unanticipated activities have been enjoyable or worthwhile, but probably more often, they have resulted in confusion, uncertainty, perhaps even frustration, and have been considered a waste of time. The popularity of group guidance activities has, in some instances, led to their scheduling without appropriate preparation, but that is not and should not be the pattern. If group guidance activities are to achieve their potential, a great deal of consideration and organization must go into their planning, conducting, and evaluation. While the organization process is very similar to group counseling, discussed earlier in this chapter, the differences, though often subtle, should be noted and the similarities should be re-emphasized. The following guidelines therefore may be helpful.

Determining That There is a Need for Group Guidance.   All too often group guidance activities are simply scheduled. On occasion, the scheduled activities may be responding to an actual need. If we are to ensure their success, it must be determined beforehand that there is a need which a group shares in common and for which a group guidance response is appropriate. Questionnaires, problem surveys, or checklists administered to specific populations often will provide a factual basis for determining possible group guidance activities.

Determining That Group Guidance is the Most Appropriate or Effective Response.   Once needs have been determined, the counseling staff must identify those for which a group guidance activity would be appropriate, in contrast to group counseling or individual counseling, or perhaps even some form of instruction. It must be emphasized that group guidance focuses on providing information or experiences and is not designed for adjustment or therapy.

Large group guidance activities are those that may be useful to nearly everyone in a specific population or setting, hence the total group would experience the activity. Examples might be a stress management program for employees in an industrial setting; a behavior workshop for public relations workers; or a career day for high school students.

Small group guidance activities, in broad general terms, are those designed for specific outcomes, which cater to the needs of smaller subgroups within the total population served by the school or agency counseling and guidance program. These activities may focus on providing information for decision making and planning purposes, activities for personal development purposes, and assistance for educational adjustments. Small group guidance activities can emphasize smaller components or follow-up activities for the larger college, career, or orientation programs. Other specific examples are guidance groups organized to develop job-seeking and interviewing skills, how-to-study techniques, assertiveness training, career education, values clarification activities, discussion groups, and experiences in nonverbal communications.

Determining the Characteristics of the Group.　Once the nature of the group guidance activity has been established, certain group characteristics must be determined. Obviously, size of the group must be one consideration. Here, the counselor must determine what size group will be most appropriate for the activities planned and outcomes anticipated. Size will also have an influence on the operational format of the group. Format planning includes determining the types of activities of the group, the length of time allotted for each group session, the number of sessions, and the setting. A final consideration affecting the group characteristics will be the role of the counselor. Will the counselor be an active participant or an inactive observer who remains in the background once the group's activities are underway? Will the counselor direct the group? Will the counselor be a group arbitrator? What information will the leader provide the group? Will roles be assigned or will roles evolve as the group progresses?

Establishing the Group.　Once the characteristics of the group have been determined, members may be selected. They may volunteer or they may be invited to participate. Invitation includes the right of the persons to refuse participation. In establishing the membership of the group, it must be verified that the planned activity will respond to the need of the individual member and that the structure or operational format will be comfortable for the group member. In large groups, such as those organized for orientation purposes, career needs, or other special information purposes, this is not necessarily essential, but for smaller, intimate groups, it is an important consideration.

Monitoring the Ongoing Activities.　Once the group has been established and the members oriented to its purpose and processes, the counselor or facilitator assumes the responsibility for keeping the group "on track." It is relatively easy, especially considering the participants' lack of experience and understanding of the group process, to deviate from the purposes of the group, to become bogged down in irrelevant discussions and activities, or to encounter personal factors that inhibit or impede the functioning of the group. The counselor must, therefore, be constantly on the alert to detect such symptoms and to use his or her skills to minimize these effects. The ongoing activities of the group are meaningful only as long as they promote the progress of the group and its members towards the goals of the group.

Evaluating Outcomes. The importance of evaluation in assessing the outcomes of groups cannot be overemphasized, and evaluation and the accountability process will be discussed in greater detail in Chapter 12. The goals or projected outcomes of the group must be stated in clear, objective, and measurable terms. The criteria for measuring goal achievement must be identified and stated, and data then collected which, when analyzed, will present an objective evaluation of outcomes. Such evaluations can assist counselors and others involved to determine which group guidance activities are most effective and which techniques within groups are most and least effective. Implications for group memberships, roles, and leadership may also result.

Values Clarification Techniques for Groups: An Overview

When we state that we believe in free speech, freedom of the press, equal rights for women, and access to education for all, we are, in effect, expressing values. Those values might appropriately reflect the consensual values of our society. Each society is characterized by well-defined, articulated values that are passed on to and practiced by the members of the society. On the other hand, when we extoll the pleasures of travel abroad, the virtues of exercise and careful diets, and the inspiration of a specific religious faith, we may, in effect, be expressing our personal values. Thus, values also represent what a person considers important in life, and these ideas of what is good or worthwhile are acquired through the modeling of the society and the personal experiences of the individual.

A discussion of values is basically a discussion of what people believe in, what they stand for, and what is important in life. They are the reasons people behave and even think the way they do. They motivate one to plan and act and serve as a standard for judging the worth of activities, achievements, things, and places. In short, it has been claimed that values give direction to one's life and, hence, one's behavior. On the other hand, people who do not know what they value often engage in meaningless, nonproductive, and usually frustrating behavior. In both individual and group counseling, then, an understanding of the client's values can facilitate the counselor's understanding of the client's behavior, goals, or lack of goals, and what is or has been of significance in the client's life.

Values Defined

The proliferation of values clarification techniques and the increasing examination of values education in the school curriculum, as with any popular movement, have clouded traditional definitions and brought forth complex explanations of what is meant by values. We do not propose to add to this confusion, but rather, to present several of the more popular definitions appropriate to those engaged in counseling. First, the dictionary defines values as ideals, customs, institutions, etc., that arouse an emotional response, for or against them in a given society or a given person—a simple, straightforward, and, we think, acceptable definition. Another equally clear definition is that proposed by Smith and Peterson (1977) that values "are those elements that show how a person has decided to use his or her life" (p. 228). Another relatively simplistic definition of values was presented by Ziegler (1972), who described values as "symbolic categories—ideas, notions, articulated feelings, if you will—which enable us to rank behaviors and events and discover which we prefer and which we don't" (p. 18).

Kluckhohn et al. (1962) reported a popular and more complex definition of values in the behavioral sciences of the Harvard Study Group, which suggested, "A value is a conception, explicit or implicit, distinctive of an individual or characteristics of a group, of the desirable which influences the selection from available modes, means, and ends of action" (p. 395). Counselors will be interested in Smith's (1962) definition, in which he refers to the value system in more psychological terms:

> The *value system* of the individual is best described as a multifactor spiral or behavior bias which molds and dominates the decision-making power of the particular person. (p. 372)

> Values seem to depend for stability or instability on beliefs. Individual beliefs are of two origins: in reference to what is or was; and to what ought to be or ought to have been. The first of these is usually referred to as *facts;* the second as valuations, judgments, or opinions.

Peterson (1970) concluded that some common principles generally agreed upon regarding values are:

1. Values are hypothetical constructs.
2. Values represent the desirable in the sense of what one "ought" to do or what he perceives is the "right" thing to do in any given circumstance.
3. Values are motivational forces. (pp. 51–52)

Another contrast of concepts that may be useful is one suggested by Mace (1972), who contrasted values with standards and behavior:

> values are the ultimate ideals and goals of mankind, which do not undergo basic change. The standards represent the attempts of human communities and groups to make rules which will ensure that the values are preserved and expressed. Behavior represents the manner in which individual men and women interact with each other, normally by conforming to the standards in order to preserve the values. (p. 17)

Kalish and Collier (1981) described the process:

> values clarification involves trying on various values to see how they fit. The process proceeds on two fronts. First, it points out that, according to a given set of values, certain things are desirable. Second, it requires you to consider whether or not you agree that these things really are valuable. Thus, you might be invited to imagine

yourself caught up in some situation. Then you'd be asked to think through the implications of certain values, always keeping in mind your own feelings about these
implications.

Notice something very important about this process. It is *not* concerned with dis-
covering what absolute values there may or may not be. Instead, it is designed to help
you clarify what values you actually hold, whether or not these values are absolute or
relative, right or wrong. This means that values clarification does not replace such
philosophical disciplines as ethics, aesthetics, and political theory. It is, however, what
might be called "applied philosophy"—that is, the application of philosophy to real
people's real problems. (p. 3)

Values Theory and Process

It is appropriate to begin this section with a statement underlining a major
hypothesis of values clarification that has significant implications for counselors
utilizing these techniques. This hypothesis suggests that the skillful and consistent use of the valuing process (explained later) by an individual increases the
likelihood that the individual will make appropriate decisions that will be satisfying both to the individual and to society.

Raths, Harmin, and Simon (1978) translated this theory into a process consisting of seven subprocesses grouped under three categories. They then suggest
that a value in one's life must meet the following criteria:

> *Choosing:*
> 1. freely
> 2. from alternatives
> 3. after thoughtful consideration of each alternative
>
> *Prizing:*
> 4. cherishing, being happy with the choice
> 5. willing to affirm the choice publicly
>
> *Acting:*
> 6. doing something with the choice
> 7. repeatedly, in some pattern of life. (p. 28)

One of the authors of this process, Simon, with deSherbinin (1975) indicated
that

> the process of values clarification involves knowing what one prizes, choosing those
> things which one cares for most and weaving those things into the fabric of daily
> living. This process is sometimes taught by working on real-life situations, at other
> times by dealing with made-up stories, but always by grappling with issues that are of
> real concern in people's lives. (p. 679)

Howe and Howe (1975) suggested a process that seemed particularly adaptable to counseling strategies. This process consisted of the following steps:

1. Developing a climate of acceptance, trust, and open communication.
2. Building self-concepts.

3. Creating awareness of prizing and publicly affirming values.
4. Helping individuals choose freely from alternatives after weighing the consequences.
5. Helping individuals learn to set goals and take actions on their values.

This process is applicable in both individual and group counseling settings.

Having broadly viewed values and their impact on behavior, noted a basis for values theory, and similarities between valuing and counseling process, let us examine further some of the relationships between values and counseling.

Values and Counseling

Historical Concerns

Rockwell and Rothney (1961) indicated that from the very beginning of the counseling and guidance movement in America, leaders in this movement have expressed concern both in their actions and writing, with values. The "father" of this movement, Frank Parsons, has been described as a "utopian social reformer," believing in the perfectibility of mankind. He viewed guidance as a means to a mutualistic society and the counselor's role as one leading to social goals by offering prescriptive advice. Davis preached the moral values of hard work, ambition, honesty, and the development of good character as assets in the business world.

Later, Carl Rogers stated his beliefs in the goodness and worthwhileness of man and man's abilities to chart his own destiny. C. Gilbert Wrenn in *The Counselor in a Changing World* (1962) and *The World of the Contemporary Counselor* (1973) discussed the values of the counselor and his or her clients. In the former book he wrote:

> It has become increasingly clear that the counselor cannot and does not remain neutral in the face of the student's value conflicts. Even the counselors who believe most strongly in letting the student work out his own solutions have firm values of their own and cannot help communicating them. They communicate their values in what they do and don't do even if they never mention their beliefs verbally. Furthermore, we expect more and more of the counselor with reference to the needs of society. Just to accept the need for the full development of abilities in the interest of a stronger nation as well as the interest of the individual is a manifest expression of a social value. Because the counselor cannot escape dealing with values and expressing values in his own behavior, he must be clear about the nature of his own values and how they influence his relationships with other people.
>
> A second developing conviction about values is that they are now seen by some psychologists as the central difficulty for many troubled people. Fifty years ago values were clearly defined, and acute maladjustment seemed to result from a willful violation of them. Psychological treatment consisted primarily of freeing the individual from an overwhelming sense of guilt over his transgression against his parents and other representatives of society. But today the picture seems almost the reverse of what it was. The maladjusted person feels himself more lost than guilty. Social expectations have become more diverse, less well defined, less insistent. The social pro-

cesses of inculcating strong values are less effective today, in part because family and community are less cohesive.

As a consequence the individual feels a lack of purpose and direction. He feels less estranged from others and even from himself; he feels worthless and unsure of his identity. He must discover character in himself for himself. Values strongly felt are the foundation upon which he can build an increasingly satisfying personal existence. Thus, clarifying values and perhaps acquiring new values becomes a major task for the individual in counseling, as in education generally. (pp. 62–63)

In the later publication, *The World of the Contemporary Counselor,* he discussed the counselor's and client's values:

The Counselor's Values

A first concern is that the counselor examine his own hierarchy of values and check it against the contemporary scene. I do not suggest that the counselor must change his values to meet changing assumptions, but rather that he attempt to increase his openness to the intrusions of change. A feeling of great certainty that what he now thinks is right and is right for all time can become a simple rigidity. It is too easy to retreat into a secure castle of one's own construction and close the gates to all that might disturb. It is healthy to be disturbed, for this means that one is required to think, to test assumptions, to question thoughtfully the bases for conduct. It is more realistic to confess confusion than to parade conviction.

On the other hand, admitting confusion could be interpreted as justifying having no convictions, no assurances of vital values. I must anticipate at this point what I want to discuss more carefully later, that one can be *committed* to values and goals even though they are tentative. In fact, one must be committed to be real, but the commitment may be to values which are seen as subject to modification, as changing with experience. "Tentativeness and commitment" paralleling each other are powerful principles. (pp. 34–35)

The Client's Values

The second area of concern is the acceptance of the client's right to be *different* in his values. This difference between the values of the client and those of the counselor is often a difference between generations or between cultures. Always, of course, the values of the client are the product of his life experience, unique to him and often markedly different from the experience of the counselor. The 30-year-old, middleclass, socially accepted, college-educated counselor cannot be expected to understand in all cases the values of a 16-year-old, ghetto-reared, socially rejected boy or girl or those of an affluent, socially amoral, parentally rejected youth. In fact, experiential understanding of another is rare. What is most important, however, is that the counselor accept the client's values as being as real and as "right" for him as the counselor's values are for the counselor. There is too frequently a tendency to protest inwardly, "He can't really *mean* that," when the value expressed by the client is in sharp contrast to a related value held by the counselor. The point is that the client does mean that; his value assumption is as justifiable to him as yours is to you.

So far I have said nothing about the counselor's responsiblity for helping the client to examine a given value assumption, particularly if the value is likely to result in behavior harmful to another or to society. He has such a responsibility, I am sure, differing widely from client to client and varying often with the client's psychological readiness to examine values. Basic to the success of any such confrontation, however, is the counselor's acceptance of the "right" of the client to have different values. If a counselor enters into a discussion of another's point of view with the implicit assumption that he is "right" and the other is "wrong," failure is assured. (p. 35)

Relationship to Counseling Theory

As we proceed to examine values clarification and its relationship and potential usefulness for counselors and other helping professionals, let us examine its relationship to some of the traditional, theoretical approaches to counseling. For example, Simon and deSherbinin (1975) noted that values clarification skills were natural companions of other skills that help people to develop their potential and live life more fully. Values clarification skills, it was suggested, go hand in hand with the work of Carl R. Rogers, emphasizing warmth and genuineness among people. Simon and deSherbinin went on to state:

> Values clarification can borrow something from Harvey Jackin's re-evaluation counseling model, in which people make commitments to help each other grow. Generally, people divide the time they have for each other into two equal segments during which each works as both client and counselor. This reciprocity generates power that penetrates deeply into people's lives; values clarification techniques can be used in exactly the same way.
>
> More and more, people working in T-groups are also coming to see that values clarification exercises rapidly advance their aims of getting people close to others' thoughts and feelings.
>
> It has also found its way into the training of Gestalt therapists. Gestalt teachers have sensed that its various strategies are useful in clarifying the way people respond to each other's problems.
>
> Other counselors simply fit a values clarification exercise into a transactional analysis technique. One way that transactional analysis workers have used values clarification is to ask a client to respond to a values question as if the child inside of him or her is speaking, then the parent inside, and then the adult. (p. 683)

Smith and Peterson (1977) noted the relationship between counseling theory and values as the common ground for "teaching human beings how to live meaningfully with self and with one another" (p. 230). It was then pointed out that a number of theoretical approaches to counseling and psychotherapy have long advocated this. For example, "All counseling and psychotherapy teaches values either directly (knowingly) or indirectly (unknowingly) . . . " (p. 230).

Smith and Peterson (1977) concluded that the actualization of consensual values in human affairs is an enormous task that requires the involvement of all persons who render guidance services.

Another concern for counselors using values clarification techniques has been the increasing criticism of these techniques in the early 1980s. These criticisms, frequently expressed in behalf of religious groups, often portrayed values clarification techniques as encouraging permissiveness, associated with secular humanism, and detracting from the role of the home and church in teaching values.

The Counselor and Values Clarification Techniques

Values clarification theory and practice has much in common with counseling theory and practice. In theory, both are seeking to assist individuals in realizing their fullest potential. In practice, both values clarification and counseling seek to assist the individual in developing better self-understandings and a positive self-concept, in making appropriate decisions and meaningful choices, and in satisfactorily adjusting to the demands of everyday living.

Because values clarification techniques are popularly practiced in groups, their potential for group counseling and guidance is considerable. For example, numerous values clarification techniques designed to promote persons getting acquainted and developing interpersonal relationship and communication skills would have their appropriate moments in group counseling and guidance. Group values exercises designed to facilitate self-assessment, self-concept clarification, and reinforcement for change would have their usefulness for the group counselor. Exercises that give a person the opportunity to compare, examine, and defend his or her behavior, values, and interests against the norms of others can also be useful in group counseling.

Summary

Today's society is group-oriented, and each person belongs to a variety of groups. These groups serve a variety of purposes, and in them one plays a variety of roles. Because of this group orientation, group guidance and counseling have become increasingly recognized as a means of assisting individuals in meeting their adjustment and developmental needs in both school and non-school settings. These group activities are distinguished by the nature of their concern and the type of group experience provided. Group guidance activities are primarily confined to school settings with an emphasis on providing information or experiences helpful in decision making. Group counseling tends to focus on routine adjustments and developmental needs or problems of individuals, whereas group therapy provides an intense experience that may last for a considerable length of time for individuals with serious adjustment, emotional, or developmental needs. The counselor's role and leadership is important to the success and accomplishment of both guidance and counseling groups. The group counselor must also be skillful and aware of the steps through which the group process moves. This process begins with the selection of members and the initial establishment of the group as a group; the identification of group goals; the clarification and exploration of the group and its individual members' problems and/or concerns; the exploration of solutions and consequences; decision making regarding solutions; implementation of the decision; and finally, termination and evaluation.

In recent years much attention has been given in the press and other media to the values of youths, the shifting values of the adult world, and the significance of personal values for satisfaction in the world of work. Values have also become increasingly important to professional counselors. Values clarification techniques can provide a helpful and nonthreatening approach for assisting clients in groups and for individual human appraisal. In a planned program of values clarification and development, the individual initially engages in exercises designed to identify his or her values, then shares them; next, examines them; confirms them, and finally, practices values. Varied group exercises are available for utilization by counselors.

Of course, for counseling—whether group or individual—to be maximally effective, it is important to know the client as well as possible. Assessment techniques which counselors may utilize for this purpose are discussed in the next two chapters.

References

Bales, R. F., & Borgatta, E. F. (1965). Size of group as a factor in the interaction profile. In A. P. Hare, E. F. Borgatta, & R. F. Bales (Eds.), *Small groups: Studies in social interaction.* New York: Alfred A. Knopf.

Bates, M., Johnson, C. D., & Blaker, K. E. (1972). *Group leadership: A manual for group counseling* (2nd ed.). Denver: Love.

Burns, J. M. (1978). *Leadership.* New York: Harper & Row.

Coleman, J. S., & James, J. (1961). The equilibrium size distribution of freely forming groups. *Sociometry, 24,* 36–45.

Dinkmeyer, D. C., & Caldwell, C. E. (1970). *Developmental counseling and guidance: A comprehensive school approach.* New York: McGraw-Hill.

Driver, H. I. (1958). *Counseling and learning through small group discussions.* Madison, WI: Monona.

Eddy, W. B., & Lubin, B. (1971). Laboratory training and encounter groups. *Personnel and Guidance Journal, 49,* 625–635.

Fischer, P. H. (1953). An analysis of the primary group. *Sociometry, 16,* 272–276.

Gazda, G. M. (1984). *Group counseling: A developmental approach* (3rd ed.). Boston: Allyn & Bacon.

Gill, S. J., & Barry, R. A. (1982). Group-focused counseling: Classifying the essential skills. *Personnel and Guidance Journal, 60,* 302–305.

Golembiewski, R. T., & Blumberg, A. (1970). *Sensitivity training and the laboratory approach.* Itasca, IL: F. E. Peacock.

Goodwin, D. K. (1978). True leadership. *Psychology Today,* October, 46–48, 50, 53–54, 57–58, 110.

Gruen, W. (1977). The stages in the development of a therapy group: Telltale symptoms and their origin in the dynamic group forces. *Group, 1,* 10–25.

Hansen, J. C., Warner, R. W., & Smith, E. M. (1980). *Group counseling: Theory and process* (2nd ed.). Chicago: Rand McNally.

Hardy, R. E., & Cull, J. G. (1974). *Group counseling and therapy techniques in special settings.* Springfield, IL: Charles C. Thomas.

Howe, L. W., & Howe, M. M. (1975). *Personalizing education: Values clarifiation and beyond.* New York: Hart.

James, W. (1890). *The principles of psychology, Vol. 1.* New York: Henry Holt.

Johnson, D. W., & Johnson, F. P. (1982). *Joining together: Group theory and group skills* (2nd ed.). Englewood Cliffs, NJ: Prentice-Hall.

Kalish, R. A., & Collier, K. W. (1981). *Exploring human values: Psychological and philosophical considerations.* Monterey, CA: Brooks/Cole.

Kluckhohn, C., and others. (1967). Values and value-orientations in the theory of action. In T. Parsons and E. Shils (Eds.), *Toward a general theory of action* (pp. 388–433). New York: Harper & Row. Cambridge MA: Harvard University Press.

Lifton, W. M. (1972). *Groups: Facilitating individual growth and societal change.* New York: John Wiley & Sons.

Luft, J. (1984). *Group processes: An introduction to group dynamics* (3rd ed.). Palo Alto, CA: Mayfield.

Mace, D. R. (1972). Values as a constant. *Penney's Forum,* Spring/Summer.

Mercurio, J. M., & Weiner, M. (1975). The mini-group in counseling. *Personnel and Guidance Journal, 54,* 227–228.

Nixon, H. L., II. (1979). *The small group.* Englewood Cliffs, NJ: Prentice-Hall.

Ohlsen, M. M. (1977). *Group counseling* (2nd ed.). New York: Holt, Rinehart & Winston.

Peterson, J. A. (1970). *Counseling and values.* Scranton, PA: International Textbook Co.

Raths, L. E., Harmin, M., & Simon, S. B. (1978). *Values and teaching: Working with values in the classroom.* Columbus, OH: Charles E. Merrill.

Rockwell, P. J., & Rothney, J. W. M. (1961). Some social ideas of pioneers in the guidance movement. *Personnel and Guidance Journal, 40,* 349–354.

Rogers, C. R. (1967). The process of the basic encounter group. In J. F. T. Bugental (Ed.), *Challenges of humanistic psychology* (pp. 261–276). New York: McGraw-Hill.

Rutan, J. S., & Alonso, A. (1978). Some guidelines for group therapists. *Group, 2,* 4–13.

Ryan, T. A. (1973). Goal setting in group counseling. In J. Vriend and W. W. Dyer (Eds.), *Counseling effectively in groups.* Englewood Cliffs, NJ: Educational Technology Publications.

Simmel, G. (1955). *The web of group affiliations.* Glencoe, IL: Free Press.

Simon, S. B., & deSherbinin, P. (1975). Values clarification: It can start gently and grow deep. *Phi Delta Kappan, 56,* 679–683.

Smith, D., & Peterson, J. (1977). Values: A challenge to the profession. *Personnel and Guidance Journal, 55,* 227–231.

Smith, D. W. (1962). Value systems and the therapeutic interview. In H. J. Peters, B. Shertzer, J. B. Heck, R. R. Stevic, and R. E. Van Atta (Eds.), *Counseling: Selected readings* (pp. 372–378). Columbus, OH: Charles E. Merrill.

Stockton, R. A. (1980). The education of group leaders: A review of the literature with suggestions for the future. *Journal for Specialists in Group Work, 5,* 55–62.

Stockton, R. A., Barr, J. E., and Klein, R. (1981). Identifying the group dropout: A review of the literature. *Journal for Specialists in Group Work, 6,* 75–82.

Tannenbaum, A. S. (1962). Reactions of member of voluntary groups: A logarithmic function of size and group. *Psychological Reports, 10,* 113–114.

Thelen, H. A. (1954). *Dynamics of groups at work.* Chicago: University of Chicago Press.

Thomas, E. J., & Fink, C. F. (1961). Models of group problem solving. *Journal of Abnormal and Social Psychology, 63,* 1.

Vriend, J., & Dyer, W. W. (Eds.). (1973). *Counseling effectively in groups.* Englewood Cliffs, NJ: Educational Technology Publications.

Wagner, C. A. (1976). Referral patterns of children and teachers for group counseling. *Personnel and Guidance Journal, 55,* 90–93.

Wrenn, C. G. (1962). *The counselor in a changing world.* Washington, D.C.: American Personnel and Guidance Association.

Wrenn, C. G. (1973). *The world of the contemporary counselor.* Boston: Houghton Mifflin.

Yalom, I. D. (1975). *The theory and practice of group psychotherapy* (2nd ed.). New York: Basic Books.

Ziegler, W. L. (1972). If we do not speak out on behalf of mankind, who will? *Penney's Forum.*

CHAPTER 7

STANDARDIZED TESTING AND HUMAN ASSESSMENT

Introduction

The objective of this chapter is to acquaint you with the role of standardized testing in assessment for counseling purposes. We will begin by acknowledging some of the controversies attending standardized testing, then move to a brief overview of test interpretation. Criteria for test selection and the different kinds of standardized tests will be presented.

Few activities in education and psychology have remained as consistent an issue over the past 50 years or have been subject to the controversy and debate that has accompanied the standardized testing movement, not only in schools, but in government agencies and business and industry as well. From statements in Cubberly, *Public Education in the United States* (1934) and Gross, *The Brainwatchers* (1963), to "Use and Misuse of Tests in Education: Legal Implications," (Nolte, 1975), "IQ Tests and Culture Issue," (Ornstein, 1976), and "Standardized Tests: Are They Worth the Cost?" (Herndon, 1976) through the more recent Nader (1980) versus ETS debates (excellently reviewed by Robinson (1983), the pros and cons of standardized test usage have been presented not only to the education profession, but to the American public as well.

Social issues have been raised and legal implications have been tested. Prominent psychologists and educators have also expressed concern over the continued uses and abuses of standardized testing. For example, Lee. J. Cronbach (1978), an internationally recognized expert on psychological and educational testing, noted: "There is a considerable risk that many students will draw inappropriate conclusions from test results." Ralph Tyler (1977) stated that standardized tests get "small answers to small questions. (p. 35)" Bernard McKenna, (1977) speaking for the National Education Association's instruction and professional development offices, noted:

Test content does not reflect local instructional objectives or specific curriculums.

Much of the content is unimportant or irrelevant to anything students need to know or understand.

Test content measures mainly recall-type learning, neglecting the higher thought processes—analyzing, synthesizing, and drawing generalizations, and applying them to new phenomena.

The tests give an incomplete picture of student learning progress, because items that all or almost all students have learned are removed from the tests in order to keep the norming procedure statistically sound.

The test maker uses a language that is not commonly used in other activities in the real world.

Test items are unduly complex and require too many different manipulations; sometimes instructions for the items are unclear.

Test vocabularies and illustrations are often unfamiliar to those who are not of white middle-class cultures or for whom English is a second language; that is, the tests are culturally and linguistically biased. (pp. 36–37)

Further evidence of this continuing concern was reflected in the results of a 1977–1978 survey sponsored by the North Central Regional Accreditation Association of Colleges and Schools (1979). In this survey, schools were asked to check problems or concerns. The responses indicated the highest single area of concern for more than 40 percent of the respondents involved problems and issues related to standardized testing.

A nationwide survey of test usage in grades 7 through 12 by Engen, Lamb, and Prediger (1982) confirmed that testing still was playing an integral role in most schools. The data indicated that nine out of ten schools provide career guidance tests, three out of four administer achievement tests, and two out of three use aptitude tests. The majority of the 547 schools administered each of these three categories of tests to all students in one or more grades.

Anastasi, an internationally recognized expert on psychological and educational testing, noted (1982):

Even well-educated laypersons have been known to confuse percentiles with percentage scores, percentiles with IQs, norms with standards, and interest ratings with aptitude scores. But a more serious misinterpretation pertains to the conclusions drawn from test scores, even when their technical meaning is correctly understood. (p. 55)

Many critics have argued that tests have a cultural and socioeconomic bias. (White middle class) college entrance examinations frequently come "under fire." On this issue in the 1970s, Robert L. Williams (1974) argued:

The primary issues in the great black-white I.Q. controversy are not those of cultural test bias, the nature of intelligence, or the heritability of I.Q. The issue is admittance to America's mainstream . . . . University admission policies have required standardized psychological tests such as the Scholastic Aptitude Test (SAT) or the Graduate Record Examination (GRE) as a criterion for admission to colleges, graduate schools, medical or law schools and other professional schools. For blacks, these tests more often mean exclusion (p. 34).

Speaking to the other side of the issue, Herbert Rudman (1977) concluded:

I believe that some of the critics and their criticisms are responsible but that others— and all too many, for a subject this important—are poorly qualified to speak with wisdom, knowledge of the facts, and insight. And unfortunately, too many of them are speaking in the name of groups that they do not faithfully represent. What started as an opportunity to stimulate discussion has developed into increasingly nonfactual rhetoric and hysteria (p. 185).

In 1984 the report of the National Commission on Excellence in Education entitled "A Nation at Risk," based much of its negative findings on standardized test results, fueling once again the controversies over the role of testing in educational evaluation.

In addition, these traditional controversies have been further complicated by the increasing popularity and attending discussions of the merits of competency-based, criterion-referenced testing and the suggestions by many educators that this is a more appropriate approach for measuring a pupil's educational progress. Although the critics of standardized testing abound and criticisms continue to be directed toward standardized measurement, much of the criticism may be as appropriately directed at the misuse and misinterpretation of the instruments as at the tests themselves. The misuse of tests in schools, especially, appears to stem from test users who are inadequately prepared in administering and interpreting standardized tests. At the same time, however, in many schools and school systems, as well as in a wide variety of agency settings, tests are used with prudence and caution by counselors and psychologists who are adequately trained in their utilization. In most institutional or agency settings where counseling takes place, including schools, standardized tests have been the counselor's basic instrument for objective assessment of the personality traits, aptitudes, interests, and other characteristics of individuals. Clearly, individual counseling demands a knowledge and recognition of the individuality of clients. Measurement of individual differences is a part of the mainstream of personnel psychology.

It therefore is most appropriate to introduce potential counselors to this important area of counselor understanding and skill, recognizing the continuing debates and issues, but assuming that a knowledge of these plus a basic understanding of these areas of testing will enable you to more effectively discriminate between uses and abuses and to retain in the counselor's repertoire a useful analytical tool.

Standardized Test Scores—What Do They Mean?

Whenever we evaluate someone, we do it in terms of some kind of comparison or point of reference. For instance, we may refer to Paul as the most handsome one in the group, Kathy as the best student in the class, and Nancy as the hardest worker in the bookstore. Here, we are comparing Paul to all others in the group; Kathy to the other students in the class, and Nancy to the other workers in the bookstore. Although we might attempt to make some predictions or deduce some other traits for Paul, Kathy, and Nancy from our observation, these would amount to nothing more than speculations, and we could justifiably be accused of unreliable procedures and data. If Kathy, Paul, and Nancy were to seek counseling, their counselor would want more objective and valid data before attempting to describe their traits and performances against the average traits and performances of others with comparable characteristics and experiences. An elementary understanding of statistics and statistically based tests, however, would enable the counselor to do this.

These basic understandings of educational and psychological statistics enable the counselor (a) to describe the characteristics of an individual or group in comparison with a specific group or population, (b) to predict the probability of future success or failure in a given area on the basis of present or past behavior, and (c) to infer the characteristics of a population from a sample of that population. It therefore follows that a good working knowledge of elementary statistical concepts is important for anyone who uses the various techniques of individual analysis and is mandatory for all who use tests and other tools of measurement. This section offers a brief overview of descriptive statistics, the basic statistical terms, and essential computational procedures, beginning with perhaps the most common—and most commonly misunderstood—of all statistical terms, *average.*

Averages

When Linda reports to her parents that she scored "70" on her history test, should they be pleased, satisfied disappointed, or what? Until they have more information, they cannot be sure how to react, because 70 could represent 70 percent of the questions answered correctly, 70 answered correctly out of 75 asked, a formula score of 70 (i.e., rights minus wrongs), or 70th in a class of 120 taking the examination. In this example, you may note that a *score* in and of itself is of little value. A score only becomes meaningful when it provides an index of how well or how poorly one performed in comparison with others taking the same test and, knowing that, what other significance can be interpreted from the results. Linda's parents are asking what is an *average* performance on this test and how does she *differ from* the average. Also, one asks to what does her score relate—what does it mean? Let us begin then by reviewing what is meant by *averages.*

Most educational and psychological evaluation is based on a person's position in a group compared with others who constitute the group. The average position in a group becomes an important point of mathematical reference in standardized testing for human assessment. It is important to note that there are three distinct statistical types of averages. These averages are known as *measures of central tendency.* These three measures are the *mean,* the *median,* and the *mode.* For most nonstatisticians, the definition of the *mean* is commonly associated with the term *average,* for the mean is defined as the mathematical average of a group of scores. The *median* is the midpoint of a set of scores with 50 percent of the scores being distributed above and 50 percent below that point. The *mode* represents the most frequent score in a set of scores. Of these three averages, the mean is the most useful and popular, and the mode, having little statistical value, is the least popular.

Variations from the Average

Once we have determined what is average, we must utilize a statistical methodology whereby we can measure the degree to which each person varies from this established average, or point of central tendency. Such statistical measures are called *measures of variability.* Two common measures of variability are the *range* and the *standard deviation.* The *range* may be defined as the spread from the lowest score to the highest score in a distribution. The actual statistical formula is the highest score in a group, minus the lowest score plus one. (The *plus one* in this formula extends the range to its real limits, which are one half of a score unit below the lowest.) The range is a relatively simple measurement device with limited descriptive value.

The *standard deviation,* on the other hand, is a statistical process that enables one to make an exact determination of distances of scores from the mean.

The mean and the standard deviation, when computed for a specific set of test scores, enable a counselor to determine how well an individual performed in relation to the group. This interpretation is made possible by the fact one can specify standard deviation distance from the mean and determine the proportion of the population that will be beyond or deviate from it, assuming that the scores are normally distributed. This normally distributed population is most popularly viewed as a *normal curve,* as shown in Figure 7–1.

In Figure 7–2, the normal curve is, in effect, sliced into bands, one standard deviation wide, with a fixed percentage of cases always falling in each band. Figure 7–2 then illustrates a significant fact: The mean plus and minus one standard deviation encompasses approximately 68 percent of a normally distributed population; the mean plus and minus two standard deviations encompasses approximately 95 percent of that population; and the mean plus and minus three standard deviations encompasses 99.74 percent of that population. This information, which remains constant for *any* normally distributed set of scores or values, enables one to make a meaningful interpretation of any score in a group. As you view the normal curve and its segmentation into standard deviations, note that these facts are handy for interpreting standard scores. Furthermore, whenever you can assume a normal distribution, you can convert standard scores to percentile scores, and vice versa. Thus, three basic facts for deriving a statistical evaluation of a person's performance on a psychological test are the person's raw score, mean, and standard deviation for the group with which the individual is being compared.

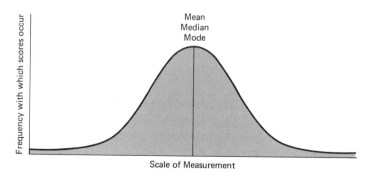

Figure 7–1. The normal curve. (Note: It rarely occurs that the mean, median, and mode are the same.)

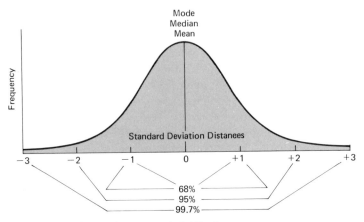

Figure 7-2. Scores in a normal distribution.

Relationships

Once you have determined the meaning of an individual's score in relation to others who have been administered the same measure, you must ask what are the other relationships or meanings of this score. The score and its comparative standing will take on meaning when it can be related to some meaningful purpose. For example, if students who score high on a college entrance examination actually perform at a high academic level in college, then one can assume that there is a relationship between scores on the examination and performance in college. The test score then becomes meaningful in terms of its prediction of college success, a meaningful purpose.

When you look for a statistical method to express relationships between two variables such as test scores and academic performance, you can compute a correlation coefficient. *Correlation coefficients* range from plus one through zero to minus one. A plus one indicates a perfect positive correlation; that is, the rank order of those taking the college entrance examination and their academic rank order in the college program are identical. On the other hand, a correlation of minus one means that the scores go in exactly the reverse direction. Thus, a correlation of minus one would indicate that persons who score highest on the entrance examination achieve the lowest in college. A zero correlation would represent a complete lack of relationship between two sets of data. A frequently computed coefficient of correlation is the Pearson product-moment coefficient.

Statistical Symbols

It is important for the counselor, teacher, or others who read test manuals, interpret test data, or in other ways seek to interpret simple statistical data to have a familiarity with basic statistical symbols. Although there is no "universal statistical language," the following are some of the more commonly recognized symbols and their meanings.

M	mean
Σ	the sum of
SD (or S)	standard deviation for a particular set of scores
X	actual or "raw" scores obtained
MD	median
x	distance (or score difference) of a score from the mean
N	number of cases
i	size of a class interval in scale units
M'	assumed mean
r	a coefficient of correlation
z	scale value of the standard normal distribution; the standard deviation of distance of a given score from the mean
f	frequency; the number of times a particular score occurs
p	percentage of persons getting a test item correct
q	percentage of persons getting a test item wrong ($p + q = 100$)

Presenting Test Scores

Inasmuch as raw test scores are in themselves meaningless, they have little value for the reporting of individual test results. As previously indicated, a raw score becomes meaningful only when it can be converted into some type of comparative score—one that enables an individual to be compared against others of a group. Most standardized tests, therefore, utilize one or more of the following methods of converting raw scores into a more meaningful method of presenting an individual's test results.

Percentiles

A *percentile score* represents the percentage of persons in the standardized sample for a given test who fall below a given raw score. A person's percentile ranking indicates his or her relative position in a normative sample. For example, if 60 percent of the students answer fewer than 30 problems correctly on an English usage test, then a raw score of 30 corresponds to the 60th percentile. Percentiles are probably the most common method of presenting scores and are relatively easy to interpret. Because of their relative ease of interpretation, however, several cautions should be noted. In working with non-test-sophisticated populations, such as parents, students, and most general populations, it is important to emphasize that percentiles do *not* represent percentages. Because percentiles represent comparison scores, it is also important to note the population with which an individual is being compared and the valid purposes for which comparisons can be made. It should also be noted that there are inequalities in percentile units.

The reason such distortion occurs is quite simple. When a raw-score distribution approximates the normal curve, there are many more moderate scores, which fall in the middle of the distribution, than either high or low scores, which occur at the ends. Since percentiles are based on the raw-score distance encompassed by a specified percentage of the total group, percentile distances near the median with its high concentration of cases will encompass a much smaller raw-score difference than the same percentile distance farther from the median. Hence the 15 points of raw-score difference between the 5th and 10th percentiles may shrink to 5 points of difference between the 40th and 45th.

These distortions make it difficult to use percentiles for profiling and other comparisons of a student's preformance on two or more tests. To overcome the limitations in test interpretation resulting from the inequality of percentiles, more and more test publishers are turning to some type of standard score for norming.

Computing Percentiles.   To expedite test interpretation, one may want to compute percentiles for a given group. Their computation is almost identical with the procedures for computing the median (which is the 50th percentile).

The formula for computing percentiles from a grouped frequency distribution is:*

$$P_x = l + \left(\frac{P_r N - \Sigma fb}{fw} \right) i$$

where P_x = the desired percentile.

Thus if the 75th percentile is desired, P_x = .75; if the 40th percentile is desired, P_x = .40. The other symbols have the same meaning as in the formula for the median.

As noted earlier, a grouped frequency table—once it is properly prepared—can be used for computing most of the elementary statistics a counselor might need for that set of scores. However, the computation of percentiles is made easier by adding to the table a column showing progressive accumulation of

Table 7-1. Computation of Percentiles from a Grouped Frequency Distribution

cf	X	f	d	fd
250	95–99	2	7	14
248	90–94	3	6	18
245	85–89	5	5	25
240	80–84	10	4	40
230	75–79	15	3	45
215	70–74	22	2	44
193	65–69	38	1	38
155	60–64	55	0	0
100	55–59	32	−1	−32
68	50–54	28	−2	−56
40	45–49	17	−3	−51
23	40–44	14	−4	−56
9	35–39	5	−5	−25
4	30–34	4	−6	−24
	$N = 250$			$\Sigma fd = -20$

frequencies. This is called a *cf (cumulative frequency) column;* it is shown at the left in Table 7–1, which uses the hypothetical Oakwood High School data.

The following steps show how one would go about finding the 25th percentile for the Oakwood High School data given in Table 7–1.

1. Multiply N by the desired percentile (converted to a decimal) to determine the class in which this percentile falls. For the Oakwood group, N is 250 and the desired percentile is 25. The product of .25 $\times$ 250 is 62.5; the *cf* column indicates that the score value of the individual ranking 62.5 from the bottom is found within the class 50–54, so it is thus established that P_{25} lies between 49.5 and 54.5.

2. Determine the necessary values for the formula:

$$P_{25}N = 62.5$$
$$\Sigma fb = 40$$
$$fw = 28$$
$$i = 5$$

3. Insert the values in the formula and perform the indicated computations:

$$P_{25} = 49.5 + \left(\frac{62.5 - 40}{28}\right)5$$
$$= 49.5 + \frac{22.5 \times 5}{28}$$
$$= 49.5 + 4.02$$
$$= 53.52 \text{ or, rounded, } 54$$

Deciles and Quartiles

Chase (1984) described deciles and quartiles as follows:

Two kinds of figures besides percentiles are also frequently used to show relative standing in a group. These are *deciles* and *quartiles,* both of which are similar to, and indeed can be read from, percentile tables. Deciles are points that divide the distribution of raw scores into segments of 10 percent each. Thus, the first decile D_1 would be that point on the distribution below which 10 percent of the cases fall, D_2 the point below which 20 percent of the cases fall, etc. Deciles can be computed in the same manner as percentiles, since D_1 is P_{10}, D_2 is P_{20}, etc.

Deciles, like percentiles, are points on a scale. Therefore, a score can be between the third and the fourth deciles, i.e., in the fourth lowest 10 percent of the group, but it cannot be *in* the third decile, since that decile is only a point on the scale.

Quartiles divide the distribution of raw scores into segments of 25 percent each. Thus, the first quartile, Q_1 is the point that cuts off the lowest 25 percent, Q_2 the lowest 50 percent of the group (what is another name for this point?), and Q_3 the lowest 75 percent of the distribution.

It should be emphasized, however, that deciles and quartiles, like percentiles, are *points* along the scale. They are not *segments* of that scale. It is wrong to say that case X *is in the third quartile* or something similar. This is an error because the third quartile is only a point on the scale. (p. 77)

Standard Scores

Standard scores have become increasingly popular with standardized test developers. A *standard score* expresses a person's distance from the mean in terms of the standardized deviation of the distribution. For example, let us return to Kathy, Paul, and Nancy and their scores on a test.

Mean of the test takers 75
Standard deviation   15
Kathy's score   90
Paul's score   65
Nancy's score   45

Using the formula $\dfrac{X(\text{raw score}) - M(\text{mean})}{SD(\text{standard deviation})}$, the following standard scores are obtained:

$$\text{Kathy:} \quad \frac{90 - 75}{15} = +1.0$$

$$\text{Paul:} \quad \frac{65 - 75}{15} = -0.7$$

$$\text{Nancy:} \quad \frac{45 - 75}{15} = -2.0$$

Because both decimal points and plus and minus signs may be confusing or easily misplaced, they can be transformed into a more convenient form by multiplying each standard score with some constant. For example, if we multiply these scores by 10, we have $+10, -7$, and -20. We can then eliminate the plus and minuses by adding a constant of 100. Thus, Kathy's score becomes 110, Paul's 93, and Nancy's 80. An example of this practice may be noted on the Scholastic Aptitude Test (SAT) of the College Entrance Examination Board, which adjusts standard scores to a mean of 500 and a SD of 100. Thus, a standard score of -2 on this test would be $(500 - 200) = 300$.

Stanines

Another variation for normalizing standard scores was developed by the United States Air Force in World War II. The name *stanine* is a contraction of standard nine, a nine-point scale having a mean of five and a standard deviation of two. The percentages of a normal distribution that fall within each of the nine stanines are as follows:

Stanine	1	2	3	4	5	6	7	8	9
Percentage	4	7	12	17	20	17	12	7	4

Relationships among various types of test scores and the normal curve may be noted in Figure 7–3.

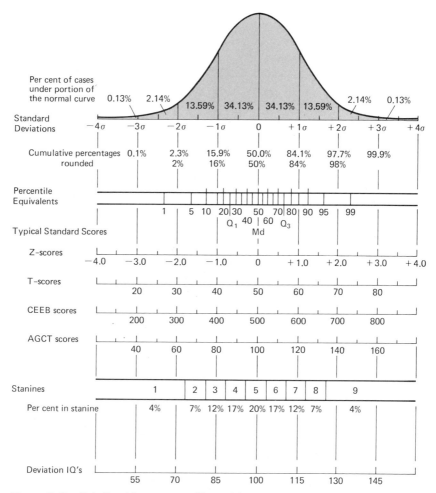

Figure 7–3. Relationships among different types of test scores in a normal distribution. *(Thorndike and Hagen, 1977, p. 133.)*

Norms

Armies over the centuries have had a favorite expression of the soldiers in the ranks—*snafu* (situation normal—all fouled up). We label persons as normal or abnormal if they deviate from our concept of normalcy, and we use such expressions as "he would normally do this," or "under normal conditions you can expect that . . . " The term *norm* or *normal* is a popular one that most persons use frequently to denote the expected, or that which can be reasonably anticipated. The concept of normal or norm as utilized in standardized testing terminology also implies normal or average performance on a given test. Norms are derived during the process of standardizing a test. As a basis for determining the norms, a test is administered to a sample (usually large) that is representative of the population for whom the test is designed. This group then comprises the standardization sample to establish the norms for the test. These norms reflect not only the average performances, but also the relative frequency of the varying degrees of deviation below and above the average.

Age Norms

The use of *age norms* or standards is a fairly popular one in the nonscientific sense. We often suggest that Joey is as big as a ten-year-old or Janie has the vocabulary of a six-year-old. The use of this concept in reporting standardized testing results became popular when the term *mental age* was used during the translations and adaptations of the original Binet scales. From this initial usage, age norms were frequently used to measure any trait that showed progressive change with age. For example, in physical development, it would be relatively simple to prepare norms for the height or weight of growing children by years. In testing, age norms represent the test performance of persons grouped and normed according to their chronological age. This type of score is more likely to be noted in the reporting of achievement tests, especially in the elementary school grades. There are two shortcomings to this concept of scoring and reporting results. First, there is a lack of agreement regarding when children should be introduced to certain basic academic subjects and at what rates, and what comprehension level should normally be expected in these subjects. Also, age norms assume uniform growth from year to year, an assumption of questionable validity.

Grade Norms

Grade norms are similar to age norms inasmuch as they are based on the average score earned by students at a specific grade level. Again, grade norms are popular for reporting achievement test results in terms of grade equivalents. This method of reporting standardized test results, however, suffers from the same shortcomings as do age norms and are more readily viewed as suggesting standards to which teachers should aspire. Table 7–2 contrasts the main type of norms for educational and psychological tests.

Table 7–2.   Main Types of Norms for Educational and Psychological Tests

Type of Norm	Type of Comparison	Type of Group
Age norms	Individual matched to groups whose performance he equals.	Successive age groups.
Grade norms	Same as above.	Successive grade groups.
Percentile norms	Percent of group surpassed by individual.	Single age or grade group to which individual belongs.
Standard score norms	Number of standard deviations individual falls above or below average of group.	Same as above.

Source: Thorndike & Hagen, 1977, p. 117.

Selecting a Test—What Criteria?

The numbers and variety of standardized tests available to counselors and other users today require a recognition and application of appropriate criteria in test selection. Furthermore, much of the criticism of standardized testing over the years has focused on poorly designed instruments and poorly prepared users, implying the need of criteria for both. Certainly, there are clinical as well as research-based reasons for concern with the trustworthiness of the data produced by our assessment devices. According to Cone (1981):

> Important decisions about clients must not be significantly influenced by random error or factors which might lead to atypical performance on a particular assessment occasion. As Cronbach (1970) has noted, erroneous decisions resulting from faulty measurement can irreparably harm an individual client or the larger community. Similarly, in the research use of assessment procedures, accurate measurement is essential for appropriate conclusions concerning relationships among variables. (p. 39)

Validity

Validity is traditionally defined as the degree to which an instrument measures what it claims to measure or is used to measure. For example, does the Whiffenpoof Mechanical Aptitude test really measure one's aptitude for mechanical activities, as claimed, or does it simply reflect one's previous experiences in the areas being tested? Or to raise a question of traditional controversy, do I.Q. tests really measure basic or native intelligence, or do they more appropriately reflect one's cultural and educational experiences? In establishing validity, one must note the appropriateness of test or interview questions and of situational samples to the evaluation objectives. Since it is impossible to include all possible questions or situations in an evaluation tool, those selected for inclusion must be representative of the content areas or behavioral patterns being assessed and must be appropriate for the individual under study and for the given circumstances. When an instrument meets these conditions, it is said to have *content* validity.

When the foregoing types of validity do not or cannot provide sufficient evidence of a test's validity, its *construct* validity may be cited. Construct validity pertains to the adequacy of the theory or concept underlying a specific instrument. In other words, it involves logically ascertaining the psychological attributes that account for variations in test scores or other derived data. Construct validity is reported in terms of the kinds of responses the test should elicit, and the ways in which those responses should be interpreted on the basis of logical inferences about the behavior the test is designed to appraise.

Reliability

The second major criterion to be applied in standardized test selection is *reliability*. Reliability represents the consistency with which a test will obtain the same results from the same population but on different occasions. An instrument's reliability enables a counselor or other user to determine the degrees to which predictions based on the established consistency of the test can be made. Two techniques are popularly used to establish reliability. One is the test-retest method. When this method is used, timing between the tests is of crucial importance because growth or decline in performance could occur if the interval is too long, whereas recall of original test items might occur if the interval is too short. A second approach for determining reliability is by establishing an instrument's internal consistency. This consistency is established by comparing persons' responses to the odd-numbered questions with the consistency of their responses to the even-numbered questions.

Practicality

A third important, but often overlooked, criterion in the selection of a standardized instrument is that of *practicality*. First and foremost of the practical considerations is whether or not trained personnel are available to administer, score, if necessary, and interpret the particular standardized test under consideration. The importance of users' understanding the fine points of interpretation cannot be overemphasized. A second and not unimportant practical consideration is the cost of the instrument and accompanying materials. The expense of scoring is included in this consideration. Additionally, many standardized tests can only be used for one testing, so replacement costs may become another factor. Time required for administration is also a practical consideration, especially, but not exclusively, in school settings. Many school administrators prefer, even insist, that any group standardized test be one that may be administered within a normal class period in order to keep disruptions at a minimum. This may be carrying practicality a bit too far, although time is a practical consideration in test selection. While a recent publication date is frequently a validity criterion, it may be a practical consideration as well, when familiarity of content is important.

Types of Standardized Tests

Having briefly examined statistical concepts, methods of scoring, and criteria for the selection of standardized tests, let us now proceed to examine the specific areas for which standardized tests are available. These include aptitude, achievement, interest, and personality testing. There is admittedly some overlap in these categories, especially in interest and personality, but let us examine them as discrete, though not exclusive, areas for the classification of standardized tests. This discussion will focus on group standardized tests. Although recognizing the value of individual tests and that counselors and psychologists in a variety of nonschool settings frequently use individual tests, beginning counselors, especially in educational settings, work almost exclusively with group tests.

Intelligence or Aptitude?

The terms *aptitude* and *intelligence* are often used synonymously. However, in the discussion of standardized tests, one should examine the subtle differences that distinguish measures of intelligence from measures of aptitude. One distinction is that intelligence tests tend to provide a broad measure of overall or general ability, primarily related to one's potential for learning, whereas aptitude measures tend to focus more narrowly on specific factors. Mehrens and Lehmann (1984) noted:

> The distinction between the terms "aptitude" and "intelligence" is not at all clear, but some distinctions have been made on two separate bases. One distinction that has been made is whether the measure we obtain is considered a *general* measure. If so, the test is frequently called an intelligence test. If the test measures *multiple* or *specific* factors, it is termed an aptitude test. Thus, we might conceptualize different measures of intelligence (aptitude) as lying on a continuum, with global measures falling at one end and specific measures at the other. At some point along the continuum we could arbitrarily change the label of the construct we are measuring, from intelligence to aptitude. Although this schema has been suggested by some, it certainly is not universally followed. It does present some difficulties, because some tests are considered measures of a general factor, yet report subscores.
>
> Another distinction between the meaning of the two terms has a historical basis. During the time intelligence tests were first being developed, psychologists thought of intelligence as being an innate characteristic not subject to change. This assumption is invalid. However, the term "intelligence" unfortunately still connotes complete innateness to some people. To avoid the implications of innateness, many test makers prefer to use the term "aptitude." Because these aptitude tests are most useful in predicting future school success, some have suggested that the phrase *scholastic aptitude tests* is the most honest and descriptive. Others prefer to refer to all such tests as measures of learning ability. (p. 372)

Intelligence Testing

The most popular area of aptitude or ability testing is the category that includes tests purporting to evaluate general academic ability, mental ability, and intelligence. Of these subsets, intelligence or IQ testing is the oldest and most controversial. Much of this controversy has centered around the various views of what constitutes intelligence, what influences it—heredity versus environment—and whether intelligence changes or not. These controversies have in recent generations led to some renaming with more popularly accepted labels such as academic ability, mental maturity, scholastic ability, or academic aptitude tests. Brown (1976–1977) pointed out that

> initially, the administrative usefulness of intelligence tests made them attractive to a great many institutions in our society, and to schools particularly. Their practical success reinforced the public's misperception of them. Most intelligence tests, after all, have been validated on school performance. They have therefore been good predictors of academic success in our school systems. They were hailed as a major advance over the much more subjective teacher's rating, which was more susceptible to bias

and error. They also provided a tool for identifying children who would probably suffer failure in the regular system of instruction but who, once identified, could undertake school programs better tailored to their educational needs (p. 17)

On the other hand, Beck (1976–1977) believed that

the most fundamental problem of general intelligence judgments is that they lead us to overlook important differences in *types* of intellectual ability and hence important distinctions between individuals who differ in the extent to which they have various intellectual abilities. (p. 29)

Beck went on to argue that other shortcomings of general intelligence assessment are that different people arrive at the same end by different intellectual means; the importance of intellectual abilities in living life well has probably been exaggerated; there has been a tendency to link judgments about intelligence with judgments about human worth, and finally, there has been a strong tendency to overlook the cultural and value relativity of intelligence judgments.

The first intelligence tests were designed for individual administering by a Frenchman, Alfred Binet, and, in the early 1900s, several American versions were developed. The most popular of these, the Stanford-Binet, based on the work of Lewis Terman at Stanford University, was published in 1916. This test has remained popular in the decades following with the most recent revisions reflected in the 1973 edition (Houghton Mifflin Company). The other popular individually administered intelligence test is the various Wechsler scales.

One of the most popular group intelligence tests over the years has been the Otis or, as currently labeled, the Otis-Lennon Mental Abilities Test (Harcourt Brace Jovanovich, 1969). The first Otis test appeared in 1918 as the Otis Group Intelligence Scale and later achieved great popularity in both industry and education as the Otis-Quick Scoring Mental Abilities Tests. The tests require 20 or 30 minutes testing time and both hand-scored and machine-scorable editions are currently available in two forms and six grade levels.

Two other popular group intelligence tests are the Lorge-Thorndike and the Henmon-Nelson Tests of Mental Ability. The Lorge-Thorndike intelligence test is available in two forms for grades 3 to 13. It provides both verbal and nonverbal batteries for those grades in a single reusable booklet. The verbal battery is made up of five subtests, using only verbal items: vocabulary, verbal classification, sentence completion, arithmetic reasoning, and verbal analogy. The nonverbal battery uses items that are either pictorial or numerical. The three subtests involved are pictorial classification, pictorial analogy, and numerical relationships. The tests in this battery yield an estimate of scholastic aptitude that is not dependent upon an ability to read. The working times are verbal battery, 35 minutes; nonverbal battery, 27 minutes.

The Henmon-Nelson Test of Mental Ability is available in two editions: Form 1 for grades 3 through 12, and a primary battery for kindergarten through grade 2. The primary battery is normatively integrated with Form 1, permitting school systems to use the Henmon-Nelson tests throughout the entire kindergarten-through-grade 12 range.

Form 1 for grades 3 through 12 has three levels (three to six, six to nine, and nine to twelve), consisting of 90 items presented in order of increasing difficulty. Form 1 of the Henmon-Nelson Tests of Mental Ability was standardized in the fall of 1972 on a national sample of 35,000 subjects in grades 3 through 12.

The primary battery for kindergarten through grade 2 consists of three separate subtests: a listening test (general information, 30 items); a picture vocabulary test (33 items); and a size and number test (23 items). These short subtests measure simple verbal and quantitative skills considered important in assessing readiness for schoolwork.

Standardization in grade 2 was carried out concurrently with the norming of the Henmon-Nelson in grades 3 through 12 during the fall of 1972. For grades kindergarten and 1, standardization was done in early 1973 on a sample of approximately 5,000 pupils drawn from the same schools that participated in the grade 2 through 12 norming program.

Counselors should also be aware that many IQ tests have for years been suspect of cultural bias—a bias that would discriminate against minorities and populations in special environments. It would therefore appear appropriate to approach the use of intelligence tests with extreme caution, *if, in fact, they are to be used at all.*

Aptitude Tests

Aptitude may be defined as a trait that characterizes an individual's ability to perform in a given area or to acquire the learning necessary for performance in a given area. It presumes an inherent or native ability that can be developed to its maximum through learning or other experiences. However, it cannot be expanded beyond this certain point, even by learning. Although that may be a debatable concept, it is stated here as a basis on which aptitude tests are developed. In theory, then, an aptitude test measures the potential of one to achieve in a given activity or to learn to achieve in that activity.

Aptitude tests may potentially be used by counselors and others because (a) they may identify potential abilities of which the person is not aware; (b) they may encourage the development of special or potential abilities of a given person; (c) they may provide information to assist a person in making educational and career decisions or other choices between competing alternatives; (d) they may serve as an aid in predicting the level of academic or vocational success a person might anticipate; and (e) they may be useful in grouping persons with similar aptitudes for developmental and other educational purposes. It should be emphasized that these are *potential* advantages only and will accrue only under optimal conditions, which include initially the use of appropriate and proper measurement instruments relevant to the client's needs.

While we usually anticipate that a person is likely to demonstrate considerable differences across a range of aptitudes, we should also be alert to the possibility that a person will not demonstrate or "measure" at the same level for a given aptitude every time. In other words, a track star may run the 100-yard dash in 10 seconds one day and the same distance under the same conditions in 10.4 seconds the next day. Aptitude measures are thus actuarial rather than absolute.

Special Aptitude Tests

Special aptitude tests usually refer to those tests that seek to measure a person's potential ability to perform or to acquire proficiency in a specific occupation or other type of activity. Tests that measure special aptitudes are sometimes referred to as single aptitude tests or component ability tests because they only secure a measure for one specific aptitude or a single special ability. Tests of special aptitude have generally declined in popularity as aptitude batteries have increased in popularity. Counselors most frequently use standardized tests to measure a single aptitude in areas of mechanical, clerical, or artistic abilities. Single aptitude tests have also been developed for use in various graduate and professional schools. Aptitude tests are also available for particular school subjects, especially in the areas of mathematics and foreign languages.

Vocational Aptitude Batteries

Multiple aptitude tests are an outgrowth of factorial studies of intelligence. Anastasi (1982) discussed the objective of factor analysis:

> The principle objective of factor analysis is to simplify the description of data by reducing the number of necessary variables, or dimensions. Thus, if we find that five factors are sufficient to account for all the common variance in a battery of 20 tests, we can for most purposes substitute five scores for the original 20 without sacrificing any essential information. The usual practice is to retain from among the original tests those providing the best measures of each of the factors. (p. 358)

According to Hopkins and Stanley (1981)

> The basic rationale underlying these tests is that various academic and occupational pursuits require different patterns of aptitude and, hence, a decision in which a profile of aptitudes is available should be more appropriate than a decision based on a single "omnibus" score. (p. 369)

These batteries typically consist of a series of subtests related in varying combinations to a series of occupations or occupationally related activities. The major advantages of batteries over single aptitude tests are (a) convenience in administration as a result of having in one package a test that can be used to measure potential in a variety of activities; (b) the norming of all of the battery's subtests on the same population, thus yielding comparable subtest norms; and (c) the opportunity to compare potential in a wide variety of areas with one test. The oldest and most widely used of these multiple aptitude batteries are the General Aptitude Test Battery (GATB), used by the United States Employment Services, and the Differential Aptitude Battery (DAT). The Flanigan Aptitude Classification Test (FACT), the Academic Promise Test (APT), and the Armed Services Vocational Aptitude Battery (ASVAB) are also extensively used. A brief examination of the characteristics of these tests may help you further understand the nature of aptitude batteries.

General Aptitude Test Battery.   The General Aptitude Test Battery, known by its initials as the GATB is administered through the United States Employment

Service. However, it is available to nonprofit institutions such as schools for counseling purposes. As may be seen in Figure 7–4, this battery has twelve subtests, which yield nine scores. It should also be noted that these aptitudes are not all independent as some of the subtests are used in determining more than one aptitude score. As might be anticipated, this battery is primarily used in career counseling for job placement for individuals 16 years of age and older.

Differential Aptitude Test. The Differential Aptitude Test consists of a battery of eight subtests. This is designed primarily for students in grades 8 through 12 and consists of eight subtests: verbal reasoning, numerical ability, abstract reasoning, clerical speed and accuracy, mechanical reasoning, space relations, language usage-spelling, and language usage-grammar. This battery has for many years been one of the most popular in common use in schools as a means of assisting counseling for vocational and educational decision making.

Flanigan Aptitude Classification Test. The Flanigan Aptitude Classification Test is one of the more time-consuming multiple aptitude tests, requiring approximately 8 hours to administer. This comprehensive aptitude test battery

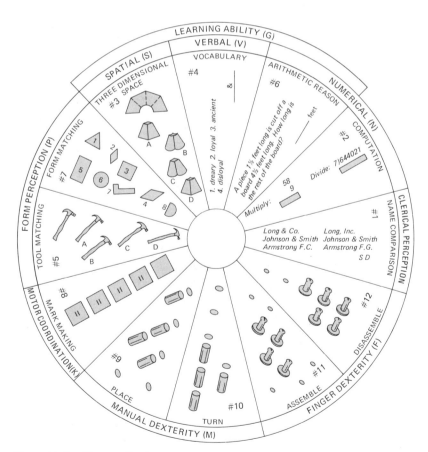

Figure 7–4. Nine aptitudes measured by twelve tests in the general aptitude test battery B1002. *(Indiana State Employment Service.)*

was based on the job elements approach basic to performance in a wide range of job classifications. The battery consists of 19 subtests:

1. Inspection.
2. Mechanics.
3. Tables.
4. Reasoning.
5. Vocabulary.
6. Assembly.
7. Judgment and comprehension.
8. Components.
9. Planning.
10. Memory.
11. Arithmetic.
12. Ingenuity.
13. Scales.
14. Expression.
15. Precision.
16. Alertness.
17. Coordination.
18. Patterns.
19. Coding.

The results of these tests are profiled for various occupational areas. Counselors may use these results as an aid in job placement or career and educational planning.

The Armed Services Vocational Aptitude Battery (ASVAB). Since 1972 approximately 1 million high school students per year have taken the Armed Services Vocational Aptitude Battery, a service that is available to local high schools at no cost or obligation to either the school or student. This battery, also used throughout the military services and the Department of Defense, consists of twelve tests, namely: general information, numerical operations, attention to detail, word knowledge, arithmetic reasoning, space perception, mathematics knowledge, electronics information, mechanical comprehension, general science, shop information, and automotive information. Approximately 3 hours administration time is needed for the current edition of the battery.

The reporting format for the ASVAB is described in the ASVAB Mini-Guide:

> Within 30 days after testing, the counselor will receive a computer-printed ASVAB score sheet for each student tested. The printout has two sections. The counselor's section can be removed and maintained for future reference. It contains the student's percentile scores by grade and by sex within grade on each of the composites, his raw scores on each composite, and his raw scores on each of the tests. The counselor's section also contains interpretative information and an explanation of the make-up of the composites.
>
> The student section of the printout is a personal copy for the individual who took the ASVAB. It has a shaded graph with a display of the student's composite scores shown as percentile scores by grade and by sex within grade. It also has the student's raw scores on the six composites. On the back of the student's section there is information to assist students in interpreting their scores.
>
> The last computer printout in the school package is a page of summary data for the school. The data contain overall means, standard deviations, and sums of the squares for each composite and test. (p. 11)

Scholastic Aptitude Tests

Scholastic or academic aptitude tests propose to measure a person's potential for performing in academic situations. Such tests as those that constitute the

SCAT and SAT batteries have much merit insofar as predicting academic performance at higher educational levels. However, more appropriate labels would be academic achievement or academic predictions, because they tend to predict future academic achievement on the basis of past learning rather than on the basis of native ability.

A popular academic aptitude test for the high school level is the advanced level of the School and College Ability Tests (SCAT III), designed for grades 9 to 12. This test, which requires 40 minutes testing time, yields a verbal, quantitative, and total score. In line with current trends in testing theory, Anastasi (1982) noted:

> SCAT undertakes to measure developed abilities. This is simply an explicit admission of what is more or less true of all intelligence tests, namely that test scores reflect the nature and amount of schooling the individual has received rather than measuring "capacity" independently of relevant prior experiences. Accordingly, SCAT draws freely on word knowledge and arithmetic processes learned in the appropriate school grades. In this respect, SCAT does not really differ from other academic intelligence tests, especially those designed for the high school and college levels; it only makes overt a condition sometimes unrecognized in other tests. (p. 313)
>
> For college-bound high school students, another application of SCAT scores is of particular interest. SCAT scores obtained in the 9th, 10th, and 11th grades can be used to predict the student's chances of scoring at or above specified levels on the College Board's Scholastic Aptitude Test (SAT). (p. 315)

Two popular tests used for the admission, placement, and counseling of college students are the Scholastic Aptitude Test (SAT) of the College Entrance Examinations Board and the American College Testing Program (ACT). The SAT measures skills in two areas, verbal and mathematics, and is administered on special dates at established centers. The SAT is restricted to the testing program administered by the College Entrance Examination Board on behalf of member colleges. The American College Testing Program (ACT), introduced in 1959, is also used by many institutions of higher education. The ACT consists of four tests: English usage, mathematical usage, social studies reading, and natural sciences reading.

Anastasi (1982) made a point frequently stated by experienced high school and college admissions counselors, noting that tests such as the SAT and the ACT

> are not intended as substitutes for high school grades in the prediction of college achievement. High school grades can predict college grades as well as most tests or slightly better. When test scores are combined with high school grades, however, the prediction of college performance is significantly improved. In part, this improvement stems from the fact that a uniform, objective test serves as a corrective for the variability in grading standards among different high schools. Moreover, such tests are not subject to the influence of irrelevant variables and possible personal biases that may enter into the assignment of course grades. (p. 318)

Achievement Tests

Achievement measurement is an area of standardized testing to which most students have been subject, not on just a single occasion or two, but probably numerous times during their educational programs. Of all the areas of standardized testing, achievement tests are the most popular in terms of numbers administered to numbers of different individuals. For example, a study reported through the North Central Association of Colleges and Schools (1979) indicated, on the average, that students graduating from secondary schools in that association would have taken standardized achievement tests twelve times during their 12 years of schooling. This study also reported that nearly 100 percent of the school systems within the associations' nineteen state region administered achievement tests at some point or points during their pupils' educational programs. Despite the widespread popularity of achievement tests, they are not infrequently confused with other measures, especially aptitude tests. Sax (1980) appropriately notes that *achievement tests* may be defined as those designed to "measure the degree of student learning in specific curriculum areas common to most schools" (p. 438). This may also include such areas as mathematics, English usage, and reading.

Achievement tests are used to provide measures of (a) the amount of learning, (b) the rate of learning, (c) comparisons with others or with achievement of self in other areas, (d) level of learning in subareas, (e) strengths and weaknesses in a subject-matter area, and, in some instances, (f) predictions of future learning. Because of their extensive use and the relatively easy task of identifying appropriate content measures, achievement tests are among the best-designed standardized measures available to counselors. There are, however, certain considerations that users of achievement tests must keep in mind if such instruments are to be used appropriately by counselors and others.

First, it is important that the content of the test is relevant to the subject-matter content the student has experienced. In other words, the test should measure what the student has had the opportunity to learn. According to Hopkins and Stanley (1981)

> The critical type of validity for achievement tests is content validity, sometimes called content relevance. Does the test reflect the reading or arithmetic objectives at a given grade level? Does the math test reflect the related curriculum? Ideally, the items on an achievement test should be a representative sample of the content and process objectives of a curriculum. (p. 387)

Further, it is important that the emphasis within the test, in terms of topical areas covered, is appropriate for the emphasis the student has experienced in the subject-matter class. Additionally, the level of difficulty of the test items must be appropriate for the age-grade level being tested. A final consideration, one that bears repeating, is the norming sample on which the test has been standardized.

If this sample is representative of the general population appropriate to the age-grade level being tested, comparisons with this general population may be appropriate. If the population of the sample is similar to the population being tested, that would usually be desirable. On the other hand, if the norming population is considerably dissimilar, it may not be an appropriate group against which to compare the group being tested.

One of the popular achievement test batteries is the Iowa Test of Basic Skills. This series is available in two forms for grades 3 through 8. Depending on which level and form are used, testing time is 60 to 80 minutes. The five major areas tested by this battery are vocabulary, reading comprehension, language skills, work-study skills, and mathematical skills. The test developers point out that this battery measures pupils' abilities to use and acquire skills, for no test or subtest is concerned with only the repetition or identification of facts.

Related to the Iowa Tests of Basic Skills are the Tests of Achievement and Proficiency. These tests are normed for grades 9 through 12 and consist of six subtests of 40 minutes each. The subtests are social studies, science, reading comprehension, mathematics, written expression, and using sources of information. Standard scores, grade equivalent scores, national percentile ranks, normal curve equivalent scores, stanines, and large city norms are available for all tests and for the composites. Local norms are available from the Riverside Scoring Service and the Riverside Publishing Company in Chicago.

The Metropolitan Achievement Test consists of eight battery levels for measuring performance from the beginning of kindergarten through grade 12. This battery consists of single tests for reading comprehension, mathematics, language, social studies, and science. The basic battery consists of the first three tests. The complete battery utilizes all five tests. This battery is available from the Psychological Corporation, a subsidiary of Harcourt Brace Jovanovich, Inc., New York.

Interest Inventories

In a discussion on career planning, one might hear such statements as "I've always been interested in nursing"; "The thought of teaching really turns me off"; "I know I'd enjoy selling cars"; or "Being a flight attendant would be the most exciting career I could imagine!"

Such pronouncements of career interests are common among adolescents and young adults. Equally common are statements of uncertainty and frustration regarding career choices, such as "I wish somebody would just tell me what career I should enter"; "I can't make up my mind between engineering or coaching"; or "I'm really upset because I can't think of any job I'm interested in."

While interest testing has, for many years, been a popular psychometric assist to adolescents and young adults in career planning, recent years have seen an increased need in interest measurement for older populations considering midlife or other career changes.

Discussions and other explorations of interests are valuable aids for career planning and related career counseling and guidance; even a simple listing in hierarchical order of possible careers may be as valid in some instances as standardized, inventoried interests. Super and Crites suggested "four approaches that can be used to ascertain individual interests: (1) direct questioning; (2) direct observation; (3) tested interests; and (4) interest inventories" (Mehrens and Lehmann, 1978, p. 466).

However, there are certain values that may result from the use of standardized interest inventories, of which counselors, teachers, and others who assist youths and adults in career and related decision making should be aware.

These potential values include:

1. A comparative and contrasting inventory of a person's interests.
2. Verification of a person's claimed interest or tentative choice.
3. Identification of previously unrecognized interests.
4. Identification of the possible level of interests for various (usually career) activities.
5. Contrast of interests with abilities and achievements.
6. Identification of problems associated with career decision making (no areas of adequate interest; high stated interest versus low inventoried interest in a career field).
7. A stimulus for career exploration or career counseling.

If, however, these values are to be realized, interest tests or inventories should, according to Holland (1975), ideally have many positive characteristics, such as:

1. Provide occupational forecasts of satisfaction and achievement. Although any information about a person or a vocation may be helpful, information with high predictive validity is especially helpful.
2. Provide the full range of vocational options by both type and level. All inventories fail to suggest all possible vocational options, even for the most favored persons in our culture (tall, white, college-educated, Protestant males, without physical or psychological difficulties).
3. Provide information or influences that are stable or reliable from one time to the next.
4. Provide an experience that is effective. Interest inventories should stimulate vocational exploration, reassure people about wise choices, upset people about unwise choices, provide long-range perspectives, provide new information (new to the person), such as more vocational alternatives, support people resisting destructive cultural forces, and promote self-reliance and understanding.
5. Provide information that is in accord with a person's life history, current circumstances, and personal potential, rather than factors such as age, race, sex, and social status.
6. Be based on a useful theory of vocational behavior, including a classification system to organize all possible alternatives. Theoretically based as opposed to empirical inventories provide a more explicit rationale that is more amenable to public examination and revision.
7. Include auxiliary materials to increase positive influence and avoid negative side effects. For example, brochures that summarize information about an inventory's strengths and weaknesses should be included with every test booklet.
8. Be oriented toward the most common occupations and to some degree toward the spectrum of the future world of work.
9. Be adaptable to new educational and occupational information. To some extent, the easier an inventory is to revise, the more likely it is that revisions will occur.
10. Be relatively resistant to client or counselor abuse and distortion. The more complete and explicit an inventory is and the more independent of the vagaries of counselors and clients, the less likely it is that its positive effects can be twisted by human hands and minds. Likewise, an inventory that lends itself to simplicity of interpretation and scoring should be less vulnerable to abuse than one that does not. (pp. 22–23)

The popular development of interest tests evolved from studies indicating that people in a given occupation seemed to be characterized by a cluster of common interests that distinguish them from people in other occupations. It was also noted that these differences in interests extended beyond those associated with job performance and that persons in a given occupation also had different nonvocational interests—hobbies and recreational activities that could distinguish them from those in other occupations. Thus, interest inventories could be designed to assess one's interests and relate them to those of various occupational areas. Two of the earlier and more popular of these inventories, still extensively used today, were the Kuder Preference Records and the Strong Vocational Interest Blanks, currently designated as the Strong-Campbell Interest Inventories.

The Kuder Preference Record is the original and most popular of the various Kuder interest inventories. It provides a series of interest items arranged in triads, from which the respondents choose the one they would like most and the one they would like least. The results are scored and profiled for the occupational areas of outdoor activities, mechanical, computational, scientific, persuasive, artistic, literary, music, social service, and clerical. Revision of the original preference record, the Kuder General Interest Survey, extends the use downward to the sixth grade by employing a simpler vocabulary that requires only a sixth-grade reading ability (the original version was usually considered appropriate for use in grades 9 through 12). The Kuder Occupational Interest Survey is still another version that provides scores showing similarities with occupational and college-level areas. This form differs from previous Kuder tests in expressing a person's score on each occupational scale as a correlation between his or her interest pattern and the pattern of a particular occupational group. The various Kuder inventories may be obtained from Science Research Associates, Inc., Chicago.

The Strong-Campbell Interest Inventory is a revision of the earlier forms of the Strong Vocational Interest Blank, which was first published in 1933:

> The SVIB introduced two principal procedures in the measurement of occupational interests. First, the items dealt with the respondent's liking or dislike for a wide variety of specific activities, objects, or types of persons that he or she commonly encountered in daily living. Second, the responses were empirically keyed for different occupations. (Anastasi, 1982, p. 536)

The various interest inventories have been suggested as usable with older adolescents and adults who may be considering higher level professional or skilled occupations. The Strong-Campbell Interest Inventory (SCII) can only be scored by computer. This later version contained 325 items grouped according to occupations, school subjects, activities, amusements, types of people, preference between activities, and personal characteristics. Results are displayed on a variety of scales (see Figure 7–5). For example, the six general occupational theme scales provide scores for realistic, investigative, artistic, social, enterprising, and conventional categories. The major and most popular scales for the Strong Vocational Interest series are the occupational scales, which, for SCII, profile scores for 124 occupations:

STRONG-CAMPBELL INTEREST INVENTORY OF THE
STRONG VOCATIONAL INTEREST BLANK

PAGE 1 PROFILE REPORT FOR: DATE TESTED:

ID: DATE SCORED:
AGE: SEX:

SPECIAL SCALES: ACADEMIC COMFORT
INTROVERSION-EXTROVERSION

TOTAL RESPONSES: INFREQUENT RESPONSES:

OCCUPATIONAL SCALES

STANDARD SCORES F M

VERY DISSIMILAR | DISSIMILAR | MODERATELY DISSIMILAR | MID-RANGE | MODERATELY SIMILAR | SIMILAR | VERY SIMILAR

REALISTIC

GENERAL OCCUPATIONAL THEME - R 30 40 50 60 70 F M

(CRS) RC	Marine Corps enlisted personnel	(CRS)	
RC RC	Navy enlisted personnel		
RC RC	Army officer		
RI RIC	Navy officer		
R R	Air Force officer		
(C) R	Air Force enlisted personnel	(C)	
R R	Police officer		
R R	Bus driver		
R R	Horticultural worker		
RC R	Farmer		
R RCS	Vocational agriculture teacher		
RI R	Forester		
(IR) RI	Veterinarian	(IR)	
RIS (SR)	Athletic trainer	(SR)	
RS R	Emergency medical technician		
RI RI	Radiologic technologist		
RI R	Carpenter		
RI R	Electrician		
RIA (ARI)	Architect	(ARI)	
RI RI	Engineer		

BASIC INTEREST SCALES (STANDARD SCORE)
AGRICULTURE F M
NATURE F M
ADVENTURE F M
MILITARY ACTIVITIES F M
MECHANICAL ACTIVITIES F M

INVESTIGATIVE

GENERAL OCCUPATIONAL THEME - I 30 40 50 60 70 F M

IRC IRC	Computer programmer		
IRC IRC	Systems analyst		
IRC IR	Medical technologist		
IR IR	R & D manager		
IR IR	Geologist		
IR (I)	Biologist	(I)	
IR IR	Chemist		
IR IR	Physicist		
IR (RI)	Veterinarian	(RI)	
IRS IR	Science teacher		
IRS IRS	Physical therapist		
IR IRS	Respiratory therapist		
IC IR	Medical technician		
IC IE	Pharmacist		
ISR (CSE)	Dietitian	(CSE)	
(SI) ISR	Nurse, RN	(SI)	
IR I	Chiropractor		
IR IR	Optometrist		
IR IR	Dentist		
I IA	Physician		
(IR) I	Biologist	(IR)	
I I	Mathematician		
IR I	Geographer		
I I	College professor		
IA IA	Psychologist		
IA IA	Sociologist		

BASIC INTEREST SCALES (STANDARD SCORE)
SCIENCE F M
MATHEMATICS F M
MEDICAL SCIENCE F M
MEDICAL SERVICE F M

ARTISTIC

GENERAL OCCUPATIONAL THEME - A 30 40 50 60 70 F M

AI AI	Medical illustrator		
A A	Art teacher		
A A	Artist, fine		
A A	Artist, commercial		
AE A	Interior decorator		
(RIA) ARI	Architect	(RIA)	
A A	Photographer		
A A	Musician		
AR (EA)	Chef	(EA)	
(E) AS	Beautician	(E)	
AE A	Flight attendant		
A A	Advertising executive		
A A	Broadcaster		
A A	Public relations director		
A A	Lawyer		
A AS	Public administrator		
A A	Reporter		
A A	Librarian		
AS AS	English teacher		
(SA) AS	Foreign language teacher	(SA)	

BASIC INTEREST SCALES (STANDARD SCORE)
MUSIC/DRAMATICS F M
ART F M
WRITING F M

CONSULTING PSYCHOLOGISTS PRESS
577 COLLEGE AVENUE
PALO ALTO, CA 94306

Figure 7–5. SVIB-SCII profile. (*Strong-Campell Intertest Inventory of the Strong Vocational Interest Blank, Form T325. Copyright © 1933, 1938, 1945, 1966, 1968, 1981, 1983, 1985 by the Board of Trustees of the Leland Stanford Junior University. All rights reserved. Printed and scored under license from Stanford University Press, Stanford, CA. Reproduced by special permission for the distributor Consulting Psychologists Press, acting for the publisher, Stanford University Press.*)

218

PAGE 2   **PROFILE REPORT FOR:**   **DATE TESTED:**

ID: **DATE SCORED:**
AGE: SEX:

OCCUPATIONAL SCALES

	STANDARD SCORES F / M	VERY DISSIMILAR	DISSIMILAR	MODERATELY DISSIMILAR	MID-RANGE	MODERATELY SIMILAR	SIMILAR	VERY SIMILAR

SOCIAL

GENERAL OCCUPATIONAL THEME - S   30 40 50 60 70   F M

BASIC INTEREST SCALES (STANDARD SCORE)

TEACHING — F / M

SOCIAL SERVICE — F / M

ATHLETICS — F / M

DOMESTIC ARTS — F / M

RELIGIOUS ACTIVITIES — F / M

F M	Occupational Scale	Score
SA (AS)	Foreign language teacher	(AS)
SA SA	Minister	
SA SA	Social worker	
S S	Guidance counselor	
S S	Social science teacher	
S S	Elementary teacher	
S S	Special education teacher	
SRI SAR	Occupational therapist	
SIA SAI	Speech pathologist	
SI (ISR)	Nurse, RN	(ISR)
SCI N/A	Dental hygienist	N/A
SC SC	Nurse, LPN	
[RIS] SR	Athletic trainer	(RIS)
SR SR	Physical education teacher	
SRE SE	Recreation leader	
SE SE	YWCA/YMCA director	
SEC SCE	School administrator	
SCE N/A	Home economics teacher	N/A

ENTERPRISING

GENERAL OCCUPATIONAL THEME - E   30 40 50 60 70   F M

BASIC INTEREST SCALES (STANDARD SCORE)

PUBLIC SPEAKING — F / M

LAW/POLITICS — F / M

MERCHANDISING — F / M

SALES — F / M

BUSINESS MANAGEMENT — F / M

F M	Occupational Scale	Score
E ES	Personnel director	
ES E	Elected public official	
ES ES	Life insurance agent	
EC E	Chamber of Commerce executive	
EC EC	Store manager	
N/A ECR	Agribusiness manager	N/A
EC EC	Purchasing agent	
EC E	Restaurant manager	
[AR] EA	Chef	(AR)
ECS E	Funeral director	
[CSE]ESC	Nursing home administrator	(CSE)
EC ER	Optician	
E E	Realtor	
E [AE]	Beautician	(AE)
E E	Florist	
EC E	Buyer	
EI EI	Marketing executive	
EIC ECI	Investments manager	

CONVENTIONAL

GENERAL OCCUPATIONAL THEME - C   30 40 50 60 70   F M

BASIC INTEREST SCALES (STANDARD SCORE)

OFFICE PRACTICES — F / M

F M	Occupational Scale	Score
C C	Accountant	
C C	Banker	
CE CE	IRS agent	
CES CES	Credit manager	
CES CES	Business education teacher	
[CS] CES	Food service manager	(CS)
[ISR] CSE	Dietitian	(ISR)
CSE (ESC)	Nursing home administrator	(ESC)
CSE CSE	Executive housekeeper	
CS [CES]	Food service manager	(CES)
CS N/A	Dental assistant	N/A
C N/A	Secretary	N/A
C (R)	Air Force enlisted personnel	(R)
CRS (RC)	Marine Corps enlisted personnel	(RC)
CRS CR	Army enlisted personnel	
CIR CIR	Mathematics teacher	

ADMINISTRATIVE INDEXES (RESPONSE %)

OCCUPATIONS	%	%	%
SCHOOL SUBJECTS	%	%	%
ACTIVITIES	%	%	%
LEISURE ACTIVITIES	%	%	%
TYPES OF PEOPLE	%	%	%
PREFERENCES	%	%	%
CHARACTERISTICS	%	%	%
ALL PARTS	%	%	%

CONSULTING PSYCHOLOGISTS PRESS
577 COLLEGE AVENUE
PALO ALTO, CA 94306

Figure 7–5. (cont.)

> Interpretations of SCII should be made only by persons with special training and
> supervised experience in assessing objective interest. Results can be faked by a sophis-
> ticated subject. Furthermore, the SCII remains applicable for use only with those
> persons who are oriented toward professional, semiprofessional, or managerial occu-
> pations that attract college graduates. For others, the relevance of the instrument is
> questionable. (Shertzer and Linden, 1979, p. 285)

The Strong-Campbell Interest Inventory may be obtained through the Stanford
University Press, Stanford, California.

The Ohio Vocational Interest Survey (OVIS) is one of a number of newer
interest inventories developed for use with high school students. This inventory
was developed after the model on which the Dictionary of Occupational Titles
is based (a cubistic model of data, people, and things). The OVIS is separated
into three parts: (a) a student questionnaire, (b) a local information survey, and
(c) the interest inventory. The OVIS reports its results on 24 scales. The Ohio
Vocational Interest Survey is available through Harcourt Brace Jovanovich,
Inc., New York.

Another approach to the assessment of career interests is the Self-Directed
Search (SDS). This instrument was developed by John Holland, whose hexag-
onal model of six occupational themes is represented in the six summary scores
of Realistic, Investigative, Artistic, Social, Enterprising, and Conventional. The
SDS is designed to be self-administered, self-scored, and self-interpreted. When
an individual completes the SDS he or she uses a summary code comprising
the types that rank first and second across all the subtests. Utilizing this code,
he or she refers to a Job Finder, which presents information about 456 jobs
listed in terms of two letter SDS codes. Once a person gets his or her lists of
careers that match a summary code, suggested next steps are listed for his or
her organized career planning. The Self-Directed Search is marketed by Consulting Psychologists Press, Palo Alto, California.

The Career Maturity Inventory, although not precisely an interest inventory,
has been designed to measure the maturity of attitudes and competencies that
are involved in career decision making. The attitude scale surveys five attitudinal clusters: (a) involvement in the career choice process, (b) orientation
toward work, (c) independence in decision making, (d) preference for career
choice factors, and (e) conceptions of the career choice process. In contrast, the
competency test measures the more cognitive variables involved in choosing an
occupation. The five parts of the competency test are (a) self-appraisal, (b) occupational information, (c) goal selection, (d) planning, and (e) problem solving.
The Career Maturity Inventory is available from McGraw-Hill Book Company,
New York.

Personality Tests

Of all the areas of standardized testing, none is more intriguing to the general
public, and perhaps to the counseling profession as well, as personality assessment. From the do-it-yourself personality test in the daily newspaper to sophisticated, projective techniques requiring highly specialized psychological train-

ing, personality testing represents a universal quest of the individual to understand what makes him or her and fellow human beings "tick." But personality testing is as complex as what it seeks to measure. Let us examine some of the questions or concerns that must be taken into consideration.

What is Personality?

Personality has been variously defined as follows:

> the visible aspects of one's character as it impresses others; a person as an embodiment of a collection of qualities; (Urdang, 1968, p. 990)
>   as the individual's unique pattern of traits; the pattern that distinguishes him as an individual and accounts for his unique and relatively consistent way of interacting with his environment. (Coleman, 1960, p. 75)

Thorpe (1960) presented definitions of personality classified into the following categories:

1. The *biosocial,* which points up the "social stimulus value" concept.
2. The *biophysical,* which emphasizes organic traits.
3. The *omnibus,* which endeavors to include everything of importance about the individual.
4. The *integrative,* which defines patterns and suggests personality as that which organizes various types of behavior into a congruent whole.
5. The *adjustment* concept, which assumes personality to be a reflection of the struggle to adjust.
6. The *uniqueness* view, which sees personality as the quality which sets each individual apart from all others.
7. The *core* or *essence* theory, in which personality to a degree is equated with the "what-a-man-really-is" concept, that is, what facets of personality are "most typical and deeply characteristic of the person." (p. 287)

You can readily discern the wide variations in viewpoints regarding this topic by asking in almost any group the question, "What is personality?" and noting the wide range of responses. It may be concluded that the concept of personality is a difficult one to treat with the precision usually associated with standardized tests. Thus, constructors of personality tests face the challenge of determining what workable definition of personality they will use and what aspect or aspects of that definition they will measure. Generally speaking, however, in conventional psychometric terminology, "personality tests are instruments for the measurement of emotional, motivational, interpersonal, and attitudinal characteristics, as distinguished from abilities." (Anastasi, 1982, p. 497)

What is "Normal" Personality?

This question will probably elicit a wide range of responses from the public. Most persons tend to view "normal" in terms of their own behavioral personality traits and values. Thus, an extremely extroverted person, viewed as normal by one group, may be viewed as "abnormal" by another group. Even if one is able to objectively identify norms for specific behavioral responses, one still must determine at what point the deviations from those norms become "abnormal."

Can Personality Be Measured?

This question has objectively been answered affirmatively by many authors of standardized personality measures and has further been affirmed by many practicing counselors, psychologists, and psychiatrists utilizing observation and other nonstandardized techniques. Some of the difficulties involved in obtaining accurate assessments are client-based and must be the concern of the test interpreter. They are:

1. The capability of a person to accurately analyze many aspects of his or her own personality is questionable. In some instances, the client may not possess the insight to respond accurately. Although the client's view of self is important, it may not be appropriate to the intent of the measuring instrument. In other instances, one must recognize that the individual's view of self can be distorted, can differ from the perceptions of others, and can be misleading to the test interpreter.
2. Some persons may deliberately falsify their responses. Sax (1980) noted that

> when an individual responds to a statement regarding some personality trait, his response is usually assumed to be either candid or deliberately deceptive. (p. 523)

Most often, deception occurs when a person responds in a manner that he or she views as more socially acceptable than perhaps his or her true response might be. For example, little children almost inevitably respond that they love their parents, even when they do not know them or when they actively dislike them. Also, one can anticipate that some respondents will project an ideal self rather than the real self in their answers. Some persons may respond as the friendly and popular person they wish they were, rather than the withdrawn individual with few friends they recognize themselves to be. The intimate nature of a question may dissuade the respondent from answering accurately. Most notable examples in this category are questions dealing with a person's sexual activities, beliefs, and values.

Several of the more popular personality inventories or standardized personality assessment instruments are the Mooney Problem Checklist, the Edwards Personal Preference Schedule, and the Minnesota Multiphasic Inventory. The latter two instruments require special training and supervised experience before their use in school or clinical settings.

The Mooney Problem Checklist consists of a series of problems to which the client reacts by underlining the problems that are of some concern, circling the problems that are of the most concern, and then writing a summary in his or her own words. It is obviously not standardized in a psychometric sense:

Designed chiefly to identify problems for group discussion or for individual counseling, this checklist drew its items from written statements of problems submitted by about 4,000 high school students, as well as from case records, counseling interviews, and similar sources. The checklist is available in junior high school, high school, college, and adult forms. The problem areas covered vary somewhat from level to level. In the high school and college forms, they include health and physical development; finances, living conditions, and employment; social and recreational activities; social-psychological relations; personal-psychological relations; courtship, sex, and marriage; home and family; morals and religion; adjustment to school work; the future—vocational and educational; and curriculum and teaching procedure. (Anastasi, 1982, p. 498)

The Mooney Problem Checklist is useful for group surveys and for identifying persons who want or need counseling assistance with personal problems.
    The Edwards Personal Preference Schedule is designed to show the relative importance to the individual of 15 key needs or motives. These are:

Achievement	Affiliation	Nurturance
Deference	Intraception	Change
Order	Succorance	Endurance
Exhibition	Dominance	Heterosexuality
Autonomy	Abasement	Aggression

Another clinically oriented instrument is the Minnesota Multiphasic Personality Inventory (MMPI). This instrument is constructed entirely on the basis of clinical criteria and contains 566 statements covering a wide range of subject matters related to the instrument's ten scales. These scales are

Hypochondriasis	Paranoia
Depression	Psychasthenia
Hysteria	Schizophrenia
Psychopathic Deviate	Hypomania
Masculinity-Femininity	Social Introversion

Four other scores are obtained: the Question score, the Lie score, the Validity score, and the K score (a suppressor variable refining the discrimination of five of the clinical variables). As mentioned earlier, the Minnesota Multiphasic Inventory requires special training and supervised experience before its utilization.

Criterion-Referenced Testing

In the 1978–1979 study by Gibson of standardized testing sponsored by the North Central Association of Colleges and Schools, one of the most frequently raised issues was that of criterion-referenced testing versus norm-referenced testing. Many educators will suggest that it is not a case of either/or; that, in fact, criterion-referenced testing complements norm-referenced testing and vice versa. The inference cannot be ignored, however, when in many school systems criterion-referenced testing has increased as norm-referenced testing has decreased. One cannot deny the rapid gains in popularity that criterion-referenced testing, aided by the accountability movement, has made in recent years.

Criterion-referenced tests have been defined by Glaser and Nitko (1971) as ones "that are deliberately constructed to yield measurements that are directly interpretable in terms of specific performance standards" (p. 653). A criterion-referenced test measures whether or not a person has attained the desired or maximum goal in a learning experience. If we were to contrast criterion-referenced testing with norm-referenced testing by using a practical example, we might note that a sixth-grade class could achieve an average score ahead of 52 percent of other sixth-grade classes in a representative nationwide sample. This information, however, might not tell those interested, such as teachers, parents, and students, more specifically how well this sixth-grade class reads or what they have learned to read. On the other hand, a typical criterion-referenced test result would indicate how many pupils in this sixth-grade class can read at a certain rate of reading, can comprehend at a certain level of comprehension, and can recall with reasonable accuracy what they have read after passage of a specific period of time. In the first instance, a class is competing against other classes to demonstrate to what degree pupils have learned or not learned to read. In the latter case, however, pupils are competing against a locally established standard, a learning objective, a criterion.

The criterion-referenced approach to measurement has guided the National Assessment of Education Progress (NAEP), a continuing nationwide survey of the knowledge, skills, understandings, and attitudes of young Americans. Currently financed by the National Institute of Education, the NAEP project has involved the periodic assessment of 20,000–32,000 people from each of four age groups (9, 13, 17, and 25–35 years) in ten subject areas. The annual plan of assessment through 1979–1980, presented in Table 7–3, shows that two or three subjects have been assessed in a given year and reassessed according to a 3- to 6-year cycle.

A stratified random-sampling procedure has been employed by NAEP in obtaining examinees: a certain number of persons of each sex, socio-educational status, and race are chosen at random from four geographical regions and four types of communities. Although a large number of questions concerning each topic are asked, the procedure of sampling both examinees and items makes only one relatively short testing period (50 minutes) necessary for each person. Adults are assessed individually, and younger people are assessed on both an individual and a group basis. Since the results are expressed in terms of the percentages of examinees at each level who possess certain skills and knowledge, the names of examinees do not appear on the test papers.

National Assessment was planned as a continuing program to provide the American public, especially legislators and educators, with information on the status and growth of educational accomplishments in the United States and the extent to which the nation's educational goals are being met. These surveys were not designed, as some have feared, to evaluate the achievements of specific schools or school districts, nor as a means of federal control over public school curricula. The findings, however, have been analyzed by geographical area, size and type of community, sex, parental

Table 7–3. Timetable for National Assessment of Educational Progress*

Learning Area	Initial or Baseline Assessment	First Measurement of Change	Second Measurement of Change
		School Year	
Art	1974–75	1978–79	
Career and Occupational Development	1973–74		
Citizenship	1969–70	1975–76	
Literature	1970–71	1979–80	
Mathematics	1972–73	1977–78	
Music	1971–72	1978–79	
Reading	1970–71	1974–75	1979–80
Science	1969–70	1972–73	1976–77
Social Studies	1971–72	1975–76	
Writing	1969–70	1973–74	1978–79

*Results are reported approximately one year after data collection.
Source: Martin, W. H., & The National Assessment of Educational Progress. *New Directions for Testing and Measurement,* 1979, 2, p. 47. Reproduced by permission of Education Commission of the States and the National Assessment of Educational Progress.

education, and race. Of particular interest are the analyses of the effects of federal support and specific types of programs on educational attainment. (Aiken, 1985, p. 117)

Rather than noting the range of individual differences in test scores, criterion-referenced tests place person in one of two groups: those who have attained the criterion and those who have not.

Writing in the November 1972 issue of *Today's Education,* Brazziel noted that the advantages of criterion-referenced tests seemed to outweigh the disadvantages. Six advantages were listed for criterion-referenced testing:

1. They permit direct interpretation of progress in terms of specific behavioral objectives.
2. They facilitate individualized instruction.
3. They eliminate a situation where half of American school children must always be below the median.
4. They enable teachers to check on student progress at regular intervals.
5. They eliminate pressures on teachers to "teach to the test" in order to have children make a good showing.
6. They enable teachers to compile a comprehensive record of the child's development and peg further instruction on clearly identified points. (pp. 52–53)

Brazziel (1972) also cited four disadvantages of criterion-referenced testing:

1. Reporting systems will vary and must be interpreted for children moving into new districts.

2. Further work must be done on constant validation on whether the given test items are measuring progress accurately.
3. Comparisons of performance of school districts are not yet readily available.
4. Materials for teaching towards specific objectives must always be available if tests are to be valid. (p. 53)

Perhaps Hawes (1973) expressed it best in noting the popularity of criterion-referenced testing when he entitled his article, "Criterion-Referenced Testing—No More Losers, No More Norms, No More Parents Raising Storms."

Summary

Standardized testing is an important tool in the counselor's array of techniques for understanding the client. Despite the historical and extensive use of standardized tests, counselors and other users must be aware of the many criticisms and concerns that have been voiced regarding their use for diagnostic purposes. An understanding of these criticisms and concerns and the degree to which they are valid will enable the careful counselor and other users to effectively but safely use standardized tests in their practices.

The importance of understanding basic statistical processes should not be underestimated. An understanding of averages and variations from the average, as expressed in statistical terminology, and of relationships as computed mathematically, are basic to the interpretation of standardized tests. It is also important that the user of standardized tests be aware of and be able to apply the criteria for test selection. These basic criteria are the validity, reliability, and practical characteristics of the test under consideration. Strengths and weaknesses of the common areas of standardized testing should be understood. It is also important that the user recognize the limitations as well as the strengths of a given instrument if it is to be intelligently used in practice. Counselors and others may also want to consider criterion-referenced tests as a substitute or supplement to their programs of standardized testing. Counselors should also be aware of the contributions which other disciplines make to the understanding of human behavior. In addition, a wide variety of nonstandardized techniques for human assessment, utilized across many disciplines, are available to the counselor who is knowledgeable in their construction and usage. The next chapter will provide an overview of these possibilities.

References

Aiken, L. R. (1985). *Psychological testing and assessment* (5th ed.). Boston: Allyn & Bacon.

Anastasi, A. (1982). *Psychological testing* (5th ed.). New York: Macmillan.

Beck, C. (1976–1977). Why general intelligence assessment should be abandoned. *Interchange, 7*(3), 29–35.

Brazziel, W. F. (1972). Criterion referenced tests. *Today's Education, 61*(8), 52–53.

Brown, A. E. (1976–1977). Intelligence tests and the politics of school psychology. *Interchange,7*(3), 17–20.

Chase, C. I. (1984). *Elementary statistical procedures* (3rd ed.). New York: McGraw-Hill.

Coleman, J. C. (1960). *Personality dynamics and effective behavior.* Glenview, IL: Scott, Foresman.

Cone, J. D. (1981). Psychometric considerations. In M. Hersen and S. Bellack (Eds.). *Behavioral Assessment: A practical handbook* (2nd ed.), (pp. 38–68). New York: Pergamon.

Cubberly, E. P. (1984). *Public education in the United States.* Boston: Houghton Mifflin.

Engen, H. B., Lamb, R. R., & Prediger, D. (1982). Are secondary schools still using standardized tests? *Personnel and Guidance Journal, 60,* 287–290.

Glaser, R., & Nitko, A. J. (1971). Measurement in learning and instruction. In R. L. Thorndike (Ed.), *Educational measurement* (2nd ed.), (pp. 625–670). Washington, D.C.: American Council on Education.

Gross, M. L. (1963). *The brainwatchers.* New York: Signet Books.

Hawes, G. R. (1973). Criterion-referenced testing—No more losers, no more norms, no more parents raising storms. *Nation's Schools, 91*(2), 35–41.

Herndon, T. (1976). Standardized tests: Are they worth the cost? *Education Digest, 42,* 13–16.

Holland, J. L. (1975). The use and evaluation of interest inventories and simulations. In E. E. Diamond (Ed.), *Issues of sex bias and sex fairness in career interest measurement* (pp. 19–44). Washington, D.C.: Department of Health, Education, and Welfare, National Institute of Education.

Hopkins, K. D., & Stanley, J. C. (1981). *Educational and psychological measurement and evaluation* (6th ed.). Englewood Cliffs, NJ: Prentice-Hall.

Martin, W. H., and The National Assessment of Educational Progress. (1979). *New directions for testing and measurement.* Washington, D.C.: Education Commission of U.S. and the National Assessment of Educational Progress.

McKenna, B. (1977). What's wrong with standardized testing? *Today's Education, 66,* 35–38.

Mehrens, W. A., & Lehmann, I. J. (1984). *Measurement and evaluation in education and psychology* (3rd ed.). New York: Holt, Rinehart & Winston.

National Committee on Excellence in Education. (1983). *A nation at risk: The imperative for educational reform.* Washington, D.C.: U.S. Government Printing Office.

Nolte, M. C. (1975). Use and misuse of tests in education: Legal implications. *Evaluation Horizons, 54,* 10–16.

North Central Association of Colleges and Schools. (1979). *Standardized testing in schools today.* Unpublished manuscript.

Ornstein, A. C. (1976). IQ tests and the culture issue. *Phi Delta Kappan, 57,* 403–404.

Robinson, S. E. (1983). Nader versus ETS: Who should we believe. *Personnel and Guidance Journal, 61,* 260–262.

Rudman, H. C. (1977). Standardized test flap. *Phi Delta Kappan, 59,* 179–185.

Sax, G. (1980). *Principles of educational & psychological measurement and evaluation* (2nd ed.). New York: Wadsworth.

Shertzer, B., & Linden, J. (1979). *Fundamentals of individual appraisal: Assessment techniques for counselors.* Boston: Houghton Mifflin.

Thorndike, R. L., & Hagen, E. (1977). *Measurement and evaluation in psychology and education* (4th ed.). New York: John Wiley & Sons.

Thorpe, L. P. (1960). *The psychology of mental health* (2nd ed.). New York: The Ronald Press.

Tyler, R. (1977). In B. McKenna, What's wrong with standardized testing? *Today's Education, 66,* 35–38.

Urdang, L. (1968) (Ed.) *The Random House dictionary of the English language,* college
    edition. (p. 990) New York: Random House.
Williams, R. L. (1974). The silent mugging of the Black community. *Psychology Today,*
    7(12), 32, 34, 37–38, 41, 101.

CHAPTER 8

NONSTANDARDIZED TECHNIQUES FOR HUMAN ASSESSMENT

Introduction

On occasion, one is called upon to explain, sometimes even justify, why one of our close friends, "behaves or acts the way he or she does." The reply may, at least subconsciously, draw upon one's knowledge of our friend's home and family background; the environment in which he or she grew up or now lives; the cultural background; the physical and psychological characteristics, as we perceive them; or the experiences of the friend. In these instances, a wealth of background information provides insights into the behavior of those we know well. Nor is this knowledge limited by our own particular occupation or discipline. Some of what we know might be classified as cultural or anthropological, some as environmental or sociological, and some as psychological.

In a similar vein, most of us feel more confident with a family physician who has looked after our ailments for years, who knows us from a broader standpoint than what we are as a physical specimen, who understands us totally. It is a situation that an equally competent, but "newcomer" physician cannot duplicate.

In the world of sporting competition there are frequent references to "psyching out the opponent." This "psyching out" of the opposition attempts to go beyond understanding the athletic skills of the opponent appropriate to the contest, suggesting that "the better we know the competition, the better we can play them."

These examples suggest the objective of this chapter, namely, a survey of nonstandardized assessment techniques for increasing and broadening our understanding of our client population. Thorough assessment increases the potential for maximum treatment efficacy. In the paragraphs that follow, interdisciplinary concepts of human assessment are presented, followed by some suggested guidelines or principles of human assessment. This chapter then focuses on the nonstandardized techniques commonly employed for individual analysis by counselors in various settings. It should be noted that standardized techniques, such as psychological testing, are those with a precise and fixed format, set of procedures, and method of scoring that enable the instrument to be used for the same purpose in a variety of settings and times. Standardization suggests uniformity and objectivity. Nonstandardization suggests a broader, variable, and more subjective approach to gathering and interpreting data for human assessment.

Concepts of Human Assessment

The most intelligent yet most complicated and difficult to understand living organism known to civilization today is the human being. When we place these complicated and often changing human beings in their environment, a rapidly changing and complex society, we cannot help but recognize the enormity of the task of those who seek to understand, predict, and assist the development of human behavior. In undertaking this responsibility, we are quick to recognize that no one discipline or area of expertise alone possesses the theoretical or technical basis for a comprehensive understanding of "modern people in modern society." To this end, then, those who study human behavior—whether from an individual or societal viewpoint; whether from the viewpoint of an anthropologist, sociologist, or psychologist; whether from the viewpoint of an American, Japanese, or German—must be willing to both learn and share with those who have this common interest. It is in this context that we suggest that counselors, regardless of the setting in which they function, can better understand the behavior of their clients through insights gained through the study of behavior in the context of other disciplines and cultures. The following is not intended to substitute for such study, but only to briefly examine these other perspectives and their implications for counselors.

Sociology

Sociology is a social science and a behavioral science that focuses on the study of individuals and groups in society and how they behave and interact with one another. The science of sociology contributes to an understanding of the social networks and their impact on individuals, individual roles, and relationships within those networks. Furthermore, sociology is concerned with the study of socialization agents or institutions. These institutions, such as the family, church, school, and government, assume the responsibility of teaching people within that environment what constitutes normal and abnormal behavior for the society. These patterns of normal and abnormal behavior are further shaped by customs, folkways, mores, and laws. Sociology also helps in understanding behavior that deviates from the norms of a group or society. The study of social deviance helps in understanding behaviors, including alcoholism and crime, that are defined as social problems. Such study also helps us to recognize that what is considered "normal" behavior in one group may be defined as deviant behavior in another group. Furthermore, study in this area can help the counselor recognize the influence of social controls or pressures on the behavior of clients, students, and others. For counselors, it is also important to keep in mind that human beings are social beings, affected by the society of which they are members and, at the same time, expected to contribute to that society.

Counselors will find sociological understandings contribute to their understanding of the groups and structures within the society of which they are a part. It is particularly important to understand the significance of the groupings and roles of clients, the influences on client behavior of the various groups of which they are members, the roles and relationships that are most significant to clients, and the restriction on clients' behavior and behavior change of the social systems of which they are a part. For the counselor, it is important to understand the various roles of people and the behavior that occurs or is anticipated as a result of these roles. That also includes an understanding of the significance of status, as already noted in many psychological studies. Some suggest that perhaps there has never been a more status-conscious society than our own. Sociologists help us understand status and its implications through the study of social stratification. Such study helps us understand social classes, social mobilities, social structures, and, in general, the ranking of social positions within society.

The sociologist, like the psychologist, is also concerned with the study of the development of a person's self-concept. Sociological study focuses upon self-concept development through the socialization process and its influence by others. It is especially important for counselors to recognize the impact of "significant others" and reference groups (both within the domain of sociological study) on the development of a person's self-concept. Who are the people whose judgments, imagined or otherwise, are significant to one's self-concept, and what are the groups that one uses to develop and test attitudes, beliefs, and so forth.

Anthropology

Anthropology is the study of the culture of a society and the characteristics of its social behavior. It involves the recording, describing, and analyzing of the cultures of humankind throughout the world and throughout history. In these studies, anthropology identifies the traditions, norms, patterns of learning, coping styles, and other behaviors, both from a current and an historical perspective. Among the understandings that the study of anthropology can provide for counselors are (a) recognizing that different cultures have different and similar concepts; (b) the importance of the ethnic and cultural background of the client; (c) the importance of the ethnic and cultural background of the counselor; and (d) the significance of recognizing subcultures within the larger societal or cultural context. The application aspects of anthropology were suggested by James Clifton (1970) when he noted that "a description of culture is a statement of what one has to know in order to understand events in a community as its members understand them and to conduct oneself in a way that they will accept as meeting their standards for themselves" (p. 221).

In this context. culture is viewed as the beliefs and practices of people within a society, including guidelines for their behavior in given situations (such as religious ceremonies, funerals, weddings, the attainment of puberty, maturity, and so forth). Human development is dependent upon environmental characteristics. The characteristics of the environment that have been developed by the past inhabitants of the environment constitute the culture with which a person interacts. That culture provides people with their initial values, behavioral guidelines, and expectancies for the future. As just noted, the self-concept is central to the study of personality and behavior by psychologists and sociologists, and the study of anthropology contributes through an understanding of the nature of self as culturally defined. We also view ourselves as influenced by the perspective we have of self in relation to culture. The study of anthropology alerts us to the fact that personality, as it develops, seeks to prepare the individual for living in his or her culture and, by the same token, that a culture only functions through the personalities of those who constitute it, thus enabling predictions regarding overt behavior on the basis of a knowledge of a culture and its traditions.

Today, we are aware that different subcultures often have different values and life-styles. For example, counselors should be able to understand the life-styles and values of such populations as Blacks, Indians, Orientals, Hispanics, Jews, Poles, and others. It is not only helpful to be able to function free of ignorance in helping relationships with clients from various bakcgrounds, but also to interact without prejudice and bias. Counselors must also recognize that ethnic and cultural affiliations do not affect all members to the same degree.

Economics

Economics is a science that studies human production, consumption, and distribution. Its significance in the creation of status and influences on our wants shapes many of our behaviors.

Economics is another social science concerned with individual behavior and human relationships. The economist's concern is with people living in various types of economic systems. Economists, like sociologists, are concerned with one's economic position, the socioeconomic status of people in a society. Economic attainment interacts with other factors in a culture to determine "status." This socioeconomic status can be significant as a determinant of client feeling, attitudes, behavior, and so forth.

Three major socioeconomic strata have been identified: upper, middle, and lower class. Within each of these levels are three sublevels of upper, middle, and lower (i.e., lower middle class). The most reliable indicators of assignment to a status are income, education, occupation, and geographic location of our residence. Since the economic environment in which people live is so closely interwoven with nearly every activity in which counselors engage, we cannot be uninvolved in this area.

C. Gilbert Wrenn (1962) noted the importance of economic learning to counselors when he commented that "the school counselor cannot afford to be a graduate student in psychology and a second-grader in economics" (p. 42). For the counselor, understanding the influences on career choices of economic systems and theories can be meaningful. In addition, the impact of economic systems on human behavior should not go unnoticed by counselors who propose to assess human behavior. The influence of the socioeconomic level of the home on the self-concept of the developing child is also of concern to the counselor.

Political Science

Political science is a discipline that is more frequently examined by accident than by a deliberate attempt to broaden our understandings of individual behavior. However, as Wasky (1970) noted:

> the focus of the behavioral approach on the individual is not sufficient; how individual decisions are aggregated is also vital, because individual preferences cannot themselves explain collective decisions. In explaining the individual we must turn to the social setting in which he is found; perhaps it is more accurate to talk of a focus on "the individual in his social environment," as when social psychologists talk of "personality in culture," not personality and culture. (p. 45)

Interdisciplinary Implications for Counselors

The preceding sections presented a brief overview of perspectives from other disciplines. From these perspectives, implications can be drawn that have relevance to counselors and their functioning in a variety of settings:

1. Counselors must reflect a greater awareness of the various cultures that may be represented within the client population they are hoping to serve.
2. To be effective and relevant, counselors must increase their understanding of the language that is vital to communicating with different cultures, which results from living in one culture and living or learning in another; the role expectancies of cultures; and cultural biases in schools and other basic institutions that create tensions, hostilities, and distrust among subcultures.
3. Counselors must have an understanding of the social structures of the communities and institutions within which they function. They must also recognize the impact of these and other social structures on how a person views himself or herself, his or her work, education, and other experiences.
4. Counselors must recognize the potential relationships between clients' socioeconomic characteristics and their behaviors and concerns.
5. Counselors should acquire a deeper understanding of the various societal influences on behavior, growth, and development of the individual based on an interdisciplinary approach.
6. Counselors must function more effectively as consultants. In this capacity, the counselor has the opportunity to interpret the social and cultural characteristics of clients and their implications for specific programs and settings.

Guidelines for Human Assessment

As we move toward an examination of specific tools and techniques available to counselors for assessing human characteristics, it is important next to recognize some basic principles or guidelines. These guidelines provide a framework for effectively and professionally functioning in the sometimes delicate task of individual assessment.

1. *Each individual human being is unique and this uniqueness is to be valued.* Although the principle of individual differences has been eulogized throughout educational and societal circles the better part of this century, in practice, constant pressures encourage conformity and standardization. Counselors must not enlarge this gap between principle and practice but should stress the principle that assessment is a means of increasing understanding of the uniqueness of the individual, a uniqueness that sets one apart from all other people, that provides each person with the basis for his or her own personal worth. That uniqueness is to be valued, not standardized.

2. *Variations exist within individuals.* Each person is unique as well as distinct from others. This principle notes that individual assessment seeks to identify, for example, the special talents, skills, and interests of a person and, at the same time, forestall tendencies to generalize from a single or several characteristics of a person, such as "anyone who excels in math can excel in anything," or "you give me an 'all-American' in one sport and I'll make them 'all-American' in another." Nor do we overlook the shortcomings. Although the emphasis on assessment is on the strengths and positive attributes of a person, all of us have our weaknesses—shortcomings that we must recognize if we are to overcome, bypass, or compensate for them.

3. *Human assessment presumes the direct participation of the person in his or her own assessment.* For human assessment to be as meaningful and accurate as possible, the person must be willingly and directly involved. This involvement includes input by the client, feedback, clarification, and interpretation, as appropriate, by both the client and counselor, and evaluation by the client. This principle presumes more than the client's one-way feeding in of data, such as taking a standardized test or completing a questionnaire. It assumes his or her right to interpretation and response to that interpretation. It presumes the client's right to clarify and expand his or her response and, as others come to know the client better, to gain better understandings of himself or herself as well.

4. *Accurate human assessment is limited by instruments and personnel.* The effective utilization of assessment techniques is dependent upon a recognition of the limitations of instruments and personnel as well as acceptance of their potential. These limitations begin with the human element—ourselves—our knowledge and skill in the techniques we would use. Counselors should not under any circumstances use assessment techniques, including standardized tests, in which they have not been thoroughly trained. Additionally, the limitations of clients in responding to individual items as well as instruments must be taken into consideration. These limitations may include an unwillingness as well as an inability to respond. In addition to these human elements, there are the limitations of the instruments themselves to consider. These include an awareness of the particular shortcomings unique to a given instrument or technique and the general recognition that any of these provide at best only a "sample," only clues, not absolutes, and results that may vary among similar instruments and techniques.

5. *Human assessment accepts the positive.* A goal of human resource assessment is the identification of the potential of each person. It is a positive process that, as noted earlier, seeks to identify the unique worth of each person. Assessment can lead to the identification of worthwhile goals and positive

planning. It should be a process clothed in optimism rather than, as so often is the case, fear of outcomes and predictions of doom. The counselor's own attitude becomes important in the establishment of the positive environment for assessment and in utilization of results for the best interests of clients.

6. *Human assessment follows established professional guidelines.* It is important for counselors, and all other helping professionals who use human assessment techniques, to be aware of the relevant ethical guidelines established by their professional organizations. These guidelines are aimed at protecting both the client and the professional practitioner. Ethical standards for counselors, which address assessment as well as other aspects of practice, are presented in Appendices B, C, F, G, H.

Doing What Comes Naturally—Observation

On any given day most of us are the subjects of informal analysis by others, and vice versa. These "analysts" are not among the handful of psychiatrists, psychologists, or counselors with whom we may be acquainted, but are amateurs doing what comes naturally—observing their fellow human beings, both friend and stranger, and drawing some conclusions about the kind of persons they are based on what is observed. Depending on what we see and how we interpret it, we may variously categorize people as executive types, models, drifters, untrustworthy, fun-loving, and so on. Furthermore, we are often prone to defend or "validate" our observations by noting, "I knew there was something that just didn't look right about her," or "You could tell he was a real athlete by the way he walked," and, on other occasions, calling upon old cliches (many of which are sexist) as back-up evidence, such as, "just another dumb blonde" or "watch out for those fiery redheads."

When we make observations "au naturel," we are, in effect, studying behavior as it is occurring in "real life." Although we must recognize—and we will help you to do this—the weaknesses of the uncontrolled observation method, we must at the same time recognize that many important questions about a person's natural social behavior cannot be determined through a controlled or clinical approach, much less be measured by standardized instruments. Ecological psychologists, such as Barker, have encouraged the study of behavior "intact" within the natural setting of the person being observed.

It is therefore appropriate as we begin an examination of the various techniques counselors use for gaining a better understanding of their clients that we begin with the most natural and popular of all these techniques—observation. As previously noted, we all employ this technique to varying degrees in drawing conclusions about others, but this is not to suggest that all observations are equally useful for human assessment. As a basis for recognizing the differing levels at which observation may take place, we suggest the following:

Levels of Observation

First Level: Casual Information Observation. The daily, unstructured, and usually unplanned observations that provide casual impressions; engaged in daily by nearly everyone. No training or instrumentation expected or required.

Second Level: Guided Observation. Planned, directed observations for a purpose. Observation at this level is usually facilitated by simple instruments such as checklists and rating scales. Some training desired.

Third Level: Clinical Level. Observations, often prolonged, and frequently with controlled conditions. Sophisticated techniques and instruments used with training, usually at a doctoral level.

Another system for classification of observational procedures suggested by Shertzer and Linden (1979) noted three types of observation as systematic, controlled, and informal. They defined these as follows:

> Systematic observation techniques employ procedures for quantifying the behavior observed in naturalistic settings.
> Controlled observation techniques are designed to evoke particular behaviors or specific responses.
> Informal observation is neither controlled in terms of what behaviors are to be observed nor systematic in the sense of observations being timed or directed to specific significant events. (p. 369)

Table 8-1. Classification of Observational Procedures

Type	Setting	Method*
Systematic	Natural	Director observation by time or event sampling of behaviors
Controlled	Controlled	The interview
	Contrived	Situational "test"
		In-Basket method
Informal	Natural	Anecdotal observation
		Developmental records
		Unobtrusive measures
		Sociometric methods

*Rating methods are not classified as they are employed in all of the settings subsumed under the three major types of observational procedures. Moreover, the case study also is not classified because it represents an integrated product of all types of observations. Both rating methods and the case study are discussed in separate chapters.
Source: Shertzer and Linden, 1979, p. 369.

Common Weaknesses of Observation

Because observation is a technique we all use and use frequently, it is only natural that we assume we are pretty accurate in our observations. However, that is a misleading assumption. Observation can be one of the most abused techniques in human assessment. Let us therefore proceed to examine some of these abuses or common weaknesses, followed by suggestions for increasing the effectiveness of this valuable assessment technique.

One of the popular questions on the written examinations for drivers' licenses in many states is to ask the applicant to identify, by shape only, the meaning of the various traffic signs. Perhaps you would like to pause and test your recall of these signs, which all of us see each day in our driving.

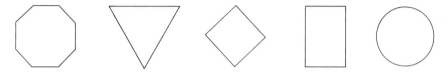

Now compare your responses to the following answers: stop, yield, warning, information, railroad. How did you do? For many at least, this points up one of the glaring weaknesses in undirected observation:

Casual observations do not lend themselves to consistent accurate recall.

Envision yourself on the witness stand in the classical courtroom scene where you are matching wits with the prosecuting attorney. In his or her best "you are guilty" voice, the prosecutor asks, "who were the first three people you observed on the morning of October 13th a year ago?" Some witnesses might have their recall saved by habit (the wife and kids) or a special event (the minister, my best friend, or my future "in-law"), but most would have difficulty recalling with accuracy and certainty the first three people they observed on "that fateful day" and even more difficulty in accurately describing what they were wearing. Although most of us have confidence in our ability to accurately recall what we have observed in the past, courtroom testimony, witnesses to accidents, observers of historical or sensational events, and even news reporters are so frequently found to be in error as to definitely suggest that we are not so accurate in our recall of the past, especially the details, as we often assume. Another weakness of undirected observations, then, would be:

Complete and accurate recall of undirected or casual observations tends to decrease with the passage of time.

Now let us involve you in another situation. Assume that you are a devout sports fan and supporter of a favorite team. Your team is involved in a close game in the closing minutes when an official calls a penalty that could conceivably cost your team the game. Regardless of how flagrant that offense or the call, it would be highly predictable that you, and those supporting your team, would have "observed" the call differently than did the officials and the supporters of the other team. It would be clear to an impartial witness that different observers were viewing the same situation differently. Similar illustrations may occur when two different observers describe the same western desert scene as "a beautiful blending by nature of sand, greenery, and beautiful hills" and "a wasteland of sand and drab plants running into bleak mountains." All of us have experienced the discrepancies that often occur as someone describes a boyfriend or girlfriend and as that same person appears to us. The point is that people differ in how they view the same event, person, or place, and also in the details they observe. We would note this as another weakness in casual and informal observations for assessment purposes:

Similar observations will be viewed differently because each person has his or her own unique frame of reference for interpreting what he or she sees.

These and other shortcomings suggest that undirected and casual observations of our clients may result in incomplete, misleading, or erroneous assessments. The values and opportunities of observation in client analysis are recognized, but it is apparent that some guidelines and instruments must be developed for increasing the accuracy and effectiveness of this technique. Here are some guiding principles for client analysis through observation, followed by a discussion of some useful instruments for reporting and recording our observations of others.

Guidelines for Client Analysis Through Observation

1. *Observe one client at a time.* Observation for individual analysis is just that; it focuses on the person. We are intent on noticing every observable detail of client behavior that may be meaningful in the counseling context. This is just as desirable an objective for observations of people in external group settings as in the more restricted setting of the counseling office.
2. *Have specific criteria for making observations.* We observe our clients for a purpose. We are observing for characteristics of the person appropriate to this purpose. These provide a basis for the identification of specific criteria, which in effect tell us "what to look for." For example, if we are observing young persons for the purpose of determining their relationships with adults, we might decide that two criteria or characteristics of this relationship that we would specifically observe would be interactions with teachers and interactions with parents. Of course, it is important that the criteria we use be appropriate to our observational objectives.
3. *Observations should be made over a period of time.* Although there is no specific time span formula for conducting observations, they should take place over a period of time that is long enough and with sufficient frequency to establish the reliability of our observation. A single sample of behavior is seldom enough for us to say with certainty that this is characteristic of the person. An illustration of this principle is to recall how your later impressions of people often differ from your first impressions, once you have had the opportunity to observe them over a period of time. Also, although concentrated periods of observation may be appropriate, the amount of observational time should not be confused with the span of time over which observations take place.
4. *The client should be observed in differing and natural situations.* Natural behavior is most likely to occur in natural situations. Although these situa-

tions vary somewhat among persons, for most youths, the school, home, neighborhood, and favorite recreational locales will be natural; with adults, the place one works will replace the school. Even within these natural settings, people will behave differently but naturally in different locales. For example, a student in school may behave differently in the classroom, the cafeteria, the gym, the hallways, and on the playground. If possible, therefore, clients should be observed in those settings and situations that are typical for them. Furthermore, this means a reasonable variety of those settings. For example, a school-aged youth may exhibit different behavior in one class at school than in others, and exhibit completely different behavior in social-recreational settings. An adult may behave differently on the job than at home and differently again in other social settings. Observing in these different settings may help us determine if some behaviors are limited to or conditioned by specific environments or situations.

5. *Observe the client in the context of the total situation.* In observation for human analysis, it is important to avoid a "tunnel vision" approach, or one in which we are so visually intent on observing just the client that we may miss noting those interactions and other factors in the setting that cause the person to behave the way he or she does. An example might be a classroom situation in which we observe that at the conclusion of nearly every math class, Nancy always leaves in tears, but we fail to observe that her classroom "neighbors" Joe and Jay appear to tease her throughout the class every day. We have observed the results but not the cause.

6. *Data from observations should be integrated with other data.* In individual analysis it is important to bring together all that we know about our client. Because we are seeking to see the client as a whole person, we would combine the impressions we gained from our observations with all other pertinent information available to us. The case study technique used by most helping professionals illustrates this point of integrating and relating data before interpretation.

7. *Observations should be made under favorable conditions.* Anyone who has tried to witness a parade three rows back or watch a key play at a game when the crowd jumps up in front can bear witness to the importance of favorable conditions for making observations. In planned observation it is desirable that we are in a position to clearly view what we are planning to report. Ideally, we should be able to conduct our observation for a sufficient period of time without either obstructions or distractions. There are also attitudinal considerations in creating favorable conditions for observation. These include an approach that is free from bias toward the client, any projections of expected behavior, or permitting one trait to predict another. It is just as important to have a clear psychological viewing point as a physical viewing point for observation for individual analysis. We should also be alert to another form of bias that may occur when the person being observed modifies his or her behavior because he or she is aware of being observed.

It has been said, "Anticipation is a wonderful thing. It often ensures that we will see what we want to see whether it is there or not."

Observation Instruments

A variety of instruments are available to counselors for use in recording their observations. Most are designed to eliminate one or more of the common weaknesses of undirected or casual observation. They provide a means of recording and preserving an impression of what was observed—an impression that is as accurate a year later as when it was initially recorded. Additionally, many instruments for reporting observations (checklists, rating scales, observation guides) provide specific directions or traits to guide the observer. Some instruments such as rating scales also provide for some degree of discrimination among the traits observed. Because many of these instruments also provide definitions or descriptions of their items that users are to accept and follow, they can also form a "mutual frame of reference" that can promote some consistency among observers viewing the same subject. The most popular of these instruments are rating scales, checklists, and observation and anecdotal reports.

Rating Scales

Rating scales, as the name implies, are scales for rating each of the characteristics or activities one is seeking to observe or assess. They enable an observer to systematically and objectively observe a person and record those observations. Although such scales are not limited to the recording and evaluating of observations, those are the common and popular uses of the instrument.

Rating scales have long been valued as an observation instrument by counselors. They are useful as a means of focusing on specific characteristics, increasing the objectivity of the rater, and providing for comparability of observations among observers; and they are easy to use.

Designing a Rating Scale

Although there are commercially designed rating scales available, counselors may find it more desirable under most circumstances to design their own. A good self-designed scale will be more appropriate for both the situation and the rater or raters, can be revised if needed, and, of course, is economical to use. The potential of any rating scale, however, is first determined by its design. There are five steps in designing a rating scale.

Determine the Purpose(s). An obvious initial step is to determine the potential population and the purpose of the observations or ratings. Usually, the purposes or objectives of such an instrument should be limited in both number and scope. This tends to prohibit the development of scales that are too lengthy and overlapping and that discourage user completion. Scales that are clear and concise and directed towards limited and precise objectives also increase the likelihood of accurate responses.

Identify the Items. Once the purposes or objectives of the scale have been established, the developer next identifies appropriate criteria or items to be rated. These items should be clearly and directly related to the objectives of the observation. Also, they should be clearly understood, easily observed, and assessed.

Identifying the Descriptors. Although there is often a subtle difference between items and descriptors, it is important to honor this difference. Items may not be ratable, so descriptors are used to effect a transition between an "identifying item or statement" and an "objective description."

Example 8-1. Developing the Rating Scale

The Beatty-Tingley Secondary School has a history of a high incidence of pupil dropout before graduation. The problem has become particularly severe in the past 3 years, and various remedial efforts have had little effect. It has therefore been determined by the school board that a concerted effort will be made to identify potential early leavers and then to design possible preventive measures. The counseling staff has been requested to design an instrument that will lead to the identification of these potential early leavers through the observation of certain behavioral traits. They proceeded to develop a rating scale by first stating the purpose as follows:

The Purpose: to identify potential dropouts.

Following a review of relevant research, the counselors agreed upon four possible criteria of potential school leavers:

1. Interest in school.
2. Relations with peers.
3. Relations with teachers.
4. Coping styles.

Having identified criteria, the next step was to agree upon descriptors appropriate for the designing of items on the rating scale. These were determined to be:

1. *Interest*
   Attention in class.
   Participation in class activities.
   Preparation for class.
2. *Relations with peers*
   Frequency of interaction with peers.
   Nature of interaction with peers.
   Attitude of peers.
   Friendships with peers.
3. Relations with teachers
   Frequency.
   Nature.
   Attitudes towards teachers.
   Attitudes of teachers.
4. *Coping styles*
   Problem-solving skills.
   Dealing with frustration and failure.
   Work habits.

They then began designing the rating scale. The first items were designed to assess the interest of students in their classes:

Rating Scale Items

Interest in School. (Check most appropriate category)

Class attention:
  Consistent and gen-
  eral alertness to
  ongoing activities
  in the subject mat-
  ter class

Never   Rarely   Sometimes   Usually   Always

Comments:

Class participation:
  Quality of participa-
  tion; knowledge-
  able and appropri-
  ate contributions
  and interactions

Poor   Below   Average   Superior   Excellent
          Average

Comments:

Frequency of partici-
    pation:

Never   Seldom   Occasionally   Often   Always

Comments:

Preparation for class:
  Readiness in terms of
  reading and other
  assignments for
  meaningful partic-
  ipation in class

Never   Seldom   Occasionally   Usually   Always

Comments:

Identifying Evaluators. As the label implies, evaluations or ratings on some kind of a scale are an anticipated characteristic of this particular technique for making and reporting observations. There are a variety of options for this purpose, such as the number of intervals or points on the scale, the defining of the evaluators, and deciding whether or not to provide space for comments.

Determining the Format. A part of the format will be determined by the identification of evaluators, as described in the previous step. Additionally, the organization usually relates items together; the length—not too long; and the directions for completion will all be items to attend to in determining the final format for the instrument.

Limitations of the Rating Scale

Limitations in using rating scales are basically those to which all instruments administered and developed by humans are subject—the limitations of the instrument and the limitations imposed by the user. The most common instrument limitations are (a) the result of poor and unclear directions for the scales' use; (b) a failure to adequately define terms; (c) limited scales for rating; (d) items that tend to prejudice how one responds; (e) overlapping items; and (f) excessive length.

The limitations that raters impose are equally prevalent and can be even more serious, because they can distort or misrepresent the characteristics of a person. The following are common examples:

1. *Ratings made without sufficient observations.* Many raters have an apparent need to complete all the items on a scale and, as a result, will "take a stab" at items with which they are unfamiliar. Others, in their haste to complete the scale, will make a rating on the basis of limited observation.
2. *Overrating.* There is a growing conviction among those who frequently use rating scales that overrating is a common practice among raters. For example, a recent review of rating scales used in conjunction with admissions to graduate work in a Big Ten university revealed that *all* 324 candidates were rated "considerably above average" or higher in three categories: appearance, social skills, and leadership.
3. *Middle rating.* Another group of raters appear to play it safe by using only the average or middle categories on a scale, thus avoiding either extremes of high or low assessments. Such ratings tend to misrepresent everyone as being just about average in everything.
4. *Biased ratings.* In addition to personal bias, bias may occur in ratings when raters permit one item that they particularly value or emphasize to set a pattern for the rating of other items.

Although the focus of this discussion has centered on the utilization of rating scales in reporting observations, it should also be noted that this instrument is not limited in use to only the reporting of observations. Rating scales are also used extensively by counselors and others for performance ratings, evaluations (both personal and institutional), and as measures of attitudes, aspirations, and experiences.

Checklists

Another instrument that may be used for recording observations is the observer checklist. This instrument is typically designed to direct the observer's attention to specific, observable personality traits and characteristics. It is relatively easy to use inasmuch as it not only directs the observer's attention to certain specific traits, but provides a simple means of indicating whether those traits are characteristic to the person being observed. Unlike the rating scale, the observer checklist does not require the observer to indicate the degree or extent to which a characteristic is present. Figure 8–1 shows an example of a simple form of a checklist.

Inventories

Self-report inventories typically consist of structured questions or statements to which the respondent answers "yes" or "no" or "yes," "?," "no" (Hopkins and

Observation Checklist

Personal characteristics of _____
(name of student)

Observed by (name or code) _____

Periods (dates of observation: from _____ to _____

Conditions under which student was observed: _____

_____

Instructions: Place a check mark in the blanks to the left of any of the following traits you believe to be characteristic of the student.

Positive Traits   Negative Traits

	Positive Traits		Negative Traits
_____	1. Neat in appearance	_____	16. Unreliable
_____	2. Enjoys good health	_____	17. Uncooperative
_____	3. Regular in attendance	_____	18. Domineering
_____	4. Courteous	_____	19. Self-centered
_____	5. Concerned for others	_____	20. Rude
_____	6. Popular with other students	_____	21. Sarcastic
_____	7. Displays leadership ability	_____	22. Boastful
_____	8. Has a good sense of humor	_____	23. Dishonest
_____	9. Shows initiative	_____	24. Resents authority
_____	10. Industrious	_____	25. A bully
_____	11. Has a pleasant disposition	_____	26. Overly aggressive
_____	12. Mature	_____	27. Shy and withdrawn
_____	13. Respects property of others	_____	28. Cries easily
_____	14. Nearly always does his/her best	_____	29. Deceitful
_____	15. Adjusts easily to different situations	_____	30. Oversolicitous

Comments: _____

_____

_____

_____

Figure 8-1. Observation checklist.

Stanley, 1981). Like rating scales, they used objective statements and responses in eliciting a person's view of self in regard to the listed items. Self-report inventories are often used to assess self-concept, study habits, and attitudes. Published and standardized instruments such as the Survey of Study Habits and Attitudes (Brown and Holtzman, 1967) and the Tennessee Self-Concept Scale are also available.

Anecdotal Reports

Anecdotal reports, as the label implies, are descriptions of a client's behavior in a given situation or event. Such reports are subjective and descriptive in nature and are recorded in a narrative form. Often a counselor will collect several of these reports, which then become an anecdotal record of a client's behavior over a period of time or situations.

Design of Anecdotal Reports

The format for anecdotal reports usually consists of three parts. They are (a) recording identifying data; (b) reporting of the observation; and (c) comments of the observer. There are serveral variations of this format, as may be noted by examining three different designs for anecdotal records. Figure 8-2 presents a format that follows in sequence the three parts previously identified. Figure 8-3 alters this format to provide space for comments alongside that are appropriate to particular statements of the anecdotal description. Figure 8-4 provides space for comments of additional observers, if desired.

Using the Anecdotal Reporting Method

The first consideration in anecdotal reporting is the selection of incidents that may be significant to report. There may be incidents that are typical of a client's behavior and are relevant for the counselor's or client's better understanding of the client. They may also be incidents so atypical of the client's behavior that their reporting and understanding may be advisable. In some situations, a series of anecdotes reporting similar behaviors over a period of time would increasingly suggest that the observed characteristics are typical of the client's behavior. Different observers making similar observations of a client's behavior on a specific occasion, or over a period of time, would have similar implications. Also, anecdotal reporting covering a period of time may identify trends or changes in client behaviors.

In school settings, teachers may be encouraged to use anecdotal reports in calling counselor attention to students who may need their assistance or in contributing to case studies or just a better understanding of individual students. The following examples illustrate uses of anecdotal reporting in school settings, as well as the counselor's interpretations of these reports.

```
Anecdotal Report Form
Henry H. Higgins High School


Name _____     Observed by _____


Where observed _____   When:  Date _____

                                            Time _____ to _____

_____

Description:




Comments:



```

Figure 8–2.   Anecdotal record: Form A.

Anecdote	Return to: Guidance Offices Nelson Elementary School
Student's name	

Description of incident observed	Comments:

Observed by _____

Time _____ Place _____

Figure 8-3. Anecdotal record: Form B.

Example 8-2. Uses of Anecdotal Reporting in School

Student's Name: Therese
Incident One
Reported by: Mr. Michael
              History Teacher

Date: January 16 (Monday)

Therese was not herself in class today. She usually is very active in the class discussions and always responds to questions when no one else seems to have the answer. However, today she sat quietly in her seat. At one point, when the discussion was bogging down, I called on Therese as always, asking her, "what were some of the factors that kept the United States from joining the League of Nations after World War I?" I could barely hear her response, but I thought she said "who cares?" and then in a louder voice which almost bordered on breaking into tears, "I'm sorry, I don't know the answer."

Anecdotal report for	
Name	Date
Situation	
Description	
Comments:	
Observor:	
Comments:	
Observor:	

Figure 8-4. Anecdotal record: Form C.

Teacher's Comments:	Therese is one of my more mature and capable students. Something is upsetting her and it would be helpful if a counselor could talk with her.
Student's Name:	Therese
Incident Two Reported by:	Ms. Haggerty Chemistry Teacher
Date:	January 18 (Wednesday)

For the first time in the two years I have known Therese as a student, she has fallen behind in her work in my class. Furthermore her behavior has been almost disruptive. For example, today, when one of her best friends, Ann, asked her if she could borrow a test tube from her, Therese snapped back at her, saying, "Don't you ever have enough stuff to do your own assignments? No, I'm not lending you anything any more!" The exchange obviously was unexpected to Ann, who didn't exchange another word with Therese for the rest of the period, while Therese seemed to spend most of the period simply staring at her lab book.

Comment:	Something is clearly wrong with this girl. This behavior is not typical at all. She needs to see a counselor.
Student's Name:	Therese
Incident Three Reported by:	Ms. Findley Physical Education Teacher
Date:	January 19 (Thursday)

Today, Therese approached me before my fifth period in which she is enrolled and said, "Ms. Findley, I am quitting the gymnastics team and I don't want to talk about it." When I put my arm around her and said, "That's O.K., Therese, I hope you're all right," she broke into tears and said, "I'll never be all right again!" and then ran into the locker room. I decided to leave her alone and didn't follow up on our conversation at this time.

Teacher's Comments:	I have noted for the past couple of weeks that Therese hasn't seemed to be herself, but today things seemed to explode. I don't know what the difficulty is, but I do intend to follow up on her problem, whatever it may be, when I see her next week. Do you have any suggestions?

In this situation it is obvious that the school counselor, by the end of the week, is able to put together a picture of a young lady who is clearly upset. Although there are no indications of cause in the incidents described, there is sufficient reason for the counselor to either call in Therese or, through consultation with Ms. Findley, attempt to provide her with appropriate help.

The previous is an example of how a series of anecdotes can lead to the identification of a student in need of counseling assistance. In some situations, however, even a single anecdote is enough to alert the counselor to a person in need of assistance.

Student's Name: Barry

Reported by: Mr. Franzen
                  English Teacher

Date: April 8

                  Barry's behavior in class today was most unusual. For example, every time a door slammed or there was any unexpected noise, he would jump as though suddenly startled. On one occasion, Sue accidently knocked her textbook on the floor, and Barry grabbed his desk tightly and exclaimed, "My God!" Most of the period he was continuously looking around the room as if expecting to be hit from all sides, and I noticed that he was in a cold sweat when he left the classroom at the end of the period. When I asked him, as he was leaving, "Barry, are you feeling O.K.?" he replied, 'We are all going to get it . . . you just wait and see."

Teacher's
Comments: Barry is usually so unobtrusive in class that he attracts little attention to himself. Today, however, everyone noticed his unusual behavior.

Advantages versus Disadvantages

Because anecdotal reports are designed to subjectively describe what has been observed, they become more lifelike than more objective measures. They present a broader, more complete viewpoint of a situation, which at the same time avoids the bleakness of the more quantitative or objective methods of reporting.

The major limitations of anecdotal reporting are those imposed by the observer-reporter. Most common of these are the reporting of "feelings about" rather than actual "behavior of" the person observed. The tendency to "read in" biases or expectancies can result in misleading reports. Overinterpretation or misinterpretation by inexperienced observers are not uncommon. The reporting of insignificant, rather than meaningful, behavior can also limit the usefulness of anecdotal reporting.

Time-Based Observations

Observations of behavior based on units or periods of time may be useful. One strategy of measuring behavior is based upon units of time rather than discrete response units. Kazdin (1981) described this as follows:

Behavior recorded during short time intervals for the total time that it is observed. With interval recording, behavior is observed for a single block of time (e.g., 30 minutes) once per day. A block of time is divided into a series of short intervals (10 or 15 seconds), and the behavior of the client is observed during each of them. The target behavior is scored as having occurred or not occurred during each interval. If a discrete behavior, such as hitting someone, occurs one or more times in a single interval, the response is scored as having occurred. Several response occurrences within an interval are not counted separately. If the behavior is ongoing with an unclear beginning or end, such as talking, playing, and sitting, or occurs for a long period of time, it is scored during each interval in which it is occurring.

A variation of interval recording is referred to as *time sampling.* This variation uses the interval method but the observations are conducted for brief periods at different times, rather than in a single block of time. (p. 107)

Another time-based method of observation is the amount of time, or duration of a particular response. Kazdin indicated that:

This method is particularly useful for ongoing responses that are continuous rather than discrete acts or responses of extremely short duration. Programs that attempt to increase or decrease the length of time a response is performed might profit from a duration method. For example, duration has been used to assess the amount of time that a claustrophobic patient spent sitting voluntarily in a small room (Leitenberg, Agras, Thompson, and Wright, 1968) and the time delinquent boys spent returning from school and errands. (Phillips, 1968).

Another measure based upon duration is not how long the response is performed, but how long it takes for the client to begin the response. The amount of elapsed time between a cue and the response is referred to as *latency.* (p. 108)

Instrument Selection

The preceding paragraphs have discussed a variety of observation techniques and instruments. In many situations, counselors and other observers will make a decision about which instrument or instruments are most appropriate for the observation task at hand. They may be aided in determining which type of types of instruments to use by considering the following:

1. Is some direction for recording observation(s) for individual analysis desired? (The answer to this is usually yes—or should be.)
2. Is a descriptive or objective report more appropriate?
3. Will more than one observer be reporting observations of the client (or potential client)?
4. Are assessments or evaluations of what has been observed desired?
5. Are comparisons among different clients or between client and other populations likely to be made?
6. Are opinions or impressions—not necessarily facts or factually based information—desired?
7. Does the instrument avoid complex observations and recording methods?
8. Will the instrument make it relatively easy to complete a report in a short period of time, even if some accuracy or depth of observation may be sacrificed?
9. Will instruments be used by counselors or others who are experienced or trained in their use?

Self-Reporting: The Autobiography and Other Techniques

Up to this point we have been discussing observaton and observation techniques for client assessment. In such techniques clients may be aware of their being observed, but rarely are they direct participants in the process.

Some of the most valuable techniques for human assessment for counseling purposes are those that call for the active involvement of the client. These techniques not only provide special insights for the counselor, but can be valuable to the clients as they engage in a process of guided self-assessment. The use of such techniques as autobiographies, self-expression essays, structured interviews, and questionnaires can facilitate both counselor and client understanding of the client's strengths, weaknesses, and uniqueness.

The Autobiography: A Popular Technique

The autobiography has been one of the most popular forms of literature throughout the ages. Humankind has consistently been interested in the personal view their fellow humans had of their own life expereinces. Additionally, almost everyone, famous or obscure, has at one time jotted down a personal view of life's experiences. Some hope for publication, whereas others only write for their own personal satisfaction. It is probably appropriate to say that there is a time or times in nearly everyone's life when they feel compelled to examine and set down in writing life's experiences. For the majority of those so inclined, it is unlikely that the desire will coincide with a need for counseling. Nonetheless, the autobiography, even when it represents a nonvoluntary effort, can be a useful source of information to the skilled counselor. Let us therefore briefly examine its use as a nonstandardized technique in human assessment.

Autobiography: A Different Technique

At this point it is probabaly appropriate to indicate that counselors should avoid the use of overlapping or similar techniques. For example, there is little to be gained in using both rating scales and observation checklists to report observations of the same type of behavior, or to use three different achievement tests to measure the same area of achievement. A feature of the autobiography is that it is different from any other technique available to the counselor, for the autobiography provides clients (or students) with the opportunity to describe their own life as they have experienced it and view it.

The autobiography lets a person express what has been important in his or her life, to emphasize likes and dislikes, identify values, describe interests and aspirations, acknowledge successes and failures, and recall meaningful personal realtionships. Such an experience, especially for the mature client, can be thought-provoking, insightful, and a stimulus for action. On occasion, the experience can also relieve tension.

The Autobiography as an Assignment

As previously indicated, there are times in most peoples lives when they reach a state of psychological readiness for writing their own life story. However, because this is unlikely to occur at the time such information may be needed by a counselor, some attention should be paid to the autobiography as a client or student assignment. If the autobiography is to be requested and used solely by the counselor, the suggestion should be presented as naturally and straight-forwardly as possible, with an indication of how it will be helpful to both the counselor and the client in the counseling process. It should also be emphasized that the contents of the autobiography will at all times (within legal limits) be treated as confidential information. The counselor should also indicate possible content and approaches for preparing this assignment. Written guidelines may also be prepared for use in such a situation. An example of one such set of guidelines provides the client three possible options for preparing an autobiography.

Example 8–3. Guidelines for Preparing an Autobiography

Purpose: 1. To provide you with the opportunity to experience the planning, organizing, and writing of your autobiography.
2. To provide you, the writer, and me, the reader, with opportunities for increased understanding, insights, and appreciations of you, the writer.

Each writer may develop and work to an outline that suits his or her own style. The emphasis and detail that you give any period, event, or person will be whatever you determine as appropriate. The following are *examples only* of outlines and topics that might be appropriate for inclusion in an auto-biography. (Note: I will be the only reader of your autobiography and will, of course, regard its contents as confidential.)

Example A.

Part I. My preschool years.
My family, where I lived, early memories, friends, likes and dislikes.
Part II. My school years.
Elementary, junior, senior high school, college, teachers, friends, subjects liked and disliked, activities, significant events, experiences, travels, concerns, and decisions.
Part III. My adult years.
Where I lived, work experiences, friends and family, travels, hobbies, continued education, concerns, and decisions.
Part IV. The current me.
Part V. My future plans.

Example B.

1. Significant people in my life.
2. Significant events and experiences in my life.
3. Significant places in my life.

Example C.

Start your autobiography as far back as you can remember—your earliest childhood memories. Tell about those things that really made an impression on you, that stood out in your memory, whether happy or sad. Try to include those events that you believe have affected your life, such as moving to another city or entering junior high school.

As you write about the event, try to show how the event affected you, what people have truly influenced your life the most and how they affected the way you feel and act today. Mention your hopes and plans for the future—what you hope to be doing ten years from now, for example.

When a counselor desires that a client emphasize a certain aspect of his or her life's experiences, that should be indicated to the writer.

In a school setting, the autobiography is often collected through a subject matter classroom. It is most frequently a written assignment in an English class at the secondary school level, and in the elementary school, as a language assignment or an assignment related to the study of famous historical figures. As a classroom assignment, the autobriography should be treated in such a way that the student will regard it as a worthwhile educational experience. This suggests that it is treated as a regular assignment for a grade, although, if grades are assigned, the teacher must emphasize that one is not receiving an A or F for their life thus far, but rather for the technical manner in which he or she described it in relation to the assignment.

Limitations

There are a number of potential limitations of the autobiography that counselors and other users must take into consideration. One obvious limitation is that many people may find the writing of an autobiography a chore; thus, it will become a brief, bleak, and usually boring document that contributes little to a better understanding of the writer. The writing ability of the author as well as the conditions under which it is written will influence the potential usefulness of this technique. Also, as with any recall-based instrument, the ability of the writer to recall past experiences accurately and in considerable detail is important. Self-insight is another important factor. The reader must also be aware of distortions that overemphasize insignificant happenings or ignore those that are important, or inject falsehoods or fantasies, which very often are descriptive of the ideal or hoped-for life experiences of a writer. Current values may also influence how an author views past experiences and associations, and these may not be consistent with how they are viewed at the time.

Interpretation

With both the possible advantages and limitations of the autobiography in mind, let us note possible analyses by the counselor. The counselor/reader may first of all prepare a checklist or summary form for those items that would be particularly relevant to the counseling needs of the client. In other situations, the counselor may simply summarize at the conclusion of the reading the most relevant aspects or, assuming that the copy will be for the counselor's viewing only, may underline or make appropriate notes in the margins. In a general reading one might use the format depicted in Figure 8–5 for analyzing an autobiography.

Autobiographical Excerpts

Two brief excerpts are presented as examples of significant statements that are often found in student autobiographies.

> When I moved from East Park High School to Newry High School I guess I had assumed that things would go on as usual. I had been a big wheel at East Park—you know what I mean—member of the Student Council, president of the "Jokers"—most popular boys' club in school; king of the Sophomore Stomp, member of about half a dozen other clubs, invites to all the parties and social activities that were of any importance. But at Newry, many of the clubs I had belonged to before didn't exist. There were no boys' social clubs and, try as I might, I couldn't seem to make friends that moved in the "popular" circles. A lot of the kids spoke to me and were pleasant enough, but they never thought of me at party time. I found as time went on I missed

I	Significant incidents
II	Organization—length, language (choice of vocabulary, depth of expression)
III	Omissions, glossing over, inaccuracies
IV	Points to check further
V	Summary comments

Figure 8–5.   Analyzing an autobiography. *(Kiley, 1975, p. 66.)*

East Park more and more, and I even began cutting school so I could drive back and visit East Park while school was in session. I had been a "B" student before at East Park, but my grades really took a beating at Newry. In fact, I think some of the kids at Newry began thinking of me as "dum-dum" and I know many of the teachers did.

The counselor in this instance found a significant clue in this portion of the client's autobiography to explain his poor grades and the subsequent difficulty he was having in securing college admission.

I guess I felt like a nobody as far back as I can remember. I think maybe my mother resented me because I wasn't a girl, because when I was born she already had five boys. I know as a kid I could never seem to do anything right, and my mother used to say I couldn't do anything right because I was a nobody. I remember that she and my Dad both began calling me "ole nobody." Then my oldest brother, the one with the sense of humor, started calling me "N.B." (for nobody). The rest of the family thought that was real "cute" and so when I started school, and all through school, I have been called "N.B" Actually, my name is James Lucifer Laswich. But I often have to stop to think what my real name is, I'm so used to N.B. I guess one reason I am so used to it is that I just seem to fit the name "Ole Nobody" so well. I sometimes don't think there is a single teacher in this school who remembers me once I leave the class, and I know most of the kids don't. I must be the only kid in school who doesn't have a "best friend."

The case of "Ole Nobody" is another example of a significant statement in a person's autobiography that provides the counselor with clues to his client's seemingly withdrawn behavior and poor self-concept.

Autobiographical Tapes

In recent years, an innovative deviation from the usual written autobiography—the autobiographical tape—has been found useful by counselors with some clients. The autobiographical tape presents the client an opportunity to orally describe and discuss one's life. In utilizing this technique, the counselor may first determine whether it is likely to be more useful than the written autobiography. Once the counselor has determined that the verbal approach is more appropriate, the counselor may then decide whether to provide the client with a structured outline to respond to or simply to describe the client's life as it comes to him or her. There may be some advantages to the autobiographical tape that will determine the circumstances under which it will be used. For example, some persons can express themselves better orally than in writing. Furthermore, because this method requires less preparation and effort on the part of the client, he or she may more freely present details that would otherwise be omitted. In addition, some clients may feel that there is less likelihood that the contents of a tape "give away one's secrets" than a written document. Voice tone on a taped autobiography may also reveal feelings and emotions of the client and, because of the nature of recording, the autobiography by tape is less likely to be subject to client editing or censoring. Finally, it should be noted it is also evident that the taping of an autobiography for some clients is a more fascinating or innovative approach than the traditional writing experience.

There are, of course, disadvantages as well, to the taping of one's autobiography. The usualy shortcomings of the written autobiography, such as lack of recall, exaggeration, and fantasy, are every bit as probable in this approach. In addition, there are some clients who lack the ability to express themselves clearly orally. Also, for some, the "unnaturalness" of this approach will be an inhibitor. Nonetheless, the taped autobiography is a tool that the counselor may wish to consider for certain clients under certain circumstances.

Self-Expression Essays

Another useful technique that counselors may want to employ on occasion is the self-expression essay. This technique seeks to solicit the client's response, usually in a short, written essay form, to a particular question or concern. The objective of this technique is to elicit spontaneous, uncensored responses to a topic or topics relevant to the counseling needs of the client. Examples of appropriate topics would include:

My biggest concern is . . .
I'll bet you don't know that . . .
I value . . .
My future plans are . . .
My job is . . .

It should be emphasized that such documents can elicit positive responses as well as descriptions of possible problems or concerns. An example, which incidentally illustrates a positive response, is the following brief essay.

Example 8–4.

"My School Problem"
    My school problem is that I have no problem! Look at us! We have a beautiful school and, just my luck, a great faculty. We can't seem to lose more than once or twice a year in any sport. The greatest gang of kids go here and the crowning blow—even the food in the cafeteria is edible. So I have a problem because I'm a natural born griper—I'm at my best when I can complain—I have a feeling of accomplishment when I can point out the weaknesses of others. I used to have a field day before I came to Lee Street High. Now I'm dejected because I'm not rejected.
    To help solve my problem I suggest that:

1. The students get busy and deface the school, mark up the restrooms, pull out the shrubbery, and all the other things that make a school more homelike.
2. The faculty get busy telling us how stupid we are; that they quit treating us like humans (I actually feel superior to my dog now), and that they get back in the old game of teacher versus student to the bitter end.
3. That our teams lose a few more games, and that our coaches get rid of their coats and ties and wear baggy sweatshirts and swear loudly at the officials so they won't be mistaken for ladies and gentlemen,

and that our student body do something pronto to get rid of that disgraceful "good sportsmanship" trophy.

4. That the students start forming cliques, avoid welcoming newcomers, and in general act more like adolescents than young adults. Oh, yes, we need a few more "kookie" dressers also.
5. Finally, that the school cafeteria manager go copy the menus and recipies from some other schools (mashed potatoes should always be served cold, and lumpy gravy should taste like glue, and fried chicken served stringy and dried out).

The Self-Description

The self description is another client-participation tool that enables the counselor to see the client as he or she sees himself or herself. The client is requested to "paint a picture of himself in words," in one page, if desired. Such a "portrait" may share whatever aspects the client wishes to have the reader know. It is usually desirable to do this in the early stages of counseling to give the counselor an additional means of getting to know the client. This differs from the self-expression essay because the self-description is one's view of one's self, whereas the essay may describe one's attitudes toward activities, events, and beliefs.

Example 8–5. Excerpts from Self-Description Essays

Sample 1

I would describe myself as a pleasant and amiable person. Others remark about my easygoing manner and happy-go-lucky personality. Honesty is a virtue I hold very dearly, and I perhaps trust others equally, thinking that they have my virtues.

My mother had always taught me that I should be conscious of others' feelings and do my best to please them. I went for many years applying this philosophy, yet found that others were not as conscious of my feelings. This led me to be hurt and used by others emotionally and mentally. I had to almost retrain myself to believe that thinking of myself was not altogether selfish and at times is the only way to think in order to lead a happy life.

Counselor's Notations: The counselor would no doubt notice the section of this self-description that indicates the client has been hurt and used by others emotionally and mentally. Also of interest to the counselor is the client's statement, "I had to almost retrain myself to believe that thinking of myself was not altogether selfish."

Sample 2

I believe that a person should not be too overtly predictable, but should possess a consistency of covert thought and feeling. I do not mean to say that I delight in the misconceptions of those who wish to categorize or predict the responses of others. I am not one to purposely masquerade, or, for some reason, to mislead those I work with or come in contact. But oftentimes an unpredictable action, comment, or response will reveal or trigger a surprising reaction on the part of an eager conversationalist. I do not become close to many, and am not always patient enough to seek out the best points of my peers or colleagues. My point of view has been said to be too sensitive at times, but I like to think that my increased sensitivity allows me to take a deeper breath of life and enjoy what beauty I may sense.

I am idealistic, serious, extremely concerned about those who need help, and a good listener.

Counselor's Notations: The counselor reading this self-description might note the fact that the client keeps his or her distance from colleagues and is considered at times to be overly sensitive. This self-description is of interest, too, for the writer's description of interactions with his or her peers.

Self-Awareness Exercises

Many persons pride themselves on their self-control; their ability "to put their feelings aside and deal in a practical manner with the situation at hand." Others simply find it difficult to express their feelings openly to others, as, for example, the often dramatized shy young man who never can work up the courage to tell his true love that he cares for her. At the other extreme we can identify persons who may express their feelings openly in such a way as to be harmful to their personal relationships with others. Even in these extremes, persons are often unaware of how their expressions of feelings and emotions may be handicapping rather than helping their relationships with others. Self-awareness exercises are designed to help people become more aware of their feelings, emotions, and values as a step toward more effectively expressing their emotions,

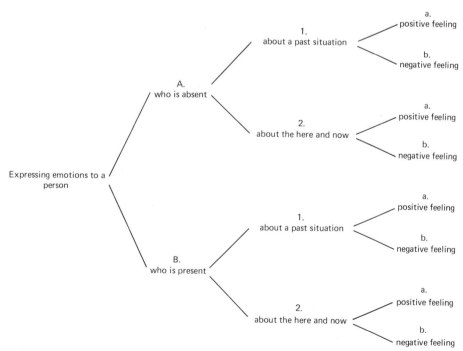

Figure 8–6. Difficulty in expressing emotion. *(Egan, 1977, p. 81.)*

feelings, and values. Egan's (1977) chart of difficulty in expressing emotion (Figure 8–6) says that in many (if not most) cases it becomes more and more difficult to express feelings and emotions the farther down the chart you go. Therefore, it's relatively easy to express a positive feeling about a past situation when the feeling is directed toward a person who is absent.

A example of such an exercise might include some of the following:

Exercise 8-1.

This exercise is designed to help you increase your awarness of how the expression of feelings/emotions affects your relationships with others. There are no right or wrong answers, so you should react to each statement as honestly as you can, recognizing that "who" and circumstances might alter your response in actual situations.

Using the scale of
1 = very annoying
2 = somewhat bothersome
3 = doesn't usually bother me
4 = feel ok
5 = will probably feel very positive

indicate in general how you feel about persons who

1. Shout at you in anger _____
2. Slap you on the back in greeting you _____
3. Cry in your presence when reading a "sad" book or news-paper item _____
4. Talk in a very loud voice when they are frustrated or upset _____
5. Laugh easily and often _____
6. Are silent and "moody" when they are mad _____
7. Are silent and moody when they are sad _____
8. Are silent when they are disappointed _____
9. Become emotional whenever things go wrong _____
10. Become emotional whenever something nice happens to them _____
11. Never show any emotions _____
12. Are inconsistent in their open displays of emotion _____

Exercise 8-2.

Indicate how you usually manage your emotions using the following scale.

1 = express my feelings openly
2 = may express my feelings openly to close friends or family
3 = would modify my expression of feelings so that they would not con-vey the real intensity of the emotion I'm feeling
4 = would keep my feelings to myself

1. I think something is funny but I doubt that others may see it that way _____

2. I am very disappointed at not achieving at a level or a goal I had hoped to   _____
3. I am very angry as a result of a great inconvenience caused me by the actions of another person   _____
4. I am frustrated by unnecessary delays and "red tape" in completing an assigned task   _____
5. I am awarded a great and unexpected honor   _____
6. I am saddened by a close personal loss   _____
7. I am a participant in an exciting event or activity   _____

In reviewing your responses to the items listed under A and B, can you identify circumstances under which emotional expressions directed at you by others or your own emotions affect how you interact with others?

Daily Schedules and Diaries

As with the autobiography, many of us have kept a diary from time to time. We may recall how we "bared our soul" in those secret pages, often protected with a little tin lock, that if reread today might help us better understand some of our present behavior and attitudes. Probably today's clients are no more willing than their predecessors to share such recordings, but when a client willingly maintains and shares diary entries with the counselor, they can provide valuable insights into understanding the client and his or her problem. Some clients will find it easier to present some aspects of their behavior and experiences in writing than in oral communication and, should this be the case, the counselor may decide to suggest the keeping of a diary for a period of time.

Another technique for systematically recording the client's daily activities is the daily schedule. This is a simple listing, usually an hour-by-hour accounting of a client's daily activities. This technique can be useful in helping the counselor and client understand how the latter is organizing and using his or her time. Whereas the diary is usually a summary of the day's activities, often with feelings and interpretations, the daily schedule is a more objective presentation or listing of the day's activities. Figure 8–7 presents an example of the less familiar of these two instruments, the daily schedule.

Questionnaire

An extremely popular nonstandardized instrument with which all of us have had many encounters is the questionnaire. Questionnaires today appear to be a part of the American way of life, since they are constantly used to inventory public reactions, solicit opinions, predict needs, and evaluate a wide range of commodities, services, and activities. This popularity does not, however, betlittle their importance as an instrument for the economical collection of data from individual clients or groups of clients.

The questionnaire has a variety of uses for the counselor. In a broad, general way, it obviously provides an opportunity to easily collect a great deal of information that may be useful in further understanding the client. Also, the ques-

Diary for _____	Week of _____	
Morning	Afternoon	Evening

Monday:
6:45 Get up
8:00 Leave for
  school
8:15–12:15 School
	12:15–1:00 Lunch in
	  school cafeteria
	1:00–3:30 More school
	4:00 Get home
	4:00–5:00 Loaf around
	  with gang
	5:00–5:30 Go to store
	  for Mom
	5:30–6:00 Read evening
	  paper, mostly sports
		6:00–7:00 Dinner
		7:00–8:00 Watch TV
		8:00–9:30 Study English
		  and history
		9:30–9:45 Take dog for
		  walk
		9:45–10:15 Study French
		10:45 Bed

Tuesday:
Same as Monday
	12:15–12:45 Lunch in
	  school cafeteria
	12:45–1:00 Talk to
	  Mr. Leonard
	1:00–3:30 Classes
	3:30–4:30 Work on
	  chemistry experiment
	4:45–6:00 Get home,
	  read paper, listen
	  to records
		6:00–7:00 Dinner
		7:00–8:00 Watch TV
		8:00–8:30 Study English
		  and chemistry
		8:30–9:00 Watch favorite
		  TV program
		9:00–9:30 Study English
		  and chemistry
		9:30–9:45 Phone call
		9:45–10:15 Study French
		10:15 Bed

Wednesday:
Same as Monday
	12:15–1:00 Bring lunch;
	  eat in Mr. Leonard's
	  class and watch experiment
	1:00–3:30 Classes
	4:00 Get home
	4:00–4:45 Study trig
	4:45–5:30 Loaf around
	  with guys who come by
		6:00–6:30 Dinner
		6:30–8:00 Study for
		  history test
		8:00–8:30 Watch TV
		8:30–9:45 Study for
		  history test
		9:45–10:00 Walk dog
		10:00–10:30 Study French
		10:50 Bed

Figure 8–7. Daily schedule.

tionnaire is a client-participation technique that promises opportunities to advance the self-understanding, at least under some circumstances, of those completing it. More specifically, questionnaires may be designed in such a way as to collect specific types of information related to specific needs of the counseling clientele. Questionnaires may also seek information for the purpose of validating other data already available to the counselor. Additionally, questionnaires can be useful in identifying problems of individuals or groups, as well as their opinions, attitudes, or values. Questionnaires can also be valuable in collecting needs assessment data as a basis for establishing program objectives and evaluation data as a basis for program improvement.

The usefulness of the instrument, however, will be determined, at least in part, by the kind of information it seeks to collect, the appropriateness of the questionnaire's design, and the skill of the person who administers it.

In questionnaire design there are certain basic considerations to keep in mind. These are briefly:

1. *Directions:* Indicate the purpose of the instrument and give glear, concise directions for its completion.
2. *Item Design:* Design items that are clear, concise, and uncomplicated. Items should solicit only one response and should be stated in such a way that the responder will not be biased or influenced in how he or she responds. Questionnaire items should also reflect the language level of the anticipated respondents.
3. *Item Content:* Questions should be designed to collect the kinds of information appropriate to the assessment purpose of the instrument. However, caution must be taken in eliciting socially sensitive, culturally restricted, or other personal-private information. Even a few such items (such as, Would you engage in sexual activity outside of marriage? Have you ever thought of committing a crime?) can arouse resentment or suspicions of some respondents that will affect their response to the total questionnaire as well. Although unsigned questionnaires may secure reasonably accurate group responses to a sensitive topic, the counselor will find such unidentified responses of considerably less value in individual counseling.
4. *Length:* A final consideration, obvious but important, is the length of the questionnaire. Often, we receive questionnaires of such length that we are discouraged from even beginning them. Clients and student populations are no exceptions in their reactions to lengthy questionnaires. Such instruments must be of reasonable length if they are to facilitate the data collection for which they are designed.

Structured Interviews

Another basic and popular technique for increasing a counselor's understanding of the client is the structured interview. This technique not only provides opportunities for client observation under certain controlled conditions, but, equally important, enables the counselor to obtain specific information and to explore in-depth behavior or responses. Interviews that are structured are usually planned to serve a particular purpose. Once the purpose has been clearly specified, questions are designed that are suitable to achieve the goal or purpose of the interview. These questions are usually arranged in some sort of a logical sequence, although the interviewer must be flexible to alter both the nature and sequence of the questions as circumstances suggest.

Although the basic principles of counseling are appropriate for the one-to-one interview (see Chapter 5), it is appropriate at this point to note that the interviewing process and setting, to be successful, should be as natural as possible, not anxiety producing. Because the interviewing setting and process may be natural and comfortable to counselors, they may, on occasion, forget that for the interviewee unfamiliar with either, it can be a frightening experience. Perhaps if you recall your own experiences when called in for an income tax audit by the Internal Revenue Service or when interviewed for a first job, you can appreciate a client's wariness. One must also recognize the possible existence of such human qualities as client forgetfulness, exaggeration, or trying too hard to give the "right" answer as limitations in some structured interviews.

For an example of a structured interview, let use go again to the Beatty-Tingley High School and its high school dropout problem. Once potential dropouts had been identified through combining the rating scale with other data, the counseling staff decided to conduct structured interviews with those students who were willing to do so. The purpose of these interviews was to further explore each individual student's views and attitudes about school in relation to their educational and career planning. They then proceeded to structure the interview as follows:

Structured Interview
1. Introduction and explanation of the purpose of the interview, how we will proceed, and the answering of any questions.
2. First, tell me how it has been going for you in school this year.
3. What have been the best things about school this year?
4. What have you disliked the most about school?
5. How do you spend your time when you're not in school?
6. Have you ever thought of dropping out? If so, what would you plan to do then?
7. How could school be made more enjoyable for you?
8. Let's talk a little about your future—what are your job or career plans? (Follow up with questions regarding reasons of choice: long-range goals and further education.)
9. Are there any questions you'd like to ask me? Anything else you'd like to say?
10. Conclude.

You will note that an intitial explanation is made of the purpose and procedures of the interview. Also, the questions are structured in such a way as to elicit discussion rather than a "yes" or "no" response. Finally, the interviewee is given the opportunity to ask questions or make additional comments before the interview is terminated.

Group Assessment Techniques

Group guidance and counseling techniques were discussed in greater detail in Chapter 6, but it is appropriate in this chapter dealing with nonstandardized assessment techniques to review briefly techniques for assessing the roles and relationships of individuals in groups. The understanding of our clients as total beings is heavily dependent on our understanding their group associations. Groups are a natural form of human association. In today's world, the hermit is an almost extinct species; persons are no longer rugged individualists, going it alone. Group associations are natural, and all of us belong to many different and diverse groups. For example, some of us may, within the brief period of 24 hours, associate with our family group, our work group, our social recreational group, a civic group, political group, and church group. In each of these several different settings, the roles and relationships are significant in shaping our behavior, both within and without the group. Also, in many of these groups, an outsider would find it difficult to accurately assess roles and relationships by only a casual observation of the group. Probably you have experienced going to a party, a class, or some activity where there are in-group jokes, a history of previous group activities that precluded you, and apparent roles and relationships that you did not understand.

Even experienced group observers such as teachers and counselors find it helpful to use structured assessment instruments on occasion to facilitate accurate understandings of persons in the group setting as well as group interactions themselves. The more popular of these techniques include sociograms, "Guess Who," communigrams, and social distance scales.

Sociometric Techniques

Sociometric techniques are basic arpproaches for the study of social relationships, such as degrees of acceptance, roles, and interactions within groups. Sociometric instruments provide a means for assessing and displaying such information as interpersonal choices made by group members.

Although sociometric devices appear to be relatively easy to devise, administer, and interpret, these impressions are deceiving. In fact, extreme caution and careful planning and analysis should be prerequisites to the use of these methods. In determining the appropriateness of conditions for using sociometric analyses, the following must be considered:

1. *The length of time the group has been together.* The longer the group has existed, the more likely that the data collected will be meaningful.
2. *The age level of the group.* A general rule of thumb is that the older the participants, the more likely that the information provided will be reliable. J. L. Moreno (1960), the acknowledged founder of modern sociometry, hypothesized that social cohesion develops with age (p. 700). He reported the cohesion of children's groups up to the age of 6 or 7 to be poor and weak; the cohesion of groups formed by children from 7 to 8 years to age 14 to be relatively high; and the cohesion of groups formed by youths between the ages of 14 and 18 to have become stabilized (p. 700–701).
3. *The size of the group.* Groups that are too large or too small will provide less valid information. It is also important to remember that all members of a group must be included in any sociometric studies.
4. *The activity provides a natural opportunity to secure responses.* In order for group members to participate willingly and honestly in sociometric analysis, the group activities for this purpose should appear logical and meaningful to the members. "What gives every sociometrically defined group its momentum is the 'criterion,' the common motive that draws persons together spontaneously, for a certain end" (Moreno, 1960, p. 97).
5. *The group chosen for study should be appropriate to the informational needs of the counselor.* For example, if it is a school counselor seeking to identify the causes of behavior problems in a given classroom, the observation of the same group of students in, for example, a recreational setting outside the classroom would not be as appropriate.

Constructing and Administering the Sociometric Test

From a construction standpoint, the sociometric test or inventory is a very simple instrument. The basic and most important aspect of its construction is the nature of the grouping situation, or criterion, upon which it is based; unless the criterion is appropriate to the particpants' ages, activites, and actual opportunities for association, the elicited responses will have little sociometric value. More specificially, a criterion or situation must be selected to elicit participants' choices that, when applied, will have practical significance, and to maintain the confidence of those participating, as previously noted, the results must be applied. Examples of school situations that lend themselves well to sociometric studies include assigning students to various committees, setting up small study groups, and organizing class projects. In these cases, and in many others, the selection of associates could appropriately be made by the participants themselves.

When the criterion has been determined, attention must next be directed to the number of choices the participant should make. Although the optimum number of choices has not been determined, if would appear that too few choices would not have the practical values of five or six where, for example, group assignments are to follow. It is recommended that sociometric techniques to be used with school groups contain only "positive" choices.

Much of the success of a sociometric test hinges upon how well it is administered. The person administering it must be respected and be on good terms with the group members. The actual administration of a sociometric test should be kept highly informal; any resemblance to a typical test situation should be avoided. The instrument itself should never be referred to as a test, nor should the group members be forewarned of its administration (in keeping with sociometric theory, which emphasizes spontaneity as an important aspect of response). For example, in a school setting, sociometric studies are more effective when the teacher merely states without prior or subsequent discussion that the class is going to engage in an activity—forming committees to give special reports, for instance—that requires small groups to be established, and that students' choices of associates are to be used as much as possible as a basis for grouping. The teacher then adds a statement about confidentiality and about the impossibility of honoring every choice of every student. Finally, the students are instructed to write their name at the top of the blank paper or card they will be given, number their paper from one to five, and list in order of preference the names of the students with whom they would like to work.

Cautions in Interpretation

The responses to sociometric questions first should be tabulated and then used to construct a sociogram—a graphic depiction of the interpersonal relationship existing in a group at the time a sociometric test is given to its members. A sociometric analysis of group structure requires that a sociogram be constructed. However, if each participant's relative degree of social acceptance is all that is desired, a simple count of the total responses each one receives is sufficient.

As previously noted, sociometric data must be interpreted with a great deal of caution. It is perhaps most appropriate to say that sociometric techniques do not analyze or provide interpretations in themselves, but rather intitiate or contribute to the assessment or understanding of persons. It is also important to remember that in many group settings the choices of group members may say more about the chooser than the chosen. Finally, we should recognize that some group members may not want to be chosen; they may prefer to be alone or with a few friends in certain group settings.

Perhaps the easiest of the different kinds of sociograms to make is that shown in Figure 8–8. This sociogram uses concentric circles in a targetlike pattern, with each student represented by a number. Only mutual positive choices are shown, and preferential rank is not considered. The highly chosen individuals, or sociometric stars, are placed in the small center circle; the sociometric isolates, students not chosen and who chose no one, are placed in the large outer circle; and all other students are place in the area between the inner and outer circles, those more frequently chosen being placed closer to the inner circle. Sex is indicated by different geometric designs: the males' number are placed within a triangle; the females' numbers are encircled. For even clearer differentiation, males are confined to one side of the figure, females to the other.

The "Guess Who?" Technique

Another useful sociometric technique is the "Guess Who?" questionnaire. This technique is best used with relatively well-established groups in which members have had the opportunity to become reasonably well acquainted. It is also most effective when the questions are positive in nature rather than negative. For

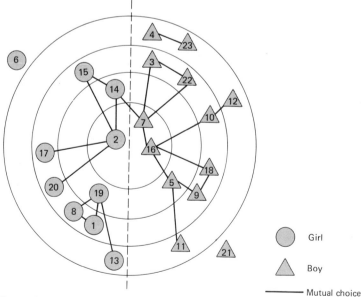

Figure 8–8. Sociogram depicting mutual choices.

example, "Who is most friendly?" is a better "Guess Who?" than "Who is the least friendly?" The "Guess Who?" questionnaire provides for the association of characteristics or activities with individuals. It can help us understand why some members of a group receive attention, behave in certain ways, or function in certain roles. We may also be able to identify those who are "popular" with group members and those who receive little, if any, recognition. The "Guess Who?" instrument is usually designed to collect specific information that counselors, teachers, or other group observers believe would be helpful in working with the group and its individual members. Figure 8–9 presents an example of a short "Guess Who?" instrument.

The directions for this technique may be altered to permit persons to list all group members they believe are, for example, funny, friendly, helpful, and so on. The teachers or other group observers may use a simple tally system that notes the total number of times each group member was mentioned for each item. A popular variation in school settings is one in which pupils are asked to assume that the class is going to put on a play. They are provided with a list of characters and asked to nominate classmates that could best portray the roles described. Examples of such characters might be as follows:

This person is known as "the arbitrator." They are always ready to try and prevent arguments from growing serious by suggesting compromises. They usually can see both sides of an argument and as a result rarely take sides.

This person is known as "the good humor person." They are always pleasant and good-natured. They smile a lot and laugh easily. They rarely show anger.

One other variation is to tell a story or describe a situation, real or fictional, in which group members are asked to assign to their peers the different characters. For example:

Group _____   Date _____

Directions: Write the name of at least one but no more than two persons whom you would identify
       as most outstanding in your group for the trait or activity listed. Your teacher (counselor, group
       leader) will use the results from your responses for planning group activities. If you cannot iden-
       tify a group member for an item, you may leave it blank. It is not necessary to sign your name.

1. Tells the funniest jokes or stories.   _____
2. Enjoys funny jokes and stories the most.   _____
3. Is the most friendly.   _____
4. Is the most helpful.   _____
5. Is the most sincere.   _____
6. Can always be depended on.   _____
7. Has the best imagination.   _____
8. Is a good organizer.   _____
9. Is optimistic.   _____
10. Is a good leader.   _____
11. Has special talents.   _____
12. Is generous.   _____

Figure 8–9. "Guess Who" example.

Example 8-6. The "Guess Who" Technique

Ron Bakersfield is a new student who has just enrolled in Snow Deep High School. In his previous school, Ron was an outstanding and all-round athlete, a good student, and popular with his fellow students. He is a handsome young man who dresses neatly and cleanly, but on this day he is a bit unsure of himself. He wonders if his new schoolmates will accept him, how long it will take him to get acquainted, who his new friends will be, what his new teachers will be like, and if he will make the teams. The school counselor, recognizing Ron as a new student, has called in two of the more popular students in the school to meet Ron and show him around. The first one to arrive is Marie Shafer, an attractive, personable girl, who greets Ron with a handshake and a big smile. The counselor suggests to Ron that Marie is known as the sunshine girl in the school because she is always smiling and has a friendly word for everyone. The next arrival is Craig Brewer, whom the counselor introduces as one of the more popular students in the school and whose hobby is photography. Craig appears also to be pleasant, but a bit more reserved that Marie. With an assurance that "we'll see that Ron gets around," Craig and Marie usher him out of the counselor's office. On the way to his first class, Ron is introduced in quick succession to Darlene, whom they refer to as 'Miss Energy'; Tom, a serious student who is taking pilot lessons; Rex, who was introduced as the most interesting storyteller in the school; and Dave, to whom they gave the label "Mr. Reliable."

At this point, Ron is beginning to feel more at home and more welcome in his new school and already sees the prospect of making some good friends with fine qualities.

After reading this brief scenario, to whom would you assign the roles of Ron, Marie, Craig, Darlene, Rex, Dave, Tom?

As Shertzer and Linden (1979) point out

The major advantage of the guess-who technique is its simplicity. It is relatively painless to administer and to score, and it can be used with persons of all age levels. Scoring is accomplished by simply counting the number of nominations received for each description. When both positive and negative descriptions are used, the number of negative nominations is subtracted from the number of positive nominations received for each characteristic. The major limitation of this method is that it does not provide very much information about patterns of interaction or communication in the group. The method is limited primarily to data on individual status and reputation (p. 446).

Communigrams

Another aspect of observation of persons in a group setting and of the group process is an assessment of the verbal participation of its members. This is perhaps the easiest communication pattern to observe and record because, in its simplest form, we are recording who talks and how often they talk over a given period of time. Figure 8–10 shows a chart in which the number of participations of each member of the group is noted with a check mark. Each check mark represents one communication, usually defined as an uninterrupted statement.

Susan Armstrong ɪɪɪɪ ɪɪɪ   Mary Smith   ɪɪɪɪ

Billy Bell   ɪɪ   Tommy Talbot   ɪɪɪ

Amy Christoph   ɪ

Figure 8–10.

Figure 8–11 illustrates an alternative that uses the same form, but indicates positions of members within the group to each other and to the group leader. Such reportings not only will identify those who frequently participate versus those who do not, but may also, for example, indicate that amount of discussion generated by certain topics and how members individually react to one topic and not another; enable comparisons between groups in terms of their frequency of communication; and, if carried one step further, as noted in Figure 8–12, will also indicate the direction of communication among members.

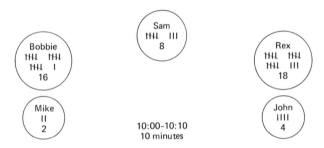

Figure 8–11.   (Myers & Myers, 1973, p. 135.)

Social Distance Scales

Another client participation technique that counselors may find useful are social distance scales. Most of the existing social distance or social acceptance scales devised for use with classroom or other school groups are patterned after the scale devised in 1925 by E. S. Bogardus (1925). The Bogardus scale was designed for measuring and comparing attitudes toward different nationalities—specifically, to determine the degrees to which various racial and nationality groups were accepted or rejected. Thus, social distance is usually defined by social psychologists as that distance a person indicates exists between other persons and himself or herself. This distance is usually identified through the reaction to statements that measure and compare attitudes of acceptance or rejection of other people. An example of a social distance item might be the following:

Tommy Rote	I would like him as a close friend	I would like him as a friend	I would like him as an acquaintance	I am indifferent toward him as a friend or acquaintance	I would prefer not to have him as a friend or acquaintance

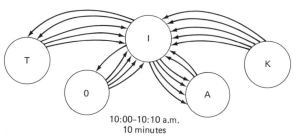

10:00–10:10 a.m.
10 minutes

Figure 8–12. (Myers & Myers, 1973, p. 137.)

Other social distance items may be built around such choices as with whom one would like to take trips, study, or go to a dance. The results from social distance scales may indicate a self social distance and group social distance. The degree of acceptance of the group by a person may be an index of "self score" and the degree of acceptance of the person by the group would be the "group score." Many studies of social distance scales in classrooms have tended to lead to the conclusion that the greatest contribution of social distance scales is in revealing the wide range of acceptance and rejection of any one student in a group. Again, as with many other client participation techniques, there is frequently a tendency to overuse or misinterpret them because of their simplicity of administration. Counselors and other users should be aware that such information does not reveal the "why" of a person's acceptance or rejection of others. Furthermore, the users of this instrument must determine how they can use negative data such as indicated group rejection to the client's advantage. (Obviously, calling the client's attention to his or her rejection by the group will create more problems than it would solve.)

Records

It has often been suggested that the first slabs of stone that our prehistoric ancestors carved out of the mountains were for the purpose of setting up personnel files. It appears that systems of recording are as old as civilization and that the primary object of much that has been recorded over the ages has been the individual. Record keeping is a reflection of the historical curiosity of humans to understand to the fullest extent possible their fellow humans (and just so we won't forget what we have already learned, we record it). Records are of importance to counselors and other helping professionals in understanding and working effectively and efficiently with their clients. It is in this context that records are discussed in the following paragraphs.

Basic Considerations

If records or a record system are to serve their potential for client understanding and assistance, certain basic considerations need to be examined before determining the nature and characteristics of the record and its attending system. These include the following.

The Extent of Record Keeping

The ever-increasing and seemingly never-ending preoccupation with record keeping may give all of us cause to wonder how many records we actually have in our name, where they are located, for what purposes, and so on. Extensive records have been maintained by the educational institutions that we attended, for even as students we become aware of the extensive and varied record data that the school maintains "to understand us better." Figure 8–13 rather accurately (but not too seriously) depicts the varying views to which the many records or types of data might, on occasion, seem to lend themselves.

In a more serious vein, Hummel and Humes (1984) pointed out that:

one of the dramatic developments in recent decades was the attention paid to student records. As class action suits developed during the 1960s, there was concern on the

Figure 8–13. "Harry High School" as seen through a multirecord system.

part of parents with regard to the use and misuse of pupil records and interpretation. This resulted in legislation in several of the state jurisdictions and culminated in the passage of federal legislation, namely, the Family Rights and Privacy Act.* Almost immediately the schools had to change their way of doing business. With the passage of this legislation, not only were parents permitted full access to pupil records and the privilege of denying access to them, but they now had the right to challenge the content of the pupil's record. Accordingly, cumulative records were purged and federal, state, and local guidelines were established for subsequent collection and use.

The new approach to record keeping posed many problems for pupil services. School psychologists, social workers, and school counselors had traditionally been prime contributors to the cumulative record through psychological reports, social case histories, and counselor notations. They now not only had to review the records for appropriateness, but also had to change ways of reporting results and contacts. Perhaps hardest hit were school psychologists who had been accustomed to writing clinical reports designed only for professional view and scrutiny. Reports now had to be written that could be also shared with parents and, at age eighteen, with students. There developed much "tooth gnashing" over watered-down reports that would contribute but little to the presenting problem. This difficulty was finally resolved through the medium of detailed oral reports, usually at team meetings, to be followed by more general written reports. (pp. 358–389)

The advent of the comptuer and other technological advances have, if anything, seemed to stimulate a challenge to gather and record data in a manner befitting these new developments in data storage, manipulation, and retrieval. Nor can school counselors belittle the importance of the decisions made on the basis of such recorded data—decisions that most frequently influence career directions and educational opportunities. Counselors working with school-aged clients through community agencies and other nonschool settings must also be aware of the extent and impact of school-maintained records.

Who Will Use the Client's Record?

The answer to that question varies across the many places in which counselors function. For example, counselors in private practice may, subject to legal limitations have exclusive access to a client's record, whereas, at the other extreme of the continuum, many school counselors may be expected to share client records with school administrative and supervisory personnel, teachers, parents, and, of course, the client. Counselors, ever concerned with client confidentiality, must at the onset determine who legally and ethically will have access to any data recorded in a systematic or institutional manner.

The use of student and client records also raises the question of record security. Although students and parents may exercise the right to examine their records, that does not lessen the counselor's reponsibility in the school, or any setting, to provide proper security for those records that are the responsibility of the counseling program. These responsibilities include provisions for the "lock and key" security of client records at all times, instructions and policies for nonprofessional (clerical) handling of records, and stated policies including ethical and legal guidelines for access to and review of records by clients, parents, and others. In determining "access" to school records, it must be noted

*Commonly referred to as the Buckley Amendment.

that certain records of students are at least quasi-public in nature. The questions that arise are who may inspect such records, for what purposes, and when?

Public records that are required to be kept and maintained by public officials are open to public inspection during reasonable office hours. Inspection of quasi-public records has been restricted mainly because of the sensitivity and confidentiality of the data contained in them. A general rule laid down by the courts may thus be stated: a person may inspect quasi-public records if the person can establish, to the satisfaction of the court, a justifiable interest in the records (Butler, Moran, and Vonderpool, 1972, p. 26).

What Are Other Legal and Ethical Considerations?

Practicing counselors, as well as those in preparation, may be confused somewhat by the apparent proliferation of statements by professional organizations providing ethical guidelines for the maintenance and use of client records. However, an examination of statements by the American Association for Counseling and Development and the American Psychological Association, to mention a few, would indicate little that is in conflict and much general agreement. These standards are presented in Appendices B and C.

In addition, your attention is directed to the American Bar Association's suggestions (1971) in regard to school policies for pupil records.

> To minimize the risk of improper disclosures, academic records should be kept separate from disciplinary records. The conditions of access to each should be set forth in an explicit policy statement. Transcripts of academic records should contain only information about academic status. Information from disciplinary or counseling files should not be available to unauthorized persons within the institution or to any person outside the institution without the express consent of the student involved, except under legal compulsion or in cases where the safety of persons or property is involved. No records should be kept which reflect political activities or beliefs of students. Special provision should be made to prevent misuse of old disciplinary records for former students. A student should have access to his records under reasonable circumstances. Administrative staff and faculty members should respect confidential information about students which they acquire in the course of their work. Students are likewise bound to respect the confidentiality of the files and records of faculty and administrators.

The primary legal concerns of counselors insofar as records and recording are concerned continue to focus upon the confidentiality of the counseling records and the right of privileged communications. Although attorneys have possessed this right by common law over the centuries and statutory law has extended this privilege to physicians, clergy, and sometimes, psychologists, counselors have limited legal guarnatee in terms of statutory provisions.

The courts generally use four fundamental conditions to determine whether a communication should be privileged (Ware, 1964):

1. The communications must originate in a confidence that they will not be disclosed.
2. This element of confidentiality must be essential to the full and satisfactory maintenance of the relation between parties.

3. The relation must be one which in the opinion of the community ought to be sedulously fostered.

4. The injury that would inure to the relation by the disclosure of the communications must be greater than the benefit thereby gained for the correct disposal of litigation. (p. 8)

School counselors must be particularly aware of the provisions of the Family Educational Rights and Privacy Act of 1974. Key statements from this act presented by Flygare (1975) point out the following:

A student (or his parents) must be given access to his records within 45 days from the time a request is made.

A student (or his parents) must be granted a hearing by the institution upon request to determine the validity of any document in the student's file.

Confidential letters or statements placed in the file prior to January 1, 1975, need not be disclosed under the law.

A student may waive his right of access to confidential letters regarding admissions, honors, or employment.

An educational institution cannot, with certain exceptions, release personally identifiable information about students.

Educational institutions must notify students and parents of their rights under the law. (p. 15)

The detailed provisions of this act are presented in Appendix D.

Furthermore, as Wilhelm and Case emphasized (1975), counselors must be aware of the implications of Title IX of the Education Amendments of 1972, effective July, 1975, which provided that:

no person . . . shall on the basis of sex be excluded from participation in, be denied the benefits of, or be subjected to discrimination under any education program receiving federal financial assistance. (p. 85)

The implications for record keeping are clear; sexual discrimination must not be maintained. That includes standardized test results based on male/female norms, and career exploration activities and counseling that reflect sex-role stereotyping.

School counselors should also be aware of other kinds of unacceptable statements often found in student records. Wilhelm and Case (1975) noted these frequent examples:

1. Libelous, unverified statements regarding the student.
2. Unverified statements regarding parents, family, or home.
3. Ambiguous, opinionated, subjective descriptions of the student, "glop" statements.
4. Factual but biased statements with negative implications.
5. Factual but inconsequential statements that add nothing to understanding the student.
6. Inferential statements with negative implications that may or may not be verifiable. (p. 85)

Counselors must bear in mind that "privileged communication" is for the benefit of the client. Thus, only the client has the option to waive that right and he or she may do so if he or she chooses, even if protected legally.

It should also be noted that privileged communications and confidentiality are not "one and the same" (Hummel and Humes, 1984).

> Litwack, Rochester, Oates, and Addison (1969) wrote that privileged communication and confidentiality have often been given the same meaning in the literature even though there is an important difference between the two terms. They explained that privileged communication refers to the right of the counselor to refuse to divulge any confidential information while testifying in a court of law (p. 108). Confidentiality, on the other hand, has an ethical meaning referring to a professional's decision that he or she should not and will not divulge what has been revealed to him in contacts with a client. (p. 108)

What Purposes Will the Client's Record Serve?

The use of the client's records will, of course, be determined to a large extent by the answer to the question previously raised—who are the users? There are certain traditional uses appropriate for almost all types of personnel records, such as:

- They provide an available pool of basic information about the person.
- They provide a means for recording and preserving meaningful information about the person for later use.
- They assist the users of the information in gaining a better understanding of the person with whom they will be interacting.
- They assist the person on whom the record is maintained to gain new insights and perspectives.

In addition, counselors use records in:

- Preparation for the counseling interview.
- The development of case studies.
- Client placement or referral.
- Consultation with other therapists, medical personnel, parents.
- Follow-up and research studies.

School counselors also use records for the following purposes:

- Identifying students who may be in need of counseling assistance.
- Identifying students who possess special talents or interests.
- Identifying students who may have special needs because of physical handicaps, for example.
- Assisting faculty and parents in gaining a better understanding of the individual student, which, it is hoped, may contribute to positive student–parent and student–teacher relationships.
- Assisting the individual student to gain self-understanding.
- Contributing to school and community needs assessments of school-aged populations.
- Facilitating the orientation of new pupils.

These listings are meant to be illustrative only and not exclusive, since any practicing counselor could readily expand on them.

Record Interpretation

The interpretation of any kind of counseling or personnel record will obviously be limited by the data recorded, and the skill and understanding of the user. Some guidelines or safeguards include the following:

- Records provide only clues to behavior—no more, and some clues will be relevant whereas others are not.
- Does the present—the time at which you are examining the record data—compare to the past—the time when the data are originally recorded?
- Look for trends or significant changes, but beware of the fact that many people have unique patterns of growth and development.
- Feelings, attitudes, and intensity of emotions seldom show in recorded information.
- Distinguish between symptoms and causes.
- Determine if record data are based on substantiated facts or merely represent opinions.
- Remember that records present only a small sample of the client's behavior.
- School records, especially, can also provide opportunities to examine certain habitual performance measures, such as attendance, grades, and health.

Summary

This chapter has presented an overview of nonstandardized techniques that may be used in human assessment. Although many nonstandardized techniques cannot lay claim to either the validity or reliability of standardized instruments, they nonetheless provide the counselor with a wide range of data collection options from which to choose, according to the dictates of the counseling situation and the assessment needs of one's clients.

Observation was noted as the most popular of the techniques usually used to assess others; however, in order that it be as accurate and meaningful as possible, it was suggested that some forms for recording observations such as anecdotal records and forms for further directing observations towards specific charcteristics such as rating scales and checklists might be used. Questionnaires and autobiographies were suggested as techniques in which useful information can be collected. Assessing behavior and roles in groups by such techniques as sociograms, communigrams, social distance scales, and role playing were suggested. There followed an examination of the role of records in human assessment and some of the legal and ethical considerations in record keeping. Assessment, both standardized and nonstandardized, can play an important role in career planning and decision making. Chapter 9 examines this important activity.

References

American Bar Association. (1971). *The confidentiality of pupil school records.* Washington, D.C.: National Assocation of American School Principals.

Bogardus, E. S. (1925). Measuring social distance. *Journal of Applied Sociology, 9,* 299–308

Brown, W.F., & Holtzman, W. H. (1967). *Survey of study habits and attitudes (SSHA).* Cleveland, OH: The Psychological Corporation, Harcourt-Brace.

Butler, H. E., Jr., Moran K. D., & Vonderpool, F. A., Jr. (1972). *Legal aspects of student records.* (Nolpe Monograph Series No. 5). Topeka, KS: National Organization on Legal Problems of Education.

Clifton, J. A. (Ed.). (1970). *Applied anthoropology: Readings into the uses of the science of man.* Boston: Houghton Mifflin.

Egan, G. (1977). *You and men: The skills of communicating and relating to others.* Monterey, CA: Brooks/Cole.

Flygare, T. (1975). *The legal rights of students.* Bloomington, IN: Phi Delta Kappa Educational Foundation.

Hopkins, K. D., & Stanley, J. C. (1981). *Educational and psychological measurement and evaluation* (6th ed.). Englewood Cliffs, NJ: Prentice-Hall.

Hummel, D. L., & Humes, C. W. (1984). *Pupil services: Development, coordination, administration.* New York: Macmillan.

Kazdin, A. E. (1981). Behavioral observation. In M. Herseu & A. S. Bellack (Eds.), *Behavioral assessment: A practical handbook* (2nd ed.), (pp. 101–124). New York: Pergamon.

Kiley, M. A. (1975). *Personal and interpersonal appraisal techniques.* Springfield, IL: Charles C. Thomas.

Leitenberg, H., Agras, W. S., Thompson, L. D., & Wright, D. E. (1968). Feedback in behavior modificaiton: An experimental analysis in two phobic cases. *Journal of Applied Behavior Analysis, 1,* 131–137.

Litwack, L., Rochester, D., Oates, R., & Addison, W. (1969). Testimonial-privileged communication and the school counselor. *The School Counselor, 17,* 108–111.

Moreno, J. L., et al. (1960). *The sociometry reader.* New York: Free Press.

Myers, G. E., & Myers, M. T. (1973). *The dynamics of human communication.* New York: McGraw-Hill.

Phillips, E. L. (1968). Achievement place: Token reinforcement procedures in a home-style rehabilitation setting for "pre-deliquent" boys. *Journal of Applied Behavior Analysis, 1,* 213–223.

Shertzer, B., & Linden, J. (1979). *Fundamentals of individual appraisal: Assessment techniques for counselors.* Boston: Houghton Mifflin.

Ware, M. L. (Ed.). (1984). *Law of guidance and counseling.* Cincinnati, OH: W. H. Anderson.

Wasky, S. L. (1970). *Political science—the discipline and its dimensions.* New York: Charles Scribner's Sons.

Wilhelm, C. D., & Case, M. (1975). Telling it like it is—Improving school records. *School Counselor, 23,* 84–90.

Wrenn C. G. (1972). *The counselor in a changing world.* Washington, D. C.: American Personnel and Guidance Association.

CHAPTER 9

COUNSELING FOR CAREER PLANNING AND DECISION MAKING

Introduction

As noted in Chapter 1, the counseling movement in America has had a long and traditional association with and concern for career development and decision making. This chapter will introduce you to this traditional area of counselor activity. The specific objectives of the chapter are (a) to inform the reader of specific interests in and influences on career planning; (b) to present popular theories of career decision making; and (c) to examine career planning and counseling in various settings.

During its early years, organized counseling efforts consisted primarily of vocational guidance. This early interest, originating with Parsons, was an outgrowth of a concern for the complexity of the world of work and the resultant difficulty in career planning, a concept that is still viable today. As originally practiced by Parsons and his associates, the concept of matching youths with jobs, based on the characteristics of both, has also had a long and traditional assocation with the counseling movement.

As this concept was broadened and other basic activities were added in the 1920s and 1930s, vocational guidance became a service activity most frequently identified with the provision of occupational and educational information. In the late 1950s and 1960s, with the original impetus from the National Defense Education Act of 1958, placement and follow-up also became significant activities of the vocational or career guidance phase of counseling programs. Thus, for nearly 60 years the counseling movement had been the caretaker for career planning in the schools and agencies of this country.

In 1971, however, the United States Office of Education, through the Commissioner of Education at that time, Sidney P. Marland, Jr., committed more than $9 million of discretionary funds to research and development projects focusing on the establishment of comprehensive career education models. With this act, the concept of career education 'as an all-school responsibility was launched, and counselors were no longer the sole designated professionals for providing career counseling and guidance for students in schools.

Definitions and Clarifications

An outgrowth of the career education movement and the attending emphasis on career counseling and guidance has been a proliferation of definitions, with attending confusion, seeking to differentiate between such terms as career education, career development, career guidance, vocational education, and human development. In this chapter and elsewhere in this text, the following definitions apply:

Career: "The totality of work one experiences in a lifetime" (Hoyt, 1974, p. 6). A more limited definition would view a career as the sum total of one's work expereinces in a general occupational category such as teaching, accounting, medicine, or sales.

Occupation: A specific job or work activity.

Career Development: That aspect of one's total development that emphasizes learning about, preparation for, entry into, and progression in the world of work.

Career Education: Those planned-for educational experiences that facilitate a person's career development and preparation for the world of work. The totality of experiences through which one learns about and prepares for engaging in work as part of a way of living. A primary responsibility of the school with an emphasis on learning about, planning for, and preparing to enter a career.

Career Guidance: Those activities that are carried out by counselors in a variety of settings for the purpose of stimulating and facilitating career development in persons over their working lifetimes. These activities include assistance in career planning, decision making, and adjustment.

Occupational Information: Data concerning training and related educational programs, careers, career patterns, and employment trends and opportunities.

Vocation: A trade or occupation.

Vocational Education: Education that is preparatory for a career in a vocational or technical field.

It should be noted that these rather limited definitions are perhaps at one end of the continuum. For example, a career is sometimes defined as the sum total of person's life experiences and life-styles, whereas career education is frequently viewed as consisting of all activities and experiences, planned or otherwise, that prepare the person for work. However, straightforward and concise, although limited, definitions are most practical in specific planning for programs of career counseling development, or education.

Current Interests in Career Planning

As previously noted, the present high level of interest in career planning was initially stimulated when Sidney Marland made his plea for "career education now" in a speech to the National Association of Secondary School Principals at its convention in Houston in 1971. Since then, the concept has swept the educational establishment in the United States. Educators from every field and discipline have been involved in the movement. Additionally, many state legislatures passed career education legislation, and career education became a mandate of the Congress of the United States when Public Law 93-380 was signed by former President Ford in August 1974. In less than a decade, more than ten major national associations endorsed career education, hundreds of publications on career education were published and distributed, and an astounding array of proponents and interpreters of the career education concept emerged. However, even with the rapid development of career education and the many and varied publications and spokespeople, certain basic concepts can be noted that may assist counselors and potential counselors in understanding the background, basic principles, and relationships of this movement.

As a rationale for the movement, Kenneth B. Hoyt, director of the Office of Career Education of the United States Office of Education, stated in his paper "An Introduction to Career Education" (1974) eleven primary criticisms of American education that career education sought to correct:

1. Too many persons leaving our education system are deficient in the basic academic skills required for adaptability in today's rapidly changing society.
2. Too many students fail to see meaningful relationships between what they are being asked to learn in school and what they will do when they leave the educational system. This is true of both those who remain to graduate and those who drop out of the educational system.
3. American education, as currently structured, best meets the educational needs of the minority of persons who will someday become college graduates. It has not given equal emphasis to meeting the educational needs of that vast majority of students who will never be college graduates.
4. American education has not kept pace with the rapidity of change in the postindustrial occupational society. As a result, when worker qualifications are compared with job requirements, we find overeducated and undereducated workers are present in large numbers. Both the boredom of the overeducated worker and the frustration of the undereducated worker have contributed to the growing presence of worker alienation in the total occupational society.
5. Too many persons leave our educational system at both the secondary and collegiate levels, unequipped with the vocational skills, the self-understanding and career decision-making skills, or the work attitudes that are essential for making a successful transition from school to work.
6. The growing need for and presence of women in the work force have been adequately reflected in neither the educational nor the career options typically pictured for girls enrolled in our educational system.
7. The growing needs for continuing and recurrent education on the part of adults are not being adequately met by our current systems of public education.

8. Insufficient attention has been given to learning opportunities outside the structure of formal education which exist and are increasingly needed by both youths and adults in our society.
9. The general public, including parents and the business-industry-labor community, has not been given an adequate role in formulation of educational policy.
10. American education, as currently structured, does not adequately meet the needs of minority, nor of economically disadvantaged persons in our society.
11. Post high school education has given insufficient emphasis to educational programs at the subbaccalaureate degree level. (pp. 1–2)

Obviously, career development, career education, and career counseling are interwoven and interrelated. One without the other is ineffective and meaningless. As career education stimulates career development, career counseling provides direction for career education and development. Furthermore, clarification of the career education movement and the related role and function of the counselor may result from noting the basic concept assumptions suggested in the United States Office of Education (USOE) policy paper of 1975:

1. Since both one's career and one's education extend from the preschool through the retirement years, career education must also span almost the entire life cycle.
2. The concept of productivity is central to the definition of work and so to the entire concept of career education.
3. Since "work" includes unpaid activites as well as paid employment, career education's concerns, in addition to its prime emphasis on paid employment, extend to the work of the student as a learner, to the growing numbers of volunteer workers in our society, to the work of the full-time homemaker, and to work activities in which one engages as part of leisure and/or recreational time.
4. The cosmopolitan nature of today's society demands that career education embrace a multiplicity of work values, rather than a single work ethic, as a means of helping each individual answer the question, "Why should I work?"
5. Both one's career and one's education are best viewed in a developmental, rather than in a fragmented, sense.
6. Career education is for all persons—the young and the old—the mentally handicapped and the intellectually gifted—the poor and the wealthy—males and females—students in elementary schools and in the graduate colleges.
7. The societal objectives of career education are to help all individuals: (a) want to work; (b) acquire the skills necessary for work in these times; and (c) engage in work that is satisfying to the individual and beneficial to society.
8. The individualistic goals of career education are to make work: (a) possible; (b) meaningful; and (c) satisfying for each individual throughout his or her lifetime.
9. Protection of the individual's freedom to choose and assistance in making and implementing career decisions are of central concern to career education.
10. The expertise required for implementing career education is to be found in many parts of society and is not limited to these employed in formal education. (pp. 7–8)

Recognizing that career education and complementary programs of career counseling should be developmental in nature and thus not limited to a particular age group, the Bureau of Occupational and Adult Education, the Office of Career Education, and the National Institute of Education engaged in research and developmental efforts that led to four operational models for career education:

1. The Employer-Based Model seeks primarily to serve teenage students through an optional out-of-school program of personalized educational experiences in an employer-based setting. The model stresses community participation, particularly by businesses and organizations, in cooperation with the schools, to offer an alternative educational program relevant to the individual's interests and needs.

2. The Home-Based Model is designed to introduce a variety of experiences using the home as a center for learning, especially for persons 18 to 25 years of age who have left school. The objectives are to develop educational systems for the home and the community; to provide a new career education programs for adults; to establish a guidance and career placement system to assist individuals in occupational and related life-roles; and to develop more competent workers. A Career Education Extension service will be established to coordinate the use of mass media and career education resources.

3. The Rural/Residential-Based Model is a research and demonstration project which will test the hypothesis that entire disadvantaged rural families can experience lasting improvement in their economic and social conditions through an intensive program at a residential center. Families are drawn from a six-state area to the project site in Glasgow, Montana. Programs will provide serivces to the entire family, including day care, health care, educational programs from kindergarten through adult, welfare, counseling, cultural and recreational opportunities. The objective is to provide rural families with employment capabilities suitable to the area, so that students will be able and ready to find employment in the area after completing the program.

4. The School-Based Model is, by far, the most common of the four models, and is the one of greatest interest to us. USOE sponsored the development of six demonstration projects through the Center for Vocational and Technical Education of the Ohio State University. The development and validation effort which was undertaken is quite extensive, and includes several school districts. . . . In all, about 115 schools, 4,200 teachers and administrators, and 85,000 students are involved. A single model [has been] developed for ALL the sites, so . . . the result [is] a model that has been tested for applicability in a variety of settings. Local educational agencies [cooperated] in the development of curricular and instructional materials to achieve specific objectives. These "treatments," along with materials located in an ongoing national search, [have been classified] and [catalogued] for dissemination to other educational agencies. Extensive in-service teacher education is part of the development program. (Florida Department of Education, 1974, p. 62)

The school-based comprehensive education model provides a theoretical base for linkages between career counseling and career education. As Ryan (1978) noted:

The School-Based Comprehensive Education Model (CCEM) has greater overall potential to make an impact on all students in grades K to 12 and was selected as the focus for linking career guidance to career education. The research and field testing related to CCEM have exerted a powerful influence on curriculum design and career guidance from 1971 to 1977. The CCEM illustrates a sequential program of career awareness in grades K–6, career exploration in 7–9, and career preparation in grades

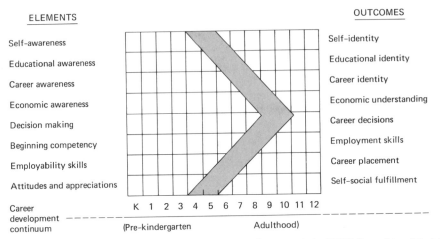

ELEMENTS   OUTCOMES

Self-awareness	Self-identity
Educational awareness	Educational identity
Career awareness	Career identity
Economic awareness	Economic understanding
Decision making	Career decisions
Beginning competency	Employment skills
Employability skills	Career placement
Attitudes and appreciations	Self-social fulfillment

Career development continuum   K 1 2 3 4 5 6 7 8 9 10 11 12

(Pre-kindergarten   Adulthood)

Figure 9–1. The comprehensive career education models (CCEM) matrix. *(Florida Department of Education, 1974, p. 61.)*

10–12. The basic model presented in Figure 9–1 identifies the eight basic elements of career education.

Underlying CCEM is the premise that intensive career guidance permeates the curriculum throughout grades K–12. Counseling and guidance are viewed as essential elements that assist the student with developing self-awareness and career awareness and with improving decision-making skills. Each element of CCEM requires a programmatic effort across all grades and strongly suggests a career guidance curriculum to assist youth in achieving the intended outcome. Each of the eight elements is defined as follows:

Self-Awareness. The student becomes aware of himself, his needs, strengths, and personal likes and dislikes so that he or she may develop self-knowledge and a positive self-identity that will aid in making effective life career decisions.

Educational Awareness. The student recognizes the significance of basic skill development and the mastery of content knowledge as a means of achieving career goals.

Career Awareness. The student realizes that career development includes progression through stages of education and occupational experiences, and understands that there are a variety of occupations found in the world of work and that there is a relationship between career and life-style.

Economic Awareness. The student understands the relationship between personal economics, life-styles, and occupations.

Decision making. The student understands that decision making includes responsible action in identifying alternatives, selecting the alternative most consistent with personal goals, and taking steps to implement the course of action. Students are proficient in using resource information to make career decisions.

Beginning Competencies. The student develops basic cognitive skills that are required to identify the objectives of a task, outline procedures, perform required operations, and evaluate the results.

Appreciations and Attitudes. The student develops an internalized value system that includes a valuing of personal career roles and the roles assumed by others. Appre-

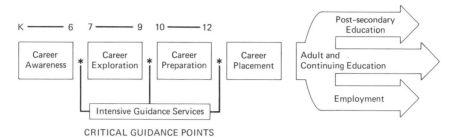

Figure 9-2. A comprehensive career education system. *(Florida Department of Education, 1974, p. 65.)*

ciation of one's personal career role should lead to an active, satisfying participation in the work of society. (pp. 12–14)

Figure 9–1 and 9–2 depict this model as presented by the Florida Department of Education (1974).

The Changing Nature of the World of Work

In addition to the needs that prompted the career education movement, there have also been other needs generated by significant changes in some of our traditional concepts of careers and work. Symptomatic of these changes are the following:

- *No longer one world—one career.*

Whereas our ancestors, perhaps even our parents, could, upon identifying their life's work, enter into their own little world and career for life, there are increasing probabilities that most persons entering the work force in the 1980s will have, at the very least, several different and significant careers over the span of their life's work. From a career standpoint, we are now living in an age in which the rapidity of technological development can affect what we do and how we do it almost literally overnight. Counselors are being more frequently reminded that such changes can result in increasing number of adults who, either by choice or necessity, will be making mid-life career decisions. This was pointed out by Ferrini and Parker (1978):

Evidence is mounting that the single career norm within the American workforce may soon become a phenomenon of the past. In the early 1970s, publications such as Striner's *Continuing Education as a National Capital Investment* (1971), Sheppard and Herrick's *Where Have All the Robots Gone* (1972) and the U.S. Department of Health, Education and Welfare's report *Work in America* (1973) began arguing for more flexible work and educational opportunities for employed adults. Career change, in particular, began to be perceived as a necessary option for many adults seeking further growth and self-renewal. (p. 3)

- *No longer is the concept "Men only—Women only" appropriate for career planning.*

The influx of women into the workplace since World War II has changed "who" is working. "Where " they are working has also changed as recent generations have witnessed the elimination of many barriers to career entry, which in the past limited certain professions and occupations exclusively to certain populations or sexes. Career exclusiveness, for example, excluded women from such traditional male professions and occupations as engineering, airline piloting, and taxicab and truck driving, to mention but a few. These once male-dominated careers and some, such as nursing for women, have been effectively challenged not only in the courts, but, more importantly, in the world of work. Additionally, the antipoverty and antidiscrimination movements have further challenged the exclusiveness of certain careers that were once limited to only racial majority members of upper socioeconomic income populations.

- *No longer the old college try and tie.*

Much has also been written in recent years regarding the decline of demand in the job market for the college graduate. Although this is not necessarily, as some claim, a rationale for declining college enrollments, it indicates that career opportunities are no longer tied directly to the level and locale of educational preparation, but may be more appropriately tied to the career relevancy of one's educational preparation and the opportunities available in a constantly shifting job market.

- *No longer can the future be predicted by the present.*

In other times it was possible for those interested in charting their future to make many appropriate preparations and predictions based on their knowledge of the present, even the past. However, changing technology plus national resource development and depletion have made it increasingly difficult, if not almost impossible, in recent years to adequately predict the future by examining only the present and past. The accelerated rate of change in modern society, prevents us from assuming, as we might have in the past, that the future will be similar to the present. In fact, we must recognize that much present planning is being based on what is anticipated in the future. Furthermore, this science of future predicting has become an increasingly precise and accurate one. Even without the scientific evidence, the one certainty we can predict for the future is that it will be different.

- *No longer is one in charge of one's own destiny.*

It is clear that the day of the rugged individualist—one who would achieve his or her own destiny—is but a memory. In today's complicated society with its many interacting forces, there are many variables affecting the destiny of people over which they have little or no control and of which many are unaware. Although people can plan and chart their futures, they must also consider alternatives and adjustments. Finally, it is evident that individual entrepreneurship and "locally owned" have given way to the corporate conglomerates with absentee ownership where a person may be known more by the group's achievements than by his or her own individual efforts.

Herr and Cramer (1984) contrasted changes in the work ethic in the 1960s and 1980s as noted in Table 9–1.

Table 9–1. Trends in the Work Ethic in the 1960s and the 1980s.

1960s	1980s
The Good Provider Theme The breadwinner—the man who provides for his family—is the real man *The Independence Theme* To make a living by working is to "stand on one's own two feet and avoid dependence on others." *The Success Theme* Hard work always pays off *The Self-Respect Theme* Hard work of any type has dignity whether it be menial or exalted. A man's inherent worth is reflected in the act of working.	*Reduced Fear of Economic Insecurity* For most people economic security continues to dominate their lives. But today people take some economic security for granted. A substantial minority say that they are now prepared to take certain risks with their own economic security for the sake of enhancing the quality of life. *Economic Division of Labor Between the Sexes* The economic discipline that maintained the rigidity of sex roles in the past has weakened. The idea of women working for purposes of self-fulfillment rather than economic motives gains wider acceptance all the time. *The Psychology of Entitlement* A broad new agenda of social rights is growing and a psychological process is developing whereby a person's wants and desires become converted into a set of presumed rights. *The Adversary Culture Challenges the Cult of Efficiency* The average American has begun to wonder whether too great a concern with efficiency and rationalization is not robbing life of the excitement and pleasure desired. *The Changing Meaning of Success* An increasing number of people are coming to feel that there is such a thing as enough money. A "big earner" who has settled for an unpleasant life style is no longer considered more successful than someone with less money who has created an agreeable life style. People are no longer as ready to make sacrifices for economic success as they were in the past.

Source: Herr and Cramer, 1984, p. 36.

Theories of Career Development and Decision Making

One of the more fascinating aspects of the study of careers, both formally and informally, is the never-ending attempt to identify why people end up in certain careers. In history we may read about the factors that resulted in a lifetime of politics for a Franklin D. Roosevelt, the multicareer talents of a Benjamin Franklin or a Thomas Jefferson, the cowboy who became O. Henry, the famous author, and more recently, the actor who became President of the United States, Ronald Reagan. At one time or another we have probably been curious about the career decisions of friends and acquaintances. But to become more personal, why are you in your present career? What influenced your career planning and decision making? You probably have been asked this question before, and as you reflected and responded, you may have analyzed a set of facts or reasons that appeared relevant to your decisions. You presented some plausible explanation. Many of us have also offered career advice to others, based on our own personal career experiences or personal "theory" of career development. Even so, one must recognize the biases and limitations of one's own experiences. To develop a theory to a usable state, it is necessary to gather data that are relevant, to study the relationships between the data, and finally, to speculate on what these mean. One's speculations are stated as hypotheses, explanations, or predictions, which can be tested. If a theory proves to have some validity, it will be built on and developed further through research and application activities.

Counselors and others who work as helping professionals with youths and adults for their career development, planning, and adjustment must have some understanding of the better recognized and researched theories of career development that have emerged in the last half of this century. An understanding of such theories gives the practicing counselor a knowledge of the studies of others, usually specialists in the field. They provide a rationale for counselor action that goes beyond personal experience and intuition.

Because many disciplines (education, economics, psychology, sociology) are interested in and actively engaged in investigating various career questions, a multitude of therories have emerged. Both the numbers of theories and the extensiveness of investigation of some preclude any attempt here to analyze the various major theories in detail. Also, it is appropriate to point out that "all theory is imperfect, a fact that is sometimes overlooked by zealous psychologists seeking to 'prove' theories. It should properly be assumed that theories will eventually die and be replaced by newer theories that deal with observed events in a more general and useful way than their predecessors" (Osipow, 1983, p. 3). In this regard, we would note that in recent years the relevancy of many of the traditional theories of career choice have been examined for their appropriateness for the high-tech information processing work world of the 1980s and 1990s. With these limitations in mind, let us explore several of the more popular categories for illustrative purposes only and without any intent to suggest or recommend a particular theoretical approach.

The Process Theories

The process theories state, in effect, that occupational choice and eventual entry is a process consisting of stages or steps that the individual will go through. For example, Ginzberg, Ginsburg, Axelrod, and Herma (1951) analyzed the process of occupational decision making in terms of three periods—fantasy choices, tentative choices, and realistic choices. This theory suggests a process that moves increasingly toward realism in career decision making as one becomes older.

In 1972, Ginzberg modified the original theory to suggest that the process of vocational choice and development is lifelong and open-ended. In the process, achieving the optimum is more appropriate to describe the ongoing efforts of persons as they seek to find the most suitable job. Originally, Ginzberg and colleagues suggested that the crystallization of occupational choice inevitably had the quality of compromise. Ginzberg's revised theory also places considerable weight on constraints such as family income and situation, parental attitudes and values, opportunities in the world of work, and value orientations. Both the early theory and Ginzberg's later revision suggest the importance of the early school years in influencing later career planning.

Osipow (1983) noted:

> The authors of the theory conclude that four important ingredients contribute to the adequacy of an individual's occupational choice process during adolescence. These are reality testing, the development of a suitable time perspective, the ability to defer gratifications, and the ability to accept and implement compromises in vocational plans. Should too many of these ingredients fail to develop properly, a deviant vocational pattern is likely to emerge. It further seems reasonable that should these four traits fail to develop adequately, the youth's overall emotional adjustment is not likely to be effective. Thus, a tie between emotional stability and vocational deviancy seems to exist, but whether of a casual or correlate nature is not clear. (p. 199)

Blau, Gustad, Jessor, Parnes, and Wilcock (1956) conceived of occupational choice as a process of compromise, continually modified, between preferences for and expectations of being able to get into various occupations. They identified eight factors determining entry into an occupation. Four of these characterize the occupation: demand, technical (functional) qualifications, personal (nonfunctional) qualifications, and rewards. Those characterizing the person were information about an occupation, technical skills, social characteristics, and value orientations. Herr and Cramer (1984) pointed out:

> Blau et al. suggest that geography, the historical moment in time, occupational characteristics, political factors, and the occupational possibility structure and its requirements affect anyone's career development. Stopping there, however, understates situational effects on choice, because while interacting with such external circumstances, the individual has also incorporated and will act on the belief system held by family, peers, neighborhood, ethnic, and religious groups that also define his or her "situation." (p. 110)

The Developmental Theories

The developmental theories relevant to career planning view career development as one aspect of a person's total development. A leading researcher in career or vocational development theory, Donald Super, formulated a theory of vocational development in 1953 that became a basis for later research and theory. Super's original propositions were as follows:

1. People differ in their abilities, interests, and personalities.
2. They are qualified, by virtue of these circumstances, each for a number of occupations.
3. Each of the occupations requires a characteristic pattern of abilities, interests, and personality traits, with tolerances wide enough, however, to allow both some variety of occupations for each individual and some variety of individuals in each occupation.
4. Vocational preferences and competencies, and situations in which people live and work, and hence their self-concepts, change with time and experience (although self-concepts are generally fairly stable from late adolescence until later maturity), making choice and adjustment a continuous process.
5. This process may be summed up in a series of life stages, characterized as those of growth, exploration, establishment, maintenance, and decline, and these stages may in turn be subdivided into (a) fantasy, tentative, and realistic phases of the exploratory stage, and (b) the trial and stable phases of the establishment stage.
6. The nature of the career pattern (that is, the occupational level attained and the sequence, frequency, and duration of trial and stable jobs) is determined by the individual's parental socioeconomic level, mental ability, and personality characteristics, and by the opportunities to which he is exposed.
7. Development through the life stages can be guided partly by facilitating the process of maturation of abilities and interests and partly by aiding in reality testing and in the development of the self-concept.
8. The process of vocational development is essentially that of developing and implementing a self-concept; it is a compromise process in which the self-concept is a product of the interaction of inherited aptitudes, neural and endocrine make-up, opportunity to play various roles, and evaluation of the extent to which the results of role playing meet with the approval of superiors and fellows.
9. The process of compromise between individual and social factors, between self-concept and reality, is one of role playing, whether the role is played in fantasy, in the counseling interview, or in real life activities such as school classes, clubs, part-time work, and entry jobs.
10. Work satisfaction and life satisfaction depend upon the exent to which the individual finds adequate outlets for his abilities, interests, personality traits, and values; they depend upon his establishment in a type of work, a work situation, and a way of life in which he can play the kind of role which his growth and exploratory experiences have led him to consider congenial and appropriate. (pp. 189–190)

As may be noted, Super (1975) pointed out that like other aspects of development, vocational development may be conceived of as beginning early in life and proceeding along a continuum until late in life, passing through the stages of growth, exploration, establishment, maintenance, and decline. At each of these stages the person must master increasingly difficult tasks. Such a concept of vocational development leads logically, according to Super, to that of vocational maturity as denoting the degree of development reached on such a continuum. In revisions to his original theory, Super, Starishevsky, Matlin, and Jordaan (1963) pointed out that one's occupation makes possible the playing of a role appropriate to the self-concept of the person. This process "requires a person to recognize himself as a distinctive individual, yet at the same time to be aware of the similarities between himself and others" (Osipow, 1983, p. 154). Role playing, stimulated by the process of identification, further facilitates the development of the vocational self-concept among youths. This does not suggest, however, that a person's characteristics or traits are so unique that only a specific "type" of person would qualify. To the contrary, Super suggested that the range of individual abilities and the latitude within occupational areas result in a multi-potential of appropriate opportunities for most people. During the process,

> the individual moves through life stages each of which calls for vocational behavior of a different sort. The adolescent is cast in the role of explorer searching for career direction. The young adult must translate the direction taken into action through training and job seeking. The more mature adult must find a place within a vocation, elaborate upon it, and secure a position. During each of these phases of vocational development, certain behaviors are more apt to result in growth than others. The degree to which the individual accomplishes the vocational tasks is a function of the adequacy with which the behaviors appropriate to each phase of development have been performed. (Osipow, 1983, p. 158)

Zaccaria (1965) has reported that those who formulate developmental tasks generally agree on the following statements:

1. Individual growth and development is continuous.
2. Individual growth can be divided into periods or life stages for descriptive purposes.
3. Individuals in each life stage can be characterized by certain general characteristics that they have in common.
4. Most individuals in a given culture pass through similar developmental stages.
5. The society makes certain demands upon individuals.
6. These demands are relatively uniform for all members of the society.
7. The demands differ from stage to stage as the individual goes through the developmental process.
8. Developmental crises occur when the individual perceives the demand to alter his present behavior and to master new learnings.
9. In meeting and mastering developmental crises, the individual moves from one developmental stage of maturity to another developmental stage of maturity.
10. The task appears in its purest form at one stage.
11. Preparation for meeting the developmental crises or developmental tasks occurs in the life stage prior to the stage in which it must be mastered.
12. The developmental task or crisis may arise again during a later phase in somewhat different form.
13. The crisis or task must be mastered before the individual can successfully move on to a subsequent developmental stage.
14. Meeting the crisis successfully by learning the required tasks leads to societal approval, happiness, and success with later crises and their correlative tasks.
15. Failing in meeting a task or crisis leads to disapproval by society. (p. 373)

Havighurst (1964) discussed vocational development as a lifelong process consisting of six stages from childhood to old age. Each age period has characteristic tasks that must be successfully achieved if a person is to attain happiness and success with tasks appropriate to the vocational stages that follow. Havighurst outlined the developmental stages as indicated in Table 9–2.

Personality Theories

Personality theories view vocational preferences as expressions of personality. They suggest that much career-seeking behavior is an outgrowth of efforts to, in effect, match one's individual characteristics with those of a specific occupational field. As one example, you may note Holland's theory of personality types and environmental models. This theory is based on major assumptions regarding personality types, their determination and relation to various out-

Table 9–2. Vocational Development: A Lifelong Process

Stages of Vocational Development	Age
I. Identification with a Worker Father, Mother, other significant persons. The concept of Working becomes an essential part of the ego-ideal.	5–10
II. Acquiring the Basic Habits of Industry Learning to organize one's time and energy to get a piece of work done. School work, chores. Learning to put work ahead of play in appropriate situations.	10–15
III. Acquiring Identity as a Worker in the Occupational Structure Choosing and preparing for an occupation. Getting work experience as a basis for occupational choice and for assurance of economic independence.	15–25
IV. Becoming a Productive Person Mastering the skills of one's occupation. Moving up the ladder with one's occupation.	25–40
V. Maintaining a Productive Society Emphasis shifts toward the societal and away from the individual aspect of the worker's role. The individual sees himself as a responsible citizen in a productive society. He pays attention to the civic responsibility attached to his job. The individual is at the peak of his occupational career and has time and energy to adorn it with broader types of activity. He pays attention to inducting younger people into stages III and IV.	40–70
VI. Contemplating a Productive and Responsible Life This person is retired from work or is in the process of withdrawing from the worker's role. He looks back over his work life with satisfaction, sees that a personal social contribution has been made, and is pleased with it. While he may not have achieved all of his ambitions, he accepts life and believes in himself as a productive person.	70–+

Source: Havighurst, 1964, p. 216.

comes and vocational choices. The concepts and assumptions that underlie the theory are as follows:

1. The choice of vocation is an expression of personality.
2. Interest inventories are personality inventories.
3. Vocational stereotypes have reliable and important psychological and socio-logical meanings.
4. The members of a vocation have similar personalities and similar histories of personal development.
5. Because people in a vocational group have similar personalities, they will respond to many situations and problems in similar ways, and they will create characteristic interpersonal environments.
6. Vocational satisfaction, stability, and achievement depend on the congru-ence between one's personality and environment (composed largely of other people) in which one works.

The following statements summarize the major assumptions of Holland's theory (1966, 1973):

1. In our culture, most persons can be categorized as one of six types: realistic, intel-lectual, social, conventional, enterprising, and artistic.
2. There are six kinds of environments: realistic, intellectual, social, conventional, enterprising, and artistic.
3. People search for environments and vocations that will permit them to exercise their skills and abilities, to express their attitudes and values, to take on agreeable problems and roles, and to avoid disagreeable ones.
4. A person's behavior can be explained by the interaction of his personality and his environment. (1966, pp. 8–12)

A summary of Holland's theory may be noted in Table 9–3, which describes the personality characteristics of the six categories and the work environments related to each.

Another popular personality theory developed by Roe (1956) and revised by Roe and Siegelmen (1964) suggests that

> there are relationships between the psychic energy, genetic propensities, and child-hood experiences that shape individual styles of behavior, and that the impulse to acquire opportunities to express these individual styles is inherent in the choices made and the ensuing career behavior. Thus, the strength of a particular need, the delay between the arousal of the need and its satisfaction, and the value that the sat-isfaction has in the individual's environment are the conditions—shaped by early childhood expereinces—that influence career development. (Herr and Cramer, 1984, p. 114)

"Chance" Theories

There are also theories of occupational choice that suggest that people arrive at a particular occupation destiny more by chance than through deliberate plan-ning or steady progress toward an earlier defined goal. Newspapers and televi-

Table 9–3. A Summary of Holland's (1959, 1966) Personality Types and Environmental Models

| | Description | |
Type	Personality Types (Modal Personal Orientation)	Environmental Models (Occupational Environments)
Realistic (Motoric)	Enjoys activities requiring physical strength; aggressive; good motor organization; lacks verbal and interpersonal skills; prefers concrete to abstract problems; unsociable.	Laborers, machine operators, aviators, farmers, truck drivers, carpenters
Intellectual (Investigative)	Task-oriented, thinks through problems; attempts to organize and understand the world; enjoys ambiguous work tasks and intraceptive activities; abstract orientation.	Physicist, anthropologist, chemist, mathematician, biologist.
Social (Supportive)	Prefers teaching or therapeutic roles; likes a safe setting; processes verbal and interpersonal skills; socially oriented; accepting of feminine impulses	Clinical psychologist, counselor, foreign missionary, teacher.
Conventional (Conforming)	Performs structured verbal and numerical activities and subordinate roles; achieves goals through conformity.	Cashier, statistician, bookkeeper, administrative assistant, post office clerk.
Enterprising (Persuasive)	Perfers verbal skills in situations which provide opportunities for dominating, selling, or leading others.	Car salesman, auctioneer, politician, master of ceremonies, buyer.
Artistic (Esthetic)	Prefers indirect personal relationships, prefers dealing with environmental problems through self-expression in artistic media.	Poet, novelist, musician, sculptor, playwright, composer, stage director.

Source: Zaccaria, 1970, p. 44.

sion reports constantly remind us of persons who seem to be "at the right place at the right time" and for no other reason end up in an unanticipated career. In a broad sense, we might include the "chance" one has for career choice as influenced by the environment, social class, culture, and other conditions one is born into or raised in; opportunities for education; observation of role models; and so forth. More narrowly we may note that chance factors result in occupational choice by an impulse or sudden emotional reaction in which unconscious forces appear to determine a person's behavior and occupation choice, such as the person who, on apparent impulse, "walks out of a good office job and is next heard from as a missionary in the African jungle." These and similar

Table 9-4.   A Synthesis of Bandura's Perspectives of Factors Influencing Chance Encounters

Personal Determinants of the Effect of Chance Encounters	Social Determinants of the Effect of Chance Encounters

Entry Skills
   Interest, skills, personal knowledge likely to gain acceptance or sustain contact with another
Emotional Ties
   Interpersonal attractiveness tending to sustain chance encounters so that certain social determinants might operate
 	
Values and Personal Standards
   Unintended influences more likely to be important if persons involved share similar standards and value systems
	Milieu Rewards
	   The types of rewards and sanctions an individual or group provides if a chance encounter alters a life path
	Symbolic Environment and Information
	   Images of reality provided by other than direct experience; different individuals or groups furnish different symbolic environments
	Milieu Reach and Closedness
	   Chance encounters with a relatively closed milieu—e.g., cults, communal groups—have the greatest potential for abruptly reordering life paths
	Psychological Closedness
	   Belief systems provide structure, directions, and purpose in life. Once persons, through chance encounter, get caught up in the belief system of a particular group, it can exert selective influence on the course of development and erect a psychological closedness to outside influence. Beliefs channel social interactions in ways that create their own validating realities.

Source: Herr and Cramer, 1984, p. 107.

evidence, as described by Caplow (1954), indicate that occupational choice may result from an accidental or unforeseen factor or factors. Accident theory, then, contends that because people may make decisions or be influenced by unforeseen or accidental circumstances, it is not possible to evaluate the decisive factors in their choices.

Bandura (1982) has expressed in recent years the view that chance encounters play a prominent role in changing the course of the lives of many of us. Herr and Cramer (1984) presented a synthesis of Bandura's perspectives (Table 9-4).

A Composite Theory for Counselors

Hoppock (1976), drawing from two prominent theories of occupational choice, suggested a "composite theory." The ten major points of his theory are as follows:

1. Occupations are chosen to meet needs.
2. The occupation that we choose is the one we believe will best meet the needs that most concern us.

3. Needs may be intellectually perceived, or they may be only vaguely felt as attractions which draw us in certain directions. In either case, they may influence choices.

4. Occupational choice begins when we first become aware that an occupation can help to meet our needs.

5. Occupational choice improves as we become better able to anticipate how well a prospective occupation will meet our needs. Our capacity thus to anticipate depends upon our knowledge of ourselves, our knowledge of occupations, and our ability to think clearly.

6. Information about ourselves affects occupational choice by helping us to discover the occupations that may meet our needs and to anticipate how well satisfied we may hope to be in one occupation as compared with another.

7. Information about occupations affects occupational choice by helping us to discover the occupations that may meet our needs, and by helping us to anticipate how well satisfied we may hope to be in one occupation as compared with another.

8. Job satisfaction depends upon the extent to which the job that we hold meets the needs that we feel it should meet. The degree of satisfaction is determined by the ratio between what we have and what we want.

9. Satisfaction can result from a job which meets our needs today, or from a job which promises to meet them in the future.

10. Occupational choice is always subject to change when we believe that a change will better meet our needs. (pp. 91–92)

Implications of Career Theories for Counselors

A review of the various theories can lead to the conclusions that career development is a process that leads to a decision; there are stages through which one passes enroute to vocational maturity and decision making; there are tasks one must accomplish at each stage; and personality traits are related to career decision making. Furthermore, there are environmental constraints on the careers to which one may aspire or recognize, and the best laid career plans may be altered by chance or accident factors.

The characteristics of these theories have certain implications for the counseling of clients with career development or adjustment needs. Counselors must understand the process and characteristics of human development, including readiness to learn and successfully complete particular tasks at certain developmental stages. Counselors must understand the basic human needs as well as the special needs of persons and their relationship to career development and decision making. Counselors must be able to assess and interpret individual traits and characteristics and to apply these assessments to a variety of counselee career-related needs. Counselors must recognize the constraints imposed by environmental and cultural factors on the career planning and decision making of clients. Counselors must recognize and assist clients to recognize that unforeseen or chance factors may, on occasion, alter career planning. Finally, counselors must recognize that the rapid changes constantly occurring in the way people work and live in this high-tech era require a constant examination and "updating" of the theory and research we use as a basis for our career counseling efforts.

Career Counseling and the Development of Human Potential

Beyond the various career choice theories is the recognition that all aspects of human development, whether they be social, physical, emotional, or educational, are but parts of one's total development—parts that are usually interwoven and often difficult to separate and distinguish from the other aspects of human development. Career development is, of course, no exception. A recognition of these relationships and the application of certain basic principles of human development are significant in the design and implementation of programs providing counseling over the life span for the development of human potential. Seven of these developmental dimensions were discussed in a publication of the National Vocational Guidance Association (1973):

1. Development occurs during the life time of an individual. It can be described in maturational terms denoting progression through life stages and the mastery of developmental tasks at each stage. Although research evidence is lacking, it seems unlikely that intervention can substantially shorten this maturational process.
2. Individual development is influenced by both heredity and environment. Psychological, sociological, educational, political, economic, and physical factors affect development. Appropriate intervention strategies which focus upon these factors can influence the quality of individual development.
3. Development is a continuous process. Individual development can best be facilitated by intervention strategies that begin in the early years and continue throughout the life of the person. Programs which focus only at certain points or at certain stages in the individual's life will have limited effectiveness.
4. Although development is continuous, certain aspects are dominant at various periods of the life span. Programs designed to facilitate career development should account for the dominant aspects at given stages.
5. Individual development involves a progressive differentiation and integration of the person's self and his perceived world. Intervention strategies need to be designed to assist individuals during normal maturational stages of career development rather than to provide remedial assistance to individuals whose development has been damaged or retarded.
6. While common developmental stages can be observed and described during childhood and adult life, individual differences in progressing through these stages can be expected. Intervention programs should provide for these differences, making no assumption that something is "wrong" with those who progress at atypical rates.
7. Excessive deprivation with respect to any single aspect of human development can retard optimal development in other areas. Optimal human development programs are comprehensive in nature, not limited to any single facet. It is recognized that those who suffer from deprivation may require special and intensive assistance. Where deprivation is long term, short-term intervention is not likely to be sufficient. (pp. 3–4)

Of course, we do not have to examine developmental theory to understand the potential that exists within the human being. The achievements of humankind from the discovery of fire to walking on the moon are testimony to the ever-present undetermined potential of human beings. While we must presume that the multiple potentials of most people will never be fully exploited, there nonetheless remains the challenge to achieve and develop to the optimum possible. It is in the selection and functioning in a person's career that the greatest opportunity may exist for the person to achieve much of his or her potential.

In career counseling for the development of human potential, the process may include a focus on encouraging clients to challenge the limitations of their present self-concept; to, in a manner of speaking, redefine their potential and to stimulate their vitality.

Kelly (1967) noted that

> the objectives of the psychotherapist must include the skillful facilitation of those human processes upon which all of us, scientist and client alike, depend as we move from stage to stage in the great human adventure. Goals, processes, and stages are often indistinguishable from each other. Indeed, the initiation and continuation of a lifetime effort to conjure up ever-fresh visions of what is worthwhile is itself a goal of psychotherapy. This is not the kind of goal at which you can hope to arrive and then stop looking further. It is, instead, a continuing series of commitments and revisions of commitments. Most of all it is a commitment to experience, with the stock-taking that honest experience requires. The person who profits from the therapeutic transaction is one who has started to make headway in this ceaseless enterprise. (p. 247)

Of course, schools are looked upon as an agency of society for developing the potential of its youths. Let us, therefore, examine in the next section, how career programs providing for career planning and decision making in schools contribute to the development of human potential.

Career Planning and Decision Making in Schools

There are three common experiences that nearly all human beings can anticipate. The first of these, development or growth, begins at birth, and is especially attended to through much of one's youth. A second common experience is education and in an informal sense, this too, begins at birth and continues throughout life, with a special societal emphasis during most of one's youth when formal schooling is provided. The third experience commonly participated in is the work experience. This experience can be anticipated to begin in one's youth and continue through most of one's adult years.

These three common experiences are significantly shaped by one common setting—the school. It is in this setting that a person's development is stimulated and shaped for the three great experiences of his or her life: learning, living with others, and working. Thus, the role of the school in what the person may become and, in turn, what society itself may become, is critical. Therefore, counselors in any setting have an interest in the impact the school experience has on their clients.

The role of the counseling program in the school setting must be one of facilitating and enhancing the school's contributions to the learning, growth and development, and preparation for work by youths. In this chapter we are particularly concerned with the latter—preparation for the world of work. This includes attending to a person's career development, planning, and decision making within the educational context.

In order to emphasize the opportunities for the student's career development, certain guiding principles are suggested as appropriate objectives for the school counseling program in general and the career guidance phase in particular. The following principles are stated within a developmental framework:

1. All students should be provided with an opportunity to develop an unbiased base from which they can make their career decisions. The shrinking of the pupil's occupational choice field as one proceeds through the school years is an educational tragedy. The first-grader seems to regard most familiar occupations in a positive light. By the time the seventh or eighth grade has been reached, pupils have begun to make decisions based on at least some general occupational considerations. Many have developed or have been educated toward biases that automatically eliminate many possibilities from further consideration. The large percentage of students who enter college preparatory courses at the ninth-grade level and never enter college or even fail to complete their secondary schooling is but one evidence of this fact. In this regard, then, the school counseling program seeks, in effective cooperation with the classroom teacher, to develop in each pupil positive attitudes and respect for all honest work. This is a formidable task, for many students are almost constantly bombarded with the biases of the adult world surrounding them. It is apparent that if they are to benefit from a true freedom of choice, the career counseling and guidance program has a vital mission in the schools.

2. The early and continuous development of positive pupil attitudes toward education is critical. The deterioration of the elementary pupil's occupational choice field is unfortunate, but the failure to maintain the pupil's continuing interest in an optimum educational development is disastrous. For objective evidence, one need only turn to the various dropout studies and the equally countless studies concerning the lack of pupil motivation and achievement commensurate with ability. In short, career development has limited meaning without parallel educational development. Any program of pupil career counseling and guidance must have as a major objective the stimulation of the student's educational development.

3. As a corollary to these previous points, the student must be taught to view a career as a *way* of life and an education as a *preparation* for life. Frequently pupils arrive at the educational decision-making stage of life viewing careers only in terms of job descriptions. At all educational levels the opportunity exists to develop—not only widen—occupational horizons. This broader approach to the eventual career choice is based on the realization that one's way of work is one's way of life. Similarly, there must be education in the concept of education itself, keeping in mind the idea of education for life rather than education only for one's eventual career. This approach—one of education for the fuller life—also has obvious implications for education's continuing efforts to reduce the percentage of school dropouts.

4. Students must be assisted in developing adequate understanding of them-

selves and must be prepared to relate this understanding to both social-personal development and career-educational planning. These understandings are significant in the fulfillment of the individual's need for self-actualization. In this context, both career guidance and pupil appraisal seek to further enrich their meaning and value to students by preparing them to look at themselves realistically in terms of continuing educational opportunities, career requirements, and the demands and relationships of society.

5. Students at all levels must be provided with an understanding of the relationship between education and careers. If pupils are to develop an attitude and belief that education is relevant, they must understand how it is relevant. Pupils need an awareness of the relationships between levels of education and related career possibilities. They should also be made aware of both the vocations and avocations that stem directly from certain subjects.

6. Pupils need an understanding of both *where* and *why* they are at a given point on the educational continuum at a given time. It is not enough for pupils to know they will be in the third grade this year and in the fourth grade next year if all goes well. If they are to gain an increased appreciation of current educational programs as well as future educational possibilities, pupils must be provided specific opportunities to gain insights into the educational process, its sequence, and its integrating of knowledge.

7. Pupils at every stage of their educational program should have career-oriented experiences that are appropriate for their levels of readiness and that are simultaneously meaningful and realistic. This means that opportunities for participation and observation will frequently take precedence over discussions and teacher or counselor lectures.

8. Students must have opportunities to test concepts, skills, and roles to develop values that may have future career application. The school career counseling and guidance program takes advantage of natural school groupings in providing "secure" opportunities for the pupil to experience and develop human relationships and other skills, variety of roles, and a system of values and concepts that are related to everyday living.

9. The school career counseling and guidance program is centered in the classroom, with coordination and consultation by the school counselor, participation by parents, and resource contributions from the community. The pupil's career counseling and guidance team needs the involvement of all those concerned with his or her development, with the teacher, counselor, and parent playing key roles.

10. The school's program of career counseling and guidance is integrated into the functioning counseling and guidance and total educational programs of the institution. The complete development of the individual is vital, and therefore the career aspects should not be separated from the whole. In fact, it is only within the total educational program framework that each segment can be strengthened by and in turn strengthen every other segment.

The Career Guidance Function

The counselor's significant role in the success of the educational system's career development program warrants a closer examination of the nature of career guidance and counseling and the counselor's attending special responsibilites. An excellent statement of the nature of career guidance is the following position paper from the 1973 National Vocational Guidance Association/American Vocational Association:

A. The Need for Career Guidance

Today there are many social factors which converge to stimulate an interest in the career development needs of persons of all ages:

1. Growing complexity in the occupational and organizational structure of society, which makes it difficult for a person to assimilate and organize the data necessary to formulate a career.
2. Evermore rapid technological change, demanding human adaptability and responsiveness.
3. Increasing national concern with the need to develop all human talent, including the talents of women and minorities.
4. An ardent search for values which will give meaning to life.
5. The need for specialized training to obtain entry jobs.
6. The apparent disenchantment expressed by students who have difficulty relating their education to their lives.

Each one of these factors impinges on the individual in ways that make achieving self-fulfillment more difficult.

In the past, some managerial personnel in business and industry have held a "non-careerism" attitude, which viewed the typical job as an isolated event in a person's life. Whether this attitude is tenable in the post-industrial period is seriously questioned today. The evolving view is that a job should be considered as a stage in an integrated, lifelong career—a step on a career lattice which involves both horizontal and vertical dimensions. On the horizontal level it involves patterns of choice at one point in time, such as: "Should I combine employment with study? Or should I engage in volunteer work along with my employment?" Vertically, it involves choices along a time line, such as: "How do my options or behavior at this point relate to options or behavior in the near, intermediate, or distant future?" As new questions are raised about the opportunities work provides for learning and self-development, the need for expanded programs of career guidance becomes apparent.

B. The Nature of Career Guidance

The nature of guidance for career development cannot be viewed as a static, tradition-based set of related services that assist individuals in making single occupational choices. The content of any career guidance program must be developed from initial assessment of the present and future career development needs of the individual; it must also account for impinging environmental factors that could affect the development and fulfillment of career expectations. Career guidance content can be organized in many ways to facilitate the individual's development. Whatever its form, the program should encourage the individual to assume responsibility for his own career development.

A career guidance program assists the individual to assimilate and integrate knowledge, experience, and appreciations related to:

1. Self-understanding, which includes a person's relationship to his own character-

istics and perceptions, and his relationship to others and the environment.

2. Understanding of the work society and those factors that affect its constant change, including worker attitudes and discipline.
3. Awareness of the part leisure time may play in a person's life.
4. Understanding of the necessity for and the multitude of factors to be considered in career planning.
5. Understanding of the information and skills necessary to achieve self-fulfillment in work and leisure.

An illumination of these content areas may include career guidance experiences to insure that each individual:

Gathers the kinds of data necessary to make rational career decisions.
Understands the necessary considerations for making choices and accepts responsbility for the decisions made.
Explores the possible rewards and satisfactions associated with each career choice considered.
Develops through work the attitude that he is a contributor to life and the community.
Determines success and failure probabilities in any occupational area considered.
Explores the possible work conditions associated with occupational options.
Shows an understanding of the varied attitudes toward work and workers held by himself and by others.
Recognizes how workers can bring dignity to their work.
Considers the possible and even predictable value changes in society which could affect a person's life.
Understands the important role of interpersonal and basic employment skills in occupational success.
Clarifies the different values and attitudes individuals may hold and the possible effects these may have on decisions and choices.
Understands that career development is lifelong, based upon a sequential series of educational and occupational choices.
Determines the possible personal risk, cost, and other related consequences of each career decision and is willing to assume responsibility for each consequence.
Systematically analyzes school and nonschool experiences as he plans and makes career-related decisions.
Explores the worker characteristics and work skills necessary to achieve success in occupational areas under consideration.
Identifies and uses a wide variety of resources in the school and community to maximize career development potential.
Knows and understands the entrance, transition, and decision points in education and the problems of adjustment that might occur in relation to these points.
Obtains necessary employability skills and uses available placement services to gain satisfactory entry into employment in line with occupational aspirations and beginning competencies. (pp. 9–11)

As has been noted, the need for career guidance and counseling is increasingly evident in the mass of data pointing to difficulties in career decision making, the underutilization of human resources, dissatisfaction with chosen careers, and such perennial problems as the hard-core unemployed. Career guidance programs are designed, in cooperation with programs of career education, to cope with such needs. To satisfactorily plan such programs, which will increase the planning and decision-making skills of students, counselors must understand how career decisions are made and the possible consequences of certain kinds of decisions. This implies an understanding of theories and related research in career decision making and the counselor's potential role in the career development of youths.

The School Counselor's Role in Student Career Development

As has been noted, the career movement in schools has been viewed as primarily a developmental and educational process. This process provides an opportunity for the school counselor to at last function in a developmental and, in a sense, a preventive capacity. Although the teacher is clearly the key person on the career education team, the school counselor, by virtue of special understandings and skills, can make a valuable contribution to the school's total effort. These contributions may be categorized under the following activities.

Career Counseling

Programs of career education are designed to prepare persons for the eventual selection of a career, but many adolescents and young adults will be unable to adequately cope with this critical decision making without the assistance of a professional counselor. Parental counseling, group counseling, and group guidance activities represent contributions of the counselor to the career development of the individual and the school's career education program.

Career Assessment

An important aspect of the career education program provides students the opportunities to assess their personal characteristics in relation to career planning and decision making. The counselor can make a significant contribution to the development of appropriate self-understandings of youths through the employment of both standardized and nonstandardized assessment techniques.

Resource Person and Consultant

The school counselor has been traditionally active in the acquisition of informational materials appropriate to career decision making and planning. The counselor is also aware of computerized information programs and such media aids as films, filmstrips, and audio and video tapes. Although it cannot be anticipated that the counselor will collect any and all materials, it is reasonable to expect that the counselor will be aware of the sources from which such materials may be obtained. In this capacity, the counselor serves as a resource person to the individual teachers involved in the career education program. The counselor also serves in a consulting capacity, utilizing his or her understanding of the pupil population and his or her understanding of career development resources and opportunities to complement the career education program.

Linkage Agent

Increasingly, the counselor will be active in collaborative efforts, not only with teachers and others in the school setting, but with community agencies and employers. Local government employment counselors and their agencies are especially important contacts.

The counselor has an important role to play in implementing and strengthening career education programs. This role does not, however, diminish the importance of the career guidance function in career planning and decision making. Let us, therefore, move on to examine some techniques for this activity.

Techniques for Career Planning and Decision Making

In counseling youths for their career development and eventual placement, counselors may employ a variety of facilitative techniques to assist persons in:

1. Self-awareness
2. Educational awareness
3. Career awareness
4. Career exploration
5. Planning and decision making

Self-Awareness

It is important from a very early age onwards that persons become aware of and respect their uniqueness as human beings. Learning about one's aptitudes, interests, values, personality traits, and so forth, is important in the development of concepts related to self and the utilization of these concepts in career exploration. Counselors may use such techniques as values clarification exercises, group guidance activities, written assignments (such as autobiographies), films and filmstrips, and standardized tests. Individual or group counseling should follow if circumstances warrant.

Educational Awareness

Awareness of the relationships between self, educational opportunities, and the world of work is an important aspect of career planning. Counselors may use films as well as printed materials for this purpose. Group guidance activities (such as "orientation days"), presentations by school alumni, and the use of educational awareness inventories can be useful. Games that relate hobbies and recreational activities to courses and careers can be stimulating for grade school and middle school pupils. Guided activities can also educate school-aged youths to the relationships between desirable school habits (i.e., responsibility, punctuality, effort, positive human relationships) and good worker traits.

Career Awareness

Counselors and counseling programs in schools should, at all educational levels, assist the pupil in the continuous expansion of knowledge and awareness of the world of work. This must include a developing recognition of the relationships between values, life styles, and careers. Many excellent films and printed materials are available for this purpose, but of course, these must be intregrated into a planned, developmental program appropriate to the student's age-grade levels. Specialized programs (i.e., career days, career shadowing, junior partners, closed circuit television "trips," and actual field trips) are useful if well planned. Excellent computer programs (noted later in this chapter) are available, and with secondary school students, standardized interest inventories can increase a student's career awareness.

Career Exploration

Career exploration represents a movement towards a systematic and planned inquiry and analysis of careers that are of interest. Comparisons, reality testing, and, again, standardized testing can be helpful. Classes in career exploration and decision making are not uncommon.

In one approach to the study of careers in classes, Wiggins and Moody (1981) noted and compared approaches to career exploration using the career cluster study approach where students studied each of the thirteen clusters listed in the *Occupational Outlook Handbook* (1979). In their studies, these students used pamphlets from the Bureau of Labor of Statistics to supplement various textbooks or career briefs, and appropriate movies and filmstrips were shown on a regular basis. Some programs also used the *Career Survey* (Wiggins, 1974) and the *Vocational Preference Inventory* (VPI) (Holland, 1978) for individual career exploration; others used the *Self-Directed Search* (Holland, 1974) with the procedures for exploration followed as outlined in the *Understanding Yourself and Your Career* booklet (Holland, 1977). The *Career Maturity Inventory* (CMI) (Crites, 1978) was also used and followed the planned exercises involving the five parts of the inventory: "Knowing Yourself," "Knowing About Jobs," "Choosing a Job," "Looking Ahead," and "What Should They Do?"

They concluded that "the cluster approach obtained poorest comparative results among the four approaches studied" and that "although there were statistically significant differences among the CMI, the SDS, and the CS-VPI approaches, no practical conclusions could be reached as to the single best career exploration method to follow" (p. 18).

Career Planning and Decision Making

At this point students need to narrow their career or career planning possibilities and then proceed to examine and test these options as critically as possible. Here again, such established techniques as values clarification activities, standardized testing, job shadowing, and group guidance activities are helpful. Many students will need to learn the process of decision making, including choosing between competing alternatives, examining the consequences of specific choices, the value of compromise, and the implementing of a decision. At this point, it is important for students to recognize the impact of their current planning and decision making on their future life. It should also be a time when students are assisted to, in a manner of speaking, "take control" of their life and become an active agent for the shaping of their own future.

Placement and Follow-up

Career Placement

Placement and follow-up services are significant to the success of career counseling programs. In recent years the high rate of youth unemployment has re-emphasized the need for a great emphasis on career placement for youths. Assistance to young people by both school and employment counselors is important if they are to avoid unnecessary difficulties and frustrations in their career search activities. Also, counselors are aware that unsatisfactory career entry can have long-term effects for youth. In this regard, it must be recognized that the current "TV generations" are often unrealistic in their expectations of career opportunities and in their viewpoints of specific careers. Pre-employment counseling may be necessary to assist these youths in obtaining a more realistic understanding of the realities of the world of work.

Earlier evidence of these problems was cited in the significant *Nationwide Study of Student Career Development* by Prediger, Roth, and Noeth (1973), which reported a sharp contrast between the need for career planning and the help received by youths. This study confirmed that youths were seriously deficient in knowledge about the world of work and career planning, and they were unable to cope with the career development tasks posed by society during the difficult high-school–to–post-high-school transition and placement period. The study recommended the reorientation of the traditional school counseling model to provide increased and more realistic assistance in career placement and to initiate significant changes that would, in effect, increase the effectiveness of counseling youths for today's world of work.

In a USOE study, "A Comparison of Common Educational-Vocational Problems of Secondary School Youth in the USA and the British Isles," Gibson and Mitchell (1970) determined that a high priority problem with youths in both countries was their concern for appropriate occupational placement upon leaving school. However, American youths, in contrast to their British counterparts, anticipated little assistance from their secondary schools in dealing with this concern.

Although these and others have testified about the importance of placement in human resources and career development, this is an often neglected and underdeveloped activity in many school counseling programs. As Buckingham and Lee (1973) stated in their study *Placement and Follow-up in Career Education,* "experience in placing students in employment and following students after they leave an institution is still largely undeveloped" (p. 1). They went on to point out:

Since career education has as its purpose the preparation of students for careers, and the successful placement of each student on the next rung of a career ladder is the only way of knowing that the preparation at one stage has been completed, placement can hardly be considered in any other way than as an integral part of the career education process, regardless of the level of education involved. (p. 3)

In another national study focusing on career placement in schools only, Gibson and Mitchell (1976) noted:

Of all the guidance placement activities, none is more important or has the potential for assisting more youth in the school setting than the job placement service. Such a service can be designed to assist both in-school and out-of-school youth, both school dropouts and school graduates. Such programs are typically involved in:

1. Assessing the needs of students regarding part-time and full-time employment, training, employability skills, and further educational desires.
2. Establishing a working relationship with business, industry, and labor representatives in order to facilitate effective cooperation and communication between these groups and educators.
3. Providing avenues and assistance to students seeking part-time or full-time employment that are compatible with their abilities and interests.
4. Establishing an efficient, participatory communication-feedback network among all involved—students, business, industry, and labor personnel, community leaders, parents, media, and school personnel. (p. 1)

With many school guidance programs currently in the process of developing or expanding the placement function, it might be helpful to note the procedural steps developed in the Indiana Model Career Placement Project for developing or expanding this phase of the school guidance program (see Figure 9–3). In

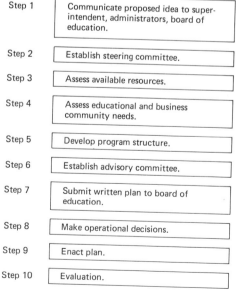

Step 1	Communicate proposed idea to superintendent, administrators, board of education.
Step 2	Establish steering committee.
Step 3	Assess available resources.
Step 4	Assess educational and business community needs.
Step 5	Develop program structure.
Step 6	Establish advisory committee.
Step 7	Submit written plan to board of education.
Step 8	Make operational decisions.
Step 9	Enact plan.
Step 10	Evaluation.

Figure 9–3. Procedural steps for program enactment. *(Shafe, Gerster, & Moore, 1976.)*

considering placement program development, the existence in many communities of well-established local governmental employment programs that often give special attention to the needs of local youths should be recognized. In such settings, the school guidance program seeks to work cooperatively and in a complementary manner with local government employment personnel to provide the best possible assistance for youthful job seekers. Even under such ideal conditions, however, it must be remembered that the important developmental aspects of school placement programs are not the responsbility of other agencies or institutions. School placement programs therefore must include activities that develop or enhance the student's skills, attitudes, and knowledge needed for job acquisition and retention.

Placement program activities may be viewed as three-dimensional. The primary activity, of course, is student development; however, student development will obviously be handicapped if job development is not also a planned program activity, and both of these activities will be less than effective without plans for program maintenance and operation. The Indiana Model Career Placement Project developed by Gibson and Mitchell (1976) suggested the following as appropriate activities:

Student Development Activities

1. Assessment of student readiness for employment—what skills, attitudes, or stereotypes does the student presently possess?
2. Preparation of student for finding and retaining a job—what skills are needed to obtain a job and, once obtained, how must one function to retain the job?
3. Individual and group career counseling—how does one develop or become competent in decision making, problem solving, and clarification of personal and career values and goals?
4. Employability skills and competencies—how does one proceed in clarifying competition for jobs? Suggested review: resumé writing, interview appearance and preparation, personal hygiene, letter of application, interpretation of job notices and terminology through job hunting clinics, employability skills and competency-building class, and/or or pre-employment job hunting materials.
5. Resources for job possibilities—where does one begin? Suggested review: yellow pages, want ads, local placement office, employment office, school counselor, relatives, and friends.
6. Post-employment adjustment counseling—what does one do if one has problems related to the job or placement situation?
7. Employer-employee relationships—what is involved in employment interactions? Suggested review: respect for authority or how to react/interact with authority, personal and social relationships, expressing criticism, work efficiency, supervision versus nonsupervision, economics of market trends, and how each affects company or business.

Job Development Activities

1. Employer lists—who are the potential employers in the general vicinity?
2. Receiving and developing job opportunities inside and outside the community—what possibilities are within a particular region or district?
3. Survey employers for needs and positions available—how can the placement program be most helpful to employers?

4. Facilitation of business and industry contacts—what are the best methods for corresponding with or keeping in touch with employers or prospective employers?
5. Screening interviews—who are the seemingly best qualified applicants for employer consideration regarding a specific available position?
6. Educational referrals for another level of training (skills) or education—in light of the needs of the student, what other "next steps" are available besides immediate employment?
7. Apprenticeships—what on-the-job training opportunities are available or could be developed for students?
8. Supervision of employed students—if work experience credit is available, how can the student interrelate his or her work experience and course offerings?
9. Summer placement program—what about equivalent services for students during the summer vacation?
10. Job data bank information—what about a system that provides the job-related information readily and easily?

Maintenance-Operational Activities

1. Gathering student data—how are student needs identified? Who needs part-time or full-time employment? What student information is needed for record keeping?
2. Gathering employer data—what is available and from whom? What are the qualifications needed and job descriptions?
3. Record keeping—what type of centralized record keeping system and/or location can best serve the student and employer needs?
4. Maintenance plan whereby employers and students are contacted after placement—what is the level of satisfaction of the student placed and of the employer?
5. Ongoing reassessment of students' and employers' needs and market trends—what can be done to modify the activities of the placement program to better serve the participating populations? (pp. 18–21)

Since placement in its broader context includes the placement of clients in a variety of settings (i.e., work, educational, environmental) for a variety of reasons and benefits, let us now proceed to examine educational and environmental placement.

Educational Placement

For years, placement in secondary schools has traditionally emphasized placement in institutions of higher education. This emphasis did not appear to be neglected even during the movement towards career placement. The previously cited study by Gibson and Mitchell (1976) indicated that in a sample of 180 secondary schools, more than 90 percent provided for some form of college or post-secondary educational placement, whereas only 57 percent had specialized provisions for career placement. Recognizing the comparative popularity of education placement, let us briefly examine some of its aspects.

In general, educational placement differs little from other forms of placement inasmuch as it represents an organized effort to match the qualifications of individuals plus personal interests and resources with the requirements of institutions and programs. Typically, school counselors, with responsbilities for college and other post-secondary educational placement, provide information to students regarding institutional entrance requirements, expenses, characteristics of the institution, and program content. They also frequently will assist students in completing the necessary application forms. An example of a form that counselors may use with high school students interested in college placement is the college checklist (see Figure 9–4).

Many school counselors are also involved in educational placement within their schools. In this capacity they are concerned with placing students in appropriate curricula and specific courses. However, scheduling activities that consist largely of a mechanical process designed to get all pupils into all slots at a given time, wtih a total disregard of individual differences, is not considered a guidance responsibility, even though counselors report that they spend many hours in such mechanical processes.

In the literature, at least, if not always in practice, placement within educational institutions has been viewed as more than just career, college, and educational placement. In its broadest sense, placement is an activity that places or facilitates the self-placement of persons in situations or settings that will enable them to benefit from needed experiences, make satisfactory adjustments, gain useful information, and, in general, contribute to their total development. As an example of this broader concept of placement, let us look at placement that focuses on giving a person experiences in different roles and environments.

Role placement assumes that experiencing different and significant roles is important for all developing pupils. Although many will experience some of these roles naturally and without planning, for the majority these developmental opportunities would be missed unless specific provisions are made. This is another opportunity for the school counselor and classroom teacher to work cooperatively in planning meaningful experiences that enhance both the instructional programs and the student's personal development. Significant role experiences would include opportunities to function periodically as a leader, a team member, an individual (isolated) worker, a teacher of others, an achiever, a responsible person, a social being, a person of authority and decision making, or one who serves others. A role assignment sheet, as illustrated in Figure 9–5, is a method of recording these experiences.

Environmental Assessment

Environmental placement can be another developmental activity. The major focus of this type of placement is to provide students with the opportunities to experience other significant, yet distinctly different, evironments from their own. An example is giving city youth opportunities to spend time in rural areas as part of farm days or "country cousins" programs. City youths may exchange places with farm youths for several days or weeks. Another example is a blend of educational preparation and environmental placement in which students spend some time in diverse collegiate settings, small and large.

Regardless of the nature of client placement, follow-up should also be planned. In the following section reasons why clients are not placed and forgotten are set forth.

Follow-up

Programs of placement activities, regardless of setting, must provide evidence of the effectiveness of their practices for both accountability and program

I. *Entrance Requirements and General Information*	Yes	No	Yes	No	Yes	No
1. Does this college offer major preparation in the field of_____ (student's planned major)?						
2. Will I be eligible for admission upon completion of my currently planned program for high school graduation?						
3. Are entrance examinations required?						
4. Must I take a physical examination?						
5. Are there other entrance requirements? (If so, list in Section VII, under Notes and Comments.)						
6. Is this a coeducational college?						
7. Is this a state- or city-supported college?						
8. Are the offerings of this college accredited by the accrediting association?						
9. Does this college have an ROTC program?						
10. What is the average enrollment?						
II. *Expenses (per school year)*						
11. Room						
12. Board						
13. Tuition						
14. Activity fees						
15. Any other special expenses: (item)_____ (item)_____						
16. Total basic cost per year	$		$		$	
III. *Room and Board*						
17. Are dormitory facilities available for boys/girls?						
18. Are noncommuting freshmen required to live in the dormitory?						
19. May you select your own roommate if you desire?						
20. Are dining facilities available (three meals per day) for students?						
IV. *Student Services and Aids*						
21. Are scholarships available?						
22. Are part-time jobs available?						
23. Are guidance services provided?						
24. Is there a freshman orientation program?						
25. Are placement services available for: (a) graduating seniors? (b) summertime jobs?						
26. Are health services provided? (a) dispensary care? (b) dental care? (c) hospitalization plan?						
27. Can I get special scholastic help (such as tutoring) if I need it?						
V. *Student Activities*						
28. Fraternities and sororities?						
29. Honorary organizations?						
30. Social dancing permitted?						
31. Are campus recreational facilities available?						
32. Is there an intramural program?						
33. Major varsity sports?						
34. A convocation series?						
35. Dramatic opportunities?						
36. Music (band and glee club)?						
37. Any others you are particularly interested in: (item)_____						

VI. Any special questions you want to ask? _____

VII. Notes and comments _____

_____　(Student's name) _____

Figure 9–4. College checklist. *(Gibson, 1960–1961, pp. 121–123.)*

_____ Grade   Class of _____ Period _____ to _____

B. D. Lewis Elementary School

Role Assignments	leader	team member	individual worker	achiever	responsibility	social leader	decision maker	server
Pupils' Names								
1. Marie Adams								
2. Rebecca Best								
3. Billy Collins								
4. Chester Dent								
5. Charles James								
6. Eleanor James								
7. Nancy Lee								
8. Archie Leedy								
9. Paul Lewis								
10. Katherine Louise								
11. Edith Miller								
12. Robert Nuzrem								
13. Jack Smith								
14. Billy Wagner								
15. Betty Watson								

* Dates are entered where role is assigned.

√ indicates student has assumed or experienced this role and further assignment is not needed at this time.

Figure 9–5. Role assignments. *(Gibson, 1972, p. 60.)*

improvement purposes. A large measure of supporting evidence for these purposes may be secured through carefully planned follow-up activities. As a complement to the guidance placement program, follow-up activities focus upon effectiveness in placing persons for a variety of purposes and settings, as viewed by not only the clients, but also by those to whom the client is responsible in such settings as job placement. Follow-up data may be obtained through questionnaires, checklists, interviews, and phone calls. Placement follow-up with those placed usually focuses upon how satisfied the persons are with their placement; how satisfied they are with the process; progress they believe they are making in their situation; adequacy of their previous preparation experience; was the placement setting as anticipated or described; future plans and recommendations. Employers may be asked to respond concerning the adequacy of preparation and experience of the employee; adaptation to work; ability to work with others; progress anticipated by employee; recommendations for improvement of placement process.

In college placement, follow-up may seek to identify adequacy of high school preparation for the particular collegiate institution and program areas of strength and weakness in entering student's preparation; degree to which the student appears to be adjusting to the collegiate environment; and recommendations for improving the placement process. As follow-up data are collected, it is equally important to anticipate and plan for systematic utilization of the data.

In recognizing the importance of planning for career placement and follow-up, we would also be cognizant of the complexities and variables involved. In an effort to assist counselors and their clients to deal more effectively with those complexities and variables, computerized assistance systems have been and continue to be developed. Several of these systems will be described in the section that follows.

Computerized Career Assistance Systems

The 1980s have witnessed the continued rapid development and public acceptance of the computer. Computers, already popular in business, industry, and higher education, are now becoming commonplace in schools at all levels, and the current boom in home computers appears likely to continue through this decade. The fascination of youths with this technological marvel is reflected not only in their patronage of video arcades and purchase of computerized video games, but in their quest for knowledge and use of even the most sophisticated of computers. In fact, it may be that our youths are the most computer knowledgeable group in our population.

The attraction of youths at all age levels to the computer has given schools unprecedented opportunities for its utilization in motivation and learning. This potential exists for school counseling programs as well, especially in providing career information and assistance.

While computer usage in counseling programs in educational settings is not new, having "been around" since the 1960s, the introduction of the microcomputer in the 1970s promoted major changes as well as opportunities for the utilization of computer-assisted career guidance systems. The economic and technical advantages of the microcomputer continue to be a major stimulus to their use in school settings for career counseling and guidance purposes.

Types of Systems

In the paragraphs that follow, two types of systems will be briefly described. These are (a) information systems, and (b) guidance systems.

Information systems are generally designed to (a) provide users with a structured search scheme for occupations, and (b) to disseminate occupational and educational information to users. These procedural steps may be used separately or in sequence. In the former, the user may complete exercises or provide ratings, even test scores indicating interests and aptitudes as a basis for the computer's search for compatible occupations. In the latter information accessing process, the user can access general information regarding specific occupations. The computer may also be programmed to respond to certain specific questions the user may ask about the occupation.

The development of information systems was greatly stimulated by grants provided by the Department of Labor and the National Occupational Information Coordinating Committee, which enabled a number of states to develop statewide career information systems. Many of these, labeled *Career Information*

Systems (CIS), emphasize local and regional information. Another, identified as the *Guidance Information System* (GIS), provides access to various kinds of national data regarding careers, educational opportunities, and the armed services. This system, marketed through Time Share of Houghton Mifflin Company, suggested in its brochures that:

> with the Guidance Information System, a massive amount of critical, decision-making information is as close as the touch of a keyboard. By typing a simple set of instructions, people can immediately zero-in on information that fits their particular needs and interests. Whether counselor or client, a GIS operator can easily match goals and expectations with the myriad of educational, occupational, and financial options available. Not only that, GIS lets users compare the results of choices and decisions they have made with the results of other choices they have made—instantly! This places the decision making where it belongs, *with the user.* (TimeShare Corporation, Houghton-Mifflin Company, The Guidance Information System, GIS brochure, 1982, p. 1)

Guidance systems are broader in scope and more instructional than information systems, providing in addition to the organized search and dissemination functions of information systems, modules such as self-assessment, instruction in decision making, future planning, and so forth. The two most popular of these systems are The System of Interactive Guidance and Information (SIGI) developed and marketed through the Educational Testing Service, Princeton, New Jersey, under the direction of Martin Katz, and the Discover System, developed by JoAnn Harris-Bowlsbey, and marketed through Discover, Inc., Hunt Valley, Maryland, and the American College Testing Program.

The SIGI system was designed primarily to assist college and college-bound students or out-of-school adults. Its subsystems are:

Subsystem	What the Client Does	Questions Answered
Introduction	Learns concepts and uses of major sections listed below.	Where do you stand now in your career decision making? What help do you need?
I. Values	Examines 10 occupational values and weighs importance of each one.	What satisfactions do you want in an occupation? What are you willing to give up?
II. Locate	Puts in specifications on 5 values at a time and gets lists of occupations that meet specifications.	Where can you find what you want? What occupations should you look into?
III. Compare	Asks pointed questions and gets specific information about occupations of interest.	What would you like to know about occupations that you are considering? Should you reduce your list?
IV. Prediction	Finds out probabilities of getting various marks in key courses of preparatory programs for occupations.	Can you make the grade? What are your chances of success in preparing for each occupation you are considering?
V. Planning	Gets displays of programs for entering each occupation,	How do you get from here to there? What steps do you take

Subsystem	What the Client Does	Questions Answered
	licensing or certification requirements, and sources of financial aid.	to enter an occupation you are considering?
VI. Strategy	Evaluates occupations in terms of the rewards they offer and the risks of trying to enter them.	Which occupations fit your values best? How do you decide between an occupation that is highly desirable but risky and one that is less desirable but easier to prepare for?

Source: Fredrickson, 1982, pp. 183–184.

The "Discover" system is designed to assist students in grades 1 through 12, college students, and adults. Its brochure describes the twelve modules of the system:

00 Entry
1a Clarifying Values
1b Values and Occupations
2a Effective Decision Making
2b Decision Making and Careers
3a Organization of the Occupational World
3b Browsing Occupations
4 Reviewing Interests and Strengths
5 Making a List of Occupations to Explore
6 Getting Information About Occupations
7 Narrowing a List of Occupations
8 Exploring Specific Career Plans
8a Local Jobs
8b Financial Aid
8c Apprenticeships
8d Four-Year College Information and Search
8e Community and Junior Colleges
8f Graduate and Professional Schools
8g Technical and Specialized Schools
8h Continuing Education
8i Military Information and Search
8j Mid-Career Job Change

Ethical Considerations

The rapid growth of computer usage in the field of counseling and its antici-pated increased usage in the future have, at the same time, raised certain ethical questions related to the use of computers in counseling. Potential problems in client confidentiality, misinterpretation of test results and other data by clients, and lack of appropriate counselor interaction with clients are but a few exam-ples of ethical implications. Sampson and Pyle (1983) suggested fourteen ethical principles in response to ethical issues involved with the use of computer-assisted counseling, testing, and guidance systems:

1. Ensure that confidential data maintained on a computer are limited to information that is appropriate and necessary for the services being provided.
2. Ensure that confidential data maintained on a computer are destroyed after it is determined that the information is no longer of any value in providing services.
3. Ensure that confidential data maintained on a computer are accurate and complete.
4. Ensure that access to confidential data is restricted to appropriate professionals by using the best computer security methods available ("appropriate professionals" are described in existing ethical standards).
5. Ensure that it is not possible to identify, with any particular individual, confidential data maintained in a computerized data bank that is accessible through a computer network.
6. Ensure that research participation release forms are completed by an individual who has automatically collected individually identifiable data as a result of using a computer-assisted counseling, testing, or guidance system.
7. Ensure that computer-controlled test scoring equipment and programs function properly thereby providing individuals with accurate test results.
8. Ensure that generalized interpretations of test results presented by microcomputer-controlled audiovisual devices accurately reflect the intention of the test author.
9. Ensure that a client's needs are assessed to determine if using a particular system is appropriate before using a computer-assisted counseling, testing, or guidance system.
10. Ensure that an introduction to using a computer-assisted counseling, testing, and guidance system is available to reduce possible anxiety concerning the system, misconceptions about the role of the computer, and misunderstandings about basic concepts or the operation of the system.
11. Ensure that a follow-up activity to using a computer-assisted counseling, testing, and guidance system is available to correct possible misconceptions, misunderstandings, or inappropriate use as well as assess subsequent needs of the client.
12. Ensure that the information contained in a computer-assisted career counseling and guidance system is accurate and up-to-date.
13. Ensure that the equipment and programs that operate a computer-assisted counseling, testing, and guidance system function properly.
14. Determining the need for counselor intervention depends on the likelihood that the client would experience difficulties that would in turn limit the effectiveness of the system or otherwise exacerbate the client's problem. It is the counselor's responsibility to decide whether the best approach to avoiding the above problems for a specific client population is direct intervention or indirect intervention through the use of workbooks, self-help guides, or other exercises. (pp. 285–286)

Certainly, we must hope that rapid developments in computer technology will not "outrun" our careful consideration of the ethical issues involved.

Career Counseling in Nonschool Settings

The initial out-of-school career contacts of many youths will be made through the assistance of their state employment services. In these offices, career guidance activities may be based on a review and discussion of the applicant's qualifications and interests in relation to available employment opportunities. Appraisal instruments, such as the General Aptitude Classification Battery, may be used to further assist the client and the counselor in career planning. Counselors in these settings are usually especially well versed in their knowledge of local job opportunities and characteristics and often have access to computerized job bank systems. These employment office counselors often work closely with high school counselors in facilitating the career planning and transitions of youths from school to work.

Career counseling and placement however, can no longer be considered an activity that focuses on youths alone. A variety of factors have resulted in significant changes in the career "habitats" of adult populations. Those changes, some of which were noted earlier in this chapter, in turn, have influenced the career counseling and placement efforts in governmental and business settings. Contributing factors to this change include the impact of technological and social change, shifts in societal values, a population that is growing older and is capable of working longer, and economic necessity.

> Probably the most general cause of the career change phenomenon is the impact of technological change on American life. Technological innovations have sparked continued economic development, which, in turn, has perpetuated the rise in this nation's standard of living. For an increasing number of Americans, this has meant greater material security and satisfaction of basic needs. As Abraham Maslow and other pscyhologists have suggested, "higher" needs such as the need for self-esteem or self-actualization are awakened when basic needs have been reasonably fulfilled. In the workplace, many Americans are no longer just asking for more salary and benefits; they are also asking for more meaningful careers which will enable them to better express their unique talents and abilities. (Ferrini and Parker, 1978, p. 4)

Moreover, technological change has resulted in related societal changes such as population shifts, altered consumer demands, and major new government policies regarding health, education, and welfare. These changes have had an impact on other occupations not directly affected by changing technologies. Human service occupations are a good example. Thousands of young adults entered educational programs in these fields. When they graduated several years later, they frequently found the labor market quite different from what it was when they began their schooling. Many of these persons could not find jobs in their career areas; others took jobs for which they were overqualified and underpaid.

Americans preparing for jobs in many other occupations have encountered similar difficulties. As technological and social changes become more rapid, the difficulty of work force forecasting increases. A 1975 Rand Corporation study by Pascal, Bell, Dougherty, Dunn, and Thompson entitled *An Evaluation of Policy-Related Research on Programs for Mid-Life Career Redirection,* concluded:

> Manpower forecasts will not give much guidance to appropriate training in a mid-life career program. They cannot give reliable estimates of the probability of being employed once training has been completed, except in very special cases. Neither can the forecasts give much information on the longevity of a career. (Volume 11, p. 76)

Ferrini and Parker (1978) went on to state:

> Given this difficulty, many career changers and younger people entering the work force are becoming more cautious about investing large amounts of time and money in preparing for occupations in which their future employment is questionable. Instead, many of these individuals are enrolling in short-term training programs or pursuing careers in which they can utilize their transferable skills. (pp. 5–6)

During recent generations, social and cultural change have also resulted in the alteration of traditional concepts and expectations that resulted in sex role stereotyping in the world of work. This has not only resulted in more female engineers, construction workers, airplane pilots, and more male nurses and elementary school teachers, but has also led to increasing numbers of women who, in the process of combining careers and marriage, interrupt their careers for child rearing before returning to the labor force. For example, Vriend (1977), indicated that:

> a woman is more likely to be in the labor force at age 45 to 54 than at age 20 to 24. This means that the average woman will have 30 to 35 active years of life starting from a mid-career point. Technological advances, more opportunities for paid employment, and social conditions such as the general movements toward human liberation and the development of individual potential, as well as the sharp rise in divorce rates, have freed women to choose employment as an alternative. Women constitute a large percentage of the mid-career crisis. Too many women don't like what they're doing, don't know what they want to do, and think they can't do anything. They need assistance to make early plans for a potentially long career outside the home, to re-enter the labor market, and to find sources of continued guidance at crucial points in the career development process. (pp. 329–330)

In short, mid-life career changes and entries are becoming commonplace for both men and women.

> Every occupation is represented, but some are more visible than others. Classic cases of midlife career change can be found in the ranks of those who put in twenty years or so in the military or in municipal activities, such as fire and police protection, and then retire at a relatively young age, free to pursue a second career. In the 1970s, thousands of engineers and scientists became unemployed because of substantial cuts in space and defense spending; these workers in declining industries were often forced to seek unrelated types of employment, or to take lesser paying jobs in the same occupation. More recently, the field of education has experienced cutbacks, causing teachers and other educational personnel to switch career paths. Whether voluntary of involuntary, it is clear that midlife career change is a visible phenomenon and that a significant proportion of workers will not fit the one life–one occupation mode. (Herr and Cramer, 1984, pp. 344–345)

Even though midlife career changes may be commonplace, even anticipated by many workers, such changes can prompt adjustment as well as decision-making difficulties. Some adjustments will be the result of adapting to a new work routine with new skills, new work associates, and possible movement to a new environment and new way of life. Also, some will view the necessity or desirability of career change as a reflection on their status as valued workers and an indication that they have erred in their earlier career planning. Marital relationships can be threatened, even when one of the spouses is not facing career change and existing problems are usually further agitated.

In counseling this more mature and work experienced group, the career counselor will want to consider the following counseling goals outlined by Herr and Cramer (1984):

1. Assist the individual to explore, specify, and evaluate the clarity of the reasons for a career shift. Is the individual confused and anxious as a result of an involuntary career shift, secure and optimistic because of the prospects of a voluntary career shift, or some combination of both? Are stress factors with which an individual has difficulty coping in a current job likely to be present in an intended job? Does the individual appear distressed, depressed, or dysfunctional? How carefully has the individual planned? These and other questions relate to the goal of shift clarification.

2. Assist the individual to acquire all necessary information relevant to a career shift. Does the individual recognize the relationship between education or training and the proposed work shift? What steps are necessary to effect the change? Where and how does one get the necessary information? One comprehensive review of the literature (Pascal et al., 1975) concluded that redirection schemes usually emphasize aptitude diagnosis, provision of realistic job information, on-the-job instruction, and placement assistance.

3. Help the individual to envision the possible effects of a career shift. Will there be financial ramifications? Will family life be affected? Will life style change appreciably? Will geographical relocation be required? What will be the immediate, intermediate, and long-range consequences?

4. Aid the individual to develop appropriate job-seeking or education-seeking behaviors. Can the person write an effective resume? Does the individual have good skills as an interviewee? Has he or she narrowed down to manageable proportions the education or training universe? Does the person have adequate information?

5. Assist the individual to clarify abilities, interests, and personal characteristics. Will the attributes of the person facilitate or impede the transition to a different career, occupation, or job? Are these characteristics germane to the person that would make his or her functioning unsatisfying in any job? Are there any physical, mental, or emotional problems to be considered?

6. Assist, if appropriate, to place the individual in a job. Certain settings wherein counselors work with midcareer shifters will have placement as a goal (such as the Employment Service or Outplacement Counseling). Other agencies that do not perform a brokerage role may well consider performing this function if no alternative is readily available. (pp. 345–346)

Many opportunities exist to provide career counseling and placement for adult career changers. The following paragraphs examine career counseling and placement in some institutional and agency settings.

It is probable that many of those seeking new careers will again seek the assistance of counselors in the Employment Security Division of the U.S. Department of Labor. A career change model (Figure 9–6) appropriate to government and other employment agencies indicates activities that counselors may find appropriate in such settings. A variety of career opportunities are provided under the provisions of the Comprehensive Employment and Training

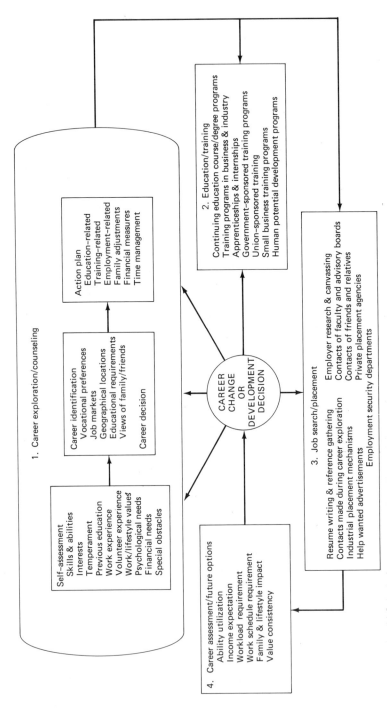

Figure 9–6. Career change model. *(Ferrini & Parker, 1978, p. 10.)*

1. Career exploration/counseling

Self-assessment
Skills & abilities
Interests
Temperament
Previous education
Work experience
Volunteer experience
Work/lifestyle values
Psychological needs
Financial needs
Special obstacles

Career identification
Vocational preferences
Job markets
Geographical locations
Educational requirements
Views of family/friends

Career decision

Action plan
Education-related
Training-related
Employment-related
Family adjustments
Financial measures
Time management

CAREER
CHANGE
OR
DEVELOPMENT
DECISION

2. Education/training
Continuing education course/degree programs
Training programs in business & industry
Apprenticeships & internships
Government-sponsored training programs
Union-sponsored training
Small business training programs
Human potential development programs

3. Job search/placement
Resume writing & reference gathering
Contacts made during career exploration
Industrial placement mechanisms
Help wanted advertisements
Employer research & canvassing
Contacts of faculty and advisory boards
Contacts of friends and relatives
Private placement agencies
Employment security departments

4. Career assessment/future options
Ability utilization
Income expectation
Workload requirement
Work schedule requirement
Family & lifestyle impact
Value consistency

Act (CETA) of 1973, as amended and extended in subsequent acts of 1974 and 1976. This program focuses largely on providing training employment and other related services to economically disadvantaged persons who are either unemployed or underemployed. Other government programs include provisions for school-to-work transition programs, senior community service employment, job corps, and work incentive programs.

While, ideally, much midlife career change and career retirement counseling would take place in the workplace, some obstacles still impede this development. However, career development and change programs that provide supporting counseling services are also beginning to emerge in business and industry. Ferrini and Parker (1978), in a survey of some 200 business and industrial firms, noted that some firms:

> had developed information resources to assist employees involved in career planning activities. For example, some firms had developed job descriptions (including skill requirements) for their jobs. These were especially valuable to employees who did not know which company jobs would best meet their needs. Career information libraries, including career change relevant publications and information about internal career opportunities, had also been established by some firms.
>
> Extensive education and training opportunities had been developed by some firms. However, those firms which had outstanding counseling-information services usually did not have outstanding education and training components, and vice versa. Most firms had some sort of tuition aid or reimbursement program enabling employees to take job-relevant courses or degree sequences at educational institutions in the community. A few firms had extended their tuition and benefits to include courses relevant to future company jobs. Other education opportunities in firms included on-the-job training options, ongoing in-house education courses, short-term training programs for specific jobs, and management training programs.
>
> A variety of placement mechanisms had also been developed in business and industry. Most firms offered some kind of job posting system for their employees. However, in many cases, employees not currently qualifying for posted jobs had difficulty using these systems. Moreover, coordination between career planning, education, and training, and job posting mechanisms appeared to be scant in most companies. Some firms had solved this problem by initiating special cross-training or lateral transfer programs which increased their participants' chances of securing career change placements. However, these programs appeared to be available only to a small number of employees. (pp. 20–21)

A comparison of support services available in business and industry and in educational institutions is presented in Figure 9–7. The second chart (Figure 9–8) depicts major career change mechanisms for employees in business and industrial settings.

Finally, it should be noted that interest and activities in career guidance in the workplace are steadily growing. Knowdell (1982) pointed out that:

> The National Vocational Guidance Association has an active commission on Career Guidance in Business and Industry; The American Society for Training and Development's Career Development Division has grown to over 2,200 members; and emerging career guidance programs are developing as integral dimensions of human resource systems rather than as isolated stop-gap measures. In addition, counselor

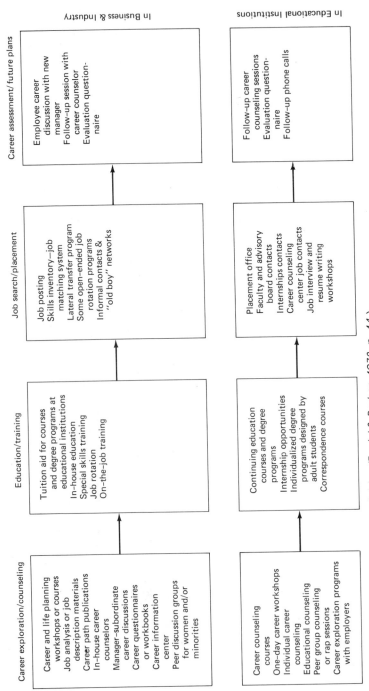

Figure 9–7. Support services available. *(Ferrini & Parker, 1978, p. 14.)*

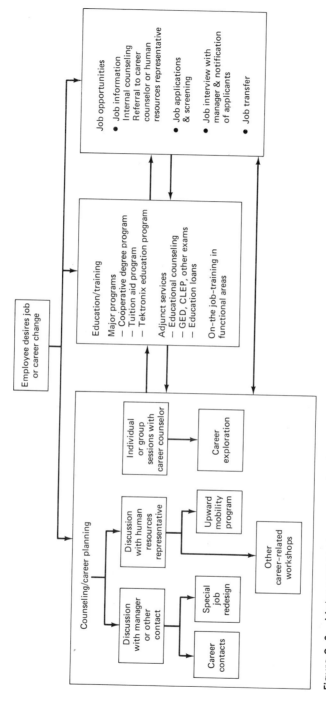

Figure 9–8. Major career change mechanisms. *(Ferrini & Parker, 1978, p. 42.)*

training programs are beginning to prepare their students for employment in the business and industrial sectors by modifying curricula and developing fieldwork and internship assignments in industry. (p. 326)

Career development opportunities are also provided for the nation's physically and mentally handicapped through state-federal programs of vocational rehabilitation. Programs of these agencies are designed to enable persons to prepare for and engage in meaningful occupations. As Norris, Hatch, Engelkes, and Winborn (1979) noted:

> Eligibility is based on a finding of a certain physical or mental problem, the existence of a substantial obstacle to employment, and a reasonable expectation that vocational rehabilitation services may enable the individual to engage in a gainful occupation. If necessary in making a decision on probable outcome, rehabilitation services can be provided during a period of extended evaluation to determine the individual's abiltiy to benefit from them.
>
> The key to the rehabilitation process is the counselor, who through his or her own professional skills enables the handicapped person to analyze problems and needs, engage in self-exploration and self-understanding, and develop a suitable plan that will lead to a productive, satisfying occupation.
>
> The state vocational rehabilitation programs across the nation reach an impressive number of handicapped people. Some are receiving and may be nearing completion of a sequence of services from other social institutions, or they may be individuals from the community at large who are blocked from vocational objectives by their problems.
>
> Special efforts of the state vocational rehabilitation programs reach target areas of highly concentrated social and economic need. These areas may be in rural America, or they may be in the severely depressed areas of cities. Such special efforts may include participation in Neighborhood Service Projects, Concentrated Employment Programs, and Model Cities Programs. (p. 312)

Moving along the maturity continuum, we are aware that the "aging of America" is another phenomenon that is increasingly challenging those responsible for providing career counseling in institutional and agency settings. As people marvel at the artistic accomplishments of a Grandma Moses at 100 or a Pablo Picasso at 90; George Burns' Academy Award-winning performance in *The Sunshine Boys* at the "youthful" age of 80; or the political activities of Ronald Reagan, the oldest President of the United States, one must be aware that age is not an inevitable barrier to career accomplishments. Coupled with this is also an awareness that life expectancy is increasing at the same time that this human physical well being and vigor are steadily improving for all age groups. It can be anticipated that increasing numbers of older and healthier citizens will be capable and desirous of work. Two projects concluded the following:

> exploring work and activity options in the post-retirement period have uncovered the need for a mix of paid employment, volunteer activities, and leisure-oriented activities to fill the "young-old years" (Katz, 1976).
>
> The Miami-Dade Project report concluded that among older persons there appears to be a need for "education for living" as well as "education for earning" (Miami-Dade Community College, 1976). The report underscored the need for leisure, vol-

unteer, and paid employment counseling to develop appropriate total activity programs for older persons. (Entine, 1977)

For many older Americans, retirement will mean a search for another career. Others may seek part-time employment. Many will simply be looking for ways to remain active and in touch with people. Volunteer work and leisure time activities may be important to this latter group. Counselors working with these senior citizens must assist their clients in planning an appropriate distribution of their time between any work activities, leisure/recreational pursuits, and "retirement living."

Summary

Changes in the world of work and the increased need for career assistance among all ages has resulted in career counseling and placement receiving a new impetus in both school and agency settings since the 1970s. In the past, career counseling was a recognized activity of most school counseling programs, but it received little curricular emphasis and, as a result, in many settings, was less than effective. The career education movement of the 1970s, however, led schools to recognize the inseparability of career education and career counseling and guidance. Career counseling programs were also encouraged to provide increased attention to placement and follow-up as a planned program activity. This emphasis has been prompted by legislative funding and recognition that career development without placement is an incomplete process. In this area, significant developments in computerized career assistance programs have been noted.

The concern over career planning and decision making has focused attention on "why people make the decisions they do and with what results." To help develop an understanding of these issues, a number of the traditional theories were reviewed in this chapter. It should be recognized that some investigators are challenging these theories as inappropriate for today's populations and careers.

Agencies and other noneducational institutions that, in the past, were primarily concerned with career placement of first-time job seekers are now recognizing the probability and importance of midlife career changes, the possiblity of employment in a new field after retirement, and the elimination of many traditional barriers to the employment of women, minorities, and older adults. These and other factors have led to a renewed interest in and examination of influences on career planning and decision making of adults. Also, the unique career assistance needs of older, retiring Americans is receiving increased attention. Career counseling across the lifetime is becoming a reality.

While, as previously noted, career counseling has been an historical traditional concern and activity of counselors, the next chapter will discuss a comparatively recent devleopment in our profession—the counselor's role as a developmental and educational consultant.

References

Bandura, A. (1982). The psychology of chance encounters and life paths. *The American Psychologist, 37*(7), 747–755.

Blau, P. M., Gustad, J. W., Jessor, R., Parnes, H. S., & Wilcock, R. G. (1956). Occupational choice: A conception framework. *Industrial and Labor Relations Review, 9,* 531–543.

Buckingham, L., & Lee, A. (1973). Placement and follow-up in career education. *Career Education Monograph No. 7.* North Carolina State University at Raleigh, NC: Center for Occupational Education.

Caplow, T. (1954). *The sociology of work.* Minneapolis, MN: University of Minnesota Press.

Crites, J. O. (1978). *Career maturity inventory.* Monterey, CA: McGraw-Hill.

Entine, A. D. (1977). Counseling for mid-life and beyond. *Vocational Guidance Quarterly, 25,* 332–336.

Ferrini, P., & Parker, L. A. (1978). *Career change.* Cambridge, MA: Technical Education Research Centers.

Florida Department of Education, Division of Vocational, Technical and Adult Education. (1974). *Career education: An introduction.* Tallahassee, FL: Author.

Fredrickson, R. H. (1982). *Career information.* Englewood Cliffs, NJ: Prentice-Hall.

Gibson, R. L. (1972). *Career development in the elementary school.* Columbus, OH: Charles E. Merrill.

Gibson, R. L., & Mitchell, M. H. (1970). Theirs and ours: Educational-vocational problems in Britain and the United States. *Vocational Guidance Quarterly, 19,* 108–112.

Gibson, R. L., & Mitchell, M. H. (1976). *Identification of effective concepts in placement and follow-up: A technical report.* Indianapolis: State of Indiana and Indiana University.

Ginzberg, E. (1972). Toward a theory of occupational choice: A restatement. *Vocational Guidance Quarterly, 20,* 169–176.

Ginzberg, E., Ginsburg, S. W., Axelrod, S., & Herma, J. L. (1951). *Occupational Choice: An approach to a general theory.* New York: Columbia University Press.

Havighurst, R. J. (1964). Youth in exploration and man emergent. In H. Borow (Ed.), *Man in a world at work,* (pp. 215–236). Boston: Houghton Mifflin.

Herr, E. L., & Cramer, S. H. (1984). *Career guidance and counseling through the life span: Systematic approaches* (2nd ed.). Boston: Little, Brown, and Co.

Holland, J. L. (1966). *The psychology of vocational choice.* Lexington, MA: Blaisdell-Ginn.

Holland, J. L. (1973). *Making vocational choices: A theory of careers.* Englewood Cliffs, NJ: Prentice-Hall.

Holland, J. L. (1974). *The self-directed search.* Palo Alto, CA: Consulting Psychologists Press.

Holland, J. L. (1977). *Understanding yourself and your career.* Palo Alto, CA: Consulting Psychologists Press.

Holland, J. L. (1978). *Vocational preference inventory.* Palo Alto, CA: Counsulting Psychologists Press.

Hoppock, R. (1976). *Occupational information.* New York: McGraw-Hill.

Hoyt, K. B. (1975). *An introduction to career education.* Washington, D.C.: U.S. Office of Education, Department of Health, Education, and Welfare.

Katz, A. M. (1976). *Employment opportunities for older adults.* First Year report submitted to the Edna McConnell Clark Foundation, NY.

Kelly, G. A. (1967). A psychology of the optimal man. In A. R. Mahrer (Ed.), *The goals of psychotherapy* (pp. 238–258). New York: Appleton-Century-Crofts.

National Vocational Guidance Association. (1973). *Career development: NVGA-AVA position paper.* Washington, D.C.: American Personnel and Guidance Association.

Norris, W., Hatch, R. N., Engelkes, J. R., & Winborn, B. B. (1979). *The career information service* (4th ed.). Chicago: Rand McNally.

Osipow, S. H. (1983). *Theories of career development.* Englewood Cliffs, NJ: Prentice-Hall.

Pascal, A. H., Bell, D., Dougherty, L. A., Dunn, W. L., & Thompson, V. M. (1975). *An evaluation of policy related research on programs for mid-life career redirection, Volumes 1 and 2.* (National Science Foundation R 1582/2NSF). Santa Monica, CA: Rand Corp.

Prediger, D., Roth, J. D., & Noeth, R. J. (1973). *Nationwide study of student career development: Summary of results.* (Research Report No. 61). Iowa City, IA: American College Testing Program.

Roe, A. (1956). *The psychology of occupations.* New York: Wiley.

Roe, A., & Siegelmen, M. (1964). *The origin of interests.* Washington, D.C.: American Personnel and Guidance Association.

Ryan, C. W. (1978). Practical linkages between career guidance and career education. *Viewpoints in Teaching and Learning, 54,* 10–19.

Sampson, J. P., Jr., & Pyle, K. R. (1983). Ethical issues involved with the use of computer-assisted counseling, testing and guidance systems. *Personnel and Guidance Journal, 61,* 283–287.

Shafe, M., Gerster, D., & Moore, B. (1976). *School based placement program.* Unpublished manuscript, State of Indiana and Indiana University.

Sheppard, H. L., & Herrick, N. Q. (1972). *Where have all the robots gone: Workers dissatisfaction in the 70's.* New York: Macmillan.

Striner, H. E. (1971). *Continuing education as a national capital investment.* New York: Upjohn Institute.

Super, D. E. (1953). A theory of vocational development. *American Psychologist, 8*(4), 189–190.

Super, D. E. (1975). *The psychology of careers.* New York: Harper & Row.

Super, D. E., Starishevsky, R., Matlin, N., & Jordaan, J. P. (1963). *Career development: Self-concept theory.* New York: College Entrance Examination Board.

Time Share Corporation. (1982). *The guidance information system (GIS).* Boston: Houghton Mifflin.

U.S. Department of Labor. (1979). *Occupational outlook handbook.* Washington, D.C.: Bureau of Labor Statistics.

Vriend, T. J. (1977). The case for women. *Vocational Guidance Quarterly, 25*(4), 329–330.

Wiggins, J. D. (1974). The career survey. Washington, D. C.: National Vocational Guidance Association.

Wiggins, J. D., & Moody, A. (1981). A field-based comparison of four career-exploration approaches. *Vocational Guidance Quarterly, 30*(1), 15–20.

Zaccaria, J. S. (1965). Developmental tasks: Implications for the goals of guidance. *Personnel and Guidance Journal, 44,* 372–375.

Zaccaria, J. S. (1970). *Theories of occupational choice and vocational development.* Boston: Houghton Mifflin.

CHAPTER 10

THE COUNSELOR AS DEVELOPMENTAL AND EDUCATIONAL CONSULTANT

Introduction

A network television news program on February 13, 1979, carried a report that a group of big business executives were going to offer their consulting services to small businesses to aid the survival chances of the small businesses. In this newscast these business people were referred to as "consultants"—a term so common in that context that the newscaster did not bother to define it. The term *consultant* is familiar to the general public as applied to the medical, legal, and business worlds. A consultant is usually an expert in a field who consults with or offers professional expertise to others both within and outside the profession. In fact, so common is the activity in the business world that we frequently hear such humorous definitions of a consultant as "anyone 50 miles from home with a briefcase," or, "one who pulls in, pops off, and pulls out."

Consultation as a mental health and educational activity is less well recognized and understood, although mental health consultation has a long tradition in the healing arts. The objective of this chapter is to introduce and describe the activity of consulting and the counselor's role as a consultant.

Caplan (1970), in a book on mental health consultation oriented to community-industrial models, restricted his use of the term *consultation* to

> the process of collaboration between two professional persons: the consultant, typically the specialist, and the consultee, who requests the consultant's help with some professional problem which he or she is having difficulty solving and which is seen as within the consultant's area of specialized competence. The professional problem may involve the management or treatment of one or more of the clients of the consultee, or the planning or implementation of a program to cater to such clients. Caplan uses the concept of *client* to denote the lay person who is the primary focus of the consultee's professional practice, such as the teacher's student, the psychologist's, psychiatrist's, or social worker's patient, the minister's parishioner, or the lawyer's client.

Caplan's definition of consultation is further restricted to those professional interactions in which the consultant has no direct responsibility for the client and the responsibility for implementing any remedial plan developed through the course of the consultation remains with the consultee. This type of consultation is aimed not only at helping the consultee with the particular problem under scrutiny, but also at increasing the general level of the consultee's competence in this area. While this definition of consultation is obviously applicable to any kind of professional work, Caplan restricts his discussion to work in the mental health field, that is, the promotion of mental health, and the prevention, treatment, and rehabilitation of mental disorders. (Goodstein, 1978, pp. 23–24)

Lewis and Lewis (1983b) suggested that:

Consultation in the human services involves helping individuals or organizations improve their effectiveness. Usually, the process has a dual aim: assisting consultees as they deal with immediate problems and helping them enhance their long-term capabilities for problem solving. Consultation may focus either on service delivery or on organizational issues. In either instance, it is characterized by a relationship that is voluntary, professional, and essentially egalitarian. (p. 173)

Block (1981) stated that a consultant is a person in a position to have some influence over an individual, group, or an organization. The recipients of this advice are called clients. Clients may be individuals, groups, departments, or organizations.

Consultation in its application to counseling as a mental health activity in schools has been even less widely recognized and defined. Most of the attention given to consultation as a school counseling activity before the 1970s seemed to suggest that it was primarily appropriate for the elementary school only. Such articles as Abbe (1961), "Consultation to a School Guidance Program," Crocker (1964) "Depth Consultation with Parents," Eckerson and Smith (1962), "Elementary School Guidance: The Consultant," and Faust (1967), "The Counselor as a Consultant to Teachers" dealt with consultation in elementary school guidance programs. Some of the popular basic guidance texts of the 1950s and 1960s such as Jones (1963) *Principles of Guidance,* Hutson (1958) *The Guidance Function in Education,* Crow and Crow (1960) *An Introduction to Guidance,* Ohlsen (1955) *Guidance: An Introduction,* and Froehlich (1958) *Guidance Services in Schools* made no mention of consultation as a school counseling activity.

In discussing consultation in *The Counselor-Consultant in the Elementary School,* Faust (1967) noted:

Although counseling has been described and researched for many years, this is not true of consultation. The latter has been practiced for as many years as counseling, if not longer, but the literature is strangely sparse in its treatment of this role. (p. 32)

Faust (1967) went on to note that:

Counseling and consultation differ in several ways. These primary differences can be found in (a) focus, and (b) the kinds of relationships that are developed within the employing school. The consultant focuses on some unit external to the consultee. In the case of a consultant to a teacher, the external unit may be a child, instructional method, course content, etc. (p. 32)

A second major difference between consultation and counseling is found in the kinds of relationships established outside the consultation and counseling settings.

Since in consultation the chief focus is on a unit external to the self of the consultee, the personal risk is not as great as it is in counseling, where internal units (the person of the counselee) receive a majority of attention. Personal investment, exposing one's personal self, is not as extensive in consultation. Therefore, risk is not as great, and the consultee need not invest as much trust in the counselor. The consultant is freer to move in many of the normal, day-to-day competitive environments of school personnel. (p. 33)

Although these early definitions focused upon consultation in community agencies, industrial settings, and the elementary school, in the past decade consultation as an appropriate counselor activity in any setting, including secondary schools and higher education institutions, has developed rapidly. This is evidenced by two consecutive special issues of the American Personnel and Guidance Association's journal, *The Personnel and Guidance Journal* (February and March 1978), and the more recent special issues of *The Counseling Psychologist* [10(1), 1982; 11(1), 1983] dealing with the counselor's role and function as a consultant at all educational levels as well as in community and other mental health settings and by an increasing number of textbooks dealing with the topic. Let us, therefore, proceed to examine some of the roles and models for consultation.

Models for Consultation

The increase in popularity and demand for consultation services has resulted in the development or identification of a variety of models or styles appropriate to the consultation process. Although differences exist among authorities in the area of consultation in terms of the organization or categorization of theories or systems for providing consultation services, similarities are far more prevalent than differences.

A traditional model that highlights the basic consultation process is a *triadic model,* as suggested by Tharp and Wetzel (1969). In this model, consultation services are offered indirectly through an intermediary to a target client or clients. The model illustrated in Figure 10–1 is described as a consultative triad, in which all effects proceed

to the target via the *mediator,* none directly from consultant to target. This analysis describes functional positions, not the people who occupy those positions. For example, any number of individuals occupying any number of social roles might serve as mediator: father, teacher, sister, minister, mother, employer, friend, and psychotherapist. Indeed, the same is true of the functions of either consultant or target. (Parker, 1975, p. 137)

Figure 10–1. The consultative triad. *(Tharp & Wetzel, 1969, p. 47.)*

Four popular consultation models, as identified by Kurpius (1978) suggest the counselor-consultant can function effectively by providing a direct service to a client identified by another party, by prescribing a solution to a specific problem identified by a consultee, by assisting others in developing a plan for problem solution, and by taking direct responsibility for defining a problem and proposing a solution. These functions are organized by Kurpius (1978) into four consulting modalities as follows:

Provision Mode

The provision mode of consultation is commonly used when a potential consultee finds himself confronted with a problem for which he or she may not have the time, interest, or competence to define objectively, to identify possible solutions, or to implement and evaluate the problem-solving strategy. Consequently, a consultant is requested to provide a direct service to the client, with little or no intervention by the consultee after the referral is accepted.

Prescriptive Mode

Sometimes consultees experience unusual work-related problems for which they request special help. Even though competent and motivated to solve the problem directly, the consultees may lack confidence in their own intervention strategy or may lack certain specific knowledge and skills for carrying out a given problem-solving plan.

In these situations, the consultee is often in need of a resource person (consultant) to support the diagnosis and treatment plan already developed by the consultee or to explore additional alternatives for defining and solving a specific problem.

There are other times, however, when a consultee is looking for an exact "pre-scription" to ameliorate a specific problem. While the prescriptive mode is quite appropriate for many situations, here are four questions that should be answered jointly by the consultant and consultee: (a) Has all the information needed to define and solve the problem been shared and is [it] accurate? (b) Has the plan prescribed by the consultant been accepted by the consultee and will it be implemented as designed? (c) Who will evaluate the "process" and "outcomes" associated with the prescriptive plan—the consultant, the consultee, or both? (d) Will adjustments in the prescription, if needed, be requested by the consultee?

Collaboration

When following the collaboration mode the consultant's goal is to facilitate the consultee's self-direction and innate capacity to solve problems. As a result, the consultant serves more as a generalist than a technical expert. His major efforts are directed toward helping people develop a plan for solving problems. Hence he acts as a catalyst and "reality tapper," helping consultees to share observations, concepts, and proven practices. He also helps consultees examine forces that are facilitative or debilitative in both the immediate and larger environments.

Mediation Mode

Mediation is uniquely different from the other three modes of consultation in which the *consultee* initiates the contact and requests help for solving a problem. In mediation, it is the *consultant* who recognizes a persisting problem, gathers, analyzes, and synthesizes existing information, defines the problem, decides on the most appropriate intervention, and then calls together the persons who have direct contact with the problem and have the greatest potential to influence a desired change. (p. 335)

Schein (1978) organizes the consultation process into three models with assumptions as follows:

Model 1: Purchase of Expertise

The core characteristic of this model is that the client has made up his or her mind on what the problem is, what kinds of help are needed, and to whom to go for this help. The client expects expert help and expects to pay for it, but not to get involved in the process of consultation itself.

In order for this model to work successfully, the following assumptions have to be met, however.

1. That the client has made a correct diagnosis of his or her own problem.
2. That the client has correctly identified the consultant's capabilities to solve the problem.
3. That the client has correctly communicated the problem.
4. That the client has thought through and accepted the potential consequences of the help that will be received.

In summary, this model of consultation is appropriate when clients have diagnosed their needs correctly, have correctly identified consultant capabilities, have done a good job of communicating what problem they are actually trying to solve, and have thought through the consequences of the help they have sought. As can be seen, this model is "client intensive," in that it puts a tremendous load on the client to do things correctly if the problem is to be solved. If problems are complex and difficult to diagnose, it is highly likely that this model will not prove helpful.

Model 2: Doctor-Patient

The core of this model is that the client experiences some symptoms that something is wrong but does not have a clue as to how to go about figuring out what is wrong or how to fix it. The diagnostic process itself is delegated completely to the consultant along with the obligation to come up with a remedy. The client becomes dependent upon the consultant until such time as the consultant makes a prescription, unless the consultant engages the client in becoming more active on his or her own behalf. Several implicit assumptions are the key to whether or not the doctor-patient model will in fact provide help to the client.

1. That the client has correctly interpreted the symptoms and the sick "area."
2. That the client can trust the diagnostic information that is provided by the consultant.
3. That the "sick" person or group will reveal the correct information necessary to arrive at a diagnosis and cure, i.e., will trust the doctor enough to "level" with him or her.
4. That the client has thought through the consequences, i.e., is willing to accept and implement whatever prescription is given.
5. That the patient/client will be able to remain healthy after the doctor/consultant leaves.

In summary, the doctor-patient model of consultation highlights the dependence of the client on the consultant both for diagnosis and prescription and thus puts a great burden on the client to correctly identify sick areas, accurately communicate symptoms, and think through the consequences of being given a prescription.

Model 3: Process Consultation

The core of this model is the assumption that for many kinds of problems that clients face, the *only* way to locate a workable solution, one that the client will accept and implement, is to involve the client in the diagnosis of the problem and the generating of that solution. The focus shifts from the content of the problem to the process by which problems are solved, and the consultant offers "process expertise" in how to help and how to solve problems, not expertise on the particular content of the client's problem. The consultant does not take the problem onto his or her own shoulders in this model. The "monkey always remains on the client's back," but the consultant offers to become jointly involved with the client in figuring out what is the problem, why it is a problem, why it is a problem right now, and what might be done about it. This consulting model is not a panacea appropriate to all problems and all situations. It also rests on some specific assumptions that have to be met if the model is to be viewed as the appropriate way to work with a client.

1. That the nature of the problem is such that the client not only needs help in making an initial diagnosis but would benefit from participation in the process of making that diagnosis.
2. That the client has constructive intent and some problem-solving ability.
3. That the client is ultimately the only one who knows what form of solution or intervention will work in his or her own situation.
4. That if the client selects and implements his or her own solution, the client's problem-solving skills for future problems will increase.

How does the consultant implement the process consultation model? The basic principle is to get into the client's world and see it initially from the client's perspective. This usually means paying attention to the "task process"—and how the problem is defined, how the agenda is set, how information is gathered, how decisions are made, all the activities that make up the "problem-solving process." (pp. 3-10–3-12)

Also in the February 1978 special issue of the *Personnel and Guidance Journal,* Werner discussed consultation in a community mental health agency. For this setting he described six possible models:

Client-Centered Case Consultation

The goal is to enable the consultee to deal more effectively with the client's problems and to improve the consultee's functioning with similar problems in the future.

Consultee-Centered Case Consultation

The goal is to collaboratively identify consultee problems in dealing with the client and to collaboratively develop the consultee's skills repertoire in dealing effectively with similar problems in the future.

Program-Centered Administration Consultation

The goal is to enable the consultee to deal more effectively with specific problems encountered in developing and providing a mental health program and to improve the consultee's functioning with similar problems in the future.

Consultee-Centered Administrative Consultation

The goal is to collaboratively identify consultee problems that have been generated in developing and providing a mental health program and to collaboratively develop the consultee's skill repertoire in dealing effectively with similar problems in the future.

Community-Centered Ad Hoc Consultation
The goal is to enable the ad hoc consultee to deal more effectively with community problems encountered in the development of a temporary program for increasing the competency of the community.

Consultee-Centered Ad Hoc Consultation
The goal is to collaboratively identify the ad hoc consultee problems that have been generated in the ad hoc consultee development in the provision of a temporary community program for increasing the competency of the community. (p. 366)

Regardless of one's choice of consultation models, Gallessich (1982) suggested certain common characteristics that apply to most consultation:

1. Consultants are professionals who are experts in specialized bodies of knowledge. Many are also experts in the process of helping peers (other professionals) solve problems.
2. Consultants work with consultees, staff members of human service organizations, to help them with their work-related concerns. Consultants do not focus on consultees' personal concerns except as they relate directly to the work situation.
3. Consultation is an indirect service. In working with an agency's staff, consultants serve a third party, the agency's clients, indirectly. Exceptions may occur, however; for example, a consulting clinician may, at times, directly examine the consultees' clients. Further client contact ordinarily moves the consultant into direct services and outside the consultant role.
4. Consultants are outsiders. The consultation relationship is a temporary one. Consultants come from external bases, such as private practice or agencies that are independent of the consultee. Sometimes, however, consultants belong to the same agency as their consultees; in these situations, the consultant role is significantly modified by the consultant's membership in the agency's authority structure and social life.
5. The consultation relationship is between peers whose areas of responsibility and expertise differ. The relationship is voluntary for both parties, and each maintains control over her or his involvement. When the agency and the consultant agree to a contract, the consultant is authorized to enter the consultee's work domain; barring a binding contractual provision, the consultee may withdraw this permission at any time. Similarly, the consultant may elect to terminate the relationship. Consultees determine the concerns to be discussed. Both consultant and consultee may introduce ideas or questions they perceive to be important and screen out irrelevant or inappropriate topics. To illustrate, a consultee might decline to discuss certain work topics even though the consultant perceived them to be related to the focal problem; or a consultant might decline to discuss a consultee's family problems. A consultant might also choose either to introduce or to withhold theories, research findings, or principles pertinent to the problem under discussion.
6. The consultee retains responsibility and authority for any action and is free to accept or reject the consultant's advice. However, two assumptions underlying the relationship are that consultees (1) will seriously consider the input of the consultant and (2) have the power to mobilize resources to effect improvements in their work situation. (pp. 11–12)

The Consultation Process

To further understand how counselors function effectively in their consulting role, let us next examine briefly the nine stages of the consulting process, as identified by Kurpius (1978):

> Stage 1. Preentry. Clarifying the consultant's values, needs, assumptions and goals about people and organizations, specifying an operational definition of consultation, and assessing the consultant's skills for performing as a consultant.
>
> Stage 2. Entry. Defining and establishing the consultation relationship, roles, ground rules and contract, including statement of presenting problem.
>
> Stage 3. Gathering Information. Gathering of additional information as an aid to clarifying the presenting problem.
>
> Stage 4. Defining the Problem. Utilizing the assessment information in order to determine the goals for change.
>
> Stage 5. Determination of the Problem Solution. Analyzing and synthesizing of information in search of the best solution to the problem as presently stated.
>
> Stage 6. Stating Objectives. Stating desired outcome that can be accomplished and measured within a stated period of time and within specified conditions.
>
> Stage 7. Implementation of the Plan. Implementing of the intervention following the guidelines clarified in the proceding steps.
>
> Stage 8. Evaluation. The monitoring of the ongoing activities (process evaluation) culminating with the measuring of the final outcomes (outcome evaluation).
>
> Stage 9. Termination. Agreeing to discontinue direct contact with the consultant, keeping in mind the effects of the consulting process are expected to continue. (p. 337)

These nine stages suggest that effective consultation draws on an organized and systematic process in which each step logically leads to the next. Consultants will also frequently find it helpful to their consultees to identify these stages as guidelines for the process they will be sharing and as a means of keeping the activity "on track."

Gallessich (1982) indicated that:

> Consultants may use facilitative strategies to stimulate consultees in generating ideas, clarifying feelings and/or values, and mobilizing resources for identifying and solving problems. In facilitative strategies—in contrast to supportive strategies—the consultant's goals and methods are explicit. Underlying facilitative strategies are these assumptions: (1) consultees' expertise is essential to achieve valid diagnoses and to plan effective solutions, (2) consultees will be more motivated to follow through on intervention plans that they help design, and (3) the facilitative approach is most likely to increase consultees' effectiveness in solving future problems. Consultants' facilitative strategies may include cognitive and/or affective components and may seek to bring about changes in consultees' cognitions, emotions, attitudes, and/or behaviors. Referent power is essential. (pp 103–104)

Goals of Consultation

Turner (1982) discussed a hierarchy of consulting goals that, though focusing on business and industrial settings, have some relevancy for counselors functioning as consultants in many settings. These are presented in Figure 10–2.

Skills for Consultation

As with all counseling and guidance activities, certain special skills are needed if the counselor is to function effectively as a consultant in either school or agency settings. Dinkmeyer and Carlson (1977) suggested that counselor training for consultation should be based on the counselors' building skills so that they can perform the following competencies:

1. Understand the purposive nature of behavior and develop skills of observation and interpretation that will facilitate problem solving.
2. Apply theories of learning to specific learning difficulties of students, that is, learning disabilities.

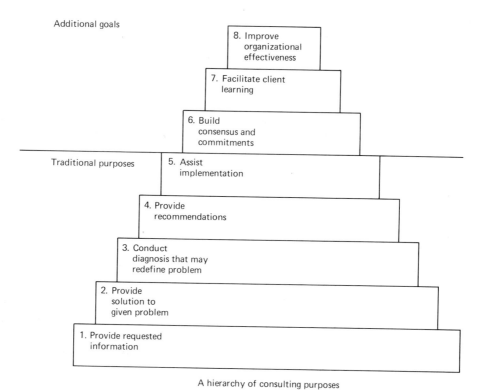

A hierarchy of consulting purposes

Figure 10–2. A hierarchy of consulting purposes. *(Turner, 1982, p. 122.)*

3. Understand and apply idiographically logical consequences and other corrective procedures for concerns presented by teachers and parents.
4. Demonstrate the ability to communicate effectively to develop effective helping relationships.
5. Demonstrate the basic group leadership competencies: structuring, universalizing, feedback, formulation of tentative hypotheses, encouraging, task setting, and commitment.
6. Understand management by objectives and be able to establish hierarchies, a plan of action, and assessment procedures needed for a systematic change.
7. Demonstrate competence in a brief, diagnostic student interview to determine the purposive nature of the individual's behavior.
8. Demonstrate effectiveness in individual teacher consultation.
9. Demonstrate effectiveness in individual parent consultation.
10. Demonstrate effectiveness in administrator consultation.
11. Develop and facilitate productive consultation groups with teachers (i.e., the consultation group collaborates, consults, clarifies, confronts, develops commitments, and is confidential).
12. Develop and facilitate effective parent education with parents.
13. Develop and facilitate productive consultation groups with parents.
14. Demonstrate knowledge and use processes and materials of the psychological or affective education programs in the classroom. (pp. 173–174)

Consultation Roles

According to Lewis and Lewis (1983):

> The human service professional, especially when he or she has moved into an administrative role, finds that consultation with others becomes a major area of involvement. In human service settings, the consultant is most likely to provide assistance through *internal consultation,* within his or her own work setting; through *networking,* or collaboration with helpers in other settings; and through *community organization,* or enhancement of the problem-solving capacities of community groups. (p. 184)

Consultation in School Settings

In school settings, counselors who function in a consulting role, are in effect giving their special expertise to teachers, school administrators, and other appropriate personnel. In this role, they become a resource professional for the developmental or adjustment needs involving third parties, usually students. For the counselor to function effectively as a consultant in the educational setting, one must possess special knowledge or skills appropriate to the consulting need. Among the relevant skills the counselor can bring to consulting with teachers and other educational providers and planners are the following:

1. An understanding of human growth and development, the problems and processes of adjustment, and the needs of the individual as he goes through those processes.
2. An understanding of psychological or affective education in the classroom, and a concern for its importance.
3. An understanding of and skills in promoting communications and other desirable human relationship skills.
4. Training in the assessment of individual charateristics and skills in relating these assessments to the development of the individual's potential.
5. Special knowledge of educational and career development and opportunities.
6. An ability to communicate, counsel, and consult with parents, fellow educators, and the community.
7. An understanding of group processes and skills useful in facilitating group motivation and change. (Gibson, 1973, p. 51)

In addition, to function effectively as a consultant, the counselor must have a background of understanding of the person or group with whom he or she is consulting, the target population for the consulting, and the characteristics of the school in which the consulting is taking place. The counselor-consultant should also be knowledgeable regarding contributing external environmental factors. Munson (1971) emphasized this:

> The consultation function, like the counseling function, is based on communication and human interaction. The relationship between the consultant and the consultee is basic. Acceptance, trust, and understanding are essential. (p. 158)

As a consultant, the school counselor has the potential to engage in a wide range of activities or roles. In discussing these roles, Faust (1967) suggested a hierarchy of first and second level of counsulting roles:

First Level:

1. Consultation with groups of teachers.
2. Consultation with the individual teacher.
3. Consultation with groups of children.
4. Consultation with the individual child.

Second Level:

5. Consultation in curriculum development.
6. Consultation with administrators.
7. Consultation with parents.
8. Consultation with school personnel specialists (psychologists, social workers, psychometrists, curriculum supervisors, nurses, psychiatrists).
9. Consultation with community agencies (family service, child guidance clinic, family physician, high school counselors, private psychotherapists, etc.). (p. 34)

Some specific examples of these activities are suggested in Table 10–1.

Table 10-1. Consulting Activities Counselors Perform

With Administrators	With Teachers	With Parents
1. Plan a schoolwide educational assessment program. 2. Identify children with special needs. 3. Facilitate community and parent–school relations.	1. Identify and analyze deficiencies in the academic and psychological development of children. 2. Develop skill in understanding child behavior, in classroom management, and in conducting parent–teacher conferences. 3. Develop remedial or prescriptive programs for individuals and groups. 4. Help develop more effective teaching strategies. 5. Help teachers develop effective career education programs.	1. Facilitate positive school–parent relationships. 2. Enhance parent understanding of children's development, abilities, and difficulties. 3. Help parent to modify child learning and behavior problems. 4. Conduct parent education groups.

Source: Blackham, 1977, p. 361.

Consulting with Teachers

As mentioned previously, the teacher is the key person and most populous professional in school settings at any level. In consultation in schools, then, the counselor must assume that he or she will most frequently consult with teachers individually or in groups. This probability is further highlighted by the fact that teachers have the most frequent contacts with pupils and that the developmental and adjustment needs of their pupils are often expressed in classroom groups. Counselors may effectively assist teachers as consultants to individualize classroom instruction.

School counselors are also experienced in collecting, organizing, and synthesizing data on individual students and in interpreting this information to identify individual differences. Through these activities, they sharpen their understanding of the individual in terms of his or her aptitudes, interests, values, personal growth, health, and ability to adjust. (Gibson, 1973, p.51)

Further, the effects of Public Law 94–142, requiring all children categorized as handicapped to be placed in regular educational programs to the fullest extent possible, has resulted in a wider diversity in the characteristics and abilities of classroom groups. As Aubrey (1978) stated:

> The consequence will be a significant change in the social system of most classrooms and a need for many physical and social alterations. As currently trained, it is doubtful if any educators are sufficiently prepared for these changes. Yet, who will teachers turn to when in trouble?
>
> In addition to mainstreaming and the enormous problems this will pose for classroom socialization and adaptation, Public Law 94–142 will provide parents with rights

and prerogatives never granted before. The law will allow any parent the right to demand a complete diagnostic workup on their child, and in addition, the right to appeal the school's appraisal. Also, schools will be held accountable for prescriptive contracts made between school and parents extending over the duration of the school year and clearly outlining the complete learning sequence for a given child. (p. 355)

Aubrey also felt that the counselor has a significant consultant role to play in assisting teachers specifically and the educational system generally in implementing this act.

As consultant in identifying and utilizing appropriate instructional resources: The classroom teacher is obviously the most knowledgeable about resources appropriate to his subject matter, but the counselor can nonetheless be profitably consulted on those occasions when specialized occupational and educational information is needed to make a class more meaningful. He can also be consulted to identify out of school resources and experiences relevant to students' learning needs. And his insights can be helpful in the development of materials and methodologies that will enable counselors and teachers to work together in special educational activities with vocational students. (Gibson, 1973, p. 51).

As consultant in the development of a classroom environment conducive to learning: The counselor's expertise in human behavior and development theory combined with the teacher's knowledge of instructional methods and materials is the basis for an excellent team effort in the crucial task of planning and establishing a productive learning environment. (Gibson, 1973, p. 54)

A basic principle of effective consultation is that the recipients must believe that they need it. Teachers and others will neither seek out nor be receptive to the counselor as a consultant if they see no value or rationale for such assistance. Many teachers, like counselors, do not understand or accept the counselor as a consultant. In each situation it is therefore important for the counselor to communicate and demonstrate his or her role as an effective consultant. As pointed out by Blackham (1977):

In educational systems, more often than not, the clients do not know what they are looking for and, indeed, should not be expected to know. All they know is that something is wrong. An important part of the consultation process is to help such clients (teacher, administrator, department) define the problem, then decide what kind of help is needed or warranted and what consultation approach would be most useful and acceptable. (p. 390)

The Counselor as a Consultant to the School Administrator

The school counselor can also make significant consultation contributions to the educational leadership of the school and the school system. The counselor has the capacity to gather data descriptive of the characteristics of the student population and their needs, which, in turn, can provide useful information for educational planning and management.

The counselor's understanding of the process and characteristics of human growth and development enables him or her to relate and to provide special counsel regarding the special needs of individuals and groups of pupils on occasion.

Consulting with Parents

The counselor can effectively consult with parents on various occasions. Many of these occasions would focus on promoting parent understanding of pupil characteristics and their relationships to pupil behavior and school achievement. Consultation can also assist parents in coping with or modifying pupil behaviors on occasion. The counselor may also serve as a consultant to interpret school programs to parents.

The Counselor as a Curriculum Consultant

Federal legislation specifying the counselor's role and importance in implementing programs of career education and education of the handicapped have already suggested that it is time for the school counselor to function actively as a consultant for curriculum development and management. In an instructional sense, the school counselor is not, of course, a curriculum specialist. However, when the curriculum is viewed as the sum of educational experiences the school proposes to provide, it follows that the counselor, because of his or her professional commitment to the total development of each student, should be actively involved, regardless of legislative mandates in curriculum planning.

Several specific examples of their function as related by Gibson (1973) describe the counselor as follows:

> *As a consultant in matters related to the career interests and concerns of students:* Comprehensive assessments of student career interests provide a basis for expanded and relevant curriculum offerings. Nor should the important area of avocational interests be overlooked. A combination of educational and avocational opportunities often provides an experience which maintains student interest and motivation. The counselor should assume major responsibility to identify and interpret these interests and concerns to all educators involved. Assessment of student interest must be translated into action, however, and it is at that point that many opportunities for curriculum development are left to founder in the sea of academic indifference.
>
> *As consultant in matters relating to the career development needs of all students:* Related to the vocational interests of students, but worth singling out, are the developmental needs of all students as they prepare for entry and progression in the world of work. Students at all grade levels need opportunities to test, compare, develop, and experience skills, concepts, roles and values as they relate to work. They need to learn to appreciate the value of all honest work and to understand the educational prerequisites for entering various careers. The more actively youth can explore and test out their abilities, interests, and work styles (especially in true, work-type situations), the more insight they will gain for later decision making. (p. 51)

School counselors and curriculum planners have a joint responsibility to see that these important aspects of the student's total development are not left to chance. In this regard, it should be noted that curricular consultation frequently points out the need for curricular change. Because the school counselor's responsibilities involve him or her with both teachers and administrators, the counselor is in a position to facilitate their cooperation and interaction in promoting curricular change. Such change usually involves the prerequisites of (a) identification of the need for change, (b) a willingness on the part of those involved to consider change, and (c) the development and acceptance of a plan for change.

Consultation in Community Mental Health Settings

Consultation has emerged, since the 1970s, as a well-established activity and specialty in mental health agencies. The general purpose

> of the consultation mandate in community mental health is for professionals to provide "indirect" services that will expand mental health personpower. In general, consultation efforts are directed to schools, clergy, criminal justice settings, industry, and other human service agencies. The classic typology of so-called mental health consultation was offered by one of its founders, Gerald Caplan (1963, 1970). He divides consultation activities in community agencies into four major categories: (1) client-centered case consultation, in which the focus is on helping the consultee deal with a particular case or client; (2) program-centered administrative consultation, in which the major aim is to help the consultee in administering a treatment or prevention program; (3) consultee-centered case consultation, in which the primary goal is to help the consultees with problems in working with clients in general; and (4) consultee-centered administrative consultation, in which the goal of the consultant is to aid the consultee or consultee agency in planning, implementing, and maintaining mental health programs. (Jeger and Slotnick, 1982, p. 141)

Mental health consultation is the major form of *indirect service* associated with the community mental health movement (Bloom, 1984, p. 155).

Bloom (1984) distinguished consultation

> from other mental health activities with which it is sometimes confused and with which it has some overlapping characteristics. Consultation can be distinguished from *supervision* on the grounds that (1) the consultant may not be of the same professional specialty as the consultee, (2) the consultant has no administrative responsibility for the work of the consultee. Consultation can be distinguished from *education* on the basis of (1) the relative freedom of the consultee to accept or reject the consultant's ideas, (2) the lack of a planned curriculum, and (3) the absence of any evaluation or assessment of the consultee's progress by the consultant. Consultation also needs to be differentiated from *psychotherapy*. In psychotherapy, there is a clear contractual relationship bebween an individual designated as a patient and another individual designated as a therapist. In this relationship, the patient acknowledges the existence of personal problems and allows the invasion of his or her privacy in order to resolve these problems. No such contractual relationship exists between consultant and consultee. The goal of consultation is improved work performance rather than improved personal adjustment. The consultant and consultee are in a peer relationship, and

each expects his or her privacy to be honored. Consultation should, finally, be distinguished from *collaboration.* Consultation carries no implication that the consultant will participate with the consultee in the implementation of any plans. The task of the consultant is to assist the consultee in meeting his or her work responsibilities more effectively. (p. 156)

Bloom (1984) also noted:

To assist community mental health centers in evaluating their consultation programs, Mannino and MacLennan (1978) reviewed how consultation services were monitored and evaluated in nearly 80 settings. They found that information being collected could be grouped into three categories: (1) information on the community being served, such as assessment of needs, survey of available resources, or characteristics of the population, (2) characteristics of the consultation program, such as target groups, frequency of contacts, financing, program descriptions, progress reports or use of staff, and (3) outcome data, such as measures of consultee satisfaction, subjective judgments by consultants, or goal-attainment measures. (p. 177)

Bloom (1984) concluded:

The usefulness of consultation as a community mental health technique is being increasingly supported. Consultation has enormous appeal among mental health professionals, and substantial time is currently allocated to the activity by mental health professionals working in community health centers. (pp. 186–187)

Summary

Booz/Allen and Hamilton noted in an advertisement in the *Chicago Tribune* March 18, 1979, that firms use their consulting services for such activities as "provide planning and strategy guidance; provide an economic and technical review of their R & D programs; perform economic and technical evaluations as they relate to proposed government regulations; provide technical marketing assistance in the chemical processing, agribusiness, engineering materials and medical fields; recommend process modifications as part of an economic evaluation/justification study."

In this same issue of the *Tribune,* other firms described their consulting services and still other firms advertised positions for consultants. These classified advertisements are only surface indications that consultation is a recognized and ongoing activity in the business world. Consultation has also been a recognized mental health activity for a number of years although not nearly as well publicized as its business counterpart. There are also consulting firms that specialize in educational matters.

However, consultation as an activity of counselors has led to an examination of various models appropriate to the consultation process and of their adaptation to counselor use. Kurpius organized these into four modalities of provision, prescription, collaboration, and remediation. Schein organized the process into three models: purchase of expertise, doctor-patient, and process consultation.

Werner described six possible agency models as client-centered case consultation; consultee-centered case consultation; program-centered administration consultation; consultee-centered administrative consultation; community-centered ad hoc consultation; and consultee-centered ad hoc consultation.

Regardless of model choice, counselor-consultants must recognize that they are involved in a process that provides structure and direction for their consultation efforts. It is naive to think that knowledge or experience in itself qualifies one to consult. An understanding of the process of consultation and the acquisition of the skills for consultation are prerequisites to success as a consultant. These are ususaly acquired through special courses in consultation.

The qualified counselor will have opportunities to consult. It is important to keep in mind however, that consultation must be wanted—must be requested—if it is to take place. Even when requested, the counselor-consultant should proceed with tact and understanding. After all, no one likes to be "told off"—even by experts!

Consultation has been increasingly utilized by counselors in the 1970s and 1980s to enhance the delivery of their services. It appears that the 1980s and 1990s will see yet another trend in our profession. Prevention and wellness has "caught the public's fancy" and serious efforts to prevent many of the disorders which have handicapped individuals and society are underway. The helping professions are responding. The next chapter discusses how our helping profession, counseling, can respond.

References

Abbe, A. E. (1961). Consultation to a school guidance program. *Elementary School Journal, 61,* 331–337.

Aubrey, R. F. (1978). Consultation, school interventions, and the elementary counselor. *Personnel and Guidance Journal, 56,* 351–354.

Blackham, G. J. (1977). *Counseling: Theory, process and practice.* Belmont, CA: Wadsworth.

Block, P. (1981). *Flawless consulting.* San Diego, CA: University Associates.

Bloom, B. L. (1984). *Community mental health: A general introduction* (2nd ed.). Belmont, CA: Brooks/Cole.

Caplan, G. (1970). *The theory and practice of mental health consultation.* New York: Basic Books.

Crocker, E. C. (1964). Depth consultation with parents. *Young Children, 20,* 91–99.

Crow, L. D. & Crow, A. (1960). *An introduction to guidance* (2nd ed.). New York: American.

Dinkmeyer, D., & Carlson, J. (1977). Consulting: Training counselors to work with teachers, parents, and administrators. *Counselor Education and Supervision, 16,* 172–177.

Eckerson. L., & Smith, H. (1962). *Elementary school guidance: The consultant* (Reprint of three articles in *School Life*). Washington, D.C.: U.S. Department of Health, Education and Welfare, Office of Education.

Faust, V. (1967). The counselor as a consultant to teachers. *Elementary School Guidance and Counseling, 1,* 112–117.

Faust, V. (1968). *The counselor-consultant in the elementary school.* Boston: Houghton Mifflin.

Froehlich, C. P. (1958). *Guidance services in schools* (2nd ed.). New York: McGraw-Hill.

Gallessich, J. (1982). *The profession and practice of consultation.* San Francisco: Jossey-Bass.

Gibson, R. L. (1973). The counselor as curriculum consultant. *American Vocational Journal, 48,* 50–51, 54.

Goodstein, L. D. (1978). *Consulting with human service systems.* Reading, MA: Addison-Wesley.

Hutson, P. W. (1958). *The guidance function in education.* New York: Appleton-Century-Crofts.

Jeger, A. M., & Slotnick, R. S. (1982). *Community mental health and behavioral-ecology: A handbook of theory, research and practice.* New York: Plenum.

Jones, A. J. (1963). *Principles of guidance* (5th ed.). New York: McGraw-Hill.

Kurpius, D. (1978). Consultation theory and process: An integrated model. *Personnel and Guidance Journal, 56,* 335–338.

Lewis, J. A., & Lewis, M. D. (1983a). *Community counseling: A human services approach* (2nd ed.). New York: John Wiley & Sons.

Lewis, J. A., & Lewis, M. D. (1983b). *Management of human service programs.* Belmont, CA: Brooks/Cole.

Mannino, F. V., & MacLennan, B. W. (1978). *Monitoring and evaluating mental health consultation and education services.* DHEW Pub. No. (ADM) 77–550. Washington, D.C.: U.S. Government Printing Office.

Munson, H. L. (1971). *Foundations of developmental guidance.* Boston: Allyn & Bacon.

Ohlsen, M. M. (1955). *Guidance: An introduction.* New York: Harcourt Brace Jovanovich.

Parker, C. A. (Ed.). (1975). *Psychological consultation: Helping teachers meet special needs.* Minneapolis: University of Minnesota, Leadership Training Institute.

Schein, E. H. (1978). The role of the consultant: Content expert or process facilitator? *Personnel and Guidance Journal, 56,* 339–345.

Tharp, R. G., & Wetzel, R. (1969). *Behavior modification in the natural environment.* New York: Academic Press.

Turner, A. N. (1982). Consulting is more than giving advice. *Harvard Business Review, 60*(5), 120–129.

Werner, J. L. (1978). Community mental health consultation with agencies. *Personnel and Guidance Journal, 56,* 364–368.

CHAPTER 11

PREVENTION AND WELLNESS

Introduction

While the old saying "An ounce of prevention is worth a pound of cure" would seem to be particularly appropriate to the health professions, the fact is that until recently, these professions, including the mental health profession, have given little more than "lip service" to prevention. However, recent generations have witnessed the pursuit of "wellness" by millions of Americans with near revolutionary zeal. At times, our whole country seems to be waking up to "jazzercise," washing down vitamin pills with instant "stay trim" breakfasts, practicing relaxation techniques on the job, jogging after work, attending stress management workshops, following the Pritikin diet, and so forth. These "signs of the times" point to our growing concern with the prevention of health disorders, including mental health. It represents, if not a shift in emphases, a sharing of emphasis between remediation and prevention. The objectives of this chapter are, therefore, to (a) present the role of prevention in counseling programs, and (b) introduce prevention through stress management, attention to nutrition, and the wise use of recreation and leisure time.

Prevention

In the field of mental health, a substantial increase in reported prevention research and professional literature appropriate for counselors is evident. These include a broad range of studies reported in such publications as *Preventive Psychology* (Felner, Jason, Moritsugu, and Farber, 1983), and special issues of the *Personnel and Guidance Journal* (April, May, 1984) focusing on primary prevention in schools, on college campuses, and in the community.

The model of prevention adopted by counselors and other mental health workers is in large part the model of prevention adopted by psychology, which in turn was borrowed from the field of public health.

Here the term "prevention" is an all-embracing one, having three separate levels: primary, secondary, and tertiary (Goldston, 1977). Tertiary prevention closely parallels traditional approaches. The focus is on the individual who has established disorder, and the goals are to reduce the residual effects of it and to rehabilitate the individual to a level where he or she may readjust to community life. Secondary prevention efforts are characterized by attempts at early identification and intervention with individuals who are displaying initial signs of disorder, but for whom it is not yet ingrained. Zax and Spector (1974) caution that it may be argued that early detection and effective treatment of mental disorder in an individual may be little more than what has long been viewed as good mental health care. (Felner, Jason, Moritsugu, and Farber, 1983, p. 5)

In planning for prevention some obvious needs may exist. Preventative programs in substance abuse are popular in schools. Premarital counseling is commonplace. Also, many counseling agencies have programs to help married couples avoid some of the anticipated problems and adjustments of marriage. In general, however, prevention has not reached the level of sophistication or popularity attained by remediation. Remer, Niguette, Anderson, and Terrell (1984) reminded us that:

> Remediation seems to be more valued, by the public in general and by mental health professionals in particular, than prevention. "Why fix that which is not broken?" We, on the other hand, are purveying a value: "mental wellness" (to borrow from the Holistic Health movement). But because the concept of mental wellness, even in contrast to that of mental health, is encompassing, the operationalization of this value is difficult. Nevertheless, we believe we must first establish a general perspective from which to operate.
>
> Some people may argue that we should address specific areas. This approach has met with resistance in the past (e.g., sex education, family planning, values education). But we believe an environment conducive to and supportive of preventive intervention must be established, an atmosphere of "good faith." Those involved can then feel they have an opportunity for input. This support is a prerequisite to the implementation of focused interventions. (p. 30)

Despite the obstacles which must be overcome, counselors and other mental health professionals are being urged, even mandated by legislation in some instances, to broaden the scope of their prevention activities in order to identify and thus intervene with even larger populations at risk. This approach recognizes the importance of significant settings and experiences that influence individual adjustment and development. The home, school, workplace, church, and community are obviously relatively stable settings over periods of time that have a significant impact on large numbers of people. It is in these settings that prevention programs should flourish.

Of course, prevention planning must be based on some systematic approach for identifying the needs of specific client populations. This involves the study of:

1. Factors associated with adjustments.
2. Characteristics of particularly susceptible people.
3. Interrelationships between 1 and 2 above.
4. Examination of how people adapt in a given environment.
5. Identification of significant events in the environment that signify success or growth outcomes.

Prevention program development should follow certain principles. Drum (1984) suggests the following as key principles:

1. Prevention programs should be designed to go beyond informing to transforming. Too often, prevention efforts rely largely on didactic presentations that fail to enable the individual to translate the information into a strategy for change. We "must transform general information into personal information for decision-making" (Schinke, Gilchrist, and Small, 1979, p. 84).

2. Design of such programs must take into account the psyche of the consumer—his or her motivation, sense of urgency, feeling of susceptibility, and so forth. Interventions built on misappraisal of the target group's readiness for and investment in change are likely to fail.

3. Preventive programs must be goal-focused in order to give coherence to the effort. Program design must accurately reflect the sequence in which information, activities, exercises, and media should be employed to help achieve the purpose of the intervention. Much like structured groups, the preparation time required to design an intervention far exceeds the time required to execute it successfully. Successful active prevention programs are probably four-fifths preparation and one-fifth implementation.

4. The problem to be addressed must be preventable. Not all problems can be anticipated prior to their being experienced.

5. The intervention must be appropriately timed. Bloom (1981) suggested that "a preventive program . . . should occur before the problem is manifested . . . but not so long before as to diffuse the effort." (p. 25) Timing the intervention to occur as close as possible to the individual's awareness of the need for change will likely ensure better results. An aversive conditioning program for teenagers enrolled in a driver education course may have more impact on changing driving habits than the same program offered several years earlier or later.

6. The intervention must be targeted to people who are susceptible (at risk) to the problem being addressed. If the consumer fully believes himself or herself to be immune to the problem, most efforts to inform, raise consciousness, and create change will be counterproductive. For example, a workshop on the art of building friendships may have more impact and be better attended by freshmen students eight weeks into the semester than during summer orientation, when they are perhaps still hoping that fortuitous circumstances will provide new relationships.

7. Once a person believes that preventive action is desirable, the intervention offered must be able to reinforce a sense of hope and movement toward the desired outcome. Far too many prevention efforts are better at raising desire for change than they are at fostering lasting change, and thus they frustrate and discourage participants even further. Many of the ills addressed by preventive programs are not solvable in any final sense, and progress is measured by positive movement or approach to complete resolution. Awakening the person to a potential or emerging problem should be followed quickly by tactics that foster risk reduction and movement toward problem solution.

8. Many prevention programs must go beyond intrapsychic solutions to inlcude removal of environmental hazards or barriers. Person–environment interaction models are important in the construction of high impact interventions. Problems are seldom exclusively a function of the individual or of the environment.

9. The environment in which the program is offered must be conducive to the changes being sought. In the campus environment, special attention needs to be paid to the social structure of the groups in which the invervention is being conducted. In particular, existing relationships among potential participants must be

considered carefully in planning the program format (exercises, activities, self-disclosure, etc.)

10. Materials, information, exercises, problem-solving strategies, and decision-making components of a program need to be paced according to the participant's motivation, coping skills, tolerance for disclosure, ability to absorb and personalize information, and other key process variables. If guidelines involving careful planning and timing have been observed, the pace of events in the change strategy should be less problematic. The pace of the material should not preclude the participants being able to identify with it or with the presenter.

11. Change involves resistance and ambivalence, which, if not carefully attended to, will frustrate and stall change efforts. Careful planning decreases the likelihood that participants will be unnecessarily resistant. It is necessary to relate decision-making and problem-solving processes to the strategies used; one-shot, short intervention efforts are likely to be ineffective in creating or maintaining change, as resistance often runs deep.

12. A well-designed preventive effort reflects a delicate balance between the challenges such programs pose to participants and the supports each participant has at his or her disposal to cope with the challenges presented. Preventive programs encourage people to adopt more functional behaviors and to eliminate maladaptive coping styles. In the process, participants often face having to let go of current semifunctional mechanisms (supports) in order to incorporate what should prove, in the long run, more effective ways of being. Therefore, it is important to avoid overwhelming participants with challenges that outstrip their supportive resources for incorporating the desired change.

13. The change technique or tactic should be well-suited to the setting (location, number of participants, demographics) of the program. Techniques such as consultation, peer or paraprofessional networks, environmental assessment, counter-conditioning, and cognitive restructuring are just a few of the many options available to the design of preventive programs for instigating change. Some techniques are ideally matched to certain types of problems and participants. For example, in a program with 300 participants, use of positive reinforcement as a change technique may prove more difficult than the use of aversive conditioning techniques.

14. Regardless of how well-planned a prevention intervention may be, it is still necessary to have legitimate access to those to be served. Points of access are often created after someone in an at-risk group has developed a problem that causes others to become aware of their own susceptibility to or complicity in the problem. For example, shortly after someone in a sorority, fraternity, or campus residence hall attempts suicide, others closely involved usually welcome the opportunity to talk as a group with a counselor or crisis intervenor about a variety of issues. What should they have done before this happened? What can be done now? Why would anyone try to kill themselves? And so on. Prior to the crisis, these same students would have had little interest in the subject. It is ironic that "postventions" are often more productive than work performed before the crisis existed. Avenues of legitimate contact with the target group often involve use of nonprofessionals in the development of interventions, especially where those in the target group perceive susceptibility to be lower than it is in reality. Use of multiple avenues of access, such as programs, brochures, peers, student affairs professionals, workshops, and media is also important.

15. Evaluation design should allow feedback about the impact of the intervention (outcome), processes used, and leadership style. Each of these three types of feedback is a necessary ingredient for refinement of future efforts. The four theme-

focused programs highlighted in this article were evaluated by participants in terms of (a) relevance and helpfulness to their needs; (b) usefulness of the materials and content of the sessions; and (c) leadership or presentation style. The results were mostly positive; however, an inspection of the materials, processes, and strategies used in the less effective sessions usually revealed a failure to address specific principles, in particular 1, 3, 7, and 12. (pp. 511–512)

Prevention programs are usually complex since they must be designed to deal with multiple factors. As an example, Table 11–1 represents a comprehensive primary prevention model for a campus alcohol education project on the University of Cincinnati campus.

To be successful, prevention programs must be able to demonstrate that some important negative outcome has indeed been prevented. An increasing number of program reports are indicating the success of these planned prevention efforts. For example, the National Consortium for Humanizing Education conducted training and research in 42 states and 7 foreign countries. Its procedures were effective in increasing both emotional and academic indices. This program represented a response to widespread recognition that schools could improve their effectiveness through programs focusing on facilitative interpersonal relations (Aspy, Roebuck, and Aspy, 1984).

The Child Development Specialist Program in Oregon has demonstrated to parents and school personnel that a school child development professional with preventive goals who provides services during the early years of education will produce positive results. The key characteristics of the child development model in Oregon were as follows:

1. All children are served.
2. The total child is served.
3. All educational partners are involved.
4. Cognitive and affective instruction is integrated.
5. Multidisciplinary-multistrategy approaches to instruction are used.
6. Both prevention and remediation are focused upon. (Sheldon and Morgan, 1984, p. 470)

While these are only two examples, a wealth of reports indicate that prevention programs do work. The section that follows will examine one of the most popular and successful techniques for prevention—stress management.

Stress Management

In recent generations the American workforce has become aware that millions of its members are "going up in smoke," that their effectiveness is handicapped by the psychological symptom labeled "burnout." While we must assume that many workers across all careers have, over the centuries, felt that their job is getting them down, the pressures are getting to them, the boss is driving them to drink, and so forth, it was not until the 1970s that a popular label, "burnout," became commonplace as a description of various psychological conditions asso-

Table 11–1. The University of Cincinnati Alcohol Education Project Design for Primary Prevention

Primary Prevention Scope

Primary Prevention Level	Extensive			Intensive		
	Method	Target	Strategy	Method	Target	Strategy
Environmental	Research findings	University community	Newspapers, campus, & city	Research findings	Student gov't, Student orgs., Faculty Senate, Campus admin., Board of Trustees	Presentation & discussion
	New alcohol policy	University community (Cell A)	Campus media; Distribution	New alcohol policy	Student gov't, Student orgs., Faculty Senate, Campus admin., Board of Trustees (Cell C)	Presentation, Discussion, & acceptance
Personal	Multilevel mass media education campaign	University student population	Use of mass media with one theme	Multisession education	Selected fraternities	Ongoing structured group experience aimed at normative change
	Students helping students	University student population (Cell B)	Establish local "BACCHUS" chapter	One-session education	Requesting groups (Cell D)	Short workshop aimed at knowledge and certain skills

Source: Conyne, 1984, p. 526.

ciated with stress and adjustment needs. In fact, today, we recognize that the term "burnout" can refer to one or a combination of factors that psychologists say contribute to a person's inability to cope with the expectancies and demands of everyday living.

> Stress affects both sexes and all ages, and is not confined to the stereotypical harried executive. People in late adolescence or their twenties may be accumulating the effects of stress, effects which may not be overtly manifested until their forties or fifties. Stress disorders are based upon the slow, developmental accumulation of psychological and physical stress responses throughout the life of the individual. Some people are vaguely aware that their personal stress is taking a heavy toll. Others are sure it is, and they have the medical bills to prove it. (Pelletier, 1977, p. 4)

Synonomous with the labeling of the disorder was the increasing awareness at management and supervisory levels that employee health is as important as other job-related concerns to the effectiveness of the organization and a further recognition that employee illness can be psychological as well as physical. As a result, one of the large-scale preventive efforts of the 1970s and 1980s has been the "stress management" movement and, not unexpectedly, counselors have been increasingly called upon to develop prevention and early intervention programs in stress prevention and management. Counselors involved in these efforts are quick to recognize the value of such prevention efforts because of the dangerously cumulative phenomenon of psycholosocial stress.

While the causes for burnout or stress may vary significantly from person to person, among the more common factors are the following:

1. Too many demanding, frustrating, or otherwise stressful situations.
2. Constant pressure to do more than can be done.
3. Too much time-consuming but not rewarding work (i.e., paperwork).
4. Constant conflicts between competing alternatives for time and effort (i.e., home and work).
5. Persistent demands for skills or knowledge that appears beyond that possessed by the individual.
6. Constant interference or interruptions of planned or anticipated activities.
7. Lack of positive feedback, recognition, reward or notice of efforts or accomplishments.
8. Lack of clarity or direction regarding work expectancies.
9. Depressing work environment.
10. Poor interpersonal relationships.
11. Constant disillusions or disappointments.
12. All work and no play, failure to lead a "balanced" life style.

Counselors may also recognize that candidates for "burnout" may be identified by the level, stage, or degree of "burnout." For example, Veninga and Spradley (1981, pp. 33–73) identified five stages of job burnout:

Stage One: The Honeymoon: A period of enthusiasm and job satisfaction that nevertheless begins to use up valuable energy reserves.

Stage Two: Fuel Shortage: Job dissatisfaction and inefficiency; fatigue coupled with sleep disturbances; escape activities such as smoking, drinking, drugs, shopping sprees.

Stage Three: Chronic Symptoms: Chronic exhaustion, physical illness; acute anger and depression.

Stage Four: Crisis: Deep pessimism and self-doubt; obsession with problems; physical illness grows from discomfort to incapacity; development of an escape mentality: the "flight response."

Stage Five: Hitting the Wall: Career, and life, are endangered.

Another view of this sequence to "burnout" is presented below.

1		2		3		4		5
Environmental demands are challenging	→	Demands are more than can be handled	→	Physical and psychological alarm	→	Frantic attempts to cope, resist, or ignore	→	Burnout

In working with clients for stress prevention or reduction, it is initially important for the counselor and the client to identify the stressors in the client's situation, their relative significance, whether they can be dealt with or not, and possible preventive or coping strategies. Among the general strategies that may be helpful to clients (and even yourself on occasion) are the following:

1. Bring "burnout" into the open—talk about it, especially with others sharing the same situation and concerns.
2. Build a support system with a small group of colleagues (including at least one optimist); help others in stress, be positive, be mutually supportive.
3. Practice time management; organize your time and stick with it. This includes the planning for and protection of your "free time" on and off the job.
4. Develop leisure time pursuits or hobbies.
5. "Get away from it all," especially when you feel the pressure beginning to build. Take real vacations regularly.
6. Shape up, both physically and psychologically; feel good about yourself!

The last point, "shaping up," brings us to an important concept in prevention—the belief that psychological prevention is enhanced by one's physical well being. This emerging area of interest to counselors is briefly examined in the next section.

Nutrition and Wellness

Nowhere has the craze for wellness and prevention manifested itself more than in the growth in popularity of health foods and healthy eating plans, exercise books, fitness equipment, and clubs. America is jogging its way through the 1980s, munching alfalfa sprouts and drinking mineral water. The concern of the individual for his or her well being cannot and should not be ignored by today's counselor. Nor should this concern be limited to our clients. As "fully functioning" counselors, we must also be concerned with our own physical well being. The advantages of a holistic health program for both clients and counselors include the following:

1. It teaches clients a total sense of personal responsibility.
2. Its effects are immediate and create a better sense of well being.
3. Wellness rather than the absence of symptoms is the main goal of therapy.
4. All modalities of healing are used.
5. The client's inner capacity for change has a distinct and clear direction to better health and well-being.
6. Clients can continue patterns that are healthy and significantly decrease problem reoccurence.
7. Self-discipline is learned and appreciated.
8. Disease prevention is enhanced for clients.
9. Conselors can benefit from all these aspects and be a significant model for clients. (Martin and Martin, 1982, p. 22)

A popular phrase is that "you are what you eat." Now, scientific inquiry seems to be further emphasizing this point as research has increasingly brought to the attention of the public at large the relationships between nutrition and behavior, between our emotions and our diet. We must pause to consider that counselors can no longer ignore this growing body of knowledge if we are to serve our clients as effectively as possible. In this regard, Martin and Martin (1982) offered the following ideas as a helpful overview to counselors:

1. Nutritional labeling on foods is relatively inadequate. Alpo dog food is more nutritious than drive-in hamburgers, pork chops, shrimp, boiled ham, and sirloin steak (Cheraskin, Ringsdorf, and Brecher, 1974). Recommend to clients that they avoid "quicky" foods or foods that have been refined and processed and that contain food additives and chemical pollutants. In attractively boxed "sugar" breakfast cereals, the box is normally more nutritious than the cereal. Chemicals increase shelf life, not your life. Teach clients how to read labels. (Reuben, 1978).
2. Recommend foods that include protein, vitamins, minerals, and essential fats. These are largely obtained from animal sources and include meat, fish, fowl, eggs, cheese, and milk. Eggs have been foolishly labeled as a cholesterol carrier and heart killer. Contrary to this misconception, 80 percent of the cholesterol in your blood does not come from the food you eat. It is manufactured by the liver and other organs (Page, 1977). Eggs furnish more nutrients per calorie than any other single food except milk. Whole egg protein has a biological value of 100 percent. Eggs are a great source of protein, minerals, and vitamins (Davis, 1954). They also contain lecithin, which emulsifies cholesterol.
3. Recommend lean varieties of meat and restrict fried meats. For complete digestion, drinking milk at breakfast or lunch is often better than other beverages. Fresh fruit should be eaten twice daily along with fruit juices that have no sugar added. These can substitute for coffee, tea, cola, and alcoholic drinks (Sheinken, Schacter, and Hutton, 1979).
4. Vegetables are the food group most absent from the average diet. Dark green and

yellow vegetables are rich in valuable nutrients and almost every vegetable has something worthwhile in it for you. They should be cooked until just tender and in as little water as possible (Lappe, 1975).

Whole grain foods, including "whole grain" breakfast cereals, 100 percent whole wheat bread, and whole wheat flour are excellent. Of the bread sold in the U.S., 95 percent is enriched white bread that is relatively worthless. In milling bread, over 26 essential nutrients are totally or partially removed from the flour. "Enrichment" means that four nutrients are replaced by synthetic chemicals and restored to the bread (Reuben, 1975; Reuben, 1978). This bread is also loaded with chemicals and pumped up with air. Bakers refer to store-bought bread as "balloon bread" (Reuben, 1978).

5. Fatty acids must be watched carefully. Dry roasted nuts without salt are preferable. Hydrogenated refined vegetable oils that are included in margarine are high cholesterol producers. Margarine contains metallic nickle, hydrogen, gas, and liquid fats. Butter and olive oil are more nutritious and less related to causing heart attacks than "unsaturated fats" (Fredericks, 1965).

6. Recommend to your clients a redirection or use stoppage of foods with the following: salt, caffeine, all sugar, white flour, hydrogenated fat, food preservatives, coloring agents, and artificial flavoring. For instance, canned vegetables have a 239,000 percent increase in sodium over fresh vegetables (Harris and Loesche, 1960).

7. Remind clients that one fourth to one third of one's total daily nutrients are received from breakfast. Much nutritional value is lost, however, as food is processed. This may necessitate a dietary supplement. Vitamin-mineral supplements should be taken before or during meals when digestive juices are flowing. This guarantees having all the essential nutrients present in the digestive track at the same time (Mindell, 1979). (Martin and Martin, 1982, pp. 23–24)

Pearson and Long (1982) identified counseling approaches that consider:

Physical as well as emotional components of mental health health are called multimodal approaches. Lazarus (1978) suggests that multimodal strategies encompass client behavior, affect, sensation, imagery, cognition, interpersonal relationships, drug use, and diet. Gerler (1979) recommends diet as a major consideration in multimodal counseling and advises that counselors focus on the interrelatedness of biological and psychological functioning.

Dwyer (1978) recommends that counselors consider themselves as part of a multidisciplinary team in addressing client health concerns and dietary issues. She suggests that counselors establish liaison with food assistance programs and use dieticians as consultants. The behaviorally oriented professions have an important contribution to make to nutrition education in the areas of attitudes, evaluation, and counseling.

Counselors can help influence client attitudes toward a healthful diet and help clients understand how certain food preferences may have emotional meanings. Schafer (1979), for example, found that self-concept is a factor in diet selection and that subjects with higher self-concepts were more receptive to nutrition information. Using their skills in tests and measurements, counselors can evaluate the emotional, social, and cognitive effects of dietary interventions. Counselors can employ behavior modification and imagery techniques to help clients avoid or select specific foods. (p. 391)

Mahoney and Caggiula (1978) offered specific suggestions for health counseling:

1. It is important for the client to take responsibility for his or her own contribution to change.
2. The identification of short-term and long-term goals must be discussed (i.e., What is it the client would like to change in the next week, within the next month?). The counselor should pay attention to realistic goals—goals that are sure to be achieved and are, therefore, self-reinforcing.
3. Outside assignments should be specific and realistic (i.e., the client should be told which food to limit, which to avoid, etc.).
4. Ask for small and comfortable changes, not an overhaul of the client's entire life-style. (Miller, 1980, p. 423)

Zifferblatt and Wilbur (1977) offered some additional suggestions:

1. Have the client systematically observe and record his or her total eating pattern: kind and amount of food eaten, times, locations, and events associated with eating.
2. Promote accurate collection of information on eating habits (keep a diary).

Miller (1980) suggested:

The counselor can request clients to read specific diet-related health books. Specific chapters can be assigned and then used for discussion topics in subsequent sessions. Books such as *Diet for a Small Planet* (Lappe, 1975) and *Let's Eat Right and Keep Fit* (Davis, 1970) are excellent for this purpose. (p. 423)

Appropriate exercise and a good diet are recognized important considerations in any program of client wellness. Perhaps not so well recognized is the importance of wise and enjoyable leisure and recreational activities in prevention and wellness.

Recreation and Leisure

If you could spend three days doing whatever you wished, how would you choose to spend your time? What do you plan to do with your vacation time this year? Chances are, your answers to these questions indicate what recreational and leisure time activities are important to you. We may also be reminded of how important this time is to us and that recreation and leisure are important activities in American society. We need but pause to consider the amount of time, money, and effort we expend in these pursuits to recognize their significance in our lives. Furthermore, as the work week continues to shrink, more and more people will find that they have additional time on their hands, time that can be expended in meaningless ways or in ways which could bring pleasure, relaxation, and improved well being for the individual. The interrelationships between a "career" and a "way of life" cannot ignore the role of recreation and leisure in the latter. Conselors concerned with the total well being of their clients must therefore become more sensitive to the role and potential of leisure time activities for enhancing their clients' quality of life and meeting their unmet or partially fulfilled needs.

As Bloland and Edwards (1981) noted:

Partial or continuing gratification of our needs leads to greater self-fulfillment and contentment with our lives. Fortunately, our society is filled with a variety of these need-reducing activities, some found in paid work and others characteristic of non-paid situations. Therefore, our psychological needs can be met by participating in some activities that are part of a paid work life, some that are leisure time activities, and still others found in both work and leisure. (p. 104)

McDowell (1981) suggested some of the potential values of leisure time activities:

- Leisure activities/experiences give one a heightened sense of or movement toward a desirable identity (Glasser, 1970)
- Leisure activities/experiences give one an increased feeling of optimism (it is good to think good thoughts, feel good feelings, do good things) (Tiger, 1979)
- Leisure activities/experiences have hedonic value.
- Leisure activities/experiences give one a heightened sense of self-expression and autonomous control (Martin, 1975; Csikszentmihalyi, 1975, Deci, 1975; Calder and Straw, 1975).
- Leisure activities/experiences offer opportunities for, but are not solely dependent on nor require, achievement learning, self-fulfillment, or self-development as standards by which to determine the value of Leisure (Lane, 1978).
- Leisure activities/experiences offer a mix of challenge striving, rest/relaxation, play/entertainment, socialization/aloneness, and construction/distraction among many other balancing involvements.
- Leisure activities/experiences allow one to explore the outer ranges of tolerance for novelty, complexity, unfamiliarity, stress, and competence.
- Leisure activities/experiences ensure one of a sense of privacy independent of socialization and otherwise public places and spaces.
- Leisure activities/experiences are compatible with the individual's conscience (however warped or virtuous it may be perceived by others) (Lane, 1978; Flugel, 1970).
- Leisure activities/experiences are chosen by the individual as something positive in themselves, and in which part or all of the individual's self-esteem may be committed to the involvement or its outcome.
- Leisure activities/experiences serve to tighten or loosen ego boundaries.
- Leisure activities/experiences allow one an opportunity for varying levels of intimacy and satisfaction with others, oneself, or the environment.
- Leisure activities/experiences complement or compensate for other life involvements (especially work and family) (p. 11).

Bloland and Edwards (1981) suggested that two themes, need deprivation and compensatory leisure, provide a useful theoretical foundation for integrating career and leisure counseling. They presented this four step model:

Step 1. Identify client needs   WHY?
   a. Survey client's past and current interests and activities
   b. Clarify client values
   c. Determine potential need-satisfying interest and activities.
Step 2. Identify activities to meet needs   WHAT?

           a. Ascertain needs fulfilled and not fulfilled by activities and interests already experienced

           b. Determine needs likely to be fulfilled by activities and interests not yet experienced

           c. Clarify client assets and limitations.

WHICH?   Step 3. Differentiate work and leisure activities

           a. List interests and activities to be investigated for need satisfying potential

           b. Conduct field research on selected activities

           c. Divide activities into work and leisure.

WHERE?   Step 4. Facilitate client's participation in selected activities

           a. Assist client to find places and ways in which to engage in chosen activities, some in work and others in leisure. (p. 105)

A rationale for leisure counseling may be based on the following:

1. The amount of time available for "leisure pursuits" is increasing.
2. Self-fulfillment includes the development of all the individual's potentials, including those which might be labelled avocational or recreational.
3. Therefore, planning for the wise and fulfilling use of leisure time is essential for the individual if their time is to be used in rewarding, enriching, and stress-reducing ways.
4. Leisure counseling can facilitate this planning by assisting individuals in identifying possible options consistent with their life styles and interests, making appropriate choices and where needed, securing the necessary education.

In concluding this brief examination of leisure counseling, we would suggest that the demands for counseling in this area will increase rapidly in the years ahead. We also believe that continued research into the role of leisure and its relationship to work will increase our knowledge and skills not only for life adjustment counseling but, perhaps more importantly, for preventive and developmental purposes as well.

Summary

This chapter has presented, in a sense, a beginning—a beginning to important new directions for counselors and the counseling profession; new directions that promise to raise the profession to heretofore unanticipated heights of societal service. To what more lofty goals can counselors aspire than the prevention of mental illness and the promotion of a happy productive life through wellness and wise, enjoyable use of leisure time?

Whereas other helping professions may concentrate on the remedial or, at best, the restoration of the client to a previous "status quo", counseling, of all the helping professions, has the prospects to advance clients to the level of "the best they've ever been" and "the best they can become!" This does not mean a de-emphasis on our traditional skills and knowledge discussed in earlier chapters (i.e., counseling, assessment, career development, and so forth). Rather, it suggests applying these skills to new opportunities; opportunities that optimistically view the positive, the possible.

The effectiveness of prevention and the other activities of counseling programs will be influenced to a large degree by how effectively programs are planned, managed, and led. The next chapter will discuss this important contribution to the delivery of counseling services.

References

Aspy, D., Roebuck, F., & Aspy, C. B. (1984). Tomorrow's resources are in today's classroom. *Personnel and Guidance Journal, 62,* 455–459.

Bloland, P. A., & Edwards, P. B. (1981). Work and leisure: A counseling synthesis. *Vocational Guidance Quarterly, 30,* 101–108.

Bloom, M. (1981). *Primary prevention: The possible science.* Englewood Cliffs, NJ: Prentice-Hall.

Calder, B. J., & Straw, B. M. (1975). Self-perception in intrinsic and extrinsic motivation. *Journal of Personality and Social Psychology, 31,* 599–605.

Cheraskin, E., Ringsdorf, N. M., & Brecher, A. (1974). *Psychodietetics.* New York: Bantam.

Conyne, R. K. (1984). Primary prevention through a campus alcohol education project. *Personnel and Guidance Journal, 62,* 524–528.

Csikszentmihalyi, M. (1975). *Beyond boredom and anxiety.* San Francisco: Jossey-Bass.

Davis, A. (1954). *Let's eat right to keep fit.* New York: Harcourt Brace.

Deci, E. L. (1975). *Intrinsic motivation.* New York: Plenum.

Drum, D. J. (1984). Implementing theme-focused prevention: Challenge for the 1980's. *Personnel and Guidance Journal, 62,* 509–514.

Dwyer, J. T. (1978). Point of view: Challenges in nutritional education of the public. *Journal of the American Dietetic Association, 72,* 53–55.

Felner, R. D., Jason, L. A., Moritsugu, J. N., & Farber, S. S. (Eds.). (1983). *Preventive psychology: Theory, research, and practice.* New York: Pergamon.

Flugel, J. C. (1970). *Man, morals and society.* New York: International University Press.

Fredericks, C. (1965). *Food facts and fallacies.* New York: Galahad Books.

Gerler, E. R., Jr. (1979). The evolving "D" in BASIC ID. *Personnel and Guidance Journal, 57,* 540–542.

Glasser, R. (1970). *Leisure: Penalty or prize?* London: Macmillan.

Goldston, S. E. (1977). Defining primary prevention. In G. W. Albee and J. M. Joffee (Eds.), *Primary prevention of psychopathology, 1, The issues.* Hanover, NH: University Press of New England.

Harris, R. S., & Loesche, H. V. (1960). *Nutritional evaluation of food processing.* New York: John Wiley & Sons.

Lane, R. E. (1978). The regulation of experience: Leisure in a market society. *Social Science Information, 17*(2), 147–184.

Lappe, F. M. (1975). *Diet for a small planet* (rev. ed.). New York: Ballantine.

Lazarus, A. A. (1978). What's multimodal therapy?: A brief overview. *Elementary School Guidance and Counseling, 13,* 6–11.

Mahoney, M. J., & Caggiula, A. W. (1978). Applying behavioral methods to nutritional counseling. *Journal of the American Dietetic Association, 72,* 373–377

Martin, A. R. (1975). Leisure and our inner resources. *Parks and Recreation, 10*(3), 1a–16a.

Martin, D., & Martin, M. (1982). Nutritional counseling: A humanistic approach to psychological and physical health. *Personnel and Guidance Journal, 61,* 21–24.

McDowell, C. F. (1981). Leisure: Consciousness, well-being & counseling. *Counseling Psychologist, 9*(3), 3–21.

Miller, M. J. (1980). Cantaloupes, carrots, and counseling: Implications of dietary interventions for counselors. *Personnel and Guidance Journal, 58,* 421–424.

Mindell, E. (1979). *Vitamin bible.* New York: Warner.

Page, I. H. (1977). *The cholesterol fallacy.* Cleveland, OH: Coronary Club.

Pearson, J. E., & Long, T. J. (1982) Counselors, nutrition, and mental health. *Personnel and Guidance Journal, 60,*(7) 389–392.

Pelletier, K. R. (1977). *Mind as healer—mind as slayer: A holistic approach to preventing stress disorders.* New York: Delacorte.

Remer, R., Niguette, G. F., Anderson, G. L., & Terrell, J. E. (1984). A meta-system for the delivery of primary preventive interventions. *Personnel and Guidance Journal, 63,* 30–34.

Reuben, D. (1975). *The save your life diet.* New York: Random House.

Reuben, D. (1978). *Everything you always wanted to know about nutrition.* New York: Simon & Schuster.

Schafer, R. B. (1979). The self-concept as a factor in diet selection and quality. *Journal of Nutrition Education, 11,* 37–39.

Schinke, S. P., Gilchrist, L. D., & Small, R. W. (1979). Preventing unwanted adolescent pregnancy: A cognitive behavioral approach. *American Journal of Orthopsychiatry, 49,* 81–88.

Scheinken, D., Schachter, M., & Hutton, R. (1979). *The food connection.* New York: Bobbs-Merrill.

Sheldon, C., & Morgan, C. D. (1984). The child development specialist: A prevention program. *Personnel and Guidance Journal, 62,* 470–474.

Tiger, L. (1979). *Optimism: The biology of hope.* New York: Simon & Schuster.

Veninga, R. L., & Spradley, J. P. (1981). *The work stress connection: How to cope with job burnout.* Boston: Little, Brown, & Co.

Zax, M., & Spector, G. A. (1974). *An introduction to community psychology.* New York: John Wiley & Sons.

Zifferblatt, S. M., & Wilbur, C. S. (1977). Dietary counseling: Some realistic expectations and guidelines. *Journal of the American Dietetic Association, 70,* 591–595.

CHAPTER 12

PROGRAM MANAGEMENT, DEVELOPMENT, AND LEADERSHIP

Introduction

Prospective counselors should be aware of the probabilities and significance of program management, development, and leadership. The objective of this chapter is to provide an introduction to the significance, principles, and practices of counseling program development, management, and leadership.

Through the centuries, a great deal has been written about the importance of management, leadership, and development to success in the worlds of business and government. The business world has long studied and contrasted the successes and failures of corporations large and small and the techniques or styles of management that have accounted for their achievements or lack of them. Leadership has played a major role in the rise and fall of nations, management is important in government effectiveness and fiscal soundness, and development is crucial in many countries, even in these modern times.

In this century, school administration in education, hospital administration in medicine, and personnel administration in business and the armed services have become areas for specialization. In the 1980s books such as *In Search of Excellence* by Peters and Waterman (1982) and *The One-Minute Manager* by Blanchard (1982) are examples of publications in this area that appeared with regularity on the "best sellers" lists. Despite a general recognition of the importance of management, leadership, and development to any organized enterprise, little attention has been given, in terms of formal preparation at least, to the "art" of developing and managing counseling programs in various settings. The complex, multiple goals required of most public agencies, institutions, and schools and school systems, emphasize the need for development and management of counselor programs and accountability to the public. Accountability means the provision of objective evidence to prove that counselors are successfully responding to identified needs. Such evidence requires recording and writing, and, perhaps, computations and tables. However, all too often those preparing to enter the profession and practice of counseling naively assume that the practice of therapy precludes any involvement with such mundane matters as program management, including administration. This is not to suggest that paperwork should replace people work or that it should be an equal priority. However, prospective counselors should be aware of the prospects and significance of their "other" responsibilities as well. Let us first define these terms:

Management: Those activities that facilitate and complement the daily, ongoing functions of the counseling staff. These include such administrative activities as recording and reporting, budgetary planning and control, facility management, and provisions for support personnel and resources.

Development: Includes needs assessment for program planning, research, evaluation, and the establishment of program accountability. Also presumes planning for program improvement.

Leadership: The providing of positive direction and motivation for personnel and program improvement. Primarily, *but not exclusively,* the responsibility of the professional designated as the chief management person for a specified unit (program, office, department, clinic).

Understanding Program Management and Development

Beginning counselors might view the prospects of program management and development responsibilities and the likelihood of being involved in administering an ongoing program as not only remote but also as potentially undesirable. Let us therefore advance some of the reasons that counselors should possess a minimal understanding of management, development, and leadership.

Administration and Your Job

A common complaint throughout all organizations today and perhaps throughout history concerns the inroads made upon professional time by nonprofessional or administrative activities. Administrative responsibilities, however, are a fact of life for all functioning professionals, including counselors in all settings. Because one cannot avoid all responsibilities for program administration, management, and development at any level, it will be beneficial if from the beginning of your professional activities as a counselor you have some minimal understandings of these matters and how you may best respond.

Recognizing the inevitability of administrative responsibilities, what can one do to discharge these responsibilities as expeditiously and effectively as possible? The following are suggestions gleaned from informal interviews with successful program managers and administrators in various settings.

1. *Be Organized.* To be organized means, among other things, having a place for everything and everything in its place. This keeps you from wasting time in search-and-find operations. Being organized also means planning the use of your time. This includes the maintaining of a daily calendar that allows sufficient time for each task for which you are responsible. Because it is not

always possible to estimate the exact amount of time a counseling interview may consume, it is better to allocate too much rather than too little time on one's calendar. Implicit in organization is an efficient filing and record-keeping system that allows ready access of items as needed. Files should contain all necessary and relevant information but should be periodically purged of outdated and nonuseful materials. Although neatness is not necessarily a guarantee of organization, there appears to be a relationship between a neat office and a well-organized office.

2. *Do It Right the First Time.* Much administration seems to focus upon the preparation of reports, the maintenance of records, and the organizing of data. As previously indicated, increasing emphasis on accountability, plus requirements mandated by state or federal statutes, has further accentuated the necessity of gathering objective data supporting the counseling enterprise. It is important to take time to understand exactly what it is you have to report and how it is to be reported. If you do not understand it, do not hesitate to ask for help if you need it. Do not waste your time and someone else's by doing it wrong the first time. You must also demand accuracy of yourself in the completing of any report or record and in the organizing of data. Long and cumbersome documents encourage guessing on the part of respondents. Other reports, especially those of an evaluative nature, may tempt one to fake or "fudge" a bit on the responses. The single word of advice is "don't." In addition to the risk of being embarrassed by someone noting your inaccuracies, you risk the more dangerous possibility of important decisions being made on the basis of inaccurate and irresponsible data.

3. *Do It On Time.* Assuming that you have been convinced to do your reporting and recording accurately, do not detract from your administrative responsibilities by being late. Usually, there is a reason that certain data are required at certain times for certain decisions. Your *delays* can handicap this process, especially when your colleagues have *all* responded on time. On those rare occasions when an emergency prevents the completion of a responsibility on time, it is important to give it the most immediate priority for completion at the earliest opportunity to avoid a domino effect in which every activity down the line will also be subject to tardiness.

4. *Plan Your Own Time.* All of us on occasion will come up against constraints on our time. By simply walking down the halls in almost any setting we can hear comments such as "all I ever do is go to meetings," or "all I get done is answer the phone," or "if people would just stop dropping in unannounced," or "I don't seem to have any time to myself any more." Time frustration seems to occur with all of us. Thus, the use and control of time are critical in one's efficient functioning, both in administration and in counseling; they also have an impact on one's morale. The objective of planning your time is to make the most of it and, at the same time, to leave you enough freedom and flexibility so you do not feel that the clock is your boss. In order to do this, there are several considerations. One is to do the things you do at the times when you do them best. For example, some may find they are most efficient in the preparation of reports if they do them the first thing in the morning. Others may find it desirable to use the first hour or so at work to complete the waking-up process with a second cup of coffee. It is also impor-

tant to do the things we do where we do them best. This may mean that for certain of our administrative responsibilities we may want to get away to some private little corner where we are uninterrupted. On the other hand, we may wish an informal setting for conferences with colleagues. In planning the use of our time, it is important that we understand ourselves in relationship to where and how we function best. We adapt our time commitment to our working style.

5. *Do It Neatly.* The effects of doing it right and doing it on time may still be lost if an interpreter is needed to translate what you have done. If you are among those grown adults whose handwriting has regressed since kindergarten days, you must develop some alternative, such as typing or printing, in preparing written reports for others. Lack of neatness can also detract from the impressions or impact of reports. A report that looks as if it had been done and re-done a dozen times may also be more subject to scrutiny and questions by superiors.

Suggestions for functioning effectively also include the following "don'ts":

1. *Don't Let it Spoil Your Day.* Although not everyone may enjoy the challenges of recording and reporting, such tasks should be accepted as inevitable responsibilities that will not be facilitated by constant complaints. The frequent suggestions of many administrators is that you do it and forget it.

2. *Don't Expect to Understand the Need for Every Report.* Frustrations frequently occur when one fails to see a rationale for the kind of data that are needed. Allied with this is the fact that we may also not understand why it has to be done "their" way instead of our "better way." When something is requested by your immediate supervisor, you are more likely to understand the need than if it is requested by the upper management, several layers removed. However, there will inevitably be occasions when reports are requested from afar that will challenge all that is rational. Again, do it and forget it.

3. *Don't Be Tempted to Become an Administrator.* In some settings, counselors appear to receive their largest number of "brownie points" from their superiors by meeting their administrative responsibilities. It therefore becomes a natural temptation to overemphasize that aspect of the job. A common complaint of many counselors is that they spend too much of their time in administrative activities. Even many program administrators claim that some counselors spend too much of their time in administrative activities. The major responsibility of a counselor in any setting, with the possible exception of a program director, is to counsel. This should be the counselor's major, time-consuming activity. Although it is important to meet one's administrative responsibilities efficiently and effectively, that does not imply they overshadow in importance or time the primary reason for which one is hired as a counselor.

As an aid to help those who may be reluctant to move from disorganization to organization, the following score pad (Table 12–1) will enable you to play the time game. It may help persons develop an awareness of their personal time management styles.

Table 12–1. The Time Game Score Pad (Object: To improve your score on a daily, weekly, or monthly basis)

Hour	What did I do?	Had I planned to do it?*	How well did I do it?**	Did I do it with a positive attitude?***	Comments to self****
8 A.M.					
9 A.M.					
10 A.M.					
11 A.M.					
12 noon					
1 P.M.					
2 P.M.					
3 P.M.					
4 P.M.					
5 P.M.					

*5 points if you had planned to do it.
3 points if you had planned to do it because it was overdue.
0 points if you hadn't planned to do it.
−3 points if you hadn't planned to do it but it was an unexpected requirement that had a higher priority than what you had planned.

**Score yourself on a scale of 0 to 5.

***3 points if you did it with enthusiasm.
2 points if you did it with a positive attitude.
1 point if you did it and then forgot about it.
0 points if you did it and then worried about it.

−1 point if you did it with frustration and/or anger.
−5 points if you did it and it drove you to drink.

****1 point for each constructive suggestion.
−1 point for statements using profanity.

Totals:
1. Subtotal A + B + C + D.
2. Subtract 5 points if you didn't take a lunch break.
3. Subtract 10 points if you didn't take a lunch break for a second day in a row.

365

Program Management

Program management as a process seeks to provide structure, order, and coordination of those activities for which it is responsible. This information, of course, will function at varying levels. For example, in educational systems, the Board of Education, the school superintendent, and the assistant superintendents represent top management. The school principal and assistant principals can be viewed as middle management, and program directors, such as the director of counseling, represent component or lower management. Figure 12–1 depicts this concept.

Regardless of the levels of management, however, the overall objective remains the same—the facilitation of the goal achievement of the organization. It is important for counselors in various settings to note that the objectives of the counseling program must be consistent with and contribute to the achievement of the objectives of the institution of which it is a part. For example, in recent years, counselors working in school settings have been called upon to indicate the contributions they are making to the *education* of school-aged youths. Although education may be viewed broadly as all growth and development, it may be more difficult for counselors to respond in those settings when education is viewed as a learning activity only. As noted by Gibson, Mitchell, and Higgins (1983):

> Helping "Harry High School" become a happy, well-adjusted (whatever this means) individual may be a commendable outcome of counseling; however, if, in the process or as a result, he does not become better educated or more effective as a student, the counseling program may be viewed by many as of questionable value to the educational institution. (p. 145)

The responsibilities and activities of program management may vary according to levels and settings, but it is possible to identify two basic areas of functioning. The first deals with the managing of basic resources, such as personnel,

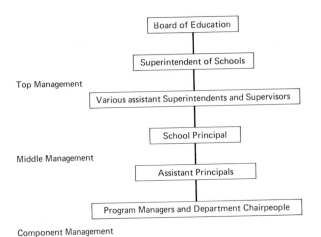

Figure 12–1. Levels of educational management.

budget, and facilities. The second focuses on organizing and facilitating such basic activities as coordination, communication, cooperation, decision making, and evaluation. The emphasis of discussions here will be on what is involved rather than on how one should do it. Following are some suggestions appropriate for entry-level counselors, who should also be aware that as one moves into management responsibilities, one's own style and techniques tend to emerge.

Managing Resources

Of all the resources that a program manager is called upon to use, the human resource is by far the most important. The manner in which this resource is managed will largely determine the success or failure of the program and also whether the manager is a program leader or simply a program administrator. The program manager's initial responsibility in many instances will begin with staffing, and this will be a consistent consideration as long as there is staff turnover. Staff selection should minimally involve four factors.

Qualifications. These are primarily but not exclusively based on training and experience in relationship to the expectancies of the position. In viewing one's training background, consideration should be given to not only the content of the training program, but also to when, where, and areas of specialization. Although academic achievements in themselves are not the sole criterion for performance on the job, one's academic achievements should not be completely ignored. There may be little difference in performance between the A and B student, but one should not anticipate that the C student will perform as well on the job as the A student.

When examining experience, program managers usually compare the type, amount, and success of previous experiences. Experience may not always be a factor, for many program managers are anxious to hire recent graduates who can bring new ideas, more up-to-date concepts, and, perhaps, needed youthful enthusiasm to their programs.

Staff Versatility. When the program manager has a staff of at least one to manage, providing for program versatility enters into staff selection. Differing backgrounds should provide a wider range of specialty skills. Also, it has frequently been noted that staffs of two or more should include one member of each sex and minority or cultural representation, as appropriate. Some range in age representation is important, especially in institutional and community settings, and the old schoolboy network (hire all graduates from the same school) should not be perpetuated at the expense of program versatility.

Adaptability. Another consideration that is often overlooked in staffing is the adaptability of a staff member to both the job setting and the community or area environment. The person must not only like the job, but the job must like the person. A staff member will function more effectively when there are congenial relationships among the staff as well as those with whom they come in frequent contact. This, of course, would include the clients that the staff is serving. It is not suggested that one form friendships with clients, but it is important to be able to relate to the client population, whether it is inner-city, suburban society, Appalachia poor, or Alaskan Eskimo. Staff members must also be able to adapt to the community or area environment that supports the job setting. It is highly unlikely that people can be unhappy in their community–home life and happy in their work life. The inability to adapt to a community environment can also have adverse effects on the public relations aspect of the counseling program. Once staffing decisions have been made and personnel are functioning on a job, management's responsibilities continue to be important. These include the following:

1. The assignment of responsibility. Each staff member should have specific activities for which they are responsible and for which the staff member knows they are responsible. In assigning these responsibilities, the program manager seeks to capitalize upon the special skills, experience, and personal characteristics of the staff member. It must be recognized that in some instances this will involve the delegation of some undesirable or less-favored tasks. Staff members must anticipate these as well as their share of the more rewarding activities. A good program manager will not delegate all the "donkey work" and keep only the "goodies" for himself or herself.

2. Provisions for staff development. The fact that counselors are providing helping services and human support to others does not mean that counselors should or can function without the support of others. A program manager must see that staff members help and support each other and, additionally, receive help and support from beyond the counseling offices. Ways in which this may be accomplished include meaningful group work or committee assignments in which members share interest in a common problem or topic with other staff members or personnel outside the counseling staff. Obviously, part of this human support system is the program manager's personal interaction with each staff member.

Budget. It is hardly possible to overemphasize the importance of budget and budget management in any setting today. Its import in any system of accountability is paramount. In effect, it enables the supporting public, whether they are taxpayers or donators, to see what they are paying for or if they are getting their money's worth. To the individual staff member, budgeting is often a mysterious, misunderstood, maddening, and far-removed process that has a direct and undeniable relationship to staff morale. It is therefore important that staff members recognize the level at which their immediate program manager is involved and the extent of that involvement. It is also helpful to understand the level at which budgeting decisions, especially those affecting staff members, are made. In many settings, lower-level managers may be limited in their budget responsibilities to recommending or requisitioning from budgets established elsewhere. Crucial budget decisions, such as salaries and salary increments, staffing additions, and equipment purchases, tend to be made at middle- and upper-management levels. These real budget managers are usually involved in budgeting for personnel, including both professional and support staff; and services, such as consultants, communications, supplies, equipment, and travel. Budget decisions for capital improvements, such as new buildings or significant remodeling, are usually made at only the highest level of management.

One form of budgeting that has in recent generations become increasingly prevalent at even the lower levels of management involves program activities supported by federal or state grants. These are usually developed in response to mandated federal or state programs. These programs have specific objectives and procedures and a budget that is directly related and accountable to those procedures and objectives.

The likelihood of beginning counselors being involved in budget management is small, but the probability of some involvement in budget expenditures is considerable. Because mismanagement or misspent monies may become your personal expense, the following suggestions are pertinent:

1. *Each budget item is related to an activity, which in turn is related to a specific goal or objective of the organization.* It is important to understand the reason for an expenditure. This also suggests that you spend only for those categories that are budgeted; for example, if professional travel is not provided for in a budget, you do not travel professionally by taking $500 from the supply item in the budget even if it is not being spent and even if the travel is to a professional meeting.

2. *Spend only what you have.* Although one may on occasion overdraw a bank account, one is usually reminded quickly and makes amends before it becomes a bankruptcy disaster. However, all too frequently, when spending someone else's money, there is an inclination to be less concerned until it is too late. Remember, any spending in which you engage that is beyond the available budget will probably end up being your own personal expense.

3. *Spend economically.* The fact that you have a budget does not mean that the sky is the limit as long as you spend it for items in the budget and as long as you do not exceed the budget. Budget managers are expected to be good shoppers. This does not mean that you sacrifice quality for economy but that you get the most for your budgetary dollar. For example, on major purchases, such as typewriters, video equipment, and tape recorders, it is customary to obtain two or three estimates including those provided by traditional discount houses before determining the place of purchase. If the expenditure is for travel, recipients are usually expected to be aware of the various bargain travel fares and to travel regular or tourist class on common carriers. If private vehicles are used, mileage rates are usually established by federal, state, or local agencies.

4. *Secure receipts.* If you are involved in the spending of budgeted funds in any amount, reimbursement is only provided when there is proof of purchase. The only acceptable proof of purchase is a receipt for the goods or service obtained (showing the item, even if it is an elephant, is not considered proof of purchase).

5. *Keep a running account.* It is important to anyone who has responsibility for any budget or segment of one to know *exactly* what has been expended and what remains at any given point during the duration of the budget. This

means keeping a daily, if necessary, running account of debits, credits, and balances.

6. *Be aware of any unusual (or usual) legal or contract restraints.* This point is perhaps most appropriate when persons have budgetary responsibilities emanating from special contracts or grants. In such instances, budget managers, when in doubt, should consult the appropriate legal or contract authority before authorizing an expenditure.

Managing Facilities

The management of facilities takes on appropriate importance when one considers that persons spend more of their waking hours in their place of work than in their home or any other facility they frequent. Facilities are important in determining whether persons will have the opportunity to do the job they are hired to do in a manner in which they are capable of doing it. In large, complex institutions, facilities are often viewed as symbols that reflect the importance with which the operation is viewed. (It is thus inevitable that a school principal's office will always be a shade larger, at least, than the school counselor's; that the college president's office and decor will be considerably larger and more luxurious than that of the institution's most distinguished professor, etc.) Facility concerns of program managers include the following:

Adequacy.   Size, furnishings, and general decor, cleanliness, and, above all for counselors, privacy are determinants of the adequacy of one's work space. These factors tend to determine the atmosphere in which one works. During a recent university visitation, a dean of students, showing the offices of the university counseling center, remarked that he had $25,000-a-year counselors in $10,000 offices turning in $5,000-a-year performances. Those who have ever worked in dingy, dreary, ill-equipped, or dirty facilities can recall the impact of these on their morale and subsequent performance. Yet, from time to time, high-level program managers seem to expect that as long as they are comfortable and their morale is good, it will spread to all levels regardless of working conditions.

Accessibility.   A person should not feel that he or she has already done a half-day's work just by getting to his or her office. Accessibility is not only important in terms of those clients it is intended to serve. Countless studies have noted that when university counseling centers or community agencies are situated in locations that are remote to the main populations they are intended to serve, their clientele does not materialize.

Individuality.   Have you ever viewed the administrative offices of large-scale enterprises or business corporations, where dozens of employees have been provided identical cubicles and furnishings as so many similar mechanical parts in a precision machine? Such facilities provide little opportunity for the individual worker to assert any individuality. Couselors are constantly reminded of the uniqueness of the individual. It would, therefore seem inconsistent with that theoretical framework to suggest that individual couselors would not have enough flexibility in their personal office facilities to express this individuality.

Supplementary Space. Program managers also are responsible for securing and managing supplementary facilities, such as conference rooms, resource or staff rooms, filing areas (security can be important here), storage and supply areas, reception areas, and support staff facilities.

Management by Objectives

Management by objectives (MBO) increased in popularity in the 1960s. This system of management was first brought to the public attention by Drucker (1954) in *The Practice of Management*, which described it as an industrial system. It

is a system in which management attempts to aim all significant activities in an organization toward the achievement of specified, agreed-upon objectives. MBO is designed to promote goal attainment, organizational clarity of action, and increased satisfaction on the part of organizational members who benefit in an environment of achievement. Although it is fairly standardized in the literature as to its general parameters, the point is often made that the application of MBO varies with the characteristics of the organization involved.

According to Miringoff (1980), essentially MBO is summarized by the following characteristics:

a. Makes objectives explicit; recognizes multiobjective situations.
b. Identifies conflicting objectives; provides for participation management.
c. Ensures a control mechanism providing for feedback and measurement of accomplishment.
d. Fosters managerial acceptance of responsibility and evaluation of managers by results.
e. Encompasses little formal administrative machinery. (p. 123)

The following (MBO) worksheet could be used for designing programs to deal with organizational concerns.

1. Describe project.
2. Identify target population.
3. Prepare goal statements.
4. Specify objective(s) within project.
5. Describe baseline data required.
6. Identify necessary programs or activities to accomplish (4).
7. Identify constraints or obstacles to be overcome.
8. Identify others who must participate or become involved to accomplish objectives.
9. Identify review periods for monitoring or feedback.
10. Identify persons involved in review.
11. Identify techniques for presentation and review. (Burgess, 1978) (Gibson, Mitchell, and Higgins, 1983, pp. 91–92)

In recent years, this system has received increasing attention as an approach to management for counseling and other human service organizations and educational institutions. In an article describing management by objectives for counseling services, Thompson and Borsari (1978) suggested that

> every program staff should assess its unique strengths and weaknesses before attempting an MBO program. Among other things, the staff must consider whether it is primarily concerned with internal program improvements or external accountability, the leadership roles to be adopted, the support for evaluation from the entire school community, time and money expenditures, the use of the data, and the commitment to personal and professional change. Development of an effective MBO system has a profound effect on all the members of the pupil-personnel team. An MBO system requires that the staff work closely together in order to develop the goals and objectives mentioned. Therefore, an MBO system should be attempted only after the basic issues listed have been fully investigated. (p. 174)

Thompson and Borsari (1978) then noted, "while each MBO effort has its own qualities that reflect the uniqueness of its creators, a generalized process for efficient development may be suggested" (p. 175).

In an abbreviated form, these processes (a) define long-range goals, or what the system wants to accomplish and set the ideal limits toward which the organization's plan will direct its efforts; (b) formulate a needs assessment to focus priorities; and (c) establish departmental objectives. Each program's activities should clearly relate to one or more systems goals. The articulation of these activities and programs and the relationships to systems goals make up the departmental objectives. Then, (d) establish individual objectives. Each staff member must develop an individual plan to help the department achieve its objectives. Individual staff members must be given the freedom to select those strategies that will make the most of the person's personal and professional strengths. Also, (e) develop action plans and assess feasibility of action plans (cost, time, personnel). Management by objectives requires the counselor to think about how he or she will achieve an objective and evaluate the activity. Counselor team members should evaluate their individual objectives in terms of how they affect client populations. Behavioral objectives keep the focus on the real test of counseling services—changes in the behaviors of clients. Finally, (f) implement action plans, monitor and evaluate operations; (g) review progress toward objectives; and (h) recycle. "The departmental objectives, activities, and their related evaluations are reviewed to direct rational decision making concerning program operation and modification." (Thompson and Borsari, 1978, p. 176)

Thompson and Borsari (1978) believed that the advantages demonstrated by the system occur in the development of goals, objectives, and measurable programs, improved feedback systems, and in personal development of the counseling staff. They caution that difficulties may occur because effective outcomes are sometimes difficult to describe and measure and because many human service specialists see the accountability and evaluation of management systems as a threat to humanistic values and procedures. They suggest that commitment, time, patience, and a willingness to learn and change are prerequisites for both the individuals and the organizations involved in adopting a management by objectives strategy.

Organizing and Facilitating Basic Activities

The program manager must also initiate and guide the organization and facilitation of the basic activities of the counseling program. This does not mean the professional activities but, rather, the basic supporting activities that complement the professional services of the organization. These include the following:

Coordination. In even less than complex organizations, some degree of coordination is necessary to prevent overlapping, conflicting, or duplicating of activities. Coordination is necessary among activities and programs, both internally and externally.

Cooperation. Cooperation is a vital ingredient in both coordination and public relations. Program managers must encourage and demonstrate a willingness to work with others in such vital counselor activities as case studies, conferences, referrals, and consultation. As suggested previously, counselors should not hesitate to ask for help when they need it. Counselors should also be willing to give help when called upon by fellow professional colleagues or support personnel in other fields as well. Cooperation is one of the basic functions in establishing and maintaining positive professional connections.

Effective Communications. Communications often determine whether or not a program is managed efficiently or not. Counselors are usually well trained in the art of personal communication, but it is surprising how frequently the communication process breaks down within a program as well as with higher-level management and external agencies and organizations. Guidelines for effective communications in management suggest care must be taken that the personal touch is not lost as a result of using impersonal means to communicate, such as memos, policy statements, and directives. When it is necessary to use such impersonal means, there must be adequate personal follow-up to ensure that such communications are understood. In addition, communication must provide for some sort of feedback. Oral communication to large groups such as staff or faculty meetings must justify the time it consumes for the number of people present.

Evaluation. A program manager is responsible for ensuring the gathering of data that provides for systematic, ongoing evaluation of the program's activities. A program manager also coordinates periodic and accreditation types of planning. At the individual staff member level, a program manager is responsible for evaluation of each member of the organization and communicating this evaluation to both the individual staff member and higher management.

Decision Making. Effective program management requires that someone be in charge. A program manager as the one in charge must have decision-making authority commensurate with the responsibilities of the decision. It is appropriate for program managers to share the decision thinking, but they cannot be expected to share all the decision making.

Program Leadership

Perhaps no single characteristic beyond the professional qualifications of the counseling staff is more significant to the success of the counseling operation than the quality of program leadership. It is desirable that counselors at least recognize those characteristics that tend to identify leaders and distinguish them from program administrators or managers. Most persons recognize the individual who is a true leader. A real leader is one who leads, not directs; real leadership gives priority to the benefit of the program and to those who are led, rather than to the leader. Some of the characteristics of program leadership include the following:

A Record of Success.   Program leaders have good track records. They justify the old concept that success breeds success. Included in the program leader's win column is previous recognition as a successful and resourceful counselor. Also the program leader is an extra competent professional. Program leadership for counseling programs can only be provided by professional counselors. It is anticipated that program leaders will contribute their competence and expert knowledge to the sucessful functioning of the counseling program, including an awareness of professional, ethical, and legal guidelines for the profession.

Inspires Confidence.   A program leader inspires confidence in himself or herself and in the individual staff members. He or she does this by being supportive and also realistic. He or she expects the possible, but not the impossible. He or she gives and shares credit publicly so that others know of the successes of individual staff members.

Shares.   The program leader shares the "ownership" of the operation and develops a feeling of "us" rather than "me and you." Active ownership does not mean that the staff runs the operation. It means that the staff shares in the running of it. Sharing the ownership of the operation creates a feeling of belonging, of being on the team. Real leadership sees that no one feels left out. There are no in-groups and out-groups.

Motivates.   All studies of leadership indicate that a common ingredient of leaders in nearly every setting is an ability to motivate others to achieve their potential, and perhaps at times, even exceed it. Although each leader has a different and unique style, the evidence is present when one observes hard-working, achieving staff members.

Creates a Positive Atmosphere.   A leader understands what makes life at the office liveable or one happy in one's work by creating professional atmospheres conducive to accomplishment. This includes effective program organization, management, and administration.

Visibility.   One cannot lead in absentia. Successful program leaders at all levels are those who are frequently and clearly visible to and available for interaction with their supporting staffs.

Forward Looking.   Leadership demands planning for the future. Program leaders are insightful and future-oriented in their planning.

Decision Makers.   Effective leadership not only accepts the decision-making responsibility and will make the hard decisions, but will also make the appropriate decision.

These characteristics can provide a checklist to identify potential counseling program leaders. As we noted in a previous publication (1983), program leaders are not likely to be chosen when the top management position is viewed as a consolation prize; a stepping stone for someone tagged to proceed up the organization; a political position to shore up support for top management; or as proof that the "Peter Principle" (Peter and Hull, 1959) really operates. (This principle suggests that one is eventually promoted to his or her level of incompetence.)

Contributing to Program Development and Improvement

All of us like to be members of "winning teams." We would also probably agree that talent alone is not enough; that winning teams require "team work" and a winning "game plan."

Upon joining a counseling staff, a counselor becomes not only a team member but also committed and involved in the continuous process of program development and improvement; the implementation of a "game plan." The effective development of any counseling program, regardless of setting, is dependent first upon an accurate and continuous assessment of the needs of the target population to be served. Such needs assessment is the key to the successful planning for goals and objectives. The accurate assessment of potential client needs is critical in establishing and maintaining program relevance and as a basis for program accountability and evaluation. The needs assessment activity, which can range from a simple to a complex process, is concerned with two data bases, as follows:

1. Target population assessment. This data gathering seeks to establish factually the needs of the target population that the counseling program has been established to serve. These data will also influence priorities among these needs.
2. Environmental assessment. This is the gathering of factual data that facilitate the counseling program's understanding of the setting from which the target population comes and within which the program functions.

Target population assessment provides a factual basis for a program's goals and objectives, and environmental assessment provides a factual basis for the procedures whereby a program achieves its goals and objectives. The personal needs are the internal factors that initiate, direct, and sustain the program's activities, whereas the environmental characteristics provide the depth of understanding for more effectively responding to the needs.

Lewis and Lewis (1983), writing from a community agency perspective, identify the generic planning process as one using the following basic steps: (a) needs assessment, (b) definition of goals and objectives, (c) identification of alternative methods for meeting goals, (d) decision making, and (e) development of plans for implementation and evaluation. "Each of these steps involves a major commitment from both agency personnel and from community members. Each step also depends on the effective completion of the previous task, beginning with the all-important process of needs assessment" (Lewis and Lewis, 1983, p. 22).

Two approaches to needs assessment are presented as examples. Although these both illustrate needs assessment for educational settings, they are equally appropriate, with minor modification, for other counseling settings. The first example illustrates a relatively simple approach and was designed by DiSilvestro (Department of Public Instruction, State of Indiana, 1974).

Step 1. Identify and list all populations to be served. To assess the guidance needs of the school and community, representatives from the following populations might be included in data collection:

Pupils.
Teachers.
Principals and other administrators.
Parents.
Pupil Personnel Service staff.

To assure an adequate representation from each of these groups, the counselor might identify the population(s) to be served in terms of the following characteristics:

Ethnic composition.
Socioeconomic strata.
Political factors.
Grade level.
Educational expectations.

Step 2. Collect data using a systematic approach that is designed to identify guidance-related needs and to identify whether current guidance practices are appropriate to these needs. Frequently used methods for collecting data include questionnaires, interviews, brainstorming sessions, school and community records, and follow-up studies. Various other methods may be developed. Also, the entire population may be surveyed, or a sample may be assessed, such as a stratified random sample.

Step 3. Develop a system for utilizing the collected data. The counselor will compile, classify, and analyze the data collected. The data will be used in determining guidance priorities.

A more complex approach is that suggested by the Department of Health, Education and Welfare (1975), in which the strategy of needs assessment was described as follows:

(i) The overall concept of educational needs assessment defines an educational need as the difference between the current status of the learner and the desired learner outcomes.

(ii) The assessment strategy includes both long- and short-range goals.

(iii) The strategy includes specific activities which have been designed to achieve each objective included in the strategy.

(iv) The strategy includes a time frame for accomplishing each activity.

(v) The strategy is sufficiently constructed so as to consider all the required elements.

(vi) Student learning goals are established for the purpose of determining children's needs through the educational needs assessment.

(vii) The student learning goals are behaviorally stated and representative of cognitive, affective, and psychomotor learning.

(viii) The student learning goals are sufficiently definitive to make them measurable objectives for student learning.

(ix) The strategy includes the elementary and secondary grade levels which will be assessed.

(x) The strategy includes provisions for collecting data about student learning objectives into three categories:

    (a) Perceptions of the community (including those in business and industry), educators, and the learners regarded as relevant and important to attaining these objectives;

    (b) Criterion-based test instruments to determine the extent to which student learning objectives have been achieved; and

    (c) Relevant demographic data about the learners.

(xi) The strategy includes provisions for a data sample from which validity can be determined; i.e., evidence that what is measured is that which purports to being measured.

(xii) The strategy includes provisions for a data sample from which reliability can be determined; i.e., that measurement is being performed accurately and consistently.

(xiii) The needs assessment strategy includes provisions for collecting appropriate information on specific sub-populations.

(xiv) The strategy includes provisions to assure that the data collected are manageable and current.

(xv) The instruments which are designed to collect data have been tested thoroughly on a pilot basis.

(xvi) Procedures for analyzing data have been thoroughly tested to determine if all data collected can be appropriately utilized and treated.

(xvii) The conclusions drawn from the interpretation of data can be supported.

(xviii) There are logical and defensible procedures established for determining the criticalness of educational needs identified by data for the State as a whole and for each distinct area of the state.

(xix) A listing of critical educational learner needs which are representative of cognitive, affective, and psychomotor learning is given. (p. 51025)

The Needs Assessment Survey

A second approach, that of your authors, begins as previously indicated with the assessment of the needs of the target population. This is a technique for factually establishing program goals and objectives. Such an assessment directly involves the target population or a sampling thereof, as well as critical support populations. For example, a school guidance program would not only gather data from students, but would also survey parents, teachers, and others who had frequent and direct contact with the student population. The direct involvement of these populations is usually secured through questionnaires or structured interviews. Figure 12–2 presents an example of a simple questionnaire used in student needs assessment and completed not only by students, but support populations as well.

In addition to questionnaire and interview data, other sources such as school and community records will provide data that substantiate or identify the needs of potential clients. Environmental assessment seeks to establish the characteristics of program and population setting through identifying the characteristics of the environment's population, economics, and geography. Community assessment may be facilitated through the use and development of certain data

Person filling out form:	Rankings: Check one for each question below					Additional Response
_____ Student	Very Important	Quite Important	Moderately Important	Somewhat Important	Not Important At All	In your opinion is this service being provided? (check one)
_____ Parent						
_____ Teacher						
_____ Business Person						
1. How important is it for the student to be able to discuss personal problems with the school counselor?						yes ___ no ___
2. How important is it for the school counselor to provide career information?						yes ___ no ___
3. How important is it for the school counselor to provide information concerning colleges, trade schools, or the armed services?						yes ___ no ___
4. How important is it for the counselor to show the relationship between education and careers?						yes ___ no ___
5. How important is it for the counselor to provide assistance to the student in job placement upon graduation?						yes ___ no ___
6. How important is it for the counselor to discuss with the student which courses he will take in school?						yes ___ no ___
7. How important is it for the counselor to work with students who are failing or dropping out?						yes ___ no ___
8. How important is it for the counselor to lead small group discussions on current student problems?						yes ___ no ___
9. How important is a counseling and guidance program in a high school?						yes ___ no ___
10. What other services for students do you think the school counselor should provide? (Please write in the space below and on the back.)						yes ___ no ___

Figure 12–2. Needs identification questionnaire.

planning instruments, as may be noted in Figures 12–3 and 12–4. Typical sources from which the previously suggested data may be gathered are noted in Figure 12–4. Figure 12–3 shows how to identify community leaders in the cat-

Community: _____   _____

Survey dates: _____   _____

Survey team: _____   _____

_____   _____

_____ 1. Political leadership

_____
_____

_____ 2. Governmental (nonpolitical) leadership
_____
_____

_____ 3. Educational leadership
_____   (School board members, superintendents, principals,
_____   education association or union officials)

_____ 4. Major religious denominations
_____   (ministers, priests, rabbis)
_____

_____ 5. Minority group (or groups) leadership
_____
_____

_____ 6. Judicial system
_____   (Chief of police, juvenile judge, lawyers, county sheriff, probationary officials)
_____

_____ 7. Business/commercial/industrial leadership
_____   (Presidents (in residence) of local corporations, plant managers, owners of
_____   prominent local businesses)

_____ 8. Labor organization leadership
_____
_____

_____ 9. Youth leadership
_____   (Student council members, athletic standouts, social club or gang leadership)
_____

_____ 10. Civic leadership
_____   (Officials of civic clubs, volunteer organizations)
_____

_____ 11. Other (indicate status and representation)
_____   _____
_____   _____
_____   _____

Note: (1) Be sure all interviewees meet the criteria for "significant contributors" as indicated in
            interviewing instructions.

       (2) Structured interview guides should be adhered to insofar as possible. Exceptions should be
            noted and reasons for deviations explained.

Figure 12–3. Community survey checklist (interview schedule).

Community: _____   _____

Survey dates: _____   _____

Survey team _____   _____

_____   _____

_____   1. Census data

_____   2. News media analysis

_____   3. Board of education (minutes of) meetings

_____   4. Annual reports of schools

_____   5. County government data

_____   6. City government data

_____   7. Employment agencies

_____   8. Church board reports

_____   9. Chamber of Commerce data

_____   10. Geographic data

_____   11. Ecological-environmental data

_____   12. Other significant data (list sources)

_____

_____

_____

_____

Note: If data are not available, place notation "NA" in blank at left of
item. Otherwise, when data are collected, place a "√."

Figure 12–4. Community survey checklist (data collection).

egories noted. Figure 12–4, on the other hand, is a checklist designed to guide
the information seeker to common sources of community information. The
form is not intended to record data, but only to provide a guide to possible
sources.

Identifying Priorities and Developing Program Relevancy

The needs assessment data that may be gathered through the previously
described procedures provide direction for determining goals and priorities and
the development of counseling program objectives that are relevant and meaningful to the target population and setting. The initial procedure is a simple
listing of goals and priorities, first as perceived by the target population. These
then may be slightly reordered, as verified by immediate support population,
and then slightly reordered again, once these base data are supplemented by
secondary populations and sources. In the school setting, the students would

represent the target population, and teachers and parents, the immediate support population. Supplementary or secondary population would include community personnel and data from student and other relevant records. This process leads to a tentative prioritizing of needs. A final reordering is established by eliminating any needs that may not be the professional responsibility of the counseling program or may require resources beyond those available to the counseling program. The final outcome of this process is the establishment of working priorities in a hierarchical order, which are then translated into goals and objectives.

The translation of priorities into goals and objectives requires their being stated in written terms. The goals of a program are typically described in broad, general terms that may not be tied to specific time constraints. On the other hand, the program objectives must be stated in objective, measurable terms and related to a time frame. Objectives are designed to describe desired performances and should contribute to the achievement of a program goal and the meeting of one or more specifically identified needs. Of course, the assessment of needs and the establishment of related goals and objectives are not, in and of themselves, a guarantee of program relevancy. A needs assessment only establishes an awareness of what a counseling program should consider in planning the utilization of its resources. The real criteria of program relevancy will result from the degree of understanding and concern and the appropriateness of the plan of action developed and executed by the counseling staff. An effective plan of action will reflect many, if not all, of the following characteristics:

1. *It should be developmental.* Program planning should be developmental, indicating immediate, intermediate, and long-range program goals. As a starting point, it may be appropriate to envision an ultimate, utopian program for the setting for which it will be designed and, once having established these long-range goals, determine those priorities that should be given immediate attention, those that may need attention within the next several years, and those that the program ultimately hopes to accomplish. Programs should never reach the point where they function simply to maintain the status quo. Programs should at all times be developmental, for development implies continuous growth and improvement.

2. *It should have a logical, sequential pattern of development.* The development of any program usually proceeds from a foundation which seems appropriate to subsequent development. As previously suggested, the appropriate foundation from which planning proceeds are its needs and readiness assessment and their relationship to the resources at hand.

3. *It should be flexible.* Counseling programs must be flexible in order to meet the changing needs of youths and other client populations. This suggests also that initial planning for program development must be limited to that which can be reasonably achieved. Programs that are overly ambitious in their design allow little room for alternate or unexpected opportunities. A part of flexibility in planning should be the identification of possible problems and alternate procedures for goal achievement.

4. *It should give a high priority to communication, coordination, and cooperation.* Like the other components of program development, these activities should

not be left to chance. It is important, for example, that there be a plan for communicating the development of the school guidance program to faculty members individually and in groups, as well as to students, parents, and others. Cooperation with other programs and persons is important if the program is to anticipate the need for reciprocal cooperation. In communicating with the various relevant groups and people in the community, different approaches must be used that recognize the uniqueness and differences of these individuals and groups. For example, techniques for communicating with youths would certainly be different in many ways than those that are effective with adults and related professionals. Often in recent years, counseling programs increasingly fail to communicate their mission clearly and effectively to others, resulting in many questioning the need for such programs. Coordination and cooperation failures have also adversely affected the positive image that counseling programs seek to portray.

5. *It should provide a basis for resource employment.* An adequate plan for program development provides a logical basis for personnel assignment, budget development, and resource allocation and utilization. This means that the plan must be a clear and concise one in which the relationships between program goals, the activities for achieving these goals, and the personnel and other resources needed to accomplish them can be readily recognized. The program director must be a resource coordinator. Program planning must therefore take into account those resources that may be available for program development and goal accomplishment. An inventory of possible resources becomes, therefore, an important activity in planning for program development.

Any plan for program initiation and development must include provisions for program accountability or evaluation. The evaluation component of a developmental plan provides a built-in mechanism for program accountability, development, and improvement.

The Counselor's Professional Development

Much has been written in recent years regarding staff development, yet, it is our observation that few counseling organizations have planned active programs for this purpose. However, it seems reasonable to assume that more programs will recognize the benefits that accrue, not only to the programs themselves, but to their professional staffs as well, from active staff development programs that increase the skills and knowledge of their counselors. Staff development can encompass a wide variety of activity, including performance appraisal, continuing education, lectures, conferences, seminars, supervisory relationships, and numerous organizational relationships that allow staff members to enhance their possession of human service technology and skills (Miringoff, 1980, p. 147).

Other activities may include quality circles, research involvement, exchange programs, sabbatical leaves, and reviews of professional literature. Of course, practicing counselors must assume the primary responsibility for their own professional development, even when benefitting from well-planned organizational staff development programs. This means one's career will be in one's own hands so to speak, and therefore one will be largely responsible for determining one's professional goals, and accomplishments or procedures needed to achieve these goals, and the resources that must be used in the process. Your professional development, of course, can contribute to the further development of your organization and the counseling profession as well.

One of the first steps beginning counselors can take to ensure their professional development is to join their appropriate professional organizations. Such organizations as the American Association for Counseling and Development and the American Psychological Association and their divisions provide excellent professional journals, newsletters, workshops, and conventions for the professional development of their members. Beyond joining the appropriate professional organizations, counselors should be an active participant in the profession's development as well. This means participating and sharing through attendance at professional meetings and conference presentations and sharing one's ideas and findings through writing and research.

The Counselor and the Law

During recent years few aspects of the counselor's role and function in any setting have remained untouched by judicial and legislative activities. For example, the Community Mental Health Centers Act of 1980, defined "community to be served" in terms of geographic and topographic characteristics. Of even greater consequence, however, is the effort

> to integrate mental health and general health services. In associating the community mental health center with physicians and hospitals, the current policy seems to assert that emotional disorders are primarily biological and require, among other responses, medical treatment, often including hospitalization. This assertion would seem inconsistent with the bulk of the evidence. At the same time, however, the policy recognizes the special role of the general hospital as the locus of what is ordinarily the highest quality community health care and serves to induce the general hospital to concern itself more with the treatment of emotionally disordered persons, even when such treatment is not medical in nature. In other words, the policy implied in the Act encourages the general hospital to broaden its view of its role in the community. (Bloom, 1984, p. 33)

Many other services that counselors and their fellow helping professionals must provide in community agency settings are specified by law. These include drug abuse treatment, the chronically mentally ill, and severely disturbed children and adolescents. Most states have enacted legislation that provides a legal basis for those who may practice or designate themselves as counselors, psychologists, marriage and family counselors, school counselors, and social workers.

Increasingly, managers of couseling programs and counselors themselves have become aware of the legal implications of their activities, the legal restrictions, and even legal conflicts with their professional conscience. This increased legal intervention is an outgrowth of a dramatic increase in litigation and attending legislation during the past 25 years. McCarthy (1976) addressed both of these points:

> Alexis de Tocqueville has noted that all important social issues in America eventually become judicial issues. This observation is verified in the field of education, as litigation in this arena has increased dramatically in recent years. Before, 1850, education was mainly ignored by both federal and state courts. Thus, practices at the local level were left largely unquestioned whether or not they conflicted with the Federal Constitution. From 1850 until 1950 education became firmly established as a state responsibility, and most adjudication during this period took place in state courts. Prior to 1954, slightly more than 100 cases involving education had been initiated in federal courts. However, since 1954 well over 1,000 cases concerning education have been litigated at the federal level, with many going all the way to the United States Supreme Court. During the past few decades the federal courts have assumed a more prominent role in ensuring that the individuals' constitutional rights are protected and balanced against the interests of the state. This increasing reliance on the federal judiciary is indicative of the growing public dissatisfaction with efforts of legislative bodies to effect reform in public education. (p. 1)

McCarthy (1976) also pointed out that:

> The increasing national interest in exploring the internal operations of schools to guarantee that the rights of children are not arbitrarily impaired also has been reflected in recent congressional legislation which has addressed certain aspects of the school's duty toward the child. The Family Rights and Privacy Act has placed restrictions on school officials' former power to indiscriminately record data about students. In addition, procedural safeguards are now required before the school can release a student's personal files. Thus, the rationale that a certain practice is "in the best interest of education" can no longer justify educational policies that arbitrarily interfere with the individual's personal liberties. Also, Title IX of the Educational Amendments of 1972 is causing some changes in the organization and administration of public schools. Title IX requires schools to eliminate discriminatory practices based on sex regarding admission policies, employment, and athletics. It is conceivable that federal legislation will continue to become more explicit in establishing standards for school policies, perhaps even in the area of instructional program adequacy. (pp. 4–5)

However, despite the increased public interest in both judicial and legislative activities with direct legal implications for schools, a study by Zirkel (1978) indicated that school leadership is abysmally ignorant of the operational dictates of Supreme Court decisions affecting education. The fact that this study was limited to Supreme Court decisions further highlights the general lack of knowledge among educators of their legal responsibilities and legal restraints.

Counselors cannot afford to be "legally ignorant." They must understand the law and its implications in arenas of counselor concern and function. These include acts or practices that might be viewed as discriminatory, compromising the constitutional and other legal rights, and prejudicing the opportunities of individuals. In this regard, note some of the legal implications for counselors of

Title IX, The Buckley Amendment, and the Education for the Handicapped Children Act.

The Counselor and Title IX

Title IX of the Education Amendments of 1972, which took effect in July, 1975, provides that

> no person . . . shall on the basis of sex, be excluded from participation in, be denied the benefits of, or be subjected to discrimination under any education program receiving federal financial assistance.

Some of the provisions that are of particular interest to counselors are as follows:

> Given the pervasiveness of dual role systems in education, employment and counseling, what are our responsibilities as counselors? As counselors it is our responsibility to "help an individual understand herself/himself and her/his world." Provision of adequate counseling services requires that we consider not only the needs, interests, and abilities of the individuals we are counseling, but also the changing nature of our society and the implications of these changes for working with students. It is our task to assist students to understand themselves, their changing options, and the implications of their decisions.
>
> One of the subtle but salient ways that differential sex socialization is perpetuated is found in the images and language provided in textbooks, newspapers, television, magazines, etc. It is not surprising, therefore, that evidence of such bias would be apparent in career materials and other counseling materials. (Office of Education, Department of Health, Education and Welfare, 1978)

In *Cracking the Glass Slipper: Peer's Guide to Ending Sex Bias in Your Schools,* Knox (1977) discussed Title IX and many of its implications for counselors:

> Nearly half of all the girls now enrolled in vocational education are enrolled in consumer and homemaking courses which do not prepare them for employment. The courses of study which do train for employment—and in which girls predominate—offer training in only 33 different occupations. In contrast, courses of study in which boys predominate offer training for paid employment in 95 different occupations. When girls do enroll in programs leading to paid employment, it is most often in areas such as office education or health services which offer relatively poor pay and relatively poor prospects for advancement. Many girls limit their own opportunities because they and their parents often approach vocational education with a narrow vision of what is appropriate and many schools have reinforced these notions with their own discriminatory policies. Schools have barred girls from certain courses of study outright and guided them away from other traditionally male fields through recruitment, admission, and counseling practices which discouraged girls' enrollment when it did not directly forbid it. The major issue in vocational education is whether girls are going to be as capable of supporting themselves as boys with the same level of education. If this is to be accomplished, a lot of past practices need to be changed. ("Vocational Education," p. 1)

Title IX requires the school to assure itself that any outside agencies, business organizations, or individuals with whom it cooperates do not discriminate against its students on the basis of sex. This might be in cooperative education, work-study programs, apprenticeships, or job placement. If the outside party refuses to give that assurance—or gives it but continues to discriminate—the school is required to end its cooperation. ("Vocational Education," p. 5)

The counselor can no longer cooperate with an outside agency, organization, or individual that wishes to discriminate against students on the basis of sex. What that boils down to is that if an employer is seeking a boy for summer employment, the counselor may not refer only one sex. For a counselor to be genuinely effective in counteracting stereotypes, the counselor will need to do more than simply not discriminate. An active attempt to expand options and opportunities is required. While Title IX does not require this kind of activity from the counselor, it is the kind of help most girls need to get past their own built-in stereotypes. ("Counseling," p. 3)

No club which is school sponsored can be limited to a single sex. Outside organizations which receive significant assistance from the school must also be nondiscriminatory. UNLESS they meet very strict criteria set up by Title IX to exempt youth service organizations such as the Girl Scouts and Campfire Girls. In order to be exempt the sponsoring organization must: be single sex; be a voluntary youth service organization; have a membership most under 19 years of age; and be tax exempt. ("Rules and Customs," p. 5)

More than one million teenagers become pregnant each year. We will need to be concerned that in teenage pregnancy, which involved two sexes to begin with, discrimination is most often directed against just one sex. More than half of all female dropouts leave school because of pregnancy. Eighty percent of the young women who become pregnant for the first time at age 17 or younger NEVER complete high school. Teenage mothers are less likely than other mothers to be working and more likely to be receiving Aid to Dependent Children. Their critical lack of education certainly plays a part in this. Under Title IX the pregnant student has the same rights and responsibilities as any other student. Solely because of pregnancy, she:

a. may not be expelled from school;
b. may not be required to attend a special school for pregnant students;
c. may not be barred from any program, course (including physical education or extracurricular activity, including competing for, or receiving, any award, honor, or elective office);
d. may not be required to take special courses in child care or related topics unless those courses are required of every other student in the school;
e. may not be required to leave school at a certain time before the birth of the child or required to remain out of school for a certain length of time afterwards:
f. may not be required to furnish notes from her physician that she is able to continue or re-enter a course of study unless such notes are required of all students (e.g., to tell when they intend to leave for surgery: or after an illness, to say that they are strong enough to return). (Knox, 1977. p. 5)

The Counselor and the Buckley Amendment

Few legislative actions have had a greater impact upon the practice of counseling and the attending record keeping than the Buckley Amendment. Before the passage in 1974 of the Family Educational Rights and Privacy Act (FERPA) as it is titled (or the Buckley Amendment as it is commonly referred to), counselors derived most of their directions for their professional functioning from the ethical guidelines provided by their professional associations. In this regard, the American Association for Counseling and Development Ethical Standards (1981) suggested that:

> ✓Records of the counseling relationship, including interview notes, test data, correspondence, tape recordings, and other documents, are to be considered professional information for use in counseling and they should not be considered a part of the records of the institution or agency in which the counselor is employed unless specified by state statute or regualtion. Revelation to others of counseling material must occur only upon the expressed consent of the client. (p. 1)

Although ethical standards were not in themselves legally binding, there are numerous instances, beginning with the case of Cherry versus the Board of Regents of the State of New York in 1942, that suggested courts might use professional ethical codes as guidelines for making judicial decisions. In the case of record keeping and confidentiality, however, the passage of the Buckley Amendment became the single most important guideline for professional conduct with regard to student records and related activities.

> The FERPA stipulates that the parents of unemancipated minor students have " ... the right to inspect and review any and all official records, files, and data directly related to their children, including all material that is incorporated into each student's cumulative record folder and intended for school use or to be available to parties outside the school or school system, and specifically including but not necessarily limited to identifying data, academic work completed, level of achievement (grades, standardized achievement scores), attendance data, scores of standardized intelligence, aptitude, and psychological tests, interest inventory results, health data, family background information, teacher or counselor ratings and observations, and verified reports of serious recurrent behavior patterns. (Getson and Schweid, 1976, p. 57)

Recognizing the conflict or, as they put it, ethical standards squeeze, Getson and Schweid (1976) suggested the following steps for school counselors to protect their counselees and students:

> First, review all existing records to assure that there is no material that predates FERPA that would violate implied or stated guarantees of privacy to the child. Second, remove all material that, because of its technical nature or vocabulary, may be inappropriate for use by lay persons. Retain only materials that can be expressed in a form unlikely to be misinterpreted. Third, initiate a policy of maintaining only records that can be reviewed with parents without threat to the welfare of a counselee. Fourth, be sure that counselees understand the legal limitation of the privacy afforded the counseling relationship relative to the rights of parents to inspect official records. Fifth, initiate a study of the full implications of the conflict between the FERPA and AACD's Ethical Standards. There may be safeguards to the right to privacy of the student implicit in FERPA of which we who are not lawyers are not aware. Sixth, if there is a clear or probable conflict between the FERPA and AACD's Ethical Standards, initiate action to change the act, the standards, or both. It would seem that, as

a minimum a provision should exist within the act that withholds from anyone except public authorized investigative bodies information under study. (pp. 57–58)

Because school counselors as well as counselors in other educational settings are frequently called upon to write letters of recommendation for college admissions or employment, it should be noted that the Buckley Amendment implications are clear that:

Unless the educator is specifically informed otherwise, he or she should assume that the student may have access to letters of recommendation. The student can be requested to sign a waiver, so that he or she will not have such access. However, unless such a waiver is signed, the student can be defended, both factually and professionally. In general, educators are on relatively safe ground when writing letters of recommendation if the following conditions are met:

1. Letters of recommendation are an expected, normal, and integral part of one's duties and responsibilities.
2. Letters are sent only to second parties (not published), who can be expected to have a reasonable interest in and concern for the person in question.
3. Letters are factual, free of malice, and reasonably objective.
4. Letters are in response to a request. (St. John and Walden, 1976, p. 683)

St. John and Walden (1976) suggested three recommendations:

First it is recommended that professional educators consult with an attorney, preferably one conversant with eduational matters, or with the school district's legal counsel, on all matters regarding confidential communications. Second, it is recommended that school districts and state departments of education cooperatively develop detailed guidelines to assist all school personnel in protecting student confidences and to respect the confidentiality of communications consistent with state and federal statutes. Third, it is recommended that the various professional organizations develop specific and up-dated codes of ethics related to this area. (p. 683)

School Counselors and Public Law 94–142

Another act of importance to school counselors is the Education for All Handicapped Children Act (PL 94–142) of November, 1975. This law guarantees the rights of all children, regardless of the severity of the handicap, to a free, appropriate education. The law further establishes a formula for providing financial aid to states and local school districts, based on the number of handicapped children receiving special education plus related services. It is this latter activity—related services—that provides for counseling by a certified counselor. In noting the implications of this act for counselors, Humes (1978) noted that

while the role of the counselor in the implementation of PL 94–142 will vary from district to district and in part will be contingent on the availability of other specialized personnel and whether the counselor has an elementary or secondary assingment, it is difficult to conceive of any situation in which a counselor will have no role to play. Some of the possible ranges of responsibility are

1. participation in team meetings.
2. development of the IEP [Individual Educational Plan].

(IEP—The core of the law is the concept of the IEP. An IEP, which is to be reviewed annually, must be developed for each handicapped child. The content of the IEP must include the present level of functioning, annual goals, short-term measurable objectives, and specific educational services required by the child.)

3. monitoring progress.
4. parental counseling.

(A section of the law that is overlooked, partly because of its traditional neglect in American public education and partly because of the ambiguous nature of the language in the statute, is the requirement for parent counseling. Parent counseling may have a variety of meanings. Parent counseling suggests a possible range of services from psychiatric assistance to advice about academic offerings and may occur in an outside agency or within the school. A conservative approach would suggest that parent counseling should occur in the school setting and satisfy the definition of counseling as opposed to therapy. If we accept this assumption, the logical person to satisfy this need would be the counselor.)

5. extracurricular planning.
6. classroom consulting.
7. in-service training.

(While it is reasonable to assume that in the early stages counselors will be the recipients of in-service training along with other pupil personnel services workers, it would be a reasonable assumption that in the middle-to-later stages of implementation the counselor will become one of the providers of in-service training.)

8. record keeping. (pp. 193–195)

Finally, we should note that counselors have, on occasion, been defendants in criminal action. As Burgum and Anderson (1975) stated, the counselor may unwittingly risk criminal liability leading to one of four possible criminal charges:

Accessory to a crime after the fact.
Encouraging an illegal abortion.
Co-conspirator in civil disobedience.
Contributing to delinquency of a minor (p. 88)

Although the counselor is honor-bound to protect the integrity and promote the welfare of his client, he also has an obligation to society at large. No area of counselor activity poses greater prospect of conflict and trouble for the counselor than when a student-client is guilty of a crime. Accessory after the fact is generally defined as "one who, knowing a felony to have been committed, receives, relieves, comforts, or assists the felon, or in any manner aids him to escape arrest or punishment."

Three elements must exist to render one an accessory after the fact:

1. A felony must have already been committed.
2. The person charged as an accessory must have knowledge that the person he is assisting committed the felony.
3. The accessory must harbor or assist the felon.

The first condition—that the felony be completed—is required because if the felon is given aid during commission of a crime the person helping him becomes a principal and not an accessory after the fact. Knowledge on the part of the defendant that a crime was committed is necessary to a charge of being an accessory after the fact. But one cannot escape guilt by merely claiming lack of knowledge. Knowledge, like intent, is a matter of fact which can be proven by inference from all facts and circumstances developed at trial. And a defendant must be able to counter any evidence that he did have knowledge of a crime. Different types of conduct can constitute sufficient "assistance" to produce judgment that the person giving such assistance was, indeed, an accessory after the fact.

Generally, evidence that a person helps to hide a felon, lends him money, gives advice, provides goods, offers transportation, blocks the path of pursuers, and, in some cases, gives false information tending to mislead the authorities has been held sufficient to sustain conviction as accessory after the fact. However, it would be inaccurate to say that just any affirmative assistance or relief would automatically result in charges that one has been an accessory. Even those acts just enumerated have not always been held sufficient to justify conviction. (pp. 89–91)

Ethical Standards and the Law

For counselors there are two basic statements of ethical practice and behavior that apply to work in the profession. These statements are: (a) "Ethical Standards of the American Association for Counseling and Development" (see Appendix B), and (b) "Ethical Principles for Psychologists," (American Psychological Association (1981) (See Appendix C). These codes of ethics and professional standards are expected to be followed by the members of these associations. Failure to abide by these standards may result in a member being expelled.

> The cited standards are basically concerned with counselor responsibilities, competence, client relationships and confidentiality. In addition, both APA and several divisions of the American Association for Counseling and Development have adopted standards for measurement and evaluation. (Hummel and Humes, 1984, p. 382)

Also available is the policy statement of the American Personnel and Guidance Association (now named the American Association for Counseling and Development) regarding the "Responsibilities of Users of Standardized Tests" (See Appendix F). Other codes of ethics of interest to counselors are the "Code of Ethics for Certified Clinical Mental Health Counselors," (National Academy of Certified Clinical Mental Health Counselors) (see Appendix G) as well as "The Code of Professional Ethics (American Association for Marriage and Family Therapy) (see Appendix H). The *American Psychologist* (1981) printed "Specialty Guidelines for the Delivery of Services by Counseling Psychologists" (See Appendix I).

Summary

Much of the success of any counseling program will be dependent upon how the program is managed, developed, and led. As educational and community institutions have become more complex in their organizational and operational structure, the necessity for special preparation of program leaders in terms of managing resources, coordinating and facilitating activities, and providing personnel motivation has become increasingly self-evident. Counselors, as organizational staff members, must also be aware of their responsibilities and knowledgeable enough to carry them out.

This chapter has also noted the importance of counselors informing themselves of the legal implications and restrictions on their professional activities and has identified codes of ethics for guiding professional practice and conduct.

The final chapter discusses an area that counseling program leaders and their staffs are giving increased attention. Accountability and evaluation are being demanded of all programs and counselors are being called upon by their profession to increase their research efforts in order to advance "the frontiers of knowledge" of our profession.

References

American Personnel and Guidance Association. (1981). *Ethical standards.* Alexandria, VA: Author.

Blanchard, K. H. (1982). *The one-minute manager.* New York: Morrow.

Bloom, B. L. (1984). *Community mental health: A general introduction* (2nd ed.). Belmont, CA: Brooks/Cole.

Burgess, J. H. (1978). *System design approaches to public services.* Cranbury, NJ: Associated University Press.

Burgum, T., & Anderson, S. (1975). *The counselor and the law.* Washington, D.C.: American Personnel and Guidance Association.

DiSilvestro, F. (1974). *The application of the planning programming, budgeting system (PPBS) concept to counseling and guidance services.* Indianapolis: Indiana State Dept. of Public Instruction.

Drucker, P. (1954). *A practice of management.* New York: Harper.

Getson, R., & Schweid, R. (1976). School counselors and the Buckley Amendment—Ethical standards squeeze. *The School Counselor, 24,* 56–58.

Gibson, R. L., Mitchell, M. H., & Higgins, R. E. (1983). *Development and management of counseling programs and guidance services.* New York: Macmillan.

Humes, C. W., II. (1978). School counselors and PL 94–142. *The School Counselor, 25,* 193–195.

Hummel, D. L., & Humes, C. W. (1984). *Pupil services: Development, coordination, administration.* New York: Macmillan.

Knox, H. (1977). *Cracking the glass slipper: Peer's guide to ending sex bias in your schools.* Washington, D.C.: The NOW Legal Defense and Education Fund.

Lewis, J. A., & Lewis, M. D. (1983). *Management of human service programs.* Belmont, CA: Brooks/Cole.

McCarthy, M. M. (1976). School law: A growing concern. *Teacher Education Forum, 4.* Bloomington, IN: Indiana University, Division of Teacher Education.

Miringoff, M. L. (1980). *Management in human services.* New York: Macmillan.

Peter, L. I., & Hull, R. (1959). *The Peter principle.* New York: Morrow.

Peters, T. J., & Waterman, R. H., Jr. (1982). *In search of excellence.* New York: Harper & Row.

St. John, W. D., & Walden, J. (1976). Keeping student confidences. *Phi Delta Kappan, 57,* 682–684.

Thompson, D. L., & Borsari, L. R. (1978). An overview of management by objectives for guidance and counseling services. *The School Counselor, 25,* 172–177.

U.S. Department of Health, Education and Welfare. (1975, November 3). *The Federal Register, 40.* Washington, D.C.: Author.

Zirkel, P. A. (1978). A test on Supreme Court decisions affecting education. *Phi Delta Kappan, 59,* 521–522, 555.

CHAPTER 13

ACCOUNTABILITY, EVALUATION, AND RESEARCH

Introduction

It is important for the beginning counselor to recognize that he or she alone is responsible—accountable—for being an effective and efficient counselor. The beginning counselor must also anticipate being the subject of professional evaluation as well as participating in organizational evaluation. Also, since both accountability and evaluation frequently imply research needs, it is important to understand basic research design and sources of research reports that may provide insights into local concerns or issues. It is therefore the objective of this chapter to introduce concepts and guidelines for the beginning counselor's involvement in program accountability, evaluation, and research.

The mere mention of the activities of accountability, evaluation, and research is said on frequent occasion to strike fear into the hearts of many honest practitioners. To mention all three of these as topics in a chapter should suffice to bring out all the traditional fears associated with these activities. These include (a) the fear of being held responsible, regardless of intervening variables, for one's activities; (b) the fear of being judged by criteria determined externally, over which one has no control; (c) the fear of being judged by unrealistic standards and expectancies; (d) the fear of being required, in the case of research, to master difficult mathematical formulae that one feels will never be used again; (e) the fear of being expected to understand and possibly even apply the results of research studies written by researchers to impress other researchers; and (f) the fear, or assumption, that evaluation is never intended to be positive.

Many of these fears will diminish to mere myths when one learns to appreciate the values and advantages of accountability, evaluation, and research for the practicing counselor.

Definitions

Although textbooks and many periodical articles have been published dealing with the separate topics of accountability, evaluation, and research, this chapter will present an overview that stresses the relationships between accountability, evaluation, and research. Let us then distinguish among these terms.

In discussing *accountability* in community mental health settings, Jeger and Slotnick (1982) stated that

> technical expertise should not be confused with accountability. As long as experts who provide services are seen as serving the local people—who decide on community priorities and evaluate the utility of services—accountability can be achieved (Rappaport, 1977) (p. 37).

Leon Lessinger (1973), who is often referred to as the "father of accountability" for the impetus given this movement during his tenure as Commissioner of Education, defines accountability as responsibility for something, to someone, with predictable consequences for the desirable and understandable performance of the responsibility.

Evaluation has been defined variously by Lessinger et al. (1973) as the "process of assessment or appraisal of value; the comparison of desired outcomes (objectives) with the actual progress made in actual accomplishments" (p. 236). Others have defined evaluation as "the task of establishing desired objectives; collecting and organizing information to assess the accomplishment of objectives; judging the adequacy of accomplishments, and making decisions for improving programs" (Wysong, 1972, p. 33); or "the process of delineating, obtaining, and providing useful information for judging decision alternatives" (Stufflebeam, Foley, Gephart, Guba, Hammond, Merriman, and Provos, 1971, p. 40).

A definition of evaluation from the National Institute of Mental Health suggests as a working definition the following:

> Program evaluation is a systematic set of data collection and analysis activities undertaken to determine the value of a program to aid management, program planning, staff training, public accountability, and promotion. Evaluation activites make reasonable judgments possible about the efforts, effectiveness, adequacy, efficiency, and comparative value of program options. (Hagedorn, Beck, Neubert, and Werlin, 1976, p. 3)

Another easily understood definition views

> evaluation as the determination of the worth of a thing. It includes obtaining information for use in judging the worth of a program, product, procedure, or objective, or the potential utility of alternative approaches designed to attain specified objectives. (Worthen and Sanders. 1973, p. 19)

We suggest that the process of evaluation seeks to provide objective evidence of a program's performance through an assessment of progress towards program objectives. The evidence collected through this process then becomes valuable as a basis for future program planning and decision making. As such, a planned and conscientious program evaluation is essential to the continuous improvement of counseling programs in any setting.

A common definition views *research* as organized scientific efforts that seek the advancement of knowledge. Galfo (1975) suggests that "research implies a systematic study of variables in order to determine if and or how they may be related to one another." (p. 8) Oetting and Hawkes (1974) believe that research is

> aimed at the advancement of scientific knowledge. There is no need for research to be immediately useful or practical and there can be great concern for making sure that the exact relationship between independent and dependent variables is known (p. 435).

According to Worthen and Sanders (1973):

> Research is the activity aimed at obtaining generalizable knowledge by contriving and testing claims about relationships among variables or describing generalizable phenomena. This knowledge, which may result in theoretical models, functional relationships, or descriptions, may be obtained by empirical or other systematic methods and may or may not have immediate application. (p. 19)

Accountability

While accountability first became a byword in education, its popularity has also spread to other tax-supported governmental institutions and agencies, including mental health agencies. Thus, with the possible exception of private practice, the likelihood is great that counselors will be employed in settings in which they will be expected to be accountable—to provide factual evidence of their accomplishments related to their costs.

A Positive View of Accountability

Recognizing that many helping professionals have negative attitudes or, at the least, uneasy feelings about accountability, let us accentuate the positive. Baker in his "Argument for Constructive Accountability" (1977) presented five positive aspects of accountability:

a. *Skill acquisition:* Whatever accountability system one uses, certain specific skills are required of the participants. Acquisition of such skills may increase one's satisfaction and confidence. Satisfaction with one's level of competence is associated with knowledge of specific skills possessed. Confidence in one's capacity to encounter new tasks, such as those related to an accountability system, increases with acquisition of new skills. Among those skills that may be acquired or improved through attention to an accountability system are the ability to envision and develop a system; developing data collection instruments; analyzing data; reporting results; making decisions based on acquired results; making plans for future actions based upon acquired results; and applying those plans to a real life setting.

b. *Program improvement:* Conscientious counselors are constantly searching for ways to improve their services. Finding useful sources of evaluative information about the existing services is a universal problem for these people. An accountability system offers the solution of this universal need because data acquired from the accountability activities may be used as the basis for program improvement. As a result, data are used constructively.

c. *Positive results:* Results acquired through an accountability system may be complimentary. Prospects of acquiring complimentary outcomes from accountability studies need to be emphasized more than is presently the case.... Such results provide intrinsic rewards for the counselor because awareness of consumer's satisfaction or of successful program outcomes provides the counselor with a feeling of satisfaction and accomplishment.

d. *A process rather than an event:* A systematic ongoing model incorporates the accountability activities and other planned enterprises with a minimum amount of drudgery and maximum efficiency.

e. *Rewards for a job well done:* The ultimate outcome for an accountability system, it seems, is to reward intrinsically those who have demonstrated that their accomplishments are extraordinary.... The reward system is viewed as the ultimate outcome because it completes the unfinished accountability model. (pp. 53–55)

Krumboltz (1974) also noted:

The potential advantages warrant counselors' efforts to construct a sound accountability system for themselves. An accountability system would enable counselors to

- Obtain feedback on the results of their work.
- Select counseling methods on the basis of demonstrated success.
- Identify clients with unmet needs.
- Devise shortcuts for routine operations.
- Argue for increased staffing to reach attainable goals.
- Request training for problems requiring new competencies.

How would counselors benefit from a sensible accountability system? By learning how to help clients more effectively and efficiently, counselors would obtain:

- More problem recognition for accomplishments.
- Increased financial support.
- Better working relationships with other professionals.
- Acknowledged professional standing.
- The satisfaction of performing a constantly improving and valued service. (pp. 639–646)

It is clear from the statements of Baker, Krumboltz, and others that conscientious counselors, dedicated to improving their skills and serving their clientele as effectively and efficiently as possible, have little to fear and much to gain from a system that will be their ally. Accountability may, at last, provide the ultimate proof that counseling programs can make a positive difference.

Developing Accountability in Counseling Programs

Krumboltz (1974) identified seven criteria to be met if an accountability system is to produce the desired results. These were as follows:

1. In order to define the domain of counselor responsibility, the general goals of counseling must be agreed to by all concerned parties.
2. Counselor accomplishments must be stated in terms of important observable behavior changes by clients.
3. Activities of the counselor must be stated as costs, not accomplishments.
4. The accountability system must be constructed to promote professional effectiveness and self-improvement, not to cast blame or punish poor performance.
5. In order to promote accurate reporting, reports of failures and unknown outcomes must be permitted and never be punished.
6. All users of the accountability system must be represented in designing it.
7. The accountability system itself must be subject to evaluation and modification. (pp. 640–641)

Rappaport (1977) described the relationship between accountability and community:

> Community control as accountability does not necessarily infer that local people run the serivce, but that experts are the employees of the local people who are the consumers. . . . The consumers would judge effectiveness and decide on continuation of the service, expansion, or reorientation of the policy and programs. One does not need to know how to help others resolve a crisis to be able to decide that that is a worthwhile service and to later evaluate if it has been helpful to one's community. . . . This is community control as accountability. It has never been fully tested. (p. 302)

Biegel and Naparstek (1982) wrote that:

> Accountability is not a one-way street; that is, not only the public sector should determine what services are delivered to a neighborhood, and whether they are delivered appropriately and effectively. Procedures for insuring mutual accountability are necessary in which consumers are accountable to providers, and providers are accountable to consumers. In this way we can help ensure that the system remains relevant. Without procedures for mutual accountability, providers are often unable to identify the strengths and needs of individuals and their families. A delivery system cannot be effective if individuals are viewed only in relation to separate programs. By building mutual accountability procedures into the system, consumers will be assured an opportunity to make their views known and to make those views count. This implies, for example, citizen involvement in the development of a mental health service from planning to evaluation stages. (pp. 276–277)

Although there is no best single approach to developing an accountability-model, most programs seem to focus upon some form of needs assessment out of which program objectives are identified and perhaps arranged according to priorities, which, in turn, lead to program activity planning and an accounting for and evaluation of the outcomes. An example of developing an accountability program in schools is described in the *American Association of School Administrators Handbook* (1973). The four phases of this planning, while intended for schools, are appropriate for other settings as well.

Phase 1. Preliminary Planning

The aim of the preliminary planning phase is to determine informally whether it is feasible to consider some form of accountability. It represents a feasibility study seeking a decision whether to move into Phase 2 or drop the matter from consideration for the present. Probably only a few key people need to be involved at this point. In framing an answer, it is expected that (a) each of the imperatives offered will have been duly considered, and (b) a positive decision to move ahead to Phase 2 is regarded as "tentative."

Phase 2. Formula Planning

The purpose of Phase 2 is two fold:

a. To place before the community and staff two questions: what *does* our school do? and what *should* it be doing?
b. To bring together an appropriate group of persons to work on these questions by (1) examining the extant data (for what they say and, sometimes shocking, for what they fail to say); (2) considering alternative ways to meet the questions; (3) of major importance, developing a consensus of the goals and objectives of an educational program.

Phase 3. Program Implementation

The major concern of Phase 3 centers on the task of further developing the staff and implementing the particular program (e.g., basic reading competency). By now, the major dimensions of the program will have been formed; through the needs assessment, specific problem areas will have been identified; a preliminary and then formal change strategy to involve people in the review of needs, the framing of general goals and performance objectives, and the design of the program will have been employed; and presumably, a generally supportive climate (in terms of attitudes, financial support, realistic time constraints, etc.) will have been established (negotiated?) through community and staff involvement.

Phase 4. Rendering the Account

The final phase of the progam deals with taking a close look at the efforts and reporting the results in accordance with the plan adopted in Phase 2. (pp. 35–44)

A summary way of viewing the development of this accountability program is shown in Table 13–1.

As we proceed from this section on accountability to the next section discussing evaluation, we would note the relationship of evaluation to accountability. As discussed by Lewis and Lewis (1983):

Most human service programs are required to submit yearly evaluation reports for the scrutiny of funding sources or public agencies, and many specially funded projects are required to spend set percentages of their total budgets on evaluation. Beyond this, however, agencies are also accountable to their communities. The "accountabil-

Table 13.1. A Process for Developing an Accountability Program

Phase 1: Preliminary Planning
Assess needs (critical).
Develop a preliminary change strategy (critical).
Consider the use of technical assistance and management systems (optional).
Make decision to move, or not to move, to Phase 2.

Phase 2: Formal Planning
Involve community/staff (critical).
 Repeat needs assessment (optional).
 Repeat change strategy devleopment (optional).
Develop goal consensus and performance objectives (critical).
Consider plan-program-budget system (optional).
Make decision to move, or not to move, to Phase 3.

Phase 3: Program Implementation
Develop program staff (critical).
Implement program procedures (critical).
Consider
 Performance contracting (internal and/or external) (optional).
 Network monitoring (optional).
Reach predetermined completion points of program efforts.

Phase 4: Rendering the Account
Evaluate program (critical).
Report the results (critical).
Use an educational program auditor (optional).
Determine level of confidence (critical).
Certify the nature of results (critical).

Source: American Association of School Administrators, 1973, p. 47.

ity model" Windle and Neigher (1978, p. 97) describe stresses this component of evaluation. The accountability model takes the position that a program should be evaluated by the public and/or those who support it. Such evaluation can have at least three purposes: (1) to let the public or other supporters make wise decisions concerning support, (2) to motivate the public and other supporters to greater program support by involving them in the goals and activities of the program, and (3) to motivate the program staff to greater public service and efficiency by their awareness that their activities are being monitored.

 Dissemination of evaluation reports describing the agency's activities and their effects can help reinforce program accountability. People concerned with agency performance can gain knowledge about the results of services, and this information undoubtedly increases community members' impact on policies and programs. (p. 146)

Evaluation

Everyone everyday constantly seeks ways to improve many daily routine chores, whether it is trying a new toothpaste or a different breakfast cereal or taking a new route to work. In a sense, people constantly evaluate many daily decisions and activities. People are also involved, usually unofficially, in many external evaluations such as the local newspaper, a current TV program, the decisions of Congress, and the teachers, courses, and textbooks with which children come in contact. Just as these evaluations are a part of the process of improving daily living or exercising a right to express one's opinions, the more formal, structured evaluations of one's professional activities and organizations should also receive daily and constant attention. As the critics of counseling have so frequently and constantly pointed out in recent years, justifiably or not, evaluative evidence and activities appear to be either missing or misleading at best (Mitchell, 1976).

Evaluation: A Process for Professional Improvement

One often reads or hears about a public office holder, a salesperson, or a teacher with 30 years' experience but with no mention of the quality of that experience. Experience does not, in and of itself, guarantee improvement and quality. Professionals must have as their own personal-ethical goal the constant and critical evaluation of their professional performance. A lack of evaluation often leads to mediocrity or failure to reach one's full potential in terms of what professionals might accomplish for the clients they serve. Evaluation, then, for counselors in a variety of settings and for other professionals, is first and foremost a process for professional improvement, a process in which one gathers objective, performance-oriented data on a systematic and nonbiased basis. These data are then used as information that leads to constantly improving, upgrading, and updating one's professional performance.

Evaluation: Providing Information for Decision Makers

Amidst the changing concepts of evaluation in recent decades, one of the most popular among evaluation experts is the view of evaluation as a process for providing information for decision makers. A leader in this decision-management approach to evaluation, D. L. Stufflebeam, developed the CIPP (context, input, process, product) evaluation model. This model affirms that "evaluation is the process of delineating, obtaining, and providing useful information for judging decision alternatives" (Stufflebeam et al., 1971, p. 40) and suggests several key points:

1. Evaluation is performed in the service of *decision making;* hence, it should provide information which is useful to decision makers.
2. Evaluation is a cyclic, continuing *process* and, therefore, must be implemented through a systematic program.
3. The evaluation process includes the three main steps of delineating, obtaining, and providing. These steps provide the basis for a methodology of evaluation.
4. The delineating and providing steps in the evaluation process are *interface* activities requiring collaboration between evaluator and decision maker, while the

obtaining step is largely a *technical* activity which is executed mainly by the evaluator.

Here evaluation is viewed as a process that can provide decision makers at all levels with objective data that will assist them in determining the relative value of competing alternatives and that will immeasurably improve their probability of making the "right decision."

Evaluation: Other Functions

The wide range of evaluation purposes may seem to rival that of the political party platforms of "promising something for everybody!" Although that is not the intent, it is important to recognize some of the values of this activity. Examples of these additional functions of evaluation are as follows:

1. Verifies or rejects practices by providing evidence for what works and what does not, or the degree to which an activity seems to be effective. This also tends to lead to the avoidance of meaningless innovations and unproven fads.
2. Measures improvement by providing evidence on a continuous basis so that both rate and level of progress may be ascertained.
3. Enhances probability of growth by providing a basis for improvements in the operation and its activities.
4. Builds credibility—by the very nature of the activity, evaluation suggests a continuous search for better ways of doing things; a constant quest for improvement; a willingness to put efforts on the line and take a look at "how we're doing!"
5. Provides for increased insights—by the fact of examining our own or an organization's functioning, we become more knowledgeable and understanding about this functioning; more aware of influencing factors and potential consequence.
6. Increases and improves participating in decision making—because evaluation involves everyone within the organizational structure, the process, by necessity, involves them in the outcomes, which in turn *should* bring about the participation of all such personnel in the planning of new directions and in implementing the findings.
7. Places responsibilities—by identifying "who is responsible for what and when," evaluation stimulates linkages between specific persons and specific activities. It decreases the probability of everyone claiming responsibility for the successes and no one claiming the failures.
8. Provides a rationality for the enterprise by improving overall accountability, including evidence of accomplishments and growth.

Principles of Evaluation

Because evaluation is a process for appraising the value or effectiveness of a program or activity, it is most effective when conducted within a framework of guiding principles. Six of these, as presented by Gibson (1977), are discussed in the following paragraphs (pp. 70–72).

Effective evaluation requries a recognition of program goals. Before any meaningful program of evaluation can be undertaken, it is essential that the goals or objectives of that program be clearly identified. These objectives provide indications of program intent, which form the basis for subsequent planning and procedures. The objectives of the program should be stated in clear and measurable terminology. This principle suggests that counseling programs be evaluated on the basis of "how well they are doing what they set out to do."

Effective evaluation requires valid measuring criteria. Once program goals are clearly defined, valid criteria for measuring progress toward those goals must be identified. The development of such criteria is crucial if the evaluation is to be both valid and meaningful. For example, if an annual program goal for a junior community college counseling program would be to provide each entering student with a series of three career interviews with a counselor, the measuring criteria could be a simple count indicating the percentage of students who did, in fact, have such an opportunity. If, on the other hand, the program goal was to provide each student with a "broadening of his career understanding," the measuring criteria would be less obvious and might be dependent on a further refinement of what is meant by "career understanding." In other words, vaguely stated goals and vaguely stated criteria lessen the effectiveness of program evaluation.

Effective program evaluation is dependent on valid application of the measuring criteria. As discussed in the previous paragraph, valid criteria for measuring progress toward the program's stated goals must be established. It is not sufficient, however, to merely establish criteria. Their ultimate validity will depend on their valid application. This implies that effective evaluation of all counseling programs should involve, in each instance, persons who are professionally competent in both evaluation techniques and understandings of such counseling programs. Too often, effective evaluation criteria are dissipated in the hands of evaluators who have, at best, only a superifical knowledge of the appropriate role and functions of counseling programs.

Program evaluation should involve all who are affected. Evaluation of a school counseling program, for example, should involve those who are participants in or who are affected by the program. This would include, in addition to the counseling staff, faculty members, and administrators, students and their parents and, on appropriate occasions, members of the community or supporting agencies. The major contribution to effective evaluation must come from those who have a first-hand knowledge or involvement in the program. External evaluators from governmental agencies, accrediting associations, or other educational institutions can, of course, be helpful, but those should not be the sole bases of evaluation.

Meaningful evaluation requires feedback and follow-through. The evaluation process and the evaluation report are not in and of themselves of great value. It is only when the results are used for program improvement and development that the evaluation process takes on meaning. This presumes, then, that the results of any program evaluation are made available to those concerned with the program management and development. It also presumes that the program manager and his or her staff will use these results for future program planning, development, and decision making.

Evaluation is most effective as a planned, continuous process. Counseling programs are most effective when planned as a continuous process. This may enable the program staff to identify at any point in time weaknesses that need correcting immediately or accomplishments that should be capitalized on. This means that there are specific plans and designated responsibilities for both the ongoing evaluation of a program's progress and the more extensive annual or semi-annual reviews.

Evaluation emphasizes the positive. Frequently, evaluation is viewed as a threatening process aimed at ferreting out hidden weaknesses and spotlighting "goofs." If program evaluation is to produce the most meaningful results possible, it must be conducted in a spirit that is positive, that is aimed at facilitating program improvement, and that emphasizes strengths as well as weaknesses.

Methods of Evaluation

Before-and-After Method. This method of evaluation seeks to identify the progress that takes place in a program's development as a result of specific program activities over a given period of time. For example, an objective of a school counseling program might be to provide each student with a weekend work experience during his or her junior year. At the beginning of the school year, before the program, it could be presumed that none had had this experience. At the end of the year, after the program, the number who actually participated would give some indication of goal achievement.

Comparison Methods. The "how-do-we-compare" process makes evaluations on the basis of comparing one group against another or against the norm of a number of groups. Different techniques for achieving the same goal can also be evaluated by this comparative method. For example, a secondary school in Bloomington, Indiana, might note that it has a counselor/pupil ratio of 1 to 258, compared with the norm for 200 midwestern secondary schools of 1 to 418. Such a comparison would indicate, of course, that the Bloomington school system is making more adequate provisions for high school counseling personnel than most other school systems in the Midwest.

The "How-Do-We-Stand" Method. This particular method is based on the identification of desirable program outcomes and related characteristics and criteria. From these criteria, rating scales, checklists, and questionnaires may be developed and used to indicate the degree to which a program measures up. For example, evaluative criteria or checklists used by most accrediting associations and many state governmental agencies and departments reflect this approach. Although this approach to evaluation may locally ignore appropriate objectives and sometimes unique and innovative practices, it does provide guidelines that enable programs to be compared with generally accepted standards.

Procedures for Evaluation

The evaluation process usually involves a series of activities in a sequence, which approximates the following.

Identification of goals to be assessed. The first step establishes the variables, or limits, for the evaluation. Evaluation can focus on the total counseling program or on only one or several particular objectives. These program objectives should be stated in clear, concise, specific, and measurable terms. Broadly stated goals (for example, "to facilitate the adjustment of the study body of J. J. Jenkins High School") are much more difficult to measure than, for example, a specifically stated goal, such as "to provide each student in Penny Junior High School with a yearly scheduled opportunity to discuss his or her career planning with a school counselor."

Development of an evaluation plan. Once the objectives for evaluation have been established, the identification and validation of criteria appropriate for measuring the program's progress toward these objectives follow. In the previous example, a simple yet valid criterion would be an indication of the percentage of the Penny Junior High School students who actually did have a scheduled career-planning interview with a school counselor. This example is illustrative of the principle that measuring criteria should also be stated in specific and objective terms. The overall evaluation plan, in addition to specifying the kinds of data to be collected, should also specify how it will be collected, when, and by whom. This plan must also give attention to how the data will be organized and reported and to whom. Finally, such a plan should conclude with provisions for using the findings for future program development.

Application of the evaluation plan. After an acceptable evaluation plan has been designed, its validity is then dependent upon the manner in which it is carried out. Once again, we stress the importance of adequate planning and a positive approach, utilizing evaluators who possess the necessary understanding and competency. Timing is also important because some aspects of a program can only be appropriately evaluated in a "longitudinal" sense, whereas other specific activities need an "immediately after" assessment.

Utilization of the findings. Evaluation as an activity is in itself of little value. It is in the application of the findings that the real worth of evaluation lies. Through the process of evaluation, programs can ascertain their strengths and weaknesses. The resulting insights may then provide directions for future program improvement. The utilization of these findings, however, cannot be left to mere chance. There must be planning, with specific responsibilities for the utilization of the findings, and subsequent follow-up to establish the degree to which the evaluation recommendations have been fulfilled.

Evaluation for Community Mental Health Counseling Programs

Community mental health center programs have also felt increased pressures in recent generations to conduct systematic program evaluations, partly as the result of the increasing demands of the federal government to verify program efficiency and effectiveness in community mental health centers. In this regard, Public Law 94-63, the Community Mental Health Centers Amendments of 1975, requires community mental health centers to allocate not less than 2 percent of their previous year's operating budgets to conducting program evaluation. The law mandates three general types of evaluation, as follows:

1. Quality assurance of clinical services.
   Each center is to establish an ongoing quality assurance of its clinical services.
2. Self-evaluation.
   Each center will collect data and evaluate its services in relation to program goals and values and to catchment area needs and resources. The data shall consist of (a) Cost of center operations; (b) Patterns of use of services; (c) Availability, awareness, acceptablity, and accessibility of services; (d) Impact of services upon the mental health of residents of the catchment area; (e) Effectiveness of consultation and education services; (f) The impact of the Center on reducing inappropriate institutionalization. (1976, p. 6)
3. Residents' review.
   Each center will at least annually publicize and make available all evaluation data of the type listed above to residents of the catchment area. In addition, it will organize and publicize an opportunity for citizens to review the Center's program of services in order to assure that services are responsive to the needs of residents of the catchment area. (p. 7)

Research

It must be acknowledged that research does not always project a popular image. It is appropriate to recognize some of the frequently stated reasons for this lack of popularity.

- Most research seems to ignore the common problems and everyday needs of practitioners.
- Most research reports are written in a manner that limits their interpretation and hence their application by practitioners.
- Research activities and resulting research reports rarely "excite the imagination."
- The research monies made available by federal and state agencies are "cornered" by universities and private research and development corporations.
- Research is too time-consuming and has very few "rewards" for most practitioners.

All of these concerns may have some basis in fact, as Goldman (1978), in his introduction to *Resarch Methods for Counselors*, wrote:

From 1969 to 1975 I was editor of the *Personnel and Guidance Journal*. I resolved from the beginning that we would publish only those articles that had something to say to counseling practitioners, that we were a reader's not a writer's journal. We found almost no research manuscripts during those years that satisfied that criterion;

quite a few research reports were received, especially in the earlier years, but almost every one of them either was so technical that it could not be truly understood except by very research-sophisticated people, or was so limited in its implications that it really had nothing to offer the practicing counselor.... I came to the realization that the problem was not "research" as a general idea but rather the *kinds* of research that have predominated in our field. I became convinced that the kinds of research methods and the kinds of research studies that prevail in the field are largely inappropriate or inadequate for most of the kinds of knowledge and insight counselors require in their daily work. (pp. 4–5)

Stockton and Hulse (1983) appropriately called attention to the fact that "Counseling is an applied discipline with an emphasis on practice; yet, if the profession does not assume responsibility for intellectual inquiry which might provide answers to basic questions concerning effective practice, the field cannot advance" (p. 303). In joining those calling for more "useable" research in our field, we would emphasize that research (a) can provide positive outcomes; (b) can be carried out by even beginning practitioners within a simple framework of research procedures; and (c) can be interesting.

Positive Outcomes of Research

For general practitioners in counseling and other helping professions, the most positive general outcome of "practitioner research" is the improvement of one's professional skills and understanding. Research can provide answers to professional questions, dilemmas, and failures. Research enables practitioners to become better at their "art." It can enable us to verify what works and what does not and, if pursued, why. It can eliminate much of the guesswork, "hunch," and uncertainty from practices. Engaging in practical research can increase our insights and deeper understandings of ourselves, our profession, and the relationships between the two. Our own research can help us as individual professionals become better at what we do.

Also, practitioner's research tends to focus on "local" problems or concerns and may therefore have opportunities to provide results that are immediately applicable. The opportunities to "make a positive difference" in one's job environment can be challenging. Furthermore, even if practitioners tend to focus on local concerns in their research activities, that still gives them the opportunities to make contributions to their profession; to exchange their ideas and findings with other similar local settings and other interested professionals. Presentations and discussions at local, state, and national conferences give the local researcher further opportunities to share findings, explore with other professionals the implications of the results, and possibly expand the interpretation of the research findings.

Finally, research can be interesting. Any new experience, learning of new knowledge, or finding an answer to an old problem can be stimulating. Research only becomes "dull" and meaningless to researchers when they investigate topics or problems that are to them dull and meaningless. Identify a professional question (problem or concern) that you would personally like answered and set out to find the answer. You may find it a surprisingly exciting quest, and you may then agree that research can be one of the most exciting and rewarding professional activities.

Some Definitions

Basic Research.   Basic research is concerned with or conducted solely for the purpose of theory development or the establishing of general principles. In educational and other settings, basic research provides the theory which, in turn, produces implications for solving problems.

Applied Research.   Applied research provides data to support theory through applying or testing the theory and evaluating its usefulness in problem solving.

Action Research.   Action research is designed to solve problems through the application of scientific method. For example:

> Action research provides a systematic framework in which the practicing counselor, therapist, or other professional in the helping field can solve problems and determine the effectiveness of his or her work. Action research provides a model for the evaluation of the effectiveness of an individual, a single program or a totality of guidance services (Goldman, 1978, p. 80).

Historical Research.
> Historical research involves studying, understanding, and explaining past events. The purpose of historical research is to arrive at conclusions concerning causes, effects, or trends of past occurrences which may help to explain present events and anticipate future events. (Gay. 1976, p. 9)

Galfo (1975) discussed four types of historical methods:

1. Cross-checking pieces of evidence against each other.
2. Establishing authorship of a document by comparative study.
3. Investigations of chronological events.
4. Word and language interpretation. (p. 15)

Descriptive Research.   Descriptive research seeks to test hypotheses or answer questions concerning the present. Three common types of descriptive studies are surveys, case studies, and comparative studies. (Galfo, 1975, p. 15)

Experimental Research.   Experimental research experiments with different variables in order to predict what will occur in the future under a given set of conditions.

> Experimental educational research has been derived from the laboratory method often used in the natural sciences. In its most elementary form, the experimental

method of science is based upon two assumptions regarding variables which may be identified in the phenomenon under investigation:

1. If two situations are equal in every respect except for a factor present in one of the situations, any difference which appears between the two situations can be attributed to the factor. This statement is referred to as the "law of the single variable."
2. If two situations are not equal but it can be demonstrated that none of the variables are significant in producing the phenomenon under investigation; or if significant variables are made equal, any difference occurring between the two situations after the introduction of a new variable to one of the systems can be attributed to the new variable. This statement is referred to as the "law of the only significant variable."

The purpose of establishing experimental-control conditions, thus, is to create a situation in which the effect of a single variable can be studied. (Galfo, 1975, pp. 17–18)

Pilot Study.   A pilot study is a preliminary trial of research methods and instruments before the development of the final research plan.

Hypotheses.   Hypotheses are predictions regarding the probable outcome of a research study which, in turn, form a basis for goals and procedures to achieve these goals.

Sampling.   Sampling is a research technique for selecting a specified number of people from a defined population as representative of that specific population.

The Research Process

Some research undoubtedly requires complex, sophisticated research skills. However, much valuable information can be obtained through research that meets the requirements of scientific inquiry but does not require a high level of research skill. In fact, "Elegance of design is not the ultimate test of the adequacy of research. The test is whether the objectives of the researcher are furthered and whether these objectives turn out to be useful." (Cramer, Herr, Morris, and Frantz, 1970, p. 2)

Thus, the following examination of research procedures is not intended to provide a basis for undertaking research, but rather to provide a better understanding of the basic factors involved in conducting research. It is hoped it will encourage practitioners to consider and become involved in relatively unsophisticated research investigations.

The first step in undertaking research is the identification of a researchable problem—a need for information. Whatever stimulates your interest or curiosity or arouses doubts in you may be a basis for the identification of a research problem. Most of us experience a constant and continuing need for information in our daily jobs. We wonder about the adequacy or effectiveness of our techniques, the various characteristics of our clients, and the nature of client needs. If we decide to initiate research in the area of techniques, we might simply seek to determine the kinds of information needed for justifying present practices or developing more effective and functional ones.

A second step in most research is to review or survey previous research and writings relevant to the possible research topic. The purposes of this review are (a) to see if adequate answers have already been found to the questions the researcher has in mind; (b) to gain a better understanding of the nature of the problem; and (c) to gain insights regarding approaches that might be used to efficiently attain the outcomes desired. Although in the past this particular step may have been one that discouraged many from considering research activities, the computer capacities of libraries with their various information retrieval systems enable even the neophyte researcher to have in hand, in a short period of time, a computerized printout of relevant research and writings, usually summarized for convenience.

The third step is to identify specifically the nature of the information desired, or to formulate the specific research problem. The problem should be stated fully and precisely in objective terminology in a complete grammatical sentence:

> One way to test your statement as a problem is to determine if it is written in such a way that anyone anywhere could read it, understand it, and react to it without the benefit of your presence. (Leedy, 1974, p. 49)

The beginning researcher should also be aware that within the main problem there may be logical subcomponents, identified as subproblems:

> By being solved separately these subproblems resolve the main problem piecemeal. By looking at the main problem through its subproblems, the researcher frequently gets a more global view of the problem. Think of a problem, therefore, in terms of its component subproblems. Rather than make a frontal attack upon the entire problem, divide and conquer it in small segments. (Leedy, 1974, p. 51)

The fourth step in the research process is to determine the kinds of information needed to permit sound conclusions about the issue (or issues) in question. In this step, the previously stated problem and related subproblems are now viewed through questions or logical constructs, called hypotheses. Hypotheses are assumptions made regarding the problem or its solution that provide the researcher with some direction for the gathering of facts that will provide the most valid answers. For example, a research investigation may be attempting to determine why a school has an unusually high dropout rate. It could be hypothesized that there are several possibilities for this dropout rate: (a) students are not interested in school; (b) students lack the ability to continue in school; (c) students are under economic pressure to leave school and obtain a job. Thus, each of these assumptions or hypotheses would provide some direction or basis for identifying facts, which would enable the investigator to determine factually why the majority of students are leaving school.

Having determined the kinds of information needed, in the fifth step, the researcher determines what procedures are most appropriate for collecting and analyzing the data. In this stage, the population or sample to be used and the means by which it is to be selected are determined, as are instruments and other data-collecting tools appropriate for the questions or hypotheses that have been stated. In this fifth step, the researcher seeks to determine the most appropriate sampling procedures and the most appropriate, efficient, and effective instruments or techniques for gathering the data needed in order to respond to the hypotheses as completely and as validly as possible.

Once the types of information and the procedures and instruments needed for collecting this information have been determined, the sixth step is the actual collection of the data.

In the seventh step, the collected data are systematically organized and analyzed. The method of data analysis should be determined before the collection of data in order to ensure that the suggested treatment is appropriate to the data collected and the manner in which it is organized. Depending upon the research design developed in step 5 of this sequence, the analysis may be no more than a simple mathematical or elementary statistical one.

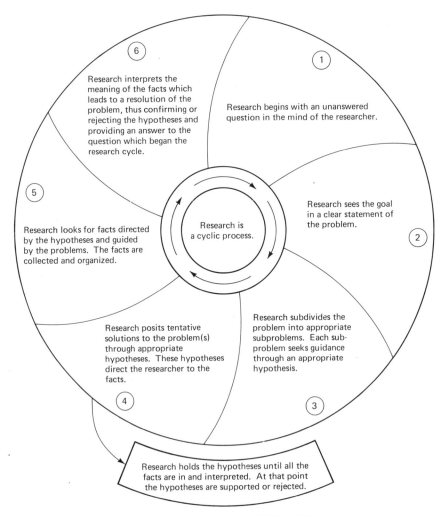

6 Research interprets the meaning of the facts which leads to a resolution of the problem, thus confirming or rejecting the hypotheses and providing an answer to the question which began the research cycle.

1 Research begins with an unanswered question in the mind of the researcher.

5 Research looks for facts directed by the hypotheses and guided by the problems. The facts are collected and organized.

Research is a cyclic process.

Research sees the goal in a clear statement of the problem.

2

4 Research posits tentative solutions to the problem(s) through appropriate hypotheses. These hypotheses direct the researcher to the facts.

3 Research subdivides the problem into appropriate subproblems. Each subproblem seeks guidance through an appropriate hypothesis.

Research holds the hypotheses until all the facts are in and interpreted. At that point the hypotheses are supported or rejected.

Figure 13-1. The research process. *(Leedy, 1974, p. 8.)*

Beginning practitioners can still engage profitably in research activities by simply recognizing their limitations in the design of their study. In the final step, the research findings are interpreted and conclusions drawn, which may lead to resolving or answering the problems. Here the previously stated hypotheses are either confirmed or rejected and answers are provided to the questions that initiated the research activity.

Figure 13–1 depicts the research process.

Summary

Accountability, evaluation, and research are all responsibilties of counseling programs and counselors in any setting. Although each is a distinct activity in its own right, the interrelationships are evident, since all can lead to program improvement. Furthermore, all three activities hold promise for the advancement of the professional and the profession. Accountability provides a model or method for the assessment of professional achievements. Evaluation enables one to gather evidence regarding the quality of a program's performance. Research enables one to advance the scientific knowledge in a field.

Whether our profession of counseling advances and achieves noble goals will not depend on the writers of textbooks, past and present, but on you, our readers, who will represent our profession in the future. You *are* our future. We wish you well!

References

American Association of School Administrators National Academy for School Executives. (1973). *An administrator's handbook on educational accountability.* Arlington, VA: Author.

Baker, S. B. (1977). An argument for constructive accountability. *Personnel and Guidance Journal, 56,* 53–55.

Biegel, D. E., & Naparstek, A. J. (Eds.). (1982). *Community support systems and mental health.* New York: Springer.

Cramer, S. H., Herr, E. L., Morris, C. N., & Frantz, T. T. (1970). *Research and the school counselor.* Boston: Houghton Mifflin.

Galfo, A. J. (1975) *Interpreting educational research* (3rd ed.). Dubuque, IA: William C. Brown.

Gay, L. R. (1976). *Educational research: Competencies for analysis and application* (2nd ed.). Columbus, OH: Charles E. Merrill.

Gibson, R. L. (1977). *Counseling and annual guidance committee report.* Unpublished manuscript, North Central Association of Colleges and Schools.

Goldman. L. (Ed.). (1978). *Research methods for counselors.* New York: John Wiley & Sons.

Hagedorn, H. J., Beck, K. J., Neubert, S. F., & Werlin, S. H. (1976). *Working manual of simple program evaluation techniques for community mental health centers.* Rockville, MD: Arthur D. Little (for National Institute of Mental Health).

Jeger, A M., & Slotnick, R. S. (1982). *Community mental health and behavioral ecology: A handbook of theory, research and practice.* New York: Plenum.

Krumboltz, J. D. (1974). An accountability model for counselors. *Personnel and Guidance Journal, 52,* 639–646.

Leedy, P. D. (1974). *Practical research: Planning and design.* (2nd ed.). New York: Macmillan.

Lessinger, L., et al. (1973). *Accountability: Systems planning in education.* Homewood, IL: ETC.

Lewis, J. A., & Lewis, M. D. (1983). *Community counseling: A human services approach* (2nd ed.). New York: John Wiley & Sons.

Mitchell, M. H. (1976). *Advancing the counseling profession through evaluation.* Unpublished manuscript; Indiana University, Annual Counseling and Guidance Workship.

National Institute of Mental Health. (1976). *A working manual of simple program evaluation techniques for community mental health centers.* Washington, D.C.: U.S. Department of Health, Education and Welfare.

Oetting, E. R., & Hawkes, F. J. (1974). Training professionals for evaluative research. *Personnel and Guidance Journal, 52,* 434–438.

Rappaport, J. (1977). *Community psychology: Values, research and action.* New York: Holt, Rinehart & Winston.

Stockton, R. & Hulse, D. (1983) The use of research teams to enhance competence in counseling research. *Counselor Education and Supervision, 22* (4), 303–310.

Stufflebeam, D. L., Foley, W. J., Gephart, W. J., Guba, E. G., Hammond, R. L., Merriman, H. O., & Provos, N. M. (Phi Delta Kappa National Study Committee on Evaluation). (1971). *Educational evaluation and decision making.* Itasca, IL: F. E. Peacock.

Worthen, B. R., & Sanders, J. R. (1973). *Educational Evaluation: Theory and practice.* Worthington, OH: Charles A. Jones.

Wysong, H. E. (1972). Accountability: Foiled fable or solution? *Impact, 2,* 33.

APPENDICES

A. The Practice of Guidance and Counseling by School Counselors—ASCA Role Statement

B. Ethical Standards—American Association for Counseling and Development

C. Ethical Principles of Psychologists—American Psychological Association

D. Protection of the Rights and Privacy of Parents and Students—Family Education Rights and Privacy Act of 1974

E. The Role of the School Counselor in Career Guidance: Expectations and Responsibilities—ASCA Role Statement

F. Responsibilities of Users of Standardized Tests—APGA Policy Statement

G. Code of Ethics for Certified Clinical Mental Health Counselors—National Academy of Certified Clinical Mental Health Counselors

H. Code of Professional Ethics—American Association for Marriage and Family Therapy

I. Specialty Guidelines for the Delivery of Services by Counseling Psychologists

APPENDIX

THE PRACTICE OF GUIDANCE AND COUNSELING BY SCHOOL COUNSELORS

ASCA Role Statement

The following role statement is an incorporation and revision of four role statements prepared separately in the 70s. "The Unique Role of the Elementary School Counselor" was originally published in Elementary School Guidance and Counseling, *Volume 8, No. 3, March 1974. It was revised and the revision, approved in August 1977 by the ASCA Governing Board, was printed in* Elementary School Guidance and Counseling, *Volume 12, No. 3, February 1978. "The Role of the Middle/Junior High School Counselor" was circulated separately in photocopy form by ASCA. "The Role of the Secondary School Counselor" first appeared in* School Counselor, *Volume 21, No. 5, May 1974; the revision, formulated by the 1976–77 ASCA Governing Board, was printed in the March 1977* School Counselor *(Volume 24, No. 4). "The Role and Function of Postsecondary Counseling" first appeared in* School Counselor, *Volume 21, No. 5, May 1974.*

The present version, incorporating all four role statements, was prepared in October 1980 by G. Dean Miller upon invitation from ASCA officers J. Thompson, H. Washburn, and J. Terrill, The role statement as it appears below was approved by the 1980–81 ASCA Governing Board in January 1981.

Reprinted with permission from the American School Counselors Association.

Professional Rationale

The national association believes that the professional identity of the school counselor is derived from a unique preparation, grounded in the behavioral sciences, with training in clinical skills adapted to the school setting. This statement attempts to identify and clarify the role of the school counselor who functions at various educational levels in United States society. The different educational levels (elementary, middle or junior high, secondary, and postsecondary) approximates the different steps of developmental growth from childhood through adolescence to adulthood. Therefore, the focus of school counselors serving different school levels is differentiated by the developmental tasks necessary for the different stages of growth the students confront going through school. This statement also commits to public records certain professional responsibilities fo school counselors and identifies a set of philosophic assumptions about the conditions under which important psychological growth occurs in the practice of guidance and counseling.

It is understood that schools in all societies are concerned with transmission of cultural heritage and socialization of the youth. Career socialization is recognized as a very important aspect of ths process. In the United States, schools are concerned about the individual student, and it is through the concept of guidance that efforts are directed toward personalizing the school experience in a developmental way.

Counselors as developmental facilitators function as school-based members of student support-services teams that include staff members from other helping professions such as school psychology, social work, and nursing. These staff, depending upon their student-staff ratios and serivce orientation, may also function in a specialized remedial way to assist with problem areas and—beginning with the very young—join counselors to intervene in a developmental way to foster psychological growth and thereby attempt collectively to prevent the costly, hard-to-change negative behavior characteristics that often begin to take form and retard growth by the middle elementary school grades.

Counselors believe that students achieve and grow in positive ways when competencies develop and the home and school strive both separately and together to establish supportive interpersonal relationships and maintain healthy environments. Counseling and guidance is an integral function in the school that is maximized when counselors provide counsultation and in-service programs for staff regarding the incorporation of developmental psychology into the curriculum. They also provide parents with additional understanding of child and adolescent development in order to strengthen the role of parents in the promotion of growth in children. Individual and small group counseling is provided to complement indirect helping through parents and teachers. Important direct interaction with students, however, is provided through a developmentally oriented guidance curriculum. Counselor interventions, regardless of their conceptual origin, aim to serve the needs of students who are expected to function in school settings in the various educational, vocational, and personal-social domains. As the student progresses through the different school levels, assistance with processing informaton, problem solving, and decision making is increased in proportion to the developmental demands made upon students and their ability to conceptualize and assume responsibility for the consequences of their behavior.

The validation of new knowledge from the behavioral sciences along with social and economic changes in society impact the role of the counselor and other members of the school staff.

Through study and retraining, the effective practicing counselor—regardless of the educational level of the students serviced—continues to be informed and competently skilled throughout the professional career.

The Nature of the Helping Process

To accommodate students at different educational levels, the organizing and specifying of various guidance programs across the life span calls for an awareness of the developmental needs identified in the pscyhology of children, adolescents, and adults. The clinical skills and knowledge base of the counselor is most effectively used if effort is directed in an organized way toward making the school, the teachers, and the curriculum sensitive to those aspects of personal development most associated with life success. Because of its association with life success the cognitive-developmental stages of psychological maturity deserve highest recognition in conceptualizing the major thrust of guidance interventions for the different educational levels. Such interventions aim to do more than inform students about problems they will face: The purpose is to promote through education important life success qualities (development of competencies, ego maturity, moral reasoning, and so forth). Counselors performing under this theoretical orientation will tend to emphasize certain interventions, no matter what the level of the educational setting—elementary, middle or junior high, secondary, or postsecondary. Major functions performed by such school counselors include the following:

- Structured developmental guidance experiences presented systematically through groups (including classrooms) to promote growth of psychological aspects of human development (e.g., ego, career, emotional, moral, and social development). Such interventions can logically become an integral part of such curriculum areas as social studies, language arts, health, or home economics. Individual or small group counseling is provided when the needs deserve more attention or privacy.
- Consultation with and in-service training for teachers to increase their communication skills, improve the quality of their interaction

with all students, and make them more sensitive to the need for matching the curriculum to developmental needs of students.

- Consultation and life-skills education for parents to assist them to understand developmental psychology, to improve family communication skills, and to develop strategies for encouraging learning in their children.

As noted above, counselors serving different school populations function differently, due primarily to the variations in the developmental stages of the students and the organization of the school. Some of the major level differences in functions include the following.

Elementary School Counselors

- Provide in-service training to teachers to assist them with planning and implementing guidance interventions for young children (preschool to 3rd grade) in order to maximize developmental benefits (self-esteem, personal relationships, positive school attitude, sex-fair choices, and so forth) in the hope of preventing serious problems or minimizing the size of such problems, if and when they do occur.
- Provide consultations for teachers who need understanding and assistance with incorporating developmental concepts in teaching content as well as support for building a healthy classroom environment.
- Accommodate parents who need assistance with understanding normal child growth and development; improving family communication skills; or understanding their role in encouraging their child to learn.
- Cooperate with other school staff in the early identification, remediation, or referral of children with developmental deficiencies or handicaps.
- As children reach the upper elementary grades, effort is directed through the curriculum toward increasing student awareness of the relationship between school and work, especially the impact of educational choices on one's life-style and career development.

Middle or Junior High Counselors

- Concentrate efforts (through group guidance, peer facilitators, and teacher in-service training) to smooth the transition for students from the more confining environment of the lower school to the middle or junior high school where students are expected to assume greater responsibility for their own learning and personal development.
- Identify, encourage, and support teachers (through in-service training, consultation, and co-teaching) who are interested in incorporating developmental units in such curriculum areas as English, Social Studies, Health, and Home Economics.
- Organize and implement a career guidance program for students that includes an assessment of their career maturity and career-planning status; easy access to relevant career information; and assistance with processing data for personal use in school-work related decision making.

Secondary Counselors

- Organize and implement through interested teachers guidance curricula interventions that focus upon important developmental concerns of adolescents (identity, career choice and planning, social relationships, and so forth).
- Organize and make available comprehensive information systems (print, computer-based, audio-visual) necessary for educational-vocational planning and decision making.
- Assist students with assessment of personal characteristics (e.g., competencies, interests, aptitudes, needs, career maturity) for personal use in such areas as course selection, post-high-school planning, and career choices.
- Provide remedial interventions or alternative programs for those students showing in-school adjustment problems, vocational immaturity, or general negative attitudes toward personal growth.

Postsecondary Counselors

- Participate in a comprehensive program of student support serivces to facilitate the meeting of transitional needs throughout adulthood (orientation activities; academic, personal, and career counseling; financial aids; independent living; job placement, career development; geriatric concerns; and so forth).
- Through individual and cooperative efforts

with other staff, offer students the opportunity to participate in deliberate psychological education that fosters maturity in such areas as ego development, moral reasoning, career development, and emotional aspects of personal relationships.

- To accommodate students with varying maturity and ability levels, provide differential assistance to help students identify and use school and community-based opportunities (internships, independent study, and travel) in order to crystalize vocational choice and career plans (e.g., choice of major, choice of vocation, lifestyle, and work values).

Professional Commitment of School Counselors

The counselor, as a school-based practitioner, is bound in relationship with others to certain practices. These counseling and guidance relationships are based on the following principles:

- It is the counselor's obligation to respect the integrity of the individual and promote the growth and development (or adjustment) of the student receiving assistance.
- Before entering any counseling relationship, the individual should be informed of the conditions under which assistance may be provided.
- The counseling relationship and information resulting from it must be kept confidential in accordance with the rights of the individual and the obligations of the counselor as a professional.
- Counselors reserve the right to consult with other competent professionals about the individual. Should the individual's condition endanger the health, welfare, or safety of self or others, the counselor is expected, in such instances, to refer the counselee to another appropriate professional person.
- Counselors shall decline to initiate or shall terminate a counseling relationship when other services could best meet the client's needs. Counselors shall refer the client to such services.

Commitment to Students

- The counselor recognizes that each student has basic human rights and is entitled to just treatment regardless of race, sex, religious preference, handicapping condition, or cultural differences.
- The counselor is available to all to provide assistance with personal understanding and use of opportunities, especially those available in the school setting.
- The counselor assumes that both cognition and perception influence behavior and the valuation process.
- The counselor in the helping relationship creates an atmostphere in which mutual respect, understanding, and confidence prevails in the hope that growth occurs and concerns are resolved.

Commitment to Parents

- The counselor recognizes that parents are the first teachers of their children and in this regard have a profound influence upon human development.
- Parents are entitled to basic human rights and their facilitative-supportive relationship to learning is recognized in the educational partnership that embraces the home and school.
- To capitalize upon the influence of parents in the educational process, the counselor involves them at strategic periods and events in order to maximinize the student's response to opportunities provided by the school.

Commitment to Teachers

- The counselor acknowledges that teachers, in creating positive, interactive relationships with students, provide the primary basis for intellectual, emotional, and social growth in the school.
- The counselor, in the consulting relationship, endeavors to acquaint teachers with applications of various theories of learning and human growth in order that a good match occurs between curriculum interventions and student developmental needs.
- The counselor recognizes that teachers need support and assistance in dealing with the normal problems of student growth and adjust-

ment, especially during the period of adolescence.

Commitment to Administrators

- The counselor acknowledges that the school administrator plays the major role in providing the support necessary for implementing and maintaining an organized team approach to guidance in the school. The counselor depends upon the school administration to support the elimination of unnecessary clerical work and other activities that detract from program delivery and counseling.
- The counselor, in recognizing the importance of the administrator's contribution, develops a close working relationship with the administrator and provides technical assistance so that appropriate assessment, planning, implementation, and evaluation occur relative to the guidance needs of the students.
- In identifying the counselor's responsibility in implementing an organized guidance program, legislative mandates and professional ethics must be taken into consideration in matters dealing with confidentiality and privileged communication as well as what duties constitute good professional practice.

Commitment to Others in the Community

- The counselor is aware that others in the community play a significant role in the overall development of children and youth.
- To capitalize upon the above contributions, the counselor maintains an ongoing set of liaison relationships with various individuals and agencies in an effort to coordinate programs and services on behalf of students in the school and those in transition status between school and some other institution.
- Ongoing relationships are formed on the premise that cooperative efforts are in the best interest of the individuals concerned when personal information is treated in an ethical manner.

The Counselor's Responsibility to the Profession

To assure good practice and continued growth in knowledge and skills for the benefit of students, parents, and teachers, as well as the profession, the counselor:

- Has an understanding of his or her own personal characteristics and their effect on counseling-consulting relationships.
- Is aware of his or her level of professional competence and represents it accurately to others.
- Is well informed on current theories and research that have impact-potential upon professional practice.
- Uses time and skills in an organized systematic way to help students and resists any effort aimed at unreasonable use of time for nonguidance activities.
- Continues to develop professional competence and maintains an awareness of contemporary trends in the field as well as influences from the world at large.
- Fosters the development and improvement of the profession by assisting with appropriate research and participating in professional association activities at local, state, and national levels.
- Discusses with professional associates (teachers, administrators, and other support staff) practices that may be implemented to strengthen and improve standards or the conditions for helping.
- Maintains constant efforts to adhere to strict confidentiality of information concerning individuals and releases such information only with the signature of the student, parent, or guardian.
- Is guided by sound ethical practices for professional counselors as embodied in the *Ethical Standards* of the American Personnel and Guidance Association—American School Counselor Assoication.
- Becomes an active member of American School Counselor Association and state and local counselor associations in order to enhance personal and professional growth.

APPENDIX B

ETHICAL STANDARDS

American Association for Counseling and Development

(Approved by Executive Committee upon referral of the Board of Directors, January 17, 1981.)

Preamble

The American Personnel and Guidance Association is an educational, scientific, and professional organization whose members are dedicated to the enhancement of the worth, dignity, potential, and uniqueness of each individual and thus to the service of society.

The Association recognizes that the role definitions and work settings of its members include a wide variety of academic disciplines, levels of academic preparation and agency services. This diversity reflects the breadth of the Association's interest and influence. It also poses challenging complexities in efforts to set standards for the performance of members, desired requisite preparation or practice, and supporting social, legal, and ethical controls.

The specification of ethical standards enables the Association to clarify to present and future members and to those served by members, the nature of ethical responsibilities held in common by its members.

The existence of such standards serves to stimulate greater concern by members for their own

Ethical Standards (revised), by the American Personnel and Guidance Association (since July 1, 1983, American Association for Counseling and Development). Copyright 1981 by the American Personnel and Guidance Association. Reprinted by permission of the American Association for Counseling and Development.

professional functioning and for the conduct of fellow professionals such as counselors, guidance and student personnel workers, and others in the helping professions. As the ethical code of the Association, this document establishes principles that define the ethical behavior of Association members.

Section A: General

1. The member influences the development of the profession by continuous efforts to improve professional practices, teaching, services, and research. Professional growth is continuous throughout the member's career and is exemplified by the development of a philosophy that explains why and how a member functions in the helping relationship. Members must gather data on their effectiveness and be guided by the findings.

2. The member has a responsibility both to the individual who is served and to the institution within which the service is performed to maintain high standards of professional conduct. The member strives to maintain the highest levels of professional services offered to the individuals to be served. The member also strives to assist the agency, organization, or institution in providing the highest caliber of professional services. The acceptance of employment in an institution implies that the member is in agreement with the general policies and principles of the institution. Therefore the professional activities of the member are also in accord with the objectives of the

institution. If, despite concerted efforts, the member cannot reach agreement with the employer as to acceptable standards of conduct that allow for changes in institutional policy conducive to the positive growth and development of clients, then terminating the affiliation should be seriously considered.

3. Ethical behavior among professional associates, both members and nonmembers, must be expected at all times. When information is possessed that raises doubt as to the ethical behavior of professional colleagues, whether Association members or not, the members must take action to attempt to rectify such a condition. Such action shall use the institution's channels first and then use procedures established by the state Branch, Division, or Association.

4. The member neither claims nor implies professional qualifications exceeding those possessed and is responsible for correcting any misrepresentations of these qualifications by others.

5. In establishing fees for professional counseling services, members must consider the financial status of clients and locality. In the event that the established fee structure is inappropriate for a client, assistance must be provided in finding comparable services of acceptable cost.

6. When members provide information to the public or to subordinates, peers or supervisors, they have a responsibility to ensure that the content is general, unidentified client information that is accurate, unbiased, and consists of objective, factual data.

7. With regard to the delivery of professional services, members should accept only those positions for which they are professionally qualified.

8. In the counseling relationship the counselor is aware of the intimacy of the relationship and maintains respect for the client and avoids engaging in activities that seek to meet the counselor's personal needs at the expense of that client. Through awareness of the negative impact of both racial and sexual stereotyping and discrimination, the counselor guards the individual rights and personal dignity of the client in the counseling relationship.

Section B: Counseling Relationship

This section refers to practices and procedures of individual and/or group counseling relationships.

The member must recognize the need for client freedom of choice. Under those circumstances where this is not possible, the member must apprise clients of restrictions that may limit their freedom of choice.

1. The member's *primary* obligation is to respect the integrity and promote the welfare of the client(s), whether the client(s) is (are) assisted individually or in a group relationship. In a group setting, the member is also responsible for taking reasonable precautions to protect individuals from physical and/or psychological trauma resulting from interaction within the group.

2. The counseling relationship and information resulting therefrom [must] be kept confidential, consistent with the obligations of the member as a professional person. In a group counseling setting, the counselor must set a norm of confidentiality regarding all group participants' disclosures.

3. If an individual is already in a counseling relationship with another professional person, the member does not enter into a counseling relationship without first contacting and receiving the approval of that other professional. If the member discovers that the client is in another counseling relationship after the counseling relationship begins, the member must gain the consent of the other professional or terminate the relationship, unless the client elects to terminate the other relationship.

4. When the client's condition indicates that there is clear and imminent danger to the client or others, the member must take reasonable personal action or inform responsible authorities. Consultation with other professionals must be used where possible. The assumption of responsibility for the client's behavior must be taken only after careful deliberation. The client must be involved in the resumption of responsibility as quickly as possible.

5. Records of the counseling relationship, including interview notes, test data, correspondence, tape recordings, and other documents, are to be considered professional information for use in counseling and they should not be considered a part of the records of the institution or agency in which the counselor is employed unless specified by state statute or regulation. Revelation to others of counseling material must occur only upon the expressed consent of the client.

6. Use of data derived from a counseing relationship for purposes of counselor training or research shall be confined to content that can be disguised to ensure full protection of the identity of the subject client.

7. The member must inform the client of the purposes, goals, techniques, rules of procedure and limitations that may affect the relationship at or before the time that the counseling relationship is entered.

8. The member must screen prospective group participants, especially when the emphasis is on self-understanding and growth through self-disclosure. The member must maintain an awareness of the group participants' compatibility throughout the life of the group.

9. The member may choose to consult with any other professionally competent person about a client. In choosing a consultant, the member must avoid placing the consultant in a conflict of interest situation that would preclude the consultant's being a proper party to the member's efforts to help the client.

10. If the member determines an inability to be of professional assistance to the client, the member must either avoid initiating the counseling relationship or immediately terminate that relationship. In either event, the member must suggest appropriate alternatives. (The member must be knowledgeable about referral resources so that a satisfactory referral can be initiated.) In the event the client declines the suggested referral, the member is not obligated to continue the relationship.

11. When the member has other relationships, particularly of an administrative, supervisory and/or evaluative nature with an individual seeking counseling services, the member must not serve as the counselor but should refer the individual to another professional. Only in instances where such an alternative is unavailable and where the individual's situation warrants counseling intervention should the member enter into and/or maintain a counseling relationship. Dual relationships with clients that might impair the member's objectivity and professional judgment (e.g., as with close friends or relatives, sexual intimacies with any client) must be avoided and/or the counseling relationship terminated through referral to another competent professional.

12. All experimental methods of treatment must be clearly indicated to prospective recipients and safety precautions are to be adhered to by the member.

13. When the member is engaged in short-term group treatment/training programs (e.g., marathons and other encounter-type or growth groups), the member ensures that there is professional assistance available during and following the group experience.

14. Should the member be engaged in a work setting that calls for any variation from the above statements, the member is obligated to consult with other professionals whenever possible to consider justifiable alternatives.

Section C: Measurement and Evaluation

The primary purpose of educational and psychological testing is to provide descriptive measures that are objective and interpretable in either comparative or absolute terms. The member must recognize the need to interpret the statements that follow as applying to the whole range of appraisal techniques including test and non-test data. Test results constitute only one of a variety of pertinent sources of information for personnel, guidance, and counseling decisions.

1. The member must provide specific orientation or information to the examinee(s) prior to and following the test administration so that the results of testing may be placed in proper perspective with other relevant factors. In so doing, the member must recognize

the effects of socioeconomic, ethnic and cultural factors on test scores. It is the member's professional responsibility to use additional unvalidated information carefully in modifying interpretation of the test results.

2. In selecting tests for use in a given situation or with a particular client, the member must consider carefully the specific validity, reliability, and appropriateness of the test(s). *General* validity, reliability and the like may be questioned legally as well as ethically when tests are used for vocational and educational selection, placement, or counseling.

3. When making any statements to the public about tests and testing, the member must give accurate information and avoid false claims or misconceptions. Special efforts are often required to avoid unwarranted connotations of such terms as *IQ* and *grade equivalent scores.*

4. Different tests demand different levels of competence for administration, scoring, and interpretation. Members must recognize the limits of their competence and perform only those functions for which they are prepared.

5. Tests must be administered under the same conditions that were established in their standardization. When tests are not administered under standard conditions or when unusual behavior or irregularities occur during the testing session, those conditions must be noted and the results designated as invalid or of questionable validity. Unsupervised or inadequately supervised test-taking, such as the use of tests through the mails, is considered unethical. On the other hand, the use of instruments that are so designed or standardized to be self-administered and self-scored, such as interest inventories, is to be encouraged.

6. The meaningfulness of test results used in personnel, guidance, and counseling functions generally depends on the examinee's unfamiliarity with the specific items on the test. Any prior coaching or dissemination of the test materials can invalidate test results. Therefore, test security is one of the professional obligations of the member. Conditions that produce most favorable test results must be made known to the examinee.

7. The purpose of testing and the explicit use of the results must be made known to the examinee prior to testing. The counselor must ensure that instrument limitations are not exceeded and that periodic review and/or retesting are made to prevent client sterotyping.

8. The examinee's welfare and explicit prior understanding must be the criteria for determining the recipients of the test results. The member must see that specific interpretation accompanies any release of individual or group test data. The interpretation of test data must be related to the examinee's particular concerns.

9. The member must be cautious when interpreting the results of research instruments possessing insufficient technical data. The specific purpose for the use of such instruments must be stated explicitly to examinees.

10. The member must proceed with caution when attempting to evaluate and interpret the performance of minority group members or other persons who are not represented in the norm group on which the instrument was standardized.

11. The member must guard against the appropriation, reproduction, or modifications of published tests or parts thereof without acknowledgement and permission from the previous publisher.

12. Regarding the preparation, publication and distribution of tests, reference should be made to:
    a. *Standards for Educational and Psychological Tests and Manuals,* revised edition, 1974, published by the American Psychological Association on behalf of itself, the American Educational Research Association and the National Council on Measurement in Education.
    b. The responsible use of test: A position paper of AMEG, APGA, and NCME. *Measurement and Evaluation in Guidance,* 1972, 5, 385–388.
    c. "Responsibilities of Users of Standardized Tests," APGA, *Guidepost,* October 5, 1978, pp. 5–8.

Section D: Research and Publication

1. Guidelines on research with human subjects shall be adhered to, such as:

a. *Ethical Principles in the Conduct of Research with Human Participants.* Washington. D.C.: American Psychological Association, Inc., 1973.

b. Code of Federal Regulations, Title 45, Subtitle A, Part 46, as currently issued.

2. In planning any research activity dealing with human subjects, the member must be aware of and responsive to all pertinent ethical principles and ensure that the research problem, design, and execution are in full compliance with them.

3. Responsibility for ethical research practice lies with the principal researcher, while others involved in the research activities share ethical obligation and full responsibility for their own actions.

4. In research with human subjects, researchers are responsible for the subjects' welfare throughout the experiment and they must take all reasonable precautions to avoid causing injurious psychological, physical, or social effects on their subjects.

5. All research subjects must be informed of the purpose of the study except when withholding information or providing misinformation to them is essential to the investigation. In such research the member must be responsible for corrective action as soon as possible following completion of the research.

6. Participation in research must be voluntary. Involuntary participation is appropriate only when it can be demonstrated that participation will have no harmful effects on subjects and is essential to the investigation.

7. When reporting research results, explicit mention must be made of all variables and conditions known to the investigator that might affect the outcome of the investigation or the interpretation of the data.

8. The member must be responsible for conducting and reporting investigations in a manner that minimizes the possibility that results will be misleading.

9. The member has an obligation to make available sufficient original research data to qualified others who may wish to replicate the study.

10. When supplying data, aiding in the research of another person, reporting research results, or in making original data available, due care must be taken to disguise the identity of the subjects in the absence of specific authorization from such subjects to do otherwise.

11. When conducting and reporting research, the member must be familiar with, and give recognition to, previous work on the topic, as well as to observe all copyright laws and follow the principles of giving full credit to all to whom credit it due.

12. The member must give due credit through joint authorship, acknowledgment, footnote statements, or other appropriate means to those who have contributed significantly to the research and/or publication, in accordance with such contributions.

13. The member must communicate to other members the results of any research judged to be of professional or scientific value. Results reflecting unfavorably on institutions, programs, services, or vested interests must not be withheld for such reasons.

14. If members agree to cooperate with another individual in research and/or publication, they incur an obligation to cooperate as promised in terms of punctuality of performance and with full regard to the completeness and accuracy of the information required.

15. Ethical practice requires that authors not submit the same manuscript or one essentially similar in content, for simultaneous publication consideration by two or more journals. In addition, manuscripts published in whole or in substantial part in another journal or published work should not be submitted for publication without acknowledgment and permission from the previous publication.

Section E: Consulting

Consultation refers to a voluntary relationship between a professional helper and help-needing individual, group or social unit in which the consultant is providing help to the client(s) in defining and solving a work-related problem or potential problem with a client or client system. (This definition is adapted from Kurpius, DeWayne. Consultation theory and process: An integrated model. *Personnel and Guidance Journal,* 1978, 56.)

1. The member acting as consultant must have a

high degree of self-awareness of his-her own values, knowledge, skills, limitations, and needs in entering a helping relationship that involves human and-or organizational change and that the focus of the relationship be on the issues to be resolved and not on the person(s) presenting the problem.

2. There must be understanding and agreement between member and client for the problem definition, change goals, and predicated consequences of interventions selected.

3. The member must be reasonably certain that she/he or the organization represented has the necessary competencies and resources for giving the kind of help that is needed now or may develop later and that appropriate referral resources are available to the consultant.

4. The consulting relationship must be one in which client adaptability and growth toward self-direction are encouraged and cultivated. The member must maintain this role consistently and not become a decision maker for the client or create a future dependency on the consultant.

5. When announcing consultant availability for services, the member conscientiously adheres to the Association's *Ethical Standards*.

6. The member must refuse a private fee or other remuneration for consultation with persons who are entitled to these services through the member's employing institution or agency. The policies of a particular agency may make explicit provisions for private practice with agency clients by members of its staff. In such instances, the clients must be apprised of other options open to them should they seek private counseling services.

Section F: Private Practice

1. The member should assist the profession by facilitating the availability of counseling services in private as well as public settings.

2. In advertising services as a private practitioner, the member must advertise the services in such a manner so as to accurately inform the public as to services, expertise, profession, and techniques of counseling in a professional manner. A member who assumes an executive leadership role in the organization shall not permit his/her name to be used in professional notices during periods when not actively engaged in the private practice of counseling.

The member may list the following: highest relevant degree, type and level of certification or license, type and/or description of services, and other relevant information. Such information must not contain false, inaccurate, misleading, partial, out-of-context, or deceptive material or statements.

3. Members may join in partnership/corporation with other members and-or other professionals provided that each member of the partnership or corporation makes clear the separate specialties by name in compliance with the regulations of the locality.

4. A member has an obligation to withdraw from a counseling relationship if it is believed that employment will result in violation of the *Ethical Standards*. If the mental or physical condition of the member renders it difficult to carry out an effective professional relationship or if the member is discharged by the client because the counseling relationship is no longer productive for the client, then the member is obligated to terminate the counseling relationship.

5. A member must adhere to the regulations for private practice of the locality where the services are offered.

6. It is unethical to use one's institutional affiliation to recruit clients for one's private practice.

Section G: Personnel Administration

It is recognized that most members are employed in public or quasi-public institutions. The functioning of a member within an institution must contribute to the goals of the institution and vice versa if either is to accomplish their respective goals or objectives. It is therefore essential that the member and the institution function in ways to (a) make the institution's goals explicit and public; (b) make the member's contribution to institutional goals specific; and (c) foster mutual accountability for goal achievement.

To accomplish these objectives, it is recognized that the member and the employer must share responsibilities in the formulation and implementation of personnel policies.

1. Members must define and describe the parameters and levels of their professional competency.
2. Members must establish interpersonal relations and working agreements with supervisors and subordinates regarding counseling or clinical relationships, confidentiality, distinction between public and private material, maintenance, and dissemination of recorded information, work load and accountability. Working agreements in each instance must be specified and made known to those concerned.
3. Members must alert their employers to conditions that may be potentially disruptive or damaging.
4. Members must inform employers of conditions that may limit their effectiveness.
5. Members must submit regularly to professional review and evaluation.
6. Members must be responsible for inservice development of self and-or staff.
7. Members must inform their staff of goals and programs.
8. Members must provide personnel practices that guarantee and enhance the rights and welfare of each recipient of their service.
9. Members must select competent persons and assign responsibilities compatible with their skills and experiences.

Section H: Preparation Standards

Members who are responsible for training others must be guided by the preparation standards of the Association and relevant Divisions(s). The member who functions in the capacity of trainer assumes unique ethical responsibilities that frequently go beyond that of the member who does not function in a training capacity. These ethical responsibilities are outlined as follows:

1. Members must orient students to program expectations, basic skills development, and employment prospects prior to admission to the program.
2. Members in charge of learning experiences must establish programs that integrate academic study and supervised practice.
3. Members must establish a program directed toward developing students' skills, knowledge, and self-understanding, stated whenever possible in competency or performance terms.
4. Members must identify the levels of competencies of their students in compliance with relevant Divison standards. These competencies must accommodate the para-professional as well as the professional.
5. Members, through continual student evaluation and appraisal, must be aware of the personal limitations of the learner that might impede future performance. The instructor must not only assist the learner in securing remedial assistance but also screen from the program those individuals who are unable to provide competent services.
6. Members must provide a program that includes training in research commensurate with levels of role functioning. Para-professional and technician-level personnel must be trained as consumers of research. In addition, these personnel must learn how to evalute their own and their program's effectiveness. Graduate training, especially at the doctoral level, would include preparation for original research by the member.
7. Members must make students aware of the ethical responsibilities and standards of the profession.
8. Preparatory programs must encourage students to value the ideals of service to individuals and to society. In this regard, direct financial remuneration or lack thereof must not influence the quality of service rendered. Monetary considerations must not be allowed to overshadow professional and humanitarian needs.
9. Members responsible for educational programs must be skilled as teachers and practitioners.
10. Members must represent thoroughly varied theoretical positions so that students may make comparisons and have the opportunity to select a position.
11. Members must develop clear policies within their educational institutions regarding field placement and the roles of the student and the instructor in such placements.
12. Members must ensure that forms of learning

focusing on self-understanding or growth are voluntary, or if required as part of the education program, are made known to prospective students prior to entering the program. When the education program offers a growth experience with an emphasis on self-disclosure or other relatively intimate or personal involvement, the member must have no administrative, supervisory, or evaluating authority regarding the participant.

13. Members must conduct an educational program in keeping with the current relevant guidelines of the American Personnel and Guidance Association and its Divisions.

APPENDIX C

ETHICAL PRINCIPLES OF PSYCHOLOGISTS

American Psychological Association

Preamble

Psychologists respect the dignity and worth of the individual and strive for the preservation and protection of fundamental human rights. They are committed to increasing knowledge of human behavior and of people's understanding of themselves and others and to the utilization of such knowledge for the promotion of human welfare. While pursuing these objectives, they make every effort to protect the welfare of those who seek their services and of the research participants that may be the object of study. They use their skills only for purposes consistent with these values and do not knowingly permit their misuse by others. While demanding for themselves freedom of inquiry and communication, psychologists accept the responsibility this freedom requires: competence, objectivity in the application of skills, and concern for the best interests of clients, colleagues, students, research participants, and society. In the pursuit of these ideals, psychologists subscribe to principles in the following areas: 1. Responsibility, 2. Competence, 3. Moral and Legal Standards, 4. Public Statements, 5. Confidentiality, 6. Welfare of the Consumer, 7. Professional Relationships, 8. Assessment Techniques. 9. Research with Human Participants, and 10. Care and Use of Animals.

Acceptance of membership in the American Psychological Association commits the member to adherence to these principles.

Psychologists cooperate with duly constituted committees of the American Psychological Association, in particular, the Committee on Scientific and Professional Ethics and Conduct, by responding to inquiries promptly and completely. Members also

Ethical Principles of Psychologists (revised edition), by the American Psychological Association. Copyright 1981 by the American Psychological Association. Reprinted by permission of the American Psychological Association.

This version of the *Ethical Principles of Psychologists* (formerly entitled *Ethical Standards of Psychologists*) was adopted by the American Psychological Association's Council of Representatives on January 24, 1981. The revised *Ethical Principles* contain both substantive and grammatical changes in each of the nine ethical principles constituting the *Ethical Standards of Psychologists* previously adopted by the Council of Representatives in 1979, plus a new tenth principle entitled "Care and Use of Animals." Inquiries concerning the *Ethical Principles of Psychologists* should be addressed to the Administrative Officer for Ethics, American Psychological Association, 1200 Seventeenth Street, N.W., Washington, D.C., 20036.

These revised *Ethical principles* apply to psychologists, to students of psychology, and to others who do work of a psychological nature under the supervision of a psychologist. They are also intended for the guidance of nonmembers of the Association who are engaged in psychological research or practice.

Any complaints of unethical conduct filed after January 24, 1981, shall be governed by this 1981 revision. However, conduct (a) complained about after January 24, 1981, but which occurred prior to that date, and (b) not considered unethical under prior versions of the principles but considered unethical under the 1981 revision, shall not be deemed a violation of ethical principles. Any complaints pending as of January 24, 1981, shall be governed either by the 1979 or by the 1981 version of the *Ethical Principles,* at the sound discretion of the Committee on Scientific and Professional Ethics and Conduct.

respond promptly and completely to inquiries from duly constituted state association ethics committees and professional standards review committees.

Principle 1: Responsibility

In providing services, psychologists maintain the highest standards of their profession. They accept responsibility for the consequences of their acts and make every effort to ensure that their services are used appropriately.

a. As scientists, psychologists accept responsibility for the selection of their research topics and the methods used in investigation, analysis, and reporting. They plan their research in ways to minimize the possibility that their findings will be misleading. They provide thorough discussion of the limitations of their data, especially where their work touches on social policy or might be construed to the detriment of persons in specific age, sex, ethnic, socioeconomic, or other social groups. In publishing reports of their work, they never suppress disconfirming data, and they acknowledge the existence of alternative hypotheses and explanations of their findings. Psychologists take credit only for work they have actually done.

b. Psychologists clarify in advance with all appropriate persons and agencies the expectations for sharing and utilizing research data. They avoid relationships that may limit their objectivity or create a conflict of interest. Interference with the milieu in which data are collected is kept to a minimum.

c. Psychologists have the responsibility to attempt to prevent distortion, misuse, or suppression of psychological findings by the institution or agency of which they are employees.

d. As members of governmental or other organizational bodies, psychologists remain accountable as individuals to the highest standards of their profession.

e. As teachers, psychologists recognize their primary obligation to help others acquire knowledge and skill. They maintain high standards of scholarship by presenting psychological information objectively, fully, and accurately.

f. As practitioners, psychologists know that they bear a heavy social responsibility because their recommendations and professional actions may alter the lives of others. They are alert to personal, social, organizational, financial, or political situations and pressures that might lead to misuse of their influence.

Principle 2: Competence

The maintenance of high standards of competence is a responsibility shared by all psychologists in the interest of the public and the profession as a whole. Psychologists recognize the boundaries of their competence and the limitations of their techniques. They only provide services and only use techniques of which they are qualified by training and experience. In those areas in which recognized standards do not yet exist, psychologists take whatever precautions are necessary to protect the welfare of their clients. They maintain knowledge of current scientific and professional information related to the services they render.

a. Psychologists accurately represent their competence, education, training, and experience. They claim as evidence of educational qualifications only those degrees obtained from institutions acceptable under the Bylaws and Rules of Council of the American Psychological Association.

b. As teachers, psychologists perform their duties on the basis of careful preparation so that their instruction is accurate, current, and scholarly.

c. Psychologists recognize the need for continuing education and are open to new procedures and changes in expectations and values over time.

d. Psychologists recognize differences among people, such as those that may be associated with age, sex, socioeconomic, and ethnic backgrounds. When necessary, they obtain training, experience, or counsel to assure competent service or research relating to such persons.

e. Psychologists responsible for decisions involving individuals or policies based on test results have an understanding of psychological or educational measurement, validation problems, and test research.

f. Psychologists recognize that personal problems and conflicts may interfere with professional effectiveness. Accordingly, they refrain from undertaking any activity in which their personal problems are likely to lead to inadequate performance or harm to a client, colleague, student, or research participant. If engaged in such activity when they become aware of their personal problems, they seek competent professional assistance to determine whether they should suspend, terminate, or limit the scope of their professional and/or scientific activities.

Principle 3: Moral and Legal Standards

Psychologists' moral and ethical standards of behavior are a personal matter to the same degree as they are for any other citizen, except as these may compromise the fulfillment of their professional responsibilities or reduce the public trust in psychology and psychologists. Regarding their own behavior, psychologists are sensitive to prevailing community standards and to the possible impact that conformity to or deviation from these standards may have upon the quality of their performance as psychologists. Psychologists are also aware of the possible impact of their public behavior upon the ability of colleagues to perform their professional duties.

a. As teachers, psychologists are aware of the fact that their personal values may affect the selection and presentation of instructional materials. When dealing with topics that may give offense, they recognize and respect the diverse attitudes that students may have toward such materials.

b. As employees or employers, psychologists do not engage in or condone practices that are inhumane or that result in illegal or unjustifiable actions. Such practices include, but are not limited to, those based on considerations of race, handicap, age, gender, sexual preference, religion, or national origin in hiring, promotion, or training.

c. In their professional roles, psychologists avoid any action that will violate or diminish the legal and civil rights of clients or of others who may be affected by their actions.

d. As practitioners and researchers, psychologists act in accord with Association standards and guidelines related to practice and to the conduct of research with human beings and animals. In the ordinary course of events, psychologists adhere to relevant governmental laws and institutional regulations. When federal, state, provincial, organizational, or institutional laws, regulations, or practices are in conflict with Association standards and guidelines, psychologists make known their commitment to Association standards and guidelines and, wherever possible, work toward a resolution of the conflict. Both practitioners and researchers are concerned with the development of such legal and quasi-legal regulations as best serve the public interest, and they work toward changing existing regulations that are not beneficial to the public interest.

Principle 4: Public Statements

Public statements, announcements of services, advertising, and promotional activities of psychologists serve the purpose of helping the public make informed judgments and choices. Psychologists represent accurately and objectively their professional qualifications, affiliations, and functions, as well as those of the institutions or organizations with which they or the statements may be associated. In public statements providing psychological information or professional opinions or providing information about the availability of psychological products, publications, and services, psychologists base their statements on scientifically acceptable psychological findings and techniques with full recognition of the limits and uncertainties of such evidence.

a. When announcing or advertising professional services, psychologists may list the following information to describe the provider and services provided: name, highest relevant academic degree earned from a regionally accredited institution, date, type, and level of certification or licensure, diplomate status, APA membership status, address, telephone number, office hours, a brief listing of the type of psychological services offered, an appropriate presentation of fee information, foreign languages spoken, and policy with regard to third-party payments. Additional relevant or important consumer information may be included if not prohibited by other sections of these Ethical Principles.

b. In announcing or advertising the availability of psychological products, publications, or services, psychologists do not present their affiliation with any organization in a manner that falsely implies sponsorship or certification by that organization. In particular and for example, psychologists do not state APA membership or fellow status in a way to suggest that such status implies specialized professional competence or qualifications. Public statements include, but are not limited to, communication by means of periodical, book, list, directory, television, radio, or motion picture. They do not contain (i) a false, fraudulent, misleading, deceptive, or unfair statement; (ii) a misinterpretation of fact or a statement likely to mislead or deceive because in context it makes only a partial disclosure of relevant facts; (iii) a testimonial from a patient regarding the quality of a psychologist's services or products; (iv) a statement intended or likely to create false or unjustified expectations of favorable results; (v) a statement implying unusual, unique, or one-of-a-kind abilities; (vi) a statement intended or likely to appeal to a client's fears, anxieties, or emotions concerning the possible results of failure to obtain the offered services; (vii) a statement concerning the comparative desirability of offered services; (viii) a statement of direct solicitation of individual clients.

c. Psychologists do not compensate or give anything of value to a representative of the press, radio, television, or other communication medium in anticipation of or in return for professional publicity in a news item. A paid advertisement must be identified as such, unless it is apparent from the context that it is a paid advertisement. If communicated to the public by use of radio or television, an advertisement is prerecorded and approved for broadcast by the psychologist, and a recording of the actual transmission is retained by the psychologist.

d. Announcements or advertisements of "personal growth groups" clinics, and agencies give a clear statement of purpose and a clear description of the experiences to be provided. The education, training, and experience of the staff members are appropriately specified.

e. Psychologists associated with the development or promotion of psychological devices, books, or other products offered for commercial sale make reasonable efforts to ensure that announcements and advertisements are presented in a professional, scientifically acceptable, and factually informative manner.

f. Psychologists do not participate for personal gain in commercial announcements or advertisements recommending to the public the purchase or use of proprietary or single-source products or services when that participation is based solely upon their identification as psychologists.

g. Psychologists present the science of psychology and offer their services, products, and publications fairly and accurately, avoiding misrepresentation through sensationalism, exaggeration, or superficiality. Psychologists are guided by the primary obligation to aid the public in developing informed judgments, opinions, and choices.

h. As teachers, psychologists ensure that statements in catalogs and course outlines are accurate and not misleading, particularly in terms of subject matter to be covered, bases for evaluating progress, and the nature of course experiences. Announcements, brochures, or advertisements describing workshops, seminars, or other educational programs accurately describe the audience for which the program is intended as well as eligibility requirements, educational objectives, and nature of the materials to be covered. These announcements also accurately represent the education, training, and experience of the psychologists presenting the programs and any fees involved.

i. Public announcements or advertisements soliciting research participants in which clinical services or other professional services are offered as an inducement make clear the nature of the services as well as the costs and other obligations to be accepted by participants in the research.

j. A psychologist accepts the obligation to correct others who represent the psychologist's professional qualifications, or associations with products or services, in a manner incompatible with these guidelines.

k. Individual diagnostic and therapeutic services are provided only in the context of a professional psychological relationship. When personal advice is given by means of public lectures or demonstrations, newspaper or magazine articles, radio or television programs, mail, or similar media, the psychologist utilizes the most current relevant data and exercises the highest level of professional judgment.

l. Products that are described or presented by means of public lectures or demonstrations, newspaper or magazine articles, radio or television programs, or similar media meet the same recognized standards as exist for products used in the context of a professional relationship.

Principle 5: Confidentiality

Psychologists have a primary obligation to respect the confidentiality of information obtained from persons in the course of their work as psychologists. They reveal such information to others only with the consent of the person or the person's legal representative, except in those unusual circumstances in which not to do so would result in clear danger to the person or to others. Where appropriate, psychologists inform their clients of the legal limits of confidentiality.

a. Information obtained in clinical or consulting relationships, or evalutive data concerning children, students, employees, and others, is discussed only for professional purposes and only with persons clearly concerned with the case. Written and oral reports present only data germane to the purposes of the evaluation, and every effort is made to avoid undue invasion of privacy.

b. Psychologists who present personal information obtained during the course of professional work in writings, lectures, or other public forums either obtain adequate prior consent to do so or adequately disguise all identifying information.

c. Psychologists make provisions for maintaining confidentiality in the storage and disposal of records.

d. When working with minors or other persons who are unable to give voluntary, informed consent, psychologists take special care to protect these persons' best interests.

Principle 6: Welfare of the Consumer

Psychologists respect the integrity and protect the welfare of the people and groups with whom they work. When conflicts of interest arise between clients and psychologists' employing institutions, psychologists clarify the nature and direction of their loyalties and responsibilities and keep all parties informed of their commitments. Psychologists fully inform consumers as to the purpose and nature of an evaluative, treatment, educational, or training procedure, and they freely acknowledge that clients, students, or participants in research have freedom of choice with regard to participation.

a. Psychologists are continually cognizant of their own needs and of their potentially influential position vis-à-vis persons such as clients, students, and subordinates. They avoid exploiting the trust and dependency of such persons. Psychologists make every effort to avoid dual relationships that could impair their professional judgment or increase the risk of exploitation. Examples of such dual relationships include, but are not limited to, research with and treatment of employees, students, supervisees, close friends, or relatives. Sexual intimacies with clients are unethical.

b. When a psychologist agrees to provide services to a client at the request of a third party, the psychologist assumes the responsibility of clarifying the nature of the relationships to all parties concerned.

c. Where the demands of an organization require psychologists to violate these Ethical Principles, psychologists clarify the nature of the conflict between the demands and these principles. They inform all parties of psychologists' ethical responsibilities and take appropriate action.

d. Psychologists make advance financial arrangements that safeguard the best interests of and are clearly understood by their clients.

They neither give nor receive any remuneration for referring clients for professional services. They contribute a portion of their services to work for which they receive little or no financial return.

e. Psychologists terminate a clinical or consulting relationship when it is reasonably clear that the consumer is not benefiting from it. They offer to help the consumer locate alternative sources of assistance.

Principle 7: Professional Relationships

Psychologists act with due regard for the needs, special competencies, and obligations of their colleagues in psychology and other professions. They respect the prerogatives and obligations of the institutions or organizations with which these other colleagues are associated.

a. Psychologists understand the areas of competence of related professions. They make full use of all the professional, technical, and administrative resources that serve the best interests of consumers. The absence of formal relationships with other professional workers does not relieve psychologists of the responsibility of securing for their clients the best possible professional service, nor does it relieve them of the obligation to exercise foresight, diligence, and tact in obtaining the complementary or alternative assistance needed by clients.

b. Psychologists know and take into account the traditions and practices of other professional groups with whom they work and cooperate fully with such groups. If a person is receiving similar services from another professional, psychologists do not offer their own services directly to such a person. If a psychologist is contacted by a person who is already receiving similar services from another professional, the psychologist carefully considers that professional relationship and proceeds with caution and sensitivity to the therapeutic issues with the client so as to minimize the risk of confusion and conflict.

c. Psychologists who employ or supervise other professionals or professionals in training accept the obligation to facilitate the further professional development of these individuals. They provide appropriate working conditions, timely evaluations, constructive consultation, and experience opportunities.

d. Psychologists do not exploit their professional relationships with clients, supervisees, students, employees, or research participants sexually or otherwise. Psychologists do not condone or engage in sexual harassment. Sexual harassment is defined as deliberate or repeated comments, gestures, or physical contacts of a sexual nature that are unwanted by the recipient.

e. In conducting research in institutions or organizations, psychologists secure appropriate authorization to conduct such research. They are aware of their obligations to future research workers and ensure that host institutions receive adequate information about the research and proper acknowledgment of their contributions.

f. Publication credit is assigned to those who have contributed to a publication in proportion to their professional contributions. Major contributions of a professional character made by several persons to a common project are recognized by joint authorship, with the individual who made the principal contribution listed first. Minor contributions of a professional character and extensive clerical or similar nonprofessional assistance may be acknowledged in footnotes or in an introductory statement. Acknowledgment through specific citations is made for unpublished as well as published material that has directly influenced the research or writing. Psychologists who compile and edit material of others for publication publish the material in the name of the originating group, if appropriate, with their own name appearing as chairperson or editor. All contributors are to be acknowledged and named.

g. When psychologists know of an ethical violation by another psychologist, and it seems appropriate, they informally attempt to resolve the issue by bringing the behavior to the attention of the pscyhologist. If the misconduct is of a minor nature and/or appears to be due to lack of sensitivity, knowledge, or experience, such an informal solution is usually appropriate. Such informal corrective efforts are made with sensitivitity to any rights to confidentiality involved. If the violation does not seem amendable to an informal solution, or is to a more serious nature, psychologists bring it to the attention of the appropriate local, state, and/or national committee on professional ethics and conduct.

Principle 8: Assessment Techniques

In the development, publication, and utilization of psychological assessment techniques, psychologists make every effort to promote the welfare and best interests of the client. They guard against the misuse of assessment results. They respect the client's right to know the results, the interpretations made, and the bases for their conclusions and recommendations. Psychologists make every effort to maintain the security of tests and other assessment techniques within limits of legal mandates. They strive to ensure the appropriate use of assessment techniques by others.

a. In using assessment techniques, psychologists respect the right of clients to have full explanations of the nature and purpose of the techniques in language the clients can understand, unless an explicit exception to this right has been agreed upon in advance. When the explanations are to be provided by others, psychologists establish procedures for ensuring the adequacy of these explanations.

b. Psychologists responsible for the development and standardization of psychological tests and other assessment techniques utilize established scientific procedures and observe the relevant APA standards.

c. In reporting assessment results, psychologists indicate any reservations that exist regarding validity or reliability because of the circumstances of the assessment or the inappropriateness of the norms for the person tested. Psychologists strive to ensure that the results of assessments and their interpretations are not misused by others.

d. Psychologists recognize that assessment results may become obsolete. They make every effort to avoid and prevent the misuse of obsolete measures.

e. Psychologists offering scoring and interpretation services are able to produce appropriate evidence for the validity of the programs and procedures used in arriving at interpretations. The public offering of an automated interpretation service is considered a professional-to-professional consultation. Psychologists make every effort to avoid misuse of assessment reports.

f. Psychologists do not encourage or promote the use of psychological assessment techniques by inappropriately trained or otherwise unqualified persons through teaching, sponsorship, or supervision.

Principle 9: Research with Human Participants

The decision to undertake research rests upon a considered judgment by the individual psychologist about how best to contribute to psychological science and human welfare. Having made the decision to conduct research, the psychologist considers alternative directions in which research energies and resources might be invested. On the basis of this consideration, the psychologist carries out the investigation with respect and concern for the dignity and welfare of the people who participate and with cognizance of federal and state regulations and professional standards governing the conduct of research with human participants.

a. In planning a study, the investigator has the responsibility to make a careful evaluation of its ethical acceptability. To the extent that the weighing of scientific and human values suggests a compromise of any principle, the investigator incurs a correspondingly serious obligation to seek ethical advice and to observe stringent safeguards to protect the rights of human participants.

b. Considering whether a participant in a planned study will be a "subject at risk" or a "subject at minimal risk," according to recognized standards, is of primary ethical concern to the investigator.

c. The investigator always retains the responsibility for ensuring ethical practice in research. The investigator is also responsible for the ethical treatment of research participants by collaborators, assistants, students, and employees, all of whom, however, incur similar obligations.

d. Except in minimal-risk research, the investigator establishes a clear and fair agreement with research participants, prior to their participation, that clarifies the obligations and responsibilities of each. The investigator has the obligation to honor all promises and commitments included in that agreement. The investigator informs the participants of all aspects of the research that might reasonably be expected to influence willingness to participate and explains all other aspects of the research about which the participants inquire. Failure to make full disclosure prior to obtaining informed consent requires additional safeguards to protect the welfare and dignity of the research participants. Research with children or with participants who have impairments that would limit understanding and/or communication requires special safeguarding procedures.

e. Methodological requirements of a study may make the use of concealment or deception necessary. Before conducting such a study, the investigator has a special responsibility to (i) determine whether the use of such techniques is justified by the study's prospective scientific, educational, or applied value; (ii) determine whether alternative procedures are available that do not use concealment or deception; and (iii) ensure that the participants are provided with sufficient explanation as soon as possible.

f. The investigator respects the individual's freedom to decline to participate in or to withdraw from the research at any time. The obligation to protect this freedom requires careful thought and consideration when the investigator is in a position of authority or influence over the participant. Such positions of authority include, but are not limited to, situations in which research participation is required as part of employment or in which the participant is a student, client, or employee of the investigator.

g. The investigator protects the participant from physical and mental discomfort, harm, and danger that may arise from research procedures. If risks of such consequences exist, the investigator informs the participant of that fact. Research procedures likely to cause serious or lasting harm to a participant are not used unless the failure to use these procedures might expose the participant to risk of greater harm, or unless the research has great potential benefit and fully informed and voluntary consent is obtained from each participant. The participant should be informed of procedures for contacting the investigator within a reasonable time period following participation should stress, potential harm, or related questions or concerns arise.

h. After the data are collected, the investigator provides the participant with information about the nature of the study and attempts to remove any misconceptions that may have arisen. Where scientific or humane values justify delaying or withholding this information, the investigator incurs a special responsibility to monitor the research and to ensure that there are no damaging consequences for the participant.

i. Where research procedures result in undesirable consequences for the individual participant, the investigator has the responsibility to detect and remove or correct these consequences, including long-term effects.

j. Information obtained about a research participant during the course of an investigation is confidential unless otherwise agreed upon in advance. When the possibility exists that others may obtain access to such information, this possibility, together with the plans for protecting confidentiality, is explained to the participant as part of the procedure for obtaining informed consent.

Principle 10: Care and Use of Animals

An investigator of animal behavior strives to advance understanding of basic behavioral principles and/or to contribute to the improvement of human health and welfare. In seeking these ends, the investigator ensures the welfare of animals and treats them humanely. Laws and regulations notwithstanding, an animal's immediate protection depends upon the scientist's own conscience.

a. The acquisition, care, use, and disposal of all animals are in compliance with current federal, state or provincial, and local laws and regulations.

b. A psychologist trained in research methods

and experienced in the care of laboratory animals closely supervises all procedures involving animals and is responsible for ensuring appropriate consideration of their comfort, health, and humane treatment.

c. Psychologists ensure that all individuals using animals under their supervision have received explicit instruction in experimental methods and in the care, maintenance, and handling of the species being used. Responsibilities and activities of individuals participating in a research project are consistent with their respective competencies.

d. Psychologists make evey effort to minimize discomfort, illness, and pain of animals. A procedure subjecting animals to pain, stress, or privation is used only when an alternative procedure is unavailable and the goal is justified by its prospective scientific, educational, or applied value. Surgical procedures are performed under appropriate anesthesia; techniques to avoid infection and minimize pain are followed during and after surgery.

e. When it is appropriate that the animal's life be terminated, it is done rapidly and painlessly.

APPENDIX D

PROTECTION OF THE RIGHTS AND PRIVACY OF PARENTS AND STUDENTS—FAMILY EDUCATIONAL RIGHTS AND PRIVACY ACT OF 1974

Public Law 93-380

Sec. 513.(a) Part C of the General Education Provisions Act is further amended by adding at the end thereof the following new section:

"Protection of the Rights and Privacy of Parents and Students"

"Sec. 438. (a) (1) No funds shall be made available under any applicable program to any State or local educational agency, any institution of higher education, any community college, any school, agency offering a preschool program, or any other educational institution which has a policy of denying, or which effectively prevents, the parents of students attending any school of such agency, or attending such institution of higher education, community college, school, preschool, or other educational institution, the right to inspect and review any and all official records, files, and data directly related to their children, including all material that is incorporated into each student's cumulative record folder, and intended for school use or to be available to parties outside the school or school system, and specifically including, but not necessarily limited to, identifying data, academic work

completed, level of achievement (grades, standardized achievement test scores), attendance data, scores on standardized intelligence, aptitude, and psychological tests, interest inventory results, health data, family background information, teacher or counselor ratings and observations, and verified reports of serious or recurrent behavior patterns. Where such records or data include information on more than one student, the parents of any student shall be entitled to receive, or be informed of, that part of such record or data as pertains to their child. Each recipient shall establish appropriate procedures for the granting of a request by parents for access to their child's school records within a reasonable period of time, but in no case more than forty-five days after the request has been made.

"(2) Parents shall have an opportunity for a hearing to challenge the content of their child's school records, to insure that the records are not inaccurate, misleading, or otherwise in violation of the privacy or other rights of students, and to provide an opportunity for the correction or delection of any such inaccurate, misleading, or otherwise inappropriate data contained therein.

"(b)(1) No funds shall be made available under any applicable program to any State or

439

local educaitonal agency, any institution of higher education, any community college, any school, agency offering a preschool program, or any other educational institution which has a policy of permitting the release of personally identifiable records or files (or personal information contained therein) of students without the written consent of their parents to any individual, agency, or organization, other than to the following—

"(A) other school officials, including teachers within the educational institution or local educational agency who have legitimate educational interests;

"(B) officials of other schools or school systems in which the student intends to enroll, upon condition that the student's parents be notified of the transfer, receive a copy of the record if desired, and have an opportunity for a hearing to challenge the content of the record;

"(C) authorized representatives of (i) the Comptroller General of the United States, (ii) the Secretary, (iii) an administrative head of an education agency (as defined in section 409 of this Act), or (iv) State educational authorities, under the conditions set forth in paragraph (3) of this subsection; and

"(D) in connection with a student's application for, or receipt of, financial aid.

"(2) No funds shall be made available under any applicable program to any State or local educational agency, any institution of higher education, any community college, any school, agency offering a preschool program, or any other educational institution which has a policy or practice of furnishing, in any form, any personally identifiable information contained in personal school records, to any persons other than those listed in subsection (b)(1) unless—

"(A) there is written consent from the student's parents specifying records to be released, the reasons for such release, and to whom, and with a copy of the records to be released to the student's parents and the student if desired by the parents, or

"(B) such information is furnished in compliance with judicial order, or pursuant to any lawfully issued subpoena, upon condition that parents and the students are notified of all such orders or subpoenas in advance of the compliance therewith by the educational institution or agency.

"(3) Nothing contained in this section shall preclude authorized representatives of (A) the Comptroller General of the United States, (B) the Secretary, (C) an administrative head of an education agency or (D) State educational authorities from having access to student or other records which may be necessary in connection with the audit and evaluation of Federally-supported education program, or in connection with the enforcement of the Federal legal requirements which relate to such programs: *Provided,* That, except when collection of personally identifiable data is specifically authorized by Federal law, any data collected by such officials with respect to individual students shall not include information (including social security numbers) which would permit the personal identification of such students or their parents after the data so obtained has been collected.

"(4) (A) With respect to subsections (c)(1) and (c)(2) and (c)(3), all persons, agencies, or organizations desiring access to the records of a student shall be required to sign a written form which shall be kept permanently with the file of the student, but only for inspection by the parents or student, indicating specifically the legitimate educational or other interest that each person, agency, or organization has in seeking this information. Such form shall be available to parents and to the school official responsible for record maintenance as a means of auditing the operation of the system.

"(B) With respect to this subsection, personal information shall only be transferred to a third party on the condition that such party will not permit any other party to have access to such information without the written consent of the parents of the student.

"(c) The Secretary shall adopt appropriate regulations to protect the rights of privacy of students and their families in connection with any surveys or data-gathering activities conducted, assisted, or authorized by the Secretary or an administrative head of an education agency. Regulations established under this subsection shall include provisions controlling the use, dissemination, and protection of such data. No survey or data-gathering activities shall be conducted by the Secretary, or an administrative head of an education agency under an applicable program, unless such activities are authorized by law.

"(d) For the purpose of this section, whenever a student has attained eighteen years of age, or is attending an institution of postsecondary education the permission or consent required of and the rights accorded to the parents of the student shall thereafter only be required of and accorded to the student.

"(e) No funds shall be made available under any applicable program unless the recipient of such funds informs the parents of students, or the students, if they are eighteen years of age or older, or are attending an institution of postsecondary education, of the rights accorded them by this section.

"(f) The Secretary, or an administrative head of an education agency, shall take appropriate actions to enforce provisions of this section and to deal with violations of this section, according to the provisions of this Act, except that action to terminate assistance may be taken only if the Secretary finds there has been a failure to comply with the provisions of this section, and he has determined that compliance cannot be secured by voluntary means.

"(g) The Secretary shall establish or designate an office and review board within the Department of Health, Education, and Welfare for the purpose of investigating, processing, reviewing, and adjudicating violations of the provisions of this section and complaints which may be filed concerning alleged violations of this section, according to the procedures contained in sections 434 and 437 of this Act."

(b)(1)(i) The provisions of this section shall become effective ninety days after the date of enactment of section 438 of the General Education Provisions Act.

(2)(i) This section may be cited as the "Family Educational Rights and Privacy Act of 1974".

Protection of Pupil Rights

Sec. 514. (a) Part C of the General Education Provisions Act is further amended by adding after section 438 the following new section:

"Protection of Pupil Rights

"Sec. 439. All instructional material, including teacher's manuals, films, tapes, or other supplementary instructional material which will be used in connection with any research or experimentation program or project shall be available for inspection by the parents or guardians of the children engaged in such program or project. For the purpose of this section 'research or experimentation program or project' means any program or project in any applicable program designed to explore or develop new or unproven teaching methods or techniques."

(b) The amendment made by subsection (a) shall be effective upon enactment of this Act.

APPENDIX E

THE ROLE OF THE SCHOOL COUNSELOR IN CAREER GUIDANCE: EXPECTATIONS AND RESPONSIBILITIES

ASCA Role Statement

Career guidance has consistently been seen as a high-priority need by youth, their parents, school boards, the private sector, and the general pubilc. Such expectations were at an all-time high in 1984. As these expectations have risen, so also has the difficulty of the task facing the professional school counselor. The certain rapidity of occupational change and the uncertain nature of the emerging service/information-oriented high-technology society have combined to change career guidance practices in significant ways. This policy statement aims to recognize and react to some of these changes.

Promises and Pitfalls of a High-Technology Approach

The professional school counselor must recognize that the promise of high technology to increase both efficiency and effectiveness of operations applies to career guidance at least as much as to any other part of the formal educational system. Thus, if the need for career guidance can be said to be greater than ever, so also is the potential for meeting this need. This potential can be recognized only if professional

Reprinted by permission of the American School Counselors Association.

school counselors are willing to broaden their roles in ways that allow them to simultaneously take advantage of the promises and avoid the pitfalls implicit in a high-technology approach to career guidance.

The promises and pitfalls to be recognized include but are not limited to the following:

- The *promise* through computer-assisted management to relieve professional school counselors of the need to spend long hours in maintaining student records, coupled with the potential *pitfall* of violating student confidentiality
- The *promise* of greatly expanding the nature, scope, and accessibility of educational/occupational information systems through the use of videodiscs and telecommunications, coupled with the potential *pitfalls* associated with assuring the validity and lack of bias found in such materials
- The *promise* of making computerized career decision-making systems available to students, coupled with the plentiful *pitfalls* of failing to use the counselor/student relationship to move toward comprehensive career planning

Thus, while high technology holds obvious promise for increasing both the efficiency and the effectiveness of career guidance, it simultaneously calls for a broadening of counselor expertise and activity. The challenge to counselors for broadening their role in career guidance is fully as great as is the need to make career guidance a high-priority item.

High-Priority Career Guidance

To make career guidance a high-priority item for professional school counselors, several basic goals must be kept clearly in mind, including the following:

- Delivering career guidance to persons in an *equitable* fashion that aims at *excellence of delivery* for each person
- Taking advantage of the obvious opportunity to utilize a wide variety of community resources in the delivery of effective career guidance
- Protecting and enhancing individual freedom of career choices for every person served
- Providing quality career guidance for *all* persons in the educational system rather than limiting it to specific portions of the student population
- Involving, to the greatest possible extent, all professional educators in the delivery of career guidance

To address this need to designate our role in career guidance as a high priority, the American School Counselor Association (ASCA) has prepared this policy statement.

Career guidance is a delivery system that systematically helps students reach the career development outcomes of self-awareness and assessment, career awareness and exploration, career decision making, career planning, and placement. The school counselor's role covers many areas within a school setting, and career guidance is one of the counselor's most important contributions to a student's lifelong development. Career guidance can best be conceptualized by the following basic concepts:

- Career development is a lifelong process.
- Career guidance is deeply rooted in the theory and research of the career development process.
- Career guidance is developmental in nature (K-postsecondary), moving from self- and career awareness to career exploration, to career decision making, to career planning, to implementation of decisions and plans. This entire developmental process can be repeated more than once during the life span.
- Career guidance recognizes and emphasizes education/work relationships at all levels of education.
- Career guidance views the work values of persons as part of their total system of personal values—and so views work as an integral part of a person's total life-style.
- Career guidance recognizes the importance of both paid and unpaid work. In doing so, it recognizes that the human need to work, for any given person, can be met by either, or both, paid or unpaid work.

The school counselor, as a career guidance professional, is the person to assume leadership in the implementation of career development outcomes. Furthermore, indirect services to parents, staff, and the greater community, as they relate to the career development outcomes for students, are also the school counselor's responsibility. Indirect services include but are not limited to staff development, parent and school board presentations, and the establishment of strong supportive linkages with business, industry, and labor.

A Five-Phased Approach to Career Guidance in an Educational System

Career guidance professionals are most needed and can gain greatest recognition through participation in process-oriented approaches to educational change. Of the several kinds of process-oriented approaches to educational change, career education represents the most logical and certainly the most ready one available for consideration by the school counselor acting in his or her capacity as a career guidance professional.

Career guidance calls for educational change beginning no later than kindergarten and extending through all publicly supported education. Concepts must be delivered in an equitable manner to all students so as to bring a sense of meaningfulness and purposefulness to both the curriculum and the services of the educational system.

Career guidance concepts have been influenced by the school counselor for many years but must now be broadened to invite support from faculty, staff, administration, students, parents, and the diverse segments of the broader community. To broaden the support base, the person in authority must make clear to all school personnel that career guidance is everyone's responsibility. No one segment is in a position to deliver all the concepts. One person must be appointed who will be held accountable and be given authority to develop, coordinate, and monitor the total effort so that a developmental delivery system is put in place and continues to function. The person responsible for this development and coordination should be a school counselor with management and organizational skills.

To implement a comprehensive career guidance program in an educational system, the initial emphasis must be on an effective process-oriented effort aimed at educational change. The following are considerations that are necessary but not sufficient to meet the needs for the educational change:

- School counselors, administrators, and faculty members must become sensitized to the concepts of career guidance.
- School counselors, administrators, and faculty members must become familiar with the concept that career infusion need not result in the loss of teaching or counseling time.
- Faculty members must be able to make the same kinds of connections between the subject(s) *taught* and the world of work that the students will make between the subject(s) *learned* and the world of work.
- Professional development and activities related to the implementation of this process shall take place during the school day, with appropriate or usual compensation provided to participants.

Based on the philosophy and the practical outcomes listed above, the following five-phased approach to career guidance will allow the school counselor to utilize his or her training and expertise in facilitating groups, coordinating activities, and identifying and developing community contacts and resources.

Phase I

The counselor as a career guidance professional develops a broad base of understanding between the faculty members and the broader community. A series of inservice programs should be developed involving faculty members and significant members of both the private and public sectors of the community. The primary goals of these inservice programs include the following:

- Developing an understanding of career guidance
- Developing a sensitivity to the concept of race, sex, and the exceptional student
- Developing a "core committee" of persons representing all levels of the educational system, with select representation from the private and public sectors

Phase II

The counselor as a career guidance professional and the core committee develop goals and objectives to form a skeleton around which subcommittees will add "flesh" in the form of faculty/counselor-developed lessons and activities.

Phase III

The counselor as a career guidance professional *facilitates* the development of workshops conducted by core committee members for the purpose of developing sample activities that relate to each goal and objective at each level. Additional staff members from each level are invited to become resource persons for the committee. Emphasis is placed on the interaction of faculty from all levels of the system who are working together to develop clearly articulated and developmentally sequenced activities.

Phase IV

The counselor as a career guidance professional, utilizing the core committee, coordinates the compilation of all the goals, objectives, and activities (the product of Phase III) and a resource appendix into one infusion document. This document, *developed with* and *delivered to* the teachers, is to be used as a guide for infusion. The document is disseminated to all faculty and administration, as well as to those community members participating in an advisory manner to the core committee.

Phase V

The counselor as a career guidance professional will call on the core committee whenever needed for the purposes of revising, updating, disseminating, and evaluating the career guidance program. It should be noted that the role of the school counselor serving as a career guidance professional is one of coordinating and facilitating, not writing or implementing, the career infusion plan for the classroom teacher.

These five phases, if implemented effectively, ensure infusion of career guidance into all curriculum areas, starting early in the educational process. The school counselor as a career guidance professional can then concentrate on the delivery of a series of common core experiences leading to career maturity through awareness, exploration, decision making, and planning. These experiences should be developmental in nature and serve as the link that ties together all of the infusion efforts and focuses on the student in relation to his or her future work experience. The common core experiences should provide the following for *all* students:

- Individual and group counseling to clarify work values and develop coping and planning skills
- Formal and informal assessment of abilities, personality traits, and interests
- Occupational/career information through community linkages such as field trips, speakers, shadowing experiences, and internships
- A career information center providing job-hunting skills, interviewing skills, educational and training opportunities, and financial aid possibilities
- Training, goal setting, and decision making for the selection of tentative career paths based on the above
- An opportunity for integrating academic and career planning, leading to the selection of a high school curriculum as it relates to the appropriate career clusters
- An opportunity for continuous evaluation and revision of the goal-setting process and action planning, including an annual review of all students' plans of study

This role statement presents a philosophy, some explanations, and a prepared plan of action concerning the role of the school counselor as a career guidance professional. This is only a beginning; much more work needs to be done to implement a proactive stance for school counselors to meet the career development needs of all students. Parents, school boards, and the public and private sectors are applying pressure on the educational system to meet these needs; we can avoid becoming victims of structural educational reform by participating in it.

RESPONSIBILITIES OF USERS OF STANDARDIZED TESTS

APGA Policy Statement

Introduction

During the past several years, individual APGA members have been under increasing pressure from their various constituencies to define, provide and employ safeguards against the misuse of standardized tests. APGA as an organization has also been challenged by individuals and agencies to provide leadership in the face of growing concern about the effects of testing on clients of all ages and all subpopulations, and in all settings.

At the 1976 APGA convention, the board of directors requested action on the development of a statement on the responsible use of standardized tests. A committee representing all APGA divisions and regions spent two years studying the issues and developing the following statement.

Target audience: The statement is intended to present the position and address the needs of the professional members of APGA divisions and regions. Although this position may provide guidance for test developers, teachers, administrators, parents, press or the general public, it is not designed to represent these audiences. The

Reprinted by permission of the American Assoication for Counseling and Development (formerly the American Personnel and Guidance Association).

statement is built on the assumption that test data of themselves are neutral and that guidelines are needed to promote constructive use of tests.

Organization and focus: The statement is organized into eight sections: Introduction, Decision Rules, Test Selection, Qualifications of Test Users, Test Administration, Scoring of Tests, Test Interpretation and Communication. Each section is directed toward the various uses and decisions that must be made by the test user (e.g., whether to test, which test(s) to use, what data to obtain, how to interpret, etc.). The committee developed a classification system for the users of standardized tests and treated only those issues that fit into the use classification scheme.

The next step was to define issues related to the classification system. Issues were sought from individuals, professional statements, literature and the popular press. Issues were examined in terms of their relevance to APGA members and to their importance in terms of the possible consequences to the person(s) tested.

Only the principles underlying each issue are specified. These principles are appropriate as standards for all APGA divisions and regions. Divisions and regions are encouraged to develop their own statements, expanding on each principle with specific procedures and examples and appropriate to their members. The principles are grouped around similar issues and are indexed for easy reference.

Composition of Committee: Each division president and the representative of each region was asked to appoint to the committee a member who was: (1) knowledgable in the use of standardized tests; (2) aware of the national concerns about the use of tests; (3) willing to involve the division/region membership in identification of the concerns, needs and propositions of the division/region as these relate to the responsible use of tests; (4) able to participate actively and to respond promptly to requests for review of draft documents; (5) capable of securing cooperation of division/region officers in developing procedures for division/region implementation of the statement; (6) willing to accept specific assignments such as providing current organizational statements.

In addition to the division/region appointment, the committee included two members-at-large and a chairperson, all appointed by the APGA president, and three test experts to serve as a core committee to assist the chairperson in analyzing and synthesizing input from committee members and in preparing draft statements for committee review.

To furnish perspective for the work of this committee, a review of relevant literature was conducted and each member of the committee received copies of numerous position papers, reports, articles and monographs that added to understanding the issues and the consequences of alternative principles.

Among these papers were the interim report of the 1975–76 APGA Committee on Standardized Testing; the 1972 APGA/AMEG Statement on the Responsible Use of Tests; position papers of individual divisions and of other professional organizations such as the American Psychological Association, the American Education Research Association and the National Council on Measurement in Education; journal articles; and conference presentations.

The committee's statement is intended to be sensitive to current and emerging problems and concerns that are generic to all APGA divisions/regions and to address these problems and concerns with principles that are specific enough to serve as a template to develop division/region statements addressed to the specific disciplines/settings of individual divisions/regions.

Decision Rules

In human service agencies, decisions about client needs may be made on the basis of direct observation or historical information alone. Further refinement of direct observation and historical data can often be obtained by employing standardized tests.

Deciding whether to test creates the possibility of three classes of errors relative to the agency functions of description, diagnosis, prescription, selection, placement, prediction, growth evaluation, etc.

First, a decision not to test can result in misjudgments that stem solely from inadequate data.

Second, tests may be used well, producing data that could improve accuracy in decisions affecting the client but that are not utilized.

Third, tests may be misused through inappropriate selection, improper administration, inaccurate scoring, incompetent interpretation or indiscriminate, inadequate, or inaccurate communication.

To reduce the chance for errors, the responsible practitioner will always determine in advance why a given test should be used. This provides protection and benefits for both the client and the agency. Having a clearly developed rationale increases the probable benefits of testing by indicating how a particular set of information, when used by an individual or set of individuals, will contribute to a sounder decision without prejudice to either the client or the agency.

The guidelines that follow are intended to provide decision rules to help agencies and practitioners avoid charge of irresponsible practice.

Defining Purposes for Testing:

1. Decide whether you will be testing to evaluate individuals, groups or both.
2. Identify your interests in the particular target population in terms of the agency's purposes and capabilities.
3. Determine limits to diagnosis, prediction or selection created by age, racial, sexual, ethnic or cultural characteristics of those to be tested.
4. Develop specific objectives and limits for the use of test data in relation to each of the component service areas of placement/selection,

prediction (expectancies), description/diagnosis and growth studies (assessing change over time).

A. Placement: If the purpose is selection or placement (selection is a simple in-out sort of placement), the test selector and interpreter must know about the programs or institutions in which the client may be placed and be able to judge the consequences of such placement or exclusion for the client.

B. Prediction/expectancies: If the purpose is prediction, the persons deciding to test and/or interpret the results must understand the pitfalls of labeling, stereotyping and prejudging people. Ways to avoid these potentially invidious outcomes should be known.

C. Description/diagnosis: If the purpose is diagnosis or description, the selector or interpreter should understand enough about the general domain being measured to be able to identify those aspects adequately measured and those not.

D. Growth/change assessment: If the purpose is to examine growth, the person designing the study and interpreting the results needs to know the many problems associated with such measurement:

1. the unreliability of change measures;
2. the pitfalls in using norms as reference points;
3. the associated problems of articulation and comparability;
4. the limitations of scoring scales, such as grade equivalents, that may not have the comparable meaning which they appear to have at different scale levels.

Determining Information Needs:

1. Assess the consequences for the clients of both testing or not testing.
2. Determine what decisions can be made with existing information to avoid unnecessary data-gathering efforts.
3. Limit data gathering to those functions or aptitude, acheivement, interests/attitudes/values and perceptual-motor skills that are directly relevant in making decisions about delivery of services to a particular individual or group.
4. Identify whether the test being considered can

provide acceptable levels of precision (reliability) for the decision being made.
5. Identify whether the data obtained can be cross-validated against other available data as a part of the decision-making process.
6. Determine the amount and form of data to be shared on the basis of maximum relevance to the agency's purposes and capabilities.

Identifying Users of Test Information:

1. Data should be prepared so that they can be comprehended by the persons using the data for decision making.
2. Limit access to users specifically authorized by the law or by the client.
3. Identify obsolescence schedules so that stored personal test data may be systematically reclassified and relocated to historical files or destroyed.
4. Process personal data used for research or program evaluation so as to assure individual anonymity.

Qualifications of Test Users

All professional personnel and guidance workers should have formal training in psychological and educational measurement and testing. Nevertheless, it is unreasonable to expect that this training necessarily makes one an expert or even that an expert always has all the knowledge and skill appropriate to any particular situation. Thus, questions of user qualifications should always arise when testing is being considered.

Those who participate in any aspect of testing should be qualified to do so. Lack of proper qualifications leads to misuse, errors and sometimes damage to clients. Each professional is responsible for making judgment on this matter in each situation and cannot leave that responsibility either to clients or to those in authority.

In many instances information or skills that may be lacking can be acquired quite readily by those with a background of professional training and experience. In all instances it is incumbent upon the individual to obtain that training or arrange for proper supervision and assistance when engaged in, or planning to engage in, testing.

The requisite qualifications for test users

depend on four factors: (1) the particular role of the user; (2) the setting in which the use takes place; (3) the nature of the test; and (4) the purpose of the testing.

These factors interact with each other but may nevertheless be considered separately for the purposes of these standards.

Roles of Test Users, Selectors, Administrators, Scorers and Interpreters:

A test user may play all of these roles or any subset of them when working with other professional personnel. In some situations each role may be the responsibility of a different person. The knowledge and skills that pertain to these roles are listed under the sections so headed. The general principle is that the test users should engage in only those testing activities for which their training and experience qualify them.

Settings and Conditions of Test Use:

Counselors and personnel workers should assess the quality and relevance of their knowledge and skills to the situation before deciding to test or to participate in a testing program.

Characteristics of Tests:

Tests differ in many ways, and users need to understand the peculiarities of the instruments they are using.

Purposes of Testing:

The purpose of the testing dictates how the test is used and thus may influence requisite qualificaitons of users beyond those entailed by their testing roles. Technically proper use for ill-understood purposes may constitute misuse.

Test Selection

Tests should be selected for a specific measurement purpose, use and interpretation. The selection of tests should be guided by information obtained from a careful analysis of the following major considerations:

—What are the characteristics of the population to be tested?

—What knowledge, skills, abilities or attitudes are to be assessed?

—What are the purposes for testing?

—How will the test scores be used and interpreted?

When complete answers to these questions have been obtained, selection or development of tests should be directed toward obtaining measures that are congruent with the stated needs for assessment in terms of the purposes, content, use, interpretation and particular characteristics of the individuals who are to be tested.

Selection of tests must also be guided by the criteria of technical quality recommended by the measurement profession and published by APA/AERA/NCME in "Standards for Educational and Psychological Tests" (1974). Full recognition and analysis of these considerations should become the focus of a process to select appropriate tests. The responsible test selector will:

Select Appropriate Test:

1. Select tests that have been demonstrated, to the satisfaction of professional specialists, as appropriate for the characteristics of the population to be tested.
2. Select tests that are within the level of skills of administration and interpretation possessed by the practitioner.
3. Determine whether a common test or different tests are required for the accurate measurement of groups with different characteristics.
4. Recognize that different tests for cultural, ethnic and racial groups constitute inefficient means for making corrections for differences in prior life experiences, except where different languages are involved.
5. Determine whether persons or groups that use different languages should be tested in either or both languages and in some instance by prior testing for bilingualism.

Relate Evidence or Validity to Particular Usage:

1. Apply tests or selection only when they show predictive validity for the specific tasks or competencies needed in an educational or employment assignment to maintain legal prescriptions for non-discriminatory practices in selection, employment or placement.

2. Determine validity of a test (whether the test measures what it claims to measure) through evidence of the constructs used in developing the measures, the correlation of the test performance with another appraisal of the characteristics being measured, or the predictions of specified behavior from the test performance.

3. Determine that the content of the test has high congruence with the users' definition of the knowledge and skills that are the desired criteria of human performance to be appraised.

4. Confirm that the criteria of human performance to be appraised are contained in the tasks and results of the testing procedure.

Employ User Participation in Test Selection:

Actively involve the persons who will be using the tests (administering, scoring, summarizing, interpreting, making decisions) in the selection of tests that are congruent with the locally determined purposes, conditions and uses of the measurement.

Select Tests to Satisfy Local Use:

1. Give specific attention to how the test is designed to handle the variation of motivation among persons taking the test, the variation or bias in response to the test content and the effects of the presence or absence of guessing in the responses to the test questions.

2. Determine whether tests standardized for nationwide use show evidence that such tests yield comparable results for individuals or groups with cultural differences.

3. Identify and analyze the effects of working speed and language facility in relation to the criteria of human performance that are expected to result from the test.

Consider Technical Characteristics of Tests:

1. Select only published or locally developed tests that have documented evidence of the reliability or consistency of the measure.

2. Select tests that have documented evidence of the effectiveness of the measure for the purpose to be served: placement/selection, predic-

tion (expectancy), description/diagnosis, or growth studies (change over time). A test is rarely equally effective for the four common test uses.

3. Consider the procedures used in standardization and norming for relevance to the local population and the desired use and interpretation.

4. Use spearate norms for men and women only when empirical evidence indicates this is necessary to minimize bias.

5. Determine the degree of reliability (or validity) demanded of a test on the basis of the nature of the decisions to be based on test scores.

6. A test for final diagnosis or selection requires a higher degree of reliability than an initial screening test.

7. Explicitly list and use the ease and accuracy of the procedures for scoring, summarizing and communicating test performance as criteria for selecting a test.

8. Recognize that the technical characteristics and norms of standardized tests may vary when used with different populations. The selection process should include trial administrations to verify that the test is functioning with the technical characteristics and desired results for the local population and local uses.

Practical constraints of cost, conditions and time for testing must be considered but not used as the primary criteria for test selection.

Test Administration

Test administration includes all procedures that are used to ensure that the test is presented consistently in the manner specified by the test developers and used in the standardization and that the individuals being tested have orientation and conditions that maximize opportunity for optimum performance.

Standardized tests should provide manuals giving specific directions for administering, scoring and interpreting tests. Tests developed for a specific local purpose, use or population should be administered in a prescribed and consistent manner to obtain optimum performance from the individuals being tested. Effective administration of tests requires that the administrator have knowledge and training with the instruments and the processes of presentation.

Orientation:

1. Inform testing candidates, relevant institutions or agencies and the community about the testing procedure. The orientation should describe the purposes and contents sampled by the test, how it is administered and how the scores will be reported and used.
2. Provide annual training for test administrators by qualified professional specialists if your agency or institution uses tests or sponsors testing programs.
3. Routinely review these test materials and administration conditions well in advance of the time for testing so that full preparation will ensure standardized administration and recognition of any irregularities that may occur.
4. Ensure that the orientation is sufficient to make the test relevant for the individual or group being tested before beginning test administration.
5. Ensure that all persons being tested have the specified practice with sample problems or test taking skills prior to their performance on the test.
6. Demonstrate the techniques and requirements for marking machine-scorable answer sheets. Check all individuals taking a test for competency in the techniques of recording their answers prior to the specific period of testing.

Qualification of Test Administrators:

1. Administer standardized tests only if you are qualified by training and experience as competent to administer particular tests.
2. Know the exact population and procedures used in standardizing the test and determine that the test is appropriate for the local population that is to be tested.
3. Acquire extensive training required to administer, score or interpret tests requiring test-specific training.

Giving Directions:

1. Administer standardized tests with the verbatim instructions, exact sequence and timing and the identical materials that were used in the test standardization.
2. Present all tests (whether standardized, published or locally constructed) in an identical manner to ensure that the test is a fair and comparable demonstration of the performance of each individual taking the test.

Recognize that taking a test may be a new and frightening experience or stimulate anxiety or frustration for some individuals. Communicate to the examinees that they should attempt each task with positive application of their skills and knowledge and the anticipation that they will do their best.

Testing Conditions:

1. Devote concentrated attention to observing the condition and reactions of the individuals being tested. Observe those being tested and identify environmental, health or emotional conditions that should be recorded and considered as invalidating elements for the test performance.
2. Possess and demonstrate clear verbal articulation, calmness and positive anticipation, empathy for and social identification with the examinees, and, impartial treatment for all being tested.
3. Determine whether the testing environment (seating, work surfaces, lighting, heating, freedom from distractions, etc.) is conducive to the best possible performance of the test-takers.
4. Administer tests in physical facilities and psychological climates that allow each individual being tested to achieve optimum performance.
5. Record any deviation from standardized test administration procedure (such as used to accommodtate handicapping conditions) and make it a permanent attachment to the test score or record.
6. Develop and complete for each test a systematic and objective procedure for observing and recording the behavior of those being tested (and recording conventional or deviant conditions of testing). Attach this record to the test scores of the persons tested.
7. Provide a written record of any circumstances that may have increased or reduced the opprotunity of an individual being tested to demonstrate his or her best performance.

8. Accept responsibility for seeing that invalid or questionable test scores are not recorded, or not recorded without written qualification of the conditions that may have affected optimum test performance.

9. Arrange assistance from trained personnel in providing uniform conditions and in observing the conduct of the examinees when large groups of individuals must be tested.

Professional Collaboration:

Recognize that in institutional settings, and wherever skill and knowledge can be pooled and responsibility shared, it is the qualifications of the team as a whole that count rather than those of individuals. However, coordination and consistency must be maintained.

Test Scoring

The measurement of human performance depends on accurate and consistent application of defined procedures for crediting the responses made by persons being tested. The procedures for scoring and recording test performance must be continuously audited for consistency and accuracy.

1. Routinely rescore a sample of the test answer sheets to verify the accuracy of the initial scoring.

2. Employ systematic procedures to verify the accuracy and consistency of machine scoring of answer sheets.

3. Obtain a separate and independent verification that appropriate scoring rules and normative conversions are used for each person tested.

4. Verify as accurate the computation of raw scores and the conversion of raw scores to normative or descriptive scales prior to release of such information to the tested person or to users of the test results.

5. Routinely check machine or manual reports of test results for accuracy. The person performing this task must be qualified to recognize inappropriate or impossible scores.

6. Develop and use systematic and objective procedures for observing and recording the conditions and behaviors of persons being tested and make this a part of the scores or test results that are reported.

7. Clearly label the scores that are reported and the date that a particular test was administered.

Test Interpretation

Test interpretation encompasses all the ways we assign value to the scores.

A test can be described as a systematic set or series of standard observations of performances that all fall in some particular domain. Typically each observation yields a rating of the performance (such as right or wrong and pass or fail), then these ratings are counted and this count becomes the basis of the scores. Such scores are usually much more stable than the result of any single performance. This score reliability creates the possibility of validity greater than can be obtained from unsystematic or nonaggregated observations.

The proper interpretation of test scores starts with understanding these fundamental characteristics of tests. Given this, the interpretation of scores from a test entails knowledge about (1) administration and scoring procedures; (2) scores, norms, and related technical features; (3) reliability; and (4) validity.

Adequate test interpretation requires knowledge and skill in each of these areas. Some of this information can be mastered only by studying the manual and other materials of the test; no one should undertake the interpretation of scores on any test without such study.

Administration and Scoring:

Standard procedure for administering and scoring the test limit the possible meanings of scores. Departures from standard conditions and procedures modify and often invalidate the criteria for score interpretation.

1. The priniciples in the section on administration and scoring need to be understood by those engaged in interpretation.

2. Ascertain the circumstances peculiar to the particular administration and scoring of the test.

A. Examine all reports from administrators, proctors and scorers concerning irregularities or conditions, such as excessive anxiety, which may have affected performance.

B. Weigh the possible effects on test scores of

examiner-examinee differences in ethnic and cultural background, attitudes and values in light of research on these matters. Recognize that such effects are probably larger in individual testing situations.

C. Look for administrators' reports of examinee behavior that indicate the responses were made on some basis other than that intended—as when a student being tested for knowledge of addition-number-facts adds by making tallies and the counting them.

3. Consider differences among clients in their reaction to instructions about guessing and scoring.

4. Recognize or judge the effect of scorer biases and judgment when subjective elements enter into scoring.

Scores, Norms and Related Technical Features:

The result of scoring a test is usually a number (or a set of numbers) called a raw score. Raw scores taken by themselves are not usually interpretable. Some additional steps must be taken.

The procedures either translate the numbers directly into descriptions of their meaning (e.g., pass or fail) or into other numbers called derived scores (e.g., standard scores) whose meaning stems from the test norms.

To interpret test scores, these procedures and the resulting descriptions or derived scores need to be thoroughly understood. Anything less than full understanding is likely to produce at least some, and probably many, serious errors in interpretation. The following are imperatives for interpreting tests:

1. Examine the test manuals, handbooks, users' guides and technical reports to determine what descriptions or derived scores are produced and what unique characteristics each may have.

2. Recognize that direct score interpretations such as mastery and nonmastery in criterion-referenced tests depend on arbitrary rules or standards.

A. Report number or percent of items right in addition to the indicated interpretation whenever it will help others understand the quality of the examinee's test performance.

B. Recognize that the difficulty of a fixed standard, such as 80 percent right, will vary widely from objective to objective. Such scores are not comparable in the normative sense.

C. Recognize that when each score is classified as pass-fail, mastery-nonmastery or the like, that each element is being given equal weight.

3. Use the derived scores that fit the needs of the current use of the test.

A. Use percentile ranks for direct comparison of individuals to the norm or reference group.

B. Use standard scores or equal unit scaled scores whenever means and variances are calculated or other arithmetic operations are being used.

4. Recognize that only those derived scores that are based on the same norm group can be compared.

5. Consider the effect of any differences between the tests in what they measure when one test or form is equated with another, as well as the errors stemming from the equating itself.

Give greater credence to growth or change shown by the same test (including level and form) than to equating measures except where practice effects or feedback have destroyed the validity of a second use.

6. Evaluate the appropriateness of the norm groups available as bases for interpreting the scores of clients.

A. Use the norms for the group to which the client belongs.

B. Consider using local norms and dervied scores based on these local norms whenever possible.

7. Acquire knowledge of specific psychological or educational concepts and theories before interpreting the scores of tests based on such knowledge.

Reliability:

Reliability is a prerequisite to validity. Generally, the greater the number of items the greater the reliability of the test. The degree to which a score or a set of scores may vary because of measurement error is a central factor in interpretation.

1. Use the standard error of measurement to obtain a rough estimate of the probable variation in scores due to unreliability.

2. Use the reliability coefficient to estimate the proportion of score variance that is not due to error.
3. Consider the sources of variance attributable to error in the particular reliability indexes reported in relationship to the uses being made of the scores.
4. Assess reported reliablities in light of the many extraneous factors that may have artificially raised or lowered these estimates, such as test speededness, sample homogeneity or heterogeneity, restrictions in range and the like.
5. Distinguish indexes of rater reliability (i.e., of objectivity) from test reliability.

Validity:

Proper test interpretation requires knowledge of the validity evidence available for the test as used. Its validity for other uses is not relevant. The purpsoe of testing dictates how a test is used. Technically proper use for ill-understood purposes may constitute misuse. The nature of the validity evidence required for a test is a function of its use.

Prediction—developing expectancies: The relationship of the test scores to an independently developed criterion measure is the basis for predictive validity.

1. Consider both the reliability and the relevance of the criterion measures used.
2. Use cross validation data to judge the validity of predictions.
3. Question the meaning of an apparently valid predictor that lacks both construct and content validity. Assess the role of underlying and concomitant variables.
4. Consider the validity of a given measure in the context of all the predictors used or available. Does the measure make an independent contribution to the prediction over and above that provided by other measures?
5. Consider the pitfalls of labeling, stereotyping and prejudging people. The self-fulfilling prophecies that may result are often undesirable.

Placement/selection: Predictive validity is the usual basis for valid placement. Consider the evidence of validity for each alternative (i.e., each placement) when inferring the meaning of scores.

1. Obtain adequate information about the programs or institutions in which the client may be placed in other to judge the consequences of such placement.
2. Estimate the probability of favorable outcomes for each possible placement (e.g., both selection and rejection) before judging the import of the scores.
3. Consider the possiblity that outcomes favorable from an institutional point of view may differ from those that are favorable from the examinees' point of view.
4. Examine the possibility that the clients' group membership (race, sex, etc.) may alter the reported validity relationships.
5. Use all the available evidence about the individual to infer the validity of the score for that indivdiual. Each single piece of information about an individual (e.g., test score, teacher report, or counselor opinion) improves the probability that proper judgments and decisions can be made.
A. Test scores should be considered in context; they do not have absolute meaning.
B. Single test scores should not be the sole basis for placement or selection.

Description/diagnosis: Distinguish between those descriptions and diagnoses using psychological constructs that can be validated only indirectly and those for which content specifications suffice.

1. Identify clearly the domain specified by those asserting content validity. Assess the adequacy of the content sampling procedures used in writing and selecting items.
2. Identify the dimensions of the construct being measured when multiple scores from a battery or inventory are used for description.
A. Examine the content validity and/or the construct validity of each score separately.
B. Consider the relative importance of the various subtests, parts, objectives or elements yielding separate scores and judge the weight they each should be given in interpretation.
C. Recognize that when scores are summed or averaged their weight is a function of their variances.

D. Recognize that when each score is classified as pass-fail, mastery-nonmastery or the like, each element is being given equal weight.

3. Examine the completeness of the description provided, recognizing that no set of test scores completely describes a human being.

Growth—Studies of change: Valid assessment of growth or change requires both a test having descriptive validity and a procedure for establishing that the scores obtained differ from those that might arise when no change has occurred.

1. Report as possibilities all the interpretations the study or evaluation design permits. Point out those interpretations that are precluded by the design used.

A. When standard procedures such as the RMC models (see Tallmadge, G.K. and Horst, D. P., A procedural guide for validating achievement gains in educational projects; Mountain View, Calif.: RMC Research Corp., Dec. 1975) for measuring growth in achievement are employed, use the descriptions of strengths and weaknesses provided.

B. Look for naturally occurring control groups not part of design whenever possible.

2. Consider the strengths and weaknesses of the particular tests used with respect to this use. Consider the possiblity of floor or ceiling effects, the content changes level to level, the adequacy of articulation in multilevel tests, the comparability of alternate forms, the adequacy of the score-equating across forms, and the comparabiltity of timing of the testing to that of the norming.

3. Recognize the unreliability of indivudal score differences as measures of change.

4. Recognize the limitations of scoring scales such as grade equivalents that may not have the comparable meaning they appear to have at different levels of the scale.

5. Recognize the need for equal interval scales when trying to assess the amount of change.

Communicating Test Results

Communication consists of reporting data in such a way that it is comprehensible and informative. The responsible practitioner reports test data with a concern for the user's need for information and the purposes of evaluating the significance of the information.

There must also be a concern for the right of the individual tested to be informed regarding how the results will be used for his or her benefit (informed consent), who will have access to the results (right to privacy), and what safeguards exist to prevent misuse.

Where standardized test data are being used to enhance decisions about an individual, the practitioner's responsibilities are as follows:

Know the Manual:

1. Become thoroughly familiar with the publisher's manual before attempting to "explain" any results.

2. Develop skills needed to communicate results of tests, using concepts that are frequently misunderstood before communicating results to clients, the public, or other recipients of the information.

Know the Limits:

1. Inform the person receiving the test information that "scores" are approximations, not absolutes, and indicate the SEM or the margin of error in some other way, such as by reporting score intervals rather than points.

2. Candidly discuss with the person receiving the test information any qualifications necessary to understand potential sources of bias for a given set of test results relative to their use with a specific individual.

3. Emphasize that test data represent just one source of information and should rarely, if ever, be used alone for decison making.

Informed Consent:

1. Inform the person receiving the test information of any circumstances that could have affected the validity or reliability of the results.

2. Inform the examinee of what action will be taken by the agency and who will be using the results.

3. Obtain the consent of the examinee before using test results for any purpose other than that advanced prior to testing.

Right to Privacy:

Inform the examinee of steps to be taken to correct any erroneous information that may be on file as a result of testing.

Where standardized test data are being used to describe groups for the purpose of evaluation, the practitioner's responsibilities are as follows:

Background Information:

1. Include background information to improve the accuracy of understanding about any numerical data.
2. Identify the purposes for which the reported data would be appropriate.

Politics:

Be aware that public release of test information provides data for all kinds of purposes and that some of these may be adverse to the interest of those tested.

Averages and Norms:

1. Clarify in particular that "average" on a standardized test is a range, not a point, and typically includes the middle 50 percent of the group being considered.
2. Qualify all group data in terms of the appropriateness of the norms for that group.

Agency Policies:

1. Work for agency test-reporting policies designed to strengthen and protect the benefits of the groups being measured.
2. Work within the agency to establish procedures for periodic review of internal test use.

APPENDIX G

CODE OF ETHICS FOR CERTIFIED CLINICAL MENTAL HEALTH COUNSELORS

National Academy of Certified Clinical Mental Health Counselors

(This code is an adaptation of the code of the Board of Licensed Professional Counselors in Virginia)

Preamble

Certified Clinical Mental Health Counselors believe in the dignity and worth of the individual. They are committed to increasing knowledge of human behavior and understanding of themselves and others. While pursuing these endeavors, they make every reasonable effort to protect the welfare of those who seek their services or of any subject that may be the object of study. They use their skills only for purposes consistent with these values and do not knowingly permit their misuse by others. While demanding for themselves freedom of inquiry and communication, certified clinical mental health counselors accept the responsibility this freedom confers: competence, objectivity in the application of skills and concern for the best

Code of Ethics for Certified Clinical Mental Health Counselors, by the National Academy of Certified Clinical Mental Health Counselors. Reprinted by permission of the American Mental Health Counselors Association.

interests of clients, colleagues, and society in general. In the pursuit of these ideals, clinical mental health counselors subscribe to the following principles:

Principle 1: Responsibility

In their commitment to the understanding of human behavior, clinical mental health counselors value objectivity and integrity, and in providing services they maintain the highest standards. They accept responsibility for the consequences of their work and make every effort to insure that their services are used appropriately.

a. Clinical mental health counselors accept ultimate responsibility for selecting appropriate areas for investigation and the methods relevant to minimize the possibility that their finding will be misleading. They provide thorough discussion of the limitations of their data and alternative hypotheses, especially where their work touches on social policy or might be misconstrued to the detriment of specific age, sex, ethnic, socio-economic, or other social categories. In publishing reports of their work, they never discard observations that may modify the interpretation of results. Clinical mental health counselors take credit only for the work they have actually done. In pursuing research, clinical mental health counselors ascertain that their efforts will not lead to changes in individuals or organizations unless such changes are part of the agreement at the time of obtaining informed consent. Clinical mental health counselors clarify in advance the expectations for sharing and utilizing research data. They avoid dual relationships which may limit objectivity, whether theoretical, political, or monetary, so that interference with data, subjects and milieu is kept to a minimum.

b. As employees of an institution or agency, clincial mental health counselors have the responsibility of remaining alert to institutional pressures which may distort reports of counseling findings or use them in ways counter to the promotion of human welfare.

c. When serving as members of governmental or other organizational bodies, clinical mental health counselors remain accountable as individuals to the Code of Ethics of the National Academy of Certified Mental Health Counselors.

d. As teachers, clinical mental health counselors recognize their primary obligation to help others acquire knowledge and skill. They maintain high standards of scholarship and objectivity by presenting counseling information fully and accurately, and by giving appropriate recognition to alternative viewpoints.

e. As practitioners, clinical mental health counselors know that they bear a heavy social responsibility because their recommedations and professional actions may alter the lives of others. They therefore remain fully cognizant of their impact and alert to personal, social, organziational, financial or political situations or pressures which might lead to misuse of their influence.

f. Clinical mental health counselors provide reasonable and timely feedback to employees, trainees, supervisors, students and others whose work they may evaluate.

Principle 2: Competence

The maintenance of high standards of professional competence is a responsibility shared by all clinical mental health counselors in the interest of the public and the profession as a whole. Clinical mental health counselors recognize the boundaries of their competence and the limitations of their techniques and only provide services, use techniques, or offer opinions as professionals that meet recognized standards. Throughout their careers, clinical mental health counselors maintain knowledge of professional information related to the services they render.

a. Clinical mental health counselors accurately represent their competence, education, training and experience.

b. As teachers, clinical mental health counselors perform their duties based on careful preparation so that their instruction is accurate, up-to-date and scholarly.

c. Clinical mental health counselors recognize the need for continuing training to prepare themselves to serve persons of all ages and cultural backgrounds. They are open to new procedures and sensitive to differences between groups of people and changes in expectations and values over time.

d. Clinical mental health counselors with the responsibility for decisions involving individuals or policies based on test results should know and understand literature relevant to the tests used and testing problems with which they deal.

e. Clinical mental health counselors/practitioners recognize that their effectiveness depends in part upon their ability to maintain sound interpersonal relations, that temporary or more enduring aberrations on their part may interfere with their abilities or distort their appraisals of others. Therefore, they refrain from undertaking any activity in which their personal problems are likely to lead to inadequate professional services or harm to a client, or, if they are already engaged in such activity when they become aware of their personal problems, they would seek competent professional assistance to determine whether they should suspend or terminate services to one or all of their clients.

Principle 3: Moral and Legal Standards

Clinical mental health counselors' moral, ethical and legal standards of behavior are a personal matter to the same degree as they are for any other citizen, except as these may compromise the fulfillment of their professional responsibilities, or reduce the trust in counseling or counselors held by the general public. Regarding their own behavior, clinical mental health counselors should be aware of the prevailing community standards and of the possible impact upon the quality of professional services provided by their conformance to or deviation from these standards. Clinical mental health counselors should also be aware of the possible impact of their public behavior upon the ability of colleagues to perform their professional duties.

a. To protect public confidence in the profession of counseling, clinical mental health counselors will avoid public behavior that is clearly in violation of accepted moral and legal standards.

b. To protect students, counselors/teachers will be aware of the diverse backgrounds of students and, when dealing with topics that may give offense, will see that the material is treated objectively, that it is clearly relevant to the course, and that it is treated in a manner for which the student is prepared.

c. Providers of counseling services conform to the statutes relating to such services as established by their state and its regulating professional board(s).

d. As employees, clinical mental health counselors refuse to participate in employer's practices which are inconsistent with the moral and legal standards established by federal or state legislation regarding the treatment of employees or of the public. In particular and for example, clinical mental health counselors will not condone practices which result in illegal or otherwise unjustifiable discrimination on the basis of race, sex, religion or national origin in hiring, promotion or training.

e. In providing counseling services to clients clinical mental health counselors avoid any action that will violate or diminish the legal and civil rights of clients or of others who may be affected by the action.

f. Sexual conduct, not limited to sexual intercourse, between clinical mental health counselors and clients is specifically in violation of this code of ethics. This does not, however, prohibit the use of explicit instructional aids including films and video tapes. Such use is within accepted practices of trained and competent sex therapists.

Principle 4: Public Statements

Clinical mental health counselors in their professional roles may be expected or required to make public statements providing counseling information, professional opinions, or supply information about the availability of counseling products and services. In making such statements, clinical mental health counselors take full account of the limits and uncertainties of present counseling knowledge and tehniques. They represent, as objectively as possible, their professional qualifications, affiliations, and functions, as well as those of the institutions or organizations with which the statements may be associated. All public statements, announcements of services, and promotional activities should serve the purpose of providing sufficient information to aid the consumer public in making informed judgments and choices on matters that concern it.

a. When announcing professional services, clinical mental health counselors limit the information to: name, highest relevant degree conferred, certification or licensure, address, telephone number, office hours, cost of services, and a brief explanation of the types of services offered but not evaluative as to their quality of uniqueness. They will not contain testimonials by implication. They will not claim uniqueness of skill or methods beyond those available to others in the profession unless determined by acceptable and public scientific evidence.

b. In announcing the availability of counseling services or products, clinical mental health counselors will not display their affiliations with organizations or agencies in a manner that implies the sponsorship or certification of the organization or agency. They will not name their employer or professional associations unless the services are in fact to be provided by or under the responsible, direct supervision and continuing control of such organizations or agencies.

c. Clinical mental health counselors associated with the development or promotion of counseling devices, books, or other products offered for commercial sale will make every effort to insure that announcements and advertisement are presented in a professional and factually informative manner without unsupported claims of superiority; [all information] must be supported by scientifically acceptable evidence or by willingness to aid and encourage independent professional scrutiny or scientific test.

d. Clinical mental health counselors engaged in radio, television or other public media activities will not participate in commercial announcements recommending to the general public the purchase or use of any proprietary or single-source product or service.

e. Clinical mental health counselors who describe counseling or the services of professional counselors to the general public accept the obligation to present the material fairly and accurately, avoiding misrepresentation through sensationalism, exaggeration or superficiality. Clinical mental health counselors will be guided by the primary obligation to aid the public in forming their own informed judgements, opinions and choices.

As teachers, clinical mental health counselors ensure that statements in catalogs and course outlines are accurate, particularly in terms of subject matter to be covered, bases for grading, and nature of classroom experiences. As practitioners providing private services, CMH counselors avoid improper, direct solicitation of clients and the conflict of interest inherent therein.

g. Clinical mental health counselors accept the obligation to correct others who may represent their professional qualifications or associations with products or services in a manner incompatible with these guidelines.

Principle 5: Confidentiality

Clincial mental health counselors have a primary obligation to safeguard information about individuals obtained in the course of teaching, practice, or research. Personal information is communicated to others only with the person's written consent or in those circumstances where there is clear and imminent danger to the client, to others or to society. Disclosures of counseling information are restricted to what is necessary, relevant, and varifiable.

a. All materials in the official record shall be shared with the client who shall have the right to decide what information may be shared with anyone beyond the immediate provider of service and to be informed of the implications of the materials to be shared.

b. The anonymity of clients served in public and other agencies is preserved, if at all possible, by withholding names and personal identifying data. If external conditions require reporting such information, the client shall be so informed.

c. Information received in confidence by one agency or person shall not be forwarded to another person or agency without the client's written permission.

d. Service providers have a responsibility to insure the accuracy and to indicate the validity of data shared with their parties.

e. Case reports presented in classes, professional meetings, or in publications shall be so disguised that no identification is possible unless the client or responsible authority has read the report and agreed in writing to its presentation or publication.

f. Counseling reports and records are maintained under conditions of security and provisions are made for their destruction when they have outlived their usefulness. Clinical mental health counselors insure that privacy and confidentiality are maintained by all persons in the employ or volunteers, and community aides.

g. Clincial mental health counselors who ask that an individual reveal personal information in the course of interviewing, testing or evaluation, or who allow such information to be divulged, do so only after making certain that the person or authorized representative is fully aware of the purposes of the interview, testing or evaluation and of the ways in which the information will be used.

h.. Sessions with clients are taped or otherwise recorded only with their written permission or the written permission of a responsible guardian. Even with guardian written consent, one should not record a session against the expressed wishes of a client.

i. Where a child or adolescent is the primary client, the interests of the minor shall be paramount.

j. In work with families, the rights of each family member should be safeguarded. The provider of service also has the responsiblity to discuss the contents of the record with the parent and/or child, as appropriate, and to keep separate those parts which should remain the property of each family member.

Principle 6: Welfare of the Consumer

Clinical mental health counselors respect the integrity and protect the welfare of the people and groups with whom they work. When there is a conflict of interest between the client and the clinical mental health counselor employing institution, the clinical mental health counselors clarify the nature and direction of their loyalties and responsiblities and keep all parties informed of their commitments. Clinical mental health counselors fully inform consumers as to the purpose and nature of any evaluative, treatment, educational or training procedure, and they freely acknowledge that clients, students, or subjects have freedom of choice with regard to participation.

a. Clinical mental health counselors are continually cognizant both of their own needs and of their inherently powerful position "vis-à-vis" clients, in order to avoid exploiting the client's trust and dependency. Clinical mental health counselors make every effort to avoid dual relationships with clients and/or relationships which might impair their professional judgement or increase the risk of client exploitation. Examples of such dual relationships include treating an employee or supervisor, treating a close friend or family relative and sexual relationships with clients.

b. Where clinical mental health counselors' work with members of an organization goes beyond reasonable conditions of employment, clinical mental health counselors recognize possible conflicts of interests that may arise. When such conflicts occur, clincial mental health counselors clarify the nature of the conflict and inform all parties of the nature and directions of the loyalties and responsibilities involved.

c. When acting as supervisors, trainers, or employers, clinical mental health counselors accord recipients informed choice, confiden-

tiality, and protection from physical and mental harm.

d. Financial arrangements in professional practice are in accord with professional standards that safeguard the best interests of the client and that are clearly understood by the client in advance of billing. This may best be done by the use of a contract. Clinical mental health counselors are responsible for assisting clients in finding needed services in those instances where payment of the usual fee would be a hardship. No commission or rebate or other form of remuneration may be given or received for referral of clients for professional services, whether by an individual or by an agency.

e. Clinical mental health counselors are responsible for making their services readily accessible to clients in a manner that facilitates the client's ability to make an informed choice when selecting a service provider. This responsibility includes a clear written description of what the client may expect in the way of tests, reports, billing, therapeutic regime and schedules.

f. Clinical mental health counselors who find that their services are not beneficial to the client have the responsibility to make this known to the responsible persons.

g. Clinical mental health counselors are accountable to the parties who refer and support counseling services and to the general public and are cognizant of the indirect or long-range effects of their intervention.

h. The clinical mental health counselor attempts to terminate a private service or consulting relationship when it is reasonably clear to the clinical mental health counselor that the consumer is not benefitting from it. If a consumer is receiving services from another mental health professional, clinical mental health counselors do not offer their services directly to the consumer without informing the professional persons already involved in order to avoid confusion and conflict for the consumer.

Principle 7: Professional Relationship

Clinical mental health counselors act with due regard to the needs and feelings of their colleagues in counseling and other professions. Clinical mental health counselors respect the prerogatives and obligations of the institutions or organizations with which they are associated.

a. Clinical mental health counselors understand the areas of competence of related professions and make full use of other professional, technical, and administrative resources which best serve the interests of consumers. The absence of formal relationships with other professional workers does not relieve clinical mental health counselors from the responsibility of securing for their clients the best possible professional service; indeed, this circumstance presents a challenge to the professional competence of clinical mental health counselors, requiring special sensitivity to problems outside their areas of training, and foresight, diligence, and tact in obtaining the professional assistance needed by clients.

b. Clinical mental health counselors know and take into account the traditions and practices of other professional groups with which they work and cooperate fully with members of such groups when research, services, and other functions are shared or in working for the benefit of public welfare.

c. Clinical mental health counselors strive to provide positive conditions for those they employ and that they spell out clearly the conditions of such employment. They encourage their employees to engage in activities that facilitate their further professional development.

d. Clinical mental health counselors respect the viability, reputation, and the proprietary right of organizations which they serve. Clinical mental health counselors show due regard for the interest of their present or prospective employers. In those instances where they are critical of policies, they attempt to effect change by constructive action within the organization.

e. In the pursuit of research, clinical mental health counselors give sponsoring agencies, host institutions, and publication channels the same respect and opportunity for giving informed consent that they accord to individual research participants. They are aware of their obligation to future research workers and insure that host institutions are given

feedback information and proper acknowledgement.

f. Credit is assigned to those who have contributed to a publication, in proportion to their contribution.

g. When a clinical mental health counselor violates ethical standards, clinical mental health counselors who know first-hand of such activities should, if possible, attempt to rectify the situation. Failing an informal solution, clinical mental health counselors should bring such unethical activities to the National Academy of Certified Clinical Mental Health Counselors.

Principle 8: Utilization of Assessment Techniques

In the development, publication, and utilization of counseling assessment techniques, clinical mental health counselors follow relevant standards. Individuals examined, or their legal guardians, have the right to know the results, the interpretations made, and where appropriate, the particulars on which final judgment was based. Test users should take precautions to protect test security but not at the expense of an individual's right to understand the basis for decisions that adversely affect that individual or that individual's dependents.

a. The client has the right to have and the provider has the responsibility to give explanations of test results in language the client can understand.

b. When a test is published or otherwise made available for operational use, it should be accompanied by a manual (or other published or readily available information) that makes every reasonable effort to describe fully the development of the test, the rationale, specifications followed in writing items analysis or other research. The test, the manual, the record forms and other accompanying material should help users make correct interpretations of the test results and should warn against common misuses. The test manual should state explicitly the purposes and applications for which the test is recommended and identify any special qualifications required to administer the test and to interpret it properly. Evidence of validity and reliability, along with other relevant research data, should be presented in support of any claims made.

c. Norms presented in test manuals should refer to defined and clearly described populations. These populations should be the groups with whom users of the test will ordinarily wish to compare the persons tested. Test users should consider the possibility of bias in tests or in test items. When indicated, there should be an investigation of possible differences in validity for ethnic, sex, or other subsamples that can be identified when the test is given.

d. Clinical mental health counselors who have the responsibility for decisions about individuals or policies that are based on test results should have a thorough understanding of counseling or educational measurement and of validation and other test research.

e. Clinical mental health counselors should develop procedures for systematically eliminating from data files test score information that has, because of the lapse of time, become obsolete.

f. Any individual or organizaton offering test scoring and interpretation services must be able to demonstrate that their programs are based on appropriate research to establish the validity of the programs and procedures used in arriving at interpretations. The public offering of an automated test interpretation service will be considered as a professional-to-professional consultation. In this the formal responsibility of the consultant is to the consultee but his/her ultimate and overriding responsibility is to the client.

g. Counseling services for the purpose of diagnosis, treatment, or personalized advice are provided only in the context of a professional relationship, and are not given by means of public lectures or demonstrations, newspaper or magazine articles, radio or television programs, mail, or similar media. The preparation of personnel reports and recommendations based on test data secured solely by mail is unethical unless such appraisals are an integral part of a continuing client relationship with a company, as a result of which the consulting clinical mental health counselor has intimate knowledge of the client's personal situation and can be assured thereby that his

written appraisals will be adequate to the purpose and will be properly interpreted by the client. These reports must not be embellished with such detailed analysis of the subject's personality traits as would be appropriate only for intensive interviews with the subjects.

Principle 9: Pursuit of Research Activities

The decision to undertake research should rest upon a considered judgment by the individual clinical mental health counselor about how best to contribute to counseling and to human welfare. Clinical mental health counselors carry out their investigations with respect for the people who participate and with concern for their dignity and welfare.

a. In planning a study the investigator has the personal responsibility to make a careful evaluation of its ethical acceptability, taking into account the following principles for research with human beings. To the extent that this appraisal, weighing scientific and humane values, suggests a deviation from any principle, the investigator incurs an increasingly serious obligation to seek ethical advice and to observe more stringent safeguards to protect the rights of the human research participants.

b. Clinical mental health counselors know and take into account the traditions and practices of other professional groups with members of such groups when research, services, and other functions are shared or in working for the benefit of public welfare.

c. Ethical practice requires the investigator to inform the participant of all features of the research that reasonably might be expected to influence willingness to participate, and to explain all other aspects of the research about which the participant inquires. Failure to make full disclosure gives added emphasis to the investigator's abiding responsibilty to protect the welfare and dignity of the research participant.

d. Openness and honesty are essential characteristics of the relationship between investigator and research participant. When the methodological requirements of a study necessitate concealment or deception, the investigator is required to insure as soon as possible the participant's understanding of the reasons for this action and to restore the quality of the relationship with the investigator.

e. In the pursuit of research, clinical mental health counselors give sponsoring agencies, host institutions, and publication channels the same respect and opportunity for giving informed consent that they accord to individual research participants. They are aware of their obligation to future research workers and insure that host institutions are given feedback information and proper acknowledgement.

f. Credit is assigned to those who have contributed to a publication, in proportion to their contribution.

g. The ethical investigator protects participants from physical and mental discomfort, harm and danger. If the risk of such consequences exists, the investigator is required to inform the participant of that fact, secure consent before proceeding, and take all possible measures to minimize distress. A research procedure may not be used if it is likely to cause serious and lasting harm to participants.

h. After the data are collected, ethical practice requires the investigator to provide the participant with a full clarification of the nature of the study and to remove any misconceptions that may have arisen. Where scientific or humane values justify delaying or withholding information the investigator acquires a special responsibility to assure that there are no damaging consequences for the participants.

i. Where research procedures may result in undesirable consequences for the participant, the investigator has the responsibility to detect and remove or correct these consequences, including, where relevant, long-term after effects.

j. Information obtained about the research participants during the course of an investigation is confidential. When the possibility exists that others may obtain access to such information, ethical research practice requires that the possibility, together with the plans for protecting confidentiality be explained to the participants as a part of the procedure for obtaining informed consent.

APPENDIX

CODE OF PROFESSIONAL ETHICS

American Assocation for Marriage and Family Therapy

Section I: Code of Personal Conduct

1. A therapist provides professional service to anyone regardless of race, religion, sex, political affiliation, social or economic status, or choice of lifestyle. When a therapist cannot offer service for any reason, he or she will make proper referral. Therapists are encouraged to devote a portion of their time to work for which there is little or no financial return.
2. A therapist will not use his or her counseling relationship to further personal, religious, political, or business interests.
3. A therapist will neither offer nor accept payment for referrals, and will actively seek all significant information from the source of referral.
4. A therapist will not knowingly offer service to a client who is in treatment with another clinical professional without consultation among the parties involved.
5. A therapist will not disparage the qualifications of any colleague.
6. Every member of the AAMFT has an obligation to continuing education and professional growth in all possible ways, including active participation in the meetings and affairs of the Association.

7. A therapist will not attempt to diagnose, prescribe for, treat, or advise on problems outside the recognized boundaries of the therapist's competence.
8. A therapist will attempt to avoid relationships with clients which might impair professional judgment or increase the risks of exploiting clients. Examples of such relationships include: treatment of family members, close friends, employees, or supervisees. Sexual intimacy with clients is unethical.
9. The AAMFT encourages its members to affiliate with professional groups, clinics, or agencies operating in the field of marriage and family life. Similarly, interdisciplinary contact and cooperation are encouraged.

Section II: Relations with Clients

1. A therapist, while offering dignified and reasonable support, is cautious in prognosis and will not exaggerate the efficacy of his or her services.

Code of Professional Ethics, by the American Association for Marriage and Family Therapy. Copyright by the American Association for Marriage and Family Therapy (no date). Reprinted by permission of the American Association for Marriage and Family Therapy.

2. The therapist recognizes the importance of clear understandings on financial matters with clients. Arrangements for payments are settled at the beginning of a therapeutic relationship.

3. A therapist keeps records of each case and stores them in such a way as to insure safety and confidentiality, in accordance with the highest professional and legal standards.

   a. Information shall be revealed only to professional persons concerned with the case. Written and oral reports should present only data germane to the purposes of the inquiry; every effort should be made to avoid undue invasion of privacy.

   b. The therapist is responsible for informing clients of the limits of confidentiality.

   c. Written permission shall be granted by the clients involved before data may be divulged.

   d. Information is not communicated to others without consent of the client unless there is clear and immediate danger to an individual or to society, and then only to the appropriate family members, professional workers, or public authorities.

4. A therapist deals with relationships at varying stages of their history. While respecting at all times the rights of clients to make their own decisions, the therapist has a duty to assess the situation according to the highest professional standards. In all circumstances, the therapist will clearly advise a client that the decision to separate or divorce is the responsibility solely of the client. In such an event, the therapist has the continuing responsibility to offer support and counsel during the period of readjustment.

Section III: Research and Publication

1. The therapist is obligated to protect the welfare of his or her research subjects. The conditions of the Human Subjects Experimentation shall prevail, as specified by the Department of Health, Education and Welfare guidelines.

2. Publication credit is assigned to those who have contributed to a publication, in proportion to their contribution, and in accordance with customary publication practices.

Section IV: Implementation

1. In accepting membership in the Association, each member binds himself or herself to accept the judgement of fellow members as to standards of professional ethics, subject to the safeguards provided in this section. Acceptance of membership implies consent to abide by the acts of discipline herein set forth and as enumerated in the Bylaws of the Association. It is the duty of each member to safeguard these standards of ethical practice. Should a fellow member appear to violate this Code, he or she may be cautioned through friendly remonstrance, colleague consultation with the party in question, or formal complaint may be filed in accordance with the following procedure:

   a. Complaint of unethical practice shall be made in writing to the Chairperson of the Standing Committee on Ethics and Professional Practices and to the Executive Director. A copy of the complaint shall be furnished to the person or persons against whom it is directed.

   b. Should the Standing Committee decide the complaint warrants investigation, it shall so notify the charged party(ies) in writing. When investigation is indicated, the Standing Committee shall constitute itself an Investigating Committee and shall include in its membership at least one member of the Board and at least two members (other than the charging or charged parties or any possible witnesses) from the local area involved. This Investigating Committee or representatives thereof shall make one or more local visits of investigation of the complaint. After full investigation following due process and offering the charged party(ies) opportunity to defend him or herself, the Committee shall report its findings and recommendations to the Board of Directors for action.

   c. The charged party(ies) shall have free access to all charges and evidence cited against him or her, and shall have full freedom to defend himself or herself before the

Investigating Committee and the Board, including the right to legal counsel.

    d. Recommendation made by the Committee shall be:

      1. Advice that the charges be dropped as unfounded.

      2. Specified admonishment.

      3. Reprimand.

      4. Dismissal from membership.

2. Should a member of this Association be expelled, he or she shall at once surrender his or her membership certificate to the Board of Directors. Failure to do so shall result in such action as legal counsel may recommend.

3. Should a member of this Association be expelled from another recognized professional association or his/her state license revoked for unethical conduct, the Standing Committee on Ethics shall investigate the matter and, where appropriate, act in the manner provided above respecting charges of unethical conduct.

4. The Committee will also give due consideration to a formal complaint by a non-member.

Section V: Public Information and Advertising

All professional presentations to the public will be governed by the Standards on Public Information and Advertising.

Standards on Public Information and Advertising

Section I: General Principles

The practice of marriage and family therapy as a mental health profession is in the public interest. Therefore, it is appropriate for the well-trained and qualified practitioner to inform the public of the availability of his/her services. However, much needs to be done to educate the public as to the services available from qualified marriage and family therapists. Therefore, the clinical members of AAMFT have a responsibility to the public to engage in appropriate informational activities and to avoid misrepresentation or misleading statements in keeping with the following general principles and specific regulations.

Selection of a marriage and family therapist

A. At a time when the Human Services field is burgeoning and becoming increasingly complex and specialized, few marriage and family therapists are willing and competent to deal with every kind of marital or family problem, and many laypersons have difficulty in determining the competence of psychotherapists in general and marriage and family therapists in particular to render different types of services. The selecton of a marriage and family therapist is particularly difficult for transients, persons moving into new areas, persons of limited education or means, and others who have had no previous experience or the degree of sophistication required to evaluate training and competence or because they are in some sort of crisis.

B. Selection of a marriage and family therapist by a layperson should be made on an informed basis. Advice and recommendation of third parties—physicians, other professionals, relatives, friends, acquaintances, business associates—and restrained publicity may be helpful. A marriage and family therapist should not compensate another person for recommending him/her, for influencing a prospective client to employ him/her, or to encourage future recommendations. Advertisements and public communications, whether in directories, announcement cards, newspapers, or on radio or television, should be formulated to convey information that is necessary to make an appropriate selection. Self-praising should be avoided. Information that may be helpful in some situations would include: (1) office information, such as name, including a group name and names of professional associates, address, telephone number, credit card acceptability, languages spoken and written, and office hours; (2) earned degrees, state licensure and/or certification, and AAMFT clinical membership status; (3) description of practice, including a statement that practice is limited to one or more fields of marriage and family therapy; and (4) permitted fee information.

C. The proper motivation for commercial publicity by marriage and family therapists lies in the need to inform the public of the availability of competent, independent marriage and family therapists. The public benefit derived from advertising depends upon the usefulness of the information provided to the community to which it is directed. Advertising marked by excesses of content, volume, scope, or frequency, or which unduly emphasizes unrepresentative biographical information, does not provide that public benefit. The use of media whose scope or nature clearly suggests that the use is intended for self-praising of the therapist without concomitant benefit to the public distorts the legitimate purpose of informing the public and is clearly improper. Indeed, this and other improper advertising may hinder informed selection of a competent, independent professional and advertising that involves excessive cost may unnecessarily increase fees for marriage and family therapy.

D. Advertisements and other communications should make it apparent that the necessity [for] and advisability of marriage and family therapy depend on variant factors that must be evaluated individually. Because fee information frequently may be incomplete and misleading to a layperson, a marriage and family therapist should exercise great care to assure that fee information is complete and accurate. Because of the individuality of each problem, public statements regarding average, minimum, or estimated fees may be deceiving as will commercial publicity conveying information as to results previously achieved, general or average solutions, or expected outcomes. It would be misleading to advertise a set fee for a specific type of case without adhering to the stated fee in charging clients. Advertisements or public claims that use statistical data or other information based on past performance or prediction of future success may be deceptive if they ignore important variables. Only factual assertions, and not opinions, should be made in public communications. Not only must commercial publicity be truthful but its accurate meaning must be apparent to the average layperson. No guarantees about the outcomes of therapy should be made or implied. Any commercial publicity or advertising for which payment is made should so indicate unless it is apparent from the context that it is paid publicity or an advertisement.

E. The desirability of affording the public access to information relevant to their needs and problems has resulted in some relaxation of the former restrictions against advertising by marriage and family therapists. Historically, those restrictions were imposed to prevent deceptive publicity that would mislead laypersons, cause distrust of the profession, and undermine public confidence in the profession, and all marriage and family therapists should remain vigilant to prevent such results. Ambiguous information relevant to a layperson's decision regarding his/her selection of a marriage and family therapist, provided in ways that do not comport with the dignity of the profession or which demean the amelioration of human problems, is inappropriate in public communications. The regulation of advertising by marriage and family therapists is rooted in the public interest. Advertising through which a marriage and family therapist seeks business by use of extravagant or brash statements or appeals to fears could mislead and harm the layperson. Furthermore, public communications that would produce unrealistic expectations in particular cases and bring about distrust of the profession would be harmful to society. Thus, public confidence in our profession would be impaired by such advertisements of professional services. The therapist-client relationship, being personal and unique, should not be established as the result of pressures, deceptions, or exploitation of the vulnerability of clients frequently experiencing significant stress at the time they seek help.

F. The Regulations recognize the value of giving assistance in the selection process through forms of advertising that furnish identification of a marriage and family therapist while avoiding falsity, deception, and misrepresentation. All publicity should be evaluated with regard to its effects on the layperson. The layperson is best served if advertisements contain no misleading information or emotional appeals, and emphasize the necessity of an individualized evaluation of the situation before conclusions as to need for a particular type of therapy and probable expenses can be made. The therapist-client relationship should result from a free and informed choice by the layperson. Unwarranted promises of benefits, over-persuasion, or vexatious or harassing conduct is improper.

G. The name under which a marriage and family therapist conducts his/her practice may be a factor in the selection process. The use of a name which could mislead laypersons concerning the identity, responsibility, source, and status of those practicing thereunder is not proper. Likewise, one should not hold oneself out as being a partner or associate of a firm if he/she is not one in fact.

H. In order to avoid the possiblity of misleading persons with whom he/she deals, a marriage and family therapist should be scrupulous in the representation of his/her professional background, training, and status. In some instances a marriage and family therapist confines his/her practice to a particular area within the field of marriage and family therapy. However, a member should not hold himself/herself out as a specialist without evidence of training, education, and supervised experience in settings which meet recognized professional standards. A marriage and family therapist may, however, indicate, if it is factual, a limitation of his/her practice or that he/she practices within one or more particular areas of marriage and family treatment in public pronouncements which will assist laypersons in selecting a marriage and family therapist and accurately describe the limited area in which the member practices.

I. The marriage and family therapist should support the creation and evolution of ethical, approved plans (such as marriage and family therapist referral systems) which aid in the selection of qualified therapists.

Section II: Regulations

A. The American Association for Marriage and Family Therapy is the sole owner of its name, its logo, and the abbreviated initials AAMFT. Use of the name, logo, and initials is restricted to the following conditions.

1. Only individual clinical members may identify their membership in AAMFT in public information or advertising materials, not associates or students of organizations.

2. The initials AAMFT may not be used following one's name in the manner of an academic degree because this is misleading.

3. Use of the logo is limited to the association, its committees and regional divisons when they are engaged in bona fide activities as units or divisions of AAMFT.

4. A regional divison or chapter of AAMFT may use the AAMFT insignia to list its individual members as a group (e.g., in the Yellow Pages). When all Clinical Members practicing within a directory district have been invited to list, any one or more member may do so.

B. A marriage and family therapist shall not knowingly make a representation about his/her ability, background, or experience, or that of a partner or associate, or about the fee or any other aspect of a proposed professional engagement, that is false, fraudulent, misleading, or deceptive, and that might reasonably be expected to induce reliance by a member of the public.

C. Without limitation, a false, fraudulent, misleading, or deceptive statement or claim includes a statement or claim which:

1. Contains a material misrepresentation of fact;

2. Omits to state any material fact necessary to make the statement, in light of all circumstances, not misleading;

3. Is intended or is likely to create an unjustified expectation;

4. Relates to professional fees other than:

   a. a statement of the fee for an initial consultation; a statement of the fee charges for a specific service, the description of which would not be misunderstood or be deceptive;

   b. a statement of the range of fees for specifically described services, provided there is a reasonable disclosure of all relevant variables and considerations so that the statement would not be misunderstood or be deceptive;

   c. a statement of specified hourly rates, provided the statement makes clear that the total charge will vary according to the number of hours devoted to the matter;

   d. the availability of credit arrangements; or

5. Contains a representation or implication that

is likely to cause an ordinary prudent person to misunderstand or be deceived or fails to contain reasonable warnings or disclaimers necessary to make a representation or implication not deceptive.

D. A member shall not, on his/her own behalf or on behalf of a partner or associate or any other therapist associated with the firm, use or participate in the use of any form of advertising of servcies which:

1. Contains statistical data or other information based on past performance or prediction of future success;
2. Contains a testimonial about or endorsement of a therapist;
3. Contains a statement of opinion as to the quality of the services or contains a representation or implication regarding the quality of services, whether therapeutic or educational, which is not susceptible of reasonable verificaton by the public;
4. Is intended or is likely to attract clients by use of showmanship or self-praising.

E. A member shall not compensate or give anything of value to a representative of the press, radio, television, or other communication medium in anticipation of or in return for professional publicity in a news item. A paid advertisement must be identified as such unless it is apparent from the context that it is a paid advertisement. If the paid advertisement is communicated to the public by use of radio or television, it shall be prerecorded, approved for broadcast by the therapist, and a recording of the actual transmission shall be retained by the therapist.

Professional Notices, Letterheads, Offices, and Directory Listings

F. A member or group of members shall not use or participate in the use of a professional card, professional announcement card, office sign, letterhead, telephone directory listing, association directory listing, or a similar professional notice or device if it includes a statement or claim that is false, fraudulent, misleading, or deceptive within the meaning

of Section II, C or that violates the regulations contained in Section II, D.

G. A member shall not practice under a name that is misleading as to the identity, responsibility, or status of those practicing thereunder, or is otherwise false, fraudulent, misleading, or deceptive within the meaning of Section II, C or is contrary to law. However, the name of a professional corporation or professional association may contain "P.C." or "P.A." or similar symbols indicating the nature of the organization.

H. A member shall not hold himself/herself out as having a partnership with one or more other qualified therapists unless they are in fact partners.

I. A partnership shall not be formed or continued between or among members in different geographical locations unless all enumerations of the members or associates of the firm on its letterhead and in other permissible listings make clear the limitations due to geographical separation of the members or associates of the firm.

J. Academic degrees earned from institutions accredited by regionally or nationally recognized accrediting agencies or assocations may be used or permitted to be used provided that the statement or claim is neither false, fraudulent, misleading, or deceptive within the meaning of Section II, C.

Solicitation of Professional Employment

K. A member shall not seek, by in-person contact, his/her employment as a therapist (or employment of a partner or associate) by a client who has not sought his/her advice regarding employment of a marriage and family therapist if:

1. The solicitation involves use of a statement or claim that is false, fraudulent, misleading, or deceptive within the meaning of Section II, C; or
2. The solicitation involves the use of undue influence; or

3. The potential client is apparently in a physical or mental condition which would make it unlikely that he or she could exercise reasonable, considered judgment as to the selection of a marriage and family therapist.

L. A member shall not compensate or give anything of value to a person or organization to recommend or secure his/her employment by a claim or as a reward for having made a recommendation resulting in his/her employment by a client.

M. A member shall not accept employment when he/she knows or it is obvious that the person who seeks his/her service does so as a result of conduct prohibited by this Section.

Suggestion of Need of Marriage or Family Therapy

N. A member who has given unsolicited advice to a layperson that he/she/they should obtain marriage or family therapy shall not accept employment results from that advice if:

1. The advice embodies or implies a statement or claim that is false, fraudulent, misleading, or deceptive within the meaning of Section II, C or that violates the regulations contained in Section II, D; or
2. The advice involves the use by the marriage and family therapist of coercion, duress, compulsion, intimidation, unwarranted promises of benefits, overreaching, [or] vexatious or harassing conduct.

APPENDIX I

SPECIALTY GUIDELINES FOR THE DELIVERY OF SERVICES BY COUNSELING PSYCHOLOGISTS

The Specialty Guidelines that follow are based on the generic *Standards for Providers of Psychological Services* originally adopted by the American Psychological Association (APA) in September 1974 and revised in January 1977 (APA, 1974b, 1977b). Together with the generic *Standards,* these Specialty Guidelines state the official policy of the Association regarding delivery of services by counseling psychologists. Admission to the practice of psychology is regulated by state statute. It is the position of the Association that licensing be based on generic, and not on specialty, qualifications. Specialty guidelines serve the additional purpose of providing potential users and other interested groups with essential information about particular services available from the several specialties in professional psychology.

Professional psychology specialties have evolved from generic practice in psychology and are supported by university training programs. There are now at least four recognized professional specialties—clinical, counseling, school, and industrial/organizational psychology.

The knowledge base in each of these specialty areas has increased, refining the state of the art to the point that a set of uniform specialty guidelines is now possible and desirable. The present Guidelines are intended to educate the public, the profession, and other interested parties regarding specialty professional practices. They are also intended to facilitate the continued systematic development of the profession.

The content of each Specialty Guideline reflects a consensus of university faculty and public and private practitioners regarding the knowledge base, services provided, problems addressed, and clients served.

Traditionally, all learned disciplines have treated the designation of specialty practice as a reflection of preparation in greater depth in a particular subject matter, together with a voluntary limiting of focus to a more restricted area of practice by the professional. Lack of specialty designation does not preclude general providers of psychological services from using the methods or dealing with the populations of any specialty, except insofar as psychologists voluntarily refrain from providing services they are not trained to render. It is the intent of these guidelines, however, that after the grandparenting period, psychologists not put themselves forward as *specialists* in a given area of practice unless they meet the qualifications noted in the Guidelines (see Definitions). Therefore, these Guidelines are

These Specialty Guidelines were prepared by the APA Committee on Standards for Providers of Psychological Services (COSPOPS), chaired by Durand F. Jacobs, with the advice of the officers and committee chairpersons of the Division of Counseling Psychology (Division 17). Barbara A. Kirk and Milton Schwebel served successively as the counseling psychology representative of COSPOPS, and Arthur Centor and Richard Kilburg were the Central Office liaisons to the committee. Norman Kagan, Samuel H. Osipow, Carl E. Thoresen, and Allen E. Ivey served successively as Division 17 presidents. Copyright 1981 by the American Psychological Association. Reprinted by permission of the publisher.

meant to apply only to those psychologists who voluntarily wish to be designated as *counseling psychologists*. They do not apply to other psychologists.

These Guidelines represent the profession's best judgment of the conditions, credentials, and experience that contribute to competent professional practice. The APA strongly encourages, and plans to participate in, efforts to identify professional practitioner behaviors and job functions and to validate the relation between these and desired client outcomes. Thus, future revisions of these Guidelines will increasingly reflect the results of such efforts.

These Guidelines follow the format and, wherever applicable, the wording of the generic *Standards*.[1] (Note: Footnotes appear at the end of the Specialty Guidelines. See pp. 661–663.) The intent of these Guidelines is to improve the quality, effectiveness, and accessibility of psychological services. They are meant to provide guidance to providers, users, and sanctioners regarding the best judgment of the profession on these matters. Although the Specialty Guidelines have been derived from and are consistent with the generic *Standards,* they may be used as separate documents. However, *Standards for Providers of Psychological Services* (APA, 1977b) shall remain the basic policy statement and shall take precedence where there are questions of interpretation.

Professional psychology in general and counseling psychology as a specialty have labored long and diligently to codify a uniform set of guidelines for the delivery of services by counseling psychologists that would serve the respective needs of users, providers, third-party purchasers, and sanctioners of psychological services.

The Committee on Professional Standards, established by the APA in January 1980, is charged with keeping the generic *Standards* and the Specialty Guidelines responsive to the needs of the public and the profession. It is also charged with continually reviewing, modifying, and extending them progressively as the profession and the science of psychology develop new knowledge, improved methods, and additional modes of psychological services.

The Specialty Guidelines for the Delivery of Services by Counseling Psychologists that follow have been established by the APA as a means of self-regulation to protect the public interest. They guide the specialty practice of counseling psychology by specifying important areas of quality assurance and performance that contribute to the goal of facilitating more effective human functioning.

Principles and Implications of the Specialty Guidelines

These Specialty Guidelines emerged from and reaffirm the same basic principles that guided the development of the generic *Standards for Providers of Psychological Services* (APA, 1977b):

1. These Guidelines recognize that admission to the practice of psychology is regulated by state statute.
2. It is the intention of the APA that the generic *Standards* provide appropriate guidelines for statutory licensing of psychologists. In addition, although it is the position of the APA that licensing be generic and not in specialty areas, these Specialty Guidelines in counseling psychology provide an authoritative reference for use in credentialing specialty providers of counseling psychological services by such groups as divisions of the APA and state associations and by boards and agencies that find such criteria useful for quality assurance.
3. A uniform set of Specialty Guidelines governs the quality of services to all users of counseling psychological services in both the private and the public sectors. Those receiving counseling psychological services are protected by the same kinds of safeguards, irrespective of sector: these include constitutional guarantees, statutory regulation, peer review, consultation, record review, and supervision.
4. A uniform set of Specialty Guidelines governs counseling psychological service functions offered by counseling psychologists, regardless of setting or form of remuneration. All counseling psychologists in professional practice recognize and are responsive to a uniform set of Specialty Guidelines, just as they are guided by a common code of ethics.
5. Counseling psychology Guidelines establish clear, minimally acceptable levels of quality for covered counseling psychological service functions, regardless of the nature of the users, purchasers, or sanctioners of such covered services.

6. All persons providing counseling psychological services meet specified levels of training and experience that are consistent with and appropriate to, the functions they perform. Counseling psychological services provided by persons who do not meet the APA qualifications for a professional counseling psychologist (see Definitions) are supervised by a professional counseling psychologist. Final responsibility and accountability for services provided rest with professional counseling psychologists.

7. When providing any of the covered counseling psychological service functions at any time and in any setting, whether public or private, profit or nonprofit, counseling psychologists observe these Guidelines in order to promote the best interests and welfare of the users of such services. The extent to which counseling psychologists observe these Guidelines is judged by peers.

8. These Guidelines, while assuring the user of the counseling psychologist's accountability for the nature and quality of services specified in this document, do not preclude the counseling psychologist from using new methods or developing innovative procedures in the delivery of counseling services.

These Specialty Guidelines have broad implications both for users of counseling psychological services and for providers of such services:

1. Guidelines for counseling psychological services provide a foundation for mutual understanding between provider and user and facilitate more effective evaluation of services provided and outcomes achieved.

2. Guidelines for counseling psychologists are essential for uniformity in specialty credentialing of counseling psychologists.

3. Guidelines give specific content to the profession's concept of ethical practice as it applies to the functions of counseling psychologists.

4. Guidelines for counseling psychological services may have significant impact on tomorrow's education and training models for both professional and support personnel in counseling psychology.

5. Guidelines for the provision of counseling psychological services in human service facilities influence the determination of accepta-

ble structure, budgeting, and staffing patterns in these facilities.

6. Guidelines for counseling psychological services require continual review and revision.

The Specialty Guidelines here presented are intended to improve the quality and delivery of counseling psychological services by specifying criteria for key aspects of the practice setting. Some settings may require additional and/or more stringent criteria for specific areas of service delivery.

Systematically applied, these Guidelines serve to establish a more effective and consistent basis for evaluating the performance of individual service providers as well as to guide the organization of counseling psychological service units in human service setting.

Definitions

Providers of counseling psychological services refers to two categories of persons who provide counseling psychological services:

A. Professional counseling psychologists.[2] Professional counseling psychologists have a doctoral degree from a regionally accredited university or professional school providing an organized, sequential counseling psychology program in an appropriate academic department in a university or college, or in an appropriate department or unit of a professional school. Counseling psychology programs that are accredited by the American Psychological Association are recognized as meeting the definition of a counseling psychology program. Counseling psychology programs that are not accredited by the American Psychological Association meet the definition of a counseling psychology program if they satisfy the following criteria:

1. The program is primarily psychological in nature and stands as a recognizable, coherent organizational entity within the institution.

2. The program provides an integrated, organized sequence of study.

3. The program has an identifiable body of students who are matriculated in that program for a degree.

4. There is a clear authority with primary responsibility for the core and specialty areas, whether or not the program cuts across administrative lines.
5. There is an identifiable psychology faculty, and a psychologist is responsible for the program.

The professional counseling psychologist's doctoral education and training experience[3] is defined by the institution offering the program. Only counseling psychologists, that is, those who meet the appropriate education and training requirements, have the minimum professional qualifications to provide unsupervised counseling psychological services. A professional counseling psychologist and others providing counseling psychological services under supervision (described below) form an integral part of a multilevel counseling psychological service delivery system.

B. All other persons who provide counseling psychological services under the supervision of a professional counseling psychologist. Although there may be variations in the titles of such persons, they are not referred to as counseling psychologists. Their functions may be indicated by use of the adjective *psychological* preceding the noun, for example, *psychological associate, psychological assistant, psychological technician,* or *psychological aide.*

Counseling psychological services refers to services provided by counseling psychologists that apply principles, methods, and procedures for facilitating effective functioning during the life-span developmental process.[4,5] In providing such services, counseling psychologists approach practice with a significant emphasis on positive aspects of growth and adjustment and with a developmental orientation. These services are intended to help persons acquire or alter personal-social skills, improve adaptablity to changing life demands, enhance environmental coping skills, and develop a variety of problem-solving and decision-making capabilities. Counseling psychological services are used by individuals, couples, and families of all age groups to cope with problems connected with education, career choice, work, sex, marriage, family, other social relations, health, aging, and handicaps of a social

or physical nature. The services are offered in such organizations as educational, rehabilitation, and health institutions and in a variety of other public and private agencies committed to service in one or more of the problem areas cited above. Counseling psychological services include the following:

A. Assessment, evaluation, and diagnosis. Procedures may include, but are not limited to, behavioral observation, interviewing, and administering and interpreting instruments for the assessment of educational achievement, academic skills, aptitudes, interests, cognitive abilities, attitudes, emotions, motivations, psychoneurological status, personality characteristics, or any other aspect of human experience and behavior that may contribute to understanding and helping the user.
B. Interventions with individuals and groups. Procedures include individual and group psychological counseling (e.g., education, career, couples, and family counseling) and may use a therapeutic, group process, or social-learning approach, or any other deemed to be appropriate. Interventions are used for purposes of prevention, remediation, and rehabilitation; they may incorporate a variety of psychological modalities, such as psychotherapy, behavior therapy, marital and family therapy, biofeedback techniques, and environmental design.
C. Professional consultation relating to A and B above, for example, in connection with developing in-service training for staff or assisting an educational institution or organization to design a plan to cope with persistent problems of its students.
D. Program development services in the areas of A, B, and C above, such as assisting a rehabilitation center to design a career-counseling program.
E. Supervision of all counseling psychological services, such as the review of assessment and intervention activities of staff.
F. Evaluation of all services noted in A through E above and research for the purpose of their improvement.

A *counseling psychological service unit* is the functional unit through which counseling psychological services are provided; such a unit may be part of a larger psychological service organization comprising psychologists of more than one specialty and headed by a professional psychologist:

A. A counseling psychological service unit provides predominantly counseling psychological services and is composed of one or more professional counseling psychologists and supporting staff.

B. A counseling psychological service unit may operate as a functional or geographic component of a larger multipsychological service unit or of a governmental, educational, correctional, health, training, industrial, or commercial organizational unit, or it may operate as an independent professional service.[6]

C. A counseling psychologcial service unit may take the form of one or more counseling psychologists providing professional services in a multidisciplinary setting.

D. A counseling psychological service unit may also take the form of a private practice, composed of one or more counseling psychologists serving individuals or groups, or the form of a psychological counsulting firm serving organizations and institutions.

Users of counseling psychological services include:

A. Direct users or recipients of counseling psychological services.

B. Public and private institutions, facilities, or organizations receiving counseling psychological services.

C. Third-party purchasers—those who pay for the delivery of services but who are not the recipients of services.

D. Sanctioners—those who have a legitimate concern with the accessibility, timeliness, efficacy, and standards of quality attending the provision of counseling psychological services. Sanctioners may include members of the user's family, the court, the probation officer, the school administrator, the employer, the union representative, the facility director, and so on. Sanctioners may also include various governmental, peer review, and accreditation bodies concerned with the assurance of quality.

Guideline 1: Providers

1.1 *Each counseling psychological service unit offering psychological services has available at least one professional counseling psychologist and as many more professional counseling psychologists as are necessary to assure the adequacy and quality of services offered.*

Interpretation: The intent of this Guideline is that one or more providers of psychological services in any counseling psychological service unit meet the levels of training and experience of the professional counseling psychologist as specified in the preceding definitions.[7]

When a professional counseling psychologist is not available on a full-time basis, the facility retains the services of one or more professional counseling psychologists on a regular part-time basis. The counseling psychologist so retained directs the psychological services, including supervision of the support staff, has the authority and participates sufficiently to assess the need for services, reviews the content of services provided, and assumes professional responsibility and accountability for them.

The psychologist directing the service unit is responsible for determining and justifying appropriate ratios of psychologists to users and psychologists to support staff, in order to ensure proper scope, accessibility, and quality of services provided in that setting.

1.2 *Providers of counseling psychological services who do not meet the requirements for the professional counseling psychologist are supervised directly by a professional counseling psychologist who assumes professional responsibility and accountability for the services provided. The level and extent of supervision may vary from task to task so long as the supervising psychologist retains a sufficiently close supervisory relationship to meet this Guideline. Special proficiency training or supervision may be provided by a professional psychologist of another specialty or by a professional from another discipline whose competence in the given area has been demonstrated by previous training and experience.*

Interpretation: In each counseling psychological service unit there may be varying levels of responsibility with respect to the nature and quality of services provided. Support personnel are considered to be responsible for their functions and behavior when assisting in the provision of counseling psychological services and are accountable to the professional counseling psychologist. Ultimate professional responsibility and accountability for the services provided require that the supervisor review reports and test protocols, and review and discuss intervention plans, strategies, and outcomes. Therefore, the supervision of all counseling psychological services is provided directly by a professional counseling psychologist in a face-to-face arrangement involving individual and/or group supervision. The extent of supervision is determined by the needs of the providers, but in no event is it less than 1 hour per week for each support staff member providing counseling psychological services.

To facilitate the effectiveness of the psychological service unit, the nature of the supervisory relationship is communicated to support personnel in writing. Such communications delineate the duties of the employees, describing the range and type of services to be provided. The limits of independent action and decision making are defined. The description of responsibility specifies the means by which the employee will contact the professional counseling psychologist in the event of emergency or crisis situations.

1.3 *Wherever a counseling psychological service unit exists, a professional counseling psychologist is responsible for planning, directing, and reviewing the provision of counseling psychological services. Whenever the counseling psychological service unit is part of a larger professional psychological service encompassing various psychological specialties, a professional psychologist shall be the administrative head of the service.*

Interpretation: The counseling psychologist who directs or coordinates the unit is expected to maintain an ongoing or periodic review of the adequacy of services and to formulate plans in accordance with the results of such evaluation. He or she coordinates the activities of the counseling psychology unit with other professional, administrative, and technical groups, both within and outside the institution or agency. The counseling psychologist has related responsibilities including, but not limited to, directing the training and research activities of the service, maintaining a high level of professional and ethical practice, and ensuring that staff members function only within the areas of their competency.

To facilitate the effectiveness of counseling services by raising the level of staff sensitivity and professional skills, the counseling psychologist designated as director is responsible for participating in the selection of staff and support personnel whose qualifications and skills (e.g., language, cultural and experiential background, race, sex, and age) are relevant to the needs and characteristics of the users served.

1.4 *When functioning as part of an organizational setting, professional counseling psychologists bring their backgrounds and skills to bear on the goals of the organization, whenever appropriate, by participation in the planning and development of overall services.*[8]

Interpretation: Professional counseling psychologists participate in the maintenance of high professional standards by representation on committees concerned with service delivery.

As appropriate to the setting, their activities may include active participation, as voting and as office-holding members, on the facility's professional staff and on other executive, planning, and evaluation boards and committees.

1.5 *Counseling psychologists maintain current knowledge of scientific and professional developments to preserve and enhance their professional competence.*

Interpretation: Methods through which knowledge of scientific and professional developments may be gained include, but are not limited to, reading scientific and professional publications, attendance at professional workshops and meetings, participation in staff development programs, and other forms of continuing education.[9] The counseling psychologist has ready access to reference material related to the provision of psychological services. Counseling psychologists are prepared to show evidence periodically that they are staying abreast of current knowledge and practices in the field of counseling psychology through continuing education.

1.6 *Counseling psychologists limit their practice to their demonstrated areas of professional competence.*

Interpretation: Counseling psychological services are offered in accordance with the providers' areas of competence as defined by verifiable training and experience. When extending services beyond the range of their usual practice, counseling psychologists obtain pertinent training or appropriate professional supervision. Such training or supervision is consistent with the extension of functions performed and services provided. An extension of services may involve a change in the theoretical orientation of the counseling psychologist, in the modality or techniques used, in the type of client, or in the kinds of problems or disorders for which services are to be provided.

1.7 *Professional psychologists who wish to qualify as counseling psychologists meet the same requirements with respect to subject matter and professional skills that apply to doctoral education and training in counseling psychology.*[10]

Interpretation: Education of doctoral-level psychologists to qualify them for specialty practice in counseling psychology is under the auspices of a department in a regionally accredited university or of a professional school that offers the doctoral degree in counseling psychology. Such education is individualized, with due credit being given for relevant course work and other requirements that have previously been satisfied. In addition, doctoral-level training supervised by a counseling psychologist is required. Merely taking an internship in counseling psychology or acquiring experience in a practicum setting is not adequate preparation for becoming a counseling psychologist when prior education has not been in that area. Fulfillment of such an individualized educational program is attested to by the awarding of a certificate by the supervising department or professional school that indicates the successful completion of preparation in counseling psychology.

1.8 *Professional counseling psychologists are encouraged to develop innovative theories and procedures and to provide appropriate theoretical and/ or empirical support for their innovations.*

Interpretation: A specialty of a profession rooted in a science intends continually to explore and experiment with a view to developing and verifying new and improved ways of serving the public and documents the innovations.

Guideline 2: Programs

2.1 *Composition and organization of a counseling psychological service unit:*

2.1.1 *The composition and programs of a counseling psychological service unit are responsive to the needs of the persons or settings served.*

Interpretation: A counseling psychological service unit is structured so as to facilitate effective and economical delivery of services. For example, a counseling psychological service unit serving predominantly a low-income, ethnic, or racial minority group has a staffing pattern and service programs that are adapted to the linguistic, experiential, and attitudinal characteristics of the users.

2.1.2 *A description of the organization of the counseling psychological service unit and its lines of responsibility and accountability for the delivery of psychological services is available in written form to staff of the unit and to users and sanctioners upon request.*

Interpretation: The description includes lines of responsibility, supervisory relationships, and the level and extent of accountability for each persons who provides psychological services.

2.1.3 *A counseling psychological service unit includes sufficient numbers of professional and support personnel to achieve its goals, objectives, and purposes.*

Interpretation: The work load and diversity of psychological services required and the specific goals and objectives of the setting determine the numbers and qualifications of professional and support personnel in the counseling psychological service unit. Where shortages in personnel exist, so that psychological services cannot be rendered in a professional manner, the director of the counseling psychological service unit initiates action to remedy such shortages. When this fails, the director appropriately modifies the scope or work load of the unit to maintain the quality of the services rendered and, at the same time, makes continued efforts to devise alternative systems for delivery of services.

2.2 *Policies:*

2.2.1 *When the counseling psychological service unit is composed of more than one person or is a component of a larger organization, a written statement of its objectives and scope of services is developed, maintained, and reviewed.*

Interpretation: The counseling psychological service unit reviews its objectives and scope of services annually and revises them as necessary to ensure that the psychological services offered are consistent with staff competencies and current psychological knowledge and practice. This statement is discussed with staff, reviewed with the appropriate administrator, and distributed to users and sanctioners upon request, whenever appropriate.

2.2.2 *All providers within a counseling psychological service unit support the legal and civil rights of the users.*[11]

Interpretation: Providers of counseling psychological services safeguard the interests of the users with regard to personal, legal, and civil rights. They are continually sensitive to the issue of confidentiality of information, the short-term and long-term impacts of their decisions and recommendations, and other matters pertaining to individual, legal, and civil rights. Concerns regarding the safeguarding of individual rights of users include, but are not limited to, problems of access to professional records in educational institutions, self-incrimination in judicial proceedings, involuntary commitment to hospitals, protection of minors or legal incompetents, discriminatory practices in employment selection procedures, recommendation for special education provisions, information relative to adverse personnel actions in the armed services, and adjudication of domestic relations disputes in divorce and custodial proceedings. Providers of counseling psychological services take affirmative action by making themselves available to local committees, review boards, and similar advisory groups established to safeguard the human, civil, and legal rights of service users.

2.2.3 *All providers within a counseling psychological service unit are familiar with and adhere to the American Psychological Association's* Standards for Providers of Psychological Services, Ethical Principles of Psychologists, Standards for Educational and Psychological Tests, Ethical Principles in the Conduct of Research With Human Participants, *and other official policy statements relevant to standards for professional services issued by the Association.*

Interpretation: Providers of counseling psychological services maintain current knowledge of relevant standards of the American Psychological Association.

2.2.4 *All providers within a counseling psychological service unit conform to relevant statutes established by federal, state, and local governments.*

Interpretation: All providers of counseling psychological services are familiar with and conform to appropriate statutes regulating the practice of psychology. They also observe agency regulations that have the force of law and that relate to the delivery of psychological services (e.g., evaluation for disability retirement and special education placements). In addition, all providers are cognizant that federal agencies such as the Veterans Administration, the Department of Education, and the Department of Health and Human Services have policy statements regarding psychological services. Providers are familiar as well with other statutes and regulations, including those addressed to the civil and legal rights of users (e.g., those promulgated by the federal Equal Employment Opportunity Commission), that are pertinent to their scope of practice.

It is the responsibility of the American Psychological Association to maintain current files of those federal policies, statutes, and regulations relating to this section and to assist its members in obtaining them. The state psychological associations and the state licensing boards periodically publish and distribute appropriate state statutes and regulations, and these are on file in the counseling psychological service unit or the larger multipsychological service unit of which it is a part.

2.2.5 *All providers within a counseling psychological service unit inform themselves about and use the network of human services in their communities in order to link users with relevant services and resources.*

Interpretation: Counseling psychologists and support staff are sensitive to the broader context of human needs. In recognizing the matrix of personal and social problems, providers make available to clients information regarding human services such as legal aid societies, social services, employment agencies, health resources, and educational and recreational facilities. Providers of counseling psychological services refer to such community resources and, when indicated, actively intervene on behalf of the users.

Community resources include the private as well as the public sectors. Consultation is sought or referral made within the public or private network of services whenever required in the best interest of the users. Counseling psychologists, in either the private or the public setting, utilize other resources in the community whenever indicated because of limitations within the psychological service unit providing the services. Professional counseling psychologists in private practice know the types of services offered through local community mental health clinics and centers, through family-service, career, and placement agencies, and through reading and other educational improvement centers and know the costs and the eligibility requirements for those services.

2.2.6 *In the delivery of counseling psychological services, the providers maintain a cooperative relationship with colleagues and co-workers in the best interest of the users.*[12]

Interpretation: Counseling psychologists recognize the areas of special competence of other professional psychologists and of professionals in other fields for either consultation or referral purposes. Providers of counseling psychological services make appropriate use of other professional, research, technical, and administrative resources to serve the best interests of users and establish and maintain cooperative arrangements with such other resources as required to meet the needs of users.

2.3 *Procedures:*

2.3.1 *Each counseling psychological service unit is guided by a set of procedural guidelines for the delivery of psychological services.*

Interpretation: Providers are prepared to provide a statement of procedural guidelines, in either oral or written form, in terms that can be understood by users, including sanctioners and local administrators. This statement describes the current methods, forms, procedures, and techniques being used to achieve the objectives and goals for psychological services.

2.3.2 *Providers of counseling psychological services develop plans appropriate to the providers' professional practices and to the problems presented by the users.*

Interpretation: A counseling psychologist, after initial assessment, develops a plan describing the objectives of the psychological services and the manner in which they will be provided.[13] To illustrate, the agreement spells out the objective (e.g., a career decision), the method (e.g., short-term counseling), the roles (e.g., active participation by the user as well as the provider), and the cost. This plan is in written form. It serves as a basis for obtaining understanding and concurrence from the user and for establishing accountability and provides a mechanism for subsequent peer review. This plan is, of course, modified as changing needs dictate.

A counseling psychologist who provides services as one member of a collaborative effort participates in the development, modification (if needed), and implementation of the overall service plan and provides for its periodic review.

2.3.3 *Accurate, current, and pertinent documentation of essential counseling psychological services provided is maintained.*

Interpretation: Records kept of counseling psychological services include, but are not limited to, identifying data, dates of services, types of services, significant actions taken, and outcome at termination. Providers of counseling psychological services ensure that essential information concerning services rendered is recorded within a reasonable time following their completion.

2.3.4 *Each counseling psychological service unit follows an established record retention and disposition policy.*

Interpretation: The policy on record retention and disposition conforms to state statutes or federal regulations where such are applicable. In the absence of such regulations, the policy is (a) that the full record be maintained intact for at least 4 years after the completion of planned services or after the date of last contact with the user, whichever is later; (b) that if a full record is not retained, a summary of the record be maintained for an additional 3 years; and (c) that the record may be disposed of no sooner than 7 years after the completion of planned services or after the date of last contact, whichever is later.

In the event of the death or incapacity of a counseling psychologist in independent practice, special procedures are necessary to ensure the continuity of active service to users and the proper safeguarding of records in accordance with this Guideline. Following approval by the affected user, it is appropriate for another counseling psychologist, acting under the auspices of the professional standards review committee (PSRC) of the state, to review the record with the user and recommend a course of action for continuing professional service, if needed. Depending on local circumstances, appropriate arrangements for record retention and disposition may also be recommended by the reviewing psychologist.

This Guideline has been designed to meet a variety of circumstances that may arise, often years after a set of psychological services has been completed. Increasingly, psychological records are being used in forensic matters, for peer review, and in response to requests from users, other professionals, and other legitimate parties requiring accurate information about the exact dates, nature, course, and outcome of a set of psychological services. The 4-year period for retention of the full record covers the period of either undergraduate or graduate study of most students in postsecondary educational institutions, and the 7-year period for retention of at least a summary of the record covers the period during which a previous user is most likely to return for counseling psychological services in an educational institution or other organization or agency.

2.3.5 *Providers of counseling psychological services maintain a system to protect confidentiality of their records.*[14]

Interpretation: Counseling psychologists are responsible for maintaining the confidentiality of information about users of services, from whatever source derived. All persons supervised by counseling psychologists, including nonprofessional personnel and students, who have access to records of psychological services maintain this confidentiality as a condition of employment and/or supervision.

The counseling psychologist does not release confidential information, except with the written consent of the user directly involved or his or her legal representative. The only deviation from this rule is in the event of clear and imminent danger to, or involving, the user. Even after consent for release has been obtained, the counseling psychologist clearly identifies such information as confidential to the recipient of the information.[15] If directed otherwise by statute or regulations with the force of law or by court order, the psychologist seeks a resolution to the conflict that is both ethically and legally feasible and appropriate.

Users are informed in advance of any limits in the setting for maintenance of confidentiality of psychological information. For instance, counseling psychologists in agency, clinic, or hospital settings inform their clients that psychological information in a client's record may be available without the client's written consent to other members of the professional staff associated with service to the client. Similar limitations on confidentiality of psychological information may be present in certain educational, industrial, military, or other institutional settings, or in instances in which the user has waived confidentiality for purposes of third-party payment.

Users have the right to obtain information from their psychological records. However, the records are the property of the psychologist or the facility in which the psychologist works and are, therefore, the responsibility of the psychologist and subject to his or her control.

When the user's intention to waive confidentiality is judged by the professional counseling psychologist to be contrary to the user's best interests or to be in conflict with the user's civil and legal rights, it is the responsibility of the counseling psychologist to discuss the implications of releasing psychological information and to assist the user in limiting disclosure only to information required by the present circumstance.

Raw psychological data (e.g., questionnaire returns or test protocols) in which a user is identified are released only with the written consent of the user or his or her legal representative and released only to a person recognized by the counseling psychologist as qualified and competent to use the data.

Any use made of psychological reports, records, or data for research or training purposes is consistent with this Guideline. Additionally, providers of counseling psychological services comply with statutory confidentiality requirements and those embodied in the American Psychological Association's *Ethical Principles of Psychologists* (APA, 1981b).

Providers of counseling psychological services who use information about individuals that is stored in large computerized data banks are aware of the possible misuse of such data as well as the benefits and take necessary measures to ensure that such information is used in a socially responsible manner.

Guideline 3: Accountability

3.1 *The promotion of human welfare is the primary principle guiding the professional activity of the counseling psychologist and the counseling psychological service unit.*

Interpretation: Counseling psychologists provide services to users in a manner that is considerate, effective, economical, and humane. Counseling psychologists are responsible for making their services readily accessible to users in a manner that facilitates the users' freedom of choice.

Counseling psychologists are mindful of their accountability to the sanctioners of counseling psychological services and to the general public, provided that appropriate steps are taken to protect the confidentiality of the service relationship. In the pursuit of their professional activities, they aid in the conservation of human, material, and financial resources.

The counseling psychological service unit does not withhold services to a potential client on the basis of that user's race, color, religion, gender, sexual orientation, age, or national origin; nor does it provide services in a discriminatory or exploitative fashion. Counseling psychologists who find that psychological services are being provided in a manner that is discriminatory or exploitative to users and/or contrary to these Guidelines or to state or federal statutes take appropriate corrective action, which may include the refusal to provide services. When conflicts of interest arise, the counseling psychologist is guided in the resolution of differences by the principles set forth in the American Psychological Association's *Ethical Principles of Psychologists* (APA, 1981b) and "Guidelines for Conditions of Employment of Psychologists" (APA, 1972).[16]

Recognition is given to the following considerations in regard to the withholding of service: (a) the professional right of counseling psychologists to limit their practice to a specific category of users with whom they have achieved demonstrated competence (e.g., adolescents or families); (b) the right and responsibility of counseling psychologists to withhold an assessment procedure when not validly applicable; (c) the right and responsibility of counseling psychologists to withhold services in specific instances in which their own limitations or client characteristics might impair the quality of the services; (d) the obligation of counseling psychologists to seek to ameliorate through peer review, consultation, or other personal therapeutic procedures those factors that inhibit the provision of services to particular individuals; and (e) the obligation of counseling psychologists who withhold services to assist clients in obtaining services from other sources.[17]

3.2 *Counseling psychologists pursue their activ-*

ities as members of the independent, autonomous profession of psychology.[18]

Interpretation: Counseling psychologists, as members of an independent profession, are responsible both to the public and to their peers through established review mechanisms. Counseling psychologists are aware of the implications of their activities for the profession as a whole. They seek to eliminate discriminatory practices instituted for self-serving purposes that are not in the interest of the users (e.g., arbitrary requirements for referral and supervision by another profession). They are cognizant of their responsibilities for the development of the profession, participate where possible in the training and career development of students and other providers, participate as appropriate in the training of paraprofessionals or other professionals, and integrate and supervise the implementation of their contributions within the structure established for delivering psychological services. Counseling psychologists facilitate the development of, and participate in, professional standards review mechanisms.[19]

Counseling psychologists seek to work with other professionals in a cooperative manner for the good of the users and the benefit of the general public. Counseling psychologists associated with multidisciplinary settings support the principle that members of each participating profession have equal rights and opportunities to share all privileges and responsibilities of full membership in human service facilities and to administer service programs in their respective areas of competence.

3.3 *There are periodic, systematic, and effective evaluations of counseling psychological services.*[20]

Interpretation: When the counseling psychological service unit is a component of a larger organization, regular evaluation of progress in achieving goals is provided for in the service delivery plan, including consideration of the effectiveness of counseling psychological services relative to costs in terms of use of time and money and the availability of professional and support personnel.

Evaluation of the counseling psychological service delivery system is conducted internally and, when possible, under independent auspices as well. This evaluation includes an assessment of effectiveness (to determine what the service unit accomplished), efficiency (to determine the total costs of providing the services), continuity (to ensure that the services are appropriately linked to other human services), availability (to determine appropriate levels and distribution of services and personnel), accessibility (to ensure that the services are barrier free to users), and adequacy (to determine whether the services meet the identified needs for such services).

There is a periodic reexamination of review mechanisms to ensure that these attempts at public safeguards are effective and cost efficient and do not place unnecessary encumbrances on the providers or impose unnecessary additional expenses on users or sanctioners for services rendered.

3.4 *Counseling psychologists are accountable for all aspects of the services they provide and are responsive to those concerned with these services.*[21]

Interpretation: In recognizing their responsibilities to users, sanctioners, third-party purchasers, and other providers, and where appropriate and consistent with the users' legal rights and privileged communications, counseling psychologists make available information about, and provide opportunity to participate in, decisions concerning such issues as initiation, termination, continuation, modification, and evaluation of counseling psychological services.

Depending on the settings, accurate and full information is made available to prospective individual or organizational users regarding the qualifications of providers, the nature and extent of services offered, and where appropriate, financial and social costs.

Where appropriate, counseling psychologists inform users of their payment policies and their willingness to assist in obtaining reimbursement. To assist their users, those who accept reimbursement from a third party are acquainted with the appropriate statutes and regulations, the procedures for submitting claims, and the limits on confidentiality of claims information, in accordance with pertinent statutes.

Guideline 4: Environment

4.1 *Providers of counseling psychological services promote the development in the service setting of a physical, organizational, and social environment that facilitates optimal human functioning.*

Interpretation: Federal, state, and local requirements for safety, health, and sanitation are observed.

As providers of services, counseling psychologists are concerned with the environment of their service unit, especially as it affects the quality of service, but also as it impinges on human functioning in the larger context. Physical arrangements and organizational policies and procedures are conducive to the human dignity, self-respect, and optimal functioning of users and to the effective delivery of service. Attention is given to the comfort and the privacy of providers and users. The atmosphere in which counseling psychological services are rendered is appropriate to the service and to the users, whether in an office, clinic, school, college, university, hospital, industrial organization, or other institutional setting.

Footnotes

[1]The footnotes appended to these Specialty Guidelines represent an attempt to provide a coherent context of other policy statements of the Association regarding professional practice. The Guidelines extend these previous policy statements where necessary to reflect current concerns of the public and the profession.

[2]The following two categories of professional psychologists who met the criteria indicated below on or before the adoption of these Specialty Guidelines on January 31, 1980, are also considered counseling psychologists: Category 1—persons who completed (a) a doctoral degree program primarily psychological in content at a regionally accredited university or professional school and (b) 3 postdoctoral years of appropriate education, training, and experience in providing counseling psychological services as defined herein, including a minimum of 1 year in a counseling setting; Category 2—persons who on or before September 4, 1974, (a) completed a master's degree from a program primarily psychological in content at a regionally accredited university or professional school and (b) held a license or certificate in the state in which they practiced, conferred by a state board of psychological examiners, or the endorsement of the state psychological association through voluntary certification, and who, in addition, prior to January 31, 1980, (c) obtained 5 post-master's years of appropriate education, training, and experience in providing counseling psychological services as defined herein, including a minimum of 2 years in a counseling setting.

After January 31, 1980, professional psychologists who wish to be recognized as professional counseling psychologists are referred to Guideline 1.7.

[3]The areas of knowledge and training that are a part of the educational program for all professional psychologists have been presented in two APA documents, *Education and Credentialing in Psychology II* (APA, 1977a) and *Criteria for Accreditation of Doctoral Training Programs and Internships in Professional Psychology* (APA, 1979). There is consistency in the presentation of core areas in the education and training of all professional psychologists. The description of education and training in these Guidelines is based primarily on the document *Education and Credentialing in Psychology II*. It is intended to indicate broad areas of required curriculum, with the expectation that training programs will undoubtedly want to interpret the specific content of these areas in different ways depending on the nature, philosophy, and intent of the programs.

[4]Functions and activities of counseling psychologists relating to the teaching of psychology, the writing or editing of scholarly or scientific manuscripts, and the conduct of scientific research do not fall within the purview of these Guidelines.

[5]These definitions should be compared with the APA (1967) guidelines for state legislation (hereinafter referred to as state guidelines), which define *psychologist* (i.e., the generic professional psychologist, not the specialist counseling psychologist) and the *practice of psychology* as follows:

A person represents himself [or herself] to be a psychologist when he [or she] holds himself [or herself] out to the public by any title or description of services incorporating the words "psychology," "psychological," "psychologist," and/or offers to render or renders service as defined below to individuals, groups, organizations, or the public for a fee, monetary or otherwise.

The practice of psychology within the meaning of this act is defined as rendering to individuals, groups, organizations, or the public any psychological service involving the application of principles, methods, and procedures of understanding, predicting, and influencing behavior, such as the principles pertaining to learning, perception, motivation, thinking, emotions, and interpersonal relationships; the methods and procedures of interviewing, counseling, and psychotherapy; of constructing, administering, and interpreting tests of mental abilites, aptitudes, interests, attitudes, personality characteristics, emotion, and motivation; and of assessing public opinion.

The application of said principles and methods includes, but is not restricted to: diagnosis, prevention, and amelioration of adjustment problems and emotional and metal disorders of individuals and groups; hypnosis; educational and vocational counseling; personnel selection and management; the evaluation and planning for effective work and learning situations; advertising and market research; and the resolution of interpersonal and social conflicts.

Psychotherapy within the meaning of this act means the use of learning, conditioning methods, and emotional reactions, in a professional relationship, to assist a person or persons to modify feelings, attitudes, and behavior which are intellectually, socially, or emotionally maladjustive or ineffectual.

The practice of psychology shall be as defined above, any existing statute in the state of_____to the contrary not withstanding. (APA, 1967, pp. 1098–1099)

[6]The relation of a psychological service unit to a larger facility or institution is also addressed indirectly in the APA (1972) "Guidelines for Conditions of Employment of Psychologists" (hereinafter referred to a CEP Guidelines), which emphasize the roles, responsibilities, and prerogatives of the psychologist when he or she is employed by or provides services for another agency, institution, or business.

[7]This Guideline replaces earlier recommendations in the 1967 state guidelines concerning exemption of psychologists from licensure. Recommendations 8 and 9 of those guidelines read as follows:

Persons employed as psychologists by accredited academic institutions, governmental agencies, research laboratories, and business corporations should be exempted, provided such employees are performing those duties for which they are employed by such organizations, and within the confines of such organizations.

Persons employed as psychologists by accredited academic institutions, governmental agencies, research laboratories, and business corporations consulting or offering their research findings or providing scientific information *to like organizaitons* for a fee should be exempted. (APA, 1967, p. 1100)

On the other hand, the 1967 state guidelines specifically denied exemptions under certain conditions, as noted in Recommendations 10 and 11:

Persons employed as psychologists who offer or provide psychological services to the public for a fee, over and above the salary that they receive for the performance of their regular duties, should not be exempted.

Persons employed as psychologists by organizations that sell psychological services to the public should not be exempted. (APA, 1967, pp. 1100–1101)

The present APA policy, as reflected in this Guideline, establishes a single code of practice for psychologists providing covered services to users in any setting.

The present position is that a psychologist providing any covered service meets local statutory requirements for licensure or certification. See the section entitled Principles and Implications of the Specialty Guidelines for further elaboration of this point.

[8]A closely related principle is found in the APA (1972) CEP Guidelines:

It is the policy of APA that psychology as an independent profession is entitled to parity with other health and human service professions in institutional practices and before the law. Psychologists in interdisciplinary settings such as colleges and universities, medical schools, clinics, private practice groups, and other agencies expect parity with other professions in such matters as academic rank, board status, salaries, fringe benefits, fees, participation in administrative decisions, and all other conditions of employment, private contractual arrangements, and status before the law and legal institutions. (APA, 1972, p. 333)

[9]See CEP Guidelines (section entitled Career Development) for a closely related statement:

Psychologists are expected to encourage institutions and agencies which employ them to sponsor or conduct career development programs. The purpose of these programs would be to enable psychologists to engage in study for professional advancement and to keep abreast of developments in their field. (APA, 1972, p. 332)

[10]This Guideline follows closely the statement regarding "Policy on Training for Psychologists Wishing to Change Their Specialty" adopted by the APA Council of Representatives in January 1976. Included therein was the implementing provision that "this policy statement shall be incorporated in the guidelines of the Committee on Accreditation so that appropriate sanctions can be brought to bear on university and internship training programs that violate [it]" (Conger, 1976, p. 424).

[11]See also APA's (1981b) *Ethical Principles of Psychologists,* especially Principles 5 (Confidentiality), 6 (Welfare of the Consumer), and 9 (Research With Human Participants); and see *Ethical Principles in the Conduct of Research With Human Participants* (APA, 1973a). Also, in 1978 Division 17 approved in principle a statement on "Principles for Counseling and Psychotherapy With Women," which was designed to protect the interests of female users of counseling psychological services.

[12]Support for this position is found in the section on relations with other professions in *Psychology as a Profession:*

Professional persons have an obligation to know and take into account the traditions and practices of other professional groups with whom they work and to cooperate fully with members of such groups with whom research, service, and other functions are shared. (APA, 1968, p. 5)

[13]One example of a specific application of this principle is found in APA's (1981a) revised *APA/CHAMPUS Outpatient Psychological Provider Manual.* Another example, quoted below, is found in Guideline 2 in APA's (1973b) "Guidelines for Psychologists Conducting Growth Groups":

The following information should be made available *in writing* [italics added] to all prospective participants:
(*a*) An explicit statement of the purpose of the group;
(*b*) Types of techniques that may be employed;
(*c*) The education, training, and experience of the leader or leaders;
(*d*) The fee and any additional expense that may be incurred;
(*e*) A statement as to whether or not a follow-up service is included in the fee:
(*f*) Goals of the group experience and techniques to be used:
(*g*) Amounts and kinds of responsibility to be assumed by the leader and by the participants. For example, (*i*) the degree to which a participant is free not to follow suggestions and prescriptions of the group leader and other group members; (*ii*) any restrictions on a participant's freedom to leave the group at any time; and
(*h*) Issues of confidentiality. (p. 933)

[14]See Principle 5 (Confidentiality) in *Ethical Principles of Psychologists* (APA, 1981b).

[15]Support for the principles of privileged communication is found in at least two policy statements of the Association:

In the interest of both the public and the client and in accordance with the requirements of good professional practice, the profession of psychology seeks recognition of the privileged nature of confidential communications with clients, preferably through statutory enactment or by administrative policy where more appropriate. (APA, 1968, p. 8)

Wherever possible, a clause protecting the privileged nature of the psychologist-client relationship be included.
When appropriate, psychologists assist in obtaining general "across the board" legislation for such privileged communications. (APA, 1967, p. 1103)

[16]The CEP Guidelines include the following;

It is recognized that under certain circumstances, the interests and goals of a particular community or segment of interest in the population may be in conflict with the general welfare. Under such circumstances, the psychologist's professional activity must be primarily guided by the principle of "promoting human welfare." (APA, 1972, p. 334)

[17]This paragraph is adapted in part from the CEP Guidelines (APA, 1972, p. 333).

[18]Support for the principle of the independence of psychology as a profession is found in the following:

As a member of an autonomous profession, a psychologist rejects limitations upon his [or her] freedom of thought and action other than those imposed by his [or her] moral, legal, and social responsibilities. The Association is always prepared to provide appropriate assistance to any responsible member who becomes subjected to unreasonable limitations upon his [or her] opportunity to function as a practitioner, teacher, researcher, administrator, or consultant. The Association is always prepared to cooperate with any responsible professional organization in opposing any unreasonable limitations on the professional functions of the members of that organization.

This insistence upon professional autonomy has been upheld over the years by the affirmative actions of the courts and other public and private bodies in support of the right of the psychologist—and other professionals—to pursue those functions for which he [or she] is trained and qualified to perform. (APA, 1968, p. 9)

Organized psychology has the responsibility to define and develop its own profession, consistent with the general canons of science and with the public welfare.

Psychologists recognize that other professions and other groups will, from time to time, seek to define the roles and responsibilities of psychologists. The APA opposes such developments on the same principle that it is opposed to the psychological profession taking positions which would define the work and scope of responsibilty of other duly recognized professions. (APA, 1972, p. 333)

[19]APA support for peer review is detailed in the following excerpt from the APA (1971) statement entitled "Psychology and National Health Care":

All professions participating in a national health plan should be directed to establish review mechanisms (or performance evaluations) that include not only peer review but active participation by persons representing the consumer. In situations where there are fiscal agents, they should also have representation when appropriate. (p. 1026)

[20]This Guideline on program evaluation is based directly on the following excerpts from two APA position papers:

The quality and availability of health services should be evaluated continuously by both consumers and health professionals. Research into the efficiency and effectiveness of the system should be conducted both internally and under independent auspices. (APA, 1971, p. 1025)

The comprehensive community mental health center should devote an explicit portion of its budget to program evaluation. All centers should inculcate in their staff attention to and respect for research findings; the larger centers have an obligation to set a high priority on basic research and to give formal recognition to research as a legitimate part of the duties of staff members.

... Only through explicit appraisal of program effects can worthy approaches be retained and refined, ineffective ones dropped. Evaluative monitoring of program achievements may vary, of course, from the relatively informal to the systematic and quantitative, depending on the importance of the issue, the availability of resources, and the willingness of those responsible to take risks of substituting informed judgment for evidence. (Smith & Hobbs, 1966, pp. 21–22)

[21]See also the CEP Guidelines for the following statement: "A psychologist recognizes that ... he [or she] alone is accountable for the consequences and effects of his [or her] services, whether as teacher, researcher, or practitioner. This responsibility cannot be shared, delegated, or reduced." (APA, 1972, p. 334).

References

American Psychological Association, Committee on Legislation. A model for state legislation affecting the practice of psychology. *American Psychologist,* 1967, *22,* 1095–1103.

American Psychological Association, *Psychology as a profession.* Washington, D.C.: Author, 1968

American Psychological Association. Psychology and national health care. *American Psychologist,* 1971, *26,* 1025–1026.

American Psychological Association. Guidelines for conditions of employment of psychologists. *American Psychologist,* 1972, *27,* 331–334.

American Psychological Association. *Ethical principles in the conduct of research with human participants.* Washington, D.C.: *Author,* 1973. (a)

American Psychological Association. Guidelines for psychologists conducting growth groups. *American Psychologist,* 1973, *28,* 933. (b)

American Psychological Association,. *Standards for educational and psychological tests.* Washington, D.C.: *Author,* 1974. (a)

American Psychological Association, *Standards for pro-*

viders of psychological services. Washington, D.C.: *Author,* 1974. (b)

American Psychological Association. *Education and credentialing in psychology II.* Report of a meeting, June 4–5, 1977, Washington, D.C.: *Author,* 1977. (a)

American Psychological Association. *Standards for providers of psychological services* (Rev. ed.). Washington, D.C.: *Author,* 1977. (b)

American Psychological Association, *Criteria for accreditation of doctoral training programs and internships in professional psychology.* Washington, D.C.: *Author,* 1979 (amended 1980).

American Psychological Association. *APA/CHAMPUS outpatient psychological provider manual* (Rev. ed.). Washington, D.C.: *Author,* 1981. (a)

American Psychological Association. *Ethical principles of psychologists* (Rev. ed.). Washington, D.C.: *Author,* 1981. (b)

Conger, J. J. Proceedings of the American Psychological Association, Incorporated, for the year 1975; Minutes of the annual meeting of the Council of Representatives. *American Psychologist,* 1976, *31,* 406–434.

Smith, M. B., & Hobbs, N. *The community and the community mental health center.* Washington, D.C.: American Psychological Association, 1966.

NAME INDEX

SUBJECT INDEX